HARD CHOICES

ALSO BY HILLARY RODHAM CLINTON

It Takes a Village

Dear Socks, Dear Buddy

An Invitation to the White House

Living History

Hillary Rodham Clinton

HARD
CHOICES

**SIMON &
SCHUSTER**

London · New York · Sydney · Toronto · New Delhi

A CBS COMPANY

First published in Great Britain by Simon & Schuster UK Ltd, 2014
A CBS COMPANY

1 3 5 7 9 10 8 6 4 2

Simon & Schuster UK Ltd
1st Floor
222 Gray's Inn Road
London WC1X 8HB

www.simonandschuster.co.uk

Simon & Schuster Australia, Sydney
Simon & Schuster India, New Delhi

A CIP catalogue record for this book
is available from the British Library

ISBN: 978-1-47113-150-9
Ebook ISBN: 978-1-47113-153-0

Interior design by Joy O'Meara
Jacket Design by Jackie Seow
Map by Robert Bull

Photo research and editing by Laura Wyss, Wyss Photo Inc., with
the assistance of Elizabeth Ceramur, Amy Hidika, and Emily Vinson.

Printed and bound in India by Replika Press Pvt. Ltd.

For America's diplomats and development experts,
who represent our country and our values so well
in places large and small, peaceful and perilous
all over the world.

and

In memory of my parents:
Hugh Ellsworth Rodham (1911–1993)
Dorothy Emma Howell Rodham (1919–2011)

CONTENTS

*Owner:
Margaret
Lofaro*

Author's Note   ix

PART ONE: A FRESH START

1 | 2008: Team of Rivals   *1*

2 | Foggy Bottom: Smart Power   *20*

PART TWO: ACROSS THE PACIFIC

3 | Asia: The Pivot   *39*

4 | China: Uncharted Waters   *65*

5 | Beijing: The Dissident   *83*

6 | Burma: The Lady and the Generals   *101*

PART THREE: WAR AND PEACE

7 | Af-Pak: Surge   *129*

8 | Afghanistan: To End a War   *150*

9 | Pakistan: National Honor   *170*

PART FOUR: BETWEEN HOPE AND HISTORY

10 | Europe: Ties That Bind   *205*

11 | Russia: Reset and Regression   *227*

12 | Latin America: Democrats and Demagogues   *246*

13 | Africa: Guns or Growth?   *269*

PART FIVE: UPHEAVAL

14 | The Middle East: The Rocky Path of Peace   *301*

15 | The Arab Spring: Revolution   *331*

16 | Libya: All Necessary Measures   *363*

17 | Benghazi: Under Attack   *382*

18 | Iran: Sanctions and Secrets   *416*

19 | Syria: A Wicked Problem   *447*

20 | Gaza: Anatomy of a Cease-fire   *471*

PART SIX: THE FUTURE WE WANT

21 | Climate Change: We're All in This Together   *491*

22 | Jobs and Energy: A Level Playing Field   *507*

23 | Haiti: Disaster and Development   *527*

24 | 21st-Century Statecraft: Digital Diplomacy in a Networked World   *545*

25 | Human Rights: Unfinished Business   *558*

Epilogue   *591*

Acknowledgments   *597*

Index   *601*

Photo Credits   *633*

AUTHOR'S NOTE

All of us face hard choices in our lives. Some face more than their share. We have to decide how to balance the demands of work and family. Caring for a sick child or an aging parent. Figuring out how to pay for college. Finding a good job, and what to do if you lose it. Whether to get married—or stay married. How to give our kids the opportunities they dream about and deserve. Life is about making such choices. Our choices and how we handle them shape the people we become. For leaders and nations, they can mean the difference between war and peace, poverty and prosperity.

I'm eternally grateful that I was born to loving and supportive parents in a country that offered me every opportunity and blessing—factors beyond my control that set the stage for the life I've led and the values and faith I've embraced. When I chose to leave a career as a young lawyer in Washington to move to Arkansas to marry Bill and start a family, my friends asked, "Are you out of your mind?" I heard similar questions when I took on health care reform as First Lady, ran for office myself, and accepted President Barack Obama's offer to represent our country as Secretary of State.

In making these decisions, I listened to both my heart and my head. I followed my heart to Arkansas; it burst with love at the birth of our daughter, Chelsea; and it ached with the losses of my father and mother. My head urged me forward in my education and professional choices.

And my heart and head together sent me into public service. Along the way, I've tried not to make the same mistake twice, to learn, to adapt, and to pray for the wisdom to make better choices in the future.

What's true in our daily lives is also true at the highest levels of government. Keeping America safe, strong, and prosperous presents an endless set of choices, many of which come with imperfect information and conflicting imperatives. Perhaps the most famous example from my four years as Secretary of State was President Obama's order to send a team of Navy SEALs into a moonless Pakistani night to bring Osama bin Laden to justice. The President's top advisors were divided. The intelligence was compelling, but far from definitive. The risks of failure were daunting. The stakes were significant for America's national security, our battle against al Qaeda, and our relationship with Pakistan. Most of all, the lives of those brave SEALs and helicopter pilots hung in the balance. It was as crisp and courageous a display of leadership as I've ever seen.

This book is about choices I made as Secretary of State and those made by President Obama and other leaders around the world. Some chapters are about events that made headlines; others are about the trendlines that will continue to define our world for future generations.

Of course, quite a few important choices, characters, countries, and events are not included here. To give them all the space they deserve, I would need many more pages. I could fill a whole book just with thanks to the talented and dedicated colleagues I relied on at the State Department. I have enormous gratitude for their service and friendship.

As Secretary of State I thought of our choices and challenges in three categories: The problems we inherited, including two wars and a global financial crisis; the new, often unexpected events and emerging threats, from the shifting sands of the Middle East to the turbulent waters of the Pacific to the uncharted terrain of cyberspace; and the opportunities presented by an increasingly networked world that could help lay the foundation for American prosperity and leadership in the 21st century.

I approached my work with confidence in our country's enduring strengths and purpose, and humility about how much remains beyond our knowledge and control. I worked to reorient American foreign policy around what I call "smart power." To succeed in the 21st century, we need to integrate the traditional tools of foreign policy—diplomacy, development assistance, and military force—while also tapping the energy and ideas of the private sector and empowering citizens, especially the activists, organizers, and problem solvers we call civil society, to meet their own challenges and shape their own futures. We have to use all of America's strengths to build a world with more partners and fewer adversaries, more shared responsibility and fewer conflicts, more good jobs and less poverty, more broadly based prosperity with less damage to our environment.

As is usually the case with the benefit of hindsight, I wish we could go back and revisit certain choices. But I'm proud of what we accomplished. This century began traumatically for our country, with the terrorist attacks on 9/11, the long wars that followed, and the Great Recession. We needed to do better, and I believe we did.

These years were also a personal journey for me, both literally (I ended up visiting 112 countries and traveling nearly one million miles) and figuratively, from the painful end of the 2008 campaign to an unexpected partnership and friendship with my former rival Barack Obama. I've served our country in one way or another for decades. Yet during my years as Secretary of State, I learned even more about our exceptional strengths and what it will take for us to compete and thrive at home and abroad.

I hope this book will be of use to anyone who wants to know what America stood for in the early years of the 21st century, as well as how the Obama Administration confronted great challenges in a perilous time.

While my views and experiences will surely be scrutinized by followers of Washington's long-running soap opera—who took what side, who opposed whom, who was up and who was down—I didn't write this book for them.

I wrote it for Americans and people everywhere who are trying to make sense of this rapidly changing world of ours, who want to understand how leaders and nations can work together and why they sometimes collide, and how their decisions affect all our lives: How a collapsing economy in Athens, Greece, affects businesses in Athens, Georgia. How a revolution in Cairo, Egypt, impacts life in Cairo, Illinois. What a tense diplomatic encounter in St. Petersburg, Russia, means for families in St. Petersburg, Florida.

Not every story in this book has a happy ending or even an ending yet—that's not the world we live in—but all of them are stories about people we can learn from whether we agree with them or not. There are still heroes out there: peacemakers who persevered when success seemed impossible, leaders who ignored politics and pressure to make tough decisions, men and women with the courage to leave the past behind in order to shape a new and better future. These are some of the stories I tell.

I wrote this book to honor the exceptional diplomats and development experts whom I had the honor of leading as America's sixty-seventh Secretary of State. I wrote it for anyone anywhere who wonders whether the United States still has what it takes to lead. For me, the answer is a resounding "Yes." Talk of America's decline has become commonplace, but my faith in our future has never been greater. While there are few problems in today's world that the United States can solve alone, there are even fewer that can be solved without the United States. Everything that I have done and seen has convinced me that America remains the "indispensable nation." I am just as convinced, however, that our leadership is not a birthright. It must be earned by every generation.

And it will be—so long as we stay true to our values and remember that, before we are Republicans or Democrats, liberals or conservatives, or any of the other labels that divide us as often as define us, we are Americans, all with a personal stake in our country.

When I began this book, shortly after leaving the State Department, I considered a number of titles. Helpfully, the *Washington Post* asked its readers to send in suggestions. One proposed "It Takes a World," a fitting sequel to *It Takes a Village*. My favorite was "The Scrunchie Chronicles: 112 Countries and It's Still All about My Hair."

In the end, the title that best captured my experiences on the high wire of international diplomacy and my thoughts and feelings about what it will take to secure American leadership for the 21st century was *Hard Choices*.

One thing that has never been a hard choice for me is serving our country. It has been the greatest honor of my life.

HARD CHOICES

PART ONE

A Fresh Start

1

2008: Team of Rivals

Why on earth was I lying on the backseat of a blue minivan with tinted windows? Good question. I was trying to leave my home in Washington, D.C., without being seen by the reporters staked out front.

It was the evening of June 5, 2008, and I was heading to a secret meeting with Barack Obama—and not the one I had hoped for and expected until just a few months earlier. I had lost and he had won. There hadn't been time yet to come to grips with that reality. But here we were. The Presidential primary campaign was historic because of his race and my gender, but it had also been grueling, heated, long, and close. I was disappointed and exhausted. I had campaigned hard to the very end, but Barack had won and now it was time to support him. The causes and people I had campaigned for, the Americans who had lost jobs and health care, who couldn't afford gas or groceries or college, who had felt invisible to their government for the previous seven years, now depended on his becoming the forty-fourth President of the United States.

This was not going to be easy for me, or for my staff and supporters who had given it their all. In fairness, it wasn't going to be easy for Barack and his supporters either. His campaign was as wary of me and my team as we were of them. There had been hot rhetoric and bruised feelings on both sides, and, despite a lot of pressure from his backers, I had refused to quit until the last vote was counted.

Barack and I had spoken two days earlier, late in the evening after the final primaries in Montana and South Dakota. "Let's sit down when it makes sense for you," he said. The next day we crossed paths backstage at a long-scheduled conference for the American Israel Public Affairs Committee in Washington. While a bit awkward, it gave our closest aides a chance to begin discussing details about a meeting. For me, that was my traveling Chief of Staff, Huma Abedin, the savvy, indefatigable, and gracious young woman who had worked for me since my time in the White House. For Obama, it was Reggie Love, the former Duke University basketball player who rarely left Barack's side. Huma and Reggie had kept open a line of communication even during the most intense days of the campaign, a hotline of sorts, in part because after every primary, no matter who won, either Barack or I called the other to concede and offer congratulations. We exchanged calls that were cordial, sometimes even lighthearted, since at least one person on the line had reason to be in a good mood. But more than a few calls were curt, just checking the box. Football coaches meet midfield after a game, but they don't always hug.

We needed a place away from the media spotlight to meet and talk, so I called my good friend Senator Dianne Feinstein of California to ask if we could use her Washington home. I'd been there before and thought it would work well for us to come and go without drawing attention. The ruse succeeded. I slid around in the van's backseat as we took the sharp left turn at the end of my street onto Massachusetts Avenue, and I was on my way.

I got there first. When Barack arrived, Dianne offered us each a glass of California Chardonnay and then left us in her living room, sitting in wing chairs facing each other in front of the fireplace. Despite our clashes over the past year, we had developed a respect for each other rooted in our shared experiences. Running for President is intellectually demanding, emotionally draining, and physically taxing. But crazy as a national campaign can be, it is our democracy in action, warts and all. Seeing that up close helped us appreciate each other for having gotten into "the arena," as Theodore Roosevelt called it, and going all the way.

By the time of our meeting I had known Barack for four years, two of which we spent debating each other. Like many Americans, I was impressed by his speech at the 2004 Democratic National Convention in Boston. Earlier that year I had supported his Senate campaign by hosting a fund-raiser at our home in Washington and attending one in Chicago. In my Senate office, to the surprise of many as time went on, I kept a photo of him, Michelle, their daughters, and me taken at that Chicago event. The photo was where I left it when I returned to the Senate full-time after the primaries. As colleagues, we had worked together on a number of shared priorities and legislation. After Hurricane Katrina, Bill and I invited Barack to join us in Houston with President George H. W. and Barbara Bush to visit evacuees from the storm and meet with emergency management officials.

We were both lawyers who got our start as grassroots activists for social justice. Early in my career I worked for the Children's Defense Fund, registered Hispanic voters in Texas, and represented poor people as a Legal Aid attorney. Barack was a community organizer on the South Side of Chicago. We had very different personal stories and experiences, but we shared the old-fashioned idea that public service is a noble endeavor, and we believed deeply in the basic bargain at the heart of the American Dream: No matter who you are or where you come from, if you work hard and play by the rules, you should have the opportunity to build a good life for yourself and your family.

But campaigns are based on highlighting differences, and ours was no exception. Despite our general agreement on most issues, we found plenty of reasons to disagree and exploited any opening to draw a contrast. And although I understood that high-stakes political campaigns are not for the fainthearted or thin-skinned, both Barack and I and our staffs had long lists of grievances. It was time to clear the air. We had a White House to win, and it was important for the country, and for me personally, to move on.

We stared at each other like two teenagers on an awkward first date, taking a few sips of Chardonnay. Finally Barack broke the ice by ribbing me a bit about the tough campaign I had run against him. Then he asked for my help uniting our party and winning the presidency. He wanted the two of us to appear together soon, and he wanted the Democratic National Convention in Denver to be unified and energized. He emphasized that he wanted Bill's help as well.

I had already decided that I would agree to his request for help, but I also needed to raise some of the unpleasant moments of the past year. Neither of us had had total control over everything said or done in our campaigns, let alone by our most passionate supporters or by the political press, including a large herd of bloggers. Remarks on both sides, including some of my own, had been taken out of context, but the preposterous charge of racism against Bill was particularly painful. Barack made clear that neither he nor his team believed that accusation. As to the sexism that surfaced during the campaign, I knew that it arose from cultural and psychological attitudes about women's roles in society, but that didn't make it any easier for me and my supporters. In response Barack spoke movingly about his grandmother's struggle in business and his great pride in Michelle, Malia, and Sasha and how strongly he felt they deserved full and equal rights in our society.

The candor of our conversation was reassuring and reinforced my resolve to support him. While I would definitely have preferred to be asking for his support instead of the other way around, I knew his success was now the best way to advance the values and progressive policy agenda I had spent the past two years—and a lifetime—fighting for.

When he asked what he needed to do to convince my supporters to join his campaign, I said he'd need to give them time, but a genuine effort to make them feel welcome would persuade the vast majority to come around. After all, he was now the standard-bearer for our agenda. If I could shift from doing my best to beat him to doing everything I could to elect him President, so could they. Eventually almost all of them did.

After an hour and a half, we'd both said what we wanted to say and talked about how to move forward. Later that night Barack emailed a proposed joint statement that would be released by his campaign confirming the meeting and our "productive discussion" about what "needs to be done to succeed in November." He also asked for a number to call Bill so that they could speak directly.

The next day, June 6, Bill and I hosted my campaign staff in the backyard of our house in D.C. It was a boiling hot day. We all tried not to overheat as we reminisced about the unbelievable twists and turns of the primary season. Being surrounded by the dedicated team that had fought so hard for me was inspiring and humbling. Some were friends who had worked with us on campaigns going all the way back to Arkansas. For many of the younger people, this was their first race. I didn't want them to be discouraged by defeat or turned off of electoral politics and public service, so I told them to be proud of the campaign we'd run and to keep working for the causes and candidates we believed in. I also knew I had to lead by example, and while my fireside chat with Barack the night before was a start, it was only that. It would take time for many to get past all that had happened, and I knew that people would be taking their cues from me. So, starting right then, I made clear I would be supporting Barack Obama 100 percent.

Despite the circumstances, people relaxed and had a good time. My dear friend Stephanie Tubbs Jones, the fearless African American Congresswoman from Ohio who resisted intense pressure and stayed by my side throughout the primaries, dangled her feet in the swimming pool and told funny stories. Two months later she would die suddenly from a brain aneurism, a terrible loss for her family and constituents and for me and my family. For this day at least, we were still sisters in arms, looking forward to better days ahead.

I signed off on the time and place for my final campaign appearance the next day and began to work on my speech. Writing this one was complicated. I had to thank my supporters, celebrate the historic significance of my campaign as the first woman to win a primary, and endorse Barack in a way that would help him in the general election. That was a lot of freight for one speech to carry, and I didn't have much time to get it right. I remembered bitter primary battles that went all the way to the Convention, especially Ted Kennedy's failed challenge to President Carter in 1980, and I would not let that history repeat itself. It would not be good for our party or for the country, so I was going to move quickly to publicly back Barack and campaign for him.

I wanted to strike the right balance between respecting my voters' support and looking toward the future. In person and over the phone, I went back and forth with speechwriters and advisors seeking the right tone and language. Jim Kennedy, an old friend with a magic touch for evocative language, had woken up in the middle of the night thinking about how the 18 million people who had voted for me had each added a hole in the ultimate glass ceiling. That gave me something to build on. I didn't want to repeat the standard bromides; this endorsement had to be in my own words, a convincing personal argument about why we should all work to elect Barack. I stayed up until the early hours of the morning, sitting at our kitchen table with Bill making revisions to draft after draft.

I gave my speech on Saturday, June 7, at the National Building Museum in Washington. We'd had trouble finding a location that could hold the expected number of supporters and press. I was relieved when we settled on what used to be called the "Pension Building," with its soaring columns and high ceilings. Originally built to serve Civil War veterans, widows, and orphans, it is a monument to the American spirit of shared responsibility. Bill, Chelsea, and my then eighty-nine-year-old mother, Dorothy Rodham, were with me as I made my way through the crowd to the podium. People were crying before I even started talking.

The atmosphere was a bit like a wake, charged with sadness and anger to be sure, but also with pride and even love. One woman wore a huge "Hillary for Pope!" button. Well, that certainly wasn't in the stars, but I was moved by the sentiment.

If the speech was hard to write, it was even harder to deliver. I felt I had let down so many millions of people, especially the women and girls who had invested their dreams in me. I started by thanking everyone who had campaigned and voted for me; I told them I believed in public service and would remain committed to "helping people solve their problems and live their dreams."

I gave a special shout-out to the women of my mother's generation, who were born before women even had the right to vote but lived long enough to see my campaign for President. One of them was eighty-eight-year-old Florence Steen of South Dakota, who insisted that her daughter bring an absentee ballot to her hospice bedside so she could vote in the Democratic primary. She passed away before the election, though, so under state law her ballot didn't count. But her daughter later told a reporter, "My dad's an ornery old cowboy, and he didn't like it when he heard mom's vote wouldn't be counted. I don't think he had voted in 20 years. But he voted in place of my mom." Being a vessel for the hopes and prayers of millions of people was a daunting responsibility, and I tried never to forget that the campaign was about them far more than it was about me.

I addressed the disappointment of my supporters directly: "Although we weren't able to shatter that highest, hardest glass ceiling this time, thanks to you, it's got about 18 million cracks in it. And the light is shining through like never before, filling us all with the hope and the sure knowledge that the path will be a little easier next time. That has always been the history of progress in America." I pledged, "You will always find me on the front lines of democracy—fighting for the future." Then I added, "The way to continue our fight now, to accomplish the goals for which we stand, is to take our energy, our passion, our strength and do all we can to help elect Barack Obama the next President of the United States."

As hard as all this was for me, I learned a lot from losing. I had experienced my share of personal and public disappointments over the years, but until 2008 I had enjoyed an unusual run of electoral successes—first as part of my husband's campaigns in Arkansas and for President, and then in my races for Senate in 2000 and 2006. The night of the Iowa caucuses, when I placed third, was excruciating.

As I moved on to New Hampshire, and then across the country, I found my footing and my voice. My spirits were lifted and my determination hardened by the many Americans I met along the way. I dedicated my victory in the Ohio primary to everyone across America "who's ever been counted out but refused to be knocked out, and for everyone who has stumbled but stood right back up, and for everyone who works hard and never gives up." The stories of the people I met reaffirmed my faith in the unbounded promise of our country but also drove home just how much we had to do to ensure that that promise was shared by all. And although the campaign was long and exhausting, and cost way too much money, in the end the process succeeded in offering voters a real choice about the future of the country.

One silver lining of defeat was that I came out of the experience realizing I no longer cared so much about what the critics said about me. I learned to take criticism seriously but not personally, and the campaign certainly tested me on that. It also freed me. I could let my hair down— literally. Once, in an interview during a trip to India when I was Secretary of State, Jill Dougherty of CNN asked about the media's obsession with my showing up in foreign capitals after long flights wearing glasses and no makeup. "Hillary Au Naturale" she called it. I had to laugh. "I feel so relieved to be at the stage I'm at in my life right now, Jill, because if I want to wear my glasses, I'm wearing my glasses. If I want to pull my hair back, I'm pulling my hair back." Some of the reporters covering me at the State Department were surprised when I occasionally ditched the diplomatic talking points and said exactly what was on my mind, whether it was telling off the leader of North Korea or pushing the Pakistanis on the whereabouts of Osama bin Laden. But I no longer had much patience for walking on eggshells.

Losing also would give me the chance to talk to leaders of other nations about how to accept difficult verdicts at home and move forward for the good of one's country. All over the world there are heads of state who claim to stand for democracy, but then do all they can to suppress it when voters protest or decide to vote them out of office. I realized I had the chance to offer a different model. Of course, I was lucky to have lost to a candidate whose views dovetailed closely with my own and who had taken such pains to include me on his team. Still, the fact that we had been fierce opponents and were now working together was a pretty impressive argument for democracy—one that I would find myself making in the years to come time and time again around the world in a job I had no idea I'd be doing.

=====

Three weeks after my speech at the Building Museum, I was on the way to Unity, New Hampshire, a town chosen for my first joint appearance with Barack not only for its name but also because we had both gotten exactly the same number of votes there in the primary: 107 votes for Barack and 107 for me. We met in Washington and flew together on his campaign plane. When we landed there was a large tour bus waiting to take us the nearly two hours to Unity. I thought back to the amazing bus tour Bill and I took with Al and Tipper Gore right after the 1992 Democratic Convention and remembered Timothy Crouse's famous book about the 1972 campaign, *The Boys on the Bus*. This time I was the "girl" on the bus, and the candidate wasn't me or my husband. I took a deep breath and got on board.

Barack and I sat together talking easily. I shared some of our experiences raising a daughter in the White House. He and Michelle were already thinking about what life might be like for Malia and Sasha if he won. The rally itself, in a big field on a gorgeous summer day, was designed to send an unmistakable message: the primary was behind us and we were now one team. People chanted both our names as we walked on stage to U2's "Beautiful Day." Large letters behind the crowd spelled out U-N-I-T-Y, and a blue banner behind the stage read, "Unite for Change." "Today and every day going forward," I told the crowd, "we stand shoulder to shoulder for the ideals we share, the values we cherish, and the country we love." When I finished, they started cheering, "Thank you, Hillary. Thank you, Hillary." Even Barack joined in. "You guys peeked at my speech. You already know the first line," he joked. Then he spoke eloquently and generously about the race I had run. Bill and Barack had a long talk a few days later, clearing up lingering issues from the primaries and agreeing to campaign together.

The biggest event of the summer was the Democratic National Convention in Denver at the end of August. I had attended every Democratic convention since 1976, and, for obvious reasons, I had particularly fond memories from 1992 in New York and 1996 in Chicago. This time Barack asked me to deliver a prime-time speech formally nominating him, and I agreed.

When the time came, Chelsea introduced me. I could not have been prouder of her or more grateful for how hard she had worked throughout the long primary campaign. She had crisscrossed the country on her own, speaking to young people and energizing crowds everywhere she went. Seeing her standing there before the packed convention hall, I couldn't get over how poised and altogether adult she had become.

Soon it was my turn. I was greeted by a sea of red-white-and-blue "Hillary" signs. For as many speeches as I'd given, this was a big one, in front of a huge audience in the arena and millions more watching on TV. I have to admit I was nervous. I tinkered with the speech right up until the very last minute, so that when my motorcade arrived one of my aides had to leap out of the van and sprint ahead to hand the thumb drive to the teleprompter operator. The Obama campaign had asked to see it much earlier, and when I didn't share it, some of his advisors worried I must be hiding something they wouldn't want me to say. But I was simply using every second I had to get it right.

It was not the speech I had long hoped to deliver at this convention, but it was an important one. "Whether you voted for me, or you voted for Barack, the time is now to unite as a single party with a single purpose. We are on the same team, and none of us can afford to sit on the sidelines. This is a fight for the future. And it's a fight we must win together," I told the crowd. "Barack Obama is my candidate. And he must be our President." Afterward Joe Biden greeted me outside the green room, falling on bent knee to kiss my hand. (Who says chivalry is dead!) Barack called from Billings, Montana, to thank me.

Earlier that day I had run into Michelle backstage at an event, and she was also appreciative of everything we were doing to help Barack. Of course, Bill was not the only spouse in the race, and Barack and I both learned that often it's your family who take attacks on you the hardest. But Michelle and I bonded over the challenges of raising a family in the public eye. Months later, over a private lunch in the Yellow Oval Room on the second floor of the White House, we talked about how the new

First Family was settling in and her plans to combat childhood obesity through healthier eating and exercise. We sat at a small table looking out the windows facing south, over the Truman Balcony, toward the Washington Monument. This was my first visit back to the family quarters since leaving on January 20, 2001. I loved seeing the residence staff, who help every President's family feel at home in the White House. When I became First Lady back in 1993, it meant so much to me to hear from Jacqueline Kennedy, Lady Bird Johnson, Betty Ford, Rosalynn Carter, Nancy Reagan, and Barbara Bush about their experiences. Only a few of us have had the privilege of living in the People's House, and I wanted to provide any support I could.

I had thought my speech to the convention would be my only role there, but a determined group of my delegates still intended to vote for me during the roll call of the states. The Obama campaign asked if I would go to the convention the next day and interrupt the roll call and instead move for an immediate declaration that Barack Obama was our party's nominee. I agreed but understood why more than a few of my friends, supporters, and delegates begged me not to do it. They wanted to finish what they had started. They also wanted history to record that a woman had won nearly two dozen primaries and caucuses and close to one thousand nine hundred delegates, something that had never happened before. They argued that if the roll call was cut short, our efforts would never be properly recognized. I couldn't help but be moved by their fierce loyalty, but I thought it was more important to show that we were completely united.

Some of my supporters were also upset that Barack had chosen Biden to be his running mate instead of me. But I was never interested in being Vice President. I was looking forward to returning to the Senate, where I hoped to help lead the charge on health care reform, job creation, and other urgent challenges. I heartily approved of Barack's choice and knew Joe would be an asset in the election and in the White House.

We kept my going to the floor a secret, so it caused quite a stir among the delegates and reporters when I suddenly appeared among the thousands of excited Democrats just as New York was called to announce its votes. Surrounded by friends and colleagues, I declared, "With eyes firmly fixed on the future, in the spirit of unity, with the goal of victory, with faith in our party and our country, let's declare together in one voice right here, right now, that Barack Obama is our candidate and he will be our

President." Then I moved to suspend the roll call and nominate Barack by acclamation. Up at the podium, Speaker of the House Nancy Pelosi asked if there was a second for my motion, and the whole convention roared its approval. The atmosphere crackled with energy and history in the making as we rallied together behind the first African American nominee of a major party.

There was one more big surprise that week. The morning after Barack addressed the convention, Senator John McCain, the presumptive Republican nominee, announced that Governor Sarah Palin of Alaska was his choice for running mate. A resounding "Who?" echoed across the nation. We would all get to know her in the coming months, but at that point she was a near-complete unknown, even to political junkies. The Obama campaign suspected that her nomination was a blatant attempt to scuttle their hope of welcoming the women who had vigorously supported me. They immediately issued a dismissive statement and reached out to me in the hopes I would follow suit. But I wouldn't. I was not going to attack Palin just for being a woman appealing for support from other women. I didn't think that made political sense, and it didn't feel right. So I said no, telling them there'd be plenty of time for criticism. A few hours later, the Obama campaign reversed itself and congratulated Governor Palin.

Over the following weeks, Bill and I attended more than one hundred events and fund-raisers in which we spoke with supporters and undecided voters and advocated for Barack and Joe. On the morning of November 4—Election Day—we went to a local elementary school near our home in Chappaqua, New York, to cast our votes. It was the end of an unbelievably long journey. That night Bill was glued to the television, doing what he always does on election nights: analyzing all the data he could find on turnout and early exit polls. Now that there was nothing more we could do to help, I tried to stay busy with other things until there was a result. It turned out to be a decisive victory, without the drawn-out waiting game we had seen in 2004 or, famously, in 2000. Huma called Reggie Love, and soon I was congratulating the President-elect. (That's how I started thinking of him, referring to him, and addressing him the moment the election was over, just as after the inauguration he would become "Mr. President.") I was elated, proud, and, frankly, relieved. It was time to exhale, and I was looking forward to getting back to the life and work I loved.

Five days after the election was a quiet Sunday afternoon, offering the perfect chance to decompress. The autumn air was crisp, and Bill and I decided to go to Mianus River Gorge, one of the many trails near where we live in Westchester County. With our hectic lives, we often seek to clear our minds with long walks together. I remember that one as particularly liberating. The election was over, and I could get back to my job in the Senate. I loved representing the people of New York, and the campaign had left me with a full agenda that I was eager to push forward. I was brimming with ideas, all of which I hoped would be strengthened by a close relationship with the incoming President.

Little did I know how close that relationship would become. In the middle of our walk, Bill's cell phone rang. When he answered he heard the voice of the President-elect, who told him he wanted to talk to both of us. Bill explained that we were in the middle of a nature preserve and needed to call back when we got home. Why was he calling? Maybe he wanted our input on the team he was putting together. Or to strategize about a major policy challenge, like economic recovery or health care reform. Or perhaps he simply wanted to line up our help for a quick burst of legislative activity in the spring. Bill, remembering his own hectic transition, guessed that he wanted to run names by us for White House and Cabinet positions.

When we got back to our house, Bill's prediction about the call proved to be accurate—for him. The President-elect picked his brain about possible members of the economic team he was assembling to tackle the financial crisis facing the country. Then he told Bill that he was looking forward to getting together with me sometime soon. I assumed he wanted to talk about working closely together on his legislative package in the Senate.

But I was curious, so I called a few members of my Senate staff to see what they thought, including my spokesman, Philippe Reines. Philippe is passionate, loyal, and shrewd. He usually knows what Washington's movers and shakers are thinking even before they do. And I can always trust him to speak his mind. This time was no different. Philippe had told me two days earlier about rumors that I would be named everything from Secretary of Defense to Postmaster General, but he had confidently predicted, "He's going to offer you Secretary of State." "That's ridiculous!" I responded immediately. "Not for a million reasons!" I thought, not for the first time, that Philippe was delusional. And frankly I was not interested in serving in the Cabinet. I wanted to go back to the Senate and my work for New York. From 9/11 to the financial crash of 2008, it had been a rough eight years for New Yorkers. They had taken a chance on me back in 2000, and now they needed a strong and committed advocate in Washington. And I liked being my own boss and setting my own schedule and agenda. Joining the Cabinet would mean giving up some of that autonomy.

When I called Philippe on Sunday, he informed me that the media had started its cycle of speculation. ABC's *This Week* mentioned rumors that President-elect Obama was considering me for the position of Secretary of State. The program added that he was attracted by the idea of having a "team of rivals" in the Cabinet, an allusion to the 2005 best-selling history by Doris Kearns Goodwin, recounting Abraham Lincoln's choice in 1860 of William Henry Seward, a Senator from New York, to be his Secretary of State after defeating him for the Republican nomination.

Over time I had become a big fan of Seward's, so this parallel was particularly intriguing to me. He was one of the leading lights of his day, a principled reformer, a strong critic of slavery, Governor and Senator from New York, and ultimately Secretary of State. He also helped President Lincoln draft the Proclamation of Thanksgiving, marking the day as an American holiday. He was described by a contemporary as "ruffled or excited never, astute, keen to perceive a joke, appreciative of a good thing, and fond of 'good victuals.'" I could relate to that.

Seward had been a well-regarded Senator from New York when he tried to get the presidential nomination, before running into a versatile, up-and-coming politician from Illinois. The parallel was not perfect; I hope no one ever describes me as a "wise macaw," which is how Seward appeared to the historian Henry Adams. And I was privately amused that the man who did more than anyone to thwart Seward's chances for President was the journalist Horace Greeley, who has a prominent statue in Chappaqua.

Seward also appealed to me for reasons that went deeper than historical coincidences. I had been to his house in Auburn, New York, a stop on the Underground Railroad for slaves fleeing to freedom from the South. It was filled with mementos of an extraordinary career and his fourteen-month trip around the world after leaving office. The diplomatic gallery includes tributes from nearly all of the world's leaders, most of whom were crowned monarchs, paying tribute to a humble servant of democracy.

For all his worldliness, Seward was deeply devoted to his constituents, and they to him. He spoke eloquently about the inclusive country America could be. And he followed up his words with actions. Harriet Tubman, the heroic conductor of the Underground Railroad, settled in a house in Seward's hometown, on land purchased from Seward himself. His friendship with Lincoln was especially moving. After conceding defeat in their contest for the nomination, Seward worked hard for Lincoln's election, crossing the country by rail and giving speeches. He soon became one of Lincoln's trusted advisors. He was there at the beginning, suggesting the breathtaking final paragraph of Lincoln's first inaugural address, which Lincoln turned into an appeal to "the better angels of our nature." And he was there at the end; the plot to kill Lincoln included a coordinated attack on Seward as well, though he survived. Lincoln and Seward traveled a great distance together, and their friendship and hard work helped save the Union.

Seward's work was not quite done when the Civil War ended. In 1867, in a final burst of statesmanship, he engineered the purchase of Alaska from Russia. The price, $7.2 million, was considered so extravagant that the deal was called "Seward's Folly," although we now realize it was one of the great land transactions in American history (and a steal at 2 cents an acre). Right after graduating from college, I spent a memorable few months in Alaska, gutting fish and washing dishes. Now, as my name began to be referenced more often in connection with the job at State, I started to wonder if Seward's ghost was following me. Still, I had to ask myself, if the President-elect asked me to serve, was it pure folly to abandon the Senate and my entire domestic agenda for a short-term assignment at State?

———

The night after President-elect Obama's phone call with Bill, a reporter at *Glamour*'s Women of the Year awards ceremony in New York City asked me on my way into the event whether I would consider accepting a position in the Obama Administration. I expressed what I was feeling at the time: "I am happy being a Senator from New York." That was true. But I was also enough of a realist to know that anything can happen in politics.

The morning of Thursday, November 13, I flew to Chicago with Huma to meet with the President-elect, and made it there uneventfully. When we arrived at the transition headquarters, I was ushered into a large wood-paneled room furnished with a few chairs and one folding table, where I would meet alone with the President-elect.

He looked more relaxed and rested than he had for months. Even though he faced the most serious economic crisis since the Great Depression, he appeared confident. As I later saw him do often, he went straight to the point by skipping the small talk and asking me to serve as his Secretary of State. He told me he had been thinking of me for the position for a while and believed I was the best person—in his words, the only person—who could serve in that role at this moment in time, with the unique challenges America faced at home and abroad.

Despite all the whispers, rumors, and point-blank questions, I was still floored. Only months before, Barack Obama and I had been locked in one of the hardest-fought primary campaigns in history. Now he was asking me to join his administration, in the most senior Cabinet post, fourth in the line of succession to the presidency. This was like a rerun of the final season of *The West Wing*; there, too, the new President-elect offers his defeated opponent the job of Secretary of State. In the TV version, the rival turns down the job at first, but the President-elect refuses to take no for an answer.

In real life, President-elect Obama presented a well-considered argument, explaining that he would have to concentrate most of his time and attention on the economic crisis and needed someone of stature to represent him abroad. I listened carefully and then respectfully declined his offer. Of course I was honored to be asked. I cared deeply about foreign policy and believed that it was essential to restore our country's damaged standing in the world. There were two wars to wind down, emerging threats to counter, and new opportunities to seize. But I also felt passionately invested in reversing the massive job losses we were seeing at home, fixing our broken health care system, and creating new opportunities for working families in America. People were hurting and needed a champion to fight for them. All of that and more was waiting for me in the Senate. Plus there were so many seasoned diplomats who I thought could also be great Secretaries. "What about Richard Holbrooke?" I suggested. "Or George Mitchell?" But the President-elect would not be put off, and I left saying that I would think about it. On the flight back to New York, I thought about nothing else.

Before I even landed back in New York, press speculation was intense. Two days later, "Obama's Talk with Clinton Creates Buzz" ran on the front page of the *New York Times*, noting that the prospect of my nomination as the nation's top diplomat could provide a "surprise ending" to the "Obama-Clinton drama" of the Presidential campaign. Out of respect for the President-elect, I avoided confirming that an offer had even been made.

I had promised to think it over, so I did. Over the course of the next week, I talked extensively with family, friends, and colleagues. Bill and Chelsea were patient listeners and urged me to carefully weigh the offer. My friends were evenly divided between enthusiasm and skepticism. I had a lot to think about and only a few days to make up my mind. The job *was* tantalizing, and I was confident I could do it well. I'd been grappling for years with the challenges facing the United States around the world, as both First Lady and Senator, and I already had relationships with many key leaders, from Angela Merkel in Germany to Hamid Karzai in Afghanistan.

John Podesta, a valued friend, the cochair of the Obama Transition Team, and a former Chief of Staff for my husband in the White House, called me on November 16 to talk over a few issues and to reinforce how much the President-elect wanted me to accept. We discussed some of the more practical concerns, like how I would pay off more than $6 million remaining from my campaign debt if I became Secretary of State and therefore would have to stay out of partisan politics. I also did not want to do anything that would limit the life-saving work Bill was doing around the world through the Clinton Foundation. Much was made in the press about possible conflicts of interest between his philanthropic efforts and my potential new position. That problem was quickly dispatched after the Presidential Transition Team vetted the Foundation's donors and Bill agreed to disclose all their names. Bill also had to give up holding overseas versions of the innovative philanthropy conference he had started, the Clinton Global Initiative, to avoid any perceived conflict. "The good you can do as Secretary of State will more than outweigh whatever work I have to cut back on," Bill assured me.

Throughout this process, and for the next four years, Bill was, as he had been for decades, my essential support and sounding board. He reminded me to focus on the "trendlines," not just the headlines, and to relish the experiences.

I sought the advice of a few of my trusted colleagues. Senators Dianne Feinstein and Barbara Mikulski and Congresswoman Ellen Tauscher encouraged me to accept, as did my fellow Senator from New York, Chuck Schumer. While many enjoyed pointing out how different Chuck and I were and how competitive we were at times, the truth is that he and I were a great team, and I respected his instincts. Senate Majority Leader Harry Reid surprised me when he told me the President-elect had asked him what he thought of the idea earlier in the fall, during a campaign stop in Las Vegas. He said that although he didn't want to lose me in the Senate, he didn't see how I could refuse the request.

And so my deliberations continued. One hour I leaned toward accepting; the next I was making plans for legislation I would introduce in the new session of Congress. I didn't know it then, but I later learned of the shenanigans my team and the President-elect's were playing to make it tough for me to say no. My staff told me it was Joe Biden's birthday so that I would call him two days earlier than the real date, giving Joe the opportunity to add to the cajoling. Incoming White House Chief of Staff Rahm Emanuel pretended the President-elect was indisposed when I tried to call to say no.

Finally, the President-elect and I spoke on the phone in the wee hours of November 20. He was attentive to my concerns, answered my questions, and was enthusiastic about the work we might do together. I told him that although Bill's charitable work and my campaign debt weighed on me, I was most worried about whether my highest and best use was serving in the Senate rather than the Cabinet. And, to be honest, I was looking for a more regular schedule after the long campaign. I laid all this out, and he listened patiently—and then assured me all my concerns could be addressed.

Shrewdly, the President-elect also steered the conversation away from the job offer and toward the job itself. We talked about the wars in Iraq and Afghanistan, the perpetual challenges posed by Iran and North Korea, and how the United States might emerge swiftly and confidently from the recession. It was great to exchange ideas in a comfortable private conversation after a year spent hammering away at each other under the hot lights of televised campaign debates. In retrospect, this conversation was even more important than it seemed at the time. We were laying the groundwork for a shared agenda that would guide American foreign policy for years to come.

Yet my answer was still no. The President-elect again refused to accept that. "I want to get to yes," he told me. "You're the best person for the job." He would not take no for an answer. That impressed me.

After I hung up, I stayed up most of the night. What would I expect if the tables were turned? Suppose I had been elected President and wanted Barack Obama to serve as my Secretary of State? Suppose I had inherited the challenges facing him? Of course I would want him to say yes—and quickly, so we could move on to other problems. I would want the most talented public servants to come together and work hard, for the good of the nation. The more I thought about it, the more I knew the President-elect was right. The country was in trouble, both at home and abroad. He needed a Secretary of State who could step immediately onto the global stage and begin repairing the damage we had inherited.

Finally, I kept returning to a simple idea: When your President asks you to serve, you should say yes. As much as I loved my work in the Senate and believed I had more to contribute there, he said he needed me in the State Department. My father served in the Navy in World War II, training young sailors to go off to fight in the Pacific. And although he often grumbled about the decisions various Presidents made in Washington, he and my mother instilled in me a deep sense of duty and service. It was reinforced by my family's Methodist faith, which taught us, "Do all the good you can, at all the times you can, to all the people you can, as long as ever you can." The call to service had helped me decide to take the plunge into elected office when I launched my first Senate campaign in 2000, and now it helped me make the hard choice to leave the Senate and accept the position of Secretary of State.

———

By the morning I had reached my decision, and I asked to speak to the President-elect one more time. He was delighted that I had come around. He guaranteed that I would have direct access to him and could see him alone whenever I needed to. He said I could choose my own team, though he would have some suggestions. As someone who had been in the White House, I knew how important both of those promises were. History had shown time and again that the State Department could be neglected by the White House, usually with negative results. The President-elect assured me that this time would be different: "I want to be sure you're successful."

He went on to say that he knew our foreign policy partnership would not be without mistakes and turbulence, but that we would strive to make the best decisions possible for our country. We had not yet developed the close relationship that would follow, but I was touched when he said, "Contrary to reports, I think we can become good friends." That comment stuck with me in the years to come.

The President fully lived up to his promises. He gave me free rein to choose my team, relied on my advice as his chief foreign policy advisor on the major decisions on his desk, and insisted on meeting often so we could speak candidly. He and I generally sat down together at least once a week when we weren't traveling. Then there were full Cabinet meetings, National Security Council meetings, and bilateral meetings with visiting foreign leaders—and those were just the meetings with the President in attendance. I also met regularly at the White House with the Secretary of Defense and the National Security Advisor. If you add it all up, despite my vigorous travel schedule, I was at the White House more than seven hundred times during my four years. After losing the election, I never expected to spend so much time there.

In the years to come, I wouldn't always agree with the President and other members of his team; some of those times you'll read about in this book, but others will remain private to honor the cone of confidentiality that should exist between a President and his Secretary of State, especially while he is still in office. But he and I developed a strong professional relationship and, over time, forged the personal friendship he had predicted and that I came to value deeply. Not too many weeks into the new administration, on a mild April afternoon, the President suggested we finish one of our weekly meetings at the picnic table outside the Oval Office on the South Lawn, right next to Malia and Sasha's new playground. That suited me perfectly. The press called it our "picnic table strategy session." I'd call it "Two folks having a good conversation."

On Monday, December 1, President-elect Obama announced me as his choice to serve as the sixty-seventh Secretary of State. As I stood next to him, he reiterated publicly what he had told me privately: "Hillary's appointment is a sign to friend and foe of the seriousness of my commitment to renew American diplomacy."

The next month, on January 20, 2009, I watched with my husband in the biting cold as Barack Obama took the oath of office. Our rivalry, once fierce, was over. Now we were partners.

2

Foggy Bottom: Smart Power

The first Secretary of State I ever met was Dean Acheson. He had served President Harry Truman at the beginning of the Cold War and was the embodiment of an imposing, old-school diplomat. I was a nervous college student about to deliver the first important public speech of my young life. It was the spring of 1969, and my Wellesley classmate and friend Eldie Acheson, the former Secretary's granddaughter, had decided our class needed its own speaker at graduation. After our college president approved the idea, my classmates asked me to speak about our tumultuous four years at Wellesley and provide a proper send-off into our unknown futures.

The night before graduation, with the speech still unfinished, I ran into Eldie and her family. She introduced me to her grandfather as "the girl who's going to speak tomorrow." The seventy-six-year-old had just completed his memoirs, *Present at the Creation*, which would go on to win the Pulitzer Prize the following year. Secretary Acheson smiled and shook my hand. "I'm looking forward to hearing what you have to say," he said. In a panic, I hurried back to my dorm to pull one last all-nighter.

I never imagined that forty years later I would follow in Acheson's footsteps at the State Department, affectionately known as "Foggy Bottom," after its D.C. neighborhood. Even my childhood dreams of becoming an astronaut would have seemed more realistic. Yet after I became Secretary of State, I often thought of the gray-haired elder statesman I met that night at Wellesley. Beneath his formal exterior, he was a highly imaginative diplomat, breaking protocol when he thought it was best for his country and his President.

America's leadership in the world resembles a relay race. A Secretary, a President, a generation are all handed the baton and asked to run a leg of the race as well as we can, and then we hand off the baton to our successors. Just as I benefited from actions taken by and lessons learned from my predecessors, initiatives begun during my years at the State Department have borne fruit since my departure, when I passed the baton to Secretary John Kerry.

I quickly learned that being Secretary of State is really three jobs in one: the country's chief diplomat, the President's principal advisor on foreign policy, and the CEO of a sprawling Department. From the start I had to balance my time and energy between competing imperatives. I had to lead our public and private diplomacy to repair strained alliances and build new partnerships. But I also had to conduct a fair amount of diplomacy within our own government, especially in the policy process at the White House and with Congress. And there was the work inside the Department itself, to get the most out of our talented people, improve morale, increase efficiency, and develop the capacities needed to meet new challenges.

A former Secretary called me with this advice: "Don't try to do everything at once." I heard the same thing from other Department veterans. "You can try to fix the policies, or you can try to fix the bureaucracy, but you can't do both."

Another piece of advice I heard frequently was: Pick a few big issues and own them. Neither admonition squared with the increasingly complex international landscape waiting for us. Perhaps there was a time when a Secretary of State could focus exclusively on a few priorities and let deputies and assistants handle the Department and the rest of the world. But those days were over. We'd learned the hard way (for example, in Afghanistan after the Soviet withdrawal in 1989) that neglecting regions and threats could have painful consequences. I would need to pay attention to the whole chessboard.

In the years since 9/11, America's foreign policy understandably had become focused on the biggest threats. And of course, we had to stay vigilant. But I also thought we should be doing more to seize the greatest opportunities, especially in the Asia-Pacific.

I wanted to deal with a range of emerging challenges that were going to require high-level attention and creative strategies, such as how to manage competition for undersea energy resources from the Arctic to the Pacific, whether to stand up to economic bullying by powerful state-owned enterprises, and how to connect with young people around the world newly empowered by social media, to name just a few. I knew there would be traditionalists in the foreign policy establishment who would question whether it was worth a Secretary of State's time to think about the impact of Twitter, or start programs for women entrepreneurs, or advocate on behalf of American businesses abroad. But I saw it all as part of the job of a 21st-century diplomat.

The newly chosen members of the incoming Obama Administration's national security team met for six hours in Chicago on December 15. It was our first discussion since the announcement of our nominations two weeks earlier. We quickly dove into some of the thorniest policy dilemmas we would face, including the status of the wars in Iraq and Afghanistan and the prospects for peace in the Middle East. We also discussed at length a problem that has proven very difficult to solve: how to fulfill the President-elect's promise to close the military prison at Guantánamo Bay, Cuba, which remains open all these years later.

I came to the Obama Administration with my own ideas about both American leadership and foreign policy, as well as about the teamwork any President should expect from the members of his National Security Council. I intended to be a vigorous advocate for my positions within the administration. But as I knew from history and my own experience, the sign on Harry Truman's desk in the Oval Office was correct: the buck did stop with the President. And because of the long primary battle, I also knew the press would be looking—even hoping—for any signs of discord between me and the White House. I intended to deprive them of that story.

I was impressed by the people the President-elect had chosen for his team. Vice President–elect Joe Biden brought a wealth of international experience from his leadership of the Senate Foreign Relations Committee. His warmth and humor would be very welcome during long hours in the White House Situation Room. Every week, Joe and I tried to meet for a private breakfast at the Naval Observatory, his official residence, which is near my home. Always the gentleman, he would meet me at the car and walk me to a sunny nook off the porch, where we would eat and talk. Sometimes we agreed, sometimes we disagreed, but I always appreciated our frank and confidential conversations.

I had known Rahm Emanuel for years. He started with my husband early in the 1992 campaign, served in the White House, and then went home to Chicago and ran for Congress. He was a rising star in the House and led the campaign that produced a new Democratic majority in 2006, but gave up his seat when President Obama asked him to be White House Chief of Staff. Later he would be elected Mayor of Chicago. Rahm was famous for his forceful personality and vivid language (that's putting it politely), but he was also a creative thinker, an expert in the legislative process, and a great asset to the President. During the hard-fought primary campaign, Rahm had stayed neutral because of his strong ties to both me and then-Senator Obama, telling his hometown *Chicago Tribune*, "I'm hiding under the desk." Now that we were all serving together, Rahm would provide some of the initial glue holding this "team of rivals" together. He offered a friendly ear and an open door in the West Wing, and we talked frequently.

The new National Security Advisor was retired Marine General James Jones, whom I had gotten to know from my time on the Senate Armed Services Committee, when he served as Supreme Allied Commander Europe. He was a dignified, levelheaded, fair broker, with a sense of humor, all important qualities in a National Security Advisor.

General Jones's Deputy and eventual successor was Tom Donilon, whom I had known since the Carter Administration. Tom had served as Secretary of State Warren Christopher's Chief of Staff, so he understood and valued the State Department. He also shared my enthusiasm for increasing our engagement in the Asia-Pacific. Tom became a valued colleague who oversaw the difficult interagency policy process that analyzed options and teed up decisions for the President. He had a knack for asking hard questions that forced us to think even more rigorously about important policy decisions.

The President's choice for UN Ambassador was Susan Rice, who had served on the National Security Council staff and then as Assistant Secretary of State for African Affairs during the 1990s. During the primaries Susan was an active surrogate for the Obama campaign and often went on TV to attack me. I knew it was part of her job, and we put the past behind us and worked together closely—for example, to round up votes at the UN for new sanctions against Iran and North Korea and to authorize the mission to protect civilians in Libya.

In a surprise to many, the President kept on Secretary of Defense Robert Gates, who had a distinguished career serving eight Presidents of both parties at the CIA and National Security Council, before President George W. Bush lured him from Texas A&M in 2006 to replace Donald Rumsfeld at the Pentagon. I had seen Bob in action from my seat on Armed Services and thought he would provide continuity and a steady hand as we dealt with two inherited wars. He was also a convincing advocate for giving diplomacy and development more resources and a bigger role in our foreign policy. You'll rarely hear any official in turf-conscious Washington suggest that some other agency should get a more generous share of funding. But Bob, looking at the larger strategic picture after many years in which U.S. foreign policy was dominated by the military, believed it was time for more balance among what I was calling the 3 Ds of defense, diplomacy, and development.

The easiest place to see the imbalance was in the budget. Despite the popular belief that foreign aid accounted for at least a quarter of the federal budget, the truth was that for every dollar spent by the federal government, just one penny went to diplomacy and development. In a 2007 speech, Bob said that the foreign affairs budget was "disproportionately small relative to what we spend on the military." As he often pointed out, there were as many Americans serving in military marching bands as in the entire diplomatic corps.

We became allies from the start, tag-teaming Congress for a smarter national security budget and finding ourselves on the same side of many internal administration policy debates. We avoided the traditional infighting between State and Defense that in many previous administrations had come to resemble the Sharks and the Jets from *West Side Story*. We held joint meetings with Defense and Foreign Ministers, and sat together for interviews to present a united front on the foreign policy issues of the day.

In October 2009, we did a joint town hall event at George Washington University, broadcast and moderated by CNN. We were asked what it was like to work together. "Most of my career, the Secretaries of State and Defense weren't speaking to one another," Bob replied, drawing laughter.

"It could get pretty ugly, actually. So it's terrific to have the kind of relationship where we can talk together. . . . We get along, we work together well. I think it starts with, frankly, based on my experience as Secretary of Defense being willing to acknowledge that the Secretary of State is the principal spokesperson for United States foreign policy. And once you get over that hurdle, the rest of it kind of falls into place."

=====

Our team inherited a daunting list of challenges at a time of diminished expectations at home and abroad about America's ability to lead the world.

If you picked up a newspaper in those days or stopped by a Washington think tank, you were likely to hear that America was in decline. Soon after the Presidential election in 2008, the National Intelligence Council, a group of analysts and experts appointed by the Director of National Intelligence, published an alarming report titled *Global Trends 2025: A Transformed World*. It offered a bleak forecast of declining American influence, rising global competition, dwindling resources, and widespread instability. The intelligence analysts predicted that America's relative economic and military strength would decrease over the coming years and that the international system we had helped build and defend since World War II would be undermined by the growing influence of emerging economic powers like China, oil-rich nations like Russia and Iran, and nonstate actors like al Qaeda. In unusually stark terms they called it "an historic transfer of relative wealth and economic power from West to East."

Shortly before President Obama's inauguration, the Yale historian Paul Kennedy wrote a column for the *Wall Street Journal* under the headline "American Power Is on the Wane." Articulating a critique heard frequently in 2008 and 2009, Professor Kennedy blamed declining U.S. power on mounting debt, the severe economic impact of the Great Recession, and the "imperial overstretch" of the wars in Iraq and Afghanistan. He offered an evocative analogy to explain how he saw America losing its place as undisputed global leader: "A strong person, balanced and muscular, can carry an impressively heavy backpack uphill for a long while. But if that person is losing strength (economic problems), and the weight of the burden remains heavy or even increases (the Bush Doctrine), and the terrain becomes more difficult (rise of new Great Powers, international terrorism, failed states), then the once-strong hiker begins to slow and stumble. That is precisely when nimbler, less heavily burdened walkers get closer, draw abreast, and perhaps move ahead."

Nonetheless I remained fundamentally optimistic about America's future. My confidence was rooted in a lifetime of studying and experiencing the ups and downs of American history and a clear-eyed assessment of our comparative advantages relative to the rest of the world. Nations' fortunes rise and fall, and there will always be people predicting catastrophe just around the corner. But it's never smart to bet against the United States. Every time we've faced a challenge, whether war or depression or global competition, Americans have risen to meet it, with hard work and creativity.

I thought these pessimistic analyses undervalued many of America's strengths, including our capacity for resilience and reinvention. Our military was by far the most powerful in the world, our economy was still the biggest, our diplomatic influence was unrivaled, our universities set the global standard, and our values of freedom, equality, and opportunity still drew people from everywhere to our shores. When we needed to solve a problem anywhere in the world, we could call on dozens of friends and allies.

I believed that what happened to America was still largely up to Americans, as had always been the case. We just needed to sharpen our tools and put them to their best use. But all this talk of decline did underscore the scope of the challenges we faced. It reconfirmed my determination to take a page from Steve Jobs and "think different" about the role of the State Department in the 21st century.

====

Secretaries come and go every few years, but most of the people at the State Department and the U.S. Agency for International Development (USAID) stay far longer. Together those agencies employ about seventy thousand people around the world, the vast majority of whom are career professionals who serve continuously over several administrations. That's far fewer than the more than 3 million working for the Defense Department, but it's still a sizable number. When I became Secretary, the career professionals at State and USAID had been facing shrinking budgets and growing demands, and they were eager for leadership that championed the important work they did. I wanted to be that leader. To do so, I would need a senior team that shared my values and was relentlessly focused on getting results.

I recruited Cheryl Mills to be my Counselor and Chief of Staff. We had become friends when Cheryl served as Deputy Counsel in the White House during the 1990s. She talked fast and thought even faster; her intellect was like a sharp blade, slicing and dicing every problem she encountered. She also had a huge heart, boundless loyalty, rock-solid integrity, and a deep commitment to social justice. After the White House, Cheryl went on to hold distinguished legal and managerial positions in the private sector and at New York University, where she was serving as senior vice president. She told me she would help with my transition to State but did not want to leave NYU for a permanent role in the government. Thankfully, she changed her mind about that.

She helped me manage "the Building," which is what everyone at State calls the bureaucracy, and directly oversaw some of my key priorities, including food security, global health policy, LGBT rights, and Haiti. She also acted as my principal liaison to the White House on sensitive matters, including personnel issues. Despite the President's pledge that I could pick my own team, there were some heated debates early on with his advisors as I tried to recruit the best possible talent.

One debate was over Capricia Marshall, who I wanted for Chief of Protocol, the senior official responsible for welcoming foreign leaders to Washington, organizing summits, engaging with the diplomatic corps, traveling with the President abroad, and selecting the gifts he and I would present to our counterparts. As First Lady, I learned how important protocol is to diplomacy. Being a generous host and a gracious guest helps build relationships, while the alternative can result in unintended snubs. So I wanted to be sure we were at the top of our game.

As White House Social Secretary in the 1990s, Capricia already knew what the job required, but the White House wanted someone who had supported the President during the primaries. I thought this was shortsighted but understood that some friction and growing pains were inevitable as we worked to merge the sprawling entities known as Obamaworld and Hillaryland. "We're going to figure this out," I assured Capricia. "I wouldn't be pushing this if you weren't the right person for the job—and you are."

The President asked me if we needed a peace process between Cheryl and Denis McDonough, one of his closest advisors, but no intervention was required. They worked it out and Capricia got the job. I knew she would not disappoint, and she didn't. Denis later recounted the story of how he and his wife, Kari, heard Capricia do an interview on NPR one morning. Kari was enchanted and asked about this "absolutely elegant" diplomat. Denis admitted that he had originally opposed appointing her. Kari thought he was crazy, and Denis agreed. He later told Cheryl, "No wonder I lost that one. And good thing I did."

Capricia's success was a microcosm of the journey we all went through, from campaign rivals to respectful colleagues. Cheryl and Denis, the two lead combatants in our early dustups, became not only colleagues but also friends. They talked constantly nearly every day and met for early-morning breakfasts on the weekends, strategizing over eggs and hot chocolate. Near the end of my tenure as Secretary, the President sent a farewell note to Cheryl, saying that we had grown from a "team of rivals" into "an unrivaled team."

═══

I also was determined to recruit Richard Holbrooke, a force of nature who was widely viewed as the premier diplomat of our generation. His hands-on efforts brought peace to the Balkans in the 1990s. As UN Ambassador, he convinced Republicans to pay our UN dues and emphasized HIV/AIDS as a security issue. Soon after accepting the job as Secretary, I asked him to serve as our Special Representative for Afghanistan and Pakistan. From the first day in office the new administration would face serious questions about the future of the war in Afghanistan, especially whether to send more troops, as the military wanted. No matter what the President decided, we would need an intensified diplomatic and development effort in both countries. Richard had the experience and moxie to pursue that goal.

Another priority was, as ever, the pursuit of peace in the Middle East. I asked former Senator George Mitchell to lead our effort. George was Holbrooke's opposite, as buttoned up as Richard was wide open, but he had a wealth of experience and expertise. He had represented Maine in the Senate for fifteen years, including six as Majority Leader. After stepping down in the mid-1990s, he worked with my husband to midwife the Irish peace process. He later headed the Sharm el-Sheikh Fact-Finding

Committee, which investigated the second intifada, the Palestinian uprising that began in 2000.

Many Presidents and Secretaries of State had used Special Envoys for targeted missions and to coordinate policy on certain matters across our government. I had seen how well that could work. Some commentators said the appointment of high-profile diplomats like Holbrooke and Mitchell would diminish my role in important policy- and decision making. That's not the way I saw it. Appointing people who were qualified to serve as Secretary themselves enhanced my reach and the administration's credibility. They would be force multipliers, reporting to me but working closely with the White House. The President agreed and came to the State Department along with the Vice President to announce both Richard and George. I was proud that men of such stature would agree to serve in these roles as part of my team. After long and distinguished careers, neither Richard nor George needed to take on what were by any measure difficult, if not impossible, assignments. But they were patriots and public servants who answered the call.

I also needed top-notch Deputy Secretaries to help run the Department. President Obama's one personnel recommendation to me was that I consider Jim Steinberg for my Deputy Secretary for Policy. Some in the press speculated that Jim would be seen as an Obama plant and predicted there would be tension between us. I thought that was just silly. I had known Jim since he served as Deputy National Security Advisor during the Clinton Administration. During the 2008 primaries he offered foreign policy advice to both campaigns and both the President and I held him in high regard. He was also a student of the Asia-Pacific, a region I wanted to prioritize. I offered him the job, and in our first meeting I made it clear that I viewed us as one team. Jim felt exactly the same way. In mid-2011, Jim left to become dean of the Maxwell School at Syracuse University. I asked Bill Burns, an exceptionally talented and experienced career diplomat, to take his place.

Traditionally there had been only one Deputy Secretary of State. I learned that a second Deputy position, for management and resources, had been authorized by Congress but never filled. I was eager to bring in a senior manager who could help me fight for the resources the Department needed up on Capitol Hill and at the White House, and to make sure they were spent wisely. I chose Jack Lew, who had served as Director of the Office of Management and Budget at the end of the 1990s. His financial and management expertise would prove invaluable as we worked together to institute policy reviews and organizational changes.

When the President asked Jack to reprise his old role at OMB in 2010, he was seamlessly succeeded by Tom Nides, who had long experience in both business and public service. His years as Chief of Staff to Speaker of the House Tom Foley and then to my friend U.S. Trade Representative Mickey Kantor prepared him well to advocate for the Department with Congress and to go to bat for U.S. companies abroad. He brought superb negotiating skills to a number of thorny issues, including a highly sensitive standoff with Pakistan that he helped resolve in 2012.

=====

As my confirmation hearing before the Senate Foreign Relations Committee approached, I dove into intensive preparation. Jake Sullivan, an earnest and brilliant Minnesotan with impeccable credentials (Rhodes scholar, Supreme Court clerk, Senate aide), had been a trusted advisor on my Presidential campaign and had assisted then-Senator Obama with debate prep during the general election. I asked Jake to work with Lissa Muscatine, my friend and a former White House speechwriter, who reprised that role at State. They helped me formulate a clear message for the hearing and answers for what we anticipated would be questions on every issue under the sun. Jake went on to become my Deputy Chief of Staff for Policy and later Director of Policy Planning and was at my side nearly everywhere I went for the next four years.

A transition team, working with career professionals at State, deluged me with thick briefing books and in-person sessions on every topic imaginable, from the budget for the Building's cafeteria to the policy concerns of every member of Congress. I've seen my fair share of briefing books, and I was impressed with the depth, magnitude, and order of these State Department products. Great care went into the smallest details, and a broad (at times byzantine) clearance process allowed experts from across the Department and the wider government to weigh in on the substance.

Beyond the formal briefing process, I spent those weeks reading, thinking, and reaching out to experts and friends. Bill and I took long walks, talking about the state of the world. Our old friend Tony Blair visited me at home in Washington in early December. He updated me on his work with the "Quartet"—the United States, United Nations, European

Union, and Russia—on Middle East peace negotiations since resigning as Prime Minister of the United Kingdom in June 2007.

Secretary of State Condoleezza Rice invited me to her apartment in the Watergate complex for a private dinner that gave us a chance to discuss policy challenges and personnel decisions I would face. She made just one request: Would I keep on her driver? I agreed and soon became as dependent on him as Condi had been.

Condi held another dinner for me with her senior staff, on the eighth floor of the State Department in one of the formal dining rooms that are tucked away there. Her advice about what I should expect in my new role proved very helpful.

I spoke with the living former Secretaries of State. This is a fascinating club that transcends partisan differences. They had each taken a leg of the relay race and were eager to help me grab the baton and get off to a fast start. Madeleine Albright was my longtime friend and partner in promoting rights and opportunities for women and agreed to chair a new public-private partnership to foster entrepreneurship and innovation in the Middle East. Warren Christopher gave me what might be the most practical advice I received: Don't plan vacations in August because something always seems to happen that month, such as Russia invading Georgia in 2008. Henry Kissinger checked in with me regularly, sharing astute observations about foreign leaders and sending me written reports on his travels. James Baker supported the State Department's efforts to preserve the ceremonial Diplomatic Reception Rooms and to realize the long-standing goal of building a museum for American diplomacy in Washington. Colin Powell provided candid assessments of individuals and ideas that the President and I were considering. Lawrence Eagleburger, the first and only career Foreign Service officer to serve as Secretary of State, joined me for the fiftieth anniversary of the Department's Operations Center (or "Ops," as everyone in the Building calls it). But it was George Shultz who gave me the best gift of all: a teddy bear that sang "Don't Worry, Be Happy" when its paw was squeezed. I kept it in my office, first as a joke, but every so often it really did help to squeeze the bear and hear that song.

I thought a lot about the experiences of my predecessors, going back to the first Secretary, Thomas Jefferson. Crafting American foreign policy has always been a high-wire balancing act between continuity and change. I tried to imagine what Dean Acheson, whom I had met all those years before at Wellesley, and his illustrious predecessor, George C. Marshall, had thought about the tumultuous international landscape of their day.

In the late 1940s the Truman Administration's mission was to create a new world—a free world—out of the destruction of World War II and in the shadow of the Cold War. Acheson described it as a task "just a bit less formidable than that described in the first chapter of Genesis." Old empires were breaking up and new powers were emerging. Much of Europe was in ruins and menaced by Communism. In what was then called the Third World, people long oppressed were finding their voice and demanding the right to self-determination.

General Marshall, a hero of World War II who served as both Secretary of State and Secretary of Defense under Truman, understood that America's security and prosperity depended on capable allies who would share our interests and buy our goods. Even more important, he knew that America had a responsibility and an opportunity to lead the world and that new challenges meant leading in new ways.

Marshall and Truman launched an ambitious plan to rebuild Europe's shattered countries and ward off the spread of Communism using every element of American power: military, economic, diplomatic, cultural, and moral. They reached across the aisle to build bipartisan support for their efforts and enlisted business leaders, labor organizers, and academics to help explain their goals to the American people.

Sixty years later, at the end of the first decade of the 21st century, our country once again found itself navigating a rapidly changing world. Technology and globalization had made the world more interconnected and interdependent than ever, and we were grappling with drones, cyber warfare, and social media. More countries—including China, India, Brazil, Turkey, and South Africa—had influence in global debates, while nonstate actors such as civil society activists, multinational corporations, and terrorist networks were playing greater roles in international affairs, for good and ill.

Although some may have yearned for an Obama Doctrine—a grand unified theory that would provide a simple and elegant road map for foreign policy in this new era, like "containment" did during the Cold War—there was nothing simple or elegant about the problems we faced. Unlike the Cold War days, when we faced a single adversary in the Soviet Union, we now had to contend with many opposing forces. So like our predecessors after World War II, we had to update our thinking to match the changes we were seeing all around us.

Foreign policy experts often refer to the system of institutions, alliances, and norms built up after World War II as "architecture." We still needed a rules-based global order that could manage interactions between states, protect fundamental freedoms, and mobilize common action. But it would have to be more flexible and inclusive than before. I came to liken the old architecture to the Parthenon in Greece, with clean lines and clear rules. The pillars holding it up—a handful of big institutions, alliances, and treaties—were remarkably sturdy. But time takes its toll, even on the greatest of edifices, and now we needed a new architecture for a new world, more in the spirit of Frank Gehry than formal Greek classicism. Where once a few strong columns could hold up the weight of the world, now a dynamic mix of materials, shapes, and structures was needed.

For decades foreign policy tools had been categorized as either the "hard power" of military force or the "soft power" of diplomatic, economic, humanitarian, and cultural influence. I wanted to break the hold of this outdated paradigm and think broadly about where and how we could use all the elements of American foreign policy in concert.

Beyond the traditional work of negotiating treaties and attending diplomatic conferences, we had to—among other tasks—engage activists on social media, help determine energy pipeline routes, limit carbon emissions, encourage marginalized groups to participate in politics, stand up for universal human rights, and defend common economic rules of the road. Our ability to do these things would be crucial measures of our national power.

This analysis led me to embrace a concept known as smart power, which had been kicking around Washington for a few years. Harvard's Joseph Nye, Suzanne Nossel of Human Rights Watch, and a few others had used the term, although we all had in mind slightly different meanings. For me, smart power meant choosing the right combination of tools—diplomatic, economic, military, political, legal, and cultural—for each situation.

The goal of smart power and our expanded focus on technology, public-private partnerships, energy, economics, and other areas beyond the State Department's standard portfolio was to complement more traditional diplomatic tools and priorities, not replace them. We wanted to bring every resource to bear on the biggest and toughest national security challenges. Throughout this book, you'll see examples of how this worked. Consider our efforts on Iran. We used new financial tools and private-sector partners to enforce stringent sanctions and cut Iran off from the global economy. Our energy diplomacy helped reduce sales of Iranian oil and drummed up new supplies to stabilize the market. We turned to social media to communicate directly with the Iranian people and invested in new high-tech tools to help dissidents evade government repression. All of that bolstered our old-fashioned shoe-leather diplomacy, and together they advanced our core national security objectives.

On January 13, 2009, I sat across the table from my Senate colleagues for my confirmation hearing with the Foreign Relations Committee. Over more than five hours I explained why and how I planned to redefine the role of Secretary, outlined positions on our most pressing challenges, and answered questions on everything from Arctic policy to international economics to energy supplies.

On January 21, the full Senate confirmed my appointment by a vote of 94 to 2. Later that day, in a small, private ceremony in my Senate office in the Russell Building, surrounded by my Senate staff, Judge Kay Oberly administered the oath to me as my husband held the Bible.

On January 22, in keeping with the tradition for all new Secretaries, I walked into the State Department through its main entrance on C Street. The lobby was full of cheering colleagues. I was overwhelmed and humbled by their enthusiastic welcome. Fluttering in a long row were the flags of every country in the world with which the United States maintains diplomatic relations. I would visit more than half of those countries, 112 in all, during the whirlwind that was about to begin. "I believe, with all of my heart, that this is a new era for America," I told the assembled throng.

Behind the crowd in the lobby, I saw etched into the marble walls the names of more than two hundred diplomats who had died while representing America overseas, going back to the earliest years of the republic. They had lost their lives to wars, natural disasters, terrorist attacks, epidemics, even shipwrecks. I knew it was possible that in the years ahead we'd lose more Americans on duty in dangerous and fragile places. (Sadly we did, from the earthquake in Haiti to the terrorist attack in Benghazi, Libya, and other places in between.) That day and every day I resolved to do everything I could to support and protect the men and women who served our country around the world.

The Secretary's office is in the seventh-floor suite known as "Mahogany Row." The hallway was lined with imposing portraits of my predecessors. I would be working under their watchful gaze. Our warren of offices and conference rooms was guarded by Diplomatic Security Service officers and routinely swept for listening devices. It was called an SCIF (Sensitive Compartmented Information Facility) and could sometimes feel as though we were working inside a giant safe. To prevent eavesdropping, nobody was allowed to bring in any outside electronic devices, even a cell phone.

After greeting my team, I walked into my private office and sat down at my desk for the first time. A letter from my predecessor, Secretary Rice, sat waiting for me. The walls of this inner office were paneled in the northern cherrywood chosen by former Secretary George Shultz, giving the small room a cozy feel very different from the grand outer office where I would receive visitors. Three phones sat on the desk, including direct lines to the White House, Pentagon, and CIA. I added a couch where I could read comfortably, even nap occasionally, and in the adjoining room there was a small kitchen and bathroom, complete with a shower.

Soon this office would become my second home, where I would spend many hours on the phone with foreign leaders while I paced the small room. But for now, on this first day, I just soaked it up.

I picked up the letter from Condi and opened it. It was brief, warm, and heartfelt. She wrote that being Secretary of State was "the best job in government" and that she was confident she was leaving the Department in good hands. "You have the most important qualification for this job—you love this country deeply." I was touched by her words.

I couldn't wait to get started.

PART TWO

Across the Pacific

3

Asia: The Pivot

My motorcade made its way through the quiet streets of Andrews Air Force Base on a bright Sunday in mid-February 2009. We rolled past guard booths, homes, and hangars, and then out onto the vast concrete expanse of the tarmac. I was embarking on my first journey as Secretary of State. The cars came to a stop beside a blue and white U.S. Air Force Boeing 757, fitted with enough advanced communications gear to coordinate global diplomacy from anywhere in the world. Emblazoned on the side, in large black letters, were the words "United States of America." I got out of the car, paused, and took it all in.

As First Lady I had flown around the world with Bill in Air Force One, the largest and grandest of government jets. I had also traveled extensively on my own, usually in a 757 much like this one, and on a variety of smaller planes as a Senator participating in Congressional delegations to places such as Iraq, Afghanistan, and Pakistan. But none of those experiences could prepare me for what it would be like to spend more than two thousand hours in the air over four years, traveling nearly a million miles. That's eighty-seven full days of recycled air and the steady vibration of twin turbofan engines propelling us forward at more than 500 miles per hour. This plane was also a powerful symbol of the nation I was honored to represent. No matter how many miles we logged or countries we visited, I never lost my sense of pride at seeing those iconic blue and white colors lit up on some far-off runway.

Inside the plane, to my left, Air Force officers were busy in a cabin full of computers and communications equipment. Beyond them the pilots performed their final checks. To the right, a narrow hallway led to my personal compartment, with a small desk, a pullout couch, a bathroom and closet, and secure and nonsecure phones.

Further on was the main cabin, which was divided into three sections for staff, security, and press and Air Force personnel. In the first section were two tables, each with four leather chairs facing each other, as in some train compartments. On one table, State Department Foreign Service officers set up a traveling office, linked to the Operations Center back in Foggy Bottom and capable of preparing everything from classified cables to detailed daily schedules, all at thirty thousand feet. Across the aisle my senior staff set up their laptops, worked the phones, or tried to get a little sleep between stops. The tables were usually covered with thick briefing books and marked-up speech drafts, but you'd often see copies of *People* magazine and *US Weekly* peeking out from underneath the official papers.

The middle section of the plane looked like a standard business-class cabin on any domestic flight. The seats were filled with policy experts from relevant State Department bureaus, colleagues from the White House and the Pentagon, a translator, and several Diplomatic Security agents. Next came the press cabin, for the journalists and camera crews who reported on our journeys.

At the back were the Air Force flight attendants who prepared our meals and always took good care of us. That was not easy when everyone's food preferences and sleep patterns were out of sync most of the time. The flight crew shopped for provisions in the countries we visited, which allowed for some unexpected treats, like Oaxaca cheese in Mexico, smoked salmon in Ireland, and tropical fruit in Cambodia. But wherever we were, we could still count on finding staff favorites on the menu, like the Air Force's famous turkey taco salad.

This packed metal tube became our home in the sky. I told the staff to dress casually, sleep as much as possible, and do whatever they could to stay sane and healthy amid the rigors of a grueling schedule. Over those two thousand hours in the air, we would celebrate birthdays, see distinguished diplomats weeping over soapy romantic comedies (and try and fail not to tease them for it), and marvel at Richard Holbrooke's bright yellow pajamas that he called his "sleeping suit."

On most flights the team carved out a lot of work time, and so did I.

But at the end of a long international tour there was a palpable sense of relief and relaxation on the flight home. We'd enjoy a glass of wine, watch movies, and swap stories. On one of those flights we watched *Breach*, a film about Robert Hanssen, an FBI agent who spied for the Russians in the 1980s and '90s. In one scene the Hanssen character complains, "Can't trust a woman in a pantsuit. Men wear the pants. The world doesn't need any more Hillary Clintons." The whole plane burst into laughter.

The plane broke down on a number of occasions. Once, stranded in Saudi Arabia with mechanical difficulties, I managed to hitch a ride home with General David Petraeus, who happened to be passing through the region. Dave generously offered me his cabin and sat with his staff. In the middle of the night we stopped to refuel at an Air Force base in Germany. Dave got off the plane and headed right to the base's gym, where he worked out for an hour, and then we were off and flying again.

On that first trip in February 2009, I walked to the back of the plane, where the journalists were settling into their seats. Many had covered previous Secretaries of State and were reminiscing about past travels and speculating about what they could expect from this new Secretary.

Some of my advisors had suggested I use my first trip to begin healing the transatlantic rifts that opened up during the Bush Administration by heading to Europe. Others suggested Afghanistan, where U.S. troops were battling a difficult insurgency. Colin Powell's first stop had been Mexico, our nearest southern neighbor, which also made a lot of sense. Warren Christopher had gone to the Middle East, which continued to demand concentrated attention. But Jim Steinberg, my new Deputy, suggested Asia, where we expected much of the history of the 21st century to be written. I decided he was right, so I was breaking with precedent and heading first to Japan, then on to Indonesia, South Korea, and finally China. We needed to send a message to Asia and the world that America was back.

═══

By the time I became Secretary, I had come to believe the United States had to do more to help shape the future of Asia and manage our increasingly complex relationship with China. The trajectory of the global economy and our own prosperity, the advance of democracy and human rights, and our hopes for a 21st century less bloody than the 20th all hinged to a large degree on what happened in the Asia-Pacific. This vast region, from the Indian Ocean to the tiny island nations of the Pacific, is home to more than half the world's population, several of our most trusted allies and valuable trading partners, and many of the world's most dynamic trade and energy routes. U.S. exports to the region helped spur our economic recovery in the wake of the recession, and our future growth depends on reaching further into Asia's expanding middle-class consumer base. Asia is also the source of real threats to our own security, most notably from North Korea's unpredictable dictatorship.

The rise of China is one of the most consequential strategic developments of our time. It is a country full of contradictions: an increasingly rich and influential nation that has moved hundreds of millions of people out of poverty, and an authoritarian regime trying to paper over its serious domestic challenges, with around 100 million people still living on a dollar or less a day. It's the world's largest producer of solar panels and also the largest emitter of greenhouse gases, with some of the world's worst urban air pollution. Eager to play a major role on the global stage but determined to act unilaterally in dealing with its neighbors, China remains reluctant to question other nations' internal affairs, even in extreme circumstances.

As a Senator, I argued that the United States would have to deal with a rising China and its growing economic, diplomatic, and military power in a careful, disciplined way. In the past, the emergence of new powers has rarely come without friction. In this case the situation was particularly complicated because of how interdependent our economies were becoming. In 2007, trade between the United States and China surpassed $387 billion; in 2013, it reached $562 billion. The Chinese held vast amounts of U.S. Treasury bonds, which meant we were deeply invested in each other's economic success. As a consequence, we both shared a strong interest in maintaining stability in Asia and around the world and in ensuring the steady flow of energy and trade. Yet beyond these shared interests, our values and worldviews often diverged; we saw it in old flash points like North Korea, Taiwan, Tibet, and human rights, and newly important ones such as climate change and disputes in the South and East China Seas.

All this made for a difficult balancing act. We needed a sophisticated strategy that encouraged China to participate as a responsible member of the international community, while standing firm in defense of our values and interests. This was a theme I carried through my campaign for President in 2008, arguing that the United States had to know both how to find common ground and how to stand our ground. I emphasized the importance of convincing China to play by the rules in the global marketplace by dropping discriminatory trade practices, allowing the value of its currency to rise, and preventing tainted food and goods from reaching consumers around the world, such as the toys contaminated by toxic lead paint that had ended up in the hands of American children. The world needed responsible leadership from China to make real headway on climate change, to prevent conflict on the Korean Peninsula, and to address many other regional and global challenges, so it wasn't in our interests to turn Beijing into a new Cold War boogeyman. Instead we needed to find a formula to manage competition and foster cooperation.

Under the leadership of Treasury Secretary Hank Paulson, the Bush Administration started a high-level economic dialogue with China that made progress on some important trade issues, but these talks remained separate from broader strategic and security discussions. Many in the region felt that the administration's focus on Iraq, Afghanistan, and the Middle East led to disengagement from America's traditional leadership role in Asia. Some of those concerns were overstated, but the perception was a problem in and of itself. I thought we ought to broaden our engagement with China and put the Asia-Pacific at the top of our diplomatic agenda.

Jim Steinberg and I quickly agreed that the person who should run the State Department's Bureau of East Asian and Pacific Affairs was Dr. Kurt Campbell. Kurt, who helped shape Asia policy at the Pentagon and the National Security Council during the Clinton Administration, became a key architect of our strategy. Besides being a creative strategic thinker and devoted public servant, he was also an irrepressible traveling companion, fond of pranks and never without a joke or a story.

During my first days on the job, I made a round of calls to key Asian leaders. One of my more candid exchanges was with Foreign Minister Stephen Smith of Australia. His boss, Prime Minister Kevin Rudd, spoke Mandarin and had a clear-eyed view of the opportunities and challenges of China's rise. Rich in natural resources, Australia was profiting by supplying China's industrial boom with minerals and other raw materials. China became Australia's largest trading partner, surpassing Japan and the United States. But Rudd also understood that peace and security in the Pacific depended on American leadership, and he put great value on the historic ties between our countries. The last thing he wanted was to see America withdraw from or lose influence in Asia. In that first call, Smith expressed his and Rudd's hope that the Obama Administration would "more deeply engage with Asia." I told him that was right in line with my own thinking and that I looked forward to a close partnership. Australia became a key ally in our Asian strategy over the coming years, under both Rudd and his successor, Prime Minister Julia Gillard.

Its neighbor New Zealand presented more of a challenge. For twenty-five years, since New Zealand prohibited all nuclear vessels from visiting their home ports, the United States and New Zealand had had a limited relationship. However, I thought our long friendship and mutual interests created a diplomatic opening for bridging the divide and shaping a new relationship between Wellington and Washington. On my visit in 2010, I signed the Wellington Declaration with Prime Minister John Key, which committed our nations to work more closely together in Asia, the Pacific, and multilateral organizations. In 2012, Secretary of Defense Leon Panetta would rescind the twenty-six-year ban on New Zealand's ships docking at American bases. In global politics, sometimes reaching out to an old friend can be as rewarding as making a new one.

All my calls with Asian leaders that first week reinforced my belief that we needed a new approach in the region. Jim and I consulted with experts about various possibilities. One option was to focus on broadening our relationship with China, on the theory that if we could get our China policy right, the rest of our work in Asia would be much easier. An alternative was to concentrate our efforts on strengthening America's treaty alliances in the region (with Japan, South Korea, Thailand, the Philippines, and Australia), providing a counterbalance to China's growing power.

A third approach was to elevate and harmonize the alphabet soup of regional multilateral organizations, such as ASEAN (the Association of Southeast Asian Nations) and APEC (the Asia-Pacific Economic Cooperation organization). Nobody was expecting anything as coherent as the European Union to spring up overnight, but other regions had learned important lessons about the value of well-organized multinational institutions. They could provide a venue for every nation and point of view to be heard and offer opportunities for nations to work together on shared challenges, resolve their disagreements, establish rules and standards of behavior, reward responsible countries with legitimacy and respect, and help hold accountable those who violated the rules. If Asia's multilateral institutions were supported and modernized, they could strengthen regional norms on everything from intellectual property rights to nuclear proliferation to freedom of navigation, and mobilize action on challenges like climate change and piracy. This kind of methodical multilateral diplomacy is often slow and frustrating, rarely making headlines at home, but it can pay real dividends that affect the lives of millions of people.

In keeping with the position I had staked out as a Senator and Presidential candidate, I decided that the smart power choice was to meld all three approaches. We would show that America was "all in" when it came to Asia. I was prepared to lead the way, but success would require buy-in from our entire government, beginning with the White House.

The President shared my determination to make Asia a focal point of the administration's foreign policy. Born in Hawaii, and having spent formative years in Indonesia, he felt a strong personal connection to the region and understood its significance. At his direction, the National Security Council staff, led by General Jim Jones, along with Tom Donilon and their Asia expert, Jeff Bader, supported our strategy. Over the next four years we practiced what I called "forward-deployed diplomacy" in Asia, borrowing a term from our military colleagues. We quickened the pace and widened the scope of our diplomatic engagement across the region, dispatching senior officials and development experts far and wide, participating more fully in multilateral organizations, reaffirming our traditional alliances, and reaching out to new strategic partners. Because personal relationships and gestures of respect are deeply significant in Asia, I made it a priority to visit almost every nation in the region. My travels would eventually take me from one of the smallest Pacific islands to the home of a long-imprisoned Nobel Peace laureate to the edge of the most heavily guarded border in the world.

Over four years, I delivered a series of speeches explaining our strategy and making the case for why the Asia-Pacific deserved greater attention from the U.S. government. In the summer of 2011, I began working on a long essay that would situate our work in the region in the broader sweep of American foreign policy. The war in Iraq was winding down, and a transition was under way in Afghanistan. After a decade of focusing on the areas of greatest threat, we had come to a "pivot point." Of course, we had to stay focused on the threats that remained, but it was also time to do more in the areas of greatest opportunity.

Foreign Policy magazine published my essay in the fall under the title "America's Pacific Century," but it was the word *pivot* that gained prominence. Journalists latched on to it as an evocative description of the administration's renewed emphasis on Asia, although many in our own government preferred the more anodyne *rebalance to Asia*. Some friends and allies in other parts of the world were understandably concerned that the phrase implied turning our back on them, but we worked to make clear that America had the reach and resolve to pivot *to* Asia without pivoting *away* from other obligations and opportunities.

═══

Our first task was to reassert America as a Pacific power without sparking an unnecessary confrontation with China. That's why I decided to use my first trip as Secretary to accomplish three goals: visit our key Asian allies, Japan and South Korea; reach out to Indonesia, an emerging regional power and the home of ASEAN; and begin our crucial engagement with China.

In early February, shortly after I took office, I invited a number of academics and Asia experts to dinner at the State Department. We ate in the elegant Thomas Jefferson State Reception Room on the ceremonial eighth floor. Painted robin's egg blue and furnished with Early American Chippendale antiques, it became one of my favorite rooms in the building, and over the years I hosted many meals and events there. We talked about how to balance America's interests in Asia, which sometimes seemed in competition. For example, how hard could we push the Chinese on human rights or climate change and still gain their support on security issues like Iran and North Korea? Stapleton Roy, a former Ambassador to Singapore, Indonesia, and China, urged me not to overlook Southeast Asia, which Jim and Kurt had also been recommending. Over the years American attention has often focused on Northeast Asia because of our alliances and troop commitments in Japan and South Korea, but countries like Indonesia, Malaysia, and Vietnam were growing in economic and strategic importance. Roy and other experts backed our plan to sign a treaty with ASEAN, which would then open the door to much greater U.S. engagement there. It seemed like a small step that could yield real benefits down the road.

A week later I went to the Asia Society in New York to deliver my first major address as Secretary on our approach to the Asia-Pacific. Orville Schell, the Asia Society's silver-haired China scholar, suggested I use an ancient proverb from Sun Tzu's *The Art of War* about soldiers from two warring feudal states who find themselves on a boat together crossing a wide river in a storm. Instead of fighting, they work together and survive. In English the proverb roughly translates as, "When you are in a common boat, cross the river peacefully together." For the United States and China, with our economic destinies bound up together in the middle of a global financial storm, this was good advice. My use of the proverb was not lost on Beijing. Premier Wen Jiabao and other leaders referenced it in later discussions with me. A few days after the speech, I boarded the plane at Andrews Air Force Base and headed out across the Pacific.

Over many years of travel I've developed the ability to sleep almost anywhere at any time—on planes, in cars, a quick power nap in a hotel room before a meeting. On the road I tried to grab sleep whenever possible since I was never sure when my next proper rest would be. When I had to stay awake during meetings or conference calls, I drank copious cups of coffee and tea, and sometimes dug the fingernails of one hand into the palm of the other. It was the only way I knew to cope with the crazy schedule and fierce jet lag. But as our plane headed across the international date line toward Tokyo, I knew there was no hope of sleep. I couldn't stop thinking about what I had to do to make the most of the trip.

I first visited Japan with Bill as part of a trade delegation from Arkansas during his governorship. The country then was a key ally but also an object of growing anxiety in the United States. Japan's "Economic Miracle" came to symbolize deep-seated fears about U.S. stagnation and decline, much as China's rise has in the 21st century. The cover of Paul Kennedy's 1987 book *The Rise and Fall of the Great Powers* featured a weary Uncle Sam stepping off a global pedestal with a determined-looking Japanese businessman scrambling up behind him. Sound familiar? When a Japanese conglomerate purchased the historic Rockefeller Center in New York in 1989, it caused a minor panic in the press. "America for Sale?" asked the *Chicago Tribune*.

In those days there were legitimate concerns about America's economic future, which helped fuel Bill's successful Presidential campaign in 1992. Yet by the time Emperor Akihito and Empress Michiko of Japan welcomed Bill and me to Tokyo's Imperial Palace in the summer of 1993, we could already see that America was regaining its economic strength. Japan, by contrast, faced a "Lost Decade" after its asset and credit bubble burst, leaving banks and other businesses loaded down with bad debt. Its economy, once feared by Americans, slowed to an anemic pace—which caused a whole different set of concerns for them and us. Japan was still one of the largest economies in the world and a key partner in responding to the global financial crisis. I chose Tokyo as my first destination to underscore that our new administration saw the alliance as a cornerstone of our strategy in the region. President Obama would also welcome Prime Minister Taro Aso to Washington later that month, the first foreign leader to meet with him in the Oval Office.

The strength of our alliance would be demonstrated dramatically in March 2011, when a 9.0-magnitude earthquake hit the east coast of Japan, setting off a tsunami with hundred-foot waves and leading to a meltdown at the Fukushima nuclear plant. The "Triple Disaster" killed nearly twenty thousand people, displaced hundreds of thousands more, and became one of the most expensive natural catastrophes in history. Our embassy and the U.S. 7th Fleet, which had a long, close partnership with the Japan Maritime Self-Defense Force, jumped quickly into action, working with the Japanese to deliver food and medical supplies, conduct search-and-rescue missions, evacuate the injured, and assist with other vital missions. It was called Operation Tomodachi, the Japanese word for "friend."

On this first visit, I landed in Tokyo amid a rush of pomp and pageantry. In addition to the normal retinue of official greeters, two women astronauts and members of Japan's Special Olympics team were at the airport to meet me.

After a few hours of sleep at Tokyo's historic Hotel Okura, a pocket of 1960s-era style and culture, straight out of *Mad Men*, my first stop was a tour of the historic Meiji Shrine. The rest of my whirlwind day featured a get-to-know-you with staff and families at the U.S. Embassy, lunch with the Foreign Minister, a heart-rending meeting with families of Japanese citizens abducted by North Korea, a lively town hall discussion with students at the University of Tokyo, interviews with American and Japanese press, dinner with the Prime Minister, and a late-night meeting with the head of the opposition party. It was the first of many jam-packed days over four years, each one full of diplomatic and emotional highs and lows.

One of the highlights was going to the Imperial Palace to see Empress Michiko again. It was a rare honor, a result of the warm personal relationship she and I had enjoyed since my time as First Lady. We greeted each other with a smile and a hug. Then she welcomed me into her private quarters. The Emperor joined us for tea and a conversation about my travels and theirs.

=====

Planning a complicated foreign trip like this takes a whole team of talented people. Huma, by now Deputy Chief of Staff for Operations, and my director of scheduling, Lona Valmoro, who juggled a million invitations without ever missing a beat, coordinated a wide-ranging process to make sure we collected the best ideas for stops and events. I made it clear that I wanted to get out beyond the Foreign Ministries and palaces and meet with citizens, especially community activists and volunteers; journalists; students and professors; business, labor, and religious leaders, the civil society that helps hold governments accountable and drives social change. This was something I had been doing since I was First Lady. In a speech at the 1998 World Economic Forum in Davos, Switzerland, I had compared a healthy society to a three-legged stool, supported by a responsible government, an open economy, and a vibrant civil society. That third leg of the stool was too often neglected.

Thanks to the internet, especially social media, citizens and community organizations had gained more access to information and a greater ability to speak out than ever before. Now even autocracies had to pay attention to the sentiments of their people, as we would see during the Arab Spring. For the United States, it was important to build strong relationships with foreign publics as well as governments. This would help ensure more durable partnerships with our friends. It would also build support for our goals and values when the government wasn't with us but the people were. In many cases civil society advocates and organizations were the ones driving progress inside countries. They were battling official corruption, mobilizing grassroots movements, and drawing attention to problems like environmental degradation, human rights abuses, and economic inequality. From the start I wanted America to be firmly on their side and to encourage and support them in their efforts.

My first town hall meeting was at the University of Tokyo. I told the students that America was ready to listen again and turned the floor over to them. They responded with a torrent of questions, and not just about the issues that were dominating the headlines, like the future of the U.S.-Japan alliance and the ongoing global financial crisis. They also asked about the prospects for democracy in Burma, the safety of nuclear power (presciently), tensions with the Muslim world, climate change, and how to succeed as a woman in a male-dominated society. It was the first of many town hall meetings I'd have with young people around the world, and I loved hearing their thoughts and engaging in a substantive back-and-forth discussion. Years later I heard that the president of the university's daughter had sat in the audience that day and decided she too wanted to become a diplomat. She went on to join Japan's Foreign Service.

A few days later, at Ewha Womans University in Seoul, South Korea, I saw how reaching out to young people was going to take me into territory well beyond traditional foreign policy concerns. As I stepped onto the stage at Ewha, the audience erupted in cheers. Then the young women lined up at the microphones to ask me some highly personal questions—respectfully, but eagerly.

Is it difficult to deal with misogynistic leaders around the world?

I responded that I would guess that many leaders choose to ignore the fact that they're dealing with a woman when they're dealing with me. But I try not to let them get away with that. (Nonetheless, it is an unfortunate reality that women in public life still face an unfair double standard. Even leaders like former Prime Minister Julia Gillard of Australia have faced outrageous sexism, which shouldn't be tolerated in any country.)

Could you tell us about your daughter, Chelsea?

I could spend hours on that question. But suffice it to say, she's an amazing person and I'm so proud of her.

How do you describe love?

On that one, I laughed and said that I now officially felt more like an advice columnist than Secretary of State. I thought for a moment and then said, "How does anybody describe love? I mean, poets have spent millennia writing about love. Psychologists and authors of all sorts write about it. I think if you can describe it, you may not fully be experiencing it because it is such a personal relationship. I'm very lucky because my husband is my best friend, and he and I have been together for a very long time, longer than most of you have been alive."

It seemed that these women felt connected to me in a personal way, and, wonderfully, they were comfortable and confident enough to talk to me as though I was a friend or mentor rather than a government official from a faraway country. I wanted to be worthy of their admiration. I also hoped that by having a conversation like this, person to person, I could reach across cultural gaps and perhaps convince them to give America a second look.

After Japan it was on to Jakarta, Indonesia, where I was welcomed by a group of young students from the primary school that President Obama attended as a young boy. During my visit, I went on *The Awesome Show*, one of the country's most popular television programs. It felt just like MTV. Loud music blared between segments, and the interviewers all looked young enough to be in school, not hosting a national talk show.

They asked me a question that I would hear all over the world: How could I work with President Obama after we had campaigned so hard against each other? Indonesia was still a very young democracy; the long-time ruler, Suharto, was ousted in 1998 through popular protests, and the first direct Presidential election was held only in 2004. So it was not surprising that people were more accustomed to political rivals being jailed or exiled rather than appointed chief diplomat. I said that it had not been easy losing a hard-fought campaign to President Obama but that democracy works only if political leaders put the common good ahead of personal interest. I told them that when he asked me to serve, I accepted because we both love our country. It was the first of many times that our partnership would serve as an example for people in other countries trying to understand democracy.

The night before, over dinner with civil society leaders at the National Archives Museum in Jakarta, we discussed the extraordinary challenges the leaders and people of Indonesia had taken on: blending democracy, Islam, modernity, and women's rights in a country with the largest Muslim population in the world. In the previous half-century Indonesia had been a relatively minor player in the region's political affairs. When I visited as First Lady fifteen years earlier, it was still a poor and undemocratic country. By 2009 it was being transformed under the forward-looking leadership of President Susilo Bambang Yudhoyono. Economic growth had lifted many people out of poverty, and Indonesia was working to share lessons from its own transition away from dictatorship with other countries across Asia.

I was impressed by Yudhoyono, who had a deep grasp of regional diplomatic dynamics and a vision for his country's continued development. In our first conversation he encouraged me to pursue a new approach toward Burma, which had been ruled by a repressive military junta for years. Yudhoyono had met twice with Burma's top general, the reclusive Than Shwe, and he told me that the junta might be willing to inch toward democracy if America and the international community helped them along. I listened carefully to Yudhoyono's wise advice, and we stayed in close touch about Burma going forward. Our engagement with that country eventually became one of the most exciting developments of my time as Secretary.

Jakarta was also the permanent home of ASEAN, the regional institution that the Asia hands back in D.C. had urged me to prioritize. In an interview in Tokyo, a Japanese reporter noted the widespread disappointment among Southeast Asians that American officials had skipped recent ASEAN conferences, which some saw as a sign of America's flagging presence in the Asia-Pacific, even as China was seeking to expand its influence. The reporter wanted to know whether I was planning to continue this trend, or if I would work to reinvigorate our engagement. It was a question that spoke to the hunger in Asia for tangible signs of U.S. leadership. I replied that expanding relations with organizations such as ASEAN was an important part of our strategy in the region, and I planned to attend as many meetings as possible. If we were going to improve our position in Southeast Asia, as China was also trying to do, and encourage nations to agree to cooperate more on trade, security, and the environment, then a good place to start would be with ASEAN.

No previous U.S. Secretary of State had ever visited the organization's headquarters. ASEAN Secretary-General Surin Pitsuwan met me with a bouquet of yellow roses and explained that Indonesians consider the color yellow a symbol of hope and new beginnings. "Your visit shows the seriousness of the United States to end its diplomatic absenteeism in the region," he said. That was a rather pointed greeting, but he was right about our intentions.

The next stop was South Korea, a wealthy, advanced democracy and key ally living in the shadow of a repressive and bellicose neighbor to the north. American troops have been on watchful guard there ever since the end of the Korean War in 1953. In my meetings with President Lee Myung-bak and other senior officials, I reassured them that although the administration in the United States had changed, our nation's commitment to South Korea's defense had not.

North Korea, by contrast, is the most tightly closed totalitarian state in the world. Many of its nearly 25 million people live in abject poverty. The political oppression is nearly total. Famine is frequent. Yet the regime, led in the early years of the Obama Administration by the aging and eccentric Kim Jong Il, and later by his young son Kim Jong Un, devotes most of its limited resources to supporting its military, developing nuclear weapons, and antagonizing its neighbors.

In 1994, the Clinton Administration negotiated an agreement with North Korea in which it pledged to halt operation and construction of facilities widely suspected of being part of a secret nuclear weapons program in exchange for assistance in building two smaller nuclear reactors that would produce energy, not weapons-grade plutonium. The agreement also provided a path to normalize relations between our two countries. By September 1999, a deal was reached with North Korea to freeze testing of its long-range missiles. In October 2000, Secretary of State Madeleine Albright visited North Korea in an effort to test the regime's intentions and negotiate another agreement on continued inspections. Unfortunately, while the North Koreans made a lot of promises, a comprehensive agreement never materialized. Once President George W. Bush took office, he quickly altered policy and referred to North Korea as part of the "Axis of Evil" in his 2002 State of the Union address. Evidence emerged that North Korea had secretly enriched uranium, and in 2003, it restarted enrichment of plutonium. By the end of the Bush Administration, Pyongyang had constructed a number of nuclear weapons that could threaten South Korea and the region.

In my public remarks in Seoul I extended an invitation to the North Koreans. If they would completely and verifiably eliminate their nuclear weapons program, the Obama Administration would be willing to normalize relations, replace the peninsula's long-standing armistice agreement with a permanent peace treaty, and assist in meeting the energy and other economic and humanitarian needs of the North Korean people. If not, the regime's isolation would continue. It was an opening gambit in a drama I was sure would continue for our entire term, as it had for decades before, and not one I thought likely to succeed. But, as with Iran, another regime with nuclear ambitions, we started off with the offer of engagement hoping it would succeed and knowing it would be easier to get other nations to pressure North Korea if and when the offer was rejected. It was particularly important for China, a longtime patron and protector of the regime in Pyongyang, to be part of a united international front.

It didn't take long to get an answer.

The next month, March 2009, a crew of American television journalists were reporting from the border between China and North Korea for Current TV, the network cofounded by former Vice President Al Gore and later sold to Al Jazeera. The journalists were there to document the stories of North Korean women who were trafficked across the border and forced into the sex trade and other forms of modern slavery. At dawn on March 17, a local guide led the Americans along the Tumen River that separates the two countries, still frozen in the early spring. They followed him out onto the ice and, briefly, as far as the North Korean side of the river. According to the journalists, they then returned to Chinese soil. Suddenly North Korean border guards appeared with guns drawn. The Americans ran, and the producer escaped along with the guide. But the two women reporters, Euna Lee and Laura Ling, were not so lucky. They were arrested and dragged back across the river to North Korea, where they were sentenced to twelve years of hard labor.

Two months later North Korea performed an underground nuclear test and announced that it no longer considered itself bound by the terms of the 1953 armistice. Just as President Obama had promised in his inaugural address, we had offered an open hand, but North Korea was responding with a closed fist.

Our first step was to see if action was possible at the United Nations. Working closely with Ambassador Susan Rice in New York, I spent hours on the phone with leaders in Beijing, Moscow, Tokyo, and other capitals drumming up support for a strong resolution imposing sanctions on the regime in Pyongyang. Everyone agreed that the nuclear test was unacceptable, but what to do about it was another story.

"I know this is difficult for your government," I told Chinese Foreign Minister Yang Jiechi in one call, "[but] if we act together, we have a chance to change North Korea's calculation about the cost to them of continuing with their nuclear and missile programs." Yang said China shared our concerns about a regional arms race and agreed that "an appropriate and measured" response was needed. I hoped that wasn't code for "toothless."

By mid-June, our efforts paid off. All the members of the UN Security Council agreed to impose additional sanctions. We had to make some concessions to get Chinese and Russian backing, but this was still the toughest measure ever imposed on North Korea, and I was pleased we were finally able to muster a unified international response.

But how to help the imprisoned journalists? We heard that Kim Jong Il would let the women go only if he received a personal visit and request from a high-ranking U.S. delegation. I discussed this with President Obama and other members of the national security team. What if Al Gore himself went? Or maybe former President Jimmy Carter, known for his humanitarian work around the globe? Maybe Madeleine Albright, who had unique experience in North Korea from her diplomacy in the 1990s? But the North Koreans already had a particular visitor in mind: my husband, Bill. It was a surprising request. On the one hand, the North Korean government was busy hurling absurd invectives at me over the nuclear issue, including calling me "a funny lady." (North Korea's propaganda operation is famous for its over-the-top and often nonsensical rhetorical attacks. They once called Vice President Biden an "impudent burglar." There's even a "random insult generator" on the internet that churns out parodies of their broadsides.) On the other hand, Kim apparently had had a soft spot for my husband ever since Bill sent a condolence letter after the death of his father Kim Il-sung in 1994. And of course he also wanted the global attention that would come from a rescue mission led by a former President.

I talked with Bill about the idea. He was willing to go if it would secure the freedom of the two reporters. Al Gore and the families of the women also encouraged Bill to take the mission. But more than a few people in the White House argued against the trip. Some may have harbored negative feelings toward Bill from the 2008 primary campaign, but most were simply reluctant to reward Kim's bad behavior with such a high-profile trip and potentially create concerns for our allies. They had a good point: we had to balance doing what was necessary to rescue the two innocent American civilians with avoiding potential geopolitical fallout.

I thought it was worth trying. The North Koreans had already gotten all the mileage they could from the incident, but they needed some reason to justify letting the women go home. Also, if we didn't do something to try to resolve the matter, our efforts on everything else with North Korea would be suspended because of their imprisonment. When I raised the idea directly with President Obama over lunch in late July, he agreed with me that it was the best chance we had.

Although it was considered a "private mission," Bill and the small team he would take along were well briefed before departing. A humorous but important part of the preparation involved coaching them not to be smiling (or frowning) when the inevitable official photos with Kim were taken.

In early August, Bill set out on his mission. After twenty hours on the ground in North Korea and a face-to-face meeting with Kim, he succeeded in winning the journalists' immediate release. They flew home with Bill to a dramatic arrival in California, greeted by family, friends, and loads of television cameras. The official images released by the regime were appropriately stilted; no smiling by any of the Americans. Afterward Bill joked that he felt like he was auditioning for a James Bond movie. But he believed that his success was proof that the insular regime would respond positively, at least on certain points, if we could find the right mix of incentives.

Unfortunately there was more trouble ahead. Late one evening in March 2010, a South Korean naval vessel, the *Cheonan*, was cruising near North Korean waters. It was a cold night, and most of the 104 South Korean sailors were belowdecks sleeping, eating, or exercising. With no warning, a torpedo fired from an unknown source detonated below the *Cheonan*'s hull. The explosion ripped the ship apart, and its remains began to sink into the Yellow Sea. Forty-six sailors died. In May, a team of UN investigators concluded that a North Korean midget submarine was likely responsible for the unprovoked attack. This time, while the Security Council unanimously condemned the attack, China blocked the naming of North Korea directly or a more robust response. Here was one of China's contradictions in full view. Beijing claimed to prize stability above all else, yet it was tacitly condoning naked aggression that was profoundly destabilizing.

In July 2010, Bob Gates and I returned to South Korea together to meet with our counterparts and demonstrate to Pyongyang that the

United States continued to stand firmly behind our allies. We drove out to Panmunjom, in the demilitarized zone (DMZ) that has divided North and South Korea since 1953. The DMZ is two and a half miles wide and follows the 38th parallel across the entire peninsula. It is the most heavily fortified and mined border in the world, and one of the most dangerous. Under an ominous sky we climbed up to a camouflaged observation point below a guard tower and the flags of the United States, the United Nations, and the Republic of Korea. A light rain fell as we stood behind sandbags and looked through binoculars into North Korean territory.

As I stared across the DMZ, it was hard not to be struck anew by how this narrow line separated two dramatically different worlds. South Korea was a shining example of progress, a country that had successfully transitioned from poverty and dictatorship to prosperity and democracy. Its leaders cared about the well-being of their citizens, and young people grew up with freedom and opportunity, not to mention the fastest broadband download speeds in the world. Just two and a half miles away, North Korea was a land of fear and famine. The contrast could not have been starker, or more tragic.

Bob and I went inside the nearby headquarters of the UN forces with our South Korean counterparts for a military briefing. We also toured a building that sits squarely on top of the border, half in the north and half in the south, designed to facilitate negotiations between the two sides. There is even a long conference table positioned exactly on the dividing line. As we walked through, a North Korean soldier stood just inches away, on the other side of a window, staring stonily at us. Maybe he was just curious. But if his goal was to intimidate, he failed. I stayed focused on our briefer, while Bob smiled merrily. A photographer captured the unusual moment in a picture that ran on the front page of the *New York Times*.

In our meetings with the South Koreans, Bob and I discussed steps we could take to put pressure on the North and discourage it from further provocative actions. We agreed to make a strong show of force to reassure our friends and make clear that the United States would protect regional security. We announced new sanctions and that the aircraft carrier USS *George Washington* would move into position off the Korean coast and join military exercises with the South Korean Navy. In all, eighteen ships, some two hundred aircraft, and about eight thousand U.S. and South

Korean troops would participate over four days. There was outrage in both Pyongyang and Beijing about the naval drills, which told us our message had been received.

That evening, South Korean President Lee Myung-bak hosted a dinner for Bob and me at the Blue House, his official residence. He thanked us for standing beside South Korea in its hour of need, and as he often did, he connected his own rise from an impoverished childhood to that of his country. South Korea had once been poorer than North Korea, but with the help of the United States and the international community it had succeeded in developing its economy—a reminder of the legacy of American leadership in Asia.

═══

Another aspect of our pivot strategy was bringing India more fully into the Asian-Pacific political scene. Having another large democracy with a full seat at the table in the region could help encourage more countries to move toward political and economic openness, rather than follow China's example of autocratic state capitalism.

I had fond memories of my first visit to India in 1995, with Chelsea by my side. We toured one of the orphanages run by Mother Teresa, the humble Catholic nun whose charity and saintliness made her a global icon. The orphanage was filled with baby girls who had been abandoned in the streets or left at the front door for the nuns to find; because they were not boys, they were not valued by their families. Our visit had prompted the local government to pave the dirt road leading up to the orphanage, which the nuns considered a minor miracle. When Mother Teresa died in 1997, I led an American delegation to her funeral in Kolkata to pay our respects to her remarkable humanitarian legacy. Her open casket was carried through the crowded streets, and Presidents, Prime Ministers, and religious leaders from many faiths placed wreaths of white flowers on the funeral bier. Later her successor invited me to a private meeting at the headquarters of their order, Missionaries of Charity. In a simple whitewashed room, lit only by tiers of flickering devotional candles, the nuns stood in a circle of quiet prayer surrounding the closed casket, which had been brought back there as its final resting place. To my surprise, they asked me to offer a prayer of my own. I hesitated, then bowed my head and thanked God for the privilege of having known this tiny, forceful, saintly woman during her time here on earth.

My first trip to India as Secretary of State was in the summer of 2009. In the fourteen years since I had first visited, trade between our countries had risen from less than $10 billion to more than $60 billion, and would continue to grow to nearly $100 billion in 2012. There were still too many barriers and restrictions, but American companies were slowly gaining access to Indian markets, creating jobs and opportunities for people in both countries. Indian companies were also investing in the United States, and lots of high-skilled Indian workers were applying for visas and helping jump-start innovative American businesses. More than 100,000 Indian students studied in the United States every year; some went home to put their skills to work in their own country, while many stayed to contribute to the American economy.

In New Delhi I met with a broad cross-section of society, including Prime Minister Manmohan Singh, business leaders, women entrepreneurs, climate and energy scientists, and students. I was happy to see Sonia Gandhi, the head of the Indian National Congress Party, whom I had gotten to know during the 1990s. She and Prime Minister Singh explained how hard it had been to show restraint toward Pakistan after the coordinated terrorist bombings in Mumbai the prior November. They made it clear to me that there would not be such restraint in the event of a second attack. Indians referred to the attack on November 26, 2008, as 26/11, in an echo of our own 9/11. In a show of solidarity with the people of India, I chose to stay at the elegant old Taj Mahal Palace Hotel in Mumbai, which had been one of the sites of the gruesome attack that killed 164 people, including 138 Indians and four Americans. By staying there and paying my respects at the memorial, I wanted to send the message that Mumbai was undeterred and open for business.

In July 2011, in sweltering summer heat, I traveled to the Indian port city of Chennai on the Bay of Bengal, a commercial hub that looks out toward the vibrant trade and energy routes of Southeast Asia. No Secretary of State had ever visited this city before, but I wanted to show that we understood India was more than Delhi and Mumbai. In Chennai's public library, the largest in the country, I spoke about India's role on the world stage, especially in the Asia-Pacific region. India has ancient ties in Southeast Asia, from the traders who sailed the Straits of Malacca to the Hindu temples that dot the region. Our hope, I said, was that India would transcend its intractable conflict with Pakistan and become a more active advocate for democracy and free-market values across Asia. As I told the audience in Chennai, the United States supported India's "Look East" policy. We wanted it to "lead east" as well.

Despite some day-to-day differences, the strategic fundamentals of our relationship with India—shared democratic values, economic imperatives, and diplomatic priorities—were pushing both countries' interests into closer convergence. We were entering a new, more mature phase in our relationship.

=====

A major goal of our strategy in Asia was to promote political reform as well as economic growth. We wanted to make the 21st century a time in which people across Asia become not only more prosperous but also more free. And more freedom would, I was confident, spur greater prosperity.

Many countries in the region were grappling with the question of which model of governance best suited their society and circumstances. China's rise, and its mix of authoritarianism and state capitalism, offered an attractive example to some leaders. We often heard that while democracy might work well elsewhere in the world, it wasn't at home in Asia. These critics suggested that it was unsuited to the region's history, maybe even antithetical to Asian values.

There were plenty of counterexamples to disprove these theories. Japan, Malaysia, South Korea, Indonesia, and Taiwan were all democratic societies that had delivered tremendous economic benefits to their people. From 2008 to 2012, Asia was the only region in the world to achieve steady gains in political rights and civil liberties, according to the nongovernmental organization Freedom House. For example, the Philippines held elections in 2010 that were widely praised as a significant improvement over previous ones, and the new President, Benigno Aquino III, launched a concerted effort to fight corruption and increase transparency. The Philippines were a valued ally for the United States, and when a terrible typhoon hit the country in late 2013, our partnership would ensure that joint relief efforts led by the U.S. Navy swung quickly into action. And, of course, there was Burma. By mid-2012 the democratic opening predicted by Indonesia's President Yudhoyono was in full swing, and Aung San Suu Kyi, who for decades had been the imprisoned conscience of her nation, was serving in Parliament.

There were other examples that were less encouraging. Too many Asian governments continued to resist reforms, restrict their people's access to ideas and information, and imprison them for expressing dissenting views. Under Kim Jong Un, North Korea remained the most closed and repressive country in the world. As hard as it is to imagine, he actually made things worse. Cambodia and Vietnam had made some progress, but not enough. On a visit to Vietnam in 2010, I learned that several prominent bloggers had been detained in the days before my arrival. In my meetings with Vietnamese officials, I raised specific concerns about arbitrary restrictions on fundamental freedoms, including arrests and the severe sentences too often imposed on political dissidents, lawyers, bloggers, Catholic activists, and Buddhist monks and nuns.

In July 2012, I took another extended tour across the region, this one designed to emphasize that democracy and prosperity go hand in hand. I started again in Japan, one of the strongest and richest democracies in the world, and then visited Vietnam, Cambodia, and Laos, where I would become the first Secretary of State to step foot in that country in fifty-seven years.

I came away with two overall impressions from my short visit to Laos. First, Laos was still in the tight grip of its Communist Party, which itself was increasingly under the economic and political control of China. Beijing took advantage of the relationship to extract natural resources and push construction of projects that did little for the average Laotian. Second, Laotians were still paying a terrible price for the extensive bombing the United States carried out over its territory during the Vietnam War. It had earned the terrible distinction of being "the most heavily bombed country in the world." This is why I visited a project in Vientiane supported by USAID to provide prosthetics and rehabilitation for the thousands of adults and children still losing limbs from the cluster-bombs littered throughout a third of the country, only 1 percent of which had been found and deactivated. I thought the United States had an ongoing obligation and was encouraged that in 2012 Congress tripled funding to speed up the removal work.

A highlight of this summer 2012 trip across Asia was Mongolia, where I had paid an unforgettable first visit in 1995. That had been a difficult time for the remote nation squeezed between northern China and Siberia.

Decades of Soviet domination had tried to impose Stalinist culture on the nomadic society. When the aid from Moscow stopped, the economy crumbled. But, like many visitors, I was enchanted by Mongolia's stark beauty, with its vast wind-swept steppes, and by the energy, determination, and hospitality of its people. In a traditional tent called a *ger*, a family of nomads offered me a bowl of fermented mare's milk, which tasted like warm, day-old plain yogurt. I was impressed by the students, activists, and government officials I met in the capital and their commitment to transforming a one-party Communist dictatorship into a pluralistic, democratic political system. It was not going to be an easy journey, but they were determined to try. I told them that, from then on, anytime someone expressed doubts that democracy could take root in unlikely places, I would tell them, "Let them come to Mongolia! Let them see people willing to hold demonstrations in subzero temperatures and travel long distances to cast their ballots in elections."

When I returned seventeen years later, a lot had changed in Mongolia and its neighborhood. China's rapid development and its insatiable demand for natural resources had created a mining boom in Mongolia, which was blessed with enormous reserves of copper and other minerals. The economy was expanding at the blistering pace of more than 17 percent in 2011, and some experts predicted faster growth in Mongolia over the next decade than in any other country on earth. Most people were still poor, and many retained their nomadic lifestyle, but the global economy that had once felt so far away had arrived in full force.

As I drove into the once sleepy capital, Ulaanbaatar, I was amazed at the transformation. Glass skyscrapers soared up from amid a jumble of traditional *gers* and old Soviet housing projects. In Sukhbaatar Square, soldiers in traditional Mongolian garb stood guard in the shadow of a new Louis Vuitton store. I walked into Government House, a large holdover from the Stalinist era, past an enormous statue of Genghis Khan, the 13th-century Mongolian warrior whose empire spanned a larger land mass than any other in history. The Soviets had suppressed the personality cult of Khan, but now he was back with a vengeance. Inside, I met with President Tsakhiagiin Elbegdorj in his ceremonial *ger*. We were sitting in a traditional nomadic tent, inside a Stalinist-era government building, discussing the future of the rapidly growing Asian economy. Talk about worlds colliding!

Since my 1995 visit, Mongolian democracy had endured. The country had held six successful Parliamentary elections. On television Mongolians from across the political spectrum openly and vigorously debated ideas. A long-awaited freedom of information law was giving citizens a clearer view into the workings of their government. Alongside this progress there was also cause for concern. The mining boom was exacerbating the problems of corruption and inequality, and China was taking a greater interest in its suddenly valuable northern neighbor. Mongolia appeared to be at a crossroads: either it was going to continue down the democratic path and use its new riches to raise the standard of living of all its people, or it was going to be pulled into Beijing's orbit and experience the worst excesses of the "resource curse." I hoped to encourage the former and discourage the latter.

The timing was good. The Community of Democracies, an international organization founded in 2000 under the leadership of Secretary Albright to nurture emerging democracies, especially those in the former Soviet bloc, was holding a summit in Ulaanbaatar. This would be an opportunity to reinforce Mongolia's progress and send a message about the importance of democracy and human rights across Asia, delivered in China's own backyard.

It's not a secret that the epicenter of the antidemocratic movement in Asia is China. The 2010 Nobel Peace Prize had been awarded to the imprisoned Chinese human rights activist Liu Xiaobo, and the world took note of his empty chair at the ceremony in Oslo. Afterward I warned that it could become "a symbol of a great nation's unrealized potential and unfulfilled promise." Things had only gotten worse in 2011. In the first few months, dozens of public interest lawyers, writers, artists, intellectuals, and activists were arbitrarily detained and arrested. Among them was the prominent artist Ai Weiwei, whose cause I and others championed.

In my speech in Ulaanbaatar I explained why a democratic future for Asia was the right choice. In China and elsewhere opponents of democracy argued that it would threaten stability by unleashing chaotic popular forces. But we had plenty of evidence from around the world that democracy actually fosters stability. It is true that clamping down on political expression and maintaining a tight grip on what people read or say or see can create the illusion of security, but illusions fade, while people's yearning for liberty does not. By contrast, democracy provides critical safety valves for societies. It allows people to select their leaders, gives those leaders legitimacy to make difficult but necessary decisions for the national good, and lets minorities express their views peacefully.

Another argument I wanted to rebut was that democracy is a privilege belonging to wealthy countries and that developing economies need to put growth first and worry about democracy later. China was often cited as the prime example of a country that had achieved economic success without meaningful political reform. But that too was a "shortsighted and ultimately unsustainable bargain," I said. "You cannot over the long run have economic liberalization without political liberalization. Countries that want to be open for business but closed to free expression will find the approach comes with a cost." Without the free exchange of ideas and strong rule of law, innovation and entrepreneurship wither.

I pledged that the United States would be a strong partner to all those across Asia and the world who were dedicated to human rights and fundamental freedoms. I had been saying "Let them come to Mongolia!" for years, and I was delighted that so many democracy activists finally had. Back home a *Washington Post* editorial declared that my speech had offered "hope that the U.S. pivot to Asia will go beyond simple muscle-flexing and become a multi-layered approach to match the complexity of China's rise as a modern superpower." In China, however, censors went right to work erasing mentions of my message from the internet.

4

China: Uncharted Waters

Like many Americans, my first real look at China came in 1972, when President Richard Nixon made his historic trip across the Pacific. Bill and I were law students without a television, so we went out and rented a portable set with rabbit ears. We lugged it back to our apartment and tuned in every night to watch scenes of a country that had been blocked from view for our entire lives. I was riveted and proud of what America accomplished during what President Nixon called "the week that changed the world."

Looking back, it's clear that both sides had taken enormous risks. They were venturing into the unknown, during the height of the Cold War no less. There could be serious political consequences at home for leaders on both sides for appearing weak or, in our case, "soft on Communism." But the men who negotiated the trip, Henry Kissinger for the United States and Zhou Enlai for China, and the leaders they represented, calculated that the potential benefits outweighed the risks. (I have joked with Henry that he was lucky there were no smartphones or social media when he made his first secret trip to Beijing. Imagine if a Secretary tried to do that today.) We do similar calculations today when we deal with nations whose policies we disagree with but whose cooperation we need, or when we want to avoid letting disagreements and competition slip into conflict.

The U.S.-China relationship is still full of challenges. We are two large, complex nations with profoundly different histories, political systems, and outlooks, whose economies and futures have become deeply entwined. This isn't a relationship that fits neatly into categories like friend or rival, and it may never. We are sailing in uncharted waters. Staying on course and avoiding the shoals and whirlpools requires both a true compass and the flexibility to make frequent course corrections, including sometimes painful trade-offs. If we push too hard on one front, we may jeopardize another. By the same token, if we are too quick to compromise or accommodate, we may invite aggression. With all these elements to consider, it can be easy to lose sight of the fact that, across the divide, our counterparts have their own pressures and imperatives. The more both sides follow the example of those intrepid early diplomats to bridge the gaps in understanding and interests, the better chance we will have of making progress.

═════

My first trip to China, in 1995, was among the most memorable of my life. The Fourth World Conference on Women, at which I declared, "Human rights are women's rights and women's rights are human rights," was a profound experience for me. I felt the heavy hand of Chinese censorship when the government blocked the broadcast of my speech, both throughout the conference center and on official television and radio. Most of my speech was about women's rights, but I also sent a message to the Chinese authorities, who had banished the events for civil society activists to a separate site in Huairou, a full hour's drive outside Beijing, and barred women from Tibet and Taiwan from attending at all. "Freedom means the right of people to assemble, organize, and debate openly," I declared from the podium. "It means respecting the views of those who may disagree with the views of their governments. It means not taking citizens away from their loved ones and jailing them, mistreating them or denying them their freedom or dignity because of the peaceful expression of their ideas and opinions." Those were more pointed words than American diplomats usually used, especially on Chinese soil, and some in the U.S. government had urged me to give a different speech or not speak at all. But I thought it was important to stand up for democratic values and human rights in a place where they were seriously threatened.

In June 1998, I returned to China for a longer stay. Chelsea and my mom accompanied Bill and me on an official state visit. The Chinese requested a formal arrival ceremony in Tiananmen Square, where tanks had crushed pro-democracy demonstrations in June 1989. Bill thought about refusing the request, so as not to appear to endorse or ignore that ugly history, but in the end he decided that his human rights message might get through more in China if he acted like a respectful guest. The Chinese, in turn, surprised us by permitting the uncensored broadcast of Bill's news conference with President Jiang Zemin, during which they had an extended exchange about human rights, including the taboo topic of Tibet. They also broadcast Bill's speech to students at Beijing University as well, in which he stressed that "true freedom includes more than economic freedom."

I came home from the trip convinced that if China over time embraces reform and modernization, it could become a constructive world power and an important partner for the United States. But it was not going to be easy, and America would have to be smart and vigilant in how we engaged this growing nation.

I returned to China as Secretary in February 2009 with the goal of building a relationship durable enough to weather the inevitable disputes and crises that would arise. I also wanted to embed the China relationship in our broader Asia strategy, engaging Beijing in the region's multilateral institutions in ways that would encourage it to work with its neighbors according to agreed-upon rules. At the same time, I wanted China to know that it was not the sole focus of our attention in Asia. We would not sacrifice our values or our traditional allies in order to win better terms with China. Despite its impressive economic growth and advances in military capacity, it had not yet come close to surpassing the United States as the most powerful nation in the Asia-Pacific. We were prepared to engage from a position of strength.

Before arriving in Beijing from South Korea, I sat down to talk with our traveling press corps. I told them I would emphasize cooperation on the global economic crisis, climate change, and security issues, such as North Korea and Afghanistan. After listing the agenda highlights, I mentioned that the sensitive issues of Taiwan, Tibet, and human rights would also be on the table and said, "We pretty much know what they're going to say."

It was true, of course. American diplomats had been raising these issues for years, and the Chinese were quite predictable in their responses. I remembered a heated discussion I had with former President Jiang about China's treatment of Tibet during the state dinner Bill and I hosted for him at the White House in October 1997. I had met previously with the Dalai Lama to discuss the Tibetans' plight, and I asked President Jiang to explain China's repression. "The Chinese are the liberators of the Tibetan people. I have read the histories in our libraries, and I know Tibetans are better off now than they were before," he replied. "But what about their traditions and the right to practice their religion as they choose?" I persisted. He forcefully insisted that Tibet was a part of China and demanded to know why Americans advocated for those "necromancers." Tibetans "were victims of religion. They are now freed from feudalism," he declared.

So I had no illusions about what Chinese officials would be saying to me when I raised these issues again. I also made the obvious point that, given the breadth and complexity of our relationship with China, our profound differences on human rights could not exclude engagement on all other issues. We had to be able to stand up forcefully for dissidents while also seeking cooperation on the economy, climate change, and nuclear proliferation. This had been our approach since Nixon went to China. Nonetheless my comments were widely interpreted to mean that human rights would not be a priority for the Obama Administration and that the Chinese could safely ignore them. Nothing could have been further from reality, as future events showed. Still, it was a valuable lesson: now that I was America's chief diplomat, every utterance would be subjected to a whole new level of scrutiny, and even seemingly self-evident observations could set off a feeding frenzy in the media.

It had been more than a decade since my previous visit, and driving through Beijing was like watching a movie in fast-forward. Where once only a handful of high-rise buildings were visible, now the sky was dominated by the gleaming new Olympic complex and endless corporate towers. Streets that had once been full of Flying Pigeon bicycles were now jammed with cars.

While in Beijing I met with a group of women activists, some of whom I had gotten to know in 1998. At that time Secretary Albright and I had crowded into a cramped legal aid office to hear about their efforts to win rights for women to own property, have a say in marriage and divorce, and be treated as equal citizens. More than ten years later the size of the group and the scope of their collective efforts had grown. Now there were activists working not just for women's legal rights but for their environmental, health, and economic rights as well.

One of them was Dr. Gao Yaojie, a diminutive eighty-two-year-old who had been harassed by the government for speaking out about AIDS in China and exposing a tainted blood scandal. When we first met I noticed her tiny feet—they had been bound—and was amazed by her story. She had persevered through civil war, the Cultural Revolution, house arrest, and forced family separation, and she never shied away from her commitment to help as many of her fellow citizens as possible protect themselves against AIDS.

In 2007, I interceded with President Hu Jintao to allow Dr. Gao to come to Washington to receive an award after local officials tried to prevent her from traveling. Here we were two years later, and she was still facing government pressure. Nonetheless she told me she planned to continue advocating for transparency and accountability. "I am already 82. I am not going to live that much longer," she said. "This is an important issue. I am not afraid." Not long after my visit, Dr. Gao was forced to leave China. She now lives in New York City, where she continues to write and speak out about AIDS in China.

Much of my time on this first visit to Beijing as Secretary was filled with get-to-know-you sessions with senior Chinese officials. I met for lunch with State Councilor Dai Bingguo at the serene and traditional Diaoyutai State Guesthouse, where President Nixon stayed on his famous visit and where we had stayed during our 1998 trip. Dai, along with Foreign Minister Yang Jiechi, would become my primary counterparts in the Chinese government. (In the Chinese system, a State Councilor is more senior than a Minister, ranking just below a Vice Premier in the hierarchy.)

A career diplomat, Dai was close to President Hu and adept at maneuvering the internal politics of the Chinese power structure. He was proud of his reputation as a man from the provinces who had risen to prominence. Small and compact, he stayed vigorous and healthy despite his advancing years by doing regular exercise and taking long walks, which he highly recommended to me. He was comfortable discussing history and philosophy as well as current events. Henry Kissinger had told me how highly he valued his relationship with Dai, whom he found to be one of the most fascinating and open-minded Chinese officials he had ever encountered. Dai thought about the grand sweep of history, and he approvingly repeated the proverb I had used in my Asia Society speech: "When you are in a common boat, cross the river peacefully together." When I told him that I thought the United States and China had to write a new answer to the age-old question of what happens when an established power and a rising power meet, he enthusiastically agreed, and frequently repeated my formulation. Throughout history, that scenario had often led to conflict, so it was our job to chart a course that avoided that end by keeping competition within acceptable boundaries and promoting as much cooperation as possible.

Dai and I hit it off right away, and we talked often over the years. Sometimes I'd be subjected to long lectures about everything the United States was doing wrong in Asia, laced with sarcasm but always delivered with a smile. At other times the two of us talked deeply and personally about the need to put the U.S.-China relationship on a sound footing for the sake of future generations. On one of my early visits to Beijing, Dai presented me with thoughtful personal gifts for Chelsea and my mother, which was above and beyond the normal diplomatic protocol. The next time he came to Washington, I reciprocated with a gift for his only grand-daughter, which seemed to please him very much. In an early meeting, he had pulled out a small photograph of the baby girl and showed it to me, saying, "This is what we're in it for." That sentiment struck a chord with me. It was concern for the welfare of children that got me into public service in the first place. As Secretary of State I had the chance to make the world a little safer and life a little better for children in America and across the globe, including in China. I viewed it as the opportunity and the responsibility of a lifetime. That Dai shared my passion became the basis of an enduring bond between us.

Foreign Minister Yang had risen up the ranks of the diplomatic corps, starting as an interpreter. His superb command of English enabled us to have long, sometimes spirited conversations during our many meetings and phone calls. He rarely dropped his careful diplomatic persona, but I could occasionally glimpse the real person behind it. Once he told me that, as a child growing up in Shanghai, he sat in an unheated classroom, shivering, his hands too cold to hold a pen. His journey from the freezing schoolhouse all the way to the Foreign Ministry was a source of his great personal pride in China's progress. He was an unapologetic nationalist, and we had our share of tense exchanges, especially about difficult topics like the South China Sea, North Korea, and territorial disputes with Japan.

Late one night, in one of our last discussions in 2012, Yang started waxing on about China's many superlative achievements, including its athletic dominance. It was just about a month after the London Olympics, and I gently pointed out that America, in fact, had won the most medals of any country. Yang, in turn, chalked up China's "decline in fortunes" at the Olympics to the absence of the injured basketball star Yao Ming. He also joked that there should be a "diplomacy Olympics" with events like "miles traveled"; that would net the United States at least one more medal.

In my first conversation with Yang in February 2009, he brought up a topic I didn't expect that was clearly bothering him. The Chinese were preparing to host a major international exposition in May 2010, like the world's fairs of an earlier era. Every country in the world was responsible for building a pavilion on the exposition grounds to showcase their national culture and traditions. Only two nations were failing to participate, Yang told me: tiny Andorra and the United States. The Chinese saw that as a sign of disrespect, and also of American decline. I was surprised to learn that we weren't pulling our weight and pledged to Yang that I would make sure the United States was well represented.

I soon discovered that the USA Pavilion was out of money, way behind schedule, and unlikely ever to be completed unless things changed dramatically. This was not a good way to project American power and values in Asia. So I made it a personal priority to get our pavilion built, which meant raising money and support from the private sector in record time.

We pulled it off, and in May 2010, I joined millions of other visitors from around the world to tour the expo. The USA Pavilion showcased American products and stories that illustrated some of our most cherished national values: perseverance, innovation, and diversity. What struck me most were the American students who volunteered to serve as hosts and guides. They represented the full spectrum of the American people, from every walk of life and background, and they all spoke Mandarin. Many Chinese visitors were stunned to hear Americans speak their language so enthusiastically. They stopped to talk, asked questions, told jokes, and swapped stories. It was another reminder that personal contacts can do as much or more for the U.S.-China relationship than most diplomatic encounters or choreographed summits.

After my discussions with Dai and Yang on that February 2009 visit, I had the opportunity to meet separately with President Hu and Premier Wen. It was the first of at least a dozen encounters over the years. The senior leaders were more scripted than Dai or Yang and less comfortable in a freewheeling discussion. The higher you went up the chain, the higher the premium the Chinese put on predictability, formality, and respectful decorum. They didn't want any surprises. Appearances mattered. With me, they were careful and polite, even a little wary. They were studying me, just as I was studying them.

Hu was gracious, expressing his appreciation for my decision to make such an early visit to China. He was the most powerful man in China, but he lacked the personal authority of predecessors such as Deng Xiaoping or Jiang Zemin. Hu seemed to me more like an aloof chairman of the board than a hands-on CEO. How in control he really was of the entire sprawling Communist Party apparatus was an open question, especially when it came to the military.

"Grandpa Wen," as the Premier (the #2 official) was called, worked hard to present a kindly, soft-spoken image to China and the world. But in private he could be quite pointed, especially when he was arguing that the United States was responsible for the global financial crisis or when he brushed aside criticism of China's policies. He was never combative, but he was more cutting than his public persona might have suggested.

In my early meetings with these leaders, I proposed making the U.S.-China economic dialogue started by former Treasury Secretary Hank Paulson a strategic dialogue as well, to cover a much wider range of issues and bring together more experts and officials from across our two governments. This wasn't an excuse for the State Department to elbow into the conversation or to set up a high-profile debating society. I knew that regular talks, in essence a high-level steering committee for the relationship, would expand our cooperation into new areas and build greater trust and resiliency. Policymakers on both sides would get to know each other and become used to working together. Open lines of communication would reduce the likelihood that a misunderstanding would escalate tensions. Future disputes would be less likely to derail everything else we needed to do together.

I had discussed this idea with Hank Paulson's successor at Treasury, Tim Geithner, over lunch at the State Department in early February 2009. I had gotten to know and like Tim when he was President of the New

York Federal Reserve. He had extensive experience in Asia and even spoke a little Mandarin, making him an ideal partner in our engagement with China. To his credit, Tim did not see my proposal for the expanded dialogue as an intrusion on Treasury's turf—turf, of course, being a precious Washington commodity. He saw it as I did: as a chance to combine our departments' strengths, especially at a time when the global financial crisis was blurring the line between economics and security more than ever. If the Chinese agreed, Tim and I would chair the new combined dialogue together.

In Beijing I was prepared for reluctance, even rejection. After all, the Chinese were not eager to discuss sensitive political topics. Yet it turned out they were also eager for more high-level contact with the United States, and were seeking what President Hu Jintao called a "positive, cooperative and comprehensive relationship." In time our Strategic and Economic Dialogue would become a model we replicated with emerging powers around the world, from India to South Africa and Brazil.

===

For decades, the guiding doctrine of Chinese foreign policy was Deng Xiaoping's counsel, "Coolly observe, calmly deal with things, hold your position, hide your capacities, bide your time, accomplish things where possible." Deng, who ruled China after the death of Chairman Mao Zedong, believed that China was not yet strong enough to assert itself on the world stage, and his "hide and bide" strategy helped avoid conflict with neighbors as China's economy took off. Bill and I met Deng briefly on his historic tour of the United States in 1979. I had never met a Chinese leader before and closely observed him as he casually interacted with the American guests at a reception and dinner at the Georgia Governor's Mansion. He was engaging and made an excellent impression, both personally and in his willingness to begin opening his country up to reform.

By 2009, however, some officials in China, especially in the military, chafed at this posture of restraint. They thought that the United States, long the most powerful nation in the Asia-Pacific, was receding from the region but still determined to block China's rise as a great power in its own right. It was, they thought, time for a more assertive approach. They were emboldened by the financial crisis of 2008 that weakened the U.S. economy, the wars in Iraq and Afghanistan that sapped American attention and resources, and a rising current of nationalism among the Chinese people. And so China started making more aggressive moves in Asia, testing how hard it could push.

In November 2009, President Obama received a noticeably luke-warm reception during his visit to Beijing. The Chinese insisted on stage-managing most of his appearances, refused to give any ground on issues such as human rights or currency valuation, and offered pointed lectures on America's budget problems. The *New York Times* described the joint press conference between President Obama and President Hu as "stilted"—so much so that it was parodied on *Saturday Night Live*. Many observers wondered whether we were seeing a new phase in the relationship, with an ascendant and assertive China no longer hiding its resources and enhanced military capabilities, moving away from "hide and bide" and toward "show and tell."

The most dramatic arena for Chinese assertiveness was at sea. China, Vietnam, the Philippines, and Japan all have coasts on the South and East China Seas. For generations they have jousted over competing ter-ritorial claims in the area, over strings of reefs, rocks, outcroppings, and mostly uninhabited islands. In the south, China and Vietnam clashed violently over contested islands in the 1970s and 1980s. China tangled with the Philippines in the 1990s over other islands. In the East China Sea, a chain of eight uninhabited islands, known as the Senkakus to the Japanese and the Diaoyus to the Chinese, have been the subject of a long and heated dispute that, as of 2014, continues to simmer and threatens to boil over at any time. In November 2013, China declared an "air defense identification zone" over much of the East China Sea, including the dis-puted islands, and demanded that all international air traffic adhere to its regulations. The United States and our allies refused to recognize this move and continued to fly military planes through what we still consider international airspace.

These conflicts may not be new, but the stakes have risen. As Asia's economy has grown, so has the trade flowing through the region. At least half the world's merchant tonnage passes through the South China Sea, including many shipments headed to or from the United States. Discover-ies of new offshore energy reserves and surrounding fisheries have made the waters around otherwise unremarkable clumps of rocks into potential treasure troves. Old rivalries heightened by the prospect of new riches make for a combustible recipe.

Throughout 2009 and 2010 China's neighbors watched with increasing alarm as Beijing accelerated a naval buildup and asserted its claim to wide swaths of water, islands, and energy reserves. These actions were the opposite of what former U.S. Deputy Secretary of State (and later president of the World Bank) Robert Zoellick had hoped for when he urged China to become a "responsible stakeholder" in a much-noted speech in 2005. Instead China was becoming what I called a "selective stakeholder," picking and choosing when to act like a responsible great power and when to assert the right to impose its will on its smaller neighbors.

In March 2009, just two months into the Obama Administration, five Chinese ships confronted a lightly armed U.S. naval vessel, the *Impeccable,* about seventy-five miles from the Chinese island province of Hainan. The Chinese demanded that the Americans leave what they claimed were exclusive territorial waters. The crew of the *Impeccable* responded that they were in international waters and had a right to free navigation. Chinese sailors threw pieces of wood in the water to block the ship's path. The Americans responded by spraying a fire hose at the Chinese, some of whom stripped to their underwear after being doused. The scene could almost be considered comical if it didn't represent a potentially dangerous confrontation. Over the next two years, similar standoffs at sea between China and Japan, China and Vietnam, and China and the Philippines threatened to spiral out of control. Something had to be done.

China prefers to resolve territorial disputes with its neighbors bilaterally, or one-on-one, because in those situations its relative power is greater. In multilateral settings where smaller nations could band together, its sway decreased. Not surprisingly, most of the rest of the region preferred the multilateral approach. They believed there were too many overlapping claims and interests to try to settle them in a patchwork, one-off fashion. Getting all the relevant players in the same room and giving them all a chance to express their views—especially the smaller countries—was the best way to move toward a comprehensive solution.

I agreed with this approach. The United States has no territorial claims in the South or East China Seas, we don't take sides in such disputes, and we oppose unilateral efforts to change the status quo. We have an abiding interest in protecting freedom of navigation, maritime commerce, and international law. And we have treaty obligations to support Japan and the Philippines.

My concerns escalated when I was in Beijing for the Strategic and

Economic Dialogue in May 2010 and for the first time heard Chinese leaders describe the country's territorial claims in the South China Sea as a "core interest" alongside traditional hot-button topics like Taiwan and Tibet. They warned that China would not tolerate outside interference. Later the meetings were disrupted when a Chinese admiral stood up and launched into an angry rant accusing the United States of trying to encircle China and suppress its rise. This was highly unusual in a carefully choreographed summit, and—although I assumed the admiral had gotten at least a tacit go-ahead from his military and party bosses—it appeared that some of the Chinese diplomats were as surprised as I was.

The confrontations in the South China Sea in the first two years of the Obama Administration reinforced my belief that our strategy in Asia must include a significant effort to upgrade the region's multilateral institutions. The available venues just weren't effective enough for resolving disputes between nations or mobilizing action. For the smaller nations, it could feel like the Wild West: a frontier without the rule of law, where the weak were at the mercy of the strong. Our goal was not just to help defuse flash points like the South or East China Sea but also to nurture an international system of rules and organizations in the Asia-Pacific that could help avoid future conflicts and bring some order and long-term stability to the region—something that began to approximate what Europe had built.

On the flight home from the talks in Beijing, I took stock with my team. I thought China had overplayed its hand. Instead of using the period of our perceived absence and the economic crisis to cement good relations with its neighbors, it had become more aggressive toward them, and that shift had unnerved the rest of the region. When times are good with few threats to security or prosperity, nations are less likely to see the appeal of expensive defense alliances, strong international rules and norms, and robust multilateral institutions. But when conflict unsettles the status quo, these agreements and protections become a lot more attractive, especially to smaller nations.

＝＝＝

Perhaps there was an opportunity to be found amid all these troubling developments. One presented itself just two months later at an ASEAN regional forum in Vietnam. I touched down in Hanoi on July 22, 2010, and went to a lunch marking the fifteenth anniversary of normalized diplomatic relations between Vietnam and the United States.

I vividly remembered the day in July 1995 when Bill made the historic announcement in the East Room of the White House, flanked by Vietnam veterans, including Senators John Kerry and John McCain. It was the beginning of a new era—healing old wounds, settling questions about prisoners of war, and charting a path of improved economic and strategic relations. In 2000, we went to Hanoi, the first visit by a U.S. President. We were prepared to find resentment, even hostility, but as we drove into the city, large crowds lined the streets to welcome us. Throngs of students, who had grown up knowing only peace between our nations, gathered at Hanoi National University to hear Bill speak. Everywhere we went we felt the warmth and hospitality of the Vietnamese people, a reflection of the goodwill that had developed between our countries in the span of a single generation and a powerful testament to the fact that the past does not have to determine the future.

Back in Hanoi as Secretary of State, I marveled at how far Vietnam had come since that visit and how our relations continued to improve. Our annual trade had grown to nearly $20 billion in 2010 from less than $250 million before relations were normalized, and it was expanding rapidly every year. Vietnam also presented a unique—though challenging—strategic opportunity. On the one hand, it remained an authoritarian country with a poor record on human rights, especially press freedoms. On the other, it was steadily taking steps to open up its economy and trying to claim a larger role in the region. Over the years Vietnamese officials had told me that, despite the war we had fought against them, they admired and liked America.

One of our most important tools for engaging with Vietnam was a proposed new trade agreement called the Trans-Pacific Partnership (TPP), which would link markets throughout Asia and the Americas, lowering trade barriers while raising standards on labor, the environment, and intellectual property. As President Obama explained, the goal of the TPP negotiations is to establish "a high standard, enforceable, meaningful trade agreement" that "is going to be incredibly powerful for American companies who, up until this point, have often been locked out of those markets." It was also important for American workers, who would benefit from competing on a more level playing field. And it was a strategic initiative that would strengthen the position of the United States in Asia.

Our country has learned the hard way over the past several decades that globalization and the expansion of international trade brings costs as well as benefits. On the 2008 campaign trail, both then-Senator Obama and I had promised to pursue smarter, fairer trade agreements. Because TPP negotiations are still ongoing, it makes sense to reserve judgment until we can evaluate the final proposed agreement. It's safe to say that the TPP won't be perfect—no deal negotiated among a dozen countries ever will be—but its higher standards, if implemented and enforced, should benefit American businesses and workers.

Vietnam also stood to gain a lot from this deal—the TPP would cover a third of world trade—so its leaders were willing to make some reforms to reach an agreement. As negotiations gained momentum, other countries in the region felt the same way. The TPP became the signature economic pillar of our strategy in Asia, demonstrating the benefits of a rules-based order and greater cooperation with the United States.

On the afternoon of July 22, the ASEAN regional meetings began in Hanoi's National Convention Center with long, formal discussions on trade, climate change, human trafficking, nuclear proliferation, North Korea, and Burma. But as the meetings stretched into the second day, there was one topic on everyone's mind: the South China Sea. The territorial disputes, already fraught with history, nationalism, and economics, had become a crucial test question: Would China use its growing power to dominate an expanding sphere of influence, or would the region reaffirm international norms that bind even the strongest nations? Naval vessels were squaring off in contested waters, newspapers were whipping up nationalist sentiments across the region, and diplomats were scrambling to prevent open conflict. Yet China kept insisting this wasn't an appropriate topic for a regional conference.

That night I gathered Kurt Campbell and my Asia team to review our plans for the next day. What we had in mind would require subtle diplomacy, calling on all the groundwork we had laid in the region over the past year and a half. We spent hours fine-tuning the statement I would make the next day and working out the choreography with our partners.

As soon as we started the ASEAN session, the drama began to build. Vietnam got the ball rolling. Despite China's objections to discussing the South China Sea in this setting, Vietnam raised the contentious issue. Then, one by one, other Ministers expressed their concerns and called for a collaborative, multilateral approach to resolving territorial disputes.

After two years of China's flexing its muscles and asserting its dominance, the region was pushing back. When the moment was right, I signaled my intention to speak.

The United States would not take sides on any particular dispute, I said, but we supported the multilateral approach being proposed, in accordance with international law and without coercion or the threat of force. I urged the nations of the region to protect unfettered access to the South China Sea and to work toward developing a code of conduct that would prevent conflict. The United States was prepared to facilitate this process because we saw freedom of navigation in the South China Sea as a "national interest." That was a carefully chosen phrase, answering the earlier Chinese assertion that its expansive territorial claims in the area constituted a "core interest."

When I was finished, I could see that Chinese Foreign Minister Yang was livid. He asked for an hour-long break before coming back to deliver his response. Staring directly at me, he dismissed the disputes in the South China Sea and warned against outside interference. Looking at his Asian neighbors, he reminded them, "China is a big country. Bigger than any other countries here." It was not a winning argument in that room.

The confrontation in Hanoi did not resolve the contests in the South and East China Seas; those remain active and dangerous as of this writing. But in subsequent years, diplomats in the region would point to that meeting as a tipping point, both in terms of American leadership in Asia and in the pushback against Chinese overreach.

As I headed back to Washington, I felt more confident about our strategy and position in Asia. When we started in 2009, many in the region doubted our commitment and our staying power. Some in China sought to take advantage of that perception. Our pivot strategy was designed to dispel those doubts. During one long discussion with Dai, he exclaimed, "Why don't you 'pivot' out of here?" I had logged more miles and sat through more awkwardly translated diplomatic speeches than I imagined possible. But it paid off. We had climbed out of the hole we found ourselves in at the beginning of the administration and reasserted America's presence in the region. The years that followed would bring new challenges, from a sudden leadership change in North Korea to a standoff with the Chinese over the fate of a blind human rights dissident hiding in the U.S. Embassy. There would be new opportunities as well. Flickers of progress in Burma would ignite a dramatic transformation and carry the promise of democracy into the heart of that formerly closed land. And thanks in part to our determined efforts to establish mutual trust and habits of cooperation, relations with China would prove more resilient than many dared hope.

=====

On the plane home from Hanoi, with my head still full of South China Sea drama, it was time to turn my attention to other urgent business. We were just over a week away from what would be one of the most important events in my life. The press was clamoring for information, and I had a lot of work to do to get ready. This time it wasn't a high-level summit or a diplomatic crisis. It was my daughter's wedding, a day I had been looking forward to for thirty years.

I was amused by how much attention Chelsea's plans were getting, and not just in the United States. In Poland in early July, an interviewer had asked me how I was juggling preparations for the wedding while representing America as Secretary of State. "How can you cope with two quite different tasks, but both of them extremely serious?" he asked. And how serious a task it was! When Bill and I got married in 1975, the ceremony took place in front of a few friends and family in the living room of our little house in Fayetteville, Arkansas. I wore a lace-and-muslin Victorian dress I had found shopping with my mother the night before. Times had changed.

Chelsea and our soon-to-be son-in-law, Marc Mezvinsky, planned an unforgettable weekend for their families and friends in Rhinebeck, New York. As mother of the bride, I was delighted to help in every way I could, including reviewing photographs of flower arrangements from the road and making time for tastings and dress selections back home. I felt lucky that my day job had prepared me for the elaborate diplomacy required to help plan a big wedding. I got such a kick out of it that I referred to myself as "MOTB" (mother of the bride) in a Mother's Day email to all State Department staff, also a nod to a necklace Chelsea had given me for Christmas with those same letters. Now that Hanoi was behind me, I was eager to get back to all the last-minute details and decisions that awaited.

On Monday I spent most of the day at the White House, meeting with President Obama in the Oval Office and with the rest of the national security team in the Situation Room and visiting with Israeli Defense

Minister Ehud Barak. I always enjoy seeing Ehud, and we were at another delicate moment for peace negotiations in the Middle East, but this time I couldn't stop thinking about when I could leave and jump on a shuttle flight up to New York.

The big day finally arrived on Saturday, July 31. Rhinebeck is a lovely town in the Hudson Valley with quaint shops and good restaurants, and it provided the perfect setting. Chelsea's and Marc's friends and family gathered at Astor Courts, an elegant Beaux Arts estate designed by the architect Stanford White for Jacob and Ava Astor around the turn of the century. Its indoor swimming pool, where Franklin Delano Roosevelt is said to have performed physical therapy for his polio, may have been the first built for a private home anywhere in America. After Jacob Astor went down with the *Titanic*, the house was passed from owner to owner and spent a number of years as a nursing home run by the Catholic Church. In 2008 it was restored to its original beauty.

Chelsea looked absolutely stunning, and watching her walk down the aisle with Bill, I couldn't believe that the baby girl I had held in my arms for the first time on February 27, 1980, had grown into this beautiful and poised woman. Bill was as emotional as I was, maybe even more so, and I was just glad he made it down the aisle in one piece. Marc was beaming as Chelsea joined him under the chuppah, a canopy of willow branches and flowers that is part of the Jewish marriage tradition. The service was led by the Reverend William Shillady and Rabbi James Ponet, and they hit just the right note. Marc stepped on a glass, in keeping with Jewish tradition, and everyone cheered. Afterward Bill danced with Chelsea to "The Way You Look Tonight." It was one of the happiest and proudest moments of my life.

So many thoughts went through my head. Our family had been through a lot together, good times and hard times, and now here we were, celebrating the best of times. I was especially glad that my mother had been able to see this day. She overcame a difficult childhood with very little love or support, and yet still figured out how to be a loving and caring mom to me and my brothers, Hugh and Tony. She and Chelsea shared a special bond, and I knew how much it meant to Chelsea to have her grandmother beside her as she planned her wedding and married Marc.

I thought about the future, and the life that Chelsea and Marc would build together. They had so many dreams and ambitions. This, I thought, is why Bill and I had worked so hard for so many years to help build a better world—so Chelsea could grow up safe and happy and one day have a family of her own, and so every other child would have the same chance. I remembered what Dai Bingguo had said to me when he pulled out the photograph of his granddaughter: "This is what we're in it for." It was our responsibility to find a way to work together to make sure our children and grandchildren inherited the world they deserved.

5

Beijing: The Dissident

Shortly after I was confirmed as Secretary, a team of engineers descended on our home in northwest Washington. They installed a bright yellow secure telephone so that even at odd hours of the night, I could speak to the President or an Ambassador in some faraway embassy about sensitive topics. It was a constant reminder that the troubles of the world were never far from home.

At 9:36 on the night of Wednesday, April 25, 2012, the yellow phone rang. It was my Director of Policy Planning and Deputy Chief of Staff Jake Sullivan, calling from his own secure line on the seventh floor of the State Department, where he'd hastily returned from a rare night off. He told me that our embassy in Beijing faced an unexpected crisis and urgently needed direction.

Unbeknownst to us, less than a week earlier, a blind, forty-year-old human rights activist named Chen Guangcheng had escaped from house arrest in Shandong Province by climbing over the wall of his home. He broke his foot but managed to elude the local police assigned to watch him. Leaving his family behind, he set out on a journey hundreds of miles to Beijing with the help of a modern-day Underground Railroad of fellow dissidents and supporters. While in hiding in Beijing he made contact with a Foreign Service officer at the American Embassy who had long ties to the Chinese human rights community. She immediately recognized the seriousness of the situation.

Chen had gained notoriety in China as the "barefoot lawyer," advocating for the rights of the disabled, helping rural villagers protest illegal land seizures by corrupt local authorities, and documenting abuses of the one-child policy such as forced sterilizations and abortions. Unlike many other high-profile Chinese dissidents, Chen was not a student at an elite university or an urban intellectual. He was a villager himself, poor and self-taught, and the public came to see him as a genuine man of the people. In 2005 he was arrested after filing a class-action lawsuit on behalf of thousands of victims of government repression. A local court sentenced him to fifty-one months in prison, supposedly for destroying property and obstructing traffic. It was a blunt miscarriage of justice, shocking even in a country with little rule of law. After serving out his full sentence, he was released into house arrest, surrounded by armed guards and cut off from the outside world.

Now he was injured, on the run, and asking for our help. At dawn in Beijing, two U.S. Embassy officers met in secret with Chen. With Chinese State Security hunting for him, he asked if he could take refuge at the embassy, at least long enough to receive medical attention and devise a new plan. They agreed to relay the request to Washington, where it quickly made its way up the chain. Chen continued to circle the Beijing suburbs in a car, waiting for a response.

A number of factors made this a particularly difficult decision. First there were the logistics. Chen had a broken foot and was a wanted man. If we didn't act quickly, he would likely be captured. To make matters worse, Chinese security regularly maintained a robust presence outside our embassy. If Chen tried to walk up to the front door, they would surely seize him before we could even unbolt the lock. The only way to get him safely inside would be to send a team out into the streets to quietly pick him up. Bob Wang, our Deputy Chief of Mission in Beijing, estimated that Chen's chances of getting in on his own were less than 10 percent. He thought it was above 90 percent if we went out and got him. That, however, would certainly increase tensions with the Chinese.

Timing was also a factor. As it happened, I was preparing to depart in five days for Beijing myself, to participate in the annual Strategic and Economic Dialogue with Treasury Secretary Tim Geithner and our Chinese counterparts. It was the culmination of an entire year's worth of painstaking diplomatic work, and we had a full agenda of important and sensitive issues, including tensions in the South China Sea, provocations from North Korea, and economic concerns like currency valuation and intellectual property theft. If we agreed to help Chen, there was a real chance that the Chinese leaders would be so angry they would cancel the summit. At the very least we could expect much less cooperation on matters of significant strategic importance.

It appeared that I had to decide between protecting one man, albeit a highly sympathetic and symbolic figure, and protecting our relationship with China. On one side of the scale were America's core values and our status as a beacon of freedom and opportunity; on the other were many of our most urgent security and economic priorities.

As I weighed this decision, I thought of the dissidents who sought refuge in American Embassies in Communist countries during the Cold War. One of them, Cardinal József Mindszenty of Hungary, stayed for fifteen years. In 1989 Fang Lizhi and his wife, Li Shuxian, Chinese physicists and prominent activists during the protests in Tiananmen Square, spent nearly thirteen months in the embassy in Beijing before finally making it to the United States. This legacy hung over the Chen case from the beginning.

I also had in mind a much more recent incident. In February 2012, just two months earlier, a Chinese police chief named Wang Lijun walked into the U.S. Consulate in Chengdu, the capital of the southwestern province of Sichuan, looking for help. Until his fall from grace, Wang had been the right-hand man of Bo Xilai, the powerful Communist Party boss of a nearby province. Wang had helped Bo run a vast network of corruption and graft. He eventually claimed to have knowledge of a cover-up of the murder of a British businessman by Bo's wife. Bo was a colorful figure and a rising star in the national Communist Party, but his spectacular abuses of power, including the alleged wiretapping of President Hu Jintao, unnerved his elders in Beijing. They began investigating both Bo and Wang. Afraid that he would end up like the poisoned Brit, Wang fled to our consulate in Chengdu with a head full of stories.

While he was inside, security forces loyal to Bo surrounded the building. It was a tense moment. Wang Lijun was no human rights dissident, but we couldn't just turn him over to the men outside; that would effectively have been a death sentence, and the cover-up would have continued. We also couldn't keep him in the consulate forever. So after asking Wang what he wanted, we reached out to the central authorities in Beijing and suggested that he would voluntarily surrender into their custody if they would listen to his testimony. We had no idea how explosive his story would prove or how seriously Beijing would take it. We agreed to say nothing about the matter, and the Chinese were grateful for our discretion.

Soon the dominoes started to fall. Bo was removed from power, and his wife was convicted of murder. Even the tightest Chinese censorship couldn't stop this from becoming an enormous scandal, and it shook confidence in the Communist Party's leadership at a sensitive time. President Hu and Premier Wen were scheduled to hand over power to a new generation of leaders in early 2013. They badly wanted a smooth transition, not a national furor over official corruption and intrigue.

Now, just two months later, we were facing another test, and I knew the Chinese leadership was more on edge than ever.

═══

I told Jake to set up a conference call with Kurt Campbell, Deputy Secretary Bill Burns, and Counselor Cheryl Mills. Kurt had been coordinating closely with our embassy in Beijing since Chen first made contact, and he told me we probably had less than an hour to make a decision. The embassy had assembled a team that was ready to move to an agreed-upon rendezvous point as soon as I gave the word. We talked it through one more time, and then I said, "Go get him."

In the end it wasn't a close call. I have always believed that, even more than our military and economic power, America's values are the greatest source of strength and security. This isn't just idealism; it's based on a clear-eyed evaluation of our strategic position. The United States had talked about human rights in China for decades, across Democratic and Republican administrations alike. Now our credibility was on the line, with the Chinese and also with other countries in the region and around the world. If we didn't help Chen, it would undermine our position everywhere.

I also was making a calculated gamble that, as the hosts of the upcoming summit, the Chinese had invested at least as much as we had in keeping it on track. Finally, with the Bo Xilai scandal and the impending leadership transition, they had their hands full and wouldn't have much appetite for a new crisis. I was willing to bet that Beijing would not blow up the entire relationship over this one incident.

Once I gave the go-ahead, things started to move fast. Bob Wang departed the embassy en route to the rendezvous. Meanwhile it fell to Jake to brief the White House. He explained my reasoning and answered skeptical questions. Some of the President's aides worried that we were about to destroy America's relationship with China. But no one was prepared to be responsible for leaving Chen to his fate by telling us to stand down. They just wanted me and the State Department to somehow make this problem go away.

While Jake was talking to the White House, a drama right out of a spy novel was unfolding in the streets of Beijing. The embassy car arrived at the rendezvous point, about forty-five minutes away, and Bob caught sight of Chen. He also saw Chinese security in the area. It was now or never. Bob hustled Chen into the car, threw a jacket over his head, and sped off. Bob reported back to Washington with an update from the car, and we all held our breath, hoping that they wouldn't be stopped before reaching the safety of the embassy grounds. Finally, at nearly 3 A.M. in Washington, Bob called back with the good news: the mission was completed, and Chen was now receiving medical attention from the embassy doctor.

Over the course of the next two days, Bill Burns, Kurt, Cheryl, Jake, and I discussed what to do next. The first step was to make contact with the Chinese, inform them that we had Chen but had made no determination about his status, and ask them to meet so we could come to a resolution before the start of the summit. We thought that if we could get them to discuss the matter in good faith, we were halfway toward a solution.

The second step was to talk with Chen himself. What did he want exactly? Was he prepared to spend the next fifteen years of his life living in the embassy, like Cardinal Mindszenty?

Once we had plotted our course, I told Kurt to get on a plane to Beijing as soon as possible so he could manage the negotiations in person. He would depart late on Friday, April 27, arriving before dawn on Sunday. Bill would follow the next day. We also recalled Ambassador Gary Locke from a family vacation in Bali and tracked down the State Department Legal Advisor, former Yale Law School Dean Harold Koh, who happened to be traveling in a remote part of China. When Cheryl reached him and asked how long it would take to get to a secure line, he said at least four hours. "Go," she said. "I'll explain when you get there."

When Kurt touched down in Beijing, he immediately made his way to the third floor of the embassy's Marine barracks. The Chinese security presence around the compound had grown significantly since the day before, and inside it felt like a siege. Chen appeared frail and vulnerable. It was hard to believe that this slight man with the large dark glasses was at the center of a brewing international incident.

I was relieved to hear from Kurt that he found at least a little good news waiting for him: The Chinese had agreed to meet. Considering we were talking about one of their own citizens, picked up on Chinese soil, that in itself was promising. What's more, Chen seemed to have already bonded with Bob and some of the other Mandarin-speaking officers at the embassy, and he was declaring his firm desire to remain in China rather than seek asylum or remain in the barracks forever. Chen talked about the abuse he suffered at the hands of the corrupt local authorities in Shandong and expressed his hope that the central government in Beijing would step in and provide justice. He had special faith in Premier Wen, who had a reputation for caring about the poor and disenfranchised. "Grandpa Wen" would surely help if he only knew what was really going on.

As we waited anxiously for negotiations to begin, there was reason to be cautiously optimistic. What was not immediately clear in those early hours was that Chen would turn out to be unpredictable and quixotic, as formidable a negotiator as the Chinese leaders outside.

=====

Kurt's counterpart on the Chinese side was an experienced diplomat named Cui Tiankai, who was later named Ambassador to the United States. Kurt and I had agreed that in his first meeting with Cui, he would start cautiously and work on establishing some common ground. There was no way we would surrender Chen, but I wanted to resolve this crisis quickly and quietly to protect the relationship and the summit. Both sides needed a win-win outcome. At least that was the plan.

The Chinese were having none of it. "I'll tell you how you solve this," Cui said. "Turn Chen over to us immediately. If you really care about the U.S.-China relationship, that's what you'll do." Kurt responded carefully, offering the Chinese the chance to come to the embassy to talk directly to Chen. This only made Cui angrier. He launched into a thirty-minute diatribe about Chinese sovereignty and dignity, growing louder and more impassioned as he went. We were undermining the relationship and insulting the Chinese people, and Chen was a coward, hiding behind American skirts. Over the following hours and days, our team endured five more negotiating sessions, all along the same lines, in ceremonial rooms at the Foreign Ministry. Behind Cui, the Chinese side included a number of senior and quite tense officials from the state security apparatus. They often huddled with Cui immediately before and after the negotiating sessions, but they never spoke in front of the Americans. At one point Kurt witnessed an intense argument between Cui and a senior security official, but he couldn't hear the details. After ten minutes a frustrated Cui waved his colleague off.

Back at the embassy our team listened as Chen talked about wanting to study law and continuing to be an advocate for reforms inside China. He was familiar with the stories of exiled dissidents who lost their influence once they left the country and lived in safe obscurity in the United States. That was not what he wanted. This was a concern Harold Koh could appreciate. His father, a South Korean diplomat, had fled Seoul after a military coup in 1961 and gone into exile in the United States. Harold spoke movingly of the difficulties Chen would face if he decided to leave China.

Besides being one of our nation's top legal scholars, Harold was also an accomplished university administrator, and his experience there now came to the fore. He developed a plan that would get Chen out of the embassy, avoid the emotionally charged question of asylum, and provide a face-saving solution for the Chinese before the start of the summit. What if Chen was admitted to study at a Chinese law school, somewhere away from Beijing, and then, after a period of time, perhaps two years, left to pursue his studies at an American university? Harold had close ties with professors and administrators at New York University, which was in the process of setting up a Shanghai campus, and overnight he persuaded the university to offer Chen a fellowship. That allowed us to present a package deal to the Chinese.

The Chinese were skeptical but didn't reject the proposal out of hand. It appeared that the Communist Party leadership was trying to walk a tightrope between working constructively with us and salvaging the Strategic and Economic Dialogue, and satisfying the concerns of more hardline elements in the security apparatus. Eventually orders came down to Cui: Do what it takes to get this resolved.

Late in the evening of Monday, April 30, five days after the initial

phone call, I boarded an Air Force jet from Andrews heading to Beijing.
That gave the negotiators roughly twenty more hours to nail down the
details. It was as tense a flight as any I can recall. From the White House
the President had sent a clear message: Don't screw up.

Slowly the outlines of a deal emerged. First Chen would be transferred to a Beijing hospital to receive medical attention for the injuries
he suffered during his escape. He would then have the opportunity to
tell appropriate authorities about the abuses he had suffered under house
arrest in Shandong. Next he would be reunited with his family, who had
faced continued harassment since his escape. Then he would leave Beijing
for two years of study elsewhere in China, followed by possible study in
the United States. The American Embassy would maintain contact with
him every step of the way. Kurt presented a list of five or six possible
Chinese universities to consider. Cui scanned the list and exploded in
anger. "There's no way he's going to East China Normal," Cui roared.
"I will not share an alma mater with that man!" That meant we were
getting somewhere.

Back at the embassy Chen himself wasn't so sure. He wanted to speak
with his family and have them come to Beijing before making any final
decisions; waiting to be reunited was not good enough. Kurt dreaded
going back with another request after the Chinese had already conceded
so much, but Chen was insistent. Sure enough, the Chinese could not
believe it. They were withering in their criticism of Kurt and the team
and refused to budge. There was no way Chen's wife and children would
be allowed to come to Beijing until the deal was finalized.

We needed to raise the stakes. The Chinese are famously sensitive to
protocol and respectful of authority. We decided to use this to our advantage. Bill Burns was the highest-ranking career diplomat in the U.S.
government, and is a widely respected former Ambassador to Jordan and
Russia. What's more, he is among the calmest and steadiest people I've
ever met, qualities that we desperately needed at the negotiating table.
When he arrived on Monday, he joined the next session. Sitting across
from Cui, Bill made a soothing and persuasive case, diplomat to diplomat:
Just deliver the family and move ahead with the summit, then we can all
put this whole incident behind us. Mollified, Cui agreed to take the matter
back to his superiors. By midnight, while I was still somewhere over the
Pacific, word came back that the family would be on the morning train
from Shandong. Now all we needed was for Chen to walk out the door.

When my plane touched down early on May 2, I sent Jake directly to the embassy with my personal encouragement to Chen. After the marathon flight, we had left most of the day open, and the first official event was a private dinner that evening with my Chinese counterpart, State Councilor Dai Bingguo.

Chen was still nervous. He felt safe in the Marine barracks, cared for by an embassy doctor. He had formed a strong relationship with the staff, especially Ambassador Gary Locke, the first Chinese American to serve in that post. Gary's grandfather had emigrated from China to Washington State, where he found work as a domestic servant, sometimes in exchange for English lessons. Gary was born in Seattle, where his family owned a small grocery store, and went on to become Governor of Washington and Secretary of Commerce. He was a living embodiment of the American Dream, and I was proud to have him as our representative at this delicate time.

Gary and Harold spent hours sitting with Chen, holding his hand, soothing his fears, and talking about his hopes for the future. Twice they arranged for Chen to talk on the phone with his wife as she sped toward Beijing by train. Finally Chen jumped up, full of purpose and excitement, and said, "Let's go." The long, difficult drama seemed to finally be coming to an end.

Leaning on the Ambassador's arm and clutching Kurt's hand, Chen emerged from the barracks and walked slowly to a waiting van. Once he was safely inside, Jake dialed me from his cell phone and handed it to Chen. After so many stressful days of waiting and worrying, we had the chance to talk at last. "I want to kiss you," he said. At that moment, I felt the same way about him.

The van arrived at nearby Chaoyang Hospital to a crush of media and security. The Chinese were scrupulous in holding up their end of the bargain: Chen was reunited with his wife and children and then whisked off to be treated by a team of doctors, accompanied by our embassy staff. I released a carefully worded press statement, my first public comment on the episode, saying, "I am pleased that we were able to facilitate Chen Guangcheng's stay and departure from the U.S. Embassy in a way that reflected his choices and our values." For their part, the Chinese denounced American interference in their internal affairs, as expected, but kept the summit on track and resisted the temptation to immediately rearrest Chen.

With Chen safely at the hospital, it was time for dinner. Dai and Cui welcomed us to the Wanshousi Temple, a 16th-century complex of quiet courtyards and ornate villas that houses a large collection of ancient artifacts. Dai proudly gave me a tour, and as we admired the jade figurines and graceful calligraphy, the sense of relief was palpable. As Dai and I liked to do, we talked expansively about the importance of the U.S.-China relationship and the sweep of history. The delegations had dinner, and then Dai and I went with Kurt and Cui into a small room for a private conversation. How long it had been since Dai had first shown me the photograph of his grandchild and we had agreed to work together to make sure they inherited a peaceful future. Now we had weathered our toughest crisis yet and the bonds had held. But Dai couldn't resist venting. He told me we had made a big mistake in trusting Chen, who he said was a manipulative criminal. Then he implored me not to raise the episode when I saw President Hu and Premier Wen later in the week. We both agreed it was time to refocus on the urgent strategic concerns of the summit, from North Korea to Iran.

=====

Across town a very different conversation was happening. The embassy staff had decided to give Chen and his wife some privacy after their long ordeal. Now that they were finally alone in the hospital room, the dissident and his family began second-guessing the choice he had made. After so much mistreatment, how could they trust the Chinese authorities to honor the deal? To Chen, the grand idea of staying in China and remaining relevant, despite the risks, may have started to seem less attractive once he was outside the protection of the embassy walls and with the loved ones he could potentially be endangering. He also spoke on the phone with friends in the human rights community worried about his safety, who urged him to get out of the country, and with reporters who questioned his decision to stay in China. As the evening went on, his answers started to change.

Back at the Wanshousi Temple, troubling press reports starting popping up on my colleagues' BlackBerrys. By the time I emerged from my meeting with Dai, it was clear something had gone wrong. Journalists were quoting Chen from his hospital bed saying he "no longer felt safe," that the Americans had abandoned him, and that he had changed his mind about remaining in China. He even denied that he had ever said he wanted to kiss me! (He later admitted to the press that "he was embarrassed by having spoken so intimately" to me.) Our carefully constructed choreography was falling apart.

When we arrived back at the hotel I convened an emergency meeting in my suite. While Chen seemed to be talking easily with every reporter and activist from Beijing to Washington, no one at the embassy could reach him on the cell phones that, ironically, we had provided. We hadn't heard anything official yet from the Chinese, but they were reading the same reports we were, and security outside the hospital was growing by the hour. I could just imagine Dai and Cui preparing to deliver an epic "I told you so."

Kurt gallantly offered me his resignation if things kept getting worse. I dismissed that out of hand and said we needed to start working on a revised plan. First we would put out a statement right away clarifying that, contrary to some of the breathless news reports, Chen had never asked for asylum and had certainly never been denied. Second, if in the morning Chen was still insisting that he wanted to go to the United States, we had to find a way to reengage the Chinese government, no matter how difficult and painful that would be, and negotiate a new deal. We couldn't afford to let this issue fester in public and overwhelm the summit. Third, I would carry on with the scheduled Strategic and Economic Dialogue events as if nothing had happened, in keeping with my understanding with Dai. With their marching orders in hand, my troops filed out of the suite looking worried and beyond tired. None of us would sleep much that night.

═══

The next day was a surreal exercise in diplomatic multitasking. Thanks to elaborate measures the government had taken in advance of the summit, the normally clogged streets and polluted air of Beijing were clearer than normal as our motorcade sped through the city that morning. But the road ahead was far from clear. A lot was riding on the next few hours.

We arrived at Diaoyutai, the sprawling complex of traditional guesthouses, gardens, and meeting rooms. It was here in 1971 that Henry Kissinger first negotiated with Zhou Enlai, laying the groundwork for President Nixon's historic visit, normalization, and everything that followed. It was also here, during our 2010 meetings, that an intemperate outburst by a Chinese admiral had exposed the deep rifts of mistrust that still divide our countries. I wondered, given the current predicament, which of those two spirits our Chinese hosts would be channeling.

The answer came as soon as the first formal speeches began. Dai and the other Chinese leaders were clearly working just as hard as Tim Geithner and I were to project a sense of normalcy and calm. They repeated their standard talking points about China's harmonious rise and the importance of other countries staying out of their internal affairs— statements that, while familiar, took on a bit more edge in light of recent events. When it was my turn, I avoided the Chen issue and focused on Iran, North Korea, Syria, and the long list of other challenges on which we needed Chinese cooperation. But, I added, "a China that protects the rights of all its citizens will be a stronger and more prosperous nation, and of course, a stronger partner on behalf of our common goals." That was as close as I got that morning to the current crisis.

Following the speeches, we moved into smaller groups to dive into the agenda in more detail. Even if our minds often wandered to the drama unfolding in a hospital room across town, this was a chance to work on important business, and we couldn't afford to waste it. So I sat through hours of presentations and discussions, asking questions and raising concerns.

Kurt, meanwhile, was constantly excusing himself so he could monitor developments with Chen. The news wasn't good. The embassy still couldn't get through to his cell phone, and the Chinese were limiting physical access to the hospital. Protesters popped up outside, some wearing Chen-style dark glasses in homage to their hero, and Chinese security was getting increasingly anxious. None of that, however, was stopping Chen from talking with American journalists, who kept trumpeting his new desire to leave China and go to the United States and questioning whether we had done enough to help him.

Back home, with election-year politics swirling, Washington was in an uproar. Republican Speaker of the House John Boehner proclaimed himself "deeply disturbed" by reports that Chen was "pressured to leave the U.S. embassy against his will amid flimsy promises and possible threats of harm to his family." Former Massachusetts Governor Mitt Romney, the Republican Presidential candidate, went even further. He said it was "a dark day for freedom" and "a day of shame for the Obama Administration." I don't know if the critics were aware that we had done what Chen said he wanted every step of the way. The White House went into full damage-control mode. The guidance to us in Beijing was simple: Fix this.

I told Kurt and Ambassador Locke to restart negotiations with Cui immediately and try to get Chen out of the country. That was easier said than done. The Chinese were absolutely incredulous that we would seek to reopen a deal that they hadn't wanted in the first place. Cui just shook his head. He said that Kurt should "go back to Washington and resign." Meanwhile Chen took his outreach to another level. Although he still had not spoken with anyone at the U.S. Embassy, he managed to call in to a Congressional hearing back in Washington. An activist close to Chen, Bob Fu, put his iPhone on speaker in front of Congressman Chris Smith's committee. "I fear for my family's lives," Chen said, and then repeated his request to travel to the United States. It was like throwing fuel on the political fire.

======

It was time for me to step in. If Cui refused to negotiate, I would put aside the pantomime and raise the issue directly with Dai. Would our years of relationship-building pay off? On Friday I was scheduled to meet with President Hu and Premier Wen in the Great Hall of the People, and it was important to both Dai and me that those encounters go smoothly. It was in both our interests to get this resolved.

On the morning of May 4, I met with Dai and thanked him for China honoring its side of the agreement. Then I explained the political firestorm back home and the difficulties it was causing us. Dai seemed surprised as I described the circus at the Congressional hearing. Nothing like that ever happened in China. What to do now? I offered what I hoped would be a face-saving solution. In the original understanding, Chen was supposed to go to school in China for a period of time and then continue his studies at an American university. Moving up that timetable wouldn't mean a whole new deal; it would simply be a refinement of the existing agreement. Dai stared at me quietly for a long while, and I wondered what thoughts were racing behind his stoic demeanor. Slowly he turned to Cui, who was visibly agitated, and directed him to try to work out the details with Kurt.

Heartened, but not yet confident, I headed off to the Great Hall of the People for my meetings with the senior leaders. True to my word, I did not raise Chen with Hu or later with Wen. I didn't need to. In our discussions they appeared distracted but pleasant. We mostly talked in circles, dancing around the big issues facing the future of our relationship, while our aides were scurrying around trying to find a way out of our common dilemma. Hu and Wen were coming to the end of their ten-year term, and we too were headed into an election that could reshape our own government. But even if the players changed, the game would remain fundamentally the same.

I left the Great Hall of the People and crossed Tiananmen Square to the National Museum of China for a dialogue about educational and cultural exchanges with State Councilor Liu Yandong, the highest-ranking woman in the Chinese government. The daughter of a former Vice Minister of Agriculture with deep ties in the Communist Party, Madame Liu rose to become one of only two women to hold a seat in the politburo. We had developed a warm relationship over the years, and I was glad to see a friendly face at a tense time.

Beijing's National Museum is enormous, designed to rival the Great Hall across the square, but its collection has never fully recovered from the removal of many of China's most precious art and artifacts to Taiwan by the retreating forces of Generalissimo Chiang Kai-shek in 1948. That's the kind of wound to national pride that takes a long time to heal. As we walked up the soaring front steps, Kurt turned to me and asked, "Do you feel like we've done the right thing?" It was a reasonable question after so much high-stakes diplomacy and nerve-wracking twists and turns. I looked back at him and said, "There are a lot of decisions I make in this job that give me a pit in my stomach. I don't have any of that here. This is a small price to pay to be the United States of America." It was what Kurt needed to hear, and it happened to be the truth.

Inside the museum we were met by a large group of Chinese and American children waving flags and offering greetings. Upstairs a chorus of Chinese and American students sang two songs of welcome, one in English, the other in Mandarin. Finally two exchange students stepped forward to speak about their experiences studying abroad. An articulate young Chinese woman talked in English about living in New York, an eye-opening, horizon-expanding, ambition-inspiring journey into an America she had only read about. The young American man was just as eloquent, describing his studies in China in Mandarin and how it had helped him better understand the relationship between our two countries.

Occasionally, amid all the diplomatic pomp and circumstance of these summits, with their prepared speeches and choreographed set pieces, an actual human moment breaks through and reminds us of what we're doing there in the first place. This was one of those moments. Listening to the students express so much empathy and excitement, I thought about all the effort we had put into what some critics dismiss as the "softer" side of diplomacy: the educational exchanges, cultural tours, and scientific collaboration. I had made it a priority to send more American students to China, with the goal of 100,000 over four years, in part because I believed it would help convince wary Chinese officials that we were serious about expanding engagement with them. These programs may garner few headlines, but they have the potential to influence the next generation of U.S. and Chinese leaders in a way no other initiative can match. If these students were any indication, it was working. I looked across the table at Liu, Cui, and the others, and I knew they could feel it too.

When Cui sat down with Kurt and his team after lunch to work out the next moves in the Chen drama, his tone was noticeably different. Despite our differences, we were working together to save the relationship and the future those two students represented. Afterward Kurt and Jake raced to put down on paper a short and carefully worded statement that would not acknowledge an explicit deal but would make it clear that an understanding had been reached. Chen, as a Chinese citizen in good standing, would apply for a visa to the United States, and it would be processed expeditiously by both sides. He could then take his family and begin his studies at New York University.

═══

Back at Diaoyutai, Tim Geithner and I joined our counterparts onstage for the closing public remarks of the Strategic and Economic Dialogue. In my comments I reviewed the substantive ground that had been covered over the past few days. I noted that there had been a number of strong disagreements, but that four years of hard work had allowed us to develop a level of trust durable enough to withstand disruptions and distractions. I quoted a bit of Taoist wisdom that roughly translates as "To lead, one must see the larger picture." We had tried to do that in this crisis and not lose sight of either the strategic concerns or our core values. Looking ahead, I told the audience, "We need to build a resilient relationship that allows both of us to thrive and meet our regional and global responsibilities without unhealthy competition, rivalry, or conflict. Zero-sum thinking will lead only to negative-sum results."

As a rule Chinese leaders refuse to take questions at these closing "press conferences," so after the formal statements, Tim Geithner and I drove back to our hotel for our first proper session with the world media since arriving in Beijing. The first question, from Matt Lee of the Associated Press, was predictable. "Madam Secretary, it won't surprise you, I think, to get the questions that you're about to get from me, which all have to do with the elephant in the room that's been dogging us," he began. I smiled at his mixed metaphor: "The elephant that has been dogging us. That's good—a good start, Matt." Laughter broke the tension in the room, just a bit. He pressed ahead: "How did the Chinese officials that you spoke to, the senior leadership, respond to your appeals on [Chen's] behalf? Are you confident that they will allow him to leave the country to go to the States with his family so that he can study? And how do you respond to critics at home and elsewhere who say that the administration has really bungled this?"

It was finally time to put this drama to rest once and for all. I began with the carefully prepared text we had agreed to with the Chinese and then added a few thoughts of my own:

> Let me start by saying that from the beginning, all of our efforts with Mr. Chen have been guided by his choices and our values. And I'm pleased that today our ambassador has spoken with him again, our Embassy staff and our doctor had a chance to meet with him, and he confirms that he and his family now want to go to the United States so he can pursue his studies. In that regard, we are also encouraged by the official statement issued today by the Chinese Government confirming that he can apply to travel abroad for this purpose. Over the course of the day, progress has been made to help him have the future that he wants, and we will be staying in touch with him as this process moves forward. But let me also add, this is not just about well-known activists. It's about the human rights and aspirations of more than a billion people here in China and billions more around the world. And it's about the future of this great nation and all nations. We will continue engaging with the Chinese Government at the highest levels in putting these concerns at the heart of our diplomacy.

As the cameras snapped away and the reporters scribbled in their notebooks, I felt good about this resolution. After the press conference I invited my team to a well-deserved celebratory dinner of Peking duck and other Chinese delicacies. Kurt and Harold recounted some of their more absurd misadventures over the past week, and we finally felt comfortable relaxing and laughing. The next day, I headed to the airport and boarded a flight to Dhaka, Bangladesh.

Chen was still in his hospital room, and we all knew there was a real chance this second deal would unravel just like the first. None of us would be truly comfortable until he was safely on American soil. Based on the understanding with the Chinese, that could take a number of weeks. But the Chinese had held up their side of the bargain throughout the crisis, and I believed they would do so again. Sure enough, on May 19 Chen and his family arrived in the United States to begin his fellowship at New York University.

=====

I was immensely proud of my team and everyone at the embassy in Beijing. This was about much more than one man. We had spent four years preparing for a crisis like this—building up the Strategic and Economic Dialogue and other diplomatic mechanisms, developing habits of trust between counterparts up and down the chain, grounding the U.S.-China relationship in a framework of mutual interest and respect, while also staking out clear markers about human rights and democratic values. It had been a delicate tightrope walk from the start, but now I felt we had proof that it had been worth it. We also had reason to believe our relationship was strong enough to withstand future crises. Given our different visions, values, and interests, they were inevitable.

One of the primary goals of the pivot plan was to increase our active involvement in Asian affairs in a way that advanced our interests in a more open democratic and prosperous region, without weakening our efforts to build a positive relationship with China. The frictions in our relationship are a reflection of both disagreements over the issues at hand and very different perceptions of how the world, or at least Asia, should work. The United States wants a future of shared prosperity and shared responsibilities for peace and security. The only way to build that future is to develop mechanisms for and habits of cooperation and to urge China toward greater openness and freedom. That's why we oppose China's suppression of internet freedom, political activists like Chen, and the Tibetan and Uighur Muslim minorities. It's why we want peaceful resolutions between China and its neighbors over their territorial claims.

The Chinese believe we don't appreciate how far they've come and how much they've changed, or how deep and constant is their fear of internal conflicts and disintegration. They resent criticism by outsiders. They claim the Chinese people are more free than they have ever been, free to work, to move, to save and accumulate wealth. They are rightly proud of moving more people out of poverty faster than any other nation in history. They believe our relationship should be formed on mutual self-interest and noninvolvement in each other's affairs.

When we disagree, they believe it's because we fear China's rise on the world stage and want to contain it. We believe disagreement is a normal part of our relationship and think if we can manage our differences it will strengthen our cooperation. We have no interest in containing China. But we do insist that China play by the rules that bind all nations.

In other words, the jury's still out. China has some hard choices to make, and so do we. We should follow a time-tested strategy: Work for the best outcome, but plan for something less. And stick to our values. As I told Kurt and Jake on that first tense night when Chen was pleading for refuge, our defense of universal human rights is one of America's greatest sources of strength. The image of Chen, blind and injured, seeking through that dangerous night for the one place he knew stood for freedom and opportunity—the embassy of the United States—reminds us of our responsibility to make sure our country remains the beacon for dissidents and dreamers all over the world.

Burma: The Lady and the Generals

She was thin, even frail, but with unmistakable inner strength. There was a quiet dignity about her, and the coiled intensity of a vibrant mind inside a long-imprisoned body. She exhibited qualities I had glimpsed before in other former political prisoners, including Nelson Mandela and Václav Havel. Like them, she carried the hopes of a nation on her shoulders.

The first time I met Aung San Suu Kyi, on December 1, 2011, we were both wearing white. It seemed like an auspicious coincidence. After so many years of reading and thinking about this celebrated Burmese dissident, we were finally face-to-face. She had been released from house arrest, and I had traveled thousands of miles to talk with her about the prospects of democratic reform in her authoritarian country. We sat down for a private dinner on the terrace of the chief U.S. diplomat's residence in Rangoon, a lovely old colonial home on Inya Lake. I felt as if we had known each other for a lifetime, even though we had just met.

I had a lot of questions. She had just as many. After years as an icon of the pro-democracy movement, she was preparing for her first experience with actual democracy. How does one move from protest to politics? What is it like to run for office and put yourself on the line in a whole new way? The conversation was easy and open, and soon we were chatting, strategizing, and laughing like old friends.

We both knew it was a delicate moment. Her country, which the ruling generals called Myanmar and the dissidents called Burma, was taking the first tentative steps toward momentous change. (For years our government maintained a strict official policy of using only the name Burma, but eventually some began using the two names interchangeably. In this book I use Burma, as I did at the time.) The country could easily fall backward into bloodshed and repression, as had happened before. Yet if we could help chart the right course, the prospects for progress were better than at any time in a generation.

For the United States, the chance to help Burma move from dictatorship to democracy and rejoin the family of nations was tantalizing. On its own, Burma was worth the effort; its millions of people deserved a chance to enjoy the blessings of freedom and prosperity. There were also outsized strategic implications. Burma was situated at the heart of Southeast Asia, a region where the United States and China were both working to increase influence. A meaningful reform process there could become a milestone of our pivot strategy, give a boost to democracy and human rights activists across Asia and beyond, and provide a rebuke to authoritarian government. If we failed, however, it could have the opposite effect. There was a risk that the Burmese generals were playing us. They might be hoping that a few modest gestures would be enough to crack their international isolation without changing much of anything on the ground. At home, many thoughtful observers believed I was making the wrong choice by reaching out when the situation was so unclear. I had my eyes open about the risks, but when I weighed all the factors, I didn't see how we could pass up this opportunity.

For two hours Suu Kyi and I sat and talked. She wanted to know how America would respond to reforms the regime was considering. I told her that we were committed to match action for action. There were many carrots we could offer, from restoring full diplomatic relations to easing sanctions and spurring investment. But we needed to see more political prisoners released, credible elections, protections for minorities and human rights, an end to military ties with North Korea, and a pathway to ending the long-running ethnic conflicts in the countryside. Every move we made, I assured her, would be aimed at nurturing further progress.

Suu Kyi was clear-eyed about the challenges ahead and the men who controlled her country. Her father, Aung San, a general himself, had led Burma's successful fight for independence from the British and Japanese, only to be assassinated in 1947 by political rivals. Suu Kyi was first imprisoned in July 1989, less than a year after entering politics during a failed democratic uprising against the military the previous year. She had been in and out of house arrest ever since. In 1990, when the military allowed an election, her political party won a resounding victory. The generals promptly nullified the vote. The next year she won the Nobel Peace Prize, which was accepted on her behalf by her husband, Dr. Michael Aris, an Oxford professor and leading scholar of Tibetan Buddhism, as well as their sons. During her years of house arrest Suu Kyi was able to see her family only a handful of times, and when Aris was diagnosed with prostate cancer, the Burmese government denied him a visa to come spend his final days with her. Instead they suggested that Suu Kyi leave the country, which she suspected would mean permanent exile. She declined and never had a chance to say good-bye. Aris died in 1999.

Suu Kyi had learned to be skeptical of good intentions and had developed a thoroughgoing pragmatism that belied her idealistic image. The possibility of a democratic opening was real, she thought, but it needed to be carefully tested. We agreed to meet again the next day to dig into more details, this time at her home.

As we parted I had to pinch myself. When I became Secretary of State in 2009, few could have imagined that this visit would be possible. Only two years before, in 2007, the world had watched in horror as Burmese soldiers fired into crowds of saffron-clad monks who were peacefully protesting against the regime. Now the country was on the brink of a new era. It was a reminder of how fast the world can change and how important it is for the United States to be ready to meet and help shape that change when it comes.

=====

Burma is a nation of close to 60 million people strategically located between the Indian subcontinent and the Mekong delta region of Southeast Asia. It was once known as "the rice bowl of Asia," and its ancient pagodas and lush beauty captured the imagination of travelers and writers like Rudyard Kipling and George Orwell. During World War II it was a battleground between Japanese and Allied forces. A sharp-tongued American general nicknamed "Vinegar Joe" Stilwell helped reopen the famed Burma Road as a vital supply route into China, and the wartime leadership of Suu Kyi's father helped to ensure Burmese independence following the end of the conflict.

Decades of military dictatorship and economic mismanagement turned the country into a poverty-stricken pariah. Now Burma ranked among the world's worst abusers of human rights. It was a source of instability and hostility in the heart of Southeast Asia, and its growing narcotics trade and military ties with North Korea represented a threat to global security.

For me, the road to Rangoon began with an unusual meeting on Capitol Hill in January 2009. I knew Mitch McConnell reasonably well after eight years together in the Senate, and we rarely saw eye to eye on anything. The conservative Republican Minority Leader from Kentucky made no secret of his intention to oppose the new Obama Administration on virtually our entire agenda. (At one point he said, "The single most important thing we want to achieve is for President Obama to be a one-term president.") But there was one area of foreign policy where I thought we might be able to work together. Senator McConnell had been a passionate champion of the pro-democracy movement in Burma since the brutal 1988 crackdown. Over the years he led the fight for sanctions against Burma's military regime and developed contacts in the dissident community, including with Suu Kyi herself.

I came into office convinced that we needed to rethink our Burma policy, and I wondered if Senator McConnell would agree. In 2008 the regime had announced a new constitution and plans to hold elections in 2010. After the failure of the 1990 elections, few observers took the prospects of a new vote very seriously. Suu Kyi was still barred from holding office, and the generals had written the rules to ensure that the military was guaranteed to hold at least a quarter of the seats in Parliament, and likely the vast majority. But even the most modest gesture toward democracy was an interesting development from such a repressive regime.

To be sure, there had been moments of false hope before. In 1995 the regime had unexpectedly released Suu Kyi from house arrest, and Madeleine Albright, then U.S. Ambassador to the UN, had flown to Rangoon to see if the military might be ready to loosen its grip. She carried with her a poster from the UN Women's Conference in Beijing that I and others had signed. But reforms proved elusive. In 1996, while visiting neighboring Thailand, I gave a speech at Chiang Mai University calling for "real

political dialogue between Aung San Suu Kyi and the military regime."
Instead, starting in 1997, the generals began sharply restricting Suu Kyi's
movements and political activities, and by 2000 she was back under house
arrest. Bill recognized her heroism by awarding her America's highest
civilian award, the Presidential Medal of Freedom, which she of course
could not accept in person. Engagement, for the moment, had failed. But
by 2009, it was hard to argue that our policy of isolation and sanctions was
working any better. Was there anything else we could do?

I told Senator McConnell I wanted to take a fresh look at our Burma
policy, from top to bottom, and I hoped he'd be part of it. He was skeptical but ultimately supportive. Our policy review would have bipartisan
backing. The Senator proudly showed me a framed note from Suu Kyi
that he kept on the wall of his office. It was clear how personal this issue
had become for him. I promised to consult him regularly as we moved
forward.

There was one more Senator I needed to see. Jim Webb was a decorated Vietnam veteran, Secretary of the Navy under President Reagan,
and now a Democratic Senator from Virginia and chair of the Senate
Foreign Relations Subcommittee on East Asian and Pacific Affairs.
He was feisty and unconventional, with strong views about U.S. policy
in Southeast Asia. Jim told me that Western sanctions had succeeded
in impoverishing Burma but that the ruling regime had only become
more entrenched and paranoid. He was also concerned that we were
inadvertently creating an opportunity for China to expand its economic
and political influence in the country. Chinese companies were investing heavily in dams, mines, and energy projects across Burma, including
a major new pipeline. Jim thought a Burma policy review was a good
idea, but he wasn't interested in going slowly. He pushed me to be creative and assertive and promised to do the same from his perch on the
subcommittee.

I also heard from the other side of the Capitol, where my friend Congressman Joe Crowley of New York had long been a leading proponent
of sanctions against the regime. Joe is an old-school straight shooter from
Queens. When I was in the Senate and we'd run into each other at New
York events, he'd serenade me with Irish ballads. He had been inspired
by his mentor on the House Foreign Affairs Committee, the late, great
Tom Lantos, to champion human rights in Burma. His support and advice would also be crucial as we moved forward.

On my first trip to Asia, in February 2009, I consulted with regional leaders for their thoughts on Burma.

The most encouraging was Indonesian President Susilo Bambang Yudhoyono. He told me that he had talked to the Burmese generals and came away convinced that progress was possible. That carried weight with me since he himself had been a general who took off the uniform and ran for office. What's more, he reported that the regime might be interested in starting a dialogue with the United States. We had not had an Ambassador in Burma in years, but there were still channels through which we occasionally communicated. The prospect of more robust discussions was intriguing.

In March I sent Stephen Blake, a senior diplomat and Director of the State Department's Office for Mainland Southeast Asia, to Burma. In a show of good faith, the regime offered Blake a rare meeting with the Foreign Minister. In return Blake agreed to be the first American official to travel from Rangoon to Nay Pyi Taw, a new capital city the military had built in a remote part of the jungle in 2005; according to a widely circulated rumor, the site was chosen on the advice of an astrologer. He was not allowed to meet Suu Kyi, however, or the country's aging and reclusive senior general, Than Shwe. Blake came home convinced that the regime was indeed interested in a dialogue and that some in the leadership were chafing at the country's deep isolation. But he was skeptical that it would lead to real progress anytime soon.

Then, in May, came one of those unpredictable quirks of history that can reshape international relations. A fifty-three-year-old Vietnam veteran from Missouri named John Yettaw had become obsessed with Suu Kyi. In November 2008 he had traveled to Rangoon and swam across Inya Lake to the house where she was imprisoned. Avoiding police boats and security guards, Yettaw climbed over a fence and reached the house undetected. Suu Kyi's housekeepers were aghast when they found him. No unauthorized visitors were allowed at the house, and Yettaw's presence put them all in danger. Reluctantly he agreed to leave without seeing Suu Kyi.

But the next spring Yettaw was back. He had lost seventy pounds, and his ex-wife reportedly feared he was suffering from post-traumatic stress disorder. Yet in early May 2009 he made the swim across Inya Lake again. This time he refused to leave and claimed to be exhausted and in poor health. Suu Kyi allowed him to sleep on the floor and then contacted the authorities. Yettaw was arrested at about 5:30 A.M. on May 6, as he attempted to swim back across the lake. Suu Kyi and her housekeepers were picked up the following week for violating the terms of her house arrest. Yettaw was eventually convicted and sentenced to seven years of hard labor. Suu Kyi and her staff were given three years, which was immediately commuted by Than Shwe to eighteen months of continued house arrest. That would ensure she remained imprisoned for the promised 2010 elections. "Everyone is very angry with this wretched American. He is the cause of all these problems. He's a fool," one of Suu Kyi's lawyers told the press.

When I heard the news, I too was furious. Suu Kyi and the progress we desperately hoped to see in Burma should not have to pay the price for the reckless actions of one misguided American. Still, because he was an American citizen, I had a responsibility to help him. I called Senator Webb and Senator McConnell to strategize. Jim offered to go to Burma to negotiate Yettaw's release, and I agreed. It was certainly worth a try.

In mid-June, there was another potentially explosive event. The U.S. Navy began tracking a 2,000-ton North Korean cargo freighter that we and our South Korean allies suspected carried military equipment, including rocket launchers and possible missile parts, bound for Burma. If true, this would be a direct violation of the ban on North Korean arms trafficking imposed by the UN Security Council in response to a nuclear test in May. Reports swirled of contacts between the Burmese military and a North Korean company with expertise in nuclear technology and of secret visits by engineers and scientists.

The Pentagon dispatched a destroyer to shadow the North Korean freighter as it sailed through international waters. The UN resolution empowered us to search the ship, but the North Koreans vowed to take that as an act of war. We reached out to other countries in the region, including China, looking for assistance. It was crucial that every port where the ship might stop along the way enforce the UN edict and thoroughly inspect the cargo. Chinese Foreign Minister Yang agreed that the resolution "should be carried out in a strict manner so that a strong unified message can be sent to the North Koreans." At the last minute, the North Koreans blinked; the ship turned around and went home.

In August Senator Webb went to Nay Pyi Taw. This time Than Shwe agreed to meet. Jim had three items on his agenda. First, he asked to bring Yettaw home on humanitarian grounds. The man was refusing to eat and suffering from a number of ailments. Second, he wanted to meet Suu Kyi, which Blake had not been allowed to do. Third, he urged Than Shwe to end her house arrest and allow her to participate in the political process; that was the only way the upcoming elections would be taken seriously. Than Shwe listened carefully and did not betray his thinking. But in the end Jim got two of his three requests. He went to Rangoon and met with Suu Kyi. Then he flew to Thailand with Yettaw on board a U.S. Air Force jet. When Jim and I spoke on the phone, I could hear the relief in his voice. But Suu Kyi remained imprisoned.

The next month I announced the results of our Burma policy review at the United Nations in New York. Our objectives had not changed: we wanted to see credible democratic reforms; the immediate, unconditional release of political prisoners, including Aung San Suu Kyi; and serious dialogue with the opposition and minority ethnic groups. But we had concluded that "engagement versus sanctions is a false choice." So going forward, we would use both tools to pursue our goals and reach out directly to senior Burmese officials.

═══

Over the next year there was discouragingly little progress. Suu Kyi remained under house arrest, although she was permitted to meet twice with Kurt Campbell. She described her solitary life to Kurt, including a daily ritual of listening to the BBC World Service and Voice of America to learn about events beyond her prison walls. The state-run newspaper cropped her out of the photo of Kurt that ran after his visit.

Unlike in 1990, there was no pro-democracy landslide in the 2010 elections. Instead the military-backed party claimed an overwhelming victory, as expected. Opposition groups and international human rights organizations joined the U.S. in condemning the vote as largely fraudulent. The regime refused to allow journalists or outside observers to monitor the election. It was all depressingly familiar and predictable. The generals had missed an opportunity to begin a transition toward democracy and national reconciliation. Meanwhile the Burmese people were falling deeper into poverty and isolation.

Though the election results were disappointing, a week after the vote in November 2010, the generals unexpectedly released Suu Kyi from house arrest. Then Than Shwe decided to retire, to be replaced by another high-ranking general, Thein Sein, who had previously served as Prime

Minister. He would put away his uniform and lead a nominally civilian government. Unlike other members of the regime, Thein Sein had traveled around the region, was well known to Asian diplomats, and had seen firsthand how Burma's neighbors were enjoying the benefits of trade and technology while his own country stagnated. Rangoon had once been one of the more cosmopolitan cities in Southeast Asia; Thein Sein knew just how far it now lagged behind places like Bangkok, Jakarta, Singapore, and Kuala Lumpur. According to the World Bank, in 2010 only 0.2 percent of the country's population used the internet. Smartphones were nonexistent because there was insufficient cellular service. The contrast to their neighbors could not have been starker.

In January 2011 I called the newly released Aung San Suu Kyi for the first time to see what she made of these developments. It was a thrill to finally hear her voice, and she seemed energized by her new freedom. She thanked me for the firm support that the United States and Presidents of both parties had given her over the years and asked about my daughter's wedding. Her political party was stepping up its organizing, testing the limits of the government's new tone, and I told her we wanted to help and were prepared to share lessons from other pro-democracy movements around the world. "I hope I can visit you one day," I said. "Or even better, you can come visit me!"

That spring Thein Sein was formally sworn in as Burma's President. Surprisingly, he invited Suu Kyi to dinner in his modest home. It was a remarkable gesture from the most powerful man in the country to the woman the military had long feared as one of their gravest enemies. Thein Sein's wife prepared the meal, and they ate under a painting of Suu Kyi's father. They would meet again that summer, in Nay Pyi Taw. The first conversations were tentative. The general and the dissident were both understandably wary of each other. But something was definitely happening.

I wanted the United States to play a constructive role in encouraging the better instincts of the new Burmese government, without rushing to embrace them prematurely or losing the leverage our strong sanctions provided. Formally returning a U.S. Ambassador to the country would be too much too soon, but we did need a new diplomatic channel to start testing Thein Sein's intentions. In our strategy sessions I asked Kurt and his team to get creative and develop various scenarios for our next steps. We appointed a veteran Asia expert named Derek Mitchell as the first Special Representative for Burma. Congress had created the position in legislation introduced by the late Congressman Tom Lantos in 2007 and signed into law by President Bush in 2008, but it had never been filled. Selecting a Special Representative to Burma would not confer the prestige of installing a permanent Ambassador, but it would open the door to better communications.

======

The Irrawaddy River cuts through Burma from north to south and has long been at the heart of the country's culture and commerce. George Orwell recalled it "glittering like diamonds in the patches that caught the sun," bounded by vast stretches of rice paddies. Bundles of teak logs, a major Burmese export, float down the river from inland forests all the way to the sea. Fed by glaciers in the eastern Himalayas, the Irrawaddy's waters run through countless canals and irrigation systems, feeding farms and villages up and down the country and across its wide and fertile delta. Like the Ganges in India and the Mekong in Vietnam, the Irrawaddy occupies a revered place in Burmese society. In the words of Suu Kyi, it is "the grand natural highway, a prolific source of food, the home of varied water flora and fauna, the supporter of traditional modes of life, the muse that has inspired countless works of prose and poetry."

None of this stopped a state-run Chinese electric power company from using Beijing's long-standing relationship with the ruling generals to win permission to build the first hydroelectric dam across the upper Irrawaddy. The massive project threatened to cause lots of damage to the local economy and ecosystem, but it held significant benefits for China. Along with six other Chinese-built dams in northern Burma, the Myitsone Dam, as it became known, would deliver electricity to energy-thirsty cities in southern China. By 2011 Chinese construction workers in hard hats had descended on the banks of the Irrawaddy's headwaters in the remote northern hills that are home to the separatist Kachin ethnic group. The Chinese began blasting, tunneling, and building. Thousands of villagers living nearby were relocated.

In a country long ruled by capricious autocrats, such a disruptive project wasn't particularly surprising. What was surprising was the reaction from the public. From the beginning, local Kachin groups had opposed the dam, but soon criticism spread to other areas of the country and even appeared in heavily censored newspapers. Activists got their hands on a nine-hundred-page environmental impact statement conducted by Chinese scientists that warned about damage to downstream fish and other wildlife, as well as proximity to a major seismic fault line, and questioned the necessity and wisdom of the project. Anger over ecological damage to the sacred Irrawaddy tapped into deep-seated popular resentment toward China, the military regime's main foreign patron. As we've seen in other authoritarian states, nationalism is often harder to censor than dissent.

A wave of unprecedented public outrage built across Burma. In August 2011 Suu Kyi, who had kept a relatively low profile since her release from house arrest, published an open letter criticizing the dam. The new, nominally civilian government appeared divided and caught off guard. The Information Minister, a retired general, held a press conference and tearfully pledged to protect the Irrawaddy. But other senior officials dismissed public concerns and insisted that the dam would continue as planned. Finally Thein Sein addressed the matter in Parliament. The government had been elected by the people, he said, so it had a responsibility to answer the concerns of the public. Construction on the controversial dam would be halted.

This was the most compelling evidence yet that the new government might be serious about reforms. It was also a surprising official repudiation of China, where the news was met with consternation.

I marveled at the success of Burma's emerging civil society, which had been persecuted for so long and prevented from organizing or speaking freely. The use of the Myitsone Dam as a galvanizing issue reminded me of a wonderful insight from Eleanor Roosevelt. "Where, after all, do universal human rights begin?" she asked in a 1958 speech to the United Nations, and then gave her answer: "In small places, close to home," in "the world of the individual person; the neighborhood he lives in; the school or college he attends; the factory, farm, or office where he works. . . . Without concerted citizen action to uphold them close to home, we shall look in vain for progress in the larger world." The people of Burma had been denied so many of their fundamental freedoms for so long. Yet it was environmental and economic abuse that ultimately sparked widespread outrage because it hit home in a direct and tangible way. We see a similar phenomenon with antipollution protests in China. What starts as a prosaic complaint can quickly become much more. Once citizens succeed in demanding responsiveness from their government on these everyday concerns, it can raise expectations for more fundamental change. It's part of what I call making "human rights a human reality."

Stopping the dam seemed to unleash a flood of new activity. On October 12 the government began freeing a few hundred of its more than two thousand political prisoners. On the 14th it legalized labor union organizing for the first time since the 1960s. These moves came on the heels of modest steps earlier in the year to ease censorship restrictions and defuse conflicts with armed ethnic minority groups in the countryside. The government also initiated discussions with the International Monetary Fund about economic reforms. A cautiously optimistic Suu Kyi spoke to supporters in Rangoon and called for more prisoners to be released and additional reforms.

In Washington we monitored these events closely and wondered how much weight to give them. We needed a better feel for what was actually happening on the ground. I asked the State Department's top human rights official, Mike Posner, to accompany Derek Mitchell to Burma and attempt to get a read on the intentions of the new government. In early November Mike and Derek met with members of Parliament and had encouraging discussions about further reforms, including allowing freedom of assembly and opening up registration for political parties. Suu Kyi's party remained banned and would not be able to participate in 2012 Parliamentary elections unless the law was changed. This was one of the top concerns of the skeptical opposition leaders who Mike and Derek met. They also cited the large number of political prisoners still being held and reports of serious human rights abuses in ethnic areas. Suu Kyi and others were urging us not to move too hastily to lift sanctions and reward the regime until we had more concrete evidence of democratic progress. That seemed sensible to me, but we also had to keep engaging the leadership and nurturing these early advances.

━━━━━

In early November, as Mike and Derek were meeting with dissidents and legislators in Burma, President Obama and I were busy planning how to take the pivot to the next level. We knew the President's upcoming trip to Asia would be our best opportunity to demonstrate what the pivot meant. We started with APEC economic meetings in Hawaii and then he went on to Australia. I stopped in the Philippines to commemorate the sixtieth anniversary of our mutual defense treaty on the deck of the destroyer USS *Fitzgerald* in Manila, and then met the President in Thailand, another key ally.

On November 17, President Obama and I both arrived in Bali, Indonesia, for a meeting of the East Asia Summit and the U.S.-ASEAN Leaders Meeting, the most important annual gathering of heads of state across Asia. It was the first time a U.S. President attended the East Asia Summit. This was a testament to President Obama's commitment to our expanded engagement in the region, and a direct result of the groundwork we had laid beginning in 2009 by signing the ASEAN Treaty of Amity and Cooperation and making multilateral diplomacy a priority in Asia. As in Vietnam the previous year, territorial disputes in the South China Sea were once again on everyone's mind. Just as at the ASEAN meeting in Hanoi, China did not want to discuss the issue in an open, multilateral setting, especially one that included the United States. "Outside forces should not, under any pretext, get involved," said Chinese Premier Wen Jiabao. The Vice Foreign Minister was more direct. "We hope the South China Sea will not be discussed at the East Asia Summit," he told reporters. But smaller countries, including Vietnam and the Philippines, were determined to have the discussion. In Hanoi we had tried to advance a collaborative approach toward peaceful resolution of disputes in the South China Sea, but in the months since that encounter Beijing had dug in its heels even deeper.

On the afternoon of November 18, I accompanied President Obama to the private leaders meeting, where we met with seventeen other heads of state and their Foreign Ministers. No other staff or journalists were allowed in. President Obama and Premier Wen both listened quietly as other leaders began the discussion. Singapore, the Philippines, Vietnam, and Malaysia were among the early speakers, all of them with an interest in the South China Sea. Speaking in turn for two hours, nearly every leader repeated the principles we had discussed in Hanoi: ensuring open access and freedom of navigation, resolving disputes peacefully and collaboratively within the framework of international law, avoiding coercion and threats, and supporting a code of conduct. Soon it was clear there was a strong consensus in the room. The leaders spoke forcefully and without equivocation, but also without acrimony. Even the Russians agreed that this was an appropriate and important issue for the group to discuss.

Finally, after sixteen other leaders had spoken, President Obama took the microphone. By now all the arguments were well aired, so he welcomed the consensus and reaffirmed U.S. support for the approach the rest of the region had articulated. "While we are not a claimant in the South China Sea dispute, and while we do not take sides," he said, "we have a powerful stake in maritime security in general, and in the resolution of the South China Sea issue specifically—as a resident Pacific power, as a maritime nation, as a trading nation and as a guarantor of security in the Asia-Pacific region." When the President finished, he looked around the room, including at Premier Wen, who was visibly displeased. This was even worse than Hanoi. He had not wanted to discuss the South China Sea at all; now he faced a united front. Unlike Foreign Minister Yang in Hanoi, Premier Wen did not ask for a recess. He responded politely but firmly, defending China's actions and again insisting that this was not the appropriate forum for such matters.

While this diplomatic theater was playing out, I was equally focused on unfolding events in Burma. In the weeks leading up to the trip, Kurt had been recommending bold new steps to engage with the regime and encourage further reforms. I had been discussing Burma with President Obama and his national security advisors, who wanted to be sure we didn't lower our guard or ease pressure on the regime prematurely. I had a strong ally in the White House helping to push engagement: Ben Rhodes, the President's longtime aide who served as Deputy National Security Advisor. Ben agreed with me that we had laid the groundwork and now needed to move forward. Ultimately, though, there was one person in particular from whom the President wanted to hear to be reassured that the time was right. I asked Kurt and Jake to speak with Suu Kyi and set up a call between her and President Obama. While flying from Australia to Indonesia on Air Force One, he got on the phone with her for the first time. She underscored the important role America could play in helping her country move toward democracy. The two Nobel Peace Prize winners also swapped stories about their dogs. After the call the President was ready to move forward. The next day I stood next to him as he stepped to the microphones in Bali and announced that he had asked me to travel to Burma to personally investigate prospects for democratic reform and closer ties between our countries. "After years of darkness, we've seen flickers of progress," he said. I would be the first Secretary of State to visit in more than half a century.

On the flight home from Indonesia, my mind was racing ahead to the upcoming trip. It would be an opportunity to size up Thein Sein for myself and to finally meet Suu Kyi in person. Could we find a way to fan those flickers of progress the President talked about and ignite truly far-reaching democratic reforms?

We stopped to refuel in Japan in a pouring rain. Two Foreign Service officers with experience in Burma stationed at our embassy in Tokyo were waiting. After hearing the President's announcement, they had brought me a stack of books about the country and a copy of a film about Suu Kyi called *The Lady*. It was just what I needed. The whole team, including the traveling press corps, watched the movie as we flew east across the Pacific back to Washington, where I immediately began planning my trip to Burma.

═══

I arrived in Nay Pyi Taw late on the afternoon of November 30, 2011. The remote capital's small airstrip is paved but does not have sufficient lighting for landings after sundown.

Just before we left Washington, Asia experts at the State Department had sent around a memo advising the traveling party not to wear white, black, or red clothing because of local cultural norms. It is not unusual to get that sort of memo before a trip; there are places where certain political parties or ethnic groups are associated with particular colors. So I diligently went through my closet trying to find outfits in the appropriate colors for Burma. I had just bought a lovely white jacket that was a perfect weight for hot climates. Would it really be culturally insensitive to bring it along? I packed it just in case the experts were wrong. Sure enough, when we stepped off the plane, we were greeted by Burmese wearing all the colors we had been warned to avoid. I hoped that wasn't a sign of deeper misconceptions on our part, but at least now I could safely wear my white jacket.

Our motorcade emerged from the airport into a landscape of vast open fields. The empty highway seemed twenty lanes wide. Occasionally we'd see a bicycle but no other cars and very few people. We passed a farmer wearing a traditional conical straw hat and riding a wagon filled with hay pulled by a white ox. It was like looking through a window into an earlier time.

In the distance we saw the towers of Nay Pyi Taw's cavernous government buildings. The city had been built in secret in 2005 by the military and was heavily fortified with walls and moats intended to defend against a hypothetical American invasion. Few people actually lived there. Many of the buildings were empty or unfinished. The whole place had the feeling of a Potemkin village.

The next morning I visited President Thein Sein in his ceremonial office. We sat on gold thrones under a massive crystal chandelier in an enormous room. Despite the setting, Thein Sein was surprisingly low-key and unassuming, especially for a head of state and leader of a military junta. He was small and slightly stooped, with thinning hair and glasses. He looked more like an accountant than a general. When he had served as Prime Minister in the military government, he had always appeared in a heavily starched green Army uniform, but now he wore a traditional blue Burmese sarong, sandals, and a white tunic.

Many people in Burma and beyond speculated that the former ruler, Than Shwe, had chosen the mild-mannered Thein Sein as his successor because he was seen as both nonthreatening to the outside world and pliable enough to be a front man for regime hard-liners. So far Thein Sein had surprised everyone by showing unexpected independence and real backbone in pushing his nascent reform agenda.

In our discussion I was encouraging, explaining the steps that could lead to international recognition and easing sanctions. "You're on the right path. As you know, there will be hard choices and difficult obstacles to overcome," I said, "[but] this is an opportunity for you to leave an historic legacy for your country." I also delivered a personal letter from President Obama, which underscored the same points.

Thein Sein responded carefully, with sparks of good humor and a sense of ambition and vision peeking through his deliberate sentences. Reforms would continue, he said. So would his détente with Suu Kyi. He was also keenly aware of the broader strategic landscape. "Our country is situated between two giants," he said, referring to China and India, and he needed to be careful not to risk disrupting relations with Beijing. Here was someone who had clearly thought long and hard about the future of his country and the role he could play in achieving it.

In my travels I met at least three kinds of world leaders: those who share our values and worldview and are natural partners, those who want to do the right thing but lack the political will or capacity to follow through, and those who view their interests and values as fundamentally at odds with ours and will oppose us whenever they can. I wondered into which category Thein Sein would fall. Even if he was sincere in his desire for democracy, were his political skills strong enough to overcome entrenched opposition among his military colleagues and actually pull off such a difficult national transformation?

My inclination was to embrace Thein Sein in the hopes that international recognition would strengthen his hand at home. But there was reason to be cautious. Before saying too much, I needed to meet Suu Kyi and compare notes. We were engaged in a delicate diplomatic dance, and it was essential not to get out of step.

After our meeting we moved into a great hall for lunch, and I sat between Thein Sein and his wife. She held my hand and talked movingly about her family and her hopes to improve life for Burma's children.

Then it was on to Parliament and meetings with a cross-section of legislators, most carefully picked by the military. They wore brightly colored traditional dress, including hats with horns and embroidered furs. Some were enthusiastic about engagement with the United States and further reforms at home. Others were clearly skeptical of all the changes going on around them and longed for a return to the old ways.

The Speaker of the Lower House of Parliament, Shwe Mann, another former general, met with me in another gigantic room, beneath a painting of a lush Burmese landscape that seemed to stretch for miles. He was chatty and good-natured. "We've been studying your country trying to understand how to run a Parliament," he told me. I asked if he'd read books or consulted with experts. "Oh no," he said. "We've been watching *The West Wing*." I laughed and promised that we would provide even more information.

Back at the hotel that evening, sitting outside at a large table with the American press corps, I tried to sum up what I had learned that day. The steps the civilian government had taken were significant, including easing restrictions on media and civil society, releasing Suu Kyi from house arrest along with some two hundred other political prisoners, and enacting new labor and election laws. Thein Sein had promised me he would build on this progress and push through even more far-reaching reforms, and I wanted to believe him. But I knew that flickers of progress could easily be extinguished. There is an old Burmese proverb: "When it rains, collect water." This was a time to consolidate reforms and lock them in for the future, so that they would become ingrained and irreversible. As

I had told Thein Sein that morning, the United States was prepared to walk the path of reform with the Burmese people if they chose to keep moving in that direction.

The flight to Rangoon took just forty minutes, but it felt like entering another world after the surreal government ghost town of Nay Pyi Taw. Rangoon is a city of more than 4 million people, with bustling streets and faded colonial charm. Decades of isolation and mismanagement had taken its toll on crumbling façades and peeling paint, but one could imagine why this place was once considered a "jewel of Asia." The heart of Rangoon is the soaring Shwedagon Pagoda, a 2,500-year-old Buddhist temple with glistening gold towers and countless golden Buddhas. As a sign of respect for the local custom, I took off my shoes and walked barefoot through the pagoda's magnificent halls. Security guards hate removing their shoes; it makes them feel less prepared in case of an emergency. But the American journalists thought it was great fun and loved getting a look at my toenail polish, which one described as "sexy siren red."

Accompanied by a throng of monks and onlookers, I lit candles and incense in front of a large Buddha. Then they brought me to one of the enormous bells that reputedly weighed forty tons. The monks handed me a gilded rod and invited me to strike the bell three times. Next, as instructed, I poured eleven cups of water over a small alabaster-white Buddha in a traditional sign of respect. "Can I make eleven wishes?" I asked. It was a fascinating introduction to Burmese culture. But this was more than sightseeing. By visiting the revered pagoda, I hoped to send a message to the people of Burma that America was interested in engaging with them, as well as with their government.

That evening I finally met Suu Kyi in person, at the lakeside villa where American Ambassadors used to live. I wore my white jacket and black pants; the cautionary clothing memo now officially forgotten. To everyone's amusement, Suu Kyi arrived in a similar outfit. We had a drink with Derek Mitchell and Kurt Campbell and then sat down for a private dinner, just the two of us. Her political party had been allowed to register in November 2011, and after numerous meetings among its leaders, they had decided to participate in the 2012 elections. Suu Kyi told me that she herself would run for Parliament. After so many years of forced solitude, it was a daunting prospect.

Over dinner I offered my impressions of Thein Sein and the other government officials I had met in Nay Pyi Taw. I also shared some memories of my first run for office. She asked me many questions about the preparation and process of becoming a candidate. This was all so intensely personal for her. The legacy of her slain father, the hero of Burmese independence, weighed on her and spurred her on. That patrimony gave her a hold on the nation's psyche, but it also created a connection to the very generals who had long imprisoned her. She was the daughter of an officer, a child of the military, and she never lost her respect for the institution and its codes. We can do business with them, she said confidently. I thought of Nelson Mandela embracing his former prison guards after his inauguration in South Africa. That had been both a moment of supreme idealism and hardheaded pragmatism. Suu Kyi had the same qualities. She was determined to change her country, and after decades of waiting, she was ready to compromise, cajole, and make common cause with her old adversaries.

Before parting for the evening, Suu Kyi and I exchanged personal gifts. I had brought a stack of American books that I thought she would enjoy and a chew toy for her dog. She presented me with a silver necklace that she had designed herself, based on a seed pod from an ancient Burmese pattern.

Suu Kyi and I met again the next morning, across the lake in her old childhood colonial home, with hardwood floors and sweeping ceilings. It was easy to forget that it had also been her prison for many years. She introduced me to the elders of her party, octogenarians who had lived through long years of persecution and could hardly believe the changes they were now seeing. We sat around a large round wooden table and listened to their stories. Suu Kyi has a way with people. She may have been a global celebrity and an icon in her country, but she showed these elders the respect and attention they deserved, and they loved her for it.

Later we walked through her gardens, resplendent with pink and red blossoms. The barbed-wire barriers that bounded the property were a pointed reminder of her past seclusion. We stood on the porch, arm in arm, and spoke to the crowd of journalists who had gathered.

"You have been an inspiration," I told Suu Kyi. "You are standing for all the people of your country who deserve the same rights and freedoms of people everywhere." I promised that the United States would be a friend to the people of Burma as they made their historic journey to a better future. She graciously thanked me for all the support and consultation we had given over the past months and years. "This will be the beginning of a new future for all of us, provided we can maintain it," she said. It was the same mix of optimism and caution that we all felt.

I left Suu Kyi's house and drove to a nearby art gallery dedicated to work by artists from Burma's many ethnic minority groups, who make up nearly 40 percent of the population. The walls were covered with photographs of the many faces of Burma. There was pride in their eyes, but sadness too. Ever since the country achieved independence in 1948, the Burmese military had waged war against armed separatist groups in the country's ethnic enclaves. Atrocities were committed on both sides, and civilians were caught in the crossfire, but the Army was the primary perpetrator. These bloody conflicts were major obstacles to the new era we hoped Burma would soon enter, and I had stressed to Thein Sein and his Ministers how important it was to bring them to peaceful conclusions. Representatives from all the major ethnic groups told me how much their people had suffered in the conflicts and hoped for cease-fires. Some wondered aloud whether Burma's new rights and freedoms would extend to them. It was a question that would haunt the reform process.

The flickers of progress were real. If Thein Sein released more political prisoners, passed new laws protecting human rights, sought cease-fires in the ethnic conflicts, cut off military contacts with North Korea, and ensured free and fair elections in 2012, we would reciprocate by restoring full diplomatic relations and naming an Ambassador, easing sanctions, and stepping up investment and development assistance in the country. As I had told Suu Kyi, it would be action for action. I hoped my visit had provided the international support that reformers needed to bolster their credibility and push ahead with their work. On the streets of Rangoon, posters went up with photographs of my walk in the garden with Suu Kyi. Her portrait was quickly becoming almost as common as her father's.

Meanwhile, I wished I could have experienced more of this picturesque country, traveling up the Irrawaddy, seeing Mandalay. I promised myself that I would return one day soon with my family.

Suu Kyi and I stayed in close touch over the following months as the reform process moved forward, speaking five times on the phone. I was delighted when, in April 2012, she won a seat in Parliament, as did more than forty of her party's candidates, winning all but one seat they contested. This time the results were not annulled, and she was allowed to serve. Now she could put her political skills to use.

In September 2012 Suu Kyi traveled to the United States for a seventeen-day tour. I remembered the wish we had shared in our first phone call. I had visited her, and now she would visit me. We sat together in a cozy nook outside the kitchen in my home in Washington, just the two of us.

The months since my visit to Burma had been full of exciting changes. Thein Sein had pulled his government slowly but surely down the path we had discussed in Nay Pyi Taw. He and I had met again over the summer at a conference in Cambodia, and he reaffirmed his commitment to reform. Hundreds of political prisoners were released, including students who organized the 1988 pro-democracy demonstrations and Buddhist monks who participated in protests in 2007. A fragile cease-fire was signed with some of the rebel groups representing ethnic minorities. Political parties were beginning to organize again, and soon privately owned newspapers would be allowed to publish for the first time in nearly half a century.

In response, the United States had begun easing sanctions and had sworn in Derek Mitchell as our first Ambassador in years. Burma was rejoining the international community and was set to chair ASEAN in 2014, a long-standing goal. While the Arab Spring was losing its luster in the Middle East, Burma was giving the world new hope that it is indeed possible to transition peacefully from dictatorship to democracy. Its progress was bolstering the argument that a mix of sanctions and engagement could be an effective tool to drive change in even the most closed societies. If the Burmese generals could be coaxed in from the cold by the lure of international trade and respect, then perhaps no regime was irredeemable.

Reassessing the conventional wisdom on Burma back in 2009 and then experimenting with direct engagement against the advice of many friends back home had been a risky choice, but it was paying off for the United States. Burma's progress, in the wake of President Obama's well-received Asian tour in November 2011, which helped erase any lingering memories from 2009 in Beijing, was making the administration's pivot look like a success. There were still plenty of questions about what would happen next, both in Burma and across the region, but in February 2012 the journalist James Fallows, who has long experience in Asia, wrote glowingly about the pivot and the President's trip in the *Atlantic*: "Much like Nixon's approach to China, I think it will eventually be studied for its skillful combination of hard and soft power, incentives and threats, urgency and patience, plus deliberate—and effective—misdirection." Professor Walter Russell Mead, a frequent critic of the administration, called our efforts "as decisive a diplomatic victory as anyone is likely to see."

Still, despite the progress we had seen in Burma, Suu Kyi looked worried when we met in Washington. When she arrived at my house, she asked to speak to me alone. The problems, she said, were that political prisoners still languished behind bars, some ethnic conflicts had actually gotten worse, and the gold rush by foreign companies was creating new opportunities for corruption.

Suu Kyi was now in Parliament, cutting deals and forming new relationships with former adversaries, trying hard to balance all the pressures on her. Shwe Mann, the Speaker of the Lower House of Parliament, was gaining stature, and Suu Kyi had developed a positive working relationship with him; she appreciated his willingness to consult with her on important matters. The political situation was complicated by the possibility that Thein Sein, Shwe Mann, and Suu Kyi were all potential Presidential candidates in 2015. The behind-the-scenes maneuvering, shifting alliances, and political competition were getting intense. Welcome to democracy!

Thein Sein had gotten Burma moving, but could he finish the job? If Suu Kyi withdrew her cooperation, there was no telling what would happen. International confidence might collapse. Thein Sein would become vulnerable to hard-liners who still hoped to roll back the reforms they resented. Suu Kyi and I discussed the competing pressures she faced. I sympathized because I too had experienced the push and pull of political life. And I knew from years of painful experiences how hard it can be to be cordial, let alone collegial, with those who had once been your political adversaries. I thought her best option was to grit her teeth, keep pushing Thein Sein to follow through on his commitments, and keep their partnership alive at least through the next election.

I know it's not easy, I said. But you are now in a position where what you're doing is never going to be easy. You have to figure out a way to keep working together until or unless there is an alternative path. This is all part of politics. You're on a stage now. You're not locked away under house arrest. So you've got to project many different interests and roles all at once, because you are a human rights advocate, you are a member of Parliament, and you may be a future Presidential candidate. Suu Kyi understood all this, but the pressure on her was enormous. She was re-vered as a living saint, yet now she had to learn to wheel and deal like any elected official. It was a precarious balance.

We moved to my dining room and joined Kurt, Derek, and Cheryl Mills. As we ate, Suu Kyi described the district she now represented in Parliament. As much as she was focused on the high drama of national politics, she was also obsessed with the minutiae of constituency service and solving problems. I remembered feeling exactly the same way when the voters of New York elected me to the U.S. Senate. If you can't get the potholes fixed, nothing else matters.

I had one more word of advice. The next day she would receive the Congressional Gold Medal in a lavish ceremony in the Rotunda of the U.S. Capitol. It would be a well-deserved recognition for her years of moral leadership. "Tomorrow, when you get that Congressional Gold Medal, I think you should say something nice about President Thein Sein," I told her.

The next afternoon I joined Congressional leaders and about five hundred others at the Capitol to honor Suu Kyi. When it was my turn to speak, I recalled the experience of meeting Suu Kyi in the house that had been her jail for so many years and compared it to walking through Robben Island with Nelson Mandela years before. "These two political prisoners were separated by great distances, but they were both marked by uncommon grace, generosity of spirit and unshakable will," I said. "And they both understood something that I think we all have to grasp: the day they walked out of prison, the day the house arrest was ended, was not the end of the struggle. It was the beginning of a new phase. Overcoming the past, healing a wounded country, building a democracy, would require moving from icon to politician." I looked at Suu Kyi and wondered whether she had thought about my suggestion from the night before. She was visibly moved by the emotion of the moment. Then she started to speak.

"I stand here now strong in the knowledge that I'm among friends who will be with us as we continue with our task of building a nation that offers peace and prosperity and basic human rights protected by the rule of law to all who dwell within its realms," she said. Then she added, "This task has been made possible by the reform measures instituted by President Thein Sein." I caught her eye and smiled. "From the depths of my heart, I thank you, the people of America, and you, their representatives, for keeping us in your hearts and minds during the dark years when freedom and justice seemed beyond our reach. There will be difficulties in the way ahead, but I am confident that we shall be able to overcome all obstacles with the help and support of our friends."

Afterward she asked me, with a twinkle in her eye, "How was that?"

"Oh, that was great, really great," I said.

"Well, I'm going to try, I'm really going to try."

The next week I met with Thein Sein at the United Nations General Assembly in New York and talked through many of the concerns Suu Kyi had raised with me. He seemed more in command than in our first conversation, in Nay Pyi Taw, and he listened carefully. Thein Sein was never going to be a charismatic politician, but he was proving to be an effective leader. In his speech at the UN he praised Suu Kyi as his partner in reform for the first time in a public setting and pledged to continue to work with her toward democracy.

=====

In November 2012 President Obama decided to see Burma's "flickers of progress" for himself. This was his first foreign trip since winning reelection, and it would be our last as a traveling team. After visiting together with the King of Thailand in his Bangkok hospital room, we flew to Burma for a six-hour stop, to be followed by the East Asia Summit in Cambodia. The President planned to meet with both Thein Sein and Suu Kyi and address students at Yangon University. Crowds jammed the streets as we drove by. Children waved American flags. People craned to see something that was impossible to imagine not long before.

Rangoon felt like a different city, although it had been just under a year since my previous visit. Foreign investors had discovered Burma and were rushing to put down stakes in what they saw as the last Asian frontier. New buildings were under construction, and real estate prices were soaring. The government had begun relaxing restrictions on the internet, and access was slowly expanding. Industry experts expected the smartphone market in Burma to grow from practically no users in 2011 to 6 million by 2017. And now the President of the United States himself had come to Burma. "We've been waiting fifty years for this visit," one man along the route told a reporter. "There is justice and law in the United States. I want our country to be like that."

For the ride from the airport, Kurt and I joined the President in the big, armored Presidential limousine that is transported everywhere the President travels (known fondly as "the Beast"), along with his close aide Valerie Jarrett. As we rolled through the city, President Obama looked out the window at the soaring golden Shwedagon Pagoda and asked what it was. Kurt told him about its central place in Burmese culture and that I had gone there to demonstrate respect for Burma's people and history. The President asked why he wasn't going there too. During the trip-planning process, the Secret Service had vetoed the idea of visiting the busy temple. They were concerned about the security risks posed by the crowds of worshippers (and they certainly didn't want to take their shoes off!), and no one wanted to close down the site and inconvenience all the other visitors. Having years of familiarity with the concerns of the Secret Service, I suggested that they might agree to an unscheduled "off the record" stop, or "OTR," as they are called. No one would know he was coming, and that would allay some of the security concerns. Plus, when the President decides he's going to go someplace, it's very difficult to say no. Soon enough, after the meeting with President Thein Sein, we were strolling through the ancient pagoda, surrounded by surprised Buddhist monks, about as close to being a couple of regular tourists as a President and a Secretary of State ever get.

Following the meeting with Thein Sein and the unscheduled stop at the pagoda, we were at Suu Kyi's house and she was welcoming the President into what had once been her jail and was now a hub of political activity. She and I embraced like the friends we had become. She thanked the President for America's support for democracy in Burma but cautioned: "The most difficult time in any transition is when we think that success is in sight. Then we have to be very careful that we are not lured by a mirage of success."

The end of Burma's story is yet to be written, and there are many challenges ahead. Ethnic strife has continued, raising alarms about new human rights abuses. In particular, spasms of mob violence against the Rohingya, an ethnic community of Muslims, rocked the country in 2013 and early 2014. The decision to expel Doctors Without Borders from the area and not to count Rohingyas in the upcoming census brought a barrage of criticism. All this threatened to undermine progress and weaken international support. The general elections in 2015 will be a major test for Burma's nascent democracy, and more work is needed to ensure that they will be free and fair. In short, Burma could keep moving forward, or it could slide backward. The support of the United States and the international community will be crucial.

It is sometimes hard to resist getting breathless about Burma. But we have to remain clear-eyed and levelheaded about the challenges and difficulties that lie ahead. Some in Burma lack the will to complete the democratic journey. Others possess the will but lack the tools. There is a long way to go. Still, as President Obama told the students at Yangon University that day in November 2012, what the Burmese people have already achieved is a remarkable testament to the power of the human spirit and the universal yearning for freedom. For me, the memories of those early days of flickering progress and uncertain hope remain a high point of my time as Secretary and an affirmation of the unique role the United States can and should play in the world as a champion of dignity and democracy. It was America at our best.

PART THREE

War and Peace

7

Af-Pak: Surge

President Obama went around the table asking each of us for our recommendation. Should we deploy more troops to join the eight-year-old war in Afghanistan? If so, how many? What should their mission be? And how long should they stay before coming home? These were some of the hardest choices he would have to make as President. The consequences would be profound for our men and women in uniform, our military families, and our national security, as well as the future of Afghanistan.

It was three days before Thanksgiving 2009, after 8 P.M. The President was sitting at the head of the long table in the White House Situation Room, flanked by his National Security Council. I sat next to National Security Advisor Jim Jones on the President's left, across the table from Vice President Biden, Defense Secretary Bob Gates, and Chairman of the Joint Chiefs of Staff Mike Mullen. In front of us the table was covered with papers and binders. (After months of watching the Pentagon brass come to our Situation Room meetings with flashy PowerPoint presentations and colorful maps, I asked the State Department to get more creative with its briefing materials. Now there were plenty of colored maps and charts to go around.)

This was my third meeting of the day at the White House with President Obama and the ninth time since September that the senior national security team had assembled to debate the way forward in Afghanistan.

We looked at the challenge from every conceivable angle. Finally we zeroed in on a plan to surge thirty thousand U.S. troops to Afghanistan by the middle of 2010, supplemented by an additional ten thousand from our allies. They would implement a new approach, focused on providing security in Afghanistan's cities, bolstering the government, and delivering services to the people, rather than waging a battle of attrition with the Taliban insurgents. There would be a full progress review at the end of the year, and we would begin to draw down troops by July 2011. How many and how fast would be up for discussion but would likely be dictated by conditions on the ground.

The team was divided about the merits of this plan. Secretary Gates and the military strongly supported it; Vice President Biden opposed it just as strongly. By now the main arguments were well reviewed, but the President wanted to hear where we each stood, one more time.

═══

Afghanistan, a mountainous, landlocked country located between Pakistan to the east and Iran to the west, is home to about 30 million of the poorest, least educated, and most battle-scarred people on earth. It has been called the "Graveyard of Empires" because so many invading armies and would-be occupiers have foundered in its unforgiving terrain. In the 1980s the United States, Saudi Arabia, and Pakistan supported an insurgency there against a Soviet puppet government. In 1989 the Soviets withdrew, and with that victory American interest in the country waned.

After a period of civil war in the 1990s, the Taliban, an extremist group with medieval cultural views, seized control of Afghanistan under the leadership of a one-eyed radical cleric named Mullah Omar. They imposed severe restrictions on women in the name of Islam: women were forced to stay out of public view, required to wear full burqas, covering them completely from head to toe with only a mesh-covered opening for their eyes, and avoid leaving their homes unless accompanied by a male family member; girls and women were banned from schools and denied social and economic rights. The Taliban inflicted severe punishments on women who violated their rules, ranging from torture to public execution. The stories that filtered out of the country were horrifying. I remember hearing about an elderly woman who was flogged with a metal cable until her leg was broken because a bit of her ankle was showing under her burqa. It seemed hard to believe that human beings could be capable of such cruelty, and in the name of God.

Sickened by what was happening, as First Lady I began speaking out in an effort to rally international condemnation. "There probably is no more egregious and systematic trampling of fundamental rights of women today than what is happening in Afghanistan under the iron rule of the Taliban," I declared at the UN's International Women's Day celebration in 1999.

The Taliban also gave safe haven to Osama bin Laden and other al Qaeda terrorists. Many of these fanatics, who had come from elsewhere, put down deep roots in the region after fighting the Soviets. In response to the bombings of our embassies in East Africa in 1998, the Clinton Administration used cruise missiles to strike an al Qaeda training camp in Afghanistan where intelligence reports said bin Laden would be. He managed to escape. Then came the terrorist attacks of September 11, 2001. After the Taliban refused to turn over bin Laden, President Bush ordered the invasion of Afghanistan and backed a rebel group called the Northern Alliance to oust the Taliban from power.

The swift victory in overthrowing the Taliban regime in Afghanistan soon gave way to a long-running insurgency, as the Taliban regrouped in safe havens across the border in Pakistan. As a Senator I visited Afghanistan three times, first in 2003, when I had Thanksgiving dinner with our troops in Kandahar, and then again in 2005 and 2007. I'll never forget the words of one American soldier I met: "Welcome to the forgotten front lines in the war against terrorism." The Taliban took advantage of the Bush Administration's preoccupation with Iraq and began reclaiming territory across Afghanistan that it had initially been forced to cede. The Western-backed government in Kabul appeared corrupt and feckless. Afghans were hungry, frustrated, and frightened. There weren't enough U.S. troops to secure the country, nor did the Bush Administration appear to have a strategy for reversing the downward slide.

During the 2008 campaign both then-Senator Obama and I called for a renewed focus on Afghanistan. It would take more troops, I argued, but also a comprehensive new strategy that addressed Pakistan's role in the conflict. "The border areas between Pakistan and Afghanistan are among the most important and dangerous in the world," I said in a speech in February 2008. "Ignoring these realities of what is happening on the ground in both Afghanistan and Pakistan has been one of the most dangerous failures of the Bush foreign policy." Attacks on American troops and those of our allies continued to climb, and 2008 became the deadliest year yet in Afghanistan, with nearly three hundred Coalition forces killed in action.

When President Obama came into office in January 2009, he found a request waiting from the Pentagon asking for thousands of additional troops to block the Taliban's expected summer offensive and provide security for the upcoming Presidential elections. We discussed the proposal in one of our first National Security Council meetings after the inauguration. Despite our campaign pledges to put more resources into the war in Afghanistan, it was reasonable to ask whether it made sense to deploy more troops before we had time to decide on a new strategy. But the military logistics necessary to deploy those forces by the summer necessitated a quick decision.

The President approved the deployment of seventeen thousand troops on February 17. He commissioned a strategy review led by Bruce Riedel, an experienced CIA analyst with extensive knowledge of the conflict, along with Michèle Flournoy, the third-ranking official at the Defense Department, and Richard Holbrooke, our Special Representative for Afghanistan and Pakistan. In the report they delivered in March, they recommended that instead of viewing them as two distinct issues, Afghanistan and Pakistan should be approached as a single regional challenge, shorthanded to Af-Pak, and that we should place greater focus on training Afghan troops to perform tasks being handled by us and our allies. In response President Obama deployed four thousand additional U.S. military trainers to work with the Afghan National Security Forces. The Riedel review emphasized the need to use "all elements of national power" in a fully resourced counterinsurgency campaign. "Not just on the military side," Riedel explained, "on the civilian side, as well." That included more intensive regional diplomacy and expanded economic development, agricultural support, and infrastructure construction. Much of that work would fall to the State Department and USAID.

The President announced his military and civilian strategy for Afghanistan and Pakistan on March 27. He set a narrow goal for the war: "To disrupt, dismantle, and defeat al Qaeda in Pakistan and Afghanistan, and to prevent their return to either country in the future." By refocusing so specifically on al Qaeda, as opposed to the Taliban insurgents who were the ones doing the vast majority of the fighting, the President was linking the war back to its source: the 9/11 attacks. He also raised the possibility of a peace and reconciliation process that would bring willing insurgents in from the cold while isolating the hardcore extremists.

Although there were now about sixty-eight thousand U.S. troops in Afghanistan, the summer fighting went badly. The Taliban insurgency continued to gain strength, and the security situation deteriorated. Reports indicated an increase in Taliban fighters over the previous three years from seven thousand to twenty-five thousand. And attacks on NATO forces rose, with more than 260 fatalities from June to September, compared to fewer than a hundred deaths over the four prior months. In May the President removed the commanding general in Afghanistan and replaced him with Lieutenant General Stanley McChrystal. Secretary Gates explained that the switch was needed to bring "fresh thinking" and "fresh eyes." Then, in August, the Afghan Presidential election was marred by widespread fraud. In September General McChrystal asked the President to consider deploying more troops. He warned that without more resources, the war effort would likely result in failure.

That was not what the White House wanted to hear. So before he would even entertain the Pentagon's request, the President wanted to be sure we thought through every option and contingency. He launched a second comprehensive strategic review, this time leading it himself. Starting on a Sunday in mid-September and continuing throughout the fall, President Obama regularly convened his top national security advisors in the White House Situation Room to debate the tough questions presented by a war that was on its way to becoming the longest in American history.

General McChrystal, with the support of General David Petraeus, the commander of all U.S. forces in the region, eventually presented three options: deploy a small additional force of around ten thousand troops to bolster training of the Afghan Army; send forty thousand troops to fight the Taliban in the most contested areas; or dispatch more than eighty thousand to secure the entire country. The generals were savvy bureaucratic warriors, and, like characters in the Goldilocks story, they often would present three options in answer to any question, expecting that the middle one would end up being favored.

━━━━

General Petraeus proved to be an effective advocate. He was clear-thinking, competitive, and politically savvy, and his arguments were informed by hard-learned lessons from Iraq. The troubled legacy of that war loomed large over our debate about Afghanistan.

Petraeus had taken command of the failing U.S. effort in Iraq in early 2007, in the middle of another deadly insurgency. He presided over the surge of more than twenty thousand additional American troops that deployed to some of the most dangerous parts of the country. In January 2007 President Bush announced the Iraq surge in a prime-time speech to a skeptical nation.

His decision to send more troops was something of a surprise, because a respected bipartisan panel, the Iraq Study Group, had issued their report recommending handing over more responsibility to Iraqi security forces, drawing down U.S. troops, and launching more intensive diplomatic efforts in the region. President Bush essentially chose to do the opposite. In his speech he mentioned regional diplomacy and doing more to encourage reconciliation among Iraq's fractured sects and political factions, but most of the emphasis was on the security more U.S. troops could provide.

I doubted that was the right decision at that time. After years of blown calls and missed opportunities, there were questions about the ability of the Bush Administration to manage a major escalation. The next night I left for a trip to Iraq with Senator Evan Bayh of Indiana and Congressman John McHugh of New York, a Republican who went on to serve as Secretary of the Army under President Obama. It was my third visit to Iraq as Senator; I had last been there in 2005 with Senators John McCain, Susan Collins, Russ Feingold, and Lindsey Graham. I wanted to see with my own eyes how things had changed and to talk to our troops and commanders to get their perspectives on the challenges we faced.

I also had other reasons to be skeptical. My lack of confidence in the Bush Administration went back to the fall of 2002, when it was boasting of ironclad intelligence about Saddam Hussein's weapons of mass destruction. After weighing the evidence and seeking as many opinions as I could inside and outside our government, Democrats and Republicans alike, I voted to authorize military action in Iraq if the diplomatic efforts, meaning the UN weapons inspections, failed.

I came to deeply regret giving President Bush the benefit of the doubt on that vote. He later asserted that the resolution gave him the sole authority to decide when the clock had run out on weapons inspections. On March 20, 2003, he decided that it had, and he launched the war, with the UN weapons inspectors pleading for just a few more weeks to finish the job. Over the years that followed, many Senators came to wish they had voted against the resolution. I was one of them. As the war dragged on, with every letter I sent to a family in New York who had lost a son or daughter, a father or mother, my mistake become more painful.

Five years later President Bush asked us to trust him again, this time about his proposed surge, and I wasn't buying it. I didn't believe that simply sending more troops would solve the mess we were in. Our military is the best in the world, and our troops give their all to succeed in whatever they're asked to do. But putting the burden on them alone, without an equally robust diplomatic strategy, wasn't fair and wasn't wise. We needed both if we were going to get at the heart of the underlying challenges: the sectarian conflicts that were tearing the country apart, as well as the regional rivalries playing out inside Iraq. Most in the Bush Administration seemed to have little interest in that sort of work, including confronting or engaging Syria or Iran, even though they were a big part of the underlying challenges we faced in Iraq. In 2003 the United States went to war in Iraq with only half a strategy, with Colin Powell's State Department all but shut out of postwar planning. We weren't going to get out with only half. Later, when I got to the State Department myself as Secretary and saw the expertise of the career professionals there, I was even more appalled that they had been largely excluded by the Bush Administration.

When Petraeus appeared before the Senate Armed Services Committee for his confirmation hearing in late January 2007, I pressed him on these points. I pointed out that the counterinsurgency manual he had written himself at the Army's Command and General Staff College in Fort Leavenworth, Kansas, said that military progress was linked to internal political progress and that one could not be achieved without the other. We had learned the same lesson trying to bring peace to the Balkans. "You are being sent to administer a policy that frankly does not reflect your experience or advice," I said. "You wrote the book, General, but the policy is not by the book. And you are being asked to square the circle, to find a military solution to a political crisis."

Fortunately, when he got to Iraq, Petraeus followed a strategy that looked a lot more like what he had advocated for in his writings and what I had pressed him on during the hearing instead of the Bush Administration's approach to date. Petraeus's comprehensive counterinsurgency strategy became known as COIN. It focused on protecting civilian population centers and winning Iraqis' "hearts and minds" through relationship-building and development projects. The slogan for the strategy became "Clear, hold, and build." The goal was to rid an area of insurgents, defend it so they couldn't return, and invest in infrastructure and governance so residents saw an improvement in their lives and would begin defending themselves. Under Petraeus, American troops in Iraq left their large, heavily fortified bases and fanned out into neighborhoods and villages, which put them more directly in harm's way but also enabled them to provide security.

Equally important, if not more consequential, there was a game-changing development on the ground that few saw coming. A number of Sunni sheiks who had formerly supported the insurgency became fed up with al Qaeda's brutality toward their people and split from the extremists. In what became known as the "Sunni Awakening," more than 100,000 tribal fighters switched sides and ended up on the American payroll. These events profoundly shifted the trajectory of the war.

Back at home, domestic politics was certainly part of the backdrop of the debate over the surge. By then it was clear just how wrong we had gotten Iraq. While the war in Iraq divided America from the start, by 2006 the American people were overwhelmingly against the war—as they made clear that November in the midterm elections. As we learned in Vietnam, it's very difficult to sustain a long and costly war without support from the American people and a spirit of shared sacrifice. I did not think we should escalate America's commitment in Iraq with such overwhelming opposition at home.

During my time in the Senate there were several Republicans whose opinion I valued highly. One of them was John Warner of Virginia. Senator Warner previously served as Secretary of the Navy under President Nixon and was the Ranking Member on the Senate Armed Services Committee, on which I sat. He voted for the Iraq Resolution in 2002, so when he returned from a visit to Iraq in late 2006 and proclaimed that in his judgment the war was now going "sideways," it sent tremors through his own party and beyond. While understated, that single word coming from John Warner was both an indictment and a demand for change.

Wherever I traveled I heard from people who were dead set against the war and, as a result, personally disappointed in me. Many had been opposed from the start; others turned against it over time. Hardest of all were the anguished military families who wanted their loved ones to come home, veterans worried about their buddies still serving tours in Iraq, and Americans of all walks of life who were heartbroken by the losses of our young men and women. They were also frustrated by a war that had weakened our country's standing in the world, was not being paid for, and set back our strategic interests in the region.

While many were never going to look past my 2002 vote no matter what I did or said, I should have stated my regret sooner and in the plainest, most direct language possible. I'd gone most of the way there by saying I regretted the way President Bush used his authority and by saying that if we knew then what we later learned, there wouldn't have been a vote. But I held out against using the word *mistake*. It wasn't because of political expediency. After all, primary voters and the press were clamoring for me to say that word. When I voted to authorize force in 2002, I said that it was "probably the hardest decision I have ever had to make." I thought I had acted in good faith and made the best decision I could with the information I had. And I wasn't alone in getting it wrong. But I still got it wrong. Plain and simple.

In our political culture, saying you made a mistake is often taken as weakness when in fact it can be a sign of strength and growth for people and nations. That's another lesson I've learned personally and experienced as Secretary of State.

Serving as Secretary also gave me a share of the responsibility for sending Americans into harm's way to protect our national security. As First Lady I watched Bill grapple with the gravity of these decisions, and as a Senator on the Armed Services Committee I worked closely with my colleagues and military leaders to conduct rigorous oversight. But there's nothing like sitting at the table in the White House Situation Room where you're debating questions of war and peace and facing the unintended consequences of every decision. And there's nothing to prepare you when people sent to serve in a dangerous place will not be coming home.

As much as I might have wanted to, I could never change my vote on Iraq. But I could try to help us learn the right lessons from that war and apply them to Afghanistan and other challenges where we had fundamental security interests. I was determined to do exactly that when facing future hard choices, with more experience, wisdom, skepticism, and humility.

=====

Generals Petraeus and McChrystal were proposing to bring COIN to Afghanistan. To do it, they needed more troops, just as they had in Iraq. But what if there were no equivalent to the Sunni Awakening this time? Was it possible we were learning the wrong lessons from Iraq?

The most vocal opponent of the Pentagon's proposals was Vice President Biden. For him, the idea of a surge was a nonstarter. Afghanistan was not Iraq. A large-scale effort at "nation-building" in a place with little infrastructure or governance was doomed to fail. He didn't think that the Taliban could be defeated, and he believed that sending more U.S. troops was a recipe for another bloody quagmire. Instead the Vice President argued for a smaller military footprint and a focus on counterterrorism. General Jones and Rahm Emanuel raised similar concerns.

The problem with this argument was that if the Taliban continued to seize more of the country, it would be that much harder to conduct effective counterterrorism operations. We wouldn't have the same intelligence networks necessary to locate the terrorists or the bases from which to launch strikes inside or outside Afghanistan. Al Qaeda already had safe havens in Pakistan. If we abandoned large parts of Afghanistan to the Taliban, they would again have safe havens there as well.

Another skeptic on sending more troops was Richard Holbrooke. We had known each other since the 1990s, when he served as my husband's chief negotiator in the Balkans. In 1996 Holbrooke proposed that I go to Bosnia to visit with religious leaders, civil society groups, and women who had borne the brunt of the violence. This was an unusual assignment for a First Lady, but, as I came to learn, Richard Holbrooke rarely wasted his time with the usual.

Holbrooke was a large and imposing figure, bursting with talent and ambition. After joining the Foreign Service in 1962 at age twenty-one, full of Kennedy-era idealism, he came of age in Vietnam. That was where he learned firsthand about the difficulties of counterinsurgency. Richard rose fast through the ranks. In the Carter Administration, when he was still in his mid-thirties, he became Assistant Secretary of State for East Asian and Pacific Affairs, helping to normalize relations with China. He secured his place in history by going toe-to-toe with the Serbian dictator Slobodan Milošević in 1995 and negotiating the Dayton Peace Accords to end the war in Bosnia.

My relationship with Richard deepened over the years. When he was Ambassador to the UN in the last couple years of the Clinton Administration, we worked together on AIDS and global health issues. I also became close with his wife, Kati Marton, a journalist and author. Richard and Kati threw wonderful dinner parties. You never knew who you were going to meet—a Nobel laureate, a movie star, maybe even a Queen. One evening he planned an unusual surprise for me. He had once heard me make a favorable comment about the Salvation Army so, in the middle of dinner, he gave a signal, the doors swung open, and in marched members of the Salvation Army Band, singing and blowing trumpets. Richard beamed from ear to ear.

When I became Secretary of State, I knew he was eager to return to service, so I asked him to take on the Afghanistan-Pakistan portfolio, which seemed in need of his outsized talents and personality. Richard had visited Afghanistan for the first time in 1971. It was the beginning of a lifelong fascination. After trips to the region in 2006 and 2008 as a private citizen, he wrote several articles urging the Bush Administration to develop a new strategy for the war, with an increased emphasis on Pakistan. I agreed with his analysis and tasked him with assembling a dedicated team made up of the best minds he could find from in and outside of government to try to put his ideas into practice. He quickly enlisted academics, experts from nongovernmental organizations, up-and-coming talent from nine federal agencies and departments, even representatives from allied governments. It was an eclectic band of quirky, bright, and very dedicated people—most of them quite young—with whom I became close, especially after Richard died.

Richard's bulldozer style took some getting used to. When he had an idea, he would pitch it relentlessly, phoning again and again, waiting outside my office, walking into meetings uninvited, even once following me into a ladies' restroom just so he could finish making his point—in Pakistan no less. If I rejected his suggestion, he would wait a few days, pretend it never happened, and then try again. Finally I would exclaim, "Richard, I've said no. Why do you keep asking me?" He would look at me innocently and reply, "I just assumed at some point you would recognize that you were wrong and I was right." To be fair, sometimes that did happen. It was exactly this tenacity that made him the best choice for this urgent mission.

Early in 2009 I invited Richard and Dave Petraeus for an evening at my home in Washington so they could get to know each other. They were men with endless energy and ideas, and I thought they would click. They dove right into the thorniest policy problems, feeding off each other. At the end of the evening they both said, "Let's do this again tomorrow night."

Richard shared Dave's interest in an aggressive counterinsurgency strategy that focused on bolstering the credibility of the government in Kabul and weakening the appeal of the Taliban as an alternative. But he wasn't sure that tens of thousands of additional troops were necessary to do it. He worried that more troops and more fighting would alienate Afghan civilians and undermine any goodwill achieved by expanded economic development and improved governance.

Drawing on his experiences in the Balkans, Richard believed that diplomacy and politics were the keys to ending the war. He wanted to lead a diplomatic offensive to change the regional dynamics that continued to fuel the conflict, especially the toxic relations between Pakistan and Afghanistan and Pakistan and India. He also pushed us to consider reconciliation among the warring Afghan combatants as a top priority.

Richard started visiting regional capitals, looking for any diplomatic opening, no matter how small, that might lead to a political solution, while also urging Afghanistan's neighbors to increase trade and contacts across their borders. He encouraged many of our allies and partners to appoint Special Representatives of their own, so he would have direct counterparts with whom to negotiate.

In February 2009, just a few weeks into our tenure, he organized an international "contact group" on Afghanistan that brought together about fifty countries, along with representatives from the UN, NATO, the European Union, and the Organization of Islamic Cooperation. He wanted every nation and group that contributed troops, donated funds, or wielded influence inside Afghanistan to share the responsibility by meeting frequently to coordinate. A month later Holbrooke and his team helped the United Nations plan a major international conference on Afghanistan at The Hague in the Netherlands. I even consented to inviting Iran in order to test the possibility of cooperating on shared interests in Afghanistan, such as improving border security and curbing drug trafficking. At lunch Holbrooke encountered the senior Iranian diplomat there in a brief exchange, one of the highest-level direct contacts between our countries since immediately after 9/11.

Within Afghanistan itself, Holbrooke advocated for a "civilian surge" that would put into practice the Riedel review's recommendations for a dramatic increase in assistance to improve life for Afghans and strengthen the government in Kabul. He pushed to shift U.S. antinarcotics operations in Afghanistan away from the farmers who eked out a living growing opium and toward the drug traffickers who were getting rich and using their wealth to help fund the insurgency. He tried to reorganize USAID's development programs in both Afghanistan and Pakistan around signature projects that would make positive impressions on the people, including hydroelectric dams in energy-starved Pakistan. And he became passionate about the propaganda war, which the Taliban was winning despite our vastly superior resources and technology. Insurgents used mobile radio transmitters mounted on donkeys, motorcycles, and pickup trucks to spread fear, intimidate local populations, and avoid detection by Coalition forces. For Richard, it was an infuriating problem.

This whirlwind of activity came with some collateral damage. At the White House some saw his efforts to coordinate among various government agencies as encroaching on their turf. Younger White House aides rolled their eyes when he invoked lessons learned in Vietnam. Officials working on the military campaign didn't understand or appreciate his focus on agriculture projects or cell phone towers. Holbrooke's old-school style of diplomacy—that mix of improvisation, flattery, and bluster that had outmaneuvered Milošević—was a bad fit in a White House intent on running an orderly policy process with as little drama as possible. It was painful to watch such an accomplished diplomat marginalized and undercut. I defended him whenever I could, including from several attempts to force him out of the job.

At one point White House aides told me point-blank to get rid of Richard. "If the President wants to fire Richard Holbrooke, he needs to tell me himself," I replied. Then, as was often the case on difficult matters, I spoke directly with President Obama. I explained why I thought Richard was an asset. The President accepted my recommendation and Richard continued his important work.

I was convinced that Richard was right about the need for both a major diplomatic campaign and a civilian surge, but I pushed back when he argued that additional troops weren't needed to make it work. "How will we force the Taliban to the peace table if they have all the momentum?" I asked him. "How do you have a civilian surge in Kandahar when the Taliban are controlling it?"

Over the course of our regular Situation Room meetings, the President seemed to be coming around to the idea of deploying the tens of thousands of additional troops the military sought, along with the new diplomats and development experts Richard and I were recommending. But he still had a lot of questions. Chief among them was how we would avoid an open-ended commitment to an endless war. What was the endgame here?

We hoped that the Afghan government and Army would eventually be strong enough to take responsibility for providing security for their own country and keeping the insurgency at bay, at which point U.S. help would no longer be needed and our troops could begin coming home. That's why we and our allies were training Afghan soldiers, modernizing Afghan government ministries, and going after the insurgents—all with the goal of paving the way for transition to Afghan control. But for this scenario to work, we needed a credible partner in Kabul who was prepared to take up these responsibilities. And in the fall of 2009 nobody around the table was confident that we had one.

———

Talking to Hamid Karzai, the President of Afghanistan, was often a frustrating exercise. He is charming, erudite, and passionate about his beliefs. He is also proud, stubborn, and quick to bristle at any perceived slight. There was, however, no way to avoid him or to take only those parts of him with which we agreed. Like it or not, Karzai was a linchpin of our mission in Afghanistan.

Karzai was the scion of a prominent Pashtun family with a long history in Afghan politics. In 2001, he was installed by the United Nations as a transitional leader after the fall of the Taliban and later chosen as interim President by a traditional grand council of tribal elders, a loya jirga. He then won a five-year term in the country's first Presidential elections in 2004. Responsible for a country riven by ethnic rivalries, devastated by decades of war, and destabilized by an ongoing insurgency, Karzai struggled to provide security and basic services beyond the capital of Kabul. He regularly frustrated his American partners with intemperate outbursts in person and in the press. Yet he was also a real political survivor who successfully played rival Afghan factions off one another and managed to form a strong personal bond with President George W. Bush. Despite his mercurial reputation, Karzai was actually quite consistent when it came

1

Surrounded by friends and supporters in the National Building Museum in Washington, D.C., I end my Presidential campaign on June 7, 2008, and endorse Barack Obama after putting "18 million cracks" in the "highest, hardest glass ceiling."

2

After a long night of writing and rewriting, Bill and I make final changes to my farewell speech before leaving our home in Washington on June 7, 2008.

Despite the hard-fought campaign, Barack and I talk easily on the bus on the way to our first joint event in June 2008 in Unity, New Hampshire, a town chosen not only for its name but also because we received exactly the same number of votes there in the primary. The rally in Unity was designed to send an unmistakable message that the primary was behind us, and we were now one team.

5

LEFT: On December 1, 2008, in Chicago, President-elect Obama announces me as his choice to serve as the sixty-seventh Secretary of State, along with the rest of his national security team. Behind us are: National Security Advisor–designate retired Marine General James Jones, Vice President-elect Joe Biden, Defense Secretary Robert Gates, Homeland Security Secretary–designate Janet Napolitano, and Attorney General–designate Eric Holder.

BELOW: Vice President Biden administers my ceremonial oath of office at the State Department on February 2, 2009, while Bill, Chelsea, and my mom, Dorothy, help hold the Bible. I was officially sworn in a few weeks earlier in my Senate office immediately after the confirmation vote so I could get right to work.

6

7

Walking through the lobby of the State Department for the first time as Secretary on January 22, 2009, I was overwhelmed and humbled by the enthusiastic welcome.

8

Vice President Biden's warmth and humor would be very welcome during our long hours in the White House Situation Room. We also tried to meet for breakfast every week at the Naval Observatory, his official residence.

I was honored to serve in President Obama's Cabinet, pictured here with President Obama and Vice President Biden in the Grand Foyer of the White House on July 26, 2012. Seated, from left, are: Transportation Secretary Ray LaHood, Acting Commerce Secretary Rebecca Blank, U.S. Permanent Representative to the United Nations Susan Rice, and Agriculture Secretary Tom Vilsack. Standing in the second row, from left, are: Education Secretary Arne Duncan, Attorney General Eric H. Holder Jr., Labor Secretary Hilda L. Solis, Treasury Secretary Timothy F. Geithner, Chief of Staff Jack Lew (who previously served as my Deputy Secretary of State), me, Defense Secretary Leon Panetta, Veterans Affairs Secretary Eric K. Shinseki, Homeland Security Secretary Janet Napolitano, and U.S. Trade Representative Ron Kirk. Standing in the third row, from left, are: Housing and Urban Development Secretary Shaun Donovan, Energy Secretary Steven Chu, Health and Human Services Secretary Kathleen Sebelius, Interior Secretary Ken Salazar, Environmental Protection Agency Administrator Lisa P. Jackson, Office of Management and Budget Acting Director Jeffrey D. Zients, Council of Economic Advisers Chair Alan Krueger, and Small Business Administration Administrator Karen G. Mills.

With some of my extraordinary State Department colleagues. My team was made up of Foreign Service officers, career civil servants, and advisors.

First Lady Michelle Obama and I bonded over our shared experiences as First Ladies—some of them humorous.

On my first full day on the job, President Obama and Vice President Biden visit the State Department to announce Richard Holbrooke (left) as Special Representative for Afghanistan and Pakistan and Senator George Mitchell (right) as Special Envoy for Middle East Peace.

Grabbing a quick lunch at the State Department cafeteria. I tried to eat regular meals but it was often a challenge, particularly on the road.

My senior advisors, from left to right, Jake Sullivan, Philippe Reines, and Huma Abedin in our home away from home, a special blue and white U.S. Air Force 757. Over four years we spent a total of eighty-seven full days in the air!

One fine day in April 2009 President Obama suggested we finish a meeting at the picnic table outside the Oval Office on the South Lawn. We tried to meet at least once every week. I surprisingly was at the White House more than seven hundred times during my four years as Secretary.

I step off the plane for the first time as Secretary of State in Tokyo, Japan, on February 16, 2009. I broke with tradition to make my first trip to Asia, signifying our "pivot" to the region.

I loved reconnecting with Japanese Empress Michiko, who was delighted that I had decided to make Japan my first stop as Secretary.

I visit with an adorable group of students from the school President Obama attended as a child in Jakarta, Indonesia, in February 2009. Indonesia is an emerging regional power and home of the Association of Southeast Asian Nations (ASEAN), an important partner in our engagement in Asia.

In August 2009, Bill secured the release of two detained American journalists working for Current TV, Laura Ling (center) and Euna Lee (right), after negotiating with North Korean dictator Kim Jong Il. Their return to the United States was an emotional moment. Standing with Bill are Current TV founders Joel Hyatt and Former Vice President Al Gore.

Secretary of Defense Bob Gates and I peer through binoculars into isolated North Korea at a guard post in the demilitarized zone (DMZ) in July 2010.

A North Korean soldier stares at us through the window as Bob Gates and I tour a building in the DMZ, the most fortified border in the world.

22

Watching traditional Indian dancers at the Kalakshetra Foundation in Chennai, India, in July 2011 reminded me of the country's rich history and culture.

23

Chinese State Councilor Dai Bingguo and I meet for the first time in February 2009 in Beijing. He once showed me a picture of his granddaughter, remarking, "This is what we're in it for."

24

Chinese Foreign Minister Yang Jiechi visits me at the State Department in March 2009. The rise of China is one of the most consequential strategic developments of our time. This isn't a relationship that fits neatly into categories like friend or rival, and it may never be. That is why I spent so much of my time working to create the right balance.

25

I join President Obama and Treasury Secretary Tim Geithner with our Chinese counterparts at the U.S. Ambassador's residence in London, where we were all attending a meeting of the G-20 in April 2009. From left to right: State Councilor Dai Bingguo, Vice Premier Wang Qishan, President Hu Jintao, President Obama, me, and Secretary Geithner.

When I learned America was one of the only countries not participating in the World Expo in Shanghai, China, I put together a team to ensure that the USA Pavilion would be a success. The best part of my May 2010 visit to the Expo was talking with the young Chinese and American students.

The proudest moment for the "MOTB" (Mother of the Bride): Chelsea's wedding on July 31, 2010, in Rhinebeck, New York. Bill and I join Chelsea and her husband, Marc, along with my mom, Dorothy. It meant so much to Chelsea to have her grandmother there as she planned the wedding and married Marc.

TOP: Chinese dissident Chen Guangcheng is escorted out of the U.S. Embassy in Beijing by, from left to right, Legal Advisor Harold Koh, U.S. Ambassador to China Gary Locke, and Assistant Secretary of State for East Asian and Pacific Affairs Kurt Campbell. BOTTOM: I had the chance to meet Chen in December 2013, in Washington, D.C.

With President Thein Sein of Burma in his ornate ceremonial office in Nay Pyi Taw in late 2011. I was the first U.S. Secretary of State to visit the formerly closed country in more than fifty years, in an attempt to nurture democratic progress.

I marvel at my surroundings as I tour the exquisite Shwedagon Pagoda during my visit to Rangoon, Burma, in December 2011.

The first time I met the Burmese Nobel Peace Prize winner Aung San Suu Kyi in December 2011, we were both wearing white. It seemed like an auspicious coincidence. I felt as if we had known each other for a lifetime, even though we had just met.

On my return trip to the Shwedagon Pagoda with President Obama, I struck the enormous bell three times. We hoped to send a message to the people of Burma that America was interested in engaging with them as well as their government. (Notice my bare feet!)

As President Obama looks on, Aung San Suu Kyi and I say farewell with an emotional hug in November 2012. Suu Kyi is an inspiration to her country and to me, and I cherish the friendship we've developed.

to his core priorities of maintaining Afghan sovereignty and unity—and his own power.

Since 9/11, I had gotten to know Karzai fairly well. In June 2004, I brought him to Fort Drum in upstate New York so he could thank soldiers from the 10th Mountain Division, one of the most deployed divisions in the U.S. Army, for their service in Afghanistan. Over the years I had the privilege of spending time with the men and women of the 10th Mountain Division, both at Fort Drum and in Iraq and Afghanistan. Whenever I visited one of those war zones as a Senator, I tried to find time to talk with soldiers from New York about what was actually happening on the ground. I heard harrowing reports about inadequate body armor and vulnerable Humvees, but also stories of bravery and perseverance. When Karzai joined me at Fort Drum, he was gracious and respectful of the sacrifices the troops were making for his country. At other times over the years, however, he seemed to blame Americans more than the Taliban for the violence in his country. That was hard to stomach.

Still, we needed Karzai, so I worked hard to connect with him. We related well on a personal and political level. And as with many other world leaders, respect and personal courtesy went a long way with Karzai. Whenever he came to Washington, I tried to find ways to make him feel like the honored guest he was. It was in those settings that he was most productive as a partner. One day we went for a walk in the rose garden at the Dumbarton Oaks estate in Georgetown, then sat down for tea in their conservatory. He talked more frankly than usual about the challenges back home, particularly the continuing threats coming from safe havens in Pakistan. In return for my gestures in Washington, he went out of his way to be hospitable during my visits to Kabul, including introducing me to his wife in their family's private quarters.

In August 2009, Karzai ran for reelection in a vote that international monitors found to be plagued with fraud. The UN called for a runoff between Karzai and his closest competitor, Abdullah Abdullah, but Karzai refused to allow it. He was angry at what he saw as foreign interference in the election (he was sure Holbrooke was scheming to oust him) and desperate not to lose his power. His pride was hurt that he hadn't been declared the victor after the first vote. By October the impasse was threatening to derail international support for his government and squander what little credibility it had with the Afghan people.

"Think about the historical consequences both for yourself, as the first democratically elected leader, and for your country," I implored over the phone, trying to broker a compromise that would preserve stability for the country and legitimacy for the regime in Kabul. "You have an opportunity to emerge with a stronger government under your leadership, but that rests on the choices that you make going forward."

Karzai dug in his heels. He was defensive about the allegations of widespread fraud in the election. "How can we tell the population that their vote was fraudulent?" he asked. After all, they had braved Taliban intimidation to participate in the election. "People's fingers and noses were cut off, people were shot, young women made sacrifices, your troops made sacrifices—to call all of that wrong and invalidated is a frightening scenario." Karzai was right about the extraordinary sacrifices Afghans had made, but wrong about how to honor them.

Over the next few days we debated back and forth. I explained to Karzai that if he accepted the runoff vote, which he would most likely win, he would gain the moral high ground and bolster his credibility with both the international community and his own citizens. I was glad that Senator John Kerry, the chairman of the Foreign Relations Committee, was planning on visiting Kabul. He would be a valuable ally on the ground, helping me convince Karzai to move forward with a second round of voting. With Kerry in the room and with me on the phone from my office at the State Department, we tag-teamed him using our own experiences to make the case. "I've run for office and so has my husband," I reminded Karzai. "I know what it's like to win and lose. Just like Senator Kerry does. We know how difficult these decisions can be."

I felt we were making progress, so when it was time for Kerry to return to Washington for Senate business, I asked him to stay in Kabul a little longer. He asked that I call Senate Majority Leader Harry Reid to request that no votes be held until he returned. When I reached Reid, he agreed to a one-day grace period but said he needed Kerry back quickly.

Finally, after four days of pressure, Karzai relented. He would accept the findings of the UN monitors and allow a second vote to be held in early November. In the end Abdullah wound up dropping out and Karzai was declared the winner. It wasn't pretty, but at least we avoided a fatal blow to Karzai's overall legitimacy, the likely collapse of his government, and grave doubts about democracy from many Afghans.

In mid-November I attended Karzai's inauguration in Kabul. The city was under exceptionally tight security as leaders from around the world gathered. Over a long dinner at the Presidential Palace on the eve of the ceremony, I pressed Karzai on several points. First, I stressed that it was time to start talking seriously about how to transition responsibility for security from the U.S.-led international Coalition to the Afghan National Army. Nobody expected this would happen overnight, but President Obama wanted assurances that the United States was not making an open-ended commitment.

I also talked with Karzai about the potential for a political settlement that might one day bring the fighting to an end. Could negotiations or incentives ever convince enough members of the Taliban to put down their guns and accept the new Afghanistan? Or were we dealing with a group of implacable extremists and dead-enders who would never compromise or reconcile? The obstacles to this kind of peace process appeared nearly insurmountable. But, I reminded Karzai, nobody was going to walk through the door if it wasn't open. Karzai was always willing to pursue negotiations with the Taliban on his own terms. One of our problems with him was that he didn't see the Taliban as his primary opponent in the war. He believed Pakistan was. He was even reluctant to visit his own forces, who were fighting the Taliban, in the field. He thought both Afghanistan and Coalition forces should direct the lion's share of their efforts against Pakistan, while he negotiated with his fellow Pashtuns in the Taliban. Unfortunately for him the Taliban did not want to reciprocate. U.S. troops and diplomats would have to lay the groundwork and then bring the parties together. In the meantime Karzai flirted with anyone who claimed to represent the Taliban.

Finally I made it clear that, after the election controversy, it was essential that he demonstrate more willingness to crack down on corruption. It was endemic in Afghanistan, sapping resources, fueling a culture of lawlessness, and alienating the Afghan people. Karzai needed a plan to go after the low-level "everyday corruption" of bribery that is a part of Afghan life and the pernicious corruption of senior officials who regularly diverted massive resources from international aid and development projects to line their own pockets. The worst example was the looting of the Kabul Bank. We didn't need Afghanistan to become a "shining city on a hill," but reducing large-scale theft and extortion was vital to the war effort.

The next day Karzai strode proudly down a red carpet flanked by an honor guard in dress uniform. If you saw only those soldiers, with their crisp white gloves and shiny boots, you would not have known that the fledgling Afghan National Army was still far from ready to lead the fight against the Taliban on its own. On that day, at least, they appeared confident and in command.

So did Karzai. As usual, he cut a dramatic figure, with his distinctive cape and jaunty hat. I was one of the few women present, and Karzai led me around to meet the Pashtun leaders from, as he said, both sides of the nonrecognized border between Afghanistan and Pakistan. Pashtuns are among the most strikingly attractive people in the world. Their sharp-featured faces and piercing, often blue eyes are set off by elaborate turbans. These are the people from whom Karzai came, and he never forgot that.

Karzai delivered his inaugural address inside the palace, flanked by Afghan flags and surrounded by a huge bed of red and white flowers. He said nearly all the right things. There was a robust pledge to take on corruption. He announced a new measure we had discussed to require government officials to register their assets so that money and influence could be more easily tracked. He also outlined steps to improve delivery of basic services, strengthen the justice system, and expand educational and economic opportunities. To the insurgents, he made this offer: "We welcome and will provide necessary help to all disenchanted compatriots who are willing to return to their homes, live peacefully and accept the Constitution," with a caveat that excluded al Qaeda and fighters directly linked to international terrorism. To show he was serious, he pledged to convene another loya jirga to discuss launching a peace and reconciliation process.

Most important of all, Karzai committed to speed efforts to stand up a capable and effective Afghan national security force that would be able to replace American and international troops over time. "We are determined that by the next five years, the Afghan forces are capable of taking the lead in ensuring security and stability across the country," he said. That was what President Obama had been waiting to hear.

———

On November 23, I met with President Obama, first in a midday Cabinet meeting, then in a late-afternoon huddle in the Oval Office with Vice President Biden, and finally in a nighttime National Security Council session in the White House Situation Room. It was the culmination of months of debate.

I updated the President on my trip to Kabul, including my discussions with Karzai. Then I laid out my thinking, beginning with the premise that we could not abandon Afghanistan. The United States had tried that in 1989, after the Soviets withdrew, and we paid a grievous price for allowing the country to become a safe haven for terrorists. Nor was the status quo acceptable. American troops were dying, and the government in Kabul was losing ground every day. Something had to change.

I supported the military's proposed troop increase, combined with a civilian surge and diplomatic efforts inside both Afghanistan and the region, to bring the conflict to an end. I believed more military forces were crucial to create space for a transition process to Afghan responsibility, to provide stability and security to help build up and strengthen the government, and to ensure leverage to pursue a diplomatic resolution.

I shared the President's reluctance about an open-ended commitment without any conditions and expectations. That's why I pressed Karzai so hard to offer a vision in his inaugural address for a transition to Afghan responsibility for security. Planning for that transition, and getting the buy-in of the international community, would have to be a priority going forward.

The President listened carefully to all the arguments presented by those of us sitting around the table. It was getting late, and he was still not ready to make a final decision. But in a few days, after a final review of the military options with Gates and Mullen, he would be.

President Obama decided to announce his new policy in a speech at West Point. After calling foreign leaders and briefing members of Congress, I joined him on Marine One for the short helicopter ride to Andrews Air Force Base, where we boarded Air Force One to New York's Stewart International Airport. Then we were back on another Marine One to West Point. As a rule, I am not fond of helicopters. They're loud and cramped and defy gravity only with fierce and jarring effort. But Marine One is different. The cabin of the iconic green and white Presidential helicopter feels more like a small plane, with white leather seats, blue curtains, and space for a dozen passengers. It's as quiet as riding in a car. Lifting off from the South Lawn of the White House, banking out over the National Mall, passing so close to the Washington Monument that it seems as if you could reach out and touch the marble—it's a unique experience.

On this ride I sat next to Gates and Mullen, facing Jones and the President, who read over the speech draft one more time. This was a President who had been elected in part because of his opposition to the war in Iraq and his pledge to end it. Now he was about to explain to the American people why he was escalating our involvement in another war in a far-off country. It had been a difficult deliberation, but I believed that the President had made the right choice.

When we arrived at West Point, I took my seat next to Secretary Gates in the Eisenhower Hall Theatre in front of a sea of gray-coated cadets. On Gates's right was General Eric Shinseki, the Secretary of Veterans Affairs. As Army Chief of Staff in 2003 he had presciently warned the Bush Administration that many more troops would be needed to secure Iraq after an invasion than were being budgeted for. As a result of his honesty, Shinseki was criticized, sidelined, and ultimately retired. Now here we were, nearly seven years later, once again debating how many troops were really needed to achieve our goals.

The President began by reminding the audience why the United States was in Afghanistan. "We did not ask for this fight," he said. But when al Qaeda attacked America on September 11, 2001—an attack planned under the protection of the Taliban in Afghanistan—war was thrust on us. He then explained how the war in Iraq had sapped resources and attention from the effort in Afghanistan. When President Obama took office, there were just over thirty-two thousand American troops in Afghanistan, compared to 160,000 in Iraq at the peak of the war. "Afghanistan is not lost, but for several years it has moved backwards," he said. "The Taliban has gained momentum." He reaffirmed our more focused mission in Afghanistan: to disrupt, dismantle, and defeat al Qaeda in Afghanistan and Pakistan and to prevent its capacity to threaten America and our allies in the future. Then he explained that he would send an additional thirty thousand U.S. troops to carry it out, along with additional contributions from our allies. "After eighteen months, our troops will begin to come home," he said.

This was a starker deadline than I had hoped for, and I worried that it might send the wrong signal to friend and foe alike. Although I strongly believed in the need for a time-bound surge and a speedy transition, I thought there was benefit in playing our cards closer to our chests. However, with the pace of withdrawal unspecified, there was enough flexibility to get the job done.

The President emphasized the importance of spurring economic development in Afghanistan and reducing corruption, directing us to focus our assistance in areas, such as agriculture, that could make an immediate impact in the lives of the Afghan people, and to put in place new standards for accountability and transparency.

Deputy Secretary Jack Lew was in charge of marshaling the staff and funds for our "civilian surge." Holbrooke and his team, along with our embassy in Kabul, mapped out its priorities: giving Afghans a stake in their country's future and providing credible alternatives to extremism and insurgency. Over the next year we would triple the number of diplomats and development experts and other civilian specialists on the ground in Afghanistan, expanding our presence out in the field nearly sixfold. By the time I left State, the Afghans had made progress. Economic growth was up and opium production was down. Infant mortality declined by 22 percent. Under the Taliban only 900,000 boys and no girls had been enrolled in schools. By 2010, 7.1 million students were enrolled, and nearly 40 percent of them were girls. Afghan women received more than 100,000 small personal loans that allowed them to start businesses and enter the formal economy. Hundreds of thousands of farmers were trained and equipped with new seeds and techniques.

That day at West Point, I was under no illusions about how difficult it would be to turn around this war. But, all things considered, I believed that the President had made the right choice and put us in the best possible position to succeed. Still, the challenges ahead were enormous. I looked around at the cadets filling every seat in the cavernous theater. They were sitting in rapt attention as their Commander in Chief spoke about a war many of them would soon find themselves fighting. These were young faces, full of promise and purpose, preparing to face a dangerous world in the hope of making America safer. I hoped we were doing right by them. When the President finished his remarks, he stepped into the crowd to shake hands, and the cadets surged around him.

8

Afghanistan: To End a War

Richard Holbrooke was, at heart, a negotiator. In the 1990s, as he described in his fascinating book, *To End a War*, he bullied, threatened, cajoled, and drank whiskey with Slobodan Milošević—whatever it took to force the Serbian dictator into a smaller and smaller corner until he finally gave in. On one difficult day during the peace talks hosted by the United States in Dayton, Ohio, when Milošević was refusing to give an inch, Richard walked him through a hangar at Wright-Patterson Air Force Base full of warplanes, providing a visual reminder of American military power. The message was clear: Compromise or face the consequences. The whole effort was a dazzling display of diplomatic skill, and a war that had appeared hopelessly intractable ended.

Richard longed to do for Afghanistan what he had done for the Balkans: reconcile the parties and negotiate a peaceful end to the conflict. He was aware how difficult that would be; he confided to his friends that this was the toughest assignment in a career full of "Mission: Impossible" moments. But as he told me from the start, he was convinced that it was worth trying to create the conditions for a peace process. If the Taliban could be persuaded or pressured to drop their ties with al Qaeda and reconcile with the government in Kabul, then peace would be possible and U.S. troops could safely come home. At the end of the day, despite all the influence and involvement of Pakistan, the United States, and others, this was not a war between nations; it was a war among Afghans to determine the future of their country. And as Richard once observed, "In every war of this sort, there is always a window for people who want to come in from the cold."

History tells us that insurgencies rarely end with a surrender ceremony on the deck of a battleship. Instead they tend to run out of steam thanks to persistent diplomacy, steady improvements in quality of life for people on the ground, and unyielding perseverance by those who want peace.

In my early conversations with Holbrooke about the possibilities of a political resolution to the conflict, we discussed two ways of approaching the problem: bottom up or top down. The former was more straightforward. There was good reason to believe that many low-level Taliban fighters were not particularly ideological. They were farmers or villagers who joined the insurgency because it offered a steady income and respect in a country wracked by poverty and corruption. If they were offered amnesty and other incentives, some of these fighters might willingly come off the battlefield and reintegrate into civilian life, especially if they grew weary of absorbing increasing American military pressure. If significant numbers could be persuaded to do so, that would leave mostly the hardcore extremists to sustain the insurgency—a much more manageable challenge for the government in Kabul.

The top-down approach was more challenging but potentially more decisive. The leaders of the Taliban were religious fanatics who had been at war practically all their lives. They had close ties with al Qaeda, relations with Pakistani intelligence officers, and deep-seated opposition to the regime in Kabul. It was unlikely they could be persuaded to stop fighting. But with enough pressure, they might realize that armed opposition was futile and the only road back to any role in Afghan public life was through negotiations. Despite the degree of difficulty, Richard thought we should pursue both approaches simultaneously, and I agreed.

In March 2009 the Riedel strategy review endorsed a bottom-up reintegration effort, but it rejected the prospect of a top-down peace process. The Taliban leaders were "not reconcilable and we cannot make a deal that includes them," it stated. Still, the review set out some core principles that would be important guides for either approach. To be reconciled, insurgents would have to lay down their arms, reject al Qaeda, and accept the Afghan Constitution. And reconciliation should not come at the expense of Afghanistan's progress on gender equality and human rights or lead to a return of reactionary social policies.

That was a concern I felt passionately about, going all the way back to my time as First Lady and continuing through my Senate service. After the fall of the Taliban in 2001, I worked with other women Senators to support First Lady Laura Bush's U.S.-Afghan Women's Council and other programs for Afghan women as they sought new rights and opportunities. When I became Secretary of State, I requested that all our development and political projects in Afghanistan take into account the needs and concerns of Afghan women. Creating opportunity for women was not just a moral issue; it was vital to Afghanistan's economy and security. While life remained difficult for most Afghan women, we did see some encouraging results. In 2001 life expectancy for women in Afghanistan was just forty-four years. By 2012 it had jumped to sixty-two. Mortality rates for mothers, infants, and children younger than five all declined significantly. Nearly 120,000 Afghan girls graduated from high school in those years, fifteen thousand enrolled in universities, and nearly five hundred women joined university faculties. Those figures are astonishing when you consider that at the beginning of the 21st century, they were close to zero across the board.

Despite this progress, Afghan women faced constant threats to their security and status, and not just from the resurgent Taliban. In the spring of 2009, for example, President Karzai signed a terrible new law that dramatically restricted the rights of women belonging to the minority Shiite population, targeting an ethnic group called the Hazara, which had conservative cultural traditions. The law, which included provisions effectively legalizing marital rape and requiring Shiite women to seek permission from their husbands before leaving the house, blatantly violated the Afghan Constitution. Karzai had backed the measure as a way of shoring up support from hard-line Hazara leaders, which was, of course, no excuse. I was appalled, and I let Karzai know it.

I called Karzai three times over the course of two days to urge him to revoke the law. If the Constitution could be ignored and the rights of this minority rolled back, then nobody's rights were secure, men's or women's. It would undermine his regime's moral case against the Taliban. I knew how much personal relationships and respect mattered to Karzai, so I also made clear that this was important to me personally. I explained that if he allowed this outrageous law to stand, it would make it very hard for me to explain why American women, including my former colleagues in Congress, should continue supporting him. Now I was speaking the language he understood. Karzai agreed to put the law on hold and send it back to the Justice Ministry for review. Changes were eventually made. Though not enough, it was a step in the right direction. To keep faith with Karzai, I generally kept this kind of personal diplomacy quiet. I wanted him to know that we could talk—and argue—without it ending up in the newspapers.

Whenever I met with Afghan women, whether in Kabul or at international conferences around the world, they movingly told me how much they wanted to help build and lead their country, as well as their fears that their hard-earned gains would be sacrificed as U.S. troops departed or Karzai cut a deal with the Taliban. That would be a tragedy, not just for Afghan women but for the entire country. So in every conversation about reintegrating insurgents and reconciling with the Taliban, I was very clear that it would not be acceptable to trade away the rights of Afghan women to buy peace. That would be no peace at all.

I made the Riedel review's criteria for reintegration—abandon violence, break with al Qaeda, support the Constitution—a mantra of my diplomacy. At our first major international conference on Afghanistan, in The Hague in March 2009, I spoke to the assembled delegates about splitting "the extremists of al Qaeda and the Taliban from those who joined their ranks not out of conviction, but out of desperation." At an international conference in London in January 2010, Japan agreed to commit $50 million to provide financial incentives to draw low-level fighters off the battlefield. I pledged that the United States would also provide substantial funding, and we convinced other countries to follow suit.

In an interview in London, I was asked if "it would be a surprise and maybe even disturbing" for Americans to hear that we were trying to reconcile with some insurgents even as the President was sending more U.S. troops to fight the very same Taliban. "You can't have one without the other," I responded. "A surge of military forces alone without any effort on the political side is not likely to succeed. . . . An effort to try to make peace with your enemies without the strength to back it up is not going to succeed. So, in fact, this is a combined strategy that makes a great deal of sense." That had been my argument during the many debates in the White House Situation Room about the troop surge, and it was in keeping with my beliefs about smart power. But I recognized that even if this was a wise strategy, it might be hard to accept. So I added, "I think underlying your question is the concern of people who say, well, wait a minute, those are the bad guys. Why are we talking to them?" That was a fair question. But at this point we weren't talking about reconciling with terrorist masterminds or the Taliban leaders who protected Osama bin Laden. I explained that all we were doing was trying to peel off nonideological insurgents who sided with the Taliban for the much-needed paycheck.

So far, at least, that was true—for us. For his part, Karzai followed up on his statements about reconciliation in his 2009 inaugural address by exploring direct talks with Taliban leaders. In the summer of 2010 he convened a traditional conference of tribal elders from across Afghanistan to back his efforts. Then he appointed a High Peace Council led by former Afghan President Burhanuddin Rabbani to lead potential negotiations. (Tragically Rabbani was assassinated in September 2011 by a suicide bomber with explosives hidden in his turban. His son agreed to take his place on the council.)

One obstacle to these early Afghan efforts was opposition from elements within the Pakistani intelligence service, known as ISI. Elements in the ISI had a long-standing relationship with the Taliban, going back to the struggle against the Soviets in the 1980s. They continued to provide safe haven for insurgents inside Pakistan, and supported the insurgency in Afghanistan as a way to keep Kabul off balance and hedge against potential Indian influence there. The Pakistanis did not want to see Karzai reach a separate peace with the Taliban that did not take their interests into account. And that was just one of the complications Karzai faced. He also had to worry about opposition from his allies in the old Northern Alliance, many of whom were members of ethnic minorities such as Tajiks and Uzbeks and were suspicious that Karzai would sell them out to his fellow Pashtuns in the Taliban. It was becoming clear that lining up all these players and interests to forge a lasting peace was going to be like solving a Rubik's Cube.

By the fall of 2010, Kabul was buzzing with reports of a new channel between Karzai and the Taliban leadership. Karzai's lieutenants held a number of meetings with a contact who crossed the border from Pakistan and was provided safe passage by Coalition troops. At one point he was flown on a NATO airplane to Kabul to meet with Karzai himself. The man claimed to be Mullah Akhtar Muhammad Mansour, a high-ranking Taliban commander, and he said he was ready to deal. Some captured

Taliban fighters reportedly were shown a photograph and confirmed his identity. This was an exciting prospect.

In October, at a NATO summit in Brussels, Belgium, Secretary Gates and I were asked about these reports. We both emphasized our support for exploring any credible reconciliation effort, but I cautioned, "There are a lot of different strains to it that may or may not be legitimate or borne out as producing any bona fide reconciliation."

Unfortunately my skepticism was warranted. In Afghanistan the story was starting to crumble. Some Afghans who had known Mansour for years claimed that this negotiator looked nothing like him. In November the *New York Times* reported that the Afghan government had determined the man was an impostor and not a member of the Taliban leadership after all. The *Times* called it "an episode that could have been lifted from a spy novel." For Karzai, it was a bitter disappointment.

While the Afghans were going down one dead end after another, Holbrooke and his team, including the noted scholar Vali Nasr, were focused on Pakistan, which they believed was one of the keys to unlocking the whole puzzle. We needed to get the Pakistanis invested in the future of Afghanistan and convince them they had more to gain from peace than from continued conflict.

Richard latched on to a stalled "transit trade agreement" between Afghanistan and Pakistan that had been languishing unfinished since the 1960s. If completed, it would lower trade barriers and allow consumer goods and commodities to flow across a border most often used in recent years for troop movements and arms shipments. He reasoned that if Afghans and Pakistanis could trade together, maybe they could learn to work together to combat the militants who threatened them both. Increased commerce would boost the economy on both sides of the border and offer people alternatives to extremism and insurgency, not to mention giving each side more of a stake in the other's success. He successfully pushed both countries to restart negotiations and resolve their outstanding differences.

In July 2010, I flew to Islamabad, the capital of Pakistan, to witness the formal signing. The Afghan and Pakistani Commerce Ministers sat next to each other, staring down at the thick green folders before them that contained the final agreement. Richard and I stood behind them, next to Pakistani Prime Minister Yousaf Raza Gilani. We looked on as the men carefully signed the accord and then stood to shake hands. Everyone applauded this tangible step, hoping that it could end up representing a new mind-set as much as a new business deal.

This was the first building block of a vision we would come to call "the new Silk Road," a network of expanded commercial and communications links that would bind together Afghanistan with its neighbors, giving them all a stake in promoting shared peace and security. Over the next few years the United States committed $70 million to significantly upgrade key roads between Afghanistan and Pakistan, including through the famous Khyber Pass. We also encouraged Pakistan to extend "most-favored nation" status to India, and India to liberalize barriers to Pakistani investment and financial flows, both of which are still moving forward. Given the distrust that exists between them, getting anything done on the Pakistan-India front was no easy task. Electricity from Uzbekistan and Turkmenistan began powering Afghan businesses. Trains started running on a new rail line from the Uzbek border to the northern Afghan city of Mazar-e-Sharif. Plans progressed for a pipeline that one day could ship billions of dollars' worth of natural gas from energy-rich Central Asia across Afghanistan to energy-hungry South Asia. All these improvements were long-term investments in a more peaceful and prosperous future for a region too long held back by conflict and rivalry. It was slow going, to be sure, but even in the short term this vision injected a sense of optimism and progress in places where they were sorely needed.

In Islamabad, on that trip in July 2010 (and on every other visit there), I pushed hard to get Pakistan's leaders to view the war in Afghanistan as a shared responsibility. We needed their help in closing the safe havens from which Taliban insurgents were staging deadly attacks across the border. As Richard kept emphasizing, there was never going to be a diplomatic solution to the conflict without Pakistani support. In a television interview with five Pakistani television journalists set up in our Ambassador's home—part of my plan to be treated like a punching bag by the hostile Pakistani press to show how serious I was about engagement—I was asked whether it was possible to pursue such a settlement while still pounding away at the other side on the battlefield. "There is no contradiction between trying to defeat those who are determined to fight and opening the door to those who are willing to reintegrate and reconcile," I replied.

In fact Richard and I still harbored hope that top Taliban leaders might one day be willing to negotiate. And there were some intriguing developments. In the fall of 2009, Richard visited Cairo and was told by senior Egyptian officials that a number of Taliban representatives, including an aide to the top leader, Mullah Omar, had recently paid them a visit. In early 2010, a German diplomat reported that he had also met with the same aide, this time in the Persian Gulf, and that he seemed to have a direct line to the elusive Taliban chief. Most interesting of all, he reportedly wanted to find a way to talk to us directly.

Richard thought this was an opening that needed to be tested, but some of our colleagues at the Pentagon, CIA, and White House were reluctant. Many agreed with the analysis in the Riedel review that the top leaders of the Taliban were extremists who could never be reconciled with the government in Kabul. Others thought the time was not yet ripe for negotiations. The surge had just begun, and it needed time to work. Some did not want to accept the political risk of engaging so directly with an adversary responsible for killing American soldiers. I understood this skepticism, but I told Richard to quietly explore what was possible.

A die-hard baseball fan, Richard started calling the Taliban contact, who was later identified by media reports as Syed Tayyab Agha, by the code name "A-Rod," and it stuck. The Germans and Egyptians both said he was the real deal, a representative empowered to speak for Mullah Omar and the Taliban high command. The Norwegians, who had contacts within the Taliban, agreed. We weren't sure, especially after other potential channels had turned out to be duds, but felt it was worth proceeding cautiously.

In the fall, even as the Afghan government was spinning its wheels with the Taliban impostor, we moved forward with a first exploratory meeting in Germany under the strictest secrecy. On a Sunday afternoon in October, Richard called his Deputy Frank Ruggiero, who had served as a civilian advisor with the military in Kandahar, and asked him to prepare to go to Munich to meet A-Rod. Ruggiero was in the car with his seven-year-old daughter, driving across the Benjamin Franklin Bridge in Philadelphia. Richard told him to remember the moment because we might be about to make history. (That was classic Holbrooke, with his irrepressible flair for the dramatic. He saw himself as wrestling with history and always believed he could win.)

The day after Thanksgiving Richard gave Ruggiero his final instructions. "The most important objective of the first meeting is to have a second meeting," he said. "Be diplomatic, clearly lay out the redlines authorized by the Secretary, and keep them negotiating. The Secretary is following this closely, so call me as soon as you walk out of the meeting." The redlines were the same conditions I had been repeating for more than a year: If the Taliban wanted to come in from the cold, they would need to stop fighting, break with al Qaeda, and accept the Afghan Constitution, including its protections for women. Those terms were nonnegotiable. But beyond that, as I told Richard, I was open to creative diplomacy that could move us toward peace.

Two days later Ruggiero and Jeff Hayes from the National Security Council staff at the White House arrived at a house arranged by the Germans in a village outside of Munich. Michael Steiner, the German Special Representative for Afghanistan and Pakistan, was the host. A-Rod was young, in his late thirties, but he had worked for Mullah Omar for more than a decade. He spoke English and, unlike many Taliban leaders, had some experience with international diplomacy. The participants all agreed on the need to maintain absolute secrecy. There could be no leaks; if the Pakistanis found out about this meeting, they might undermine the talks just as they had Karzai's early efforts.

The group talked for six intense hours, feeling one another out and stepping carefully around the massive issues on the table. Could sworn enemies actually come to some kind of understanding that would end a war and rebuild a shattered country? After so many years of fighting, it was hard enough to sit together and talk face-to-face, let alone trust one another. Ruggiero explained our conditions. The Taliban's top concern seemed to be the fate of its fighters being held at Guantánamo Bay and other prisons. In every discussion about prisoners, we demanded the release of Army Sergeant Bowe Bergdahl, who had been captured in June 2009. There would not be any agreement about prisoners without the sergeant coming home.

The next day Richard drove out to Dulles Airport to meet Ruggiero's plane. He couldn't wait to get a firsthand report, which he would then relay to me. The two sat down at Harry's Tap Room in the airport, and Ruggiero talked while Richard tore into a cheeseburger.

=====

A few days after Ruggiero's return from Munich, on December 11, 2010, he and Richard came up to my office on the seventh floor of the State

Department to meet with Jake Sullivan and me about how to proceed. We were also in the final stages of the one-year policy review that President Obama had promised when he approved the troop surge. No one would say that things were going well in Afghanistan, but there was some encouraging progress to report. The extra troops were helping blunt the Taliban's momentum. Security was improving in Kabul and in key provinces like Helmand and Kandahar. Our development efforts were starting to make a difference in the economy, and our diplomacy with the region and the international community was picking up steam.

In November I had gone with President Obama to a summit of NATO leaders in Lisbon, Portugal. The summit reaffirmed the shared mission in Afghanistan and agreed to a trajectory for transitioning responsibility for security to Afghan forces by the end of 2014, along with an enduring NATO commitment to the country's security and stability. Most important, the summit sent a strong message that the international community was united behind the strategy President Obama had announced at West Point. The increase in American forces, supplemented by those from our NATO and Coalition partners, was helping create conditions for political and economic transitions, as well as a security handoff and the basis for a diplomatic offensive. There was a clear road map for the end of U.S. combat operations and the continuing support that we knew would be necessary for Afghan democracy to survive. Now we had a secret channel to the Taliban leadership that appeared genuine and might one day lead to real peace talks among Afghans. (My spokeswoman Toria Nuland, with her talent for quotable lines, started short-handing our three mutually reinforcing lines of effort as "Fight, talk, build," which I thought summed it up nicely.)

Richard was excited about our momentum coming out of Lisbon, and throughout the policy review process he repeatedly made his case to all who would listen that diplomacy needed to be a central element of our strategy going forward. On December 11, he was late to the meeting in my office, explaining that he had been tied up first with the Pakistani Ambassador and then at the White House. As usual, he was full of ideas and opinions. But as we talked, he grew quiet and his face suddenly turned an alarming bright red. "Richard, what's the matter?" I asked. I knew immediately it was serious. He looked back at me and said, "Something horrible is happening." He was in such physical distress that I insisted he go see the State Department medical staff, located on the building's lower

level. Reluctantly he agreed, and Jake, Frank, and Claire Coleman, my
executive assistant, helped him get there.

The medical staff quickly sent Richard to nearby George Washington
University Hospital. He took the elevator down to the garage and got
into an ambulance for the short drive. Dan Feldman, one of Richard's
closest aides, rode over with him. When they got to the emergency room,
doctors found a tear in his aorta and sent him directly to surgery, which
lasted twenty-one hours. The damage was severe and his prognosis was
not good, but Richard's doctors would not give up.

I was at the hospital when the surgery ended. The doctors were "cautiously optimistic" and said that the next few hours would be crucial.
Richard's wife, Kati, their children, and his many friends were keeping
vigil at the hospital. His State Department team volunteered to take shifts
in the lobby to help manage the flow of visitors and run interference
for Kati. Even as the hours stretched on, none of them would leave the
hospital. The Operations Center was fielding lots of incoming calls from
foreign leaders concerned about Richard. Pakistani President Asif Ali
Zardari was particularly anxious to speak to Kati to express his concern.
He reported that people all over Pakistan were praying for her husband.

The next morning, with Richard still clinging to life, the doctors decided another surgery was necessary to try to stop the continued bleeding. We were all praying. I was staying close to the hospital, as were so
many others who loved Richard. Around 11 A.M. President Karzai tele-
phoned from Kabul and spoke to Kati. "Please tell your husband that we
need him back in Afghanistan," he said. As they talked, Kati's call waiting chimed. It was President Zardari, who promised to call right back.
Richard would have been delighted that so many illustrious people were
spending hour after hour talking about nothing but him. He would hate
to have missed it.

By late afternoon Richard's surgeon, who by coincidence was from Lahore, Pakistan, reported that Richard was "inching in the right direction,"
although he remained in critical condition. The doctors were impressed
by his resilience and marveled at the fight he was putting up. For those
of us who knew and loved him, that was no surprise at all.

By Monday afternoon, with the situation much the same, Kati and
the family decided to join me and President Obama at the State Department for a long-scheduled holiday reception for the diplomatic corps. I
welcomed everyone to the Benjamin Franklin Room on the eighth floor

and began with a few words about our friend, who was fighting for his life only a few blocks away. I said that the doctors were "learning what diplomats and dictators around the world have long known: There's nobody tougher than Richard Holbrooke."

Just a few hours later things took a turn for the worse. Around 8 P.M. on December 13, 2010, Richard Holbrooke died. He was just sixty-nine years old. His doctors were visibly upset that they had not been able to save his life, but remarked that Richard had entered the hospital with uncommon dignity for someone who had suffered such a traumatic event. I visited quietly with the family—Kati; Richard's sons, David and Anthony; his stepchildren, Elizabeth and Chris; and his daughter-in-law, Sarah—and then went to be with the crowd of friends and colleagues downstairs. Teary-eyed people held hands and talked about the need to celebrate Richard's life, while also continuing the work to which he was so devoted.

I read aloud to those gathered the formal statement I had just issued: "Tonight America has lost one of its fiercest champions and most dedicated public servants. Richard Holbrooke served the country he loved for nearly half a century, representing the United States in far-flung war zones and high-level peace talks, always with distinctive brilliance and unmatched determination. He was one of a kind—a true statesman—and that makes his passing all the more painful." I thanked the medical staff and everyone who had offered their prayers and support over the past few days. "True to form, Richard was a fighter to the end. His doctors marveled at his strength and his willpower, but to his friends, that was just Richard being Richard."

Everyone started swapping their favorite Richard stories and reminiscing about this remarkable man. After a while, in a move I think Richard would have approved of, a large group of us headed over to the bar of the nearby Ritz-Carlton Hotel. For the next few hours we held an impromptu wake and celebration of Richard's life. Everyone had great stories to tell, and we laughed and cried in equal measure, sometimes all at once. Richard had trained an entire generation of diplomats, and many of them spoke movingly about what having him as a mentor meant to their lives and careers. Dan Feldman shared with us that on the way to the hospital, Richard had said that he considered his team at the State Department "the best he had ever worked with."

In mid-January, Richard's many friends and colleagues from across the world gathered at the Kennedy Center in Washington for a memorial service. Among the eulogists were President Obama and my husband. I spoke last. Looking out at the large crowd, a testament to Richard's genius for friendship, I was reminded how keenly I would miss having him by my side. "There are few people in any time, but certainly in our time, who can say, I stopped a war. I made peace. I saved lives. I helped countries heal. Richard Holbrooke did these things," I said. "This is a loss personally and it is a loss for our country. We face huge tasks ahead of us, and it would be better if Richard were here, driving us all crazy about what we needed to be doing."

═══

I couldn't let Richard's death derail the work to which he was so committed. His team felt the same way. We had been discussing the idea of a major speech on the prospects for peace and reconciliation in Afghanistan. I was sure Richard would want us to go ahead with it. So we put aside our grief and got to work.

I asked Frank Ruggiero to serve as acting Special Representative and sent him to Kabul and Islamabad in the first week of January 2011 to brief Karzai and Zardari on what I was planning to say. I was about to put a lot of weight and momentum behind the idea of reconciliation with the Taliban, and we wanted them to be prepared. Karzai was in equal measure engaged, encouraging, and suspicious. "What are you really discussing with those Taliban?" he asked. Just like the Pakistanis, he was worried that we would cut a deal without him that might leave him exposed.

While I worked on the speech with the team in Washington, Ruggiero headed to Qatar for a second meeting with A-Rod, our Taliban contact. We still had concerns about his legitimacy and ability to deliver results, so Ruggiero proposed a test. He asked A-Rod to have the Taliban propaganda arm release a statement with some specific language in it. If they did, we'd know he had real access. In return Ruggiero told A-Rod that in my upcoming speech, I would open the door to reconciliation with stronger language than any American official had yet used. A-Rod agreed and promised to send the message back to his superiors. Later the statement came out with the promised language.

Before I finalized my speech, I needed to decide on a permanent successor to Holbrooke. It would be impossible to fill his shoes, but we needed another senior diplomat to lead his team and carry the effort forward. I turned to a widely respected retired Ambassador, Marc Grossman, whom I had met when he served in Turkey. Marc is quiet and self-effacing, a dramatic departure from his predecessor, but he brought uncommon skill and subtlety to the job.

In mid-February I flew to New York and went to the Asia Society, where Richard had once served as chairman of the board, to deliver a memorial lecture in his name, which would in time become an annual tradition. I began by providing an update on the military and civilian surges that President Obama had announced at West Point. Then I explained that we were conducting a third surge, a diplomatic one, aimed at moving the conflict toward a political outcome that would shatter the alliance between the Taliban and al Qaeda, end the insurgency, and help produce a more stable Afghanistan and a more stable region. This had been our vision from the beginning, and it was what I had argued for in President Obama's strategic review process in 2009. Now it was moving front and center.

To understand our strategy, it was important for Americans to be clear about the difference between the al Qaeda terrorists, who attacked us on 9/11, and the Taliban, who were Afghan extremists waging an insurgency against the government in Kabul. The Taliban had paid a heavy price for their decision in 2001 to defy the international community and protect al Qaeda. Now the escalating pressure from our military campaign was forcing them to make a similar decision. If the Taliban met our three criteria, they could rejoin Afghan society. "This is the price for reaching a political resolution and bringing an end to the military actions that are targeting their leadership and decimating their ranks," I said, including a subtle but important shift in language, describing these steps as "necessary outcomes" of any negotiation rather than "preconditions." It was a nuanced change, but it would clear the way for direct talks.

I acknowledged, as I had many times before, that opening the door to negotiations with the Taliban would be hard to swallow for many Americans after so many years of war. Reintegrating low-level fighters was odious enough; negotiating directly with top commanders was something else entirely. But diplomacy would be easy if we had to talk only to our friends. That's not how peace is made. Presidents throughout the Cold War understood that when they negotiated arms control agreements with the Soviets. As President Kennedy put it, "Let us never negotiate out of fear. But let us never fear to negotiate." Richard Holbrooke had made this his life's work, negotiating with an ugly tyrant like Milošević because that was the best way to end a war.

I closed the speech by urging Pakistan, India, and other nations in the region to support a process of peace and reconciliation that would isolate al Qaeda and give everyone a new sense of security. If Afghanistan's neighbors kept viewing Afghanistan as an arena for playing out their own rivalries, peace would never succeed. It was going to take a lot of painstaking diplomacy, but we needed to play an inside game with the Afghans and an outside game with the region.

The speech made a few headlines at home, but its real impact was in foreign capitals, especially Kabul and Islamabad. All sides now knew we were serious about pursuing a peace process with the Taliban. One diplomat in Kabul described the effect as a "seismic shift" that would encourage all sides to more actively pursue peace.

═══

The successful U.S. Navy SEAL raid that killed Osama bin Laden at his compound in Abbottabad, Pakistan, in May 2011, was a major victory in the battle against al Qaeda and another low point in our already badly strained relationship with Pakistan. But I thought it might also provide us some new leverage with the Taliban. Five days after the raid, Ruggiero met for a third time with A-Rod, this time back in Munich. I told him to pass along a direct message from me: bin Laden was dead; this was the time for the Taliban to break from al Qaeda once and for all, save themselves, and make peace. A-Rod did not seem distressed about losing bin Laden, and he remained interested in negotiating with us.

We began discussing confidence-building measures that both sides could take. We wanted the Taliban to make public statements disassociating themselves from al Qaeda and international terrorism and committing to participate in a peace process with Karzai and his government. The Taliban wanted to be allowed to open a political office in Qatar that would provide a safe place for future negotiations and engagement. We were open to this idea, but it raised a number of challenges. Many Taliban leaders were considered terrorists by the international community and could not appear in the open without facing legal jeopardy. Pakistan also had to agree to allow them to come and go openly. And there was a good chance Karzai would see a Taliban outpost in Qatar as a direct threat to his legitimacy and authority. All these concerns seemed manageable, but they would require careful diplomacy.

As a first step, we agreed to begin working with the United Nations to remove a few key Taliban members from the terrorist sanctions list, which imposed a travel ban. Soon the UN Security Council agreed to split the Taliban and al Qaeda lists and treat them separately—a direct manifestation of the distinction drawn in my speech—which gave us considerably more flexibility. The Taliban still wanted their fighters released from Guantánamo, but that was not a step we were willing to take yet.

In mid-May Afghan officials in Kabul leaked word of our secret talks and named Agha as our Taliban contact to the *Washington Post* and *Der Spiegel*, a German newsweekly. Privately the Taliban understood that the leak was not from us, but publicly they expressed outrage and suspended future talks. Pakistani authorities, already outraged over the bin Laden raid, were livid that they had been left out of our discussions with the Taliban. We had to scramble to pick up the pieces. I went to Islamabad and talked to the Pakistanis for the first time about the extent of our contacts and requested that there be no retribution against A-Rod. I also asked Ruggiero to fly to Doha and pass a message through the Qataris to the Taliban urging them to return to the table. In early July the Qataris reported that Agha was willing to return.

Talks resumed in Doha in August. A-Rod presented Ruggiero with a letter for President Obama that he said was from Mullah Omar himself. There was some debate inside the administration about whether Mullah Omar was still alive, let alone in charge of the Taliban and directing the insurgency. But whether it was from Omar or from other senior leaders, its tone and content were encouraging. The letter said that now was the time for both sides to make tough choices on reconciliation and work to end the war.

There were constructive discussions about an office in Doha and possible prisoner swaps. Marc Grossman joined the talks for the first time, and his personal touch helped move things along.

In October, on a visit to Kabul, Karzai told me and our highly regarded and experienced Ambassador Ryan Crocker, with whom he had a good relationship, that he was enthusiastic about what we were doing. "Go faster," he said. In Washington serious discussions began about the viability of limited prisoner releases, although the Pentagon was not sup-

portive and I was unsure whether we could secure the conditions necessary to agree to a Taliban office in Qatar. By late fall, however, the pieces
seemed finally in place. A major international conference on Afghanistan
was scheduled to take place in Bonn, Germany, in the first week of December. Our goal was to announce the opening of the office following
the conference. It would be the most tangible sign yet that a real peace
process was under way.

Bonn was part of the diplomatic offensive I had described in my Asia
Society speech, aimed at mobilizing the broader international community
to help Afghanistan take responsibility for meeting its many challenges.
Grossman and his team helped organize a series of summits and conferences in Istanbul, Bonn, Kabul, Chicago, and Tokyo. In Tokyo, in 2012,
the international community committed $16 billion in economic assistance
through 2015 to help Afghanistan prepare for a "decade of transformation" marked less by aid and more by trade. Starting in 2015, estimated
financing for the Afghan National Security Forces would be more than
$4 billion per year. The Afghans' ability to take responsibility for their
own security was and remains a prerequisite for everything else they hope
to achieve in the future.

The Bonn conference in December 2011 turned into a disaster for
our peace efforts. Karzai, ever unpredictable, turned against the idea of
a Taliban office, berating Grossman and Crocker. "Why have you not
kept me informed of these talks?" he demanded, despite the fact that
just a few months earlier he had urged us to accelerate them. Karzai was
once again afraid of being left behind and undercut. Our plan had always
been for these U.S.-Taliban talks to lead to parallel negotiations between
the Afghan government and the insurgents. That was the sequence we
had agreed to with A-Rod and discussed with Karzai. But now Karzai
insisted he wanted his own people in the room for any future meetings
between the Taliban and us. A-Rod balked when Grossman and Ruggiero broached this proposal. From his perspective, we were changing
the rules of the game. In January 2012 the Taliban once again pulled out
of our talks.

This time it was not so easy to coax them back. The peace process went
into a deep freeze. Still, based on various public statements throughout
2012, there appeared to be a renewed debate under way within the ranks
of the Taliban over the benefits of talking versus fighting. Some key figures publicly accepted that a negotiated solution was inevitable, reversing

nearly a decade of rejection. Others, however, were committed to violent opposition. At the end of 2012 the door to reconciliation remained open, but only part way.

======

In January 2013, just before I left office, I invited President Karzai to have dinner with me, Secretary of Defense Leon Panetta, and a few other senior officials at the State Department in Washington. Karzai brought along the chair of his High Peace Council and other key advisors. We gathered in the James Monroe Room on the eighth floor, surrounded by antiques from the early days of the American republic, and talked about the future of Afghanistan's democracy.

It had been more than three years since Karzai and I had dined on the eve of his inauguration. Now I was about to hand the reins of the State Department over to Senator Kerry, and another Afghan election would soon select Karzai's successor, or at least that was the plan. Karzai had publicly pledged to abide by the Constitution and leave office in 2014, but many Afghans wondered if he would actually follow through on that promise. The peaceful transfer of power from one ruler to the next is a crucial test of any democracy, and it is not unusual in that part of the world (and many others) for leaders to find ways to extend their tenure.

In a long one-on-one meeting before dinner, I urged Karzai to keep his word. If the government in Kabul could build more credibility with its citizens, deliver services, and administer justice fairly and effectively, it would help undercut the appeal of insurgency and improve the prospects for national reconciliation. That depended on all government officials, but especially Karzai, to uphold the Constitution and the rule of law. Presiding over a constitutional transition would be an opportunity for Karzai to cement his legacy as the father of a more peaceful, secure, and democratic Afghanistan.

I recognized how difficult this might be for him. The Rotunda of the Capitol Building in Washington is home to a series of soaring patriotic paintings that depict proud moments from our own democracy's early days, from the voyage of the Pilgrims to the victory at Yorktown. There is one painting in particular that I have always thought spoke to the democratic spirit of our country. It shows General Washington turning his back on the offered throne and giving up his commission as commander in chief of the Army. He went on to serve two terms as a civilian President and then voluntarily stepped down. More than any election victory or inaugural parade, that selfless act was the hallmark of our democracy. If Karzai wanted to be remembered as Afghanistan's George Washington, he had to follow this example and give up the throne.

The other topic I raised with Karzai was the stalled peace process with the Taliban. Karzai had effectively pulled the plug in late 2011; I wanted him to reconsider. If we waited until after U.S. troops started coming home, we and he would have less leverage with the Taliban. Better to negotiate from a position of strength.

Over dinner Karzai ran through a litany of familiar concerns: How would we verify if Taliban negotiators actually spoke for the leadership? Would Pakistan be pulling the strings from Islamabad? Would Americans or Afghans lead the talks? One by one I answered his questions. I tried to impart the sense of urgency I felt to get the process moving again and suggested a plan that did not require him to directly reach an agreement with the Taliban on opening the office. All he had to do, I said, was make a public statement supporting the idea. I would then arrange for the Emir of Qatar to invite the Taliban to move forward. The goal would be to open the office and organize a meeting between the Afghan High Peace Council and representatives of the Taliban within thirty days. If that failed to happen, the office would be closed. After much discussion, Karzai agreed.

In June 2013, a few months after I left the State Department, the Taliban negotiating office finally opened. But the new understanding, which had taken years to reach, collapsed in little more than a month. The Taliban staged a flag-raising ceremony at the office and proclaimed that it represented the "Islamic Emirate of Afghanistan," the official name of the country in the 1990s when the Taliban were in power. We had been clear from the beginning that using the office in this way would be unacceptable. Our objective had always been to strengthen the constitutional order in Afghanistan and, as I had assured Karzai, we were vested in the sovereignty and unity of the country. Understandably, Karzai was apoplectic. To him it looked more like the headquarters of a government-in-exile than a negotiating venue. It was everything he had always feared. The Taliban refused to back down, relations ruptured, and the office was forced to close.

Watching all this now as a private citizen, I am disappointed but not surprised. If making peace were easy, it would have been done long ago. We knew the secret channel with the Taliban was a long shot, with failure more likely than success. But it was worth testing. I believe that we laid a positive foundation that might help future peace efforts. There are now a range of contacts between Afghans and the Taliban, and we exposed debates inside the Taliban that I suspect will only intensify over time. The need for reconciliation and a political settlement isn't going away. If anything, it is more pressing than ever. The benchmarks we put down could still guide the way.

I wondered what Richard would have thought. Up until the end, he never lost his confidence in the power of diplomacy to untangle even the toughest knots. I wish he were still with us, twisting arms and slapping backs and reminding everyone that the way to start ending a war is to begin talking.

9

Pakistan: National Honor

The secure videoconference room in the basement of the West Wing fell silent. Next to me, Secretary Bob Gates sat in his shirtsleeves with his arms folded and his eyes fixed intently on the screen. The image was fuzzy, but unmistakable. One of two Black Hawk helicopters had clipped the top of the stone wall surrounding the compound and crashed to the ground. Our worst fears were coming true.

Although President Obama sat stoically watching the screen, we were all thinking the same thing: Iran 1980, when a hostage-rescue mission ended in a fiery helicopter crash in the desert, leaving eight Americans dead and badly scarring our nation and our military. Would this end the same way? Bob had been a senior official at the CIA then. The memory surely was weighing on him, and on the man across the table, President Obama. He had given the final order, directly staking the lives of a team of Navy SEALs and Special Operations helicopter pilots and perhaps the fate of his presidency on the success of this operation. Now all he could do was watch the grainy images beamed back to us.

It was May 1, 2011. Outside the White House, Washington was enjoying a spring Sunday afternoon. Inside, the tension had been building since the helicopters took off from a base in eastern Afghanistan about an hour earlier. Their target was a fortified compound in Abbottabad, Pakistan, which the CIA believed might be sheltering the world's most wanted man, Osama bin Laden. Years of painstaking work by the intelligence community, followed by months of soul-searching debate at the highest levels of the Obama Administration, had brought us to this day. Now it all rested on the pilots of those state-of-the-art helicopters and the Navy SEALs they carried.

The first test had been crossing the Pakistani border. These Black Hawks were equipped with advanced technology designed to allow them to operate undetected by radar, but would it work? Our relationship with Pakistan, America's nominal ally in the fight against terrorism, was already very troubled. If the Pakistani military, always on a hair trigger out of fear of a surprise attack from India, discovered a secret incursion into their airspace, it was possible they'd respond with force.

We had debated whether to inform Pakistan about the raid ahead of time in order to avoid this scenario and the complete breakdown in relations that could follow. After all, as Bob Gates often reminded us, Pakistani cooperation would continue to be needed to resupply our troops in Afghanistan and pursue other terrorists in the border region. I had invested considerable time and energy in the Pakistan relationship over the years, and I knew how offended they would be if we did not share this information with them. But I also knew that elements in the Pakistani intelligence service, the ISI, maintained ties to the Taliban, al Qaeda, and other extremists. We had been burned by leaks before. The risks of blowing the whole operation were just too great.

At one point another senior administration official asked if we needed to worry about irreparably wounding Pakistani national honor. Maybe it was the pent-up frustration from dealing with too much double-talk and deception from certain quarters in Pakistan, or the still-searing memories of the smoking pile in Lower Manhattan, but there was no way I was going to let the United States miss our best chance at bin Laden since we lost him at Tora Bora, Afghanistan, in 2001. "What about *our* national honor?" I said, in exasperation. "What about *our* losses? What about going after a man who killed three thousand innocent people?"

The road to Abbottabad ran from the mountain passes of Afghanistan through the smoking ruins of our embassies in East Africa and the shattered hull of the USS *Cole*, through the devastation of 9/11 and the dogged determination of a handful of U.S. intelligence officers who never gave up the hunt. The bin Laden operation did not end the threat of terrorism or defeat the hateful ideology that fuels it. That struggle goes on. But it was a signal moment in America's long battle against al Qaeda.

=====

September 11, 2001, is indelibly etched in my mind, just as it is for every American. I was horrified by what I saw that day, and as New York's Senator, I felt an intense responsibility to stand with the people of our wounded city. After a long, sleepless night in Washington, I flew to New York with Chuck Schumer, my partner in the Senate, on a special plane operated by the Federal Emergency Management Agency. The city was in lockdown, and we were the only ones in the sky that day, except for the Air Force fighters patrolling overhead. At La Guardia Airport we boarded a helicopter and flew toward Lower Manhattan.

Smoke was still rising from the smoldering wreckage where the World Trade Center once stood. As we circled above Ground Zero, I could see twisted girders and shattered beams looming above the first responders and construction workers searching desperately through the rubble for survivors. The TV images I'd seen the night before didn't capture the full horror. It was like a scene out of Dante's *Inferno*.

Our helicopter set down on the West Side near the Hudson River. Chuck and I met up with Governor George Pataki, Mayor Rudy Giuliani, and other officials and started walking toward the site. The air was acrid, and the thick smoke made it hard to breathe or see. I was wearing a surgical mask, but the air burned my throat and lungs and made my eyes tear up. Occasionally a firefighter would emerge out of the dust and gloom and trudge toward us, exhausted, dragging an axe, covered in soot. Some of them had been on duty nonstop since the planes hit the Towers, and they had all lost friends and comrades. Hundreds of brave emergency responders lost their lives while trying to save others, and more would suffer painful health effects for years to come. I wanted to embrace them, thank them, and tell them everything was going to be all right. But I wasn't sure yet that it was.

In the makeshift command center at the Police Academy on Twentieth Street, Chuck and I were briefed on the damage. It was crushing. New Yorkers were going to need a lot of help to recover, and it was now our job to make sure they got it. That night I caught the last train south before they closed Penn Station. First thing in the morning in Washington I went to see Senator Robert Byrd of West Virginia, the legendary chairman of the Appropriations Committee, to make the case for emergency relief funding. He heard me out and said, "Think of me as the third Senator from New York." In the days ahead he was as good as his word.

That afternoon Chuck and I headed to the White House, and in the Oval Office we told President Bush that our state would need $20 billion. He quickly agreed. He too stood by us through all the political maneuvering that was required to deliver that emergency aid.

Back at my office the phones were ringing with callers asking for help to track down missing family members or to seek aid. My extraordinary Chief of Staff, Tamera Luzzatto, and my Senate teams in D.C. and New York were working around the clock, and other Senators began sending aides to help out.

The next day Chuck and I accompanied President Bush on Air Force One back to New York, where we listened as he stood on a pile of rubble and told a crowd of firefighters, "I can hear you, the rest of the world hears you! And the people who knocked these buildings down will hear all of us soon!"

In the days that followed, Bill, Chelsea, and I visited a makeshift missing persons center at the 69th Regiment Armory and a family assistance center on Pier 94. We met with families cradling photos of their missing loved ones, hoping and praying that they might still be found. I visited wounded survivors at St. Vincent's Hospital and at a rehabilitation center in Westchester County where a number of the burn victims had been taken. I met a woman named Lauren Manning; although more than 82 percent of her body was terribly burned, giving her a less than 20 percent chance of survival, through fierce willpower and intense effort she fought her way back and reclaimed her life. Lauren and her husband, Greg, who are raising two sons, became vocal advocates on behalf of other 9/11 families. Another amazing survivor is Debbie Mardenfeld, who was brought to New York University Downtown Hospital as an unidentified Jane Doe after falling debris from the second plane crushed her legs and caused extensive injuries. I visited her several times and got to know her fiancé, Gregory St. John. Debbie told me that she wanted to be able to dance at her wedding, but the doctors doubted that she'd survive, let alone walk. After nearly thirty surgeries and fifteen months in the hospital, Debbie confounded all expectations. She lived, she walked, and, miraculously, she even danced at her wedding. Debbie had asked me to do a reading at the ceremony, and I will always remember the joy on her face as she walked down the aisle.

With equal measures of outrage and determination, I spent my years in the Senate fighting to fund health care for first responders harmed by their time near Ground Zero. I helped create the 9/11 Victims Compensation Fund and the 9/11 Commission, and supported the implementation of their recommendations. I did all I could to urge the pursuit of bin Laden and al Qaeda and improve our nation's efforts against terrorism.

During the 2008 campaign both Senator Obama and I criticized the Bush Administration for taking its eye off the ball in Afghanistan and losing focus on the hunt for bin Laden. After the election we agreed that aggressively going after al Qaeda was crucial to our national security and that there should be a renewed effort to find bin Laden and bring him to justice.

I thought we needed a new strategy in Afghanistan and Pakistan and a new approach to counterterrorism around the world, one that used the full range of American power to attack terrorist networks' finances, recruitment, and safe havens, as well as operatives and commanders. It would take daring military action, careful intelligence gathering, dogged law enforcement, and delicate diplomacy all working together—in short, smart power.

All these memories were in my mind as the SEALs approached the compound in Abbottabad. I thought back to all the families I had known and worked with who had lost loved ones in the 9/11 attacks nearly a decade before. They had been denied justice for a decade. Now it might finally be at hand.

=====

Our national security team began grappling with the urgency of the threat posed by terrorists even before President Obama walked into the Oval Office for the first time.

On January 19, 2009, the day before his inauguration, I joined senior national security officials of the outgoing Bush Administration and incoming Obama Administration in the White House Situation Room to think through the unthinkable: What if a bomb goes off on the National Mall during the President's address? Is the Secret Service going to rush him off the podium with the whole world watching? I could see from the look on the faces of the Bush team that nobody had a good answer. For two hours we discussed how to respond to reports of a credible terrorist threat against the inauguration. The intelligence community believed that Somali extremists associated with Al Shabaab, an al Qaeda affiliate, were trying to sneak across the Canadian border with plans to assassinate the new President.

Should we move the ceremony indoors? Cancel it altogether? There was no way we were going to do either. The inauguration had to go forward as planned; the peaceful transfer of power is too important a symbol of American democracy. But that meant everyone had to redouble efforts to prevent an attack and ensure the safety of the President.

In the end the inauguration went off without incident, and the Somali threat proved to be a false alarm. But the episode served as yet another reminder that even while we were trying to turn the page on many aspects of the Bush era, the specter of terrorism that defined those years required constant vigilance.

Intelligence reports painted a troubling picture. The U.S.-led invasion of Afghanistan in 2001 had overthrown the Taliban regime in Kabul and dealt a blow to its al Qaeda allies. But the Taliban had regrouped, staging insurgent attacks on U.S. and Afghan forces from safe havens across the border in Pakistan's lawless tribal areas. Al Qaeda's leaders were likely hiding there as well. The border region had become the epicenter of a global terrorist syndicate. As long as those safe havens remained open, our troops in Afghanistan would be fighting an uphill battle and al Qaeda would have the chance to plan new international attacks. This was my logic for appointing Richard Holbrooke as Special Representative for both Afghanistan *and* Pakistan. Those safe havens were also fueling increasing instability within Pakistan itself. A Pakistani branch of the Taliban was waging its own bloody insurgency against the fragile democratic government in Islamabad. An extremist takeover there would be a nightmare scenario for the region and the world.

In September 2009 the FBI arrested a twenty-four-year-old Afghan immigrant named Najibullah Zazi, who they believed had trained with al Qaeda in Pakistan and was planning a terrorist attack in New York City. He later pled guilty to conspiring to use weapons of mass destruction, conspiracy to commit murder in a foreign country, and providing material support to a terrorist organization. It was yet another reason to be concerned about what was happening in Pakistan.

I looked into the sorrowful eyes of Asif Ali Zardari, the President of Pakistan, and then down at the aging photograph he held out to me. It was fourteen years old, but the memories it evoked were as vivid as the day it was taken in 1995. There was his late wife, Benazir Bhutto, the astute and elegant former Prime Minister of Pakistan, resplendent in a bright red suit and white headscarf, holding the hands of their two young children. Standing next to her was my own teenage daughter, Chelsea, her face full of wonder and excitement about meeting this fascinating woman and exploring her country. And there I was, on my first extended trip overseas as First Lady without Bill. How young I was then, with a different haircut and a different role, but just as proud to be representing my country in a difficult place halfway around the world.

A lot had happened in the years since 1995. Pakistan had endured coups, a military dictatorship, a brutal extremist insurgency, and escalating economic hardship. Most painful of all, Benazir was assassinated while campaigning to restore democracy to Pakistan in 2007. Now, in the fall of 2009, Zardari was the first civilian President in a decade, and he wanted to renew the friendship between us and between our nations. So did I. That's why I had come to Pakistan as Secretary of State at a time when anti-American sentiments were surging across the country.

Zardari and I were about to go into a formal dinner with many of Pakistan's elite. But first we reminisced. Back in 1995 the State Department had asked me to go to India and Pakistan to demonstrate that this strategic and volatile part of the world was important to the United States and to support efforts to strengthen democracy, expand free markets, and promote tolerance and human rights, including the rights of women. Pakistan, which split from India in a tumultuous partition in 1947, the year I was born, was a longtime Cold War ally of the United States, but our relationship was rarely warm. Three weeks before I arrived on that 1995 trip, extremists killed two U.S. Consulate workers in Karachi. One of the main plotters in the 1993 World Trade Center bombing, Ramzi Yousef, was later arrested in Islamabad and extradited to the United States. So the Secret Service was understandably nervous about my intention to leave the safety of official government compounds and visit schools, mosques, and health clinics. But the State Department agreed with me that there was real value in that kind of direct engagement with the Pakistani people.

I was looking forward to meeting Benazir Bhutto, who had been elected Prime Minister in 1988. Her father, Zulfikar Ali Bhutto, had served as Prime Minister during the 1970s before being deposed and hanged in a military coup. After years of house arrest, Benazir emerged in the 1980s as the head of his political party. Her autobiography is aptly titled *Daughter of Destiny*. It tells a riveting story of how determination, hard work, and political smarts enabled her to rise to power in a society where many women still lived in strict isolation, called *purdah*. They were never seen by men outside their immediate family and left their homes only when fully veiled, if at all. I experienced that firsthand when I paid a call on Begum Nasreen Leghari, the traditionalist wife of President Farooq Ahmad Khan Leghari.

Benazir was the only celebrity I ever stood behind a rope line to see. During a family vacation to London in the summer of 1987, Chelsea and I noticed a large crowd gathered outside the Ritz Hotel. We were told that Benazir Bhutto was expected to arrive there shortly. Intrigued, we waited in the crowd for her motorcade to arrive. She emerged from the limousine, elegantly swathed from head to toe in yellow chiffon, and glided into the lobby, looking graceful, composed, and intent.

Just eight years later, in 1995, I was First Lady of the United States and she was Prime Minister of Pakistan. It turned out Benazir and I had mutual friends from her time at Oxford and Harvard. They had told me she had a sparkle about her: bright eyes, a ready smile, and good sense of humor, along with a sharp intellect. All that was true. She talked candidly with me about the political and gender challenges she faced and how committed she was to education for girls, an opportunity then and now limited largely to the wealthy upper class. Benazir wore a *shalwar kameez*, the national dress of Pakistan, a long, flowing tunic over loose pants that was both practical and attractive, and she covered her hair with lovely scarves. Chelsea and I were so taken with this style that we wore it for a formal dinner in Lahore held in our honor. I wore red silk, and Chelsea chose turquoise green. At the dinner I was seated between Benazir and Zardari. Much has been written and gossiped about their marriage, but I witnessed their affection and banter and watched how happy he made her that night.

The following years were marked by pain and conflict. General Pervez Musharraf seized power in a military coup in 1999, forcing Benazir into exile and Zardari into prison. She and I stayed in touch, and she sought my help to obtain her husband's release. He was never tried on the assortment of charges against him and finally was released in 2004. After 9/11, under heavy pressure from the Bush Administration, Musharraf allied with the United States in the war in Afghanistan. Yet he had to know that elements of Pakistan's intelligence and security services maintained ties to the Taliban and other extremists in Afghanistan and Pakistan that dated back to the struggle against the Soviet Union in the 1980s. As I often told my Pakistani counterparts, this was asking for trouble, like keeping poisonous snakes in your backyard and expecting them to bite only your neighbors. Sure enough, instability, violence, and extremism swelled, and the economy crumbled. Pakistani friends I'd met in the 1990s told me, "You can't imagine what it's like now. It's so different. We're scared to go to some of the most beautiful parts of our country."

In December 2007, after returning from eight years of exile, Benazir Bhutto was assassinated at a campaign rally in Rawalpindi, not far from the headquarters of the Pakistani military. After her murder, Musharraf was forced out by public protests and Zardari swept into office as President on a wave of national grief. But his civilian government struggled to manage Pakistan's escalating security and economic challenges, and the Pakistani Taliban began expanding their reach from the remote border region into the more heavily populated Swat Valley, just a hundred miles from Islamabad. Hundreds of thousands of people fled their homes as the Pakistani military moved in to beat back the extremists. A cease-fire agreement between President Zardari's government and the Taliban in February 2009 fell apart after only a few months.

As their country's problems worsened, many Pakistanis directed their anger at the United States, fueled by a rambunctious media that trafficked in wild conspiracy theories. They blamed us for stirring up trouble with the Taliban, exploiting Pakistan for our own strategic ends, and showing favoritism toward their traditional rival, India. And those were the most rational claims. In some polls, approval of America fell below 10 percent, despite the billions of dollars in aid that we had contributed over the years. In fact, a massive new assistance package passed by Congress became a lightning rod for criticism in Pakistan because it was seen as having too many strings attached. It was maddening. All the public anger made it harder for the Pakistani government to cooperate with us in counterterrorism operations and easier for the extremists to find shelter and recruits. But Zardari proved more politically adept than expected. He worked out a modus vivendi with the military, and his was the first democratically elected government to complete its full term in the history of Pakistan.

In the fall of 2009 I decided to go to Pakistan and take on the anti-American sentiments. I told my staff to plan a trip heavy on town halls, media roundtables, and other forms of public engagement. They warned, "You'll be a punching bag." I smiled and replied, "Punch away."

I have faced my share of hostile public opinion over the years and have learned it can't be wished away or papered over with happy talk. There will always be substantive disagreements between peoples and nations, and we shouldn't be surprised about that. It makes sense to engage directly with people, hear them out, and offer a respectful exchange of views. That might not change many minds, but it's the only way to move toward constructive dialogue. In today's hyperconnected world our ability to communicate with publics as well as governments has to be part of our national security strategy.

My years in politics prepared me for this phase of my life. I'm often asked how I take the criticism directed my way. I have three answers: First, if you choose to be in public life, remember Eleanor Roosevelt's advice and grow skin as thick as a rhinoceros. Second, learn to take criticism seriously but not personally. Your critics can actually teach you lessons your friends can't or won't. I try to sort out the motivation for criticism, whether partisan, ideological, commercial, or sexist, analyze it to see what I might learn from it, and discard the rest. Third, there is a persistent double standard applied to women in politics—regarding clothes, body types, and of course hairstyles—that you can't let derail you. Smile and keep going. Granted, these words of advice result from years of trial and error and mistakes galore, but they helped me around the world as much as they did at home.

To help us better tell America's story and take on the critics, I turned to one of the country's smartest media executives, Judith McHale, to come on board as Under Secretary for Public Diplomacy and Public Affairs. She had helped found and lead MTV and the Discovery Channel, and is the daughter of a career Foreign Service officer. In that capacity she helped us explain our policies to a skeptical world, push back against extremist propaganda and recruiting, and integrate our global communications strategy with the rest of our smart power agenda. She also was my representative to the Broadcasting Board of Governors, which oversees the Voice of America and other U.S.-funded media around the world. During the Cold War, this was an important part of our outreach, giving people locked behind the Iron Curtain access to uncensored news and information. But we had not kept up with the changing technological and market landscape. Judith and I agreed we needed to overhaul and update our capabilities, but it proved to be an uphill struggle to convince either Congress or the White House to make this a priority.

———

I saw my job as pushing Pakistan to be more committed and coopera-tive in the fight against terrorists and helping its government strengthen democracy and deliver economic and social reforms that offered citizens a viable alternative to radicalism. I had to pressure and criticize with-out losing Pakistan's help in the struggle that was critical to both our futures.

Shortly after I arrived in Islamabad in late October 2009, a car bomb exploded in a busy marketplace in Peshawar, a city just ninety miles northwest of us. More than a hundred people were dead, many of them women and children. Local extremists had demanded that women be banned from shopping in the market, and the blast seemed designed to target those who had refused to be intimidated. Pictures of badly burned bodies and smoking ruins filled television screens across Pakistan. Was the timing coincidental, or were the extremists sending a message? Either way, the stakes had just been raised on an already delicate trip.

The first stop on my itinerary was a meeting with Pakistani Foreign Minister Shah Mahmood Qureshi, a short drive away from the U.S. Em-bassy through Islamabad's well-manicured diplomatic quarter. Islamabad is a planned city of wide avenues rimmed by low green mountains, built in the 1960s to move the government away from the commercial hub in Karachi and closer to the military headquarters in Rawalpindi. Even when a civilian government is nominally in charge, the influence of the Army remains pervasive. One of our traveling journalists asked me on the plane ride over, Was I convinced that the Pakistani military and intel-ligence services had cut off all ties with terrorists? No, I said, I was not.

For years most Pakistanis had regarded the unrest on their northwest frontier as distant. The region had never been under the full control of the national government, and they had been much more concerned with the practical and immediate problems of electricity shortages and unemployment. But now that the violence was spreading, attitudes were starting to change.

At the press conference following our meeting, Qureshi was distressed by the bombing and directed his words to the extremists. "We will not buckle. We will fight you," he said. "You think by attacking innocent people and lives, you will shake our determination? No, sir, you will not." I joined him in condemning the bombing in strong terms and said, "I want you to know that this fight is not Pakistan's alone." I also announced a major new assistance project to help with the chronic energy shortages bedeviling the Pakistani economy.

Later that evening I sat down with a group of Pakistani television reporters to continue the discussion. From the first minute, their questions were suspicious and hostile. Like many other people I met that week, they pressed me on the conditions attached to the large new aid package approved by Congress. One might have thought, given the generosity of the package, especially at a time of economic hardship of our own, that there would have been statements of appreciation. Instead all I heard was anger and suspicion about why the money came with "strings attached." The bill tripled our assistance, yet many Pakistanis took issue with its requirement that military aid be tied to the country's efforts to fight the Taliban. That seemed a reasonable request, but the Pakistani military reacted negatively to being told what it could and could not do with our money. The condition was seen by many Pakistanis as an insult to their sovereignty and pride. I was surprised at the degree of vitriol and misunderstanding generated around this issue, and how many people seemed to be scrutinizing every word of the legislation for possible slights. Very few Americans ever read our own laws so carefully. "I think your PR and charm offensive is fine, explaining your position is fine," one of the journalists said, but "we believe that the bill had a sort of hidden agenda." I tried to stay patient and calm. This was aid meant to help people, nothing more. "I am very sorry you believe that, because that was not the intention," I replied. "Let me be very clear: You do not have to take this money. You do not have to take any aid from us."

Clearly our approach to development aid in Pakistan was not working. Either the toxic politics of our relationship had infected the aid, or the aid wasn't being allocated and spent in a way that made a positive impression on the Pakistani people, or both.

When I became Secretary, the United States was funding over a hundred projects in Pakistan, most of them relatively small and targeted. Some were run directly by USAID, but most were outsourced for implementation to for-profit contractors, as well as nonprofits, including private NGOs, faith-based charities, and research institutes. The contractors were paid whether or not their programs produced verifiable results or furthered our country's interests and values. There were so many American-funded projects that our embassy couldn't determine the total number. It was no wonder Pakistanis were telling me they could not see the impact of American efforts.

Both before and after my trip, I worked with Richard Holbrooke on a strategy to address these concerns. We agreed that the entire effort needed to be streamlined. USAID needed to consolidate programs into signature projects with support among Pakistanis and measurable impacts for both our countries. Since we were spending ten times more money in Pakistan than all other countries combined, it seemed an easily achievable objective.

Nothing moved quickly enough for my taste, but USAID announced in April 2012 that it had developed a more focused and strategic plan for Pakistan that centered on a reduction in the number of programs, from 140 in 2009 to thirty-five in September 2012, emphasizing energy, economic growth, stabilization, health, and education. That was at least a step in the right direction.

Throughout my October 2009 visit, Pakistanis emphasized the human and financial costs they were bearing in the fight against terrorism, which many viewed as America's war that had been unfairly imposed on them. Was it worth the lives of their thirty thousand civilian and military victims? Couldn't they just make a separate peace with the extremists and live in peace? "You had one 9/11, and we are having daily 9/11s in Pakistan," one woman in Lahore said to me. I recognized their feelings, and everywhere I went I paid tribute to the sacrifices of the Pakistani people. I also tried to explain why this struggle was as important to Pakistan's future as to our own, especially now that the extremists were expanding their reach beyond the border region. "I don't know any country that can stand by and look at a force of terrorists intimidating people and taking over large parts of your territory," I told the students. I asked them to imagine how the United States would react if terrorists crossed the border from Canada and took control of Montana. Would we accept it because Montana is remote and sparsely populated? Of course not. We would never allow such a scenario anywhere in our country, and neither should Pakistan.

I also heard a lot of questions about drones. The use of remotely pi-loted aircraft was fast becoming one of the most effective and controversial elements of the Obama Administration's strategy against al Qaeda and like-minded terrorists in hard-to-reach areas. President Obama would eventually declassify many of the details of the program and explain his policies to the world, but in 2009 all I could say was "No comment" whenever the subject came up. Yet it was widely known that dozens of senior terrorists had been taken off the battlefield, and we later learned that bin Laden himself worried about the heavy losses that drones were inflicting.

Within the administration we intensely debated the legal, ethical, and strategic implications of drone strikes and worked hard to establish clear guidelines, oversight, and accountability. Congress provided a domestic legal basis for counterterrorism operations when it authorized the use of military force against al Qaeda after 9/11, and we had an international legal basis under the laws of war and self-defense. The administration began briefing all strikes occurring outside of Iraq and Afghanistan to the appropriate committees of Congress. The preference remained to detain, interrogate, and prosecute terrorists when those options were available. But when there was not the ability to capture individual terrorists who posed a real threat to the American people, drones provided an important alternative.

I agreed with the President when he said that "this new technology raises profound questions—about who is targeted, and why; about civil-ian casualties, and the risk of creating new enemies; about the legality of such strikes under U.S. and international law; about accountability and morality." I spent time talking about the complexities of these is-sues with Harold Koh, the State Department Legal Advisor, a former Dean of Yale Law School, and a renowned expert on international law. Harold argued that, as with any new weapon, we needed to put in place transparent processes and standards governing their use, in accordance with domestic and international law and the interests of U.S. national security. That America is a nation of laws is one of our great strengths, and the Supreme Court has been clear that the fight against terrorism cannot occur in a "legal black hole."

Every individual decision to carry out a strike was subjected to a rigorous legal and policy review. There were times when I supported a particular strike because I believed it was important to the national security of the United States and met the criteria the President set out. There were other times when I dissented; my good friend Leon Panetta, the Director of the Central Intelligence Agency, and I had a shouting match over one proposed strike. But in every case I thought it was crucial that these strikes be part of a larger smart power counterterrorism strategy that included diplomacy, law enforcement, sanctions, and other tools.

The administration did everything it could to achieve near certainty that civilians would not be killed or injured. Despite those efforts, reports of civilian casualties from drone strikes—often, but not always, untrue—fueled anger and anti-American sentiments. Because the program remained classified, I could not confirm or deny the accuracy of these reports. Nor was I free to express America's sympathies for the loss of any innocent life, or explain that our course of action was the one least likely to harm civilians, especially when compared to more conventional military action, such as missiles or bombers—or the costs of leaving terrorists in place.

Another common question in Pakistan was how, after backing Musharraf for so long, America expected to be taken seriously about wanting to promote development and democracy. One TV journalist called our behavior "rolling out the red carpet for a dictator." He and I went back and forth a bit about George Bush, Musharraf, and who was responsible for what. Finally I said, "Look, we can either argue about the past—which is always fun to do, but can't be changed—or we can decide we're going to shape a different future. Now, I vote that we shape a different future." I'm not sure I convinced him, but by the end of the session the steam seemed to have come out of the group's anger, at least a bit.

After I wrapped up with the journalists, it was time for meetings and dinner with President Zardari. That's when, in a quiet moment before we went into the formal dining room in the Presidential Palace, he produced the fourteen-year-old photo of me and Chelsea with Benazir and their children.

The next day I flew to Lahore, an ancient city full of fantastic Mogul architecture. Thousands of police lined the road as we sped into town. I saw some welcome banners hanging along the streets, but we also passed crowds of young men who held signs with messages like "Hillory go back" and "Drone attack is terror."

At a meeting with university students, I fielded more questions: Why does America always support India instead of Pakistan? What can America do to help with energy shortages and poor education in Pakistan, and why, again, does the aid package come with so many strings attached? Why are Pakistani exchange students in America stereotyped as terrorists? How can we trust America when you've let us down so many times before? I tried to provide full and respectful answers. "It is difficult to go forward if we're always looking in the rearview mirror," I pointed out. The mood in the room was sullen and aggrieved, with little of the positive energy I had encountered in other university visits around the world.

Then a young woman stood up. She was a medical student and a member of Seeds of Peace, an organization I have long supported that is dedicated to bringing young people together across cultural divides and conflicts. She generously thanked me for serving as an inspiration to young women around the world. Then she pivoted to a sharp-edged question about the use of drones. She noted the collateral damage inflicted on Pakistani civilians and asked why, if these strikes were so important, the United States couldn't just share the necessary technology and intelligence with the Pakistani military and let them handle it. I was a little taken aback by the shift in tone. But looking at her, I thought back to my own days as a student who was quick to question authority figures. Young people often fearlessly say what the rest of us are thinking but are too cautious to speak out loud. If I had been born in Pakistan, who knows, perhaps I would be standing where she was now.

"Well, I will not talk about that specifically," I responded, mindful of the limits of what I could legally say at that point about drones, "but generally, let me say that there's a war going on. And thankfully, there is a very professional and successful military effort that has been undertaken by the Pakistani military. And I'm hoping that the support that the United States provides and the courage of the Pakistani military will bring much of this to a conclusion. Now, there will, unfortunately, always be those who seek to inflict terror, but eventually they can be eliminated and they can be deterred if society just abruptly turns against them. So I think that the war that your government and your military is waging right now is a very important one for the future of Pakistan, and we are going to continue to assist the government and the military to be successful in that war."

I doubt that satisfied her. It was true, but I couldn't say what else was in my head: Yes, Pakistanis had borne a terrible price in this fight against extremism, civilians and soldiers alike. Those sacrifices should never be forgotten. And thankfully the Pakistani Army was finally moving into contested areas like the Swat Valley. But too many leaders of the Pakistani military and intelligence services were obsessed with India and either turning a blind eye to the Taliban insurgency and other terrorist groups or, worse, aiding and abetting them. Al Qaeda was operating from Pakistani soil with seeming impunity. So Pakistanis had some hard choices to make about what kind of country they wanted to live in and what they were willing to do to secure it.

I answered all the questions I could. Even if they didn't like what I had to say, I wanted to be sure everyone understood that America was listening and responding to their concerns.

Next it was on to another sit-down with local journalists, and once again I was playing the role of punching bag. I heard all the same questions about America's lack of respect for Pakistani sovereignty, and I engaged as honestly and respectfully as I could. As the press described it, I "sounded less like a diplomat than a marriage counselor." Trust and respect are two-way streets, I reminded my questioners. I was prepared to take an honest view of America's record in the region and to take responsibility for the consequences of our actions. For example, the United States had been too quick to walk away from Afghanistan after the Soviets withdrew in 1989. Pakistanis also had to take responsibility and apply the same scrutiny to their own leaders that they applied to us. "I don't believe in dancing around difficult issues, because I don't think that benefits anybody," I said.

After answering a question about why we were forcing Pakistan to fight America's war without enough help, I looked around at these journalists, many of whom were so quick to blame the United States for all their troubles. "Let me ask *you* something," I said. "Al Qaeda has had safe haven in Pakistan since 2002. I find it hard to believe that nobody in your government knows where they are and couldn't get them if they really wanted to. . . . The world has an interest in seeing the capture and killing of the people who are the masterminds of this terrorist syndicate, but so far as we know, they're in Pakistan."

For a moment the room was completely silent. I had just said what every American official believed to be true but never uttered out loud. Bin Laden and his key lieutenants, in all likelihood, were hiding in Pakistan. Somebody had to know where. That evening my statement was repeated endlessly on Pakistani television, and government officials in Islamabad hurried to deny that they knew anything at all. Back in Washington, Robert Gibbs, the White House Press Secretary, was asked, "Does the White House think it was appropriate for Secretary Clinton to be as blunt as she was towards Pakistan in the comments she made about Pakistan's unwillingness to find terrorists within their borders?" Gibbs responded, "Completely appropriate."

The next day, in yet another round with the Pakistani press, I made the point again: "Somebody, somewhere in Pakistan, must know where these people are."

A few months after I returned from Pakistan, Leon Panetta invited me to visit him at CIA headquarters in Langley, Virginia. I had known Leon and his wife, Sylvia, for decades. As Director of the Office of Management and Budget in the Clinton Administration, Leon played a big role in crafting and passing Bill's successful economic plan. Then, as Chief of Staff, he helped steer the Clinton White House through the difficult period between the Republican takeover of Congress in 1994 and Bill's reelection in 1996. A proud Italian American, Leon is a shrewd, blunt, and colorful Washington operator with fantastic instincts and judgment. I was delighted when President Obama asked him to return to government as CIA Director and later as Secretary of Defense. Now Leon was reaching out to strategize about our fight against al Qaeda. The administration's military, diplomatic, and intelligence operations against the terrorist network were showing results, but he and I both thought we needed to do a better job of combating extremist propaganda and cutting off al Qaeda's access to finances, recruits, and safe havens.

I drove out to Langley in early February 2010. The storied lobby in the headquarters, re-created in countless spy thrillers, contains a solemn memorial. Nearly one hundred small stars are carved into the marble, each one memorializing a CIA officer who died in the line of duty, including many whose identities remain classified. I thought back to my first visit to Langley, representing my husband at a memorial service in early 1993 for two CIA officers shot and killed at a traffic light just down the street. The murderer was a Pakistani immigrant named Mir Aimal Kansi, who fled the country but was later caught in Pakistan, extradited, convicted, and executed. I had been First Lady just a few weeks, and the service at Langley left a lasting impression on me of the quiet dedication of those who serve in the CIA.

Now, seventeen years later, the CIA was grieving again. On December 30, 2009, seven officers were killed in a suicide bombing at a base in eastern Afghanistan. Security and Intelligence officers at the compound were about to meet with a potentially high-value al Qaeda informant when he detonated concealed explosives. The attack was a terrible blow for the tight-knit Agency and for Leon himself, who met the flag-draped caskets of the fallen at Dover Air Force Base in Delaware.

Leon published an op-ed in the *Washington Post* defending his people against unwarranted criticisms of "poor tradecraft" and explaining, "Our officers were engaged in an important mission in a dangerous part of the world. They brought to that mission their skills, expertise and willingness to take risks. That's how we succeed at what we do. And sometimes in a war, that comes at a very high price." Leon was right, both about the importance of serving our country in dangerous places and the reality of the risks involved. Most Americans understand that our troops often must be in harm's way. But the same is also true for our intelligence officers, diplomats, and development experts, as we were tragically reminded during my years at State.

When I arrived at Langley for our meeting, Leon brought me to his seventh-floor office, which looked out over the woods and sprawl of suburban Virginia and the Potomac.

Soon we were joined by analysts from the Agency's Counterterrorism Center for a briefing on the fight against al Qaeda. We discussed how the State Department could work more closely with the intelligence community to counter violent extremism in Afghanistan, Pakistan, and other hotspots around the world. The CIA team was especially eager for our help in the information wars online and in the airwaves. I agreed. I still had the angry complaints of Pakistanis ringing in my ears. And it drove me crazy that, as Richard Holbrooke once said, we were losing the communications battle to extremists living in caves. Most important, we had to find ways to slow the spread of radicalization or more terrorists would spring up to replace those we were taking off the battlefield. We also needed to bring more countries into the fight against al Qaeda, especially Muslim-majority nations who could help counter extremist propaganda and recruiting. Leon and I directed our teams to work together to draw up concrete proposals that we could bring to the President. Over the next few months, thanks to the leadership of my counterterrorism advisor Danny Benjamin, we developed a four-pronged strategy.

First, to do a better job contesting the online space, including media websites and chat rooms where al Qaeda and its affiliates spread their propaganda and recruited followers, we wanted to create a new Center for Strategic Counterterrorism Communications housed at the State Department but drawing on experts from across the government. This nerve center in Washington would link with military and civilian teams around the world and serve as a force multiplier for our embassies' communications efforts to preempt, discredit, and outmaneuver extremist propagandists. We would expand our small "digital outreach team" into a battalion of communications specialists fluent in Urdu, Arabic, Somali, and other languages who could do battle with extremists online and answer anti-American misinformation.

Second, the State Department would lead a diplomatic offensive to better coordinate with partners and allies around the world who shared our interest in combating violent extremism. Remarkably, nearly a decade after 9/11 there was still no dedicated international venue to regularly convene key counterterrorism policymakers and practitioners. So we envisioned a Global Counterterrorism Forum that would bring together dozens of countries, including many from the Muslim world, to share best practices and address common challenges, such as how to strengthen porous borders and respond to ransom demands from kidnappers.

Third, we wanted to step up training of foreign law enforcement and counterterrorism forces. The State Department already worked with nearly seven thousand officials from more than sixty countries each year, and we had experience building counterterrorism capacity in Yemen, Pakistan, and other frontline states. We wanted to do even more.

Fourth, we wanted to use targeted development programs and partnerships with local civil society to try to tip the balance away from extremism in specific terrorist-recruiting hotspots. Over time we had found that recruits tended to come in clusters, influenced by family and social networks. We might not be able to end poverty or bring democracy to every country in the world, but by focusing on specific neighborhoods, villages, prisons, and schools, we might be able to break the cycle of radicalization and disrupt the recruiting chains.

I thought that these four initiatives, along with aggressive efforts by the Treasury Department to disrupt terrorist-financing networks, added up to a coherent, smart power approach to counterterrorism that would complement what the intelligence community and the military were doing. I asked Danny Benjamin to brief the White House staff on our plans and to find a time for me to present our strategy to the President and the rest of the National Security Council.

Some of the White House national security aides supported our plan, but others were concerned. They wanted to be sure that State wasn't trying to usurp the White House's role as the primary coordinator of activity across the various agencies, especially when it came to communications. Danny patiently explained that this was intended to be a highly targeted initiative to combat extremist propaganda. To clear the air, as had already been necessary a number of times, I decided to present it directly to the President.

In early July, at a regularly scheduled meeting with President Obama and his full homeland security and counterterrorism teams, I presented our strategy. Danny brought a detailed PowerPoint presentation that described the four initiatives and the resources and authorities we'd need to execute them. Panetta immediately backed me up, telling the President that this was exactly what was needed. Secretary Gates agreed. Attorney General Eric Holder and Secretary of Homeland Security Janet Napolitano also spoke in favor. Then we turned to the President. I could see he was a little upset. "I don't know what I have to do around here to get people to listen to me," he said, with exasperation. Not a good start. "I've been asking for this kind of plan for more than a year!" That was a green light from the top. "We have everything we need," I told Danny afterward. "Let's get started."

"We've got a lead."

It was early March 2011, and Leon Panetta and I were having lunch in a private dining room on the eighth floor of the State Department.

Not long before, he had taken me aside after a meeting in the Situation Room and said he had something important to talk about privately. No staff, no notes. I had offered to pay another visit to his office at Langley, but this time he insisted on coming to the State Department. So here we were at lunch. I was eager to hear what was on his mind.

Leon leaned in and said that the CIA had been tracking the best lead they'd had in years about the possible whereabouts of Osama bin Laden. The Agency had been quietly working this for some time. Leon had slowly started telling senior administration officials, starting at the White House. He went and saw Bob Gates at the Pentagon in December. In February, he brought in the Joint Chiefs and Admiral Bill McRaven, commander of the Joint Special Operations Command, whose troops might be called upon to lead a raid if the intelligence was strong enough. Now he was telling me, because he wanted me to join a small group at the White House to discuss what to do.

I knew that President Obama had told Leon shortly after the inauguration that he wanted the CIA to refocus its efforts on al Qaeda and finding bin Laden. Agents and analysts worked triple-time in Langley and out in the field, and now it seemed their efforts were yielding results. It had been nearly a decade since I stood at the smoldering pile at Ground Zero, and Americans still wanted justice. But I also knew that intelligence is an uncertain business and that previous leads had failed to pan out.

I couldn't tell anyone at the State Department—or anywhere, for that matter—what was happening, which created some awkward moments with my staff. It has been more than twenty years since I've been able to do much of anything without at least a dozen people noticing, but with a little misdirection, I pulled it off.

Our small group met at the White House multiple times in March and April. Leon and his team presented the case that led them to suspect that a "high-value target," possibly bin Laden, was living in a walled compound in the Pakistani city of Abbottabad, not far from the country's premier military training academy, the equivalent of our West Point. Some of the intelligence analysts were highly confident they finally had their man. Others were far less confident, especially those who had lived through the failed intelligence process that concluded that Saddam Hussein possessed weapons of mass destruction. We sifted through the reports, listened to the experts, and weighed the probabilities on both sides.

We also debated our options. One was sharing intelligence with the Pakistanis and conducting a joint raid, but I and others thought we could not trust Pakistan. The President immediately took that option off the table. Another was to bomb the compound from the air. That would pose little risk to U.S. personnel but was likely to cause significant collateral damage in a densely populated neighborhood, and there would be no way to determine with absolute certainty if bin Laden had really been there at all. Using a targeted missile fired from a drone or other platform might limit the damage, but there would still be no way to recover and identify the body or to collect any other useful intelligence on the premises. Worse yet, it could miss, or not do the trick. The only way to be certain he was there, and equally certain that he would be captured or killed, would be to insert Special Operations forces deep into Pakistan to raid the compound. Admiral McRaven's special operators were highly skilled and experienced, but there was no doubt that this option posed by far the greatest risk, especially if our men ended up in conflict with Pakistani security forces, hundreds of miles from a safe haven.

The President's top advisors were split on the wisdom of a raid. Leon and Tom Donilon, by then National Security Advisor, ultimately recommended launching the operation. Bob Gates, who had spent decades as a CIA analyst, wasn't sold. He thought the intelligence was circumstantial, and he worried that a blowup with the Pakistanis would jeopardize the war effort in Afghanistan. Bob also carried painful memories of Operation Eagle Claw, the disastrous botched rescue attempt of hostages in Iran in 1980 that left eight U.S. servicemen dead when a helicopter collided with a transport aircraft. That was a nightmare scenario that nobody wanted to see repeated. He thought the risks of a raid were just too high and preferred a strike from the air, although he would eventually change his mind. Vice President Biden remained skeptical.

These were difficult and emotional discussions. Unlike most matters I handled as Secretary of State, because of the extreme secrecy of this case there was no trusted advisor I could turn to or expert I could call.

I took that seriously, as President Obama found out when, after the raid was over but before he went on television to inform the country, he called all four living ex-Presidents to tell them personally. When he reached Bill, he began, "I assume Hillary's already told you . . ." Bill had no idea what he was talking about. They told me not to tell anyone, so I didn't tell anyone. Bill later joked with me, "No one will ever doubt you can keep a secret!"

I respected Bob and Joe's concerns about the risks of a raid, but I came to the conclusion that the intelligence was convincing and the risks were outweighed by the benefits of success. We just had to make sure it worked.

That would be the job of Admiral McRaven. He was a Navy man who had come up through the ranks, including a stint leading an underwater demolition SEAL team. The more I got to know him and watch him plan this mission, the more confident I felt. When I asked about the dangers of the raid on the compound, Admiral McRaven assured me that his Special Operations forces had conducted hundreds of similar missions in Iraq and Afghanistan, sometimes two, three, or more in a single night. Operation Eagle Claw had been a disaster, but the Special Operations forces learned from it. The complicated part would be reaching Abbottabad without triggering Pakistani radar and a response from its security forces stationed nearby. Once his Navy SEALs were on the ground, they would get the job done.

The SEALs and the Night Stalkers, the pilots of the Army's 160th Special Operations Aviation Regiment, trained extensively for the mission, including two rehearsals on full-sized replicas of the compound conducted at two different secret locations in the United States. There was also a specially trained Belgian Malinois dog named Cairo who worked alongside the SEALs.

On April 28, 2011, President Obama convened our group for one last meeting in the White House Situation Room. He went around the table and asked everyone for their final recommendation. The President and I are both lawyers, and I had learned over time how to appeal to his highly analytical mind. So I methodically laid out the case, including the potential damage to our relationship with Pakistan and the risks of a blown operation. But, I concluded, the chance to get bin Laden was worth it. As I had experienced firsthand, our relationship with Pakistan was strictly transactional, based on mutual interest, not trust. It would survive. I thought we should go for it.

There was also the question of timing and logistics. Because the raid had to be conducted under cover of darkness, Admiral McRaven recommended launching on the soonest moonless night, which would be Saturday, April 30, just two days away. Some officials raised an unexpected concern. The annual White House Correspondents' Dinner, a high-profile black-tie event at which the President usually tells jokes in front of a room full of reporters and celebrities, was scheduled for Saturday night. These officials worried about how it would look to have the President doing a stand-up routine in case he was needed while the mission was under way. And if he canceled or left early, it would look suspicious and might jeopardize the secrecy of the operation. Admiral McRaven, always the good soldier, gamely promised to make Sunday work if that was the final decision, although any further delays would be a major problem.

I've sat through a lot of absurd conversations, but this was just too much. We were talking about one of the most important national security calls the President would ever make. The mission was already compli-cated and dangerous enough. If the commander of Special Operations wanted to move on Saturday, then that's what we should do. While I don't remember exactly what I said, some in the media have quoted me using a four-letter word to dismiss the Correspondents' Dinner as a concern. I have not sought a correction.

The President agreed. He said that if worst came to worst and he had to bow out in the middle of the dinner, they could just blame a stomach-ache. In the end, fog was predicted for Abbottabad on Saturday night, and the mission had to be postponed to Sunday anyway. But at least it wasn't for a Washington party.

After the final meeting the President took time to think it over. The team was still divided. It was a decision only he could make. Then he gave the order. The operation, code-named Neptune Spear, was a go.

═══════

I spent Saturday night at the wedding of a close friend of my daughter's. The bride, a bright young military strategist fluent in Mandarin who studies the Chinese military, and her friends are all smart and engaging young people. It was a cool spring night, and at the reception on a rooftop overlooking the Potomac, I stood off to the side looking at the river and thinking about what the next day would bring. Guests kept coming up and talking to me, and soon I had about a dozen clustered around. One of them asked, "Secretary Clinton, do you think we'll ever get bin Laden?" I barely suppressed a double take, startled that he had asked me that question on this night of all nights. I responded, "Well, I sure hope so."

At 12:30 P.M. the next day, Sunday, May 1, I took the fifteen-minute drive from my home to the White House and joined other senior members of the national security team in the Situation Room. White House staff had brought in food from a local deli, and everyone was dressed informally. Two of the CIA officers who had chased bin Laden for more than a decade joined us; it was hard to believe their hunt might soon be over. We reviewed the details of the operation again, including the calls we would make afterward.

At 2:30 P.M. Washington time, two Black Hawk helicopters carrying Navy SEALs took off from a base in Jalalabad, in eastern Afghanistan, where it was 11 P.M. Once they crossed into Pakistan, three large Chinook transport helicopters followed with reinforcements ready to deploy if needed.

The whir of the Black Hawks' rotors cut into the silence of the Abbottabad night about two minutes before they swooped in over the compound. Their approach was visible, fast and low, on the video screen in a small conference room where we had gathered, across from the larger Situation Room. Then, instead of hovering in the air while the SEALs "fast-roped" to the ground, as the plan had called for, one of the Black Hawks quickly began to lose lift. The pilot "landed hard," and the helicopter's tail hit the compound wall. (Later the military was able to pinpoint the problem: the full-scale practice model of the compound had a chain-link fence instead of a stone wall, which changed the airflow dynamics enough to compromise the Black Hawk's operability.) As if this were not alarming enough, a second helicopter, which was supposed to land and drop SEALs on the roof of the compound, had to improvise, flew past without stopping, and landed instead on the ground outside the compound.

That was as tense a moment as any I can remember. It conjured up ghosts, not just of the tragic accident in Iran that Bob had presciently feared from the outset, but also the infamous "Black Hawk Down" incident in Somalia in 1993, in which eighteen American soldiers were killed in Mogadishu. Were we about to witness another disaster for the United States? I thought about the men risking their lives out there in the middle of the night on the other side of the world, and I held my breath. There is a famous photograph of that day that shows me holding my hand over my mouth as we all stared at the screen. I can't say for sure at what moment that picture was taken, but it does capture how I felt.

Finally we could exhale: the damaged Black Hawk landed and the

SEALs jumped out, ready to begin the assault. It was the first of many heroic acts that night. Admiral McRaven was right: his team knew how to handle every bump in the road. The operation was still a go.

We watched on the video feed as the SEALs improvised, sweeping through the courtyard of the compound and heading inside to look for bin Laden. Contrary to some news reports and what you see in the movies, we had no means to see what was happening inside the building itself. All we could do was wait for an update from the team on the ground. I looked at the President. He was calm. Rarely have I been prouder to serve by his side as I was that day.

After what seemed like an eternity, but was actually about fifteen minutes, word came from McRaven that the team had found bin Laden and he was "E-KIA," enemy killed in action. Osama bin Laden was dead.

One of the backup helicopters had arrived to help ferry the SEALs to safety, along with bin Laden's body and a treasure trove of captured intelligence. But first they had to blow up the disabled helicopter they were leaving behind so none of its advanced technology could be recovered and studied. While some of the team planted explosives, others gathered up all the women and children who were living in the compound—the families of bin Laden and the others—and led them to safety behind a wall so they would be shielded from the blast. Amid all the dangers and pressures of the day, this humane gesture by our military spoke volumes about America's values.

===

Once he knew the SEALs were back in Afghanistan and the body had been confirmed as bin Laden's, it was time for the President to address the nation. I walked with him, Biden, Panetta, Donilon, Mike Mullen, and Jim Clapper, the Director of National Intelligence, to the East Room, a place I had been countless times for announcements, musical performances, and state dinners. Now I was in a small audience watching the President deliver historic remarks. I was drained from the emotions and unrelenting tension of the day, not to mention the weeks and months that had led up to it. Listening to the President describe the successful operation made me both proud and grateful. As we walked back through the colonnade that borders the Rose Garden, we heard an unexpected roar coming from beyond the gates. Then I saw a huge crowd of young people, many of them students from nearby universities, gathered outside the White House in a spontaneous celebration, waving American flags, chanting, "USA! USA!" Most had been children when al Qaeda attacked the United States on 9/11. They had grown up in the shadow of the War on Terror; it had been part of their consciousness for as long as they could remember. Now they were expressing the emotional release our entire country felt after so many years waiting for justice.

I stood still and let the shouts and cheers wash over me. I thought about the families I knew back in New York who still grieved for their loved ones lost on that terrible day. Would they find some measure of solace tonight? Would survivors like Lauren Manning and Debbie Mardenfeld, who had been so badly injured, face the future with renewed optimism and confidence? I also thought about the CIA officers who never gave up the hunt, even when the trail went cold, and about the SEALs and pilots who performed even better than Admiral McRaven had promised. And every one of them came home.

_____

I was not looking forward to the difficult conversations ahead with the Pakistanis. As expected, when news spread, the country was in an uproar. The military was humiliated and the public inflamed by what they viewed as a violation of Pakistani sovereignty. But when I connected with President Zardari, he was more philosophical than hostile. "People think I am weak," he said, "but I am not weak. I know my country and I have done everything possible. I cannot deny the fact that the most wanted man in the world was in my country. It is everyone's failure that we did not know." He emphasized that Pakistan had been a friend to the United States for six decades, and he described the fight against terrorism in deeply personal terms. "I am fighting for my life and for the future life of my children," he said. "I am fighting the people who killed the mother of my children."

I commiserated with Zardari and told him that a number of senior American officials were on their way to meet with him in person. I would come myself when the time was right. But I was also firm with him: "Mr. President, I believe strongly that there can be a way forward that meets both our interests. We would both be worse off if our close cooperation ended. But I want to be clear, as a close friend and someone with high regard for you, that finding this path will require you and your country to make choices. We want greater cooperation."

I would devote intense energy over the coming months to holding together our fragile relationship, as did our Ambassador in Islamabad, Cameron Munter, and his team. We came close to a serious rupture quite a few more times, but the fundamental shared interests that I had described to my colleagues in our White House deliberations continued to bring our two countries back together. Even without bin Laden, terrorism would remain a threat neither nation could ignore. Pakistan still faced a deadly Taliban insurgency and mounting social and economic problems.

In November 2011, six months after the Abbottabad operation, twenty-four Pakistani soldiers were killed by U.S. forces in a tragic accident along the border with Afghanistan. The United States quickly offered condolences, but Pakistani emotions ran high. In response Pakistan's government closed NATO's supply lines into Afghanistan, and the Parliament launched a review of relations with the United States. The Pakistanis wanted a direct apology, and the White House was unwilling to give it. Military shipping containers sat idle for months, creating logistical challenges for our troops, adding financial costs for us—$100 million a month—and depriving the Pakistanis of much-needed revenue.

With no progress on reopening the supply lines by the time of the NATO Summit in Chicago in May 2012, I suggested to President Obama that we needed a different approach to resolve the impasse. He agreed, over objections from both the National Security Council and Defense, to let me try. Some of the President's advisors, keeping their eyes on the reelection campaign, were allergic to the idea of any apology, especially to the country that had harbored bin Laden. But to help supply Coalition troops we needed to sort it out. I told the President I would absorb any incoming political attacks. I met with President Zardari in Chicago and told him I needed his help to get the supply lines open, just as his government needed the payments it received for permitting convoys to traverse Pakistan. I dispatched Deputy Secretary Tom Nides, an experienced negotiator, to sit down in private with Pakistan's Finance Minister. This was one of those calls where a willingness to recognize error is not a sign of weakness but a pragmatic compromise. So I gave Tom clear instructions: Be discreet, be reasonable, and get a deal done.

The back channel helped soothe Pakistani feelings. When I met with

Foreign Minister Hina Rabbani Khar, who had replaced Qureshi, in Istanbul in June, I could tell we were close to a resolution. By early July we sealed an agreement. I acknowledged the mistakes that resulted in the loss of Pakistani military lives and again offered our sincere condolences. Both sides were sorry for losses suffered in the struggle against terrorism. The Pakistanis reopened the border, allowing us to conduct the planned drawdown of Coalition forces at a much lower cost than if we had had to take a different route. Tom and the Finance Minister kept their dialogue going and even published a joint op-ed exploring possible areas of cooperation, especially in economic development.

The negotiations and eventual agreement over the supply lines offer lessons for how the United States and Pakistan can work together in the future to pursue shared interests. As U.S. combat troops leave Afghanistan, the nature of our relationship will change. But both countries will still have interests that depend upon the other. So we'll need to find ways to work together constructively. Future disagreements and distractions are inevitable, but if we want results we have no choice other than to stay focused and pragmatic.

Meanwhile al Qaeda had been dealt a serious blow, though it was not yet defeated. Because of the operation in Abbottabad, the SEALs returned with extensive new intelligence about the inner workings of al Qaeda. It would add to what we already understood about the spread of affiliated organizations: Somalia's Al Shabaab, North Africa's al Qaeda in the Islamic Maghreb, and al Qaeda in the Arabian Peninsula, which were becoming bigger threats every day. The death of bin Laden, and the loss of so many of his top lieutenants, would certainly degrade the capacity of al Qaeda's core in Afghanistan and Pakistan to stage new attacks against the West. At the same time, however, this would shift influence and momentum to the affiliates, creating a more diffuse and complex threat.

Faced with this evolving challenge, I felt even more certain that we needed to pursue the smart power approach to counterterrorism I had described to the President in 2010. At the State Department we had been quietly working to develop the tools and capabilities we would need, including expanding our counterterrorism office into a full-fledged bureau headed by an Assistant Secretary of State. But working with the rest of the government could be frustratingly slow. We had to fight for every penny of funding, and despite the President's pointed comments in July 2010, it took more than a year to get the White House to issue an executive order establishing the Center for Strategic Counterterrorism Communications. We finally received it on September 9, 2011. That same day I visited the John Jay College of Criminal Justice in New York and delivered a major speech explaining our strategy to bulk up the civilian side of counterterrorism.

Twelve days later, on the sidelines of the United Nations General Assembly, I inaugurated the Global Counterterrorism Forum. Turkey served as cochair, and nearly thirty other nations joined us, including Middle Eastern and other Muslim-majority countries. Early results over the following two years were encouraging. The United Arab Emirates agreed to host an international center focused on countering violent extremism, and a center on justice and the rule of law is set to open in Malta. These institutions will train police, educators, religious and community leaders, and policymakers. They'll bring together experts on communications who understand how to undermine extremist propaganda, and law enforcement agents who can help governments and communities learn to protect themselves from terrorists. They'll also work with educators who can devise curricula free of hatred and give teachers the tools to protect at-risk children from recruitment by extremists.

An early focus of the Global Counterterrorism Forum was kidnapping for ransom, which emerged as a top funding tool for al Qaeda affiliates in North Africa and around the world, especially as other financial avenues were closed off to them. With strong U.S. support, the Forum developed a code of conduct that would stop nations from paying ransoms, which only encourages more kidnapping. The United Nations Security Council backed the code, and the African Union set up trainings to help security forces across the region develop alternative tactics.

We made some progress on the communications front as well. For example, as the Arab Spring swept through the Middle East, our new Center for Strategic Counterterrorism Communications worked hard to show that al Qaeda was on the wrong side of history. One short video clip the team produced and circulated online began with a recording of al Qaeda's new leader, Ayman al-Zawahiri, claiming that peaceful action would never bring about change in the Middle East, followed by footage of peaceful protests in Egypt and celebrations after the fall of Mubarak. The video stirred up a flurry of responses across the region. "Zawahiri has no business with Egypt; we will solve our problems ourselves," wrote one commentator on the website Egypt Forum.

This kind of ideological battle is slow and incremental but important, because al Qaeda and its terrorist affiliates cannot survive without a steady flow of new recruits to replace the terrorists who are killed or captured and because unchecked propaganda can ignite instability and inspire attacks. We saw this in September 2012, when extremists whipped up outrage across the Muslim world over an offensive but obscure internet video about the Prophet Muhammad. U.S. embassies and consulates in many countries were targeted as a result.

If we step back and take a broader view, we can see that violent extremism is bound up with nearly all of today's complex global problems. It can take root in zones of crisis and poverty, flourish under repression and in the absence of the rule of law, spark hatred between communities that have lived side-by-side for generations, and exploit conflict within and between states. That is an argument for America to be engaged in the hardest places with the toughest challenges around the world.

PART FOUR

Between Hope
and History

10

Europe: Ties That Bind

There's a Girl Scouts song I learned in elementary school: "Make new friends, but keep the old. One is silver, and the other gold." For America, our alliance with Europe is worth more than gold.

When the United States was attacked on September 11, 2001, European nations stood with us without hesitation. A headline in the French newspaper *Le Monde* proclaimed, "We are all Americans." The day after the attack, NATO (the North Atlantic Treaty Organization) invoked Article V of the Washington Treaty for the first time in history, which stipulates that an attack on one ally is an attack on all of the allies. After decades of Americans standing alongside Europeans in places ranging from Utah Beach to Checkpoint Charlie to Kosovo, the Europeans were letting us know that they wanted to be right there beside us in our hour of need.

Unfortunately, from that high-water mark, the relationship deteriorated. Most of our European allies disagreed with the decision to invade Iraq. Many were put off by the "you're either with us or against us" style of President George W. Bush's Administration, exemplified by Secretary of Defense Donald Rumsfeld's dismissive description of France and Germany as "Old Europe" at the height of the Iraq debate in early 2003. By 2009 positive views of America across Europe had eroded significantly, from 83 percent approval in the United Kingdom and 78 percent in Germany in 2000 to 53 and 31 percent, respectively, at the end of 2008. Clearly, the new Obama Administration had our work cut out for us.

Probably our greatest asset in turning the tide of European public opinion was "the Obama Effect." Across the continent many Europeans were incredibly excited about our new President. As a candidate in July 2008, he had electrified an enormous crowd of nearly 200,000 people in Berlin. The day after the election a French newspaper headline proclaimed, "An American Dream." In fact expectations ran so high that managing them and channeling all that positive energy into lasting progress became an early challenge.

Despite Bush-era strains, our bonds ran far deeper than any disagreements about particular policies. Our European allies remained America's partners of first resort on nearly every challenge. And above all, this was an alliance of values, rooted in a deep commitment to liberty and democracy. The scars of two world wars and the Cold War were receding into history, but many Europeans were still mindful of the great sacrifices that Americans had made to keep them free. More than sixty thousand American soldiers lay buried in France alone.

The vision of Europe as whole, free, and at peace had been a goal of every U.S. administration since the end of the Cold War. At its heart was the notion that peoples and countries could move beyond old conflicts to chart a peaceful and prosperous future. I had seen how difficult this could be, how tightly the chains of history bound entire generations and societies. I once asked an official from southern Europe how things were going in her country. She started her answer by saying, "Since the Crusades . . ." That's how deep memories ran in many parts of Europe and indeed around the world, as if the 20th and 21st centuries were just so much topsoil. Even as memory bound together neighbors and allies and saw them through difficult times, it also kept old hatreds alive and prevented people from turning their focus to the future. Yet the people of Western Europe had shown that it was possible to shake off the burdens of the past when they reconciled in the years after World War II. We saw it again after the fall of the Berlin Wall, when Central and Eastern Europe began the process of integration with each other and with the nations of the European Union.

By 2009 historic progress had been achieved across much of the continent, and in many ways we were closer than ever to the vision of a whole, free, peaceful Europe. But it was more fragile than many Americans may have realized. Along Europe's periphery, southern European economies reeled from the financial crisis, the Balkans struggled still with the scars of war, democracy and human rights were under threat in too many former Soviet republics, and Russia under Putin had invaded Georgia, reawakening old fears. My predecessors had worked to build our alliances in Europe and to support the movement toward greater unity, freedom, and peace across the continent. Now it was my turn to pick up the baton and do everything I could to renew old ties and manage old conflicts.

Relations between nations are based on shared interests and values—but also on personalities. The personal element matters more in international affairs than many would expect, for good or ill. Think of the famous friendship between Ronald Reagan and Margaret Thatcher that helped win the Cold War or the feud between Khrushchev and Mao that helped lose it. It was with this in mind that I began reaching out to key European leaders starting on my first full day at the State Department. Some I already knew and liked from my time as First Lady and Senator. Others would become new friends. But all of them would be our valuable partners in the work we hoped to do.

I began every call with a message of America's reassurance and renewed commitment. David Miliband, the British Foreign Secretary, caused me to gulp and smile simultaneously when he said, "My goodness, your predecessors have left you with a world of problems. It's a Herculean job, but I think you're the right Hercules for this task." I was flattered (as I was meant to be) but made clear that what I thought we needed was renewed partnership and common action, not a lone mythological hero.

David proved to be an invaluable partner. He was young, energetic, smart, creative, and attractive, with a ready smile. We found our views on how the world was changing remarkably similar. He believed in the importance of civil society and shared my concern for the growing numbers of out-of-work and disconnected young people in Europe, the United States, and around the world. In addition to becoming good professional colleagues, we developed a genuine friendship.

David's boss was the embattled Labour Prime Minister Gordon Brown, Tony Blair's successor. Gordon, an intelligent and dogged Scotsman, ended up presiding over the economic recession that hit Britain hard. He was dealt a bad hand, including the baggage of Tony's unpopular support of Bush's decision to invade Iraq. When he hosted the

G-20 meeting in London in April 2009, I could see the strain he was under. He went on to lose the next election and was replaced by David Cameron, a Tory. President Obama and Cameron took to each other right off, starting with a private meeting before Cameron's electoral victory. They had an easy rapport and enjoyed each other's company. Cameron and I met together a number of times over the years, both with and without President Obama. He was intellectually curious and eager to exchange ideas about world events, from the unfolding Arab Spring to the crisis in Libya and the ongoing debate over economic austerity versus growth.

For Foreign Secretary, Cameron chose William Hague, a former leader of the Tory Party and an implacable political foe of Tony Blair in the late 1990s. Before the election, when he was still the Shadow Foreign Secretary, he came to see me in Washington. We both started off a bit cautiously with each other, but, much to my delight, I found him a thoughtful statesman with good sense and good humor. He also became a good friend. I was a fan of his biography of William Wilberforce, the chief advocate for ending slavery in 19th-century England. Hague brought to his job the understanding that diplomacy is slow and often boring but absolutely necessary. At a farewell dinner he hosted for me in 2013 at the British Embassy in Washington, his toast included the following gem: "It was a great former British Foreign Secretary and Prime Minister Lord Salisbury who said that diplomatic victories 'are made up of a series of microscopic advantages: of a judicious suggestion here, of an opportune civility there, of a wise concession at one moment and a far-sighted persistence at another, of sleepless tact, immovable calmness, and patience that no folly, no provocation, no blunder can shake.'" That pretty well summed up my experience as America's chief diplomat. It also reminded me that Hague was the David Beckham of toasting!

Across the English Channel I found other memorable partners. Bernard Kouchner, the French Foreign Minister, was a Socialist physician serving Nicolas Sarkozy, a Conservative President. Bernard had started Médecins Sans Frontières, or Doctors Without Borders, which provides medical care in disaster and conflict zones in some of the poorest places on earth. He was a key player after the devastating earthquake in Haiti in January 2010. I also worked closely with his successor, Alain Juppé, and later with Laurent Fabius, appointed by Sarkozy's successor, François Hollande, who was elected in May 2012. Although from opposing political parties, Juppé and Fabius were both consummate professionals and enjoyable company.

Most leaders are quieter in person than they appear to be on the stage. Not Sarkozy. He was even more dramatic—and fun—in person. Sitting in a meeting with him was always an adventure. He'd jump up and gesture dramatically as he made his points, with his intrepid female interpreter struggling to keep up but usually managing to mimic him flawlessly, inflections and all. Sarkozy's rapid-fire, almost stream-of-consciousness soliloquies covered the waterfront of foreign policy, sometimes making it challenging to get a word in edgewise, but I never tired of trying. He would gossip, casually describing other world leaders as crazy or infirm; one was a "drug-addled maniac"; another had a military "that didn't know how to fight"; yet another came from a long line of "brutes." Sarkozy was forever asking why all the diplomats who came to see him were so unforgivably old, gray, and male. We would laugh, debate, and argue, but most of the time we would end up agreeing on what needed to be done. Sarkozy was intent on reasserting France's place as a top world power and eager to shoulder more of an international burden, which I saw in action in Libya. And despite his exuberance, he was always a gentleman. One chilly day in January 2010, as I was walking up the steps of the Élysée Palace in Paris to greet him, I stepped out of my shoe, leaving me barefoot in front of the press, who gleefully snapped pictures. He gracefully took my hand and helped me regain my footing. Later I sent him a copy of the photograph inscribed, "I may not be Cinderella but you'll always be my Prince Charming."

The most powerful leader in Europe, though, was a woman with a temperament nearly the opposite of Sarkozy's: Chancellor Angela Merkel of Germany. I first met Angela in 1994, during a visit with Bill to Berlin. She came from the former East Germany and was already serving as Minister of Women and Youth under Chancellor Helmut Kohl. When she was introduced to me, she was described as "a young woman who will go far"—words that proved prophetic. She and I stayed in touch over the years, even appearing together on a German television show in 2003. In 2005 she was elected Chancellor, the first woman leader of her country. For all of its vaunted progressivism on matters like health care and climate change, Europe can still feel like the world's most venerable old boys' club, and it was heartening to see Angela shaking things up.

My admiration for Angela grew during my term as Secretary of State.

She was decisive, astute, and straightforward, and she always told me exactly what was on her mind. As an accomplished scientist, having studied physics and earned a doctorate with a dissertation on quantum chemistry, she was particularly knowledgeable on technical issues like climate change and nuclear power. She brought her curiosity about the world to every discussion, armed with questions about events, people, and ideas—a welcome change from some other world leaders who seemed to think they already knew everything worth knowing.

When the Chancellor visited Washington for a state visit in June 2011, I hosted a lunch for her at the State Department and toasted her warmly. In response she presented me with a framed German newspaper covering a recent visit I had made to Berlin. As soon as I saw it, I started to laugh. The front page featured a large photo of the two of us standing side-by-side, but with our heads cropped out. Two sets of hands clasped in front of two similar pantsuits in just the same way. The paper challenged its readers to guess which one was Angela Merkel and which one was me. I had to admit that it was hard to tell. The framed newspaper hung in my office for the remainder of my time as Secretary.

During the worst years of the global financial crisis, Angela's leadership was put to the test. Europe was hit hard by the crash and faced unique challenges because of the single currency shared by many of its nations, the euro. The weakest economies—Greece, Spain, Portugal, Italy, and Ireland—faced staggering public debt, anemic growth, and high unemployment, but they did not have the monetary policy tools at their disposal that come from controlling your own currency. In exchange for emergency help, Germany, the strongest economy in the Eurozone, insisted that these countries take drastic measures to reduce spending and reform their budgets.

The crisis posed a difficult policy dilemma. If these weak economies failed to get out from under their debts, the entire Eurozone might collapse, which would throw the world and our own economy into turmoil. Yet I also worried that too much austerity in Europe would slow growth even further, making it harder for them and the rest of the world to climb out of the hole. In the United States, President Obama responded to the recession by pushing an aggressive investment program through Congress to get growth going again, while working to reduce the national debt over the long term. It was reasonable to suggest that Europe should take similar steps rather than just cutting spending, which would contract the economy even more.

I spent a lot of time talking to European leaders about these challenges, including Merkel. One could agree or not with her fiscal and monetary policies, but it was impossible not to be impressed with her steely determination. As I observed in 2012, she was "carrying Europe on her shoulders."

The strongest link in the transatlantic chain was NATO, the military alliance that included Canada as well as our European partners. (Many Americans may take our relationship with Canada for granted, but our northern neighbor is an indispensable partner in nearly everything we do around the world.) Beginning at the start of the Cold War, NATO succeeded in containing the Soviet Union and Warsaw Pact nations for four decades. After the end of the Cold War, the Alliance prepared for new threats to the security of the transatlantic community. Virtually all of the former Soviet republics, other than Russia itself, felt vulnerable without some security guarantees from the West, given their fear that Russia might someday revert to aggressive, expansionist behavior. Led by the United States, NATO decided to open the door to any of the countries to the East. The Alliance also established a network of partnerships with many former Soviet republics and a consultative council with Russia itself. As the Clinton Administration made clear at the time, NATO, while dealing with new challenges, would still retain what was called a "hedge" capacity should a future Russia once again threaten its neighbors.

While NATO forces were fighting to bring peace to Kosovo, Bill and I celebrated its fiftieth anniversary with a summit of its leaders in April 1999, hosting the largest gathering of heads of state ever to meet in Washington. The meeting marked great optimism about the future for Europe and NATO. Václav Havel, the first post–Cold War President of the Czech Republic and a fierce and compelling democracy advocate, remarked, "This is the first summit of the Alliance that is attended by representatives of . . . countries that were members of the Warsaw Pact no more than ten years ago. . . . Let us hope that we are thus entering a world in which the fates of nations are not decided by powerful foreign dictators but by the nations themselves." If not, he might have added, let us be prepared to defend the freedom we have gained.

In 2004, seven more former Eastern bloc nations joined, expanding NATO's reach even farther. Two more, Albania and Croatia, did so on April 1, 2009, bringing the total membership to twenty-eight. Others, including Ukraine, Bosnia, Moldova, and Georgia, were exploring the possibilities of future European Union and NATO membership.

In the wake of Russia's illegal annexation of Crimea in early 2014, some have argued that NATO expansion either caused or exacerbated Russia's aggression. I disagree with that argument, but the most convincing voices refuting it are those European leaders and people who express their gratitude for NATO membership. It gives them greater confidence about their future in light of the ambitions of Russia's President, Vladimir Putin. They understand that Putin's claim that NATO's open door is a threat to Russia reflects his refusal to accept the idea that Russia's relations with the West could be based on partnership and mutual interests, as Boris Yeltsin and Mikhail Gorbachev believed. Those who give credence to Putin's position should ponder how much more serious the crisis would be—and how much more difficult it would be to contain further Russian aggression if Eastern and Central European nations were not now NATO allies. The NATO door should remain open, and we should be clear and tough-minded in dealing with Russia.

By the time President Obama took office, NATO had become a democratic community of nearly a billion people stretching from the Baltics in the East to Alaska in the West. At my first visit to NATO's Brussels headquarters in March 2009, the hallways resounded with excitement about the "return" of American engagement. I shared the feeling and spent many hours with the NATO Foreign Ministers and NATO's Secretary-General, Anders Fogh Rasmussen, the former Prime Minister of Denmark, the kind of experienced and skillful leader that the Alliance needed.

Sometimes there were growing pains, not all of them serious. Bulgaria, for example, which joined NATO in 2004, was a faithful partner in Afghanistan and other missions. Yet when I visited its capital, Sofia, in February 2012, Prime Minister Boyko Borisov was clearly nervous about our meeting. I knew we had serious matters to discuss and hoped nothing was wrong. After all, we were allies now. "Madam Secretary, I was very worried when I saw television footage of you getting off the plane," he began. "I was briefed by my chief of staff that when your hair is pulled back, it means you're in a bad mood." My hair was in fact pulled back at that very moment (perhaps invoking bad memories of KGB agents and Communist Party apparatchiks). I looked at the mostly bald Prime Minister, smiled, and said, "It just takes me a little longer to do my hair than it takes you." He laughed, and with that out of the way, we went on to have a productive meeting.

The long war in Afghanistan had taxed NATO's capacities and exposed gaps in its preparedness. Some allies were slashing their defense budgets, leaving others (mostly the United States) to pick up the slack. Everyone was suffering from the economic crisis. There were voices on both sides of the Atlantic asking whether NATO was still relevant twenty years after the end of the Cold War.

I thought NATO remained essential for meeting the evolving threats of the 21st century. America can't and shouldn't do everything by ourselves; that's why building partnerships around common interests and goals was so important. NATO was still by far our most capable partner, especially since its members voted to act "out of area" for the first time in Bosnia in 1995, a recognition that our collective security could be threatened beyond direct attacks on NATO countries themselves. And NATO allies sacrificed their blood and treasure in Afghanistan, a commitment we should never forget.

In 2011 we were able to show what a relevant 21st-century NATO looks like as the Alliance took the lead in the military intervention to protect civilians in Libya, working in concert for the first time with the Arab League and its member nations. Fourteen allies and four Arab partners contributed naval and air forces to the mission. Contrary to the views of some critics, this proved to be a successful joint operation. The United States provided unique capabilities but our allies—not us—flew 75 percent of the sorties and were responsible for striking 90 percent of the more than six thousand targets destroyed in Libya. That was a nearly exact reversal of the distribution of labor a decade before, during NATO's intervention in Kosovo, when the United States was responsible for 90 percent of the bombing of air defenses and military targets. And though Britain and France led the way with their capable militaries, the effort extended beyond them. Italy dedicated seven air bases to hosting hundreds of allied jets. Belgian, Canadian, Danish, Dutch, and Norwegian planes, as well as jets from the United Arab Emirates (UAE), Qatar, and Jordan, all contributed to the more than twenty-six thousand sorties. The Greek,

Spanish, Turkish, and Romanian navies helped enforce the arms embargo at sea. It was a true team effort, just as NATO was intended to be.

If NATO is one of the most successful military alliances in history, the European Union (EU) is one of the most successful political and economic organizations. In a remarkably short period of time, countries that had fought two world wars in the 20th century agreed to make decisions by consensus and elect representatives to a shared Parliament. Despite the EU's unwieldy bureaucracy, it is nothing short of miraculous that it exists and persists.

The EU's many contributions to peace and prosperity within and beyond its borders were honored with a Nobel Peace Prize in 2012. Individually and collectively our European partners accomplish so much around the world. Norway is second to none in supporting global public health projects. Ireland, a land once ravaged by famine, leads the way on ending hunger. The Netherlands sets the standard for working on poverty and sustainable development. The Baltic states, Estonia, Latvia, and Lithuania, provide invaluable support and expertise to pro-democracy activists around the world. The Danes, Swedes, and Finns are champions on climate change. The list could go on and on.

I wanted to expand our partnership with the EU, especially on energy and economics. Early on in President Obama's first term, I urged the EU to start the U.S.-EU Energy Council to coordinate transatlantic efforts to help vulnerable countries, particularly in Eastern and Central Europe, develop their own energy resources, where possible, and reduce dependency on Russian gas. The U.S. and EU also began discussing a comprehensive economic agreement that would harmonize regulations, increase trade, and spur growth on both sides of the Atlantic.

———

None of our relationships in Europe needed more tending than Turkey, a country of more than 70 million people, overwhelmingly Muslim, with one foot in Europe and one in Southwest Asia. Modern Turkey, established by Mustafa Kemal Atatürk out of the disintegration of the Ottoman Empire after World War I, was intended to be a secular democracy oriented toward the West. It joined NATO in 1952 and was a reliable ally throughout the Cold War, sending troops to fight alongside ours in Korea and hosting U.S. forces for decades. Yet the Turkish military, which saw itself as the guarantor of Atatürk's vision, intervened a number of times over the years to topple governments it saw as too Islamist, too left-wing, or too weak. Maybe that was good for the Cold War, but it delayed democratic progress.

Unfortunately the Bush years took a toll on our relations, and by 2007 approval of the United States had collapsed to just 9 percent in Turkey, the lowest in any of the forty-seven countries surveyed by the Pew Research Center's Global Attitudes Project that year.

Meanwhile, Turkey's economy was booming, with one of the fastest growth rates in the world. As the rest of Europe staggered under the financial crisis and the Middle East stagnated, Turkey emerged as a regional powerhouse. Like Indonesia, Turkey was testing whether democracy, modernity, women's rights, secularism, and Islam could all coexist, and people across the Middle East were watching. It was strongly in the interest of the United States that this experiment succeed and that relations between our countries get back on firmer footing.

I visited Turkey as part of my first trip to Europe as Secretary. In addition to meetings with top Turkish officials, including Prime Minister Recep Tayyip Erdoğan and President Abdullah Gül, I reached out directly to the Turkish people, as I tried to do everywhere. This was particularly important in countries where governments wanted to work with us but large segments of the population were generally distrustful or anti-American. By taking my case directly to the people, via the mass media, I was trying to influence attitudes, which, in turn, could give governments greater political cover to cooperate with us.

A popular television talk show called *Haydi Gel Bizimle Ol*, or *Come and Join Us*, invited me to appear as a guest. Similar in format to *The View*, it appealed to a wide cross-section of Turkish society, especially women. The hosts, a diverse collection of women, asked me about serious policy issues as well as more personal questions. The discussion was warm, funny, and wide-ranging.

"When was the last time you fell in love and felt like a simple person with a simple life?" one of them wanted to know. This wasn't normal fodder for a Secretary of State, but it was exactly the kind of topic that might help me connect to viewers. I talked about meeting my husband in law school, falling in love, and building a life together, and also about the challenge of raising a family in the public eye. "I think that my favorite times are when my husband and my daughter and I are together and we do simple things," I said. "I mean, we go to the movies, we talk and play games together, card games and board games. We go for long walks. I try to do that every chance I can with my husband. And my daughter is busy with her own life now, but when she can, she joins us. So it's not easy, but I work really hard to find those quiet times when the spotlights aren't on and when you can just be yourself and be with people that you enjoy and love. And those are the best times in life."

The audience in the room warmly applauded, and the feedback collected afterward by our embassy staff was encouraging. For many Turks who had become distrustful of America and its leaders, it apparently was a pleasant surprise to see the U.S. Secretary of State as a normal person with cares and concerns similar to their own. Maybe as a result they'd be more receptive to what I had to say about the future of U.S.-Turkish relations.

One man in particular held the key to the future of Turkey and of our relationship: Prime Minister Erdoğan. (In the Turkish system, the President is largely a ceremonial post and the Prime Minister actually runs the government.) I first met him when he was Mayor of Istanbul in the 1990s. He was an ambitious, forceful, devout, and effective politician. Turks first elected his Islamist Party in 2002 and reelected them in 2007 and 2011. Prime Minister Erdoğan viewed all three elections as mandates for sweeping change. His government aggressively went after alleged coup plotters in the military and managed to gain a tighter grip on power than any of its civilian predecessors. (The term *Islamist* generally refers to people and parties who support a guiding role for Islam in politics and government. It covers a wide spectrum, from those who think Islamic values should inform public policy decisions to those who think all laws should be judged or even formulated by Islamic authorities to conform to Islamic law. Not all Islamists are alike. In some cases, Islamist leaders and organizations have been hostile to democracy, including some who have supported radical, extremist, and terrorist ideology and actions. But around the world, there are political parties with religious affiliations— Hindu, Christian, Jewish, Muslim—that respect the rules of democratic politics, and it is in America's interest to encourage all religiously based political parties and leaders to embrace inclusive democracy and reject violence. Any suggestion that faithful Muslims or people of any faith cannot thrive in a democracy is insulting, dangerous, and wrong. They do it in our own country every day.)

Some of the changes under Erdoğan's leadership were positive. Motivated by the requirements of potential EU membership (which up to now has remained out of reach), Turkey abolished state security courts, reformed the penal code, expanded the right to legal counsel, and eased restrictions on teaching and broadcasting in Kurdish. Erdoğan also announced an intention to pursue a "Zero Problems with Neighbors" foreign policy. The initiative to resolve old regional conflicts and take a more active role in the Middle East was advocated by Ahmet Davutoğlu, one of Erdoğan's advisors who later became Foreign Minister. Zero Problems sounded good, and in many cases it was constructive. But it also made Turkey overeager to accept an inadequate diplomatic agreement with its neighbor, Iran, that would have done little to address the international community's concerns about Tehran's nuclear program.

Despite positive developments under Erdoğan, there was growing cause for concern, even alarm, about his government's treatment of political opponents and journalists. Decreasing room for public dissent raised questions about the direction Erdoğan was taking the country and his commitment to democracy. Opponents were suspicious that his ultimate goal was to turn Turkey into an Islamic state with no room for dissent, and some of his actions gave support to that fear. His government jailed journalists at a troubling rate in his second and third terms and cracked down hard on protesters for questioning certain decrees. Corruption remained a massive problem, and the government was not able to keep up with the rapidly rising expectations of its increasingly worldly and middle-class citizens.

Religious and cultural issues were particularly sensitive in a country where Islam and secularism had lived in uneasy balance and different faith traditions sometimes felt squeezed. Over the years I had gotten to know the Patriarch of the Greek Orthodox Church, His All Holiness Ecumenical Patriarch Bartholomew, and I respected his sincere commitment to interfaith dialogue and religious freedom. Patriarch Bartholomew viewed Erdoğan as a constructive partner, but the Church was still waiting for the government to return seized Church property and allow the long-shuttered Halki Seminary to reopen. I supported the Patriarch's goal and made a number of runs at getting Halki reopened, which sadly hasn't happened yet.

When Erdoğan talked about giving women students the right to wear head scarves at university, some saw it as a step forward for religious freedom and a woman's right to choose her own course. Others saw it as a blow to secularism, a sign of creeping theocracy that would ultimately curtail women's rights. It speaks to the deep contradictions in 21st-century Turkey that both views may be correct. Erdoğan himself was very proud of his own accomplished daughters, who wore veils, and he asked my advice about one of them pursuing graduate studies in the United States.

I spent hours talking with Erdoğan, often accompanied only by Davutoğlu, who served as our interpreter. Davutoğlu is an exuberant academic turned diplomat and politician, and his writings about how Turkey could regain a position of global importance dovetailed with Erdoğan's own thoughts. He brought passion and erudition to his position, and we developed a productive and friendly working relationship that, though strained numerous times, never ruptured.

In my four years as Secretary, Turkey proved to be an important and at times frustrating partner. Sometimes we agreed (working closely together on Afghanistan, counterterrorism, Syria, and other issues), and other times we did not (Iran's nuclear program).

Time and attention from both President Obama and me helped stabilize our relationship, but external events, especially heightened tensions with Israel, presented new challenges. And Turkey's internal dynamics continued to roil. Large protests against Erdoğan's increasingly heavy-handed rule erupted in 2013, followed by a wide-ranging corruption investigation that ensnared a number of his senior Ministers. As of this writing, despite his increasing authoritarianism, Erdoğan's support in more conservative areas of Turkey remains strong. Turkey's future direction is uncertain. But what is certain is that Turkey will continue to play a significant role in both the Middle East and Europe. And our relationship will remain of vital importance to the United States.

A Zero Problems foreign policy was an ambitious goal, especially because Turkey was entangled in a number of long-running disputes with its neighbors. There was the bitter standoff with Greece over the Mediterranean island nation of Cyprus that had dragged on for decades. There was also the emotionally charged conflict with Armenia, a small, landlocked former Soviet republic in the Caucasus to Turkey's east. These were both examples of how old enmities could hold back new progress.

Turkey and Armenia never established official diplomatic relations when Armenia emerged as an independent nation after the breakup of the Soviet Union. Tensions were further heightened by Armenia's war in the early 1990s with Turkey's ally Azerbaijan over a contested strip of land called Nagorno-Karabakh. That dispute still occasionally flares into hostilities between soldiers on both sides of the border.

Disputes such as Turkey-Armenia and Nagorno-Karabakh are sometimes called "frozen conflicts" because they have been going on for years with little hope of resolution. When I looked at all the challenges we faced in Europe and around the world, it was tempting to just ignore these trouble spots as insoluble. But they each had broader strategic consequences. For example, conflict in the Caucasus posed problems for our plans for piping Central Asian natural gas to European markets to lessen their dependence on Russian energy. Collectively these conflicts represented obstacles to the Europe we were trying to help build. I thought Turkey's Zero Problems strategy might create an opening to negotiate—and perhaps even resolve—some of these frozen conflicts, so I asked my Assistant Secretary for European and Eurasian Affairs Phil Gordon to see what we could do.

Throughout 2009 we worked closely with European partners, including Switzerland, France, Russia, and the EU, to support negotiations between Turkey and Armenia, which we hoped would lead to establishing formal diplomatic relations and opening the border to trade. I spoke on the phone with officials from both countries nearly thirty times in my first several months on the job and conferred in person with Davutoğlu and the Armenian Foreign Minister Edward Nalbandian.

Hard-liners in both countries were implacably opposed to compromise and put considerable pressure on each government not to make a deal. Yet over the spring and summer, thanks largely to the efforts of the Swiss, the terms of an agreement that would jointly open the border were coming into focus. Plans were made for a formal signing ceremony in Switzerland in October, after which the agreement would be submitted to both countries' Parliaments for ratification. As the date approached, we stepped up our encouragement, including a call from President Obama to the President of Armenia. Everything seemed to be falling into place.

On October 9, I flew to Zurich to witness the accord signing alongside the Foreign Ministers of France, Russia, and Switzerland and the EU High Representative. The next afternoon I left my hotel and headed to the University of Zurich for the ceremony. But there was a problem. Nalbandian, the Armenian Minister, was balking. He was worried about what Davutoğlu planned to say at the signing and suddenly was refusing to leave the hotel. It seemed as if months of careful negotiations might fall apart. My motorcade turned around and raced back to Zurich's Dolder Grand Hotel. While I waited in the car, Phil Gordon went upstairs along with the lead Swiss negotiator to find Nalbandian and take him to the signing ceremony. But he wouldn't budge. Phil came back downstairs to report and joined me in the car, which was now parked behind the hotel. I started working the phones. On one cell I dialed Nalbandian, and I got Davutoğlu on a second line. We went back and forth for an hour, trying to bridge the gap and coax Nalbandian out of his room. "This is too important, this has to be seen through, we have come too far," I told them.

Finally I went upstairs to talk to Nalbandian in person. What if we simply canceled the speaking portion of the event? Sign the document, make no statements, and leave. Both sides agreed, and Nalbandian at last emerged. We walked downstairs, and he got in my sedan to drive to the university. It took another hour and a half of hand-holding and arm-twisting at the site to get them to actually walk onstage. We were three hours late, but at least we were there. We held the expedited signing ceremony, and then, with a huge sense of relief, everyone left as fast as they could. To date, neither country has ratified the protocols, and the process remains stalled; however, at a December 2013 conference, the Turkish and Armenian Foreign Ministers met for two hours to discuss how to move forward, and I still hope for a breakthrough.

On my way to the airport after the signing, President Obama called to offer his congratulations. It hadn't been pretty, but we'd taken a step forward for a sensitive region. Later the *New York Times* described my efforts that afternoon as "down-to-the-wire, limousine diplomacy." My car wasn't a limousine, but apart from that, it was an apt description.

═══

The Balkan wars of the 1990s provide a searing reminder that old hatreds in Europe can erupt into new and devastating violence.

When I visited Bosnia in October 2010 as part of a three-day trip through the Balkans, I was both pleased by the progress I saw and sobered by how much there still was to do. Children could now go to school in safety and parents could go to work, but there weren't enough good jobs, and economic hardship and discontent simmered. The virulent ethnic and religious hatreds that fueled the wars had cooled, but dangerous currents of sectarianism and nationalism persisted. The country was a federation of two republics, one dominated by Bosnian Muslims and Croats, the other dominated by Bosnian Serbs. The Bosnian Serbs thwarted all attempts to remove roadblocks to growth and good governance, in the stubborn hope that they could one day become a part of Serbia or even an independent country. The promise of greater stability and opportunity represented by integration into the EU or NATO remained out of reach.

In Sarajevo I participated in an open discussion with students and civil society leaders at the historic National Theater, which had escaped serious damage in the war. One young man rose to speak about his visit to the United States as part of an exchange program sponsored by the State Department and hosted by American colleges and universities. He called it "easily one of the best experiences" of his life and implored me to keep supporting and expanding academic exchanges. When I asked him to elaborate on why he thought it was so important, he said, "The main thing that we learned was to choose tolerance over intolerance, to work with each other to respect everyone equally. . . . We had participants from Kosovo and from Serbia at the same time, and they didn't care about the issues that their countries are going through because they realized . . . we are friends, we can have a dialogue, we can interact together; it's not a problem if you really want to do it." I loved the simple phrase "choose tolerance over intolerance." It captured perfectly the transition the people of the Balkans were still making. It was the only way to heal their—or any—old wounds.

Next it was on to Kosovo. In the 1990s, Kosovo was part of Serbia, and its majority–ethnic Albanian population faced brutal attacks and forced expulsion by Milošević's forces. In 1999, a U.S.-led NATO air campaign bombed Serbian troops and cities, including Belgrade, to stop the ethnic cleansing. In 2008, Kosovo declared its independence and was recognized as a new nation by much of the international community. But Serbia refused to recognize Kosovo's independence and continued to exert significant influence in the northern border region, where many ethnic Serbs lived. The majority of hospitals, schools, and even courts there continued to be run and financed from Belgrade, and Serbian security forces provided protection, all of which undermined Kosovo's sovereignty, exacerbated the country's internal divisions, and strained relations between the two neighbors. The tense situation was getting in the way of the economic and social progress both countries needed to make on their own, including moving toward EU membership. But old histories and hatreds were proving difficult to transcend. One goal of my visit was to nudge both sides toward a resolution.

When I arrived in Pristina, Kosovo's capital, enthusiastic crowds waving American flags lined the road from the airport, cheering as our motorcade passed, often with children sitting on adults' shoulders so they could see. By the time we reached the plaza in town, which features a monumental statue of Bill, the crowds were so dense our motorcade had to stop. I was glad it did; I wanted to say hello. So I jumped out and started shaking hands and hugging and being hugged. Across the plaza was an adorable little clothing boutique with a familiar name: Hillary. I couldn't resist a quick visit. The shopkeeper said they named the store after me "so that Bill wouldn't be lonely in the square."

A few months later, in March 2011, representatives from Kosovo and Serbia sat down together in Brussels under the auspices of the European Union. It was the first time they had ever talked directly and at length with each other in this way. American diplomats were present for every meeting, urging both sides to make the compromises that could lead to normalized relations and open the door to eventual EU membership. That was possible only if the border issues were resolved. The talks continued for eighteen months. Negotiators reached modest agreements on freedom of movement, customs, and border management. While Serbia still wouldn't recognize Kosovo's independence, it dropped its objections to Kosovo's participating in regional conferences. At the same time, I was urging NATO to continue its military mission in Kosovo, where around five thousand peace-supporting troops from thirty-one countries have remained since June 1999.

The main issues remained unresolved when a new nationalist government was elected in Serbia in the spring of 2012. Cathy Ashton, the EU's top foreign policy official (its first High Representative for Foreign Affairs and Security Policy), and I decided to travel together to both countries to see if we could break the impasse and speed a final settlement.

Cathy was an invaluable partner on this and many other issues. In Britain she had served as leader of the House of Lords and Lord President of the Council under Prime Minister Gordon Brown. Then, following a year as the European Commissioner of Trade, she was selected for the EU foreign affairs position—a bit of a surprise because, like me, she was not a traditional career diplomat, but she turned out to be an effective and creative partner. Down-to-earth (especially for a Baroness, I would kid her), she was easy to get along with, and we worked closely together not only on European issues but also on Iran and the Middle East. We'd also catch each other's attention in a large meeting when one of our male colleagues unintentionally, even unconsciously, slipped in a sexist remark, and we slowly roll our eyes together.

In October 2012, we made the rounds in the Balkans together. We urged each country to advance concrete measures to normalize relations. Kosovar Prime Minister Hashim Thaçi told us, "Today Kosovo is still not the Kosovo of our dreams. We are persistently working for a European Kosovo, for a Euro-Atlantic Kosovo. We are conscious that we need to do more." Cathy and I also met with representatives of the ethnic Serbian minority at a Serbian Orthodox church in Pristina, which had been torched during anti-Serb riots in 2004. They worried about their future in an independent Kosovo. They were grateful for recent efforts by the government to be more inclusive and to offer jobs to ethnic Serbs. That was the kind of grassroots reconciliation that we wanted to promote. Kosovo's impressive female Muslim President, Atifete Jahjaga, was our ally in pushing for change and reconciliation inside her country. As Cathy put it, this diplomacy was not just about normalizing relations between countries; it was about "normalizing life so that the people who live in the north can go about their daily lives feeling part of a community."

In April 2013, thanks to Cathy's continued hard work building on the foundation we had laid together, Kosovo's Prime Minister Thaçi and Serbia's Prime Minister Ivica Dačić reached a landmark agreement to resolve the disputes along their border, move toward normalization, and open the door to EU membership. Kosovo agreed to give more autonomy to local Serbian communities in the north, and Serbia agreed to pull back its forces. Both sides pledged not to interfere in the other's quest for greater European integration. If they proceed to implement the agreements, the people of Kosovo and Serbia finally have a chance to build the peaceful, prosperous future they deserve.

My final trip as Secretary of State in December 2012 brought me again to
Northern Ireland, a place where people have worked hard and suffered
much to leave their past conflicts behind. They would be the first to tell
you, from both sides of their Catholic-Protestant sectarian divide, that
their work is far from over and that their biggest challenge is stimulating enough economic activity to create inclusive prosperity that benefits
each community. Still, at a luncheon in Belfast, happily surrounded by
old friends and acquaintances, we reminisced about how far we'd come
together.

When Bill was first elected President, the Troubles in Northern Ireland had been raging for decades. Most Protestants wanted to remain
part of the United Kingdom, while most Catholics wanted to join with
the Republic of Ireland to the south, and long years of violence had left
both sides embittered and dug in. Northern Ireland was an island within
an island. Street by street, the old touchstones of identity loomed large—
which church a family went to, which school the children attended, which
soccer jersey they wore, which street they walked down, at which hour
of the day, with which friends. Everybody noticed everything. And that
was on a normal day.

In 1995, Bill appointed former Senator George Mitchell as Special
Envoy for Northern Ireland. Bill became the first U.S. President to visit
Northern Ireland when he and I traveled to Belfast later that year, and
turned on the lights of Belfast's Christmas tree in front of a vast crowd.

I returned to Northern Ireland nearly every year for the rest of the
decade and stayed actively involved as a Senator in the years that followed. In 1998 I helped organize the Vital Voices Conference of women
in Belfast who were pressing for a peace agreement. Their whispers of
"Enough!" had become a rallying cry that could no longer be ignored.
As I spoke from the podium, I looked up and saw Gerry Adams, Martin
McGuinness, and other leaders of Sinn Féin, the political wing of the Irish
Republican Army, sitting in the front row of the balcony. Behind them I
saw leading Unionists who refused to talk with Sinn Féin. The fact that
they were both there—at a women's conference for peace—exemplified
their openness to compromise.

The Good Friday Agreement, which was signed that year and put
Northern Ireland on the path toward peace, was a triumph of diplomacy,

especially for Bill and George Mitchell, who did so much to bring the parties together. Most of all, though, it was a testament to the courage of the people of Northern Ireland. It felt like one of those moments when "hope and history rhyme," in the words of the great Irish poet Seamus Heaney. Implementation would be bumpy, but peace began to bring benefits. Unemployment fell, home values rose, and the number of American companies investing in Northern Ireland increased.

By the time I returned as Secretary of State in 2009, the global financial crisis had taken a heavy toll on the celebrated "Celtic Tiger." Roadblocks and barbed wire were gone from the streets, but the process of disarmament and "devolution," which was supposed to grant increasing autonomy to Northern Ireland, was in danger of stalling. Many Catholics and Protestants still lived segregated lives, in separate neighborhoods, some still divided by actual walls—which had the Orwellian name "peace walls."

In March 2009, two British soldiers were killed in County Antrim and a policeman was killed in County Armagh. Rather than sparking violence, the murders had the opposite effect. Catholics and Protestants marched together in vigils, attended interfaith services, and declared with one voice their refusal to go back to the old ways. The killings could have been the start of a backward slide. Instead they proved how far Northern Ireland had come. On a visit in October 2009 and in frequent phone calls to Northern Ireland's First Minister Peter Robinson, Deputy First Minister Martin McGuinness, and other leaders, I urged them to continue disarmament by paramilitary groups and take the final steps of devolution, especially on putting the vital areas of policing and justice under the control of the Northern Irish government.

Addressing a full session of the Northern Ireland Assembly, I reminded them, "There have been many moments in Northern Ireland's peace journey when progress seemed difficult, when every route forward was blocked, and there seemed to be nowhere to go. But you have always found a way to do what you believed was right for the people of Northern Ireland." Because of this perseverance, "Northern Ireland stands as an example to the world of how even the staunchest adversaries can overcome differences to work together for the common and greater good. So I encourage you to move forward now with that same spirit of unstoppable grit and resolve. And I pledge that the United States will be behind you all the way, as you work toward peace and stability that lasts."

Just weeks after my visit, a car bomb seriously injured another police-man, and it again seemed as if the carefully stitched fabric of peace might unravel. But once again it held. In February 2010, the parties reached a new deal on policing powers, called the Hillsborough Agreement. Prog-ress toward a lasting peace was back on track, despite the best efforts of extremists on both sides to derail the process. In June 2012, we saw the most remarkable sign of change yet: Queen Elizabeth visited Northern Ireland and shook hands with Martin McGuinness. It was a gesture that would have been unimaginable just a few years before.

In December 2012, seventeen years since my first visit to Belfast, I was back there and I ran into an old friend, Sharon Haughey. In 1995, when she was just fourteen years old, she sent Bill a deeply moving letter about the future she dreamed of for herself and for Northern Ireland. He read an excerpt at the Christmas tree lighting in Belfast. "Both sides have been hurt. Both sides will have to forgive," she wrote. When Sharon got a little older, she worked as an intern in my Senate office, helping serve New York, with its large and proud Irish American community. She learned a lot in Washington, and when she went home she ran for office and was elected Lord Mayor of Armagh. When she showed up at that lunch in 2012, she was wearing her ceremonial chain of office and told me she had plans to be married later that month. I thought about the family Sharon would start and about all the children growing up in Northern Ireland after the Good Friday Agreement. They had a chance at lives uncolored by the pain of the Troubles. I hoped they would never turn back and that their peace and progress would be an inspiration for the rest of Europe and the world.

11

Russia: Reset and Regression

Hard men present hard choices—none more so than Vladimir Putin, the President of Russia. Putin's worldview is shaped by his admiration for the powerful czars of Russian history, Russia's long-standing interest in controlling the nations on its borders, and his personal determination that his country never again appear weak or at the mercy of the West, as he believes it was after the collapse of the Soviet Union. He wants to reassert Russia's power by dominating its neighbors and controlling their access to energy. He also wants to play a larger role in the Middle East to increase Moscow's influence in that region and reduce the threat from restive Muslims within and beyond Russia's southern borders. To achieve these goals, he seeks to reduce the influence of the United States in Central and Eastern Europe and other areas that he considers part of Russia's sphere, and to counter or at least mute our efforts in the countries roiled by the Arab Spring.

All of that helps explain why Putin first pressured Ukrainian President Viktor Yanukovych to walk away from closer ties with the European Union in late 2013, and why, after Yanukovych's government disintegrated, Putin invaded and annexed Crimea. If Putin is restrained and doesn't push beyond Crimea into eastern Ukraine, it will not be because he has lost his appetite for more power, territory, and influence.

Putin sees geopolitics as a zero-sum game in which, if someone is winning, then someone else has to be losing. That's an outdated but still dan-

gerous concept, one that requires the United States to show both strength
and patience. To manage our relationship with the Russians, we should
work with them on specific issues when possible, and rally other nations
to work with us to prevent or limit their negative behavior when needed.
That's a difficult but essential balance to strike, as I found over my four
years as Secretary.

Winston Churchill observed, "In a true unity of Europe, Russia must
have her part," and in 1991, when the Soviet Union collapsed, there was
great hope that it would happen. I remember the thrill of watching Boris
Yeltsin standing on a tank in Moscow as he turned back a coup by old
Soviet hard-liners that threatened Russia's new democracy. Yeltsin was
willing to quit pointing nuclear weapons toward American cities, destroy
fifty tons of plutonium, and sign a cooperation pact with NATO. But he
faced stiff opposition to his policies at home from those who wanted to
keep their distance from Europe and the United States, keep as much
control over their neighbors as possible, and keep the unruly force of
Russian democracy at bay.

After Yeltsin underwent heart surgery in 1996, he never regained
the energy and powers of concentration required to manage the unruly
Russian political system. He unexpectedly retired on New Year's Eve in
1999, six months before his term expired, clearing the way for his chosen
successor, a little-known former KGB officer from St. Petersburg named
Vladimir Putin.

Most people assumed that Putin was chosen because he would be loyal,
protecting Yeltsin and his family, and because he would govern more
vigorously than Yeltsin had. He was disciplined and fit, a practitioner
of judo, and he inspired hope and confidence among Russians still reeling from so much political change and economic adversity. But he also
proved over time to be thin-skinned and autocratic, resenting criticism
and eventually cracking down on dissent and debate, including from a
free press and NGOs.

In June 2001, when President Bush met Putin for the first time, he
famously said, "I was able to get a sense of his soul." The two leaders made
common cause in the "Global War on Terror," as Putin found it useful
to align his brutal campaign in the restive Muslim-majority republic of

Chechnya with America's fight against al Qaeda. But it didn't take long for relations to sour. The Iraq War, Putin's increasingly authoritarian behavior at home, and Russia's invasion of Georgia in August 2008 increased tension.

As Russia's economy grew, driven by oil and gas revenues, Putin allowed the wealth to concentrate in the hands of politically connected oligarchs rather than investing broadly in the talents of the Russian people and the country's infrastructure. He pursued an aggressive vision of a "Greater Russia" that unnerved his neighbors and conjured up bad memories of Soviet expansionism. And he used Russia's natural gas exports to intimidate Ukrainians and others in January 2006 and again in January 2009 by cutting off supplies and raising prices.

Among the most egregious developments in the new Russia were the attacks on the press. Newspapers, television stations, and bloggers faced intense pressure to toe the Kremlin line. Since 2000, Russia has been the fourth most dangerous place in the world to be a journalist—not as bad as Iraq but worse than Somalia or Pakistan. Between 2000 and 2009 nearly twenty journalists were killed in Russia, and in only one case was the killer convicted.

When I visited Moscow in October 2009, I thought it important to speak out in support of press freedoms and against the official campaign of intimidation. At a reception at Spaso House, the stately home of American Ambassadors to Russia since 1933, I met with journalists, lawyers, and other civil society leaders, including one activist who told me that he had been badly beaten by unidentified thugs. These Russians had seen friends and colleagues harassed, intimidated, even killed, yet they went on working, writing, and speaking, refusing to be silenced. I assured them that the United States would publicly and privately raise human rights concerns with the Russian government.

Where you say something can be as important as what you say. I could talk with activists in Spaso House all I wanted, but most Russians would never hear my words. So I asked the embassy if they could find an independent broadcaster who would host me. One possibility, a radio station called Ekho Moskvy, or "Echo of Moscow," sounded more like an awkwardly named propaganda outlet than a bastion of a free press. But our diplomats on the ground assured me that the station was one of the most independent, fair-minded, and hard-hitting in Russia.

In my live interview, I was asked about some of the pressing issues in the U.S.-Russia relationship, including Georgia and Iran, and then we turned to the question of human rights inside Russia. "I have no doubt in my mind that democracy is in Russia's best interests," I said, "and that respecting human rights, an independent judiciary, a free media are in the interests of building a strong, stable political system that provides a platform for broadly shared prosperity. We will continue to say that and we will continue to support those who also stand for those values." We talked about the imprisonment, beatings, and killings of journalists. "I think people want their government to stand up and say this is wrong, and they're going to try to prevent it and they're going to make sure the people are brought to justice who are engaged in such behavior," I said. The station remains on the air and continues to maintain its independence. Unfortunately, during the crackdown on dissent surrounding the invasion of Crimea in 2014, the radio station's website was temporarily blocked. It appears the Kremlin is moving to further stamp out all dissenting voices.

=====

After eight years as President, Putin faced constitutionally mandated term limits, leading him in 2008 to swap jobs with his Prime Minister, Dmitry Medvedev. At first the switch seemed like a farce, a way for Putin to keep a hold on power from a different perch, and there was certainly an element of that. But Medvedev surprised many by bringing a new tone to the Kremlin. He seemed more open to dissenting views at home, more conciliatory abroad, and more interested in diversifying Russia's economy beyond oil, gas, and other commodities.

I came into office skeptical of Russia's leadership duet but hopeful that we could find areas where we could work together. As a Senator I had been a frequent critic of Putin's rule, but I knew it was counterproductive for us to see Russia only as a threat when there were issues we needed to pursue with them.

The question of nations working together on some issues while clashing on others is part of a classic debate within foreign policy circles. Should the United States stop negotiating on arms control or trade because we objected to Russia's aggression in Georgia? Or should issues proceed on parallel tracks? Straight up transactional diplomacy isn't always pretty, but often it's necessary.

In 2009, President Obama and I thought we could achieve key U.S.

national interests with Russia through an approach with three elements: finding specific areas for cooperation where our interests aligned, standing firm where our interests diverged, and engaging consistently with the Russian people themselves. This approach became known as "the reset."

As we formulated this approach at State, Bill Burns, who had served three years as U.S. Ambassador to Russia, led our planning, offering insights into the opaque machinations of the Kremlin's personalities. Medvedev was a young leader who had come to power without excessive Cold War baggage. Putin, by contrast, had cut his teeth in the KGB in the 1970s and 1980s, the ultimate Cold War résumé. In my view, despite the office shuffle, Putin remained a formidable power who would make attempts at expanding cooperation more difficult. If there were opportunities to do so—and I thought there were—it would be because both sides made a clear-eyed assessment of shared interests.

My first meeting with Russian Foreign Minister Sergey Lavrov was in March 2009. Richard Holbrooke, who had known him when they both served as Ambassadors at the UN in the late 1990s, told me Lavrov was the consummate diplomat, serving his masters in Moscow with intellect, energy, and no small amount of arrogance. (Coming from Richard, that was really saying something!) Lavrov, perpetually tanned and well-tailored, spoke fluent English and had a taste for fine whiskey and the poetry of Pushkin. He had a turbulent relationship with my predecessor, Condoleezza Rice, especially (and for good reason) after Russia invaded Georgia. Those tensions had not disappeared, but if we wanted progress on nuclear arms control, sanctions on Iran, or access to Afghanistan's northern border, we needed to cooperate. Perhaps a joke could break the ice.

In politics a sense of humor is essential. There are countless reasons why you have to be able to laugh at yourself. How many times, as Senator from New York, did I go on David Letterman's show to deliver a pantsuit joke? (The answer is three.) During the 2008 campaign I made a surprise appearance on *Saturday Night Live* alongside Amy Poehler, who had perfected a hilarious "Hillary Clinton" with a memorably boisterous laugh. In diplomacy, with its carefully scripted conversations across language and cultural divides, there's less room for humor. But occasionally it comes in handy. This felt like one of those times.

In a speech at the Munich Security Conference in February, Vice President Biden had said, "It is time to press the reset button and to revisit the many areas where we can and should be working together with Russia." I liked the idea of a "reset"—not as a way of ignoring our real disagreements but to embed them in a broader agenda alongside areas of common interest. Talking it over with my team in the run-up to meeting Lavrov in Geneva, Switzerland, we hit on an idea. Why not present Lavrov with an actual reset button? It might get people laughing—including Lavrov—and ensure that our commitment to a fresh start, not our disagreements, made the headlines. A little unconventional, maybe, but worth a try.

Lavrov and I met in the InterContinental Hotel's Salon Panorama, named for its panoramic view of Geneva. Before we sat down, I presented him with a small green box, complete with a ribbon. While the cameras snapped away, I opened it and pulled out a bright red button on a yellow base that had been pulled off the whirlpool in the hotel. It was labeled with the Russian word *peregruzka*. We both laughed and pushed the button together. "We worked hard to get the right Russian word. Do you think we got it?" I asked. The Foreign Minister took a closer look. The other Americans in the room, especially the Russian-speaking ones who had chosen the word, held their breath. "You got it wrong," he said. Was this light moment about to become an international incident? I just kept laughing. Then so did Lavrov, and everyone relaxed. "It should be *perezagruzka*," he explained. "This means overcharged." "Well," I responded, "we won't let you do that to us, I promise."

It was not the finest hour for American linguistic skills. But if our goal had been to break the ice and make sure no one would ever forget the "reset," then our translation error had certainly done that. Lavrov said he would take the button home and keep it on his desk. Later that night, Philippe Reines, who had helped dream up the joke in the first place, made a last-ditch effort to correct the spelling error. He approached the Russian Ambassador to Switzerland, who was holding the button, and asked to replace the label. "I don't think I can do that until I talk with my minister," the cautious Ambassador replied. "Well, if your minister doesn't give that back to us, my minister is going to send me to Siberia!" Philippe exclaimed. I must admit, it was a tempting thought.

At President Obama's first meeting with Medvedev, in London in April 2009, the American and Russian delegations faced each other across the formal dining table at Winfield House, the residence of our U.S. Ambassador. I was the only woman on either side of the table. This was President Obama's first overseas trip since taking office, a strategic swing through Europe to attend a G-20 meeting, a NATO summit, and visits to key allies, and I was glad to be by his side. Our time on the road together over the years, from that first visit to London all the way to our historic final trip to Burma in late 2012, gave us a chance to consult and strategize far away from the daily hubbub of Washington. Before one of our meetings in Prague, on that same April trip, he pulled me aside and said, "Hillary, I need to talk to you." He put his arm around me and walked me over toward a window. I wondered what sensitive policy matter he wanted to discuss. Instead he whispered in my ear, "You've got something in your teeth." It was embarrassing, to be sure, but also the kind of thing only a friend would say and a sign that we were going to have each other's backs.

During that first meeting with the Russians, the two Presidents broached the idea of a new treaty to cut the number of nuclear weapons on both sides and managed to find common ground on Afghanistan, terrorism, trade, and even Iran, despite disagreements on missile defense and Georgia. Medvedev said that Russia's experience in Afghanistan in the 1980s had been "pitiful" and that they were willing to allow the United States to transport lethal cargo across their territory to supply our troops. That was important because it would give us leverage with Pakistan, which otherwise controlled the only route for troops and equipment into Afghanistan. Medvedev also acknowledged, to my surprise, that Russia had underestimated Iran's growing nuclear capacity. "Turns out you were right," he said. Russia had a complicated relationship with Iran. It was selling Tehran weapons and even helping it build a nuclear power plant, but the Russians did not want to see nuclear proliferation or instability on their already volatile southern flank. As you'll read later, Medvedev's comment opened a door for stronger cooperation on Iran and eventually led to a landmark vote at the UN to impose tough new sanctions. He did not, however, alter his opposition to our plans for missile defense in Europe, despite the fact that, as we said many times, it was designed to protect against potential threats from Iran rather than from Russia.

President Obama emphasized the positive and promised a quick follow-up on a new nuclear arms treaty, as well as deeper cooperation regarding Afghanistan, terrorism, and Russia's entry into the World Trade Organization. All in all, it was a thorough, candid discussion of difficult issues—what we came to expect from Medvedev. The reset seemed to be on track.

A team of State Department negotiators, led by Under Secretary Ellen Tauscher and Assistant Secretary Rose Gottemoeller, worked for a year with their Russian counterparts to iron out every detail of the New Strategic Arms Reduction Treaty, or New START, which set limits on numbers of Russian and American nuclear warheads on missiles and bombers. After President Obama and Medvedev signed the treaty in April 2010, I began making the case to persuade my former Senate colleagues to ratify it, working closely with my Assistant Secretary for Legislative Affairs Rich Verma, a longtime aide to Senate Majority Leader Harry Reid and an astute student of Capitol Hill's often impenetrable ways. I called key Senate Republicans, who told me they didn't trust the Russians and worried the United States would not be able to verify compliance. I explained that the treaty gave us mechanisms to do just that and if the Russians didn't live up to their word, we could always withdraw. I reminded them that even President Reagan, with his philosophy of "trust but verify," had signed disarmament agreements with the Soviets. And I stressed that time was of the essence; the old START had expired, so for nearly a year we hadn't had any weapons inspectors on the ground in Russia checking what was happening in their missile silos. That was a dangerous lapse we couldn't let continue.

In the weeks leading up to the vote, I spoke with eighteen Senators, nearly all of them Republicans. As Secretary of State I worked with Congress on many matters, especially the Department's budget, but this was my first experience twisting arms on behalf of the White House since leaving the Senate myself. It was helpful to call on my relationships with former colleagues built over eight years of reaching across the aisle to write legislation and consult on committees. We also had on our side a master Senate operator, Vice President Biden, and the bipartisan tag-team at the helm of the Senate Foreign Relations Committee, Chairman John Kerry of Massachusetts and Ranking Member Richard Lugar of Indiana.

We kept getting closer to the two-thirds majority of the Senate required under the Constitution to ratify a treaty, but the final votes were hard to find. Our prospects dimmed after the midterm elections in November 2010, when Republicans took control of the House, winning sixty-three more seats, and narrowed the Democratic majority in the Senate, picking up six seats. Despite that setback, Senator Lugar urged me to come up to the Hill in person to make the final sale. With the outlook for passage grim, I kept working the phones and visited the Capitol again just before Christmas to make a final appeal. That night the Senate voted successfully to end debate, and the next day the treaty passed 71 to 26. It was a victory for bipartisanship, U.S.-Russia relations, and a safer world.

Over time, President Obama and President Medvedev developed a personal relationship that offered further opportunities for cooperation. At a long meeting I had with Medvedev outside Moscow in October 2009, he raised his plan to build a high-tech corridor in Russia modeled after our own Silicon Valley. When I suggested that he visit the original in California, he turned to his staff and told them to follow up. He included a stop there on his 2010 visit to the United States, and, by all accounts, was impressed with what he saw. That could have been the start of realizing Medvedev's vision for a diversified Russian economy—if Putin had permitted it.

The reset led to a number of early successes, including imposing strong sanctions on Iran and North Korea, opening a northern supply route to equip our troops in Afghanistan, bringing Russia into the World Trade Organization, winning UN backing for the no-fly zone in Libya, and expanding counterterrorism cooperation. But the tone began to shift in late 2011. In September Medvedev announced that he would not run for reelection; instead Putin would reclaim his old job in 2012. This shuffle confirmed what I had said four years before: that Medvedev was just keeping Putin's chair warm.

Then, in December, Russia's Parliamentary elections were marred by widespread reports of fraud. Independent political parties were denied the right to register, and there were reported attempts to stuff ballot boxes, manipulate voter lists, and other blatant irregularities. Independent Russian election observers were harassed, and their websites faced cyber attacks. At an international conference in Lithuania, I expressed serious concerns about these reports. "The Russian people, like people everywhere, deserve the right to have their voices heard and their votes counted," I said, "and that means they deserve fair, free, transparent elections and leaders who are accountable to them." Tens of thousands of Russian citizens reached the same conclusion and took to the streets to protest. When chants of "Putin is a thief" filled the air, Putin lashed out—directly at me. "She set the tone for some actors in our country and gave them a signal," he claimed. If only I had such power! The next time

I saw President Putin, I chided him about his remarks: "I can just see people in Moscow waking up and saying Hillary Clinton wants us to go demonstrate. That's not how it works, Mr. President." Still, if I had helped even a few people find the courage to speak out for real democracy, then it was all to the good.

In May 2012, Putin formally reclaimed the title of President and shortly afterward declined President Obama's invitation to a G-8 summit at Camp David. A cool wind was blowing from the east. In June, I sent a memo to President Obama outlining my views. He was no longer dealing with Medvedev and needed to be ready to take a harder line. Putin was "deeply resentful of the U.S. and suspicious of our actions," I argued, and intent on reclaiming lost Russian influence in its neighborhood, from Eastern Europe to Central Asia. He might call his project "regional integration," but that was code for rebuilding a lost empire. I was with President Obama when he sat down with Putin for the first time as two heads of state on the sidelines of a G-20 meeting in Los Cabos, Mexico. "Bargain hard," I advised, because Putin will "give no gifts."

Russia soon took a less constructive approach on many key issues, especially the conflict in Syria, where it propped up the Assad regime in its brutal war and blocked all attempts at the United Nations to organize a strong international response. The Kremlin cracked down hard on dissidents, NGOs, and LGBT citizens at home and went back to bullying its neighbors.

For those who expected the reset to open a new era of goodwill between Russia and the United States, it proved to be a bitter disappointment. For those of us who had more modest expectations—that de-linking tough issues and toning down rhetoric on both sides could create space for progress on specific priorities—the reset delivered. Later, after the invasion of Crimea in 2014, some in Congress blamed the reset for emboldening Putin. I think this view misunderstands both Putin and the reset. After all, he had invaded Georgia in 2008 and faced few consequences, from the United States or others. Putin invaded Georgia and Crimea for his own reasons, on his own timetable, in response to events on the ground. Neither the Bush Administration's tough rhetoric and doctrine of preemptive war nor the Obama Administration's focus on pragmatic cooperation on core interests deterred or invited these acts of aggression. The reset was not a reward; it was a recognition that America has many important strategic and security interests, and we need to make progress where we can. That remains true today.

═════

To understand the complexities of our relationship with Russia during the reset and what we were trying to achieve, consider just one example: Central Asia and the challenge of supplying our troops in Afghanistan.

In the aftermath of 9/11, as the United States prepared to invade Afghanistan, the Bush Administration leased former Soviet air bases in two remote but strategically located Central Asian countries, Uzbekistan and Kyrgyzstan. They were used to fly soldiers and supplies into the Afghan theater. Given the extraordinary international dynamics at the time, Russia did not object, despite the fact that it viewed these underdeveloped former Soviet republics as within its sphere of influence. But soon the Kremlin was encouraging the Uzbek and Kyrgyz governments to make sure the Americans did not stay permanently. For Putin, Central Asia was Russia's backyard. He was wary of both growing Chinese economic influence and an American military presence.

By 2009, President Obama was in the early stages of planning a troop surge into Afghanistan, to be followed by a phased withdrawal beginning in 2011. That meant the U.S. military once again needed to move large amounts of troops and matériel into and out of the mountainous, land-locked country. The most direct supply line into Afghanistan was through Pakistan, but this route was vulnerable to attacks by Taliban insurgents and temper tantrums by Pakistani officials. Pentagon planners wanted a second land route, even if it was longer and more expensive, to ensure that our troops were never cut off. The natural place to look was Central Asia. Cargo could be off-loaded at ports in the Baltic Sea and then shipped thousands of miles by rail through Russia, to Kazakhstan and Uzbekistan, and finally across Afghanistan's northern border. Meanwhile troops could be flown in through the still-open air base in Kyrgyzstan. The Northern Distribution Network, as it came to be known, would provide lavish revenues to corrupt regimes, but it would also significantly aid the war effort. It was one of those classic compromises of foreign policy. But before it could get going, we had to get Russia to agree to let us transport military equipment across its territory.

In President Obama's first meeting with Medvedev, he emphasized that, as part of the reset, the Northern Distribution Network would be a top priority for us. In response, Medvedev said that Russia was open to cooperating (and profiting from the transit fees). In July 2009, when President Obama visited Moscow, an agreement was formally signed to allow the transport of lethal military equipment through Russia to Afghanistan.

Medvedev's agreement on lethal transit masked another agenda, however. For the Kremlin, influence in Central Asia was still turf to be guarded, jealously. So even as Russia allowed U.S. cargo to move through its territory, it worked to expand its own military footprint across Central Asia, using our presence as its excuse to increase control over the region's regimes and undermine their growing ties with Washington. It was like a modern-day version of the "Great Game," the elaborate 19th-century diplomatic contest between Russia and Britain for supremacy in Central Asia—except that America had a narrowly focused interest in the region and was not seeking dominance.

In early December 2010, I traveled to Kyrgyzstan, Kazakhstan, and Uzbekistan, meeting with leaders to keep things on track. In a town hall meeting with students and journalists in Bishkek, I answered questions about relations with Moscow. "Where does Kyrgyzstan come in your reset with Russia?" one young man asked. I explained that while our countries disagreed on many topics—I mentioned Georgia and human rights in particular—our goal was to work together on a positive agenda and overcome a long legacy of mistrust.

One of the journalists followed up with a question about whether the reset would come at the cost of Kyrgyzstan and Central Asia: "Is there any rivalry going on between Russia and the U.S., I mean, in the region, particularly in Kyrgyzstan?" I replied that we were trying to avoid such a scenario and that the goal of the reset was to reduce tensions between Washington and Moscow, which should help countries like Kyrgyzstan that sometimes feel trapped in the middle. But, I added, it was true that Kyrgyzstan was a fledgling democracy in a region of autocracies. Democracy was in retreat in Russia. It was nonexistent in China, the other big player in the region. So this was not going to be easy. "I think it's important for you to have relations with many, but not be dependent on any," I said. "Try to balance off all the different relations you have, and get the best help you can."

When Putin was preparing to take back the presidency in Moscow, he published an essay in the fall of 2011 in a Russian newspaper announcing plans to regain lost influence among former Soviet republics and create "a powerful supra-national union capable of becoming a pole in the modern world." Putin said that this new Eurasian Union would "change the geo-political and geo-economic configuration of the entire continent." Some dismissed these words as campaign bluster, but I thought they revealed Putin's true agenda, which was effectively to "re-Sovietize" Russia's periphery. An expanded customs union would be just the first step.

Putin's ambitions weren't limited to Central Asia. In Europe he used every bit of leverage he had to keep former Soviet republics from building ties to the West, including cutting off gas to Ukraine, banning imports of Moldovan wine, and boycotting Lithuanian dairy products. His acquisitive gaze extended north, to the Arctic Circle, where melting ice was opening up new trade routes and opportunities for oil and gas exploration. In a symbolic move in 2007, a Russian submarine deposited a Russian flag on the floor of the ocean near the North Pole. More ominously, Putin was reopening old Soviet military bases across the Arctic.

President Obama and I discussed Putin's threats and how to counter them. I also made a point of traveling to countries that felt threatened. In Georgia, which I visited twice, I called on Russia to end its "occupation," a word that caused some consternation in Moscow, and withdraw from the territories it had seized in 2008.

====

For many Americans, the crisis in Ukraine and the Russian invasion of Crimea in early 2014 was a wake-up call. A part of the world that many had not thought much about since the end of the Cold War was suddenly back on the radar. But far from being a surprise, the Ukrainian crisis was in fact the latest reminder of Putin's long-standing aims. With these ambitions in mind, the Obama Administration and our European allies had quietly begun working for years to reduce Putin's leverage and counter his machinations.

On January 1, 2009, Gazprom, Russia's powerful state-owned energy conglomerate, halted natural gas exports to Ukraine. That, in turn, restricted energy flowing to part of Europe. Eleven people froze to death in the first ten days, ten of them in Poland, where temperatures fell below −10 degrees Fahrenheit. It wasn't the first time this had happened. In fact it had happened exactly three years earlier, in the middle of another cold winter.

Ukraine, which has a sizable ethnic Russian and Russian-speaking minority, has had a close but conflicted relationship with Moscow for centuries. The Orange Revolution, following disputed Ukrainian elections in 2004, brought a pro-Western government to power that sought closer ties with the European Union, angering Putin. Shutting off the gas in 2006 was his way of sending a not-so-subtle message to the independent-minded leaders in Kyiv. In 2009, he was trying to jack up the prices for Russian energy and remind everyone of his power. The move sent a chill across Europe. Much of the continent relied on Russian gas; if Ukraine could be cut off, so could anyone. After nineteen days a new agreement was signed, and gas began to flow again into Ukraine by the time of President Obama's inauguration.

In my confirmation testimony before the Senate Foreign Relations Committee that same January, in the middle of the crisis, I talked about the importance of strengthening NATO and the transatlantic alliance and emphasized my intention to give energy security "a much higher priority in our diplomacy." I cited the problems in Eastern Europe as "only the most recent example of how energy vulnerability constrains our foreign policy options around the world, limiting effectiveness in some cases and forcing our hand in others."

In my first telephone conversation with Polish Foreign Minister Radosław Sikorski, a week after taking office, we discussed the challenge. "We want a new policy and a new source," Sikorski told me. He favored a pipeline through the Balkans and Turkey that could give Europe access to natural gas holdings in the Caspian Sea. It had become known as the Southern Corridor pipeline and emerged as one of our most important energy diplomacy initiatives. I appointed Ambassador Richard Morningstar as my special envoy to negotiate the necessary agreements to get the project going. This was complicated by the fact that Azerbaijan, the key source country on the Caspian, had a long-running conflict with its neighbor Armenia. Morningstar developed a constructive working relationship with the President of Azerbaijan, Ilham Aliyev, to the point that I recommended Morningstar be nominated as our ambassador there. I twice visited Azerbaijan to encourage regional peace efforts, promote democratic reforms, and move the pipeline forward, including by meeting industry leaders at the annual Caspian Oil & Gas Show in Baku in 2012. As I left the State Department, deals were falling into place and construction is expected to begin in 2015 with the goal of getting gas flowing by 2019.

When I met with EU leaders in March 2009, I urged them to elevate energy as an urgent priority for action. I later worked with the EU's Cathy Ashton to create the U.S.-EU Energy Council. Teams of U.S. energy experts fanned out across Europe to help countries explore alternatives to Russian gas. When I visited Poland in July 2010, Foreign Minister Sikorski and I announced Polish-American cooperation on a global shale gas initiative to capitalize on new extraction technologies in a safe, environmentally sustainable manner. Exploration has now started there.

America's own expanding natural gas supplies helped loosen Russia's grip on Europe's electricity—not because we started exporting lots of gas, but because we no longer need to import it ourselves. Gas once destined for the United States started finding its way to Europe. Consumers there got cheaper gas, and Gazprom was forced to compete, no longer dictating supply and demand.

These efforts may not have made big news back home, but they were not lost on Putin. By 2013, when Ukraine was negotiating for closer trade ties with the EU, he must have felt Russia's influence slipping. Putin threatened to increase gas prices if the deal went through. Ukraine's debt to Russia was already more than $3 billion, and the country's finances were in shambles. In November, Ukraine's President Yanukovych abruptly walked away from the nearly completed EU agreement and soon accepted a $15 billion bailout package from the Kremlin.

Many Ukrainians, especially those living in the capital, Kyiv, and the non-Russian-speaking sections of the country, were inflamed by the about-face. They dreamed of living in a prosperous European democracy, and now they faced the prospect of coming once again under Moscow's thumb. Massive protests broke out and intensified when the government fired on demonstrators. Under pressure, Yanukovych agreed to constitutional reforms and new elections. A deal was brokered between the government and opposition leaders through the mediation of diplomats from Poland, France, and Germany. (The Russians participated in the talks but then refused to sign the agreement.) The crowds in the streets, however, rejected the compromise and demanded Yanukovych's resignation. Surprisingly he then abandoned his palace and fled Kyiv for the east, ultimately ending up in Russia. In response the Ukrainian Parliament asked opposition leaders to form a new government.

All this unsettled Moscow. Under the guise of protecting Russian citizens and Ukrainians of Russian descent from what he said was anarchy and violence in Ukraine, Putin sent Russian troops to occupy the Black Sea peninsula of Crimea, which had been part of Russia until the 1950s and was still home to many ethnic Russians and major Russian naval installations. Despite warnings from President Obama and European leaders, the Kremlin engineered a rump referendum for secession in Crimea that was largely boycotted by the non-Russian-speaking citizens. The UN General Assembly condemned the referendum in late March by an overwhelming margin.

As of this writing, Ukraine's future is in jeopardy. The whole world will be watching to see how this plays out, especially other former Soviet states and satellites fearful for their own independence. All our work since 2009 to reinvigorate NATO, restore strained transatlantic relations, and reduce Europe's dependence on Russian energy has put us in a stronger position to meet this challenge, though Putin has many cards to play, too. And we have to keep working at it.

═══

I spent time over the years thinking about ways to understand Putin.

On a visit to his dacha outside of Moscow in March 2010, we engaged in a contentious debate about trade and the World Trade Organization that kept going in circles. Putin wasn't giving an inch. He was hardly even listening. In exasperation, I tried a different tack. I knew that one of his personal passions is wildlife conservation, which I also care about deeply. So out of the blue, I said, "Prime Minister Putin, tell me about what you're doing to save the tigers in Siberia." He looked up in surprise. Now I had his attention.

Putin stood and asked me to follow him. Leaving our aides behind, he led me down a long corridor to his private office. We surprised a number of beefy security guards who had been lounging about. They jumped to attention as we passed. Behind an armored door, we reached his desk and a nearby wall containing a large map of Russia. He launched into an animated discourse in English on the fate of the tigers in the east, polar bears in the north, and other endangered species. It was fascinating to see the change in his engagement and bearing. He asked me if my husband wanted to go with him in a few weeks to tag polar bears on Franz Josef

Land. I told him I'd ask, and that if he couldn't go, I'd check my schedule. Putin raised an eyebrow in response. (As it turned out, neither of us went.)

Another memorably unscripted conversation with Putin occurred in September 2012 at the Asia-Pacific Economic Cooperation meeting he hosted in Vladivostok. President Obama couldn't attend because of his campaign schedule, so I represented him. Putin and Lavrov resented the President's absence and my strong criticism of Russia's support for Bashar al-Assad in Syria. They would not agree to a meeting between Putin and me until fifteen minutes before the dinner started. But, in accordance with protocol, the representative of the United States, as the former host of APEC, would be seated next to that year's host, which meant Putin and I would sit together.

We discussed his challenges, from Russia's long border with China in the east to the restive Muslim states inside Russia and across its borders. I told Putin about my recent visit in St. Petersburg to a memorial for the victims of the Nazis' siege of the city (then called Leningrad), which lasted from 1941 to 1944 and killed more than 600,000 people. That struck a chord with the history-conscious Russian leader. He launched into a story about his parents that I had never heard or read about. During the war Putin's father came home from the front lines for a short break. When he approached the apartment where he lived with his wife, he saw a pile of bodies stacked in the street and men loading them into a waiting flatbed truck. As he drew nearer, he saw a woman's legs wearing shoes that he recognized as his wife's. He ran up and demanded his wife's body. After an argument the men gave in, and Putin's father took his wife in his arms and, after examining her, realized she was still alive. He carried her up to their apartment and nursed her back to health. Eight years later, in 1952, their son Vladimir was born.

When I reported this story to our U.S. Ambassador to Russia Mike McFaul, a prominent Russia expert, he said he too had never heard it before. Obviously I have no way to verify Putin's story, but I've thought of it often. For me, it sheds some light on the man he has become and the country he governs. He's always testing you, always pushing the boundaries.

In January 2013, as I prepared to leave the State Department, I wrote President Obama a final memo about Russia and what he might expect from Putin in the second term. It had been four years since the reset first allowed us to make progress on nuclear arms control, Iranian sanctions, Afghanistan, and other key interests. I still believed it was in America's long-term national interest to have a constructive working relationship with Russia, if possible. But we had to be realistic about Putin's intentions and the danger he represented to his neighbors and the global order, and design our policy accordingly. In stark terms, I advised the President that difficult days lay ahead and that our relationship with Moscow would likely get worse before it got better. Medvedev may have cared about improving relations with the West, but Putin was under the mistaken impression that we needed Russia more than Russia needed us. He viewed the United States primarily as a competitor. And he was running scared because of his own resurgent domestic opposition and the collapse of autocracies in the Middle East and elsewhere. This was not a recipe for a positive relationship.

With all this in mind, I suggested we set a new course. The reset had allowed us to pick off the low-hanging fruit in terms of bilateral cooperation. And there was no need to blow up our collaboration on Iran or Afghanistan. But we should hit the pause button on new efforts. Don't appear too eager to work together. Don't flatter Putin with high-level attention. Decline his invitation for a Presidential-level summit in Moscow in September. And make clear that Russian intransigence wouldn't stop us from pursuing our interests and policies regarding Europe, Central Asia, Syria and other hotspots. Strength and resolve were the only language Putin would understand. We should send him a message that his actions have consequences while reassuring our allies that the United States will stand up for them.

Not everyone at the White House agreed with my relatively harsh analysis. The President accepted Putin's invitation for a bilateral summit in the fall. But over the summer it became harder to ignore the negative trajectory, especially with Edward Snowden, the contractor who leaked National Security Agency secrets to journalists, given asylum by Putin in Russia. President Obama canceled the Moscow summit and began taking a harder line with Putin. By 2014, and the Ukrainian crisis, relations had plummeted.

Beyond Crimea and other international consequences of Putin's rule, Russia itself has become a study in squandered potential. Talented people and money are leaving. It doesn't have to be this way. Russia is blessed not just with vast natural resources but also a well-educated workforce. As I've discussed with Putin, Medvedev, and Lavrov over the years, Russia could be charting a peaceful and profitable future as part of Europe rather than as its antagonist. Think of the more expansive trade deals Russia could negotiate with a different attitude. Instead of intimidating Ukraine and other neighbors, it could be engaged in greater scientific cooperation with EU and U.S. partners, expanding innovation and developing advanced technologies, trying to build its own high-tech world-class business center, as Medvedev envisioned. Think also of the long-term strategic interests Russia could pursue if Putin weren't fixated on reclaiming the Soviet Empire and crushing domestic dissent. He might realize that Russia's hand in dealing with extremists along its southern border, as well as with China in the east, would be strengthened by closer ties with Europe and the United States. He might see Ukraine as it wants to be seen—as a bridge between Europe and Russia that would increase prosperity and security for all of them. Unfortunately, as of now, Russia under Putin remains frozen between the past they can't let go of and the future they can't bring themselves to embrace.

12

Latin America:
Democrats and Demagogues

Here's a question whose answer may surprise you: What part of the world is the destination for more than 40 percent of all U.S. exports? It's not China, which accounts for just 7 percent. It's not the European Union, at 21 percent. It's the Americas. In fact the two largest single destinations for our exports are our closest neighbors: Canada and Mexico.

If that's news to you, you're not alone. Many of us in the United States have an outdated picture of what's happening in our hemisphere. We still think of Latin America as a land of coups and crime rather than a region where free markets and free people are thriving, as a source of migrants and drugs rather than a destination for trade and investment.

Our southern neighbors have made remarkable economic and political progress over the past twenty years. Latin America is a region with thirty-six countries and territories (nearly all of them democracies), with about 600 million people, rapidly expanding middle classes, abundant energy supplies, and a combined GDP of more than $5 trillion.

Because of our proximity, the economies of the United States and our neighbors have long been deeply entwined. Supply chains crisscross the region; so do family, social, and cultural networks. Some see those close ties as a threat to sovereignty or identity, but I see our interdependence as a comparative advantage to be embraced, especially at a time when we need to spur more growth at home. There's a lot we can learn from the story of Latin America's transformation and what it means for the United States and the world, especially if we are going to make the most of this "power of proximity" in the years ahead.

=====

Many of our current misconceptions about Latin America have their roots in a century of difficult history. Latin America was a battleground of the ideological competition between the United States and the Soviet Union. Cuba was the most prominent example of a Cold War flash point, but proxy battles raged in one form or another up and down the hemisphere.

The collapse of the Soviet Union and the end of the Cold War helped usher in a new era for the region. Long and brutal civil wars wound down. Elections brought new democratic governments to power. Economic growth began lifting people out of poverty. In 1994 my husband invited all the region's democracies to the first Summit of the Americas in Miami, where we all committed to meet every four years to continue our economic integration and political cooperation.

The Summit was just one of many efforts the Clinton Administration made to forge a broader partnership with our neighbors. The United States provided crucial assistance to Mexico and Brazil during their financial crises. With bipartisan backing in Congress, we developed and funded Plan Colombia, an ambitious campaign to help defend South America's oldest democracy from narcotraffickers and guerrilla groups, and in Haiti, helped reverse a coup and restore constitutional democracy. In a sign of how far the region had come, many of Latin America's other democracies provided troops for the UN mission in Haiti. According to the Pew Research Center, approval of the United States in Latin America reached 63 percent in 2001.

As a Governor of Texas who supported increasing trade and immigration reform, President George W. Bush came in with good standing in the region. He developed strong personal relationships with Mexican President Vicente Fox and his successor, Felipe Calderón. The Bush Administration supported and strengthened Plan Colombia and started the Mérida Initiative to assist Mexico in its fight against drug cartels. The administration's broader approach to foreign policy, however, did not win many friends in the region. Nor did its tendency to view the hemisphere through a left vs. right ideological lens that was a remnant of the Cold War. By 2008 just 24 percent of Mexicans and 23 percent of Brazilians approved of the United States. The average across the region, according to Gallup, was 35 percent. When the Obama Administration came into office in early 2009, we knew it was time for a new start.

President Obama explained our "equal partnership" approach in a speech in April 2009 at the Summit of the Americas in Trinidad and Tobago. He pledged that there would no longer be a "senior partner and junior partner in our relations"; instead the people of Latin America could expect "engagement based on mutual respect and common interests and shared values." As he often did, the President reflected on the need to move beyond "stale debates" and "false choices," in this case between "rigid, state-run economies or unbridled and unregulated capitalism; between blame for right-wing paramilitaries or left-wing insurgents; between sticking to inflexible policies with regard to Cuba or denying the full human rights that are owed to the Cuban people." On Cuba in particular he promised a new beginning. In a first step to modernize a policy that had "failed to advance liberty or opportunity for the Cuban people," the United States would begin allowing Cuban Americans to visit the island and send larger amounts of money back to their families there. The President also said he was prepared to engage directly with the Cuban government on a wide range of issues, including implementing democratic reforms and working together on drug trafficking and migration challenges, so long as it led to concrete progress. "I didn't come here to debate the past," he said. "I came here to deal with the future."

It was going to be my job, along with a top-notch group of Latin America experts at the State Department, to put the President's promise into practice. I decided to begin with a bold gesture to signal that we were serious about a new tone in the hemisphere. The place to do it was Mexico, our closest southern neighbor, which represented so much of both the promise and the peril of a region at a crossroads.

———

The United States and Mexico share a border that is nearly two thousand miles long, and our economies and cultures, especially in the areas around that border, are highly integrated. After all, much of the southwestern United States was once part of Mexico, and decades of immigration have only strengthened the familial and cultural ties between our nations. My firsthand experience in this area began in 1972, when the Democratic National Committee sent me to register voters in the Rio Grande Valley of Texas in support of George McGovern's campaign for President. Some people were understandably wary of a blond girl from Chicago who didn't speak a word of Spanish, but soon I was welcomed into homes and communities where citizens of Mexican ancestry were eager to participate fully in our democracy.

I also made some trips across the border with my new friends for dinner and dancing. It was a whole lot easier to cross back and forth in those days. I ended up working alongside a guy from Yale whom I'd been dating named Bill Clinton. After McGovern lost the election in a landslide, Bill and I decided to decompress at a small resort on the Pacific Coast, and we discovered that we loved Mexico so much that we went back often over the years, including on a honeymoon trip to Acapulco in 1975.

Because of the overheated rhetoric of our domestic immigration debate, many Americans still think of Mexico as an impoverished land that people are desperate to leave behind when they head north. But the truth is Mexico's economy has thrived in recent years, its middle class has swelled, and its democracy has made significant strides. I was impressed that, to take one example, under President Felipe Calderón, Mexico built 140 tuition-free universities to meet the needs of its growing economy.

At the start of the Obama Administration, one of the biggest hurdles standing in the way of Mexico's continued democratic and economic development was an epidemic of drug-related violence. Rival cartels battled one another and the nation's security forces, often catching entire communities in the crossfire. After assuming office in December 2006, President Calderón had deployed the army in a major offensive against the cartels. The violence escalated, and despite some successes by the government, the cartels continued to operate. By the time I became Secretary of State, drug gangs had metastasized into paramilitary organizations and thousands of people were dying every year. Though the crime rate was down in areas untouched by drug trafficking, where the cartels did operate, car bombings and kidnappings became commonplace. Border cities such as Tijuana and Ciudad Juárez started to resemble war zones. And the violence threatened to spill into El Paso and other nearby American communities.

In 2008, gunmen attacked the U.S. Consulate in Monterrey with small arms and a grenade. Thankfully no one was injured. In March 2010, however, three people connected to our consulate in Ciudad Juárez were murdered. An American employee of the consulate, Lesley Enriquez, was shot in her car along with her husband, Arthur Redelfs. At nearly the same time, across town, the Mexican husband of a locally employed staff member of the consulate, Jorge Alberto Salcido Ceniceros, was also shot. These murders were another reminder of the risks the men and women representing our country face all over the world, not just in places like Iraq, Afghanistan, or Libya. The incidents also underscored the need to help Mexico restore order and security.

The basic fact of the drug war was that the cartels were fighting one another for the right to export narcotics to the United States. An estimated 90 percent of all the drugs used in America flowed through Mexico, and roughly 90 percent of the weapons used by the cartels came from the United States. (The ban on assault weapons that Bill signed in 1994 expired ten years later and was not renewed, opening the door to increased arms trafficking across the border.) It was hard to look at these facts and not conclude that America shared responsibility for helping Mexico stop the violence. In March 2009, in one of my first trips as Secretary, I flew to Mexico City for consultations on how we might expand our cooperation amid the growing violence.

I met with Calderón and his Foreign Secretary Patricia Espinosa, a career diplomat who became one of my favorite colleagues and a good friend. They outlined their needs, including for more Black Hawk helicopters to respond to the increasingly well-armed cartels. Calderón was passionate about stopping the violence against his people, and he radiated the intensity of a man on a very personal mission. The brazenness of the drug cartels offended him and undermined his plans for jobs and education. He was also angry about the mixed messages he believed he received from the United States. How am I supposed to stop the well-armed drug traffickers, he would ask, when you won't stop the weapons they buy across the border and you have states starting to legalize the use of marijuana? Why should my citizens, law enforcement, or military put their lives on the line under such circumstances? Those were uncomfortable but fair questions.

I told Calderón and Espinosa that we would expand the Bush Administration's Mérida Initiative to help law enforcement. We asked Congress to allocate more than $80 million for helicopters, night-vision goggles, body armor, and other equipment. We also requested funding to deploy hundreds of new border guards on our side to crack down on gunrunning and drug smuggling. This was an effort by the whole administration, including Secretary of Homeland Security Janet Napolitano, Attorney General Eric Holder, and John Brennan, the President's Assistant for Homeland Security and Counterterrorism.

After our meeting Espinosa and I held a joint press conference. I explained that the Obama Administration viewed drug trafficking as a "shared problem" and that we recognized the challenge of reducing demand for illegal drugs in the United States and stopping the flow of illegal guns across the border into Mexico. The next day I flew north to Monterrey. In a speech at TecMilenio University, I reiterated this commitment. "The United States recognizes that drug trafficking is not only Mexico's problem," I told the students. "It is also an American problem. And we, in the United States, have a responsibility to help you address it."

I thought that was a pretty obvious thing to say. It was demonstrably true. It was also a key tenet of the new approach the Obama Administration intended to take in Latin America. But I knew that this kind of candor could come with a cost back home. Certain media outlets could be expected to react with hysteria and talk of "apologizing for America." Political concerns are not irrelevant in foreign policy; the United States is strongest when we face the world united, so building and maintaining public support for our policies at home is important. But in this case I was prepared to absorb the criticism in order to do what was right and advance our agenda. Sure enough, the *New York Post* headline screamed, "Hillary's Drug Shock." I had long since stopped taking such criticism personally, and I felt strongly that if we wanted to improve our standing around the world and actually solve problems, we would have to tell some hard truths and face the world as it is.

Soon our expanded cooperation began to produce dividends. Mexico extradited more than a hundred fugitives to the United States in 2009. Nearly two dozen high-level drug traffickers were captured or killed thanks to improved intelligence and targeting. The Obama Administration tripled funding to reduce demand for illegal drugs in the United States to more than $10 billion a year, and the FBI stepped up arrests of cartel members operating north of the border. We helped train thousands of Mexican police officers, judges, and prosecutors and formed new partnerships across Central America and the Caribbean to make citizen security a priority of our diplomacy in Latin America.

Our relationship became strained in late 2010, when secret reports from our Ambassador to Mexico Carlos Pascual were published as part of the WikiLeaks affair. When I returned for another visit in January 2011, Calderón was livid. The *New York Times* reported that he was particularly upset by one leaked report "that quoted Mr. Pascual questioning the Mexican Army's reluctance to act on American intelligence about a drug cartel leader." Calderón told the press that the leaks caused "severe damage" to Mexico's relationship with the United States. He complained to the *Washington Post*, "It's difficult if suddenly you are seeing the courage of the army [questioned]. For instance, they have lost probably 300 soldiers . . . and suddenly somebody in the American embassy, they [say] the Mexican soldiers aren't brave enough." Espinosa advised me to meet with the President to explain and apologize. When I did, Calderón told me that he no longer wanted to work with Carlos and insisted that he be replaced. It was one of the tougher meetings I've ever sat through. Afterward I told Carlos that I had no choice but to bring him home, but assured him I'd find a new assignment to utilize his skills and experience. He officially resigned from his post in March and shortly afterward took charge of our new bureau on global energy issues. Espinosa and I worked hard to repair the damage, and our cooperation continued.

===

There was a good model for how an ambitious effort like Mexico's could succeed: Colombia. This was a country that had captured my imagination ever since my brother Hugh served in the Peace Corps there in the early 1970s. He described it as the most rewarding experience of his life, and after he came home he used to regale us with stories of his adventures. Bill thought they sounded right out of his favorite novel, Gabriel García Márquez's *One Hundred Years of Solitude*, but Hugh swore they were all true. Sadly, by the 1990s, Colombia was one of the most violent countries on earth, terrorized by drug traffickers and guerrillas who controlled vast swaths of territory and who could strike at will in any major city. Foreign policy experts routinely referred to it as a failed state.

Bill worked with President Andrés Pastrana to provide more than $1 billion to fund Colombia's campaign against the drug cartels and the leftist rebel faction known as the FARC. Over the following decade, Pastrana's successor, President Álvaro Uribe, whose father was killed by

FARC guerrillas in the 1980s, expanded Plan Colombia with strong support from the Bush Administration. But even as the government made progress, new concerns began to arise about human rights abuses, violence against labor organizers, targeted assassinations, and the atrocities of right-wing paramilitary groups. When the Obama Administration came into office, we made the choice to continue America's bipartisan support for Plan Colombia, but we broadened our partnership with the government beyond security to work more on governance, education, and development.

By the time I visited Bogotá in June 2010, violence was down dramatically, the insurgency was on the road to defeat, and citizens enjoyed an unprecedented measure of security and prosperity. By a happy coincidence in our hectic schedules, Bill was traveling through Colombia on Clinton Foundation business while I was there. We met in Bogotá and went out for dinner with friends and staff at a local steakhouse, and toasted Colombia's progress. As we walked through the streets, we marveled at how far the country had come. A quiet evening stroll like this would have been unthinkable even a few years earlier.

When I sat down with President Uribe, we discussed Colombia's remaining security challenges, but they were only one part of the agenda. We spent time talking about how Colombia and the United States could work together at the UN Security Council on global issues, how to expand trade, and prepare for the upcoming Summit of the Americas. Uribe was a hard-nosed, hands-on leader. The end of his term was approaching, and he reminisced about the long road his country had traveled. "You know, when I was inaugurated eight years ago," he told me, "we couldn't even hold the ceremony outside because there were so many attacks, there were snipers and bombs. We've come such a long way."

Uribe's successor, Juan Manuel Santos, who studied in the United States in 1980 on a Fulbright scholarship, moved to consolidate this progress and in 2012 began negotiations with what was left of the FARC. These talks offer the promise of bringing lasting peace to Colombia. I spoke by phone with President Santos and congratulated him. "It's very important and symbolic and I hope we can achieve a good ending in this process," he replied.

The credit for Colombia's progress goes to its courageous people. But I am proud of the role that the United States has played over three administrations to help to reverse the country's disintegration, strengthen human rights and the rule of law, and promote economic development.

After my comments in Mexico in March 2009 about shared responsibility and President Obama's speech in Trinidad and Tobago in April about equal partnership, it was starting to feel as though we had laid a foundation for the new chapter of engagement we sought in the hemisphere. Little did we know that the month of June would test our efforts and intentions in unexpected ways.

For me, June began in the smallest country in Central America, El Salvador, where I attended the inauguration of the country's new President and a regional conference on promoting broad-based economic growth and reducing economic inequality. Both events spoke to the promise and potential we hoped would come to define our relationship with Latin America.

The combined economy of Latin America was nearly three times the size of India's or Russia's and not far behind China's and Japan's. The region was poised to accelerate out of the global recession with growth of nearly 6 percent in 2010, and unemployment would fall to its lowest rate in two decades by 2011. According to the World Bank, the middle class in Latin America had grown by 50 percent since 2000, including an increase of more than 40 percent in Brazil and 17 percent in Mexico. That translated to increased prosperity for them and more than 50 million new middle-class consumers eager to buy U.S. goods and services.

So we worked hard to improve and ratify trade agreements with Colombia and Panama and encouraged Canada and the group of countries that became known as the Pacific Alliance—Mexico, Colombia, Peru, and Chile—all open-market democracies driving toward a more prosperous future to join negotiations with Asian nations on TPP, the trans-Pacific trade agreement. The Alliance stood in stark contrast to Venezuela, with its more authoritarian policies and state-controlled economy.

Yet for all this progress, economic inequality in Latin America was still among the worst in the world. Despite rapid development in many areas, parts of Latin America remained locked in persistent poverty. At the conference in El Salvador, which was organized under the banner of a regional initiative started by the Bush Administration called "Pathways to Prosperity," I argued that a key challenge for Latin America in the years ahead would be to make sure that the benefits of economic growth were broadly shared and that the region's democracies delivered concrete results for their citizens. "Rather than defining economic progress simply by profit margins and GDP, our yardstick must be the quality of human lives," I suggested, so we should be measuring "whether families have enough food on the table, whether young people have access to schooling from early childhood through university, whether workers earn decent wages and have safe conditions at their jobs."

A number of Latin American countries, notably Brazil, Mexico, and Chile, had already found success in reducing inequality and lifting people out of poverty. Some of the most effective tools were "conditional cash transfer" programs. In the 1990s Brazil under President Fernando Cardoso began providing regular small payments to millions of poor families if they kept their children in school. Later, President Luiz Inácio Lula da Silva expanded the program to include regular medical checkups and classes on nutrition and disease prevention. These incentives empowered women, increased school attendance, improved child health, and spurred economic growth. As the program expanded, so did the results. In Brazil the percentage of the population living below the poverty line fell from 22 percent in 2003 to just 7 percent in 2009, and similar programs spread across the hemisphere.

One area of economic cooperation that I thought was particularly important was energy. The United States already sourced more than 50 percent of our imported energy from our own hemisphere. Further expanding cooperation on energy and climate change could serve as a vehicle for bridging divides between nations, creating economic opportunity, and improving the environment all at the same time. My team helped develop a proposal for an Energy and Climate Partnership of the Americas to support innovation and build on the region's strengths. There were many examples to learn from. Brazil was a leader on biofuels. Costa Rica generated nearly all of its electricity from hydropower. Colombia and Peru were developing clean energy mass-transit systems. Mexico was closing landfills, capturing the methane for power generation, and improving the air quality of Mexico City, greening the roofs and walls of its buildings, and planting a massive number of new trees in the area. Barbados was unlocking the potential of solar water heaters. And islands such as Saint Kitts and Nevis and Dominica were developing their geothermal resources.

Over the coming years we would build on this foundation and put special emphasis on linking different national and regional electrical grids from northern Canada all the way to the southern tip of Chile, as well as out to the Caribbean, which pays some of the highest electricity costs in the world. Because the costs are so high, the Caribbean could achieve access and independence through solar, wind, and biomass fuel production with zero subsidies if the governments have the will to shift their spending from imported oil to homegrown clean power. The same is true in Central America. All this was particularly important because 31 million people across the hemisphere still lacked access to reliable and affordable electricity. (Worldwide the number is 1.3 billion people.) That held back progress in so many ways. How can you run a successful business or school in the 21st century without power? The easier access people have to energy, the better their chances of climbing out of poverty, educating their children, and staying healthy. So we set a goal of seeing every community in the region gain access to electricity by the year 2022.

The other highlight of my visit to El Salvador at the beginning of June 2009 was the inauguration of a new President, Mauricio Funes. It was an occasion to reflect on the profound political transformation that had swept Latin America since the end of the Cold War. Constitutional democracies had taken root where right-wing military dictatorships and left-wing demagogues had once dominated the political landscape. In 2013 the NGO Freedom House labeled the Americas, which includes the United States and Canada, "second only to Western Europe in levels of freedom and respect for human rights."

The region's political and economic success (despite a few holdouts) made it a model for emerging democracies elsewhere, including in the Middle East. And, to my great satisfaction, Latin America was also showcasing the power of women leaders. In a part of the world often known for its machismo culture, powerful and accomplished women have led Argentina, Brazil, Chile, Costa Rica, Guyana, Jamaica, Nicaragua, Panama, and Trinidad and Tobago and have served as interim leaders in Ecuador and Bolivia.

═══════

I left El Salvador and flew to Honduras for the annual meeting of the Organization of American States. Honduras, roughly the size of Mississippi, is home to about 8 million of the poorest people in Latin America. Its history has been marked by a seemingly endless parade of discord and disasters. The President of Honduras was Manuel Zelaya, a throw-back to the caricature of a Central American strongman, with his white cowboy hat, dark black mustache, and fondness for Hugo Chavez and Fidel Castro.

I woke up early on the morning of June 2 and prepared for a long day of multilateral diplomacy, which, thanks to all the set-piece speeches and procedural mumbo-jumbo, can often be deadly boring. This day at the OAS, however, promised drama. We expected a number of nations to put forward a resolution lifting the 1962 suspension on Cuba's membership in the organization. By tradition the OAS operates by consensus, meaning that even a single country's objection to a measure can hold it up. But, technically, a two-thirds majority was all it took to adopt a resolution, if it came to that. Every vote counter believed a big majority of nations would support lifting the Cuba ban because they generally viewed it as an outdated artifact of the Cold War and believed that engaging Cuba and bringing it inside the family of nations was the best way to encourage reforms on the island. A few countries, including Venezuela, Nicaragua, Bolivia, and Ecuador, would characterize the ban more harshly as an ex-ample of U.S. bullying, and they saw bringing Cuba back into the OAS as a way both to stick it to the United States and weaken democratic norms across the region. That worried me. The OAS had adopted a charter in 2001 codifying strong democratic principles, and it stood as a landmark of the region's journey away from its dictatorial past. We couldn't let Chavez and his cronies make a show of gutting that charter.

For the new Obama Administration, this presented an early test. We could stick to our old policy and refuse to support lifting Cuba's suspen-sion because a dictatorship has no place in an association of democracies, but then we would likely alienate many of our neighbors and make the United States look isolated in our own backyard. Or we could cave and admit that Cuba's suspension was a Cold War anachronism, but that could make a mockery of the region's hard-won democratic norms and create a firestorm back home. Neither option was at all appealing.

As I was getting ready in my hotel room, I turned on CNN and saw a story about a Cuban father living and working in the United States who hadn't seen his baby boy in a year and a half because of the restrictions on traveling between the two countries. Thanks to the Obama Admin-istration's easing of those restrictions, father and son were finally able to reunite. Following up on those changes, we offered to begin talks with the

Cuban government about restoring direct mail service and cooperation on immigration processes. In the run-up to this summit in Honduras, the Cubans accepted. In short, the United States was living up to the President's promise of a new beginning. But welcoming Cuba back to the OAS without dramatic democratic reforms was simply a nonstarter.

For fifty years Cuba had been ruled as a Communist dictatorship by Fidel Castro. He and his regime denied its people fundamental freedoms and human rights, repressed dissent, kept a tight hold of the state-controlled economy, and worked to spread "the revolution" to other countries across the region and beyond. Despite advancing age and declining health, Castro and his brother, Raul, continued to rule Cuba with absolute power.

Since 1960, the United States had maintained an embargo against the island in hopes of squeezing Castro from power, but it only succeeded in giving him a foil to blame for Cuba's economic woes. In late 1995 the Clinton Administration offered Castro quiet talks to explore the possibility of improving relations. Those discussions were under way when, in February 1996, a Cuban Air Force jet shot down two small unarmed planes, killing four crew members. The planes were owned by a group of Cuban exiles in Miami called Brothers to the Rescue, who flew periodic missions to drop anti-Castro leaflets over Cuba. My husband called the incident "a blatant violation of international law." The UN Security Council condemned Cuba's actions, and the U.S. Congress passed legislation, with large bipartisan majorities in both houses, strengthening the embargo against Cuba and requiring Congressional approval for any future changes. The experience taught me to keep my eyes wide open when it came to dealing with the Castros.

Since the Castro brothers were implacably opposed to the democratic principles enshrined in the OAS charter and did not hide their disdain for the institution, it was hard to see how giving them a seat at that table would be good for democracy or for the OAS. In fact, given the tradition of making decisions by consensus, it could give Cuba an effective veto over important regional matters.

The Castro brothers were not in Honduras to argue their case. In fact they expressed no interest in joining the OAS. The charge was led by the government of Hugo Chavez in Venezuela (although it had wide support from others). A self-aggrandizing dictator who was more of an aggravation than a real threat, except to his own citizens, Chavez had shouted and schemed against the United States for years and worked to subvert democracy in his own country and across the region. He represented so much of the negative history that the region was trying to transcend. Chavez had stifled political opposition and the press in Venezuela, nationalized companies and seized their assets, squandered the country's oil wealth, and was busy turning the country into a dictatorship.

In April, President Obama had crossed paths with Chavez at the Summit of the Americas. At the time Chavez seemed delighted to shake President Obama's hand, and he made a big show of presenting the President with a gift as a gesture of his goodwill. It turned out to be a book about U.S. imperialism and exploitation in Latin America—so not much of a gesture.

I regularly criticized Chavez and defended those in Venezuela brave enough to stand up to him. But I also tried not to say anything that might give Chavez an excuse to puff himself up and ride his high horse all over the region complaining about U.S. bullying. On Venezuelan television he once entertained a huge crowd by singing "I'm not loved by Hillary Clinton . . . and I don't love her either" to the tune of a popular local song. It was hard to argue with that.

My day in Honduras began with an early breakfast with Foreign Ministers from across the Caribbean. We had a lot to talk about, especially plans to respond to growing drug violence and for greater cooperation on energy. Most Caribbean nations were both starved for energy and vulnerable to the effects of climate change, from rising sea levels to extreme weather. So they were eager to work with us to find solutions. But, of course, the conversation also came around to Cuba. "We do look forward to the day when Cuba can join the OAS," I assured the Ministers. "But we believe that membership in the OAS must come with responsibility. And we owe it to each other to uphold our standards of democracy and governance that have brought so much progress to our hemisphere. It's not about reliving the past; it's about the future and being true to the founding principles of this organization."

After breakfast it was on to the main event, the OAS General Assembly. Secretary-General José Miguel Insulza, a Chilean diplomat, and President Zelaya, our Honduran host, welcomed us to the hall and invited all the Ministers to pose for a "family photo." How many of these leaders would join us in defending the organization's democratic principles?

Brazil was key. Under the leadership of President Luiz Inácio Lula da Silva, Brazil had emerged as an important global player. Lula, as he's known, a charismatic former trade union leader elected in 2002, was the face of the dynamic new Brazil, which boasted one of the fastest growing economies in the world and a rapidly expanding middle class. Perhaps more than any other country, Brazil's rise symbolized Latin America's transformation and its promise for the future.

When I first traveled to Brazil, as First Lady in 1995, it was still a relatively poor nation with a fragile democracy and massive economic inequality. Years of military dictatorship and a leftist insurgency had given way to a succession of weak civilian governments, which had not produced many results for the people. Brazil started to modernize with the election of President Fernando Henrique Cardoso, who had been inaugurated a few months before my visit. He set the country's economic awakening in motion, and his wife, Ruth, an accomplished sociologist, started a poverty-reduction agency and conditional cash transfers to improve the lives of women and poor families. Cardoso was succeeded by the wildly popular Lula, who continued his economic policies, expanded the social safety net to reduce poverty, and slowed annual destruction in the Amazon rain forest by 75 percent.

As Brazil's economy grew, so did Lula's assertiveness in foreign policy. He envisioned Brazil becoming a major world power, and his actions led to both constructive cooperation and some frustrations. For example, in 2004 Lula sent troops to lead the UN peacekeeping mission in Haiti, where they did an excellent job of providing order and security under difficult conditions. On the other hand, he insisted on working with Turkey to cut a side deal with Iran on its nuclear program that did not meet the international community's requirements.

Still, overall I welcomed Brazil's growing influence and considerable capacities to help solve problems. Later I would enjoy working with Dilma Rousseff, Lula's protégée, Chief of Staff, and eventual successor as President. On January 1, 2011, I attended her inauguration on a rainy but festive day in Brasília. Tens of thousands of people lined the streets as the country's first woman President drove by in a 1952 Rolls-Royce. She took the oath of office and accepted the traditional green and gold Presidential sash from her mentor, Lula, pledging to continue his work on eradicating poverty and inequality. She also acknowledged the history she was making. "Today, all Brazilian women should feel proud and happy." Dilma is a formidable leader whom I admire and like. In the early 1970s she was a member of a left-wing guerrilla group and was imprisoned and tortured by the military dictatorship. She may not have Lula's colorful bravado or Cardoso's technical expertise, as some observers argued, but she has a strong intellect and true grit, two characteristics necessary for leadership in these challenging times. She showed her mettle in 2013, when Brazilians, frustrated by slowing growth, rising prices, and the perception that the government was more focused on preparing for high-profile events like the 2014 World Cup and 2016 Olympics than improving life for average citizens, took to the streets in protest. Instead of rebuffing or beating and jailing the protestors, as many other countries have done, including Venezuela, Dilma met with them, acknowledged their concerns, and asked them to work with the government to solve the problems.

On Cuba, I knew convincing the Brazilians would be an uphill battle. Lula would be inclined to support lifting the OAS suspension. But I wondered if his desire to play the role of regional statesman might work in our favor and encourage him to help us broker a compromise. I would have to feel out his Foreign Minister Celso Amorim and see what was possible.

Another important player would be Chile. Like Brazil, Chile was a Latin American success story, transitioning to democracy in the 1990s from the brutal military dictatorship of General Augusto Pinochet. The role of the United States in the 1973 coup that brought Pinochet to power and our support for his right-wing regime is a dark chapter in our involvement in the region, but our more recent relationship was strong and productive. Michelle Bachelet, elected in 2006 as Chile's first woman President, was trained as a pediatrician. Like Dilma Rousseff in Brazil, she faced persecution under her country's military dictatorship and eventually went into political exile. She returned after the fall of Pinochet and began her ascent through Chile's political ranks. As President she worked to unite the country and address the human rights abuses of its past, opening a Museum of Memory and establishing the National Institute for Human Rights. Bachelet's efforts on behalf of women in her country earned widespread praise and, after the end of her term as President in 2010, led to her appointment as the executive director of the newly created United Nations Entity for Gender Equality and the Empowerment of Women, known as UN Women. She and I became allies and friends in the ongoing struggle for the rights of women and girls. She returned to Chile and ran successfully for a second term as President in late 2013.

Chile favored reducing Cuba's isolation and had urged the United

States to lift our embargo. In early 2009, Bachelet became the first Chilean President in decades to visit Havana and meet with the Castro brothers. Afterward Fidel published a column taking Bolivia's side in a territorial dispute with Chile dating from the 1870s and criticizing the "Chilean oligarchy" for exploiting the Bolivians. It was a reminder of how capricious and nasty he could be. I hoped Chile would decide to uphold its own democratic principles and help us defuse this crisis.

My top advisor on Latin America was Assistant Secretary for Western Hemisphere Affairs Tom Shannon, a highly respected senior Foreign Service officer who had served in five administrations. Tom had held the top Latin America job under Secretary Rice, and I asked him to stay on until he could be confirmed to serve as our Ambassador to Brazil. Ever since Tom laid out the pros and cons of Cuba's rejoining the OAS and explained what a difficult diplomatic position we were in, he and I had been brainstorming ways out of the crisis. Eventually the outlines of a plan came into focus.

Given what President Obama had said about moving past the stale debates of the Cold War, it would be hypocritical of us to continue insisting that Cuba be kept out of the OAS for the reasons it was first suspended in 1962, ostensibly its adherence to "Marxism-Leninism" and alignment "with the communist bloc." It would be more credible and accurate to focus on Cuba's present-day human rights violations, which were incompatible with the OAS charter. What if we agreed to lift the suspension, but with the condition that Cuba be reseated as a member only if it made enough democratic reforms to bring it in line with the charter? And, to expose the Castro brothers' contempt for the OAS itself, why not require Cuba to formally request readmittance? Perhaps that was a compromise that Brazil, Chile, and others would accept. We didn't necessarily need to win over the hard-liners like Venezuela because maintaining the status quo would be a win in itself. But if they saw the region moving toward a compromise, even they might want to get on board.

After the pomp and circumstance of the opening session was over, I went into a side meeting of several Foreign Ministers and presented our compromise resolution as an alternative to the version that lifted the suspension with no conditions. The proposal was met with considerable surprise in the room because it was quite different from the line the United States had previously taken, although in my view it achieved the same goals. Tom and I began making the rounds, buttonholing Foreign

Ministers and making the case for our plan. At midday I addressed the General Assembly and argued that the organization's democratic principles and Latin America's democratic progress were too important to surrender. I also reminded my colleagues that the Obama Administration was already taking steps to engage Cuba.

Cuba's backers were making their case as well. Zelaya called the original 1962 vote to suspend Cuba "that other day that will live in infamy" and urged the assembly to "correct that mistake." Nicaraguan President Daniel Ortega said the suspension was "imposed by tyrants" and, showing his true colors, declared that "the OAS continues to be an instrument of domination of the United States." Along with the Venezuelans, the Nicaraguans were threatening either to call a vote, which would put everyone on the spot, or to walk out and quit the organization.

As the day wore on I was keenly aware of the clock. I was supposed to leave Honduras in the early evening to fly to Cairo, where I was meeting President Obama for his major address to the Muslim world. Before I left we needed to make sure that there wasn't a two-thirds majority ready to admit Cuba without conditions. We argued to everyone who would listen that this would not be in the best interests of the OAS. At one point President Obama called Lula directly, encouraging him to help push through our compromise. I pulled Zelaya aside into a small room and played up his role and responsibilities as host of the conference. If he backed our compromise, he could help save not just this summit but the OAS itself. If not, he would be remembered as the leader who presided over the organization's collapse. These appeals seemed to make a difference. By late afternoon, though we were far from consensus, I felt confident that things were moving in the right direction. Even if our resolution didn't pass, neither would the other one, and I thought it was unlikely that the OAS would disintegrate over the issue. I headed for the airport and asked Tom to keep me closely updated. "Bring it home," I told him as I got into the car.

A few hours later Tom called to tell me that it looked like a deal might be at hand. Our team was negotiating on final language for the conditions, but it seemed our compromise was gaining support. By the end of the evening only Venezuela, Nicaragua, Honduras, and a few allies were holding out for their clean resolution. Instead of the United States being isolated, as we had originally feared, now it was Chavez and his crew facing a unified region. According to some reports, Zelaya called

Chavez and suggested they bow to the will of the majority and accept the compromise. Whatever the reason, in the morning they reversed course, and we were able to achieve consensus on our resolution. The Ministers broke into applause when it was adopted.

In Havana, the Castro regime reacted angrily and refused to petition for entry into the OAS or to accept any conditions or democratic reforms. So in effect, the suspension remained in place. But we succeeded in replacing an outdated rationale with a modern process that would further strengthen the OAS commitment to democracy.

True to form, in December 2009, the Castros created new problems by arresting a USAID contractor named Alan Gross for bringing computer equipment to the small, aging Jewish community in Havana. Cuban authorities subjected him to a rump trial and then sentenced him to fifteen years in prison. One of my regrets as Secretary was our failure to bring Alan home. The Department and I stayed in close touch with his wife, Judy, and his daughters. I spoke out publicly about Alan and asked numerous other countries to intervene with Cuba. But despite the direct engagement with Cuban officials and numerous efforts by third parties, the Cubans refused to release him unless the United States released five convicted Cuban spies serving time in prison. It is possible that hard-liners within the regime exploited the Gross case as an opportunity to put the brakes on any possible rapprochement with the United States and the domestic reforms that would require. If so, it is a double tragedy, consigning millions of Cubans to a kind of continued imprisonment as well.

In the face of a stone wall from the regime in Havana, President Obama and I proceeded to engage the Cuban people rather than the government. Based on lessons learned all over the world, we believed that the best way to bring change to Cuba would be to expose its people to the values, information, and material comforts of the outside world. Isolation had only strengthened the regime's grip on power; inspiring and emboldening the Cuban people might have the opposite effect. In early 2011, we announced new rules to make it easier for American religious groups and students to visit Cuba and to allow U.S. airports to allow charter flights. We further raised the limit on remittances Cuban Americans could send back to family members. Hundreds of thousands of Americans now visit the island annually. They are walking advertisements for the United States and for the benefits of a more open society.

Every step of the way, we faced vocal opposition from some members of Congress who wanted to keep Cuba in a deep freeze. But I remained convinced that this kind of people-to-people engagement was the best way to encourage reform in Cuba and that it was profoundly in the interests of the United States and the region. So I was pleased when we started to see change slowly creeping into the country, no matter how hard the regime hard-liners tried to stop it. Bloggers and hunger-strikers added their voices and examples to the demands for freedom. I was particularly moved by the courage and determination of the Cuban women known as Damas de Blanco, "Ladies in White." Starting in 2003, they marched every Sunday after Catholic mass to protest the continuing detention of political prisoners. They endured harassment, beatings, and arrests, but they kept marching.

Near the end of my tenure, I recommended to President Obama that he take another look at our embargo. It wasn't achieving its goals, and it was holding back our broader agenda across Latin America. After twenty years of observing and dealing with the U.S.-Cuba relationship, I thought we should shift the onus onto the Castros to explain why they remained undemocratic and abusive.

═══

The end of the summit in San Pedro Sula was not the end of the drama that June. Just a few weeks later the ghosts of Latin America's troubled past resurfaced in Honduras. On Sunday, June 28, 2009, the Supreme Court of Honduras ordered the arrest of President Zelaya amid allegations of corruption and fears that he was preparing to circumvent the Constitution and extend his term in office. Zelaya was seized and, still in his pajamas, hustled onto a plane to Costa Rica. A temporary government headed by National Congress President Roberto Micheletti assumed power.

I was at home in Chappaqua enjoying a quiet Sunday morning when I received word of the crisis from Tom Shannon. He told me what we knew, which still wasn't much, and we discussed how to respond. One immediate issue was Zelaya's wife and daughters, who were asking to take refuge in the residence of our Ambassador to Honduras. I told Tom to make sure they were protected and well cared for until the crisis could be resolved. I also spoke with General Jones and Tom Donilon at the White House and called the Spanish Foreign Minister for a quick consultation.

The forced exile of Zelaya presented the United States with another dilemma. Micheletti and the Supreme Court claimed to be protecting Honduran democracy against Zelaya's unlawful power grab and warned that he wanted to become another Chavez or Castro. Certainly the region did not need another dictator, and many knew Zelaya well enough to believe the charges against him. But Zelaya had been elected by the Honduran people, and exiling him under cover of darkness sent a chill through the region. No one wanted to see a return to the bad old days of frequent coups and unstable governments. I didn't see any choice but to condemn Zelaya's ouster. In a public statement I called on all parties in Honduras to respect the constitutional order and the rule of law and to commit themselves to resolve political disputes peacefully and through dialogue. As required by our laws, our government began moving to suspend aid to Honduras until democracy was restored. Our view was shared by other countries in the region, including Brazil, Colombia, and Costa Rica. Soon it became the official position of the OAS as well.

In the subsequent days I spoke with my counterparts around the hemisphere, including Secretary Espinosa in Mexico. We strategized on a plan to restore order in Honduras and ensure that free and fair elections could be held quickly and legitimately, which would render the question of Zelaya moot and give the Honduran people a chance to choose their own future.

I began looking for a respected elder statesman who could act as a mediator. Óscar Arias, the President of Costa Rica, which has one of the highest per capita incomes and greenest economies in Central America, was a natural choice. He was a seasoned leader, having earned the respect of the entire world and the 1987 Nobel Peace Prize for his work to end conflicts across Central America. After sixteen years out of office, he successfully ran for President again in 2006 and became an important voice for responsible governance and sustainable development. In early July, I called him. We discussed the need to ensure that elections occurred as scheduled in November. He was game to try to broker an agreement, but he was concerned that Zelaya would not accept him as a mediator and asked me to push the deposed President to take a leap of faith.

That afternoon I hosted Zelaya at the State Department. He arrived in better shape than when he first addressed the world from Costa Rica; the pajamas were gone and the cowboy hat was back. He even joked a bit about his forced flight. "What have Latin American presidents learned from Honduras?" he asked me. I smiled and shook my head. "To sleep with our clothes on and our bags packed," he replied.

Jokes aside, Zelaya was frustrated and impatient. Reports from Honduras of clashes between protesters and security forces only heightened the tension. I told him that we should all do everything we could to avoid bloodshed and urged him to participate in the mediation process to be led by Arias. By the end of the conversation, Zelaya was on board. I knew that Micheletti would not accept the mediation if he thought Zelaya had the upper hand, so I wanted to announce the new diplomatic effort alone, without Zelaya by my side. As soon as we finished talking, I asked Tom to take Zelaya into an empty office and have the Operations Center place a call to Arias so the two of them could speak. Meanwhile I hurried down to the State Department press briefing room to make an official announcement.

The first few days brought no breakthroughs. Arias reported that Zelaya was insisting on being fully restored as President, while Micheletti maintained that Zelaya had violated the Constitution and refused to stand aside until the next scheduled elections. In other words, neither side showed any inclination to compromise.

I stressed to Arias, "Our bottom line is free, fair, and democratic elections with a peaceful transfer of power." He agreed that firm talk was needed and expressed frustration at the intransigence he was encountering. "They are not willing to give concessions," he explained. Then he echoed a sentiment I think many of us felt: "I'm doing this and am in favor of Zelaya to be restored because of principles, Mrs. Clinton, not because I like these people. . . . If we allow the de facto government to stay, the domino effect goes all around Latin America." That was an interesting reformulation of the domino theory, the famous Cold War fear that if one small nation went Communist, its neighbors would soon follow.

Zelaya returned to the State Department in early September for additional negotiations. Then, on September 21, he secretly returned to Honduras and resurfaced at the Brazilian Embassy, a potentially explosive development.

The negotiations dragged on. By late October it was clear that Arias was making minimal progress in bringing the two sides to an agreement. I decided to send Tom to Honduras to make it clear that America's patience had run out. On October 23, just after 9 P.M., I received a call from Micheletti. "There is a growing sense of frustration in Washington and elsewhere," I warned him. Micheletti tried to rationalize that they were "doing everything in [their] power to reach an agreement with Mr. Zelaya."

About an hour later I reached Zelaya, still holed up in the Brazilian Embassy. I informed him that Tom would be arriving soon to help resolve the matter. I promised that I would stay closely involved personally and that we were going to try to settle the crisis as soon as possible. We knew we had to develop a process that allowed the Hondurans themselves to resolve this problem in a way that both sides could accept—a tall order, but not, as it turned out, impossible. Finally, on October 29, Zelaya and Micheletti signed an agreement to set up a national unity government to run Honduras until the upcoming elections and establish a "truth and reconciliation" commission to investigate the events leading to Zelaya's removal from office. They agreed to leave to the Honduran Congress the question of Zelaya's return to office as part of the national unity government.

Almost immediately there were arguments about the structure and purpose of the unity government, and both sides threatened to pull out of the agreement. Then the Honduran Congress voted overwhelmingly not to restore Zelaya to office, dealing him a painful and unexpected setback. He had greatly overestimated the depth of support in the country for his cause. After the vote he flew to the Dominican Republic and spent the next year in exile. The elections, however, went ahead. In late November voters chose Porfirio Lobo, who had been runner-up to Zelaya in 2005, as the new President of Honduras. Many South American countries did not accept this outcome, and it took a year of additional diplomacy before Honduras was accepted back into the OAS.

This was the first time in Central American history that a country that suffered a coup and was on the verge of major civil conflict was able to restore its constitutional and democratic processes through negotiation, without imposition from the outside.

If ever there were a region where we need to look beyond the headlines to focus on the trendlines, it's Latin America. Yes, there are still big problems that have to be solved. But on the whole, the trends are toward democracy, innovation, more broadly shared opportunities, and positive partnerships among the countries themselves and with the United States. That's the future we want.

13

Africa: Guns or Growth?

Will Africa's future be defined more by guns and graft or growth and good governance? Across this vast continent, there is rising prosperity and terrible poverty, responsible governments and total lawlessness, lush fields and forests and drought-stricken states. That one region can encompass all these extremes prompts the question that guided our work at the State Department: How can we help support the tremendous progress happening in so many places across Africa, while also helping to turn the tide in those places where chaos and privation still dominate?

The legacy of history hangs heavy over this question. Many of the continent's conflicts and challenges stem from colonial-era decisions that drew borders without regard for ethnic, tribal, or religious differences. Poor governance and faulty economic theories in the postcolonial era perpetuated divisions and promoted corruption. Rebel leaders, as is often the case everywhere, knew how to fight but not govern. The Cold War made much of Africa an ideological and sometimes real battleground between forces backed by the West and those backed by the Soviet Union.

The continent's challenges remain acute, to be sure, but there is another side to Africa emerging in the 21st century. Several of the fastest-growing economies in the world are in sub-Saharan Africa. Since 2000, trade between Africa and the rest of the world tripled. Private foreign investment surpassed official aid, and it is expected to continue growing. Between 2000 and 2010, nonpetroleum exports from across Africa to the

United States quadrupled, from $1 billion to $4 billion, including clothing and crafts from Tanzania, cut flowers from Kenya, yams from Ghana, and high-end leather goods from Ethiopia. Over the same period, child mortality rates declined while primary school enrollment increased. More people gained access to clean water and fewer died in violent conflicts. Africa now boasts more cell phone users than either the United States or Europe. Economists expect consumer spending in sub-Saharan Africa to grow from $600 million in 2010 to $1 trillion by 2020. All of this means that a different kind of future is possible. In many places, that future has already arrived.

President Obama and I knew that helping Africa tip toward opportunity instead of conflict was not likely to make big headlines back home, but it could yield big benefits for the United States down the road. To that end, he visited sub-Saharan Africa earlier in his term than any American President before him, making a trip to Ghana in July 2009. In a speech at the Parliament in Accra describing a new vision for America's support for democracy and expanded trade in Africa, the President memorably said, "Africa doesn't need strongmen. It needs strong institutions." He also acknowledged that historically Western powers had too often seen Africa as a source of resources to be exploited or as a charity cause in need of patronage. He issued a challenge to Africans and Westerners alike: Africa needs partnership, not patronage.

For all the progress being made, however, there were too many African nations where workers earned less than a dollar a day, mothers and fathers died of preventable diseases, children were schooled with guns instead of books, women and girls were raped as a tactic of war, and greed and graft were the dominant currency.

The Obama Administration's engagement in Africa would be built around four pillars: promoting opportunity and development; spurring economic growth, trade, and investment; advancing peace and security; and strengthening democratic institutions.

Our approach was in sharp contrast to the way other nations engaged across Africa. Chinese companies, many of them state-owned, responding to their own immense domestic demand for natural resources, were buying up concessions for African mines and forests. Starting in 2005, their direct investment across the continent increased thirtyfold, and by 2009, China had replaced the United States as Africa's largest trading partner. A pattern developed: Chinese companies would enter a market and sign lucrative contracts to extract resources and ship them back to Asia. In return they built eye-catching infrastructure projects like soccer stadiums and superhighways (often leading from a Chinese-owned mine to a Chinese-owned port). They even built a massive new headquarters for the African Union in Addis Ababa, Ethiopia.

There was no doubt that these projects were welcomed by many African leaders and that they were helping modernize infrastructure in a continent where just 30 percent of the roads were paved. But the Chinese brought their own laborers rather than hire local workers who needed jobs and sustainable incomes, and they paid little attention to the health and development challenges Western nations and international organizations worried about. They also turned a blind eye to human rights abuses and antidemocratic behavior. Strong Chinese support for the regime of Omar al-Bashir in Sudan, for example, significantly reduced the effectiveness of international sanctions and pressure, which led some activists concerned with the genocide in Darfur to call for boycotting the Beijing Olympics in 2008.

I grew increasingly concerned about the negative effects of foreign investment in Africa, and frequently raised the issue with Chinese and African leaders. On a visit to Zambia in 2011, I was asked by a TV journalist about the effects of this kind of investment. "Our view is that over the long run, investments in Africa should be sustainable and for the benefit of the African people," I responded. We were sitting together in a U.S.-funded medical center focused on pediatric HIV/AIDS. I had just met a young mother who was HIV-positive, but because of the treatment she was able to receive at the center, her eleven-month-old daughter was HIV-negative. To me, it was a great example of the kind of investment in Africa that America was making. Were we doing that to make money? No. We were doing it because we wanted to see a healthy, prospering Zambian people, which would ultimately be in American interests. "The United States is investing in the people of Zambia, not just the elites, and we are investing for the long run," I said.

The journalist followed up with a question about China in particular. Could the Chinese economic and political system serve as a model for African nations, he asked, "as opposed to the notion of good governance which is largely seen in Africa as being imposed by the West?" I would be the first to applaud the job China has done lifting millions of people out of poverty, but in terms of good governance and democracy, it leaves a lot to be desired. For example, the Chinese policy of noninterference in a nation's internal affairs meant ignoring or abetting the corruption that was costing African economies an estimated $150 billion a year, scaring away investment, stifling innovation, and slowing trade. Accountable, transparent, and effective democratic governance was a better model. But to give the Chinese their due, they have the capacity to get big projects done, at home and abroad. If we wanted to do a better job of creating opportunity and reducing corruption, we had to do more to increase countries' capacity to deliver results.

I talked about some of these challenges in a speech in Senegal in the summer of 2012. I emphasized that America was pursuing "a model of sustainable partnership that adds value rather than extracts it." I hoped African leaders would become smart shoppers and prioritize the long-term needs of their people over the short-term benefits of a quick payday.

Democracy was under pressure across much of Africa. Between 2005 and 2012, the number of electoral democracies in sub-Saharan Africa fell from twenty-four to nineteen. That was still far better than in the 1990s, when there were hardly any, but it was not an encouraging trend. Over my years as Secretary, we saw coups in Guinea-Bissau, where no elected President has ever successfully served a full five-year term, the Central African Republic, Côte d'Ivoire, Mali, and Madagascar.

The United States devoted considerable diplomatic effort to resolving these crises. In June 2011, I visited the headquarters of the African Union in Ethiopia and issued a challenge directly to the continent's leaders: "The status quo is broken; the old ways of governing are no longer acceptable; it is time for leaders to lead with accountability, treat their people with dignity, respect their rights, and deliver economic opportunity. And if they will not, then it is time for them to go." I invoked the upheaval of the Arab Spring, which was washing away stagnant governments across the Middle East and North Africa, and suggested that without change and a positive vision for the future, that wave could roll across sub-Saharan Africa as well.

When I visited Senegal, long viewed as a model of African democracy that had never suffered a military coup, it had recently weathered a constitutional crisis. In 2011, President Abdoulaye Wade, the country's idiosyncratic eighty-five-year-old leader, attempted to circumvent constitutional limits and run for a third term, sparking widespread protests. This problem was all too familiar in Africa: aging leaders, especially former heroes of national liberation movements who saw themselves as the fathers of their countries, refused to retire when the time came or allow their country to move forward into the future without them. The most famous example of that is Robert Mugabe of Zimbabwe who clings to power while his country suffers.

In Senegal, when Wade decided to remain in office, a handful of musicians and young activists helped build a mass movement with a simple slogan: "We're Fed Up." Johnnie Carson, my Assistant Secretary for African Affairs, tried to convince Wade to put the good of the country first, but he wouldn't listen. Senegal's civil society demanded the President honor the Constitution and step down. They got to work registering and educating voters. Students marched in the streets proclaiming, "My voting card is my weapon." The Senegalese military, true to its tradition, stayed clear of politics.

In the February 2012 elections, long lines of citizens waited to vote. Activists fanned out to observe more than eleven thousand polling stations, texting vote counts and reports of irregularities to an independent clearinghouse in Dakar, called the Situation Room by the Senegalese women who ran it. All in all, it was perhaps the most sophisticated election monitoring program ever deployed in Africa. At the end of the day Wade was defeated. He finally acceded to the will of the voters, and there was a peaceful transfer of power. I called President-elect Macky Sall to commend him on his victory and told him, "Even more than your personal victory, the peaceful transfer of power is an historic victory for democracy." The day after the vote, Sall visited the Situation Room to thank the activists who had worked so hard to protect Senegal's Constitution.

In my speech in Dakar that August, I congratulated the people of Senegal and emphasized that promoting democratic progress was at the heart of America's approach in Africa:

> *I know there is sometimes an argument that democracy is a privilege belonging to wealthy countries, and that developing economies must put economic growth first and worry about democracy later. But that's not the lesson of history. Over the long run, you can't have effective economic liberalization without political liberalization. . . . The United States will stand up for democracy and universal human rights, even*

when it might be easier or more profitable to look the other way, to keep the resources flowing. Not every partner makes that choice, but we do and we will.

=====

As much as any place, Liberia represents the ongoing struggle for so many countries in Africa between a painful past and a hopeful future—between guns or growth.

Americans often worry about partisan warfare in Washington and wonder why our elected leaders can't seem to get along. But our Congressional feuds pale in comparison to the battles fought by members of the Legislature of Liberia. When I visited in August 2009, the chamber was full of lawmakers who had literally taken up arms against one another for years. Here was Senator Jewel Taylor, ex-wife of the former Liberian dictator Charles Taylor, who was then on trial at The Hague for war crimes. There was the former warlord turned Senator Adolphus Dolo, known on the battlefield as General Peanut Butter (many Liberian generals had colorful nicknames), whose election slogan was "Let him butter your bread." The fact that they were sitting together as the elected representatives of a nation finally at peace would have been hard to imagine during Liberia's long and bloody civil war. Between 1989 and 2003 roughly 250,000 Liberians were killed and millions fled their homes. The story of how Liberians finally managed to put that dark chapter behind them is one of hope, and a testament to the role that women can (and often must) play in making peace, restitching the torn fabric of society, and working together for a better future.

In 2003 Liberian women began saying to one another, "Enough is enough." Activists like the future Nobel Peace Prize winner Leymah Gbowee formed a movement to agitate for peace. That spring thousands of women from all walks of life, Christians and Muslims together, flooded the streets, marching, singing, and praying. Dressed all in white, they sat in a fish market in the hot sun under a banner that read, "The women of Liberia want peace now." The warlords tried to ignore them. Then they tried to disperse them. But the women wouldn't leave. Finally the warlords agreed to begin peace negotiations. But the talks dragged on and on, so a group of the women traveled to the peace conference in neighboring Ghana and staged a sit-in. They linked arms and blocked the doors and windows until the men inside reached an agreement. This story is captured in a remarkable documentary, *Pray the Devil Back to Hell*, which I highly recommend.

A peace agreement was finally signed, and the dictator Charles Taylor fled. Still the women of Liberia did not rest. They turned their energies to making sure the peace would endure and deliver results for their families and reconciliation for their nation. In 2005 they helped elect one of their own, another future Nobelist, Ellen Johnson Sirleaf, as the first woman President in Africa.

Like Nelson Mandela, President Johnson Sirleaf grew up as the grandchild of a chief. As a young woman, she studied economics and public policy in the United States, receiving a Master of Public Administration degree from Harvard's Kennedy School in 1971. Her career in Liberian politics was a high-wire act. She served as an Assistant Minister of Finance but fled the country in 1980 when a coup toppled the government. After stints at the World Bank and Citibank, she returned in 1985 and ran for Vice President. But she was promptly jailed for criticizing the repressive regime of dictator Samuel Doe. She was pardoned amid an international outcry, and then ran for and won a seat in the Senate, but refused it in protest. After being arrested and imprisoned once again, she sought exile in the United States in 1986. In 1997, she was back, this time running for president of Liberia against Charles Taylor. Finishing a distant second, she was once more forced into exile. After the civil war ended in 2003 and Taylor resigned, Johnson Sirleaf returned and finally won the presidency in 2005, and was reelected to a second term in 2011.

Under Johnson Sirleaf's leadership, the country started to rebuild. The government adopted more responsible fiscal policies and began to attack corruption and promote transparency. Liberia made progress on debt relief and land reform, and the economy grew despite the global economic crisis. Soon there was free and compulsory education for primary school children, including girls. Johnson Sirleaf worked hard to reform the security services and provide the rule of law that citizens could trust.

By the time I stood before the Legislature in 2009, I was able to congratulate the people of Liberia and declare that, if they kept making progress, their country had the opportunity "to be a model not just for Africa, but for the rest of the world."

That August I also visited Kenya. With U.S. Trade Representative Ron Kirk, I flew into Nairobi's Jomo Kenyatta International Airport, named after the founder of modern Kenya. On the day his country was born, December 12, 1963, he gave a famous speech that used the word *harambee*, Swahili for "all pull together," and asked his country's newly independent citizens to unite as one. The phrase was on my mind as we drove into town from the airport and saw the hundreds of little mom-and-pop businesses lining the roads and then the office towers of downtown Nairobi.

Ron and I were there to attend the annual trade and investment meeting held under the African Growth and Opportunity Act (AGOA), legislation signed by my husband in 2000 to increase African exports to the United States. The United States imported hundreds of thousands of barrels of oil from Nigeria and Angola per day, and we worked persistently to support greater transparency and accountability for oil revenues. But we also wanted to encourage greater nonpetroleum exports, especially from small and medium-sized businesses.

Corruption was the major impediment to growth in most of Africa, so I was smiling when I entered the campus of the University of Nairobi and saw large crowds waving and holding banners of welcome, one of which announced, "You are entering a no-corruption zone." Inside I held a raucous town hall discussion with students and activists, moderated by the American journalist Fareed Zakaria.

One of the participants was Wangari Maathai, the Kenyan Nobel Peace Prize winner who had led a grassroots movement of poor women to plant trees across Africa and reforest the continent. I was a fan and a friend of Wangari and was delighted to see her, and pained when she passed away too soon in 2011. At one point Zakaria turned to her for a comment about China's growing influence and investment in Africa, noting that she had told the press that China was "willing to do business without conditions like respect for human rights." In her response Wangari said something that has stayed with me ever since. "We are in a continent that is extremely rich. Africa is not a poor continent. Anything you want in the world is on this continent. It's like the gods were on our side when the world was being created," she said, to applause. "Yet we are considered among the poorest people on the planet. There's something seriously wrong." Africans, she urged, needed to demand good governance

and accountability from their leaders, and also from the foreign investors
and partners seeking to do business there.

I agreed completely and offered the example of Botswana as a model
of how good choices could lead to good outcomes. In the mid-20th century that landlocked nation just north of South Africa was among the
poorest places in the world. When it gained independence from Britain
in 1966, it had only two miles of paved roads and one public secondary
school. The next year the future of the country changed forever when a
massive diamond mine was discovered. Botswana's new government, led
by President Seretse Khama, was faced with an influx of new wealth and
powerful outside actors with their own agendas.

Many countries in this situation have fallen victim to the "resource
curse," squandering their potential windfalls due to corruption and poor
governance. Leaders have lined their own pockets or grasped for short-
term profits at the expense of long-term sustainability. Foreign governments and corporations have exploited weak institutions while leaving
most people as poor as before. But not in Botswana. Its leaders set up a
national trust fund that invests diamond revenues in the country's people
and infrastructure. As a result Botswana has thrived. USAID and the
Peace Corps were able to pack up shop and go home. Democracy took
root, with regular, free, and fair elections and a strong human rights
record. The country boasts some of the best highways in Africa—which
I saw when Bill and I visited in 1998—nearly universal primary education, clean water, and one of the longest life expectancies on the continent.
Botswana's leaders have stressed the 5 Ds: Democracy, Development,
Dignity, Discipline, and Delivery.

If more African nations followed the example of Botswana, many of
Africa's challenges could finally be surmounted. As I told the audience
in Nairobi, "Africa's best days can be ahead if we get a hold of this whole
question of the use of natural resources and who benefits and where the
revenues go."

After many more questions about the choices facing Africa's people,
Zakaria turned to a lighter topic. Five years earlier a Kenyan city coun-
cilman had written Bill a letter offering forty goats and twenty cows in
exchange for our daughter's hand in marriage. As I prepared to return to
Nairobi, he made a stir in the local press by announcing that the offer was
still on the table. To the delight of the crowd, Zakaria wanted to know
what I thought of the proposal. I paused. I'd answered a lot of questions

all over the world, but this was a first. "Well, my daughter is her own person. She's very independent," I said. "So I will convey this very kind offer." The students laughed and applauded.

Despite the good feelings in the hall, the mood outside was complex and uncertain. The paroxysm of violence that followed the controversial December 2007 elections led to an uneasy alliance between former opponents, President Mwai Kibaki and Prime Minister Raila Amolo Odinga (a newly created position). Their government included a Deputy Prime Minister, Uhuru Kenyatta, who would later be elected President himself despite being indicted for the violence by the International Criminal Court.

President Kibaki and Prime Minister Odinga brought together their Cabinet to meet with me in the hope I would tell them that President Obama would visit soon. I explained instead that the President and I were concerned about the flawed election, political violence, and rampant corruption, and that the President expected more from them. My comments led to a spirited discussion, and I offered U.S. help to improve Kenya's election system. Along with the United Kingdom, the United States offered assistance registering voters and electronically counting votes, which would work well both when the country voted in favor of a new Constitution in 2010, and when Kenyatta won the 2013 election. The United States also stepped up our support to the Kenyan military as it joined the fight in Somalia against Al Shabaab, a terrorist group with ties to al Qaeda.

Kenya is an economic and strategic hub for East Africa, so what happens there matters not just to Kenyans. Improving governance and growth are key to their stability and prosperity, and a key priority is increasing agricultural productivity. That's why I visited the Kenya Agricultural Research Institute with U.S. Secretary of Agriculture Tom Vilsack. We toured a soil-testing lab and exhibitions on agricultural improvements made possible by U.S. development aid. For three decades, despite the fact that farming remained the dominant form of employment across Africa, agricultural exports declined. The lack of roads, inconsistent irrigation, poor storage facilities, and ineffective farming practices, including poor seeds and fertilization, undermined the hard work of farmers in the field and threatened food supplies. Unless this problem could be solved, neither Kenya nor Africa would ever achieve full economic or social potential.

Historically the U.S. government has sent large amounts of food aid to fight hunger in developing countries in Africa and around the world. Delivering free rice and wheat and other essentials helped feed hungry families, but it also undercut the market viability of indigenous agriculture, encouraged dependency, and did little to create homegrown, sustainable solutions. We decided to take a new approach, focused more on building up the capacity of local farmers and making sure the right infrastructure was in place to get their produce to consumers. The result was a program we called Feed the Future. I later visited successful programs in Tanzania, where it had the strong support of President Jakaya Kikwete, and in Malawi, where President Joyce Banda stressed the importance of improving the country's agricultural productivity. To date Feed the Future has reached more than 9 million households, and its nutrition programs have served more than 12 million children under five. I'm hoping that we will see the time when African farmers (most of whom are women) will be able to produce enough to feed the continent and export the rest.

===

Alongside much progress, Africa still offered many cautionary tales of countries that have tipped into conflict and chaos. There was probably no place on the map more grim than the eastern Congo.

In May 2009, Senator Barbara Boxer, a longtime champion of women's rights, chaired a hearing of the Senate Foreign Relations Committee on violence against women in war zones. She focused on the long-running civil war in the Democratic Republic of Congo (DRC), where soldiers on both sides raped women as a way of dominating communities and gaining tactical advantage. At least 5 million people had died over fifteen years of fighting, and millions of refugees had fled their homes, destabilizing the Great Lakes region of Central Africa. The eastern city of Goma was full of displaced people and had become known as the rape capital of the world. Roughly thirty-six women a day, 1,100 a month, reported rapes, and there was no telling how many went unreported.

Following the hearing, Senator Boxer and two of her colleagues, Russ Feingold and Jeanne Shaheen, sent me a letter with a series of recommendations about how the United States could show greater leadership in the DRC. Horrified by the reports coming from Goma and concerned about the broader strategic stakes, I asked Johnnie Carson whether a personal visit from me could help deliver tangible results for the women of Goma.

He thought that if I could convince the embattled Congolese President Joseph Kabila to accept help to crack down on gender-based violence, it would be worth the trip. Plus there was no better way to draw the attention of the world and galvanize a more robust response from international institutions and aid organizations. So we decided to go.

In August 2009, I landed in Kinshasa, the DRC's sprawling capital on the Congo River. The NBA star Dikembe Mutombo, towering over me, led me on a tour of the pediatric ward of the Biamba Marie Mutombo Hospital, which he had built and named in his late mother's honor.

At a town hall meeting at St. Joseph's School, I encountered an air of sullen resignation among the young people of Kinshasa. They had reason to feel hopeless. The government was feckless and corrupt, roads were nonexistent or barely passable, hospitals and schools were woefully inadequate. For generations their country's rich resources had been plundered, first by the Belgians, then by the notorious dictator Mobutu (who, I am sorry to say, profited extensively from his manipulation of U.S. aid), and then by the rulers who succeeded him.

It was hot and stuffy in the auditorium, adding to the sour mood. A young man stood up and asked a question about a controversial Chinese loan to the government. He was nervous and stumbled a bit, but the translation I was hearing came through as, "What does Mr. Clinton think through the mouth of Mrs. Clinton?" It sounded like he wanted me to share my husband's thoughts rather than my own. In a country where too many women were abused and marginalized, the question infuriated me. "Wait, you want me to tell you what my husband thinks?" I snapped. "My husband is not the Secretary of State. I am. So you ask my opinion, I will tell you my opinion. I'm not going to be channeling my husband." The moderator quickly turned to another question.

After the event the young man came over and apologized. He said he had meant to ask about President Obama, not President Clinton, and that the translation had been garbled. I was sorry I had snapped at him, not least because the moment dominated the headlines and overshadowed the message I wanted to send about improving governance and protecting women in the Congo.

The next day I left Kinshasa on a UN transport plane and flew more than three hours east to Goma. My first stop was to meet President Kabila in a tent behind the governor's house on the shore of Lake Kivu.

Kabila was distracted and unfocused, seemingly overwhelmed by the many challenges plaguing his country. One crucial issue was figuring out how to pay the government's soldiers. Undisciplined and unpaid, they had become as much a threat to the people of the region as the rebels who attacked from the jungle. It wasn't enough to allocate money in Kinshasa. By the time it filtered down through the ranks, nearly all of it would be pocketed by corrupt senior officers, leaving nothing for the enlisted men. I offered to help his government set up a mobile banking system to make it easier to transfer money directly into accounts for each soldier. Kabila was amazed at the potential of this technology and agreed. By 2013 the system was being hailed as "just short of a miracle," although corruption remained endemic.

After seeing Kabila, I headed to the Mugunga camp for internally displaced people, refugees in their own country. More than a decade of war had devastated towns and villages, forcing families to abandon their homes and belongings in search of any shelter that offered relative security. But as is so often the case in refugee crises, this and other camps were plagued by problems. Access to clean water, sanitation, and other basic services was a continuing challenge. The security personnel hadn't been paid in months. Disease and malnutrition ran rampant.

I began by meeting with aid workers to learn more about their experiences in the camp. Then a Congolese man and woman, introduced as the "elected leaders" of the camp, gave me a tour through the long rows of tents, small market, and health clinic. It reminded me of why I had become impatient about many refugee camps. While I appreciate the need to give people temporary shelter during a conflict or after a disaster, too often camps turn into semi-permanent de facto detention centers, awash with disease, poverty, and hopelessness.

I asked the woman leading the tour what the people there needed most. "Well, we'd like our children to go to school," she said. "What?" I asked, appalled. "There is no school? How long have you been here?" "Nearly a year," she said. That drove me crazy. The more I learned, the more questions I had: Why were women being raped when they went out to get firewood and water? Why couldn't the camp organize patrols of the men to protect the women coming and going? Why were babies dying from diarrhea when medical supplies were available? Why couldn't we donors do a better job of learning and applying lessons from our experiences in helping refugees and internally displaced people in other places?

In brightly colored clothing and with exuberant, undaunted energy, the people of the camp crowded around everywhere I went, waving and smiling and shouting out comments. It was inspiring to feel the force of their spirited endurance in the face of so much pain and destruction. The NGO workers, doctors, counselors, and UN officials were all doing what they could under extremely difficult circumstances. They worked every day to repair the broken bodies and spirits of women who had been raped, often by gangs, and often in such brutal fashion that they could no longer bear children, work, or even walk. Despite my criticism of conditions in the camp, I admired the resilience I saw.

From the camp I headed to HEAL Africa, a hospital built to treat victims of rape and sexual attacks. In a small room there I had heartrending conversations with two women who had survived brutal sexual attacks that had left each suffering from horrible physical and mental wounds.

If I had seen the worst of humanity on this visit, I had also seen the best, especially those women who, after they had recovered from being raped and beaten, went back into the forest to rescue other women left to die. During my trip to the DRC, I heard an old African proverb: "No matter how long the night, the day is sure to come." These people were doing their best to make that day come faster, and I wanted to do all I could to help.

I announced that the United States would provide more than $17 million to combat sexual violence in the DRC. The money would fund medical care, counseling, economic assistance, and legal support for survivors. Nearly $3 million would be used to recruit and train police officers to protect women and girls, to investigate sexual violence, and to dispatch technology experts to help women and frontline workers use cell phones to document and report abuses.

Back home we also supported legislation targeting the extraction and sale of "conflict minerals" that helped fund the militias that kept the conflict going. Some of these minerals eventually found their way into high-tech consumer goods, including mobile phones.

A little more than a month after my trip to Goma, in late September 2009, I presided over a meeting of the United Nations Security Council focused on women, peace, and security, where I proposed making the protection of women and children from the kinds of rampant sexual violence I witnessed in the Congo a priority for UN peacekeeping missions around the world. All fifteen Council members agreed. It wasn't going to solve the problem overnight, but it was a start.

One country that embodied hopes for the future but seemed weighted down by its troubled past and present was South Sudan. It was the newest country in the world, having gained its independence from Sudan in July 2011, after decades of struggle and conflict. But when I visited in August 2012, South Sudan and Sudan were once again locked in a deadly dispute.

Sudan had been riven by religious, ethnic, and political divisions since the mid-20th century. Since 2000, genocide in the Darfur region and intense fighting over land and resources between the Arab north and the Christian south had claimed more than 2.5 million lives, subjected civilians to unspeakable atrocities, and sent refugees fleeing into neighboring countries. A Comprehensive Peace Agreement was finally signed in 2005, and it included a promise that the South could eventually hold a referendum on independence. But in 2010, talks broke down, and preparations for the referendum stalled. The peace agreement appeared close to collapse, and a return to open conflict seemed likely. With lots of encouragement from the United States, the African Union, and other members of the international community, the two sides pulled back from the brink. The independence vote was held at last, in January 2011, and in July, South Sudan became Africa's fifty-fourth nation.

Unfortunately the 2005 peace agreement left some important issues unresolved. Both sides claimed certain border regions and were ready to occupy them by force. Even more crucial was the issue of oil. By a quirk of geography, South Sudan was blessed with extensive reserves, while Sudan itself was not; however, the South was landlocked and lacked refining and shipping facilities, which the North did have. That meant the two bitter rivals needed each other, stuck in a symbiotic but dysfunctional partnership.

The Sudanese government in Khartoum, still smarting over the loss of their southern dominions, began demanding exorbitant prices to process and transport the South's oil, and it confiscated crude when the South refused payment. In January 2012, South Sudan retaliated by shutting down production altogether. For months the two sides stuck to their guns. Both economies, already fragile, began to crumble. Inflation soared. Millions of families faced food shortages. Soldiers readied for renewed fighting and clashes broke out in oil-rich border areas. It seemed like the definition of a lose-lose scenario.

So in August I flew to Juba, the new capital of South Sudan, to try to broker a deal. It had taken years of patient diplomacy to end the civil war and midwife the birth of a new nation, and we couldn't let that achievement fall apart now. What's more, with intense efforts under way around the world to convince energy-hungry nations to reduce consumption of Iranian oil and shift to new suppliers, we could ill afford to see Sudanese oil go off the market.

But the new President of South Sudan, Salva Kiir, wouldn't budge. I listened to him explain all the reasons why South Sudan couldn't compromise with the North on an oil deal. Behind all the arguments about pricing and refining was a simple human reality: these battle-scarred freedom fighters couldn't bring themselves to move beyond the horrors of the past, even if it meant starving their new nation of the resources it needed to thrive. When the President paused, I decided to try a different tack. I took out a copy of an op-ed that had run in the *New York Times* just a few days before and slid it across the table. "Before we go any further, I would appreciate you reading this," I told him. President Kiir was curious; this was unusual behavior in a high-level diplomatic meeting. As he began to read, his eyes widened. Pointing to the byline, he said, "He was a soldier with me." "Yes," I replied, "but now he's a man of peace. And he remembers that you fought together for freedom and dignity, not for oil."

Bishop Elias Taban is one of the most remarkable people I've ever met. He was born in 1955 in the city of Yei in South Sudan, when it was still under British colonial rule. That same day forces from the North massacred dozens of people in town, and Elias's mother fled into the jungle with her screaming infant. His umbilical cord was freshly cut, and his mother used crushed leaves to stop the bleeding. For three days they hid, before finally returning home. As he grew, Elias was caught up in the country's endless civil war. He became a child soldier at age twelve, alongside his father. Eventually the elder Taban managed to get Elias to the Ugandan border and told him to flee. He was found on the other side by UN relief workers.

By 1978 Elias was back in southern Sudan, living in Juba. He met a group of evangelists from Kenya and felt called to become a man of faith. He earned degrees in civil engineering and theology and learned to speak English, Lingala, Arabic, Bari, and Swahili. When war broke out again in the 1980s, Bishop Taban and his wife, Anngrace, both joined the Sudan People's Liberation Movement and fought for southern Sudan's independence. After the peace agreement in 2005, he devoted himself to promoting reconciliation and sustainable development. He and his followers build schools, orphanages, hospitals, and clean water wells.

In July 2012, dismayed by the continuing conflict between North and South, Bishop Taban published a plea for peace. His op-ed made a significant impression on me. "There must always come a point," he wrote, "where we look forward and recognize the need to stop fighting over past wrongs so we can build toward a new future." That is one of the hardest lessons for people to learn on any level, personal or political, but it is profoundly important in a world where so many societies are still held back by old enmities and conflicts.

I watched President Kiir read his old comrade's words, and his defiance seemed to soften. Perhaps now we could get down to business. I kept emphasizing that "a percentage of something is better than a percentage of nothing." Finally President Kiir agreed to reopen negotiations with the North to try to find a compromise on oil pricing. At 2:45 A.M. the next day, after a marathon negotiation in Ethiopia, the two sides reached a deal so that the oil could begin flowing again.

It was a step in the right direction, but hardly the end of the story. Tensions continued to simmer between the neighbors and within South Sudan itself. In late 2013, tribal divisions and personal feuds erupted in a spasm of violence that threatens to tear the country apart. As of 2014, the future of Africa's youngest nation is full of uncertainty.

Before leaving Juba that August, I asked to meet Bishop Taban so I could thank him in person for his powerful words. When he and his wife came to the U.S. Embassy, they proved to be even more dynamic and inspiring than I had expected, and they got a big kick out of hearing my story about distributing his op-ed in the Presidential Palace.

In September 2013, I was honored to invite Bishop Taban to the Clinton Global Initiative meeting in New York and present him with a Global Citizen Award for his peacemaking efforts. He told the audience that American engagement in the oil dispute had been "an answer for prayers" and that, while many challenges remained for his country, the fragile peace was holding. Then he pointed to an eight-month-old baby sitting on his wife's lap. The boy had been discovered in the jungle near Yei in February. The police had called Bishop Taban and Anngrace for help. After some soul-searching, Anngrace said, "If it is a call of God in our life, we have no choice. Let them bring the child." The police were relieved, but then they said, "Bishop, wait a minute. The cord is not cut. We want to rush to the hospital and make sure that it's cut." The Bishop and his wife took this echo of his own birth as a sign, and they brought Little John home to live with their four other adopted children in a country still struggling to grow beyond its own difficult birth.

======

For decades Somalia has been one of the poorest, most war-torn nations in the world, a classic failed state. Persistent conflict between rival warlords and extremists, prolonged drought, widespread hunger, and periodic disease outbreaks left roughly 40 percent of the population in need of emergency humanitarian aid. For Americans, the name Somalia conjures up painful memories of the troubled UN humanitarian mission launched by President George H. W. Bush in late 1992 to ensure that food aid reached starving Somalis without interference by clashing warlords. My husband continued the mission when he became President. The tragic "Black Hawk Down" incident, in which eighteen American soldiers were killed in Mogadishu, became a lasting symbol of the dangers of American involvement in messy global hotspots. Bill pulled our troops out of Somalia, and for the next fifteen years the United States remained reluctant to commit military resources to Africa, although we remained active with political and humanitarian efforts.

Yet, by 2009, Somalia's problems were too great for the United States to ignore. The violent extremist group Al Shabaab, which has links to al Qaeda, represented a growing threat to the entire region. The terrorist attacks of 9/11 had driven home the lesson that failed states could become staging grounds for strikes far beyond their borders. Pirates based in Somalia were also posing an increasing threat to international shipping in the Gulf of Aden and the Indian Ocean, highlighted by the April 2009 hijacking of the *Maersk Alabama*, dramatized in the 2013 movie *Captain Phillips*. So the United States and the international community had a compelling interest in arresting Somalia's slide into oblivion and helping bring some semblance of order and stability to the Horn of Africa. Here was a guns-or-growth question with major implications for our own national security.

In the spring and summer of 2009 Al Shabaab was on the offensive, overwhelming the forces of Somalia's weak transitional government in the capital of Mogadishu and the African Union troops deployed to protect it. The extremists reached within a few city blocks of the Presidential Palace. I told Johnnie Carson, "We can't let the Somali government fail and we can't let Al Shabaab win." Johnnie later told me that he lay awake that night racking his brain for ideas of how we could act quickly and effectively enough to prevent a terrorist victory. The most urgent need was to get the government cash to pay its troops and purchase ammunition to fight off the extremists. I encouraged Johnnie to be creative in providing what the beleaguered Somali troops needed. Over that summer, Johnnie arranged to deliver the needed funds and hired accountants to track the money. The State Department also arranged for a contractor to fly in a few planeloads of small arms and ammunition from Uganda. It wasn't much, but it provided the beleaguered Somali troops the support they needed to take a stand and begin to push Al Shabaab back.

In August, I arranged to meet with the President of Somalia's transitional government, Sheikh Sharif Sheikh Ahmed. He flew to Nairobi to sit down with me at the U.S. Embassy. Sheikh Sharif was a strictly religious Islamic scholar who had fought an unsuccessful war to replace the government with a system of religious law courts (although he also won acclaim for negotiating the release of kidnapped children). After losing on the battlefield, he had won at the ballot box and, for the moment, appeared to be focused on protecting Somalia's tenuous democracy and improving life for its people. Not that it would matter much if his government was defeated by Al Shabaab.

I found Sheikh Sharif, a young-looking forty-five-year-old, to be intelligent and forthright. He wore a white Islamic prayer hat and a blue business suit with a lapel pin depicting Somali and American flags. I thought that nicely captured the delicate balance he was trying to strike. In our conversation he was candid about the enormous challenges facing his country and fragile government. I told him that the United States would continue to send millions of dollars of military aid to his beleaguered forces and step up training and other support. But in return, his government would have to commit to making real progress toward establishing an inclusive democracy that brought together the country's divided factions. Doing that would take substantial political will, especially from Sheikh Sharif himself.

As we talked, I wondered: Would he shake my hand? That was not a question I had to ask very often as the chief diplomat of the most powerful nation on earth, despite the sexism still rampant in many parts of the world. Even in the most conservative countries where women had little contact with men outside their families, I was nearly always received respectfully. But would this conservative Islamic scholar risk alienating his supporters by shaking the hand of a woman in public, even if it was the U.S. Secretary of State?

When we finished, we walked outside and held a joint press conference. I shared my belief that Sheikh Sharif's government represented "the best hope we've had in quite some time" for the future of Somalia. (Privately I told Johnnie we were going to have to redouble our efforts to help the country get back on track.) As we parted, to my delight, Sheikh Sharif grabbed my hand and gave it an enthusiastic shake. A Somali journalist in the crowd shouted a question about whether such a gesture was against Islamic law. Sheikh Sharif just shrugged him off and kept smiling.

Throughout 2009 the Obama Administration increased support for the transitional government and allied African Union forces. Nearly $10 million in targeted aid began to turn the tide against Al Shabaab. Working together, the State Department and the Pentagon stepped up training of thousands of Somali troops in Uganda, sending them back into Mogadishu supplied with food, tents, gasoline, and other essentials. We also increased our training and assistance for the African peacekeepers fighting alongside the Somali troops. We flew in reinforcements directly from Uganda, Burundi, Djibouti, Kenya, and Sierra Leone.

To combat piracy, we set up a task force with the Department of Defense and other agencies and worked with allies and partners around the world to create an international naval force to patrol the most dangerous waters. Even China, usually reluctant to participate in such efforts, joined in. By 2011 pirate attacks off the Horn of Africa had declined by 75 percent.

To help bolster the still relatively weak transitional government, we embedded technical advisors to oversee the distribution of increased economic development assistance. Eventually the lights came back on in Mogadishu and the streets started being cleaned again. Our emergency humanitarian aid kept hungry Somalis alive and gave people the hope and strength needed to reject the extremist insurgency and begin rebuilding their country.

To provide a plan for the future, we launched a diplomatic offensive to bring together Somalia's East African neighbors and the international community behind a single road map for political reconciliation and the establishment of a permanent democratic government that represented all of the country's clans and regions. (The "transitional" government had been in place for years, with few signs of forward movement.)

In the years that followed, Somalia weathered several crises and made halting progress in strengthening democratic institutions and implementing the international road map. There were several times when the process seemed stalled and Al Shabaab rebounded and made tactical gains on the battlefield. The extremists continued to carry out terrorist attacks, including a suicide bombing in October 2011 in Mogadishu that killed more than seventy people, many of whom were young students waiting in line to receive test results. But in September 2011 key leaders from across Somalia's fractured political spectrum pledged to implement the road map, finalize a new Constitution, and select a new government by mid-2012. There was a lot to get done in a short amount of time, but at least there was a plan and a commitment.

In August 2012, just weeks before Somalia was supposed to hold elections and hand over power to new leaders, I once again met with Sheikh Sharif in Nairobi. We were joined by other leaders from Somalia's various clans and factions. I praised them for the progress they had achieved but emphasized how important it was to proceed with the elections and a peaceful transfer of power. That would send a powerful message about Somalia's trajectory toward peace and democracy.

In September, Somalis elected Hassan Sheikh Mohamud President of the new, permanent government. Sheikh Sharif finished a distant second and, admirably, bowed out gracefully.

Our diplomatic work to support Somalia and to coordinate a military campaign against Al Shabaab also had ancillary benefits in the region, helping us develop closer ties to East African partners and improving the capacity of the African Union to take the lead in providing African solutions to African problems.

In August 2012, I visited the Kasenyi Military Base, near Lake Victoria in Uganda, and talked with U.S. Special Operations troops helping train and support the African forces. They showed me some of the small Raven unmanned surveillance drones that were helping the African Union troops go after Al Shabaab. They looked like a child's model airplane, and when I picked one up, it was surprisingly light. Yet it was loaded with sophisticated cameras, and the Ugandans were delighted to have them.

I was glad that American innovation was making a difference in this important fight, and I told the American and Ugandan soldiers that I hoped we could use this new technology also to speed the capture of the notorious warlord Joseph Kony. He and his murderous Lord's Resistance Army (LRA) had been wreaking havoc across Central Africa for years. Kony kidnapped children from their homes, forcing girls into sexual slavery and boys into service in his rebel army. His murderous rampage displaced tens of thousands of Africans and forced countless more to live in perpetual fear. Kony's atrocities became infamous in 2012 through a documentary that became a worldwide internet sensation. I had long been disgusted and outraged by what this monster was doing to children in Central Africa and was eager to see him brought to justice. I urged the White House to help coordinate diplomatic, military, and intelligence resources to track down Kony and the LRA.

President Obama decided to deploy a hundred U.S. Special Operations troops to support and train African forces hunting for Kony. To work with them, I sent State Department experts from our new Bureau of Conflict and Stabilization Operations, which I had created to increase the Department's ability to work in crucial hotspots. Our civilian team arrived on the ground a few months before the troops and began building relationships in local communities. With their encouragement, village chiefs and other leaders started actively encouraging defections from the LRA, including through a new radio station we helped set up for them. It was a small mission, but I thought it showed the potential of what we could achieve when soldiers and diplomats lived in the same camps, ate the same MREs (Meals, Ready-to-Eat), and focused on the same goals. That's smart power in action. Now, if we could use those drones I was inspecting to see through the thick jungle canopy, we might finally be able to locate Kony and end his atrocities. In March 2014, President Obama announced that the United States would send additional Special Operations forces and aircraft to find him. The international community should not rest until he is found and defeated.

Meanwhile, in Somalia, Al Shabaab has lost most of the territory it once controlled. But the group remains a lethal threat, both to Somalia and the wider region. We saw this with tragic consequences in September 2013, when Al Shabaab terrorists attacked a shopping mall in Nairobi and killed more than seventy people. Among the dead was Elif Yavuz, a thirty-three-year-old Dutch nurse working for CHAI, the Clinton Health

Access Initiative, which combats HIV/AIDS and other diseases. She was eight-and-a-half-months pregnant. Elif's Australian partner, Ross Langdon, and their unborn child were also killed. My husband had met Elif on a trip to Tanzania just six weeks earlier and remembered her as beloved by her colleagues. "This beautiful woman comes up to me, very pregnant. She was so pregnant that I assured her that I had been a Lamaze father and could be pressed into service at any moment," he recalled afterward. When Bill reached Elif's grieving mother to offer our condolences, she told him the family had decided to name her unborn child and they were looking at the Swahili words for *life* and *love*. It was heartbreaking for all of us at the Foundation and a reminder that terrorism remains an urgent challenge for our country and the world.

=====

Like so many development workers, Elif Yavuz dedicated her life to helping overcome the scourge of HIV/AIDS and other diseases, including malaria. For Africa, this is a pivotal challenge, with implications for long-term development, prosperity, and peace. In 2003, President George W. Bush launched the ambitious President's Emergency Plan for AIDS Relief (PEPFAR). There are more than 35 million people living with HIV around the world, more than 70 percent of them in sub-Saharan Africa.

When I became Secretary, I was determined to support and expand PEPFAR. I began by convincing Dr. Eric Goosby to head the program as our Global AIDS Coordinator. As a physician in San Francisco in the early 1980s, he had started treating patients with a mysterious disease that would one day be recognized as AIDS. He later joined the Clinton Administration and ran the program named for Ryan White, a young American who contracted the disease from a blood transfusion.

In August 2009, Eric and I traveled to a PEPFAR clinic outside Johannesburg, South Africa. Inside we met with the new South African Minister of Health, Dr. Aaron Motsoaledi. With Motsoaledi's appointment that May, South African President Jacob Zuma signaled a shift away from his predecessor's denial of South Africa's enormous HIV/AIDS problem and toward an aggressive new effort to combat and treat the disease. In that first meeting Motsoaledi told me that South Africa would not have enough money to buy the drugs to treat patients in all nine provinces and asked for our help.

This was a problem I was familiar with. Starting in 2002, Bill and a team at CHAI led by Ira Magaziner worked with pharmaceutical makers to reduce the cost of HIV/AIDS drugs and help millions of people afford the medicine they needed. By 2014 more than 8 million patients around the world have access to HIV/AIDS medicine at much lower cost in no small part because of CHAI's efforts. And not just a little cheaper—up to 90 percent cheaper.

Yet by 2009, even though South Africa was a large manufacturer of generics, the government was still buying large quantities of brand-name antiretroviral drugs. PEPFAR, CHAI, and the Gates Foundation worked with them to complete a shift to generics, which now constitute a vast majority of their purchases. The Obama Administration invested $120 million in 2009 and 2010 to help South Africa buy the less costly medicine. As a result more than double the number of people have been treated. By the end of my tenure, many more people were on antiretroviral drugs in South Africa, and the government had saved hundreds of millions of dollars in the process, all of which it put back into improving health care. When I returned to South Africa in August 2012, the government was preparing to take over management of all the HIV/AIDS programs in the country and to oversee a large-scale expansion of treatment with a goal of treating 80 percent of those in need by 2016.

I knew that we had to build on PEPFAR's success with fewer resources in an age of shrinking aid budgets. Through the use of generic antiretroviral drugs, consolidation of clinics, and more efficient administration and distribution, PEPFAR was able to save hundreds of millions of dollars, which allowed us to expand the program without asking Congress for additional funding. The number of patients treated with antiretroviral drugs paid for by PEPFAR together with country investments and support from the Global Fund rose from 1.7 million in 2008 to nearly 6.7 million in 2013.

The results were above and beyond what I had hoped for. According to the United Nations, since 2000 the rate of new HIV infections has dropped by more than half in many parts of sub-Saharan Africa. People are living longer and accessing more and better treatments. HIV/AIDS, a disease that used to kill 100 percent of patients, is no longer a death sentence.

Because of these successes and the advances of science, I declared an ambitious new goal on World AIDS Day in 2011: an AIDS-free generation. That means a generation in which no child is born with the virus, young people are at far lower risk of being infected throughout their lives, and those who do contract HIV have access to treatment that will prevent them from developing AIDS and from passing the virus on to others. HIV may be with us well into the future, but AIDS need not be.

To achieve this goal, we have to focus on targeting key populations, identifying people at risk, and getting them the prevention and care they need as quickly as possible. If we continue to drive down the number of new infections and drive up the number of people on treatment, eventually we will be able to treat more people than become infected every year. That will be the tipping point. It's treatment as prevention.

In August 2012, I visited the Reach Out Mbuya Health Center in Kampala, Uganda, where I met a patient named John Robert Engole. Eight years earlier, having contracted AIDS, John Robert was near death, having dropped ninety-nine pounds and developed tuberculosis. He became the first person in the world to receive life-saving medication through PEPFAR. Miraculously he was still alive and thriving—a living and breathing example of the promise that American support can bring to the people of the world. And he proudly introduced me to two of his children.

=====

Nobody symbolizes the pain of Africa's past or the promise of its future more than Nelson Mandela. Mandela is rightly hailed as a larger-than-life hero. But he was, in fact, deeply human and full of complexity: a freedom fighter and also a champion of peace; a prisoner and a President; a man of anger and forgiveness. Madiba, as his clan, family, and friends called him, spent all those years in prison learning to reconcile these contradictions and become the leader he knew his country needed.

I first went to South Africa in 1994 for Mandela's inauguration. For those of us who witnessed the ceremony, it was an unforgettable moment. Here was a man who had spent twenty-seven years as a political prisoner now being sworn in as President. And his journey represented something even larger: a long but steady march toward freedom for all South Africa's people. His moral example helped a system born out of violence and division end in truth and reconciliation. It was the ultimate guns-or-growth decision.

That day I had breakfast with outgoing President F. W. de Klerk at his official residence and then returned for lunch with the new President. In the course of a few hours the entire history of a nation had changed. At the lunch President Mandela stood to greet the many high-level delegates from around the world. Then he said something that has stayed with me always (I'm paraphrasing here): "The three most important people to me, here in this vast assembly, are three men who were my jailers on Robben Island. I want them to stand up." Mandela called them by name and three middle-aged white men stood up. He explained that in the midst of the terrible conditions in which he was held for so many years, each of those men saw him as a human being. They treated him with dignity and respect. They talked to him; they listened.

In 1997, I returned to South Africa, this time with Chelsea, and Mandela took us to Robben Island. As we retraced his steps through the cells, he said that when he was finally released, he knew he had a choice to make. He could carry the bitterness and hatred of what had been done to him in his heart forever, and he would still be in prison. Or he could begin to reconcile the feelings inside himself. The fact that he chose reconciliation is the great legacy of Nelson Mandela.

Before that visit my head was preoccupied with all the political battles and hostility in Washington, but listening to Madiba talk, I felt those troubles falling back into perspective. I also loved watching Chelsea's face light up around him. They developed a special bond that lasted for the rest of his life. Whenever he and Bill talked on the phone, Madiba would ask to talk to Chelsea, and he stayed in touch with her as she went off to Stanford and Oxford and then moved to New York.

On my first visit to South Africa as Secretary, in August 2009, I paid a call on Madiba at his office in a suburb of Johannesburg. At ninety-one he was frailer than I remembered, but his smile still lit up the room. I pulled my chair close and held his hand, and we talked for half an hour. I also was delighted to see Madiba's remarkable wife, my friend Graça Machel. Before marrying Mandela, she was a political activist and a Minister in Mozambique's government, married to Samora Machel, the President of Mozambique, who helped guide that war-torn country toward peace. He died in a suspicious plane crash in 1986.

Together Graça and I walked through the Nelson Mandela Foundation Centre of Memory and Dialogue, where I examined some of Madiba's prison diaries and letters, early photographs, and even his Methodist Church membership card from 1929. As a fellow Methodist, I was struck by his commitment to self-improvement, a topic he mentioned often, and his unshakable discipline.

Mandela's successors, Thabo Mbeki and Jacob Zuma, struggled with translating his legacy into reality for a nation that was still too violent and too poor. Both men harbored suspicions of the West left over from the decades when the United States supported the apartheid government as a bulwark against Communism during the Cold War. They wanted South Africa to be respected as the most powerful nation in the region and taken seriously on the world stage. That's what we wanted too, and I hoped that a strong and prosperous South Africa would be a force for peace and stability. But respect comes from taking responsibility.

In some instances South Africa could be a frustrating partner. President Mbeki's denial of the science around the HIV/AIDS epidemic was a tragic mistake, and South Africa usually opposed international humanitarian intervention, even in dire cases such as Libya and Côte d'Ivoire, when civilians were under attack. Sometimes it was difficult to interpret the reasons behind the government's actions. Just before my final visit to the country, in August 2012, the South Africans refused at the last minute to allow my Diplomatic Security team to bring the vehicles and weapons they needed into the country. My plane sat on the tarmac in Malawi, waiting to hear how the negotiations unfolded. In the end the matter was resolved, and we were finally able to take off. I was leading a delegation of American business leaders from FedEx, Chevron, Boeing, General Electric, and other companies who were looking to expand their investments in South Africa.

We had worked with the U.S. Chamber of Commerce to organize the trip because more trade between America and South Africa promised to create jobs and opportunities in both countries. More than six hundred American businesses had already put down roots in South Africa. In 2011, for example, Amazon opened a new customer care center in Cape Town that employed five hundred people, with plans to hire as many as a thousand more. A renewable energy company based in Louisville, Kentucky, called One World Clean Energy, signed a $115 million deal for a biorefinery in South Africa to simultaneously produce electricity, natural gas, ethanol, and biodiesel from organic material. The facility was built in the United States and shipped to South Africa in 2012, employing 250 people in South Africa and up to a hundred skilled trade workers in Kentucky. The American executives I brought along had a chance to meet two hundred South African business leaders to talk about prospects for similar mutually beneficial investments.

At a dinner in Pretoria we were greeted by a rare snowfall (August is winter in the Southern Hemisphere), and some South Africans started calling me Nimkita, "The one who brought the snow." There was a lot to discuss with my diplomatic counterpart, International Relations and Co-operation Minister Maite Nkoana-Mashabane. She is a strong woman with a good sense of humor and firm views on her country's prerogatives, who became a friend. Maite hosted dinners for me on both my visits. The guests were predominantly women leaders, including Nkosazana Dlamini-Zuma, who became the first woman elected to head the African Union. During the 2012 visit a talented South African jazz and pop singer got us all up on our feet. We danced, sang, and laughed together on that snowy night.

On that trip I also paid a final visit to my old friend Madiba, who was living in his ancestral village of Qunu, in the Eastern Cape province of South Africa. There he had spent much of his boyhood, and according to his autobiography, it was the scene of his happiest years. As I walked into his modest house among the rolling hills, I was struck, as always, by his incredible smile and uncommon grace. Even in failing health, Mandela was the embodiment of dignity and integrity. He was, until the end, the captain of his "unconquerable soul," as described in his favorite poem, "Invictus" by William Ernest Henley.

My spirits were still soaring from our time together when I arrived at the University of the Western Cape in Cape Town for a speech about the future of South Africa and the continent. In my closing sentences I tried to evoke for the young people there just how far they and we had all come because of Mandela. Recalling his humanity toward his former jailers, I asked them to help us create a world of mutual understanding and justice, where every boy and girl can have a fighting chance. I reminded them that the great burden of coming from a country admired by the rest of the world, as both the United States and South Africa are, requires adherence to a set of higher standards. It was his willingness to accept that heavy burden that always set Nelson Mandela apart.

On December 5, 2013, Nelson Mandela died at the age of ninety-five. Like so many others around the world, I grieved the passing of one of the greatest statesmen of our time, and the loss of a dear friend. He had meant so much to our whole family for so long. President Obama asked us to accompany him to the funeral, along with Michelle and George W. and Laura Bush. I joined them, and Bill and Chelsea, who were in Brazil, flew to meet us there.

On the flight over in Air Force One, the President and Mrs. Obama occupied their cabin at the front of the plane. Its two beds, shower, and office make the long flight more bearable for any First Family. The Bushes were assigned the room usually occupied by the medical team. I was in the senior staff room. The Obamas invited the Bushes and me to join them in the big conference room. George, Laura, and I talked about "life after the White House," and George described his newfound passion for painting. When I asked him if he had any photos of his work, he fetched his iPad to show us his latest subjects, bleached animal skulls found on his ranch. He explained that he was practicing how to paint different shades of white. It was clear he had a natural talent and had worked hard to learn the art. The atmosphere was warm and relaxed. Regardless of politics, we've had a unique experience, and finding time to catch up and trade stories is invariably educational and often entertaining.

The memorial ceremony was held in a stadium in Soweto under a steady rain. Present and former Kings, Queens, Presidents, Prime Ministers, and dignitaries from around the world joined thousands of South Africans to pay tribute to the man President Obama called "a giant of history."

After the public ceremony, Bill, Chelsea, and I visited privately with Graça, other family members, and close staff at their home in Johannesburg. We signed a book of memories in Mandela's honor and recalled stories of his remarkable life. Another friend, the rock star and activist Bono, had also come to the public memorial. He had become a passionate and effective advocate for fighting poverty across the world, and he developed a partnership and deep friendship with Mandela. Back at the hotel where we were staying, he sat down at a big white piano and played a song in Madiba's memory. I'm no Condi Rice on the piano, but Bono was generous enough to let me sit next to him and hit a few keys, which delighted my more musical husband.

I thought back to Madiba's inauguration in 1994 and marveled at all he and his nation had accomplished. But I also hoped that South Africa would take this sad moment to recommit itself to following the course Mandela had begun, toward a stronger, more inclusive democracy and a more just, equal, and humane society. I hoped the same for all of us around the world. When he accepted the Nobel Peace Prize, Mandela shared his dream of "a world of democracy and respect for human rights, a world freed from the horrors of poverty, hunger, deprivation and ignorance." With that kind of vision, anything is possible, and one of my fondest hopes is that a 21st-century Africa will emerge that creates opportunity for its young people, democracy for its citizens, and peace for everyone. That would be an Africa worthy of Nelson Mandela's long walk to freedom.

PART FIVE

Upheaval

14

The Middle East:
The Rocky Path of Peace

The Palestinian flag has three horizontal stripes, black, white, and green, with a red triangle jutting out from the hoist. From the time of the Six Day War in 1967 until the Oslo Peace Accords in 1993, it was banned in the Palestinian territories by the Israeli government. It was seen by some as an emblem of terrorism, resistance, and the intifada, the violent uprising against Israeli rule that rocked the Palestinian territories in the late 1980s. Even seventeen years after Oslo, the flag remained a controversial and inflammatory symbol among some conservative Israelis. So it was a surprise to arrive in mid-September 2010 at the official residence in Jerusalem of Prime Minister Benjamin "Bibi" Netanyahu, leader of the right-wing Likud Party, and find the black, white, green, and red colors of the Palestinians hanging next to the familiar blue and white flag of Israel.

Flying the Palestinian flag, which Bibi had criticized when his predecessor, Ehud Olmert, had done it some years before, was a conciliatory gesture from the Prime Minister to his other guest that day, Palestinian Authority President Mahmoud Abbas. "I'm glad you came to my house," Bibi said, as he greeted Abbas. The Palestinian President stopped in the entryway to sign the Prime Minister's guest book: "Today I returned to this house after a long absence, to continue the talks and negotiations, hoping to reach an eternal peace in the entire region and especially peace between the Israeli and Palestinian peoples."

The exchange of kind words could not paper over the pressure we all felt that day. As we sat down in Netanyahu's small private study and began to talk, a deadline hung over our heads. In less than two weeks a ten-month moratorium on the construction of new Israeli settlements in the West Bank would expire. Unless we could reach an agreement to extend the freeze, Abbas had pledged to withdraw from the direct negotiations we had only just begun—and Netanyahu was holding firmly to his position that ten months was more than enough. It had taken nearly two years of difficult diplomacy to get these two leaders to agree to negotiate face-to-face on resolving a conflict that had plagued the Middle East for decades. They were finally grappling with core issues that had eluded all previous efforts at peacemaking, including the borders of a future Palestinian state; security arrangements for Israel; refugees; and the status of Jerusalem, a city both sides claimed as their capital. Now it looked like they might walk away from the table at a crucial moment, and I was far from confident that we would find a way out of the impasse.

═══

I visited Israel for the first time in December 1981 on a church trip to the Holy Land with Bill. While my parents babysat for Chelsea back in Little Rock, we spent more than ten days exploring the Galilee, Masada, Tel Aviv, Haifa, and the ancient streets of Jerusalem's Old City. We prayed at the Church of the Holy Sepulchre, where Christians believe Jesus was buried and resurrected. We also paid our respects at some of the holiest sites for Christians, Jews, and Muslims, including the Western Wall, the Al-Aqsa Mosque, and the Dome of the Rock. I loved Jerusalem. Even amid all the history and traditions, it was a city pulsing with life and energy. And I deeply admired the talent and tenacity of the Israeli people. They had made the desert bloom and built a thriving democracy in a region full of adversaries and autocrats.

When we left the city and visited Jericho, in the West Bank, I got my first glimpse of life under occupation for Palestinians, who were denied the dignity and self-determination that Americans take for granted. Bill

35

On December 1, 2009, sitting across from President Obama and National Security Advisor Jim Jones, and next to Defense Secretary Bob Gates and Chairman of the Joint Chiefs Mike Mullen aboard Marine One, the Presidential helicopter, on the way to West Point, where President Obama announced his decision to send additional troops to Afghanistan.

General Stanley McChrystal, commander of Coalition forces in Afghanistan; Ambassador Richard Holbrooke; and U.S. Ambassador to Afghanistan Karl Eikenberry look on as I shake hands with a NATO soldier upon my arrival at the airport in Kabul, Afghanistan, on November 18, 2009.

37

Richard Holbrooke speaks at an April 2010 conference in Kabul with Afghan President Hamid Karzai and General David Petraeus.

38

Eating with President Karzai at the Dumbarton Oaks estate in Washington, D.C., in May 2010. I worked hard to connect with Karzai. As with many world leaders, respect and personal courtesy went a long way.

39

I meet with Afghan women activists at an international conference in Bonn, Germany, in December 2011. After the fall of the Taliban in 2001, I began supporting Afghan women as they sought new rights and opportunities.

The day after the 9/11 terrorist attacks, I tour the devastation in Lower Manhattan with New York Governor George Pataki (left) and New York City Mayor Rudolph Giuliani (center). President Obama and I both felt that defeating al Qaeda was crucial to our national security, and that there should be a renewed effort to find Osama bin Laden and bring him to justice.

Students protest my visit in Lahore, Pakistan, in October 2009. My staff warned me that I would be a "punching bag" in Pakistan because of the rising tide of anti-American sentiment, but I thought it was important to engage. "Punch away," I said.

42

I make final edits to a speech in Pakistan in October 2011. I told the Pakistanis that supporting Taliban insurgents was asking for trouble, like keeping poisonous snakes in your backyard and expecting them to bite only your neighbors. With, from left to right, Huma Abedin, Ambassador to Pakistan Cameron Munter, speechwriter Dan Schwerin, Special Representative for Afghanistan and Pakistan Marc Grossman (seated), spokeswoman Toria Nuland, and Philippe Reines.

In one of the most iconic photos—and one of the most dramatic moments—of my four years, we watch the Osama bin Laden raid on May 1, 2011. Seated around the table (from left): Vice President Biden, President Obama, Brigadier General Marshall B. "Brad" Webb, Deputy National Security Advisor Denis McDonough, me, and Secretary Gates. Standing (from left): Admiral Mike Mullen, Chairman of the Joint Chiefs; National Security Advisor Tom Donilon; Chief of Staff Bill Daley; National Security Advisor to the Vice President Tony Blinken; Audrey Tomason, Director for Counterterrorism; John Brennan, Assistant to the President for Homeland Security; and Director of National Intelligence Jim Clapper.

May 1, 2011: The end of a very long day. The national security team listens as President Obama tells the nation that Osama bin Laden has been brought to justice. Joining me are, seated from left to right: James Clapper, Director of National Intelligence; National Security Advisor Tom Donilon; CIA Director Leon Panetta; Admiral Mike Mullen, Chairman of the Joint Chiefs of Staff; and Vice President Joe Biden.

After President Obama announced that Osama bin Laden had been killed, crowds gathered outside the White House in celebration. We could hear the chants of "USA! USA!"

Pictured here with me at the State Department in July 2009, British Foreign Secretary David Miliband was an invaluable partner and friend. On our first call he flattered me as "the right Hercules for this task."

Miliband's successor as British Foreign Secretary, William Hague, and I talk during a United Nations Security Council meeting on peace and security in the Middle East in September 2012. The eloquent Hague would also become a close colleague and a good friend.

ABOVE: I admire a painting while on a tour of Buckingham Palace in London, May 2011. Spending a night at the palace was like stepping into a fairy tale.

RIGHT: Walking up the steps of the Élysée Palace in Paris in January 2010 to greet French President Nicolas Sarkozy, I stepped out of my shoe, leaving me barefoot in front of the press corps. He gracefully took my hand and helped me regain my footing. Later, I sent him a copy of the photograph inscribed, "I may not be Cinderella, but you'll always be my Prince Charming."

German Chancellor Angela Merkel has a great sense of humor. During a lunch at the State Department in June 2011, Vice President Biden and I laugh as she presents me with a framed German newspaper. The front page featured a photo of the two of us standing side by side looking nearly identical, but with our heads cropped out. The paper challenged its readers to guess which is Merkel and which is me.

I host my G-8 counterparts at Blair House in Washington in April 2012. From left to right: Koichiro Gemba of Japan, Guido Westerwelle of Germany, Sergey Lavrov of Russia, William Hague of the United Kingdom, Alain Juppé of France, John Baird of Canada, Giulio Terzi di Sant'Agata of Italy, and Catherine Ashton of the European Union.

52

Meeting with Turkish Prime Minister Recep Tayyip Erdoğan at the Dolmabahce Palace in Istanbul, Turkey, in April 2012. Turkey was a growing power in the region, and I spent hours talking with Erdoğan about everything from Iran to Libya to Syria.

53

Standing with Turkish President Abdullah Gül (left), and Turkish Foreign Minister Ahmet Davutoğlu (right) overlooking Istanbul. I developed a productive and friendly working relationship with Davutoğlu that, though strained numerous times, never ruptured.

54

With Russian Prime Minister Vladimir Putin at his dacha just outside Moscow in March 2010. Putin sees geopolitics as a zero-sum game in which, if someone is winning, then someone else has to be losing. President Obama and I discussed Putin's threats and how to counter them.

55

In June 2012, meeting with Russian Foreign Minister Sergey Lavrov in St. Petersburg. We went from a high point of working on a reset in our relationship to a standoff over Syria. The reset led to a number of early successes, including imposing strong sanctions on Iran and North Korea, before relations cooled when Putin returned.

56

Waiting in my car outside a hotel in Zurich, Switzerland, in October 2009, I work the phones with my Assistant Secretary for European and Eurasian Affairs Phil Gordon to try to coax the Armenian Foreign Minister out of his room to sign an agreement with Turkey. The *New York Times* described my efforts as "down-to-the-wire, limousine diplomacy."

57

I wave to the crowds in Pristina, Kosovo, in front of a huge statue of Bill, who is revered for his role in ending the war there in the 1990s. Across the plaza was an adorable boutique with a familiar name: Hillary. The shopkeeper said they named the store after me "so that Bill wouldn't be lonely in the square."

58

Celebrating with the newly inaugurated Brazilian President Dilma Rousseff on January 1, 2011. She has a strong intellect and true grit, two characteristics necessary for leadership in these challenging times.

59

Dressed in a green jacket, I'm thrilled and surprised when a whale comes quite close to our small boat off the coast of Mexico in February 2012, with other G-20 Foreign Ministers. Next to me is our host, Mexican Foreign Secretary Patricia Espinosa.

60

My time as Secretary wasn't all business. While in Cartagena, Colombia, for the Summit of the Americas in April 2012, I joined staff for a birthday celebration for my Assistant Secretary for Western Hemisphere Affairs, Roberta Jacobson. Later a State Department spokesman was asked by the media to quantify precisely how much fun I had had and gave the official response: "A lot."

61

Greeting Chilean President Michelle Bachelet at the airport in Santiago after a major earthquake in early 2010.

In Monrovia, Liberia, I consult with Liberian President Ellen Johnson Sirleaf during a visit in August 2009. The first woman to serve as President of an African country, Johnson Sirleaf is an impressive leader, and I admire her passion and perseverance.

One of the most heartbreaking trips I took as Secretary was to a refugee camp in Goma in the Democratic Republic of Congo in August 2009. Here I tour the camp and talk to people who face deplorable conditions and an epidemic of sexual violence.

Somalia's transitional President Sheikh Sharif Sheikh Ahmed surprised many in his conservative religious society by shaking my hand after our August 2009 meeting in Nairobi, Kenya. Helping his government beat back Al Shabaab terrorists was a top national security priority in Africa.

It was a privilege to meet Bishop Elias Taban in Juba, South Sudan, in August 2012. Bishop Taban's inspirational story touched me deeply, and I took a copy of his powerful op-ed to my meeting with South Sudanese President Salva Kiir earlier that day.

TOP: Tanzanian Prime Minister Mizengo Pinda and I do some planting at a women's cooperative in Mlandizi, Tanzania, in June 2011 as part of our Feed the Future initiative. BOTTOM: I sing and applaud with Malawian women at the Lumbadzi Milk Bulking Group in Lilongwe, Malawi, in August 2012. Fighting hunger and extreme poverty was both the right and the smart thing to do.

Finding out that there is a Hillary Clinton Shop in Karatu, Tanzania, puts a smile on my face.

Visiting HIV/AIDS patients at a health clinic in Kampala, Uganda, in August 2012. I set an ambitious new goal of achieving an "AIDS-free generation." HIV may be with us well into the future, but AIDS need not be.

After Nelson Mandela's December 2013 memorial service in South Africa, we sat telling stories and celebrating his life and legacy, joined by our friend Bono. Here Bono sits with me at the piano. Bill got a kick out of my attempt to hit a few keys.

and I both came home from that trip feeling a strong personal bond to the Holy Land and its peoples, and over the years we held on to the hope that one day Israelis and Palestinians might resolve their conflict and live in peace.

Over the next thirty years I would return to Israel again and again, making friends and getting to know and work with some of Israel's great leaders. As First Lady I developed a close friendship with Prime Minister Yitzhak Rabin and his wife, Leah, although I don't think Yitzhak ever forgave me for banishing him to the cold air of the White House balcony when he wanted to smoke. (After Rabin accused me of endangering the peace process with this policy I finally relented and said, "Well, if it will further the effort toward peace, I will rescind the rule, but only as it applies to you!") The signing of the Oslo Accords by Rabin and Arafat, accompanied by their famous handshake on the South Lawn of the White House, made September 13, 1993, one of the best days of Bill's presidency. Rabin's assassination on November 4, 1995, was one of the worst. I will never forget sitting with Leah and listening to their granddaughter Noa's heartrending eulogy at his funeral in Israel.

Nor will I forget the Israeli victims of terrorism I met over the years. I've held their hands in hospital rooms and listened to doctors describe how much shrapnel was left in a leg, arm, or head. I visited a bombed-out pizzeria in Jerusalem in February 2002 during some of the darkest days of the second intifada, in which a few thousand Palestinians and about a thousand Israelis were killed between 2000 and 2005. And I've walked along the security fence near Gilo and talked to families who knew a rocket could fall on their home at any moment. These experiences will always be with me.

Here's just one story of an Israeli who touched my life. In 2002, I met Yochai Porat. He was only twenty-six but already a senior medic with MDA, Israel's emergency medical service. He oversaw a program to train foreign volunteers as first responders in Israel. I attended the program's graduation ceremonies and remember the pride in his face as yet another group of young people set off to save lives. Yochai was also a reservist with the Israel Defense Forces. A week after we met, he was killed by a sniper near a roadblock, along with other soldiers and civilians. MDA renamed its overseas volunteer program in his memory. When I visited again in 2005, I met with Yochai's family, who spoke passionately about how important it was to continue supporting the MDA and its mission. I went home and began a campaign to convince the International Red Cross to admit MDA as a full voting member after half a century of exclusion. In 2006, they agreed.

I am not alone in feeling so personally invested in Israel's security and success. Many Americans admire Israel as a homeland for a people long oppressed and a democracy that has had to defend itself at every turn. In Israel's story we see our own, and the story of all people who struggle for freedom and the right to chart their own destinies. That's why President Harry Truman waited only eleven minutes to recognize the new nation of Israel in 1948. Israel is more than a country—it's a dream nurtured for generations and made real by men and women who refused to bow to the toughest of odds. It's also a thriving economy that's a model for how innovation, entrepreneurship, and democracy can deliver prosperity even in unforgiving circumstances.

I was also an early voice calling publicly for Palestinian statehood. During satellite remarks to the Seeds of Peace Middle East Youth Summit in 1998, I told the young Israelis and Palestinians that a Palestinian state would "be in the long-term interest of the Middle East." My comments received considerable media attention, coming two years before Bill, near the end of his presidency, proposed statehood in a plan Israeli Prime Minister Ehud Barak accepted but Arafat didn't, and three years before the Bush Administration made statehood official U.S. policy.

The Obama Administration came into office during a perilous time in the Middle East. Throughout December 2008, militants from the Palestinian extremist group Hamas fired rockets into Israel from the Gaza Strip, which it had controlled since forcing out its rival Palestinian faction, Fatah, in 2007. In early January 2009, the Israeli military invaded Gaza to stop the rocket attacks. In the final weeks of the Bush Administration, Israeli troops battled Hamas gunmen in the streets of densely populated areas. "Operation Cast Lead" was deemed a military victory for Israel—Hamas suffered heavy casualties and lost much of its stockpile of rockets and other weapons—but it was also a public relations disaster. More than one thousand Palestinians died, and Israel faced widespread international condemnation. On January 17, just days before President Obama's inauguration, Prime Minister Ehud Olmert announced a cease-fire beginning at midnight, if Hamas and another radical group in Gaza, the Palestinian

Islamic Jihad, stopped firing rockets. The next day the militants agreed. The fighting stopped, but Israel maintained a virtual siege around Gaza, closing the borders to most traffic and commerce. Hamas, using secret smuggling tunnels that went under the border with Egypt, immediately began rebuilding its arsenal. Two days later President Obama took the oath of office in Washington.

With the crisis in Gaza dominating world attention, my first call to a foreign leader as Secretary of State was to Olmert. We immediately turned to how to preserve the fragile cease-fire and protect Israel from further rocket fire, as well as address the severe humanitarian needs inside Gaza. We also talked about restarting negotiations that could end the broader conflict with the Palestinians and deliver a comprehensive peace to Israel and the region. I told the Prime Minister that President Obama and I would announce former Senator George Mitchell as a new Special Envoy for Middle East Peace later that day. Olmert called Mitchell "a good man" and expressed his hope that we could work together on all the areas we discussed.

At the start of March, I joined representatives from other international donor countries at a conference in Egypt to raise humanitarian aid for needy Palestinian families in Gaza. It was a step toward helping traumatized Palestinians and Israelis put the latest violence behind them. Whatever you thought of the tangled politics of the Middle East, it was impossible to ignore the human suffering, especially the children. Palestinian and Israeli children have the same right as children everywhere in the world to a safe childhood with a good education, health care, and the chance to build a bright future. And parents in Gaza and the West Bank share the same aspirations as parents in Tel Aviv and Haifa for a good job, a secure home, and better opportunities for their kids. Understanding that is a vital starting point for bridging the gaps that divide the region and providing the foundation for lasting peace. When I made this point at the conference in Egypt, members of the normally hostile Arab media broke into applause.

In Jerusalem I had the pleasure of seeing my old friend President Shimon Peres, a lion of the Israeli left who had helped build the new state's defense, negotiated Oslo, and carried forward the cause of peace after Rabin's assassination. As President, Peres had a largely ceremonial role, but he served as the moral conscience of the Israeli people. He still believed passionately in the need for a two-state solution, but he recognized how hard it would be to achieve. "We don't take it lightly, the burden that is now lying on your shoulders," he told me. "But I think they are strong, and you will find in us a real and sincere partner in the double purpose to prevent and stop terror and achieve peace for all of the people in the Middle East."

I also consulted with Olmert and his smart, tough Foreign Minister Tzipi Livni, a former Mossad agent, on defusing tensions in Gaza and strengthening the cease-fire. With sporadic rocket and mortar attacks continuing, it seemed that full-fledged conflict could flare up again at any time. I also wanted to reassure Israel that the Obama Administration was fully committed to Israel's security and its future as a Jewish state. "No nation should be expected to sit idly by and allow rockets to assault its people and its territories," I said. For years, under both Democratic and Republican administrations, the United States had been committed to helping Israel maintain a "qualitative military edge" over every competitor in the region. President Obama and I wanted to take it to the next level. Right away, we got to work expanding security cooperation and investing in key joint defense projects, including Iron Dome, a short-range missile defense system to help protect Israeli cities and homes from rockets.

Olmert and Livni were determined to move toward a comprehensive peace in the region and a two-state solution to the conflict with the Palestinians, despite the many disappointments over decades of halting negotiations. But they were soon on their way out of power. Olmert had announced his resignation under a cloud of corruption charges, mostly stemming from his earlier service as Mayor of Jerusalem. Livni assumed the leadership of their Kadima Party and ran in new elections against Netanyahu and Likud. Kadima actually won one more seat in the Israeli Parliament, the Knesset, than Likud (twenty-eight seats for Kadima, compared to twenty-seven for Likud), but Livni couldn't put together a viable majority coalition among the fractious smaller parties that held the balance of power. So Netanyahu was given a chance to form a government.

I talked to Livni about the idea of a unity government between Kadima and Likud that might be more open to pursuing peace with the Palestinians. But she was dead set against it. "No, I'm not going into his government," she told me. So Netanyahu put together a majority coalition of smaller parties and, at the end of March 2009, returned to the Prime Minister's office he had occupied from 1996 to 1999.

I had known Netanyahu for years. He is a complicated figure. He spent his formative years living in the United States, studied at both Harvard and MIT, and even worked briefly at the Boston Consulting Group with Mitt Romney in 1976. Netanyahu has been deeply skeptical of the Oslo framework of trading land for peace and a two-state solution that would give the Palestinians a country of their own in territory occupied by Israel since 1967. He is also understandably fixated on the threat to Israel from Iran, especially the possibility of Tehran acquiring nuclear weapons. Netanyahu's hawkish views were shaped by his own experience in the Israel Defense Forces, especially during the Yom Kippur War of 1973; the memory of his brother Yonatan, a highly respected commando killed leading the Entebbe raid of 1976; and the influence of his father, Benzion, an ultranationalist historian who had favored a Jewish state encompassing all of the West Bank and Gaza since before the birth of the State of Israel. The elder Netanyahu held fast to that position until he died in 2012 at age 102.

In August 2008, after the end of my Presidential campaign, Netanyahu came to see me in my Senate office on Third Avenue in New York. After a decade in the political wilderness following his defeat in the 1999 elections, Bibi had climbed his way back up to the top of Likud and was now poised to retake the Prime Minister's office. Sitting in my conference room above Midtown Manhattan, he was philosophical about his twists of fortune. He told me that after being voted out, he received some advice from Prime Minister Margaret Thatcher, the Iron Lady herself: "Always expect the unexpected." Now he was giving me the same advice. A few months later, when President-elect Obama first said the words "Secretary of State" to me, I thought back to what Bibi had predicted.

Later we would both look back on that conversation as a new beginning in our relationship. Despite our policy differences, Netanyahu and I worked together as partners and friends. We argued frequently, often during phone calls that would go on for over an hour, sometimes two. But even when we disagreed, we maintained an unshakeable commitment to the alliance between our countries. I learned that Bibi would fight if he felt he was being cornered, but if you connected with him as a friend, there was a chance you could get something done together.

With the region still reeling from the Gaza conflict, and a skeptic back at the helm in Israel, the prospects for reaching a comprehensive peace agreement seemed daunting, to say the least.

There had been nearly a decade of terror, arising from the second intifada, which started in September 2000. About a thousand Israelis were
killed and eight thousand wounded in terrorist attacks from September
2000 to February 2005. Three times as many Palestinians were killed and
thousands more were injured in the same period. Israel began construct-
ing a long security fence to physically separate Israel from the West Bank.
As a result of these protective measures, the Israeli government reported
a sharp decline in suicide attacks, from more than fifty in 2002 to none
in 2009. That was, of course, a great source of relief for Israelis. But it
also lessened the pressure on them to seek even greater security through
a comprehensive peace agreement.

On top of that, the number of Israeli settlers in the West Bank continued to grow, and most of them were adamantly opposed to giving
up any land or closing any settlements in what they called "Judea and
Samaria," the biblical name for the land on the West Bank of the Jordan
River. Some settlers who moved to these outposts across the 1967 "Green
Line" were simply trying to avoid a housing crunch in expensive Israeli
cities, but others were motivated by religious zeal and a belief that the
West Bank had been promised to Jews by God. Settlers were the political
base of Netanyahu's main coalition partner, the Yisrael Beiteinu Party, led
by Avigdor Lieberman, a Russian émigré who became Foreign Minister
in the new government. Lieberman viewed negotiating concessions as a
sign of weakness and had a long history of opposition to the Oslo peace
process. Bibi and Lieberman also believed that Iran's nuclear program
was a bigger and more urgent threat to Israel's long-term security than
the Palestinian conflict. All of this contributed to a reluctance among
Israel's leaders to make the hard choices necessary to achieve a lasting
peace.

═══

After visiting with both the outgoing and the incoming Israeli leadership
in Jerusalem in early March 2009, I crossed into the West Bank and headed
to Ramallah, the headquarters of the Palestinian Authority (PA). Under
previous agreements, the PA administered parts of the Palestinian territories and maintained its own security forces. I visited a classroom where
Palestinian students were learning English through a U.S.-sponsored
program. They happened to be studying Women's History Month and

learning about Sally Ride, America's first woman astronaut. The students, especially the girls, were captivated by her story. When I asked for a single word to describe Sally and her accomplishments, one student responded, "Hopeful." It was encouraging to find such a positive attitude among young people growing up under such difficult circumstances. I doubted one would hear the same sentiment in Gaza. For me, that summed up the divergence of fortunes between the two Palestinian territories.

For nearly twenty years two factions, Fatah and Hamas, have vied for influence among the Palestinian people. When Arafat was alive, his Fatah party was ascendant and his personal stature was enough to largely keep the peace between the two. But after he died in 2004, the schism burst into open conflict. To those disillusioned by a peace process that had failed to deliver much concrete progress, Hamas peddled the false hope that a Palestinian state could somehow be achieved through violence and uncompromising resistance. By contrast, Arafat's successor as head of Fatah and the Palestinian Liberation Organization, Mahmoud Abbas (also known as Abu Mazen), maintained a platform of nonviolence and urged his people to keep pushing for a negotiated political solution to the conflict, while building up the economy and institutions of a future Palestinian state.

In early 2006, Hamas won legislative elections in the Palestinian territories that had been pushed by the Bush Administration over objections by some members of Fatah and the Israelis. The upset victory led to a new crisis with Israel and a violent power struggle with Fatah.

After the election results came in, I released a statement from my Senate office condemning Hamas and stressing, "Until and unless Hamas renounces violence and terror, and abandons its position calling for the destruction of Israel, I don't believe the United States should recognize Hamas, nor should any nation in the world." The outcome was a reminder that genuine democracy is about more than winning an election, and that if the United States pushes for elections, we have a responsibility to help educate people, and parties, about the process. Fatah had lost several seats because it ran two candidates in districts when Hamas fielded only one. It was a costly mistake. The next year Hamas led a coup in Gaza against the authority of Abbas, who continued to serve as President despite his party's losses in the legislative elections. With Fatah still in control in the West Bank, the Palestinian people were split between two competing power centers and two very different visions for the future.

This division made the prospects of resuming peace talks more remote and increased Israeli reluctance. However, as a result of this unusual arrangement, both sides were able to test their approach to governing. The results could be seen every day in Palestinian streets and neighborhoods. In Gaza, Hamas presided over a crumbling enclave of terror and despair. It stockpiled rockets while people fell deeper into poverty. Unemployment ran to nearly 40 percent, and was even higher among young people. Hamas impeded international assistance and the work of humanitarian NGOs and did little to promote sustainable economic growth. Instead Hamas sought to distract Palestinians from its failure to govern effectively by stoking new tensions with Israel and inciting popular anger.

Meanwhile, in the West Bank, Abbas and Prime Minister Salam Fayyad, an able technocrat, produced very different results in a relatively short period of time. They got to work addressing a history of corruption and building transparent and accountable institutions. The United States and other international partners, especially Jordan, helped improve the effectiveness and reliability of PA security forces, which was a key priority for Israel. Reforms began to increase public confidence in the courts, and in 2009 they handled 67 percent more cases than in 2008. Tax revenues were finally being collected. The PA began building schools and hospitals and training teachers and medical staffs. It even started work on a national health insurance program. More responsible fiscal policies, support from the international community—including hundreds of millions of dollars each year from the United States, the PA's largest bilateral donor—and improving security and the rule of law led to significant economic growth. Despite ongoing economic challenges, more Palestinians in the West Bank were finding jobs, starting businesses, and reversing the economic stagnation that followed the outbreak of the second intifada in 2000. The number of new business licenses issued in the West Bank in the fourth quarter of 2009 was 50 percent higher than in the same period in 2008, as Palestinians opened everything from venture capital funds to hardware stores and luxury hotels. Unemployment in the West Bank fell to less than half the rate in Gaza.

Even with this progress, there was much more work to do. Too many people remained frustrated and out of work. Anti-Israeli incitement and violence were still problems, and we hoped to see greater reforms to crack down on corruption, instill a culture of peace and tolerance among Palestinians, and reduce dependence on foreign assistance. But it was becoming easier to envision an independent Palestine able to govern itself, uphold its responsibilities, and ensure security for its citizens and its neighbors. The World Bank reported in September 2010 that if the Palestinian Authority maintained its momentum in building institutions and delivering public services, it would be "well-positioned for the establishment of a state at any point in the near future."

I saw the progress firsthand on visits to the West Bank in 2009 and 2010. Well-equipped Palestinian security officers, many of them trained with U.S. and Jordanian assistance, lined the road. Driving into Ramallah, I could see new apartment buildings and office towers rising from the hills. But as I looked at the faces of the men and women who came out of their shops and homes, it was impossible to forget the painful history of a people who have never had a state of their own. Economic and institutional progress is important, indeed necessary, but it is not sufficient. The legitimate aspirations of the Palestinian people will never be satisfied until there is a two-state solution that ensures dignity, justice, and security for all Palestinians and Israelis.

I will always believe that in late 2000 and early 2001, Arafat made a terrible mistake in refusing to join Prime Minister Barak in accepting the "Clinton Parameters," which would have given the Palestinians a state in the West Bank and Gaza, with a capital in East Jerusalem. Now we were trying again with President Abbas. He had worked long and hard to realize the dreams of his people. He understood those dreams could be achieved only through nonviolence and negotiation. And he believed an independent Palestine living side by side with Israel in peace and security was both possible and necessary. I sometimes thought that while Arafat had the circumstances required to make peace but not the will, Abbas may have had the will but not the circumstances, though at some of our more frustrating moments, I wondered about his will, too.

=====

Coaxing the Israelis and the Palestinians back to the negotiating table was not going to be easy. There was no great mystery about what a final peace deal might look like and the compromises that would have to be struck; the challenge was mobilizing the political will on both sides to make the choices and sacrifices necessary to accept those compromises and make peace. Our diplomatic efforts had to focus on building trust and confidence on both sides, helping the leaders carve out political space to negotiate with each other, and making a persuasive case that the status quo was unsustainable for everyone.

I was convinced that was true. For the Palestinians, decades of resistance, terrorism, and uprisings had not produced an independent state, and more of the same was not going to do anything to advance their legitimate aspirations. Negotiations offered the only credible path to that goal, and waiting just meant prolonging the occupation and suffering on both sides.

For the Israelis, the case was harder because the status quo was less obviously and immediately problematic. The economy was booming, improved security measures had dramatically reduced the threat of terrorism, and many Israelis felt that their country had tried to make peace and received nothing in return but heartbreak and violence. In their eyes, Israel had offered generous deals to Arafat and Abbas, and the Palestinians had walked away. Under Prime Minister Ariel Sharon, Israel had unilaterally withdrawn from Gaza (without a negotiated peace agreement), which had turned into a terrorist enclave that lobbed rockets into southern Israel. When Israel pulled back from southern Lebanon, Hezbollah and other militant groups, with Iranian and Syrian support, used the territory as a base for attacking northern Israel. What reason did Israelis have to think that giving up more land would lead to actual peace?

I was sympathetic to those fears and to the threats and frustrations behind them. But as someone who cares deeply about Israel's security and future, I thought there were compelling demographic, technological, and ideological trends that argued for making another serious attempt at a negotiated peace.

Because of higher birth rates among Palestinians and lower birth rates among Israelis, we were approaching the day when Palestinians would make up a majority of the combined population of Israel and the Palestinian territories, and most of those Palestinians would be relegated to second-class citizenship and unable to vote. As long as Israel insisted on holding on to the territories, it would become increasingly difficult and eventually impossible to maintain its status as both a democracy and a Jewish state. Sooner or later, Israelis would have to choose one or the other or let the Palestinians have a state of their own.

At the same time, the rockets flowing into the hands of Hamas in Gaza and Hezbollah in Lebanon were increasingly sophisticated and capable of reaching Israeli communities far from the borders. In April 2010, there were reports that Syria was transferring long-range Scud missiles to Hezbollah in Lebanon, which could reach all of Israel's major cities. In the spring of 2014, Israel intercepted a ship carrying Syrian-made M-302 surface-to-surface rockets bound for Palestinian militants in Gaza that could reach all of Israel. We would continue building up Israel's air defenses, but the best missile defense system of all would be a just and lasting peace. And the longer the conflict dragged on, the more it would strengthen the hand of extremists and weaken moderates across the Middle East.

For all these reasons, I believed it was necessary for Israel's long-term security to give diplomacy another chance. I had no illusions that it would be any easier to reach an agreement than it had been for previous administrations, but President Obama was ready to invest his own personal political capital, and that counted for a lot. Netanyahu, precisely because of his well-known hawkishness, had the credibility with the Israeli public to cut a deal, like Nixon's going to China, if he were convinced it was in Israel's security interests. Abbas was aging and there was no telling how long he could hold on to power; we couldn't take for granted that his successor, whomever it would be, would be as committed to peace. With all his political baggage and personal limitations, Abbas might well be the last, best hope for a Palestinian partner committed to finding a diplomatic solution and determined enough to sell one to his people. Yes, there was always a danger in diving back into the quagmire of Middle East peace negotiations. Trying and failing could well discredit moderates, embolden extremists, and leave the parties more distrustful and estranged than before. But success was impossible if we didn't try, and I was determined to do so.

The first step toward jump-starting the peace process in January 2009 was appointing George Mitchell as Special Envoy so he could try to repeat the success he had achieved with the Good Friday Agreement in Northern Ireland. The soft-spoken former Senator from Maine was always quick to point out the differences between the two conflicts, but he also drew encouragement from the fact that Northern Ireland had once been deemed as intractable as the Middle East and had been resolved through painstaking negotiations. "We had 700 days of failure and one day of success," he often said. On the other hand, when Mitchell remarked to an audience in Jerusalem that it took eight hundred years of conflict before peace finally came to Northern Ireland, one elderly gentleman scoffed, "Such a recent argument—no wonder you settled it!"

President Obama agreed with me that Mitchell possessed the international prestige, negotiating skills, and patient temperament to take on this crucial task. I also asked Dennis Ross, who had served as Middle East Special Envoy during the 1990s, to come back to the State Department to work on Iran and regional issues. President Obama was so impressed with Ross that he soon asked him to move to the White House to advise him more closely, including on the peace process. There were sometimes tensions between Ross and Mitchell, given their overlapping responsibilities and the high stakes of the assignment, but I valued both of their perspectives and was grateful to have two such experienced foreign policy thinkers as part of our team.

Only days after his appointment, Mitchell headed out to the region for a multistop tour. The Israelis were still sorting out their new government, so Mitchell made the rounds of the Arab capitals. His mandate included working for peace not just between Israel and the Palestinians but also between Israel and all its neighbors. The basis for a comprehensive regional peace would likely be a plan proposed in 2002 by King Abdullah of Saudi Arabia. The plan was unanimously endorsed by all Arab League members, including Syria, in March 2002. Under the Arab Peace Initiative, as it's called, all those countries, and some Muslim-majority nations outside the region, agreed that in return for a successful peace agreement with the Palestinians, they would normalize relations with Israel, including economic, political, and security cooperation. If this could be achieved, it would have profound implications for the strategic dynamics of the Middle East. Because of their shared suspicion of Iran and their partnerships with the United States, Israel and many of the Arab states, especially the Gulf monarchies, should have been natural allies. Enmity over the Palestinian conflict prevented that. Before the 2008–2009 war in Gaza, Turkey had been trying to broker peace talks between Israel and Syria. If Syria could be pried away from its toxic alliance with Iran in exchange for progress on the Golan Heights—the territory it lost to Israel in 1967—that too would have significant strategic consequences.

In nearly every capital Mitchell heard the same thing: Israel needed to stop building settlements on land that would one day become part of a Palestinian state. Each new settlement beyond the old 1967 lines would make it harder to reach a final agreement. For decades the United States had opposed the expansion of settlements as counterproductive to peace efforts. President George H. W. Bush and his Secretary of State, Jim Baker, considered suspending loan guarantees to Israel over the issue. President George W. Bush called for a full construction freeze in his "Roadmap for Peace." But given Netanyahu's political ties to the settlers, he could be expected to balk at any limitations.

After his initial consultations, Mitchell suggested that we ask all three parties—the Israelis, the Palestinians, and the Arab states—to take specific constructive steps to show good faith and lay the foundation for a return to direct peace negotiations.

For the Palestinian Authority, we wanted it to do more to crack down on terrorism and reduce anti-Israeli incitement. Examples of incitement included renaming a public square in the West Bank after a terrorist who murdered Israeli civilians, whipping up conspiracy theories claiming that Israel was planning to destroy Muslim holy places, and actions that glorified and encouraged further violence. As for Hamas, its isolation would continue until it renounced violence, recognized Israel, and pledged to abide by previous signed agreements. Without those basic steps, Hamas would not get a seat at the table. We also demanded the immediate release of Gilad Shalit, a kidnapped Israeli soldier being held in Gaza.

For the Arab states, we hoped to see steps toward normalization with Israel as envisioned under the Arab Peace Initiative, including allowing overflight rights for Israeli commercial air traffic, reopening trade offices, and establishing postal routes. Netanyahu pressed me on this over dinner at the State Department in May 2009. He especially wanted to see action from Saudi Arabia, whose role as "Custodian of the Two Holy Mosques" would give its gestures outsized significance in the region. In June 2009, President Obama traveled to Riyadh and personally raised this issue with King Abdullah.

For the Israelis, we requested that they freeze all settlement construction in the Palestinian territories without exception. In retrospect, our early hard line on settlements didn't work.

Israel initially refused our request, and our disagreement played out in public, becoming a highly personal standoff between President Obama and Netanyahu, with the credibility of both leaders on the line. That made it very hard for either one to climb down or compromise. The Arab states were happy to sit on the sidelines and use the dustup as an excuse for their own inaction. And Abbas, who had consistently called for a halt to settlement construction for years, now claimed it was all our idea and said that he wouldn't come to the peace table without a moratorium on settlement construction.

The President and his advisors had debated the wisdom of making a demand for a settlement freeze. The strongest voice in favor of doing so was Rahm Emanuel's, the White House Chief of Staff. Rahm, a former civilian volunteer with the Israel Defense Forces, had a deep personal commitment to Israel's security. Drawing on his experiences in the Clinton Administration, he thought that the best way to deal with Netanyahu's new coalition government was to take a strong position right out of the gate; otherwise he'd walk all over us. The President was sympathetic to that argument, and he thought insisting on a settlement freeze was both good policy and smart strategy since it would help reestablish America as an honest broker in the peace process, softening the perception that we always took the side of the Israelis. Mitchell and I worried we could be locking ourselves into a confrontation we didn't need, that the Israelis would feel they were being asked to do more than the other parties, and that once we raised it publicly Abbas couldn't start serious negotiations without it. A senior Israeli official once explained to me that for Israelis, the worst thing in the world is to be a *freier*, the Hebrew slang word for "sucker." Israeli drivers would rather end up in the hospital than let someone cut them off on the highway, he told me. Bibi himself was once quoted as saying, "We are not *freiers*. We don't give without receiving." I feared that in this light, our demands for a settlement freeze would not be well-received. But I agreed with Rahm and the President that if we were going to revive a moribund peace process, we had to take some risks. So that spring I delivered the President's message as forcefully as I could, then tried to contain the consequences when both sides reacted badly.

In June 2009, two important speeches reshaped the diplomatic landscape. First, in Cairo, President Obama offered an ambitious and eloquent recalibration of America's relationship with the Islamic world. In the wide-ranging address, he reaffirmed his personal commitment to pursue a two-state solution that would meet the aspirations of both Israelis and

Palestinians. Before the speech the President and I made time to take a private tour of the city's cavernous Sultan Hassan Mosque, one of the biggest in the world. We removed our shoes, and I put on a headscarf as we looked in wonder at the intricate medieval craftsmanship and listened to explanations from an Egyptian American art historian. It was a lovely, quiet moment together in the middle of all the madness of a Presidential trip and a major policy rollout. It made me smile when later that day the President said in his speech, "Islamic culture has given us majestic arches and soaring spires; timeless poetry and cherished music; elegant calligraphy and places of peaceful contemplation."

Ten days later Bibi went to Bar-Ilan University outside Tel Aviv and, while he continued to reject a settlement freeze, he endorsed the idea of the two-state solution for the first time. It seemed like a seminal turn, that Netanyahu wanted to be remembered as a leader who could take bold risks and deliver a historic deal.

Mitchell and I spent the summer and early fall working with both the Israelis and the Palestinians to break the logjam over settlements. In fairness, we shared responsibility for creating that logjam by allowing the issue to turn into a test of wills. President Obama decided that the best way to move forward was to insist that both leaders sit down with him together when they were in New York for the UN General Assembly in September. These wouldn't be formal negotiations, but they would provide a first opportunity for the leaders to talk to each other and perhaps build some momentum toward a more substantive process. The meeting in New York was awkward; both leaders were blunt about their positions and showed little willingness to compromise, especially on the issue of settlements. "We all must take risks for peace," President Obama told them. "It's difficult to disentangle ourselves from history, but we must do so."

We came out of New York with little to show for the effort. But Mitchell and I kept working on Netanyahu, and finally he agreed to a partial halt on building permits for future West Bank settlements. We still had to sort out how long the freeze would last and which areas would be covered, but this was an important start—and it was more than any previous Israeli government had been willing to do. The sticking point would be Jerusalem. East Jerusalem had been captured along with the West Bank in 1967, and Palestinians dreamed of one day establishing the capital of their future state there. The Palestinians therefore sought to halt construction in East Jerusalem. That was a nonstarter for Bibi, who refused to restrict building in any part of Jerusalem.

In early October I spoke with Ehud Barak, who was Netanyahu's coalition partner, as well as Minister of Defense and the most important voice for peace in the government. Barak was endlessly optimistic, despite living in a region where so much seemed to go wrong. He was also one of the most decorated war heroes in a nation of war heroes. As lore has it, he even dressed in drag during a daring commando assault into Beirut in the 1980s. We got along famously. From time to time he would call me and say, "Hillary, let's strategize," and then launch into a whirlwind of rapid-fire ideas and arguments. He was eager to help me reach an accommodation over settlements that could move the process forward. "We'll be ready to listen, to be sensitive and to be responsive," he told me. The Israelis eventually agreed to a freeze on new construction in the West Bank for ten months but held firm against including Jerusalem.

I called Abbas to discuss the Israeli offer. The initial Palestinian reaction was to reject it out of hand as inadequate, "worse than useless," but I thought this was the best deal they were going to get and we should seize the opportunity to move forward to direct negotiations. "I want to stress to you again, Mr. President, that our policy on settlement activity is and will remain unchanged," I assured him, "and although the Israeli settlement moratorium as described to you by George Mitchell will be significant and will be an unprecedented step by any Israeli government, it will not be a substitute for Israel's roadmap commitments." Abbas did not take issue with my use of the word *unprecedented*, but he wasn't happy about the Jerusalem exclusion or other limitations and did not agree to enter negotiations.

To show his own good faith, though, Abbas made a concession as well. He offered that the Palestinians would delay a vote at the United Nations on the controversial Goldstone Report, which accused Israel of war crimes during the 2008 war in Gaza. Abbas received swift and sharp criticism for his decision from across the Arab world, including relentless personal attacks against him on Al Jazeera, a satellite news network owned by Qatar. Abbas was beside himself and confided in me that he feared for his safety and that of his grandchildren, who had been harassed at school. I thanked him for his "very courageous and important decision," but I could tell he was starting to waver. About a week later he reversed himself and called for a UN vote on the Goldstone Report. Later, in 2011, Richard Goldstone himself retracted some of the most inflammatory charges in the report, including that the Israeli military intentionally targeted civilians, but the damage had been done.

At the end of October 2009 I was intensely focused on getting the proposed settlement moratorium in place, in the hopes that it would clear the way for direct negotiations between the parties. I met with Abbas in Abu Dhabi and then with Netanyahu in Jerusalem. Standing next to Bibi at a late-night press conference, I described the construction freeze as "unprecedented," just as I had said to Abbas. But this time my use of the word caused outrage in Arab countries, where people thought that I was being too generous toward an offer that was qualified, short term, and excluded East Jerusalem. It was not the first time, nor the last, that telling a hard truth would cause me trouble.

Many in the region would later look quite wistfully at that much-maligned moratorium. But the immediate imperative was to defuse the situation and refocus the region on getting to direct negotiations. Over the coming days I did damage control in Morocco and Egypt. In Cairo, I explained privately to President Hosni Mubarak and also in public that our official policy on settlements had not changed. We still opposed all construction and would have preferred a longer, comprehensive freeze. But I stood by my description of the offer "to halt all new settlement activities and to end the expropriation of land, and to issue no permits or approvals" as "unprecedented." Because the fact of the matter is, it was.

In late November the freeze went into effect, and the clock started ticking. We had ten months to move the parties toward direct negotiations and a comprehensive peace agreement.

═══

One by one the months slipped by. As promised, the Israelis halted new settlement construction in the West Bank, but the Palestinians held out for East Jerusalem to be included and continued to refuse to join direct negotiations, although they did agree to what were called "proximity talks," with Mitchell shuttling back and forth between the two sides to discuss their vision for the negotiations.

In March 2010, the Israelis managed to make the Palestinian case for them with an unnecessarily provocative act. Vice President Biden was visiting Israel on a goodwill tour, reaffirming the administration's strong support for the country's security and trying to put the unpleasantness of our row over settlements behind us. While he was still on the ground, the Israeli Interior Ministry announced plans for 1,600 new housing units in East Jerusalem, a move certain to inflame Palestinian sensitivities. Netanyahu said that he had nothing to do with the unfortunate timing of the announcement, but it was taken by many as a snub of the Vice President and the United States.

Biden was, characteristically, even-tempered about the whole kerfuffle. But both President Obama and Rahm were furious, and they asked me to make that clear to Bibi. In a long and heated telephone conversation, I told the Prime Minister that President Obama viewed the news about East Jerusalem "as a personal insult to him, the Vice President, and the United States." Strong stuff for a diplomatic conversation. I didn't enjoy playing the bad cop, but it was part of the job. "Let me assure you and the President that the timing was entirely unintentional and unfortunate," he replied, but he refused to reverse the decision.

By coincidence, this incident occurred just before the annual conference in Washington of the American Israel Public Affairs Committee, a prominent pro-Israel advocacy organization. Netanyahu was scheduled to visit D.C. and address the conference. It would be up to me to represent the administration. I went first. The big crowd gathered at the Washington Convention Center was a little wary at first. They had wanted to hear how I would address the controversy and if I'd keep up the criticism of Netanyahu. I knew I had to speak to that, but I also wanted to step back and make the broader case for why we viewed a negotiated peace agreement as crucial to Israel's future.

I talked about my own personal devotion to Israel's security and to the two-state solution and explained our concerns about the trends in demography, technology, and ideology. It was my most comprehensive public argument to date as Secretary about why the status quo was unsustainable and the need for peace undeniable. Then I turned to the contretemps over East Jerusalem. Our objection was not based on wounded pride, I said, or on any judgment about the final status of East Jerusalem, which would have to be decided at the negotiating table. New construction in East Jerusalem or the West Bank would undermine the mutual trust we needed to build between the parties, expose daylight between Israel and the United States that others in the region might try to exploit, and diminish America's unique ability to play the role of honest broker. "Our credibility in this process depends in part on our willingness to praise both sides when they are courageous, and when we don't agree, to say so, and say so unequivocally," I said.

My speech helped cool some of the tensions, at least in the room, but the relationship between Netanyahu and President Obama continued to deteriorate. Later that afternoon I met with Bibi for more than an hour at his hotel. He told me he planned to come out swinging in his speech to the conference that evening, and he was as good as his word. "Jerusalem is not a settlement—it is our capital," he declared defiantly. (We had never referred to Jerusalem as a settlement; our argument was that the city's final status should be determined by good-faith negotiations, and building new homes for Israelis in Palestinian neighborhoods would not be helpful to that end.) The next day Netanyahu had a charged meeting with the President at the White House. At one point during the discussion, the President reportedly left him waiting in the Roosevelt Room for about an hour while he took care of other matters. It was an unusual move, but one that effectively telegraphed his displeasure. One positive outcome of this mini-crisis was that the Israelis got a lot better about warning us before any new, potentially controversial housing projects were announced, and they became much more sensitive about East Jerusalem. At least while the ten-month moratorium remained in place, there was little if any additional construction there.

As if the tensions over settlements weren't enough, things went from bad to worse at the end of May. Israeli commandos raided a flotilla of ships from Turkey carrying pro-Palestinian activists trying to break the Israeli blockade of Gaza. Nine Turkish citizens were killed, including one American with dual citizenship. I received an urgent call from Ehud Barak while I was marching in the Chappaqua Memorial Day parade, one of my favorite annual traditions in our small town. "We're not happy with the results, but we had to make tough choices. We couldn't avoid it," Ehud explained. "There will be unforeseen repercussions," I warned him.

Turkey had long been one of Israel's only partners in the region, but in the wake of this debacle, I had to convince the enraged Turks not to take serious actions against Israel in response. The day after the raid Foreign Minister Davutoğlu came to see me, and we talked for more than two hours. He was highly emotional and threatened that Turkey might declare war on Israel. "Psychologically, this attack is like 9/11 for Turkey," he said, demanding an Israeli apology and compensation for the victims. "How can you not care?" he asked me. "One of them was an American citizen!" I did care—quite a lot—but my first priority was to calm him down and put aside all this talk of war and consequences. Afterward I advised President Obama to call Turkish Prime Minister Erdoğan as well. Then I relayed the Turkish concerns and demands to Netanyahu. He said he wanted to patch things up with Turkey but refused to apologize publicly. (My efforts to convince Bibi to apologize to Turkey seesawed back and forth for the remainder of my tenure. On several occasions he told me he would finally do it, only to be stopped by other members of his center-right coalition. I even enlisted Henry Kissinger to make the strategic case to him in August 2011. Finally, in March 2013, with a re-elected President Obama at his side during a visit to Jerusalem, Bibi called Erdoğan to apologize for "operational mistakes" and to express regret for the unintentional loss of life that resulted. The Turks and Israelis are still working to rebuild the trust lost in this incident.)

Back to the summer of 2010. With the ten-month settlement freeze winding down, we faced the urgency of getting the parties back to the negotiating table. Mitchell and I enlisted Jordan and Egypt to pressure the Palestinians to relent on their preconditions. President Obama met with Abbas in June and announced a major new aid package for the West Bank and Gaza. Finally, in August, Abbas agreed to attend direct negotiations in Washington about all the core issues of the conflict, so long as the settlement moratorium remained in place. If it expired as planned at the end of September, he would walk away again. An exasperated George Mitchell asked Abbas, "How is it that something which you described as worse than useless eight months ago has now become indispensable?" We all understood that Abbas had to manage his own difficult politics, both with his own people and with the Arab states, but it was frustrating nonetheless.

There was no way we were going to resolve all the core issues in a single month—Mitchell optimistically suggested a one-year deadline for the talks—but we hoped that we could build enough momentum either to convince Netanyahu to extend the freeze or persuade Abbas to keep negotiating without it. If we could make enough progress on the question of final borders for the two states, then that would significantly ease the settlement issue because it would be clear to everyone which areas would ultimately stay with Israel and which would go to the Palestinians. It wasn't going to be as simple as just returning to the 1967 lines. The heavy growth of settlements along the border had made that a nonstarter. Land swaps could carve out the settlement blocks and provide Palestinians with a roughly equal amount of land elsewhere. But, as always, the devil would be in the details.

=====

On the first day of September, President Obama welcomed Netanyahu and Abbas to the White House, along with King Abdullah II of Jordan and President Mubarak of Egypt. He hosted a small working dinner in the Old Family Dining Room. Tony Blair, the former British Prime Minister, and I joined the group. Blair served as a Special Envoy for the Quartet, which was established in 2002 by the United Nations, the United States, the European Union, and Russia to coordinate diplomatic efforts on behalf of Middle East peace. The seven of us gathered around the dining-room table beneath an elegant crystal chandelier in the bright yellow room that was largely unchanged from the days when I used to host private meals there as First Lady. Bibi and Abbas sat next to each other, flanked by me and Blair, across from President Obama, Mubarak, and the King.

President Obama set the tone in remarks before dinner, reminding the leaders, "Each of you are the heirs of peacemakers who dared greatly—Begin and Sadat, Rabin and King Hussein—statesmen who saw the world as it was but also imagined the world as it should be. It is the shoulders of our predecessors upon which we stand. It is their work that we carry on. Now, like each of them, we must ask, do we have the wisdom and the courage to walk the path of peace?"

The atmosphere was warm, despite the many difficult months that had led up to this moment, but still cautious. Everyone was aware of the time pressure we faced, and no one wanted to appear ungracious at President Obama's dinner table, yet their fundamental disagreements were not easy to hide.

The next day the drama moved to the State Department. I convened the leaders and their negotiating teams in the ornate Benjamin Franklin

Room on the eighth floor. It was time to roll up our sleeves and see what we could accomplish. "By being here today, you each have taken an important step toward freeing your peoples from the shackles of a history we cannot change, and moving toward a future of peace and dignity that only you can create," I told Netanyahu and Abbas. "The core issues at the center of these negotiations—territory, security, Jerusalem, refugees, settlements, and others—will get no easier if we wait. Nor will they resolve themselves. . . . This is a time for bold leadership and a time for statesmen who have the courage to make difficult decisions." Sitting on either side of me, Netanyahu and Abbas sounded ready to accept the challenge.

Bibi invoked the biblical story of Isaac (father of the Jews) and Ishmael (father of the Arabs), the two sons of Abraham who, despite their differences, came together to bury their father. "I can only pray, and I know that millions around the world, millions of Israelis and millions of Palestinians and many other millions around the world, pray that the pain that we have experienced—you and us—in the last hundred years of conflict will unite us not only in a moment of peace around a table of peace here in Washington, but will enable us to leave from here and to forge a durable, lasting peace for generations."

Abbas reminisced about the famous handshake in 1993 between Rabin and Arafat and spoke of reaching "a peace that will end the conflict, that will meet all the demands, and start a new era between the Israeli and the Palestinian people." The gaps we had to overcome were substantial and time was running short, but at least everyone was saying the right things.

After a long afternoon of formal negotiations, I invited the two leaders to my office on the seventh floor. Senator Mitchell and I talked with them for a while, and then we left them alone. They sat in two high-backed chairs in front of the fireplace and agreed to meet again face-to-face in two weeks. We hadn't made much substantive progress, but I was encouraged by both their words and their body language. It was a moment of optimism and ambition that, sadly, would not be matched by action.

Two weeks later we reconvened in Sharm el-Sheikh, a sun-soaked Egyptian resort town on the Red Sea. (One of the ironies of international diplomacy is that we often travel to places like Sharm or Bali or Hawaii but then have no time at all to enjoy them, or even venture outside the formal conference rooms. I sometimes felt like Tantalus, the hungry wretch of Greek mythology doomed to stare at delicious fruit and refreshing water for all eternity but never able to taste it.) This time our host was President Mubarak, who, despite being an autocrat at home, was a steadfast proponent of the two-state solution and peace in the Middle East. Because Egypt shared borders with Gaza and Israel, and was the first Arab country to sign a peace agreement with Israel, back in 1979, its role was crucial. Mubarak had a close relationship with Abbas and helped get the Palestinians to the table in the first place. Now I hoped he could help keep them there.

Mubarak and I began the day by meeting separately with the Israelis and the Palestinians. Then we brought Netanyahu and Abbas together, and they talked for an hour and forty minutes. Both sides reaffirmed their intention to participate in good faith and with seriousness of purpose. Then we started drilling down on some of the core issues of the conflict. It was slow going—there was a lot of positioning, posturing, and taking the measure of the other side—but it felt good to finally be talking about the heart of the matter. After more than twenty months of false starts, we were engaging with the key questions that held out the promise of ending the conflict once and for all. After a lunch for all of us, we decided to meet again, and Netanyahu delayed his departure so we could keep talking.

The next day the conversation continued at Netanyahu's home in Jerusalem, where he displayed the Palestinian flag as a sign of respect to Abbas. Beit Aghion, the Prime Minister's official residence, was built by a wealthy merchant in the 1930s and served as a hospital for fighters in the 1948 Arab-Israeli War. It sits on a quiet, partially closed-off street in the well-to-do neighborhood of Rehavia. Outside, its façade is covered with Jerusalem limestone, like the Western Wall and much of the Old City. Inside it is surprisingly cozy. The four of us—Netanyahu, Abbas, Mitchell, and I—crammed into the Prime Minister's personal study for intense discussions. In the back of everyone's mind was the approaching deadline; the settlement freeze would expire and the talks would collapse in less than two weeks if we didn't find a way forward. The ticking of this clock was deafening.

Among other tough questions, our discussion focused on how long the Israeli military would maintain a presence in the Jordan Valley, which would become the border between Jordan and a future Palestinian state. Mitchell and I offered suggestions about how to reconcile the continuing needs of Israeli security with Palestinian sovereignty. Netanyahu insisted that Israeli troops remain along the border for many decades without a fixed date for withdrawal so future decisions could be based on conditions on the ground. At one point Abbas said that he could live with an Israeli military deployment in the Jordan Valley for a few years beyond the establishment of a new state, but no longer and it had to be a set period of time, not an open-ended stay. Despite the obvious disagreement, I thought that was a potentially significant opening; if the conversation was about years, not decades or months, then perhaps the right mix of international security support and advanced border protection tactics and technologies could bridge the gap, if we could keep the talks going.

They debated back and forth as the hours went by. Outside, the American press corps grew restless, and many of the journalists decamped to a nearby hotel bar. Inside, I was frustrated that we weren't making the kind of progress I knew would be needed to survive the end of the settlement freeze. But Mitchell, the veteran of the interminable Northern Ireland negotiations, offered some helpful perspective. "The negotiations there lasted for twenty-two months," he observed. "And it was many, many months into the process before there was a single, serious, substantive discussion on the major issues that separated the parties." Here we were already deep into the most difficult and sensitive issues of the conflict.

After the meeting finally broke up, nearly three hours later, I stayed behind to talk to Netanyahu alone. Surely he didn't want to be responsible for halting these talks now that they were under way and delving into the core issues. Could he agree to a brief extension of the moratorium to allow us to press ahead and see what could be achieved? The Prime Minister shook his head. He had given ten months, and the Palestinians had wasted nine of them. He was ready to keep talking, but the settlement freeze would end on schedule.

That night in Jerusalem was the last time Netanyahu and Abbas would sit and talk face-to-face. As of this writing, despite intensive efforts between the parties in 2013 and 2014, there has not yet been another session between the two leaders.

=====

Over the following weeks we launched a full-court press to persuade Bibi to reconsider extending the freeze. Much of the action played out in New York, where everyone had gathered once again for the UN General Assembly. The year before, President Obama had hosted the first direct meeting between Netanyahu and Abbas. Now we were fighting to forestall total collapse of the negotiations. There were long nights at the Waldorf Astoria hotel, strategizing with President Obama and our team and then working with the Israelis, the Palestinians, and the Arabs to try to find a solution. I met with Abbas twice, had a private meeting with Ehud Barak, had breakfast with a group of Arab Foreign Ministers, and spoke with Bibi by phone, each time making the case that walking away from the talks, settlement freeze or no, would only set back the aspirations of the Palestinian people.

In his speech to the General Assembly, President Obama called for the moratorium to be extended, and he urged both sides to stay at the table and keep talking: "Now is the time for the parties to help each other overcome this obstacle. Now is the time to build the trust—and provide the time—for substantial progress to be made. Now is the time for this opportunity to be seized, so that it does not slip away."

After the initial stonewalling, it appeared that Netanyahu was willing to discuss the idea of an extension, but only if we met an ever-expanding list of demands that included providing new state-of-the-art fighter planes. For his part, Abbas insisted that Israel had to "choose between peace and the continuation of settlements."

On the night before the deadline, I reminded Ehud Barak that "the collapse of the moratorium would be a disaster for Israel and the United States." Also for the Palestinians, he replied. Barak did everything he could to help me work out a compromise, but he was never able to bring Netanyahu or the rest of the Israeli Cabinet along.

The deadline came and went. Direct negotiations were over, for now. But my work wasn't. I thought it was crucial that we not allow the collapse of talks to lead to a collapse of public confidence—or to violence, as had happened in the past. Over the final months of 2010, I threw myself into efforts to keep both sides from doing anything provocative and to explore whether we could close some of the gaps revealed in our negotiating sessions through proximity talks and creative diplomatic proposals. "I'm increasingly worried about the way ahead," I told Netanyahu in a call in early October. "We're trying very hard to keep things on track and avoid any precipitous collapse. You know how disappointed we are we couldn't avoid an end to the moratorium." I urged him to show restraint when approving new construction or talking about future plans. Reckless talk would only inflame a tense situation. Bibi promised to be judicious, but warned me against allowing the Palestinians to "play brinksmanship."

Abbas, always worried about his precarious standing with the divided Palestinian public and his Arab patrons, was searching for a way to restore his credibility, which took a hit with the end of the settlement freeze. One idea he was considering was to go to the United Nations and ask for statehood. That would be an end-run around negotiations and put the United States in a difficult position. We would feel obligated to veto the issue in the Security Council, but a vote might expose how isolated Israel had become. "I know you're fed up, Mr. President, and I'm sure you wonder if what we are trying to do now will lead anywhere," I told Abbas. "I would not be calling you if I didn't think what we are doing had a chance of succeeding for us as partners. We are working tirelessly and as you have said yourself, there is no alternative path to peace, but through negotiations." He was in a corner and didn't know how to get out of it, but this was a predicament of his and our own making.

In my calls and meetings with the leaders, I probed to see if we could narrow the gaps on territory and borders enough to move beyond the settlement issue. I told Netanyahu in mid-October, "The question is, as-suming your needs on security are met: What could you offer Abu Mazen on borders? I need to know this with some specificity because the Palestin-ians know the ballpark." Netanyahu responded, "What concerns me is not Abu Mazen's territorial demands, but his understanding and acceptance of my security needs. . . . I'm a realist. I know what's needed to close the deal." Our call went on like this for an hour and twenty minutes.

In November I spent eight hours with Netanyahu at the Regency Hotel in New York City. It was my longest single bilateral meeting as Secretary. We talked everything over, again and again, including the old ideas for restarting a settlement moratorium in exchange for military hardware and other security assistance. Eventually he agreed on a pro-posal to bring to his Cabinet that would halt construction in the West Bank (but not East Jerusalem) for ninety days. In exchange, we pledged a $3 billion security package and promised to veto any resolutions at the UN that would undercut direct negotiations between the parties.

When news of the deal became public, it caused consternation on all sides. Netanyahu's right-wing coalition partners were irate, and to placate them, he emphasized that construction would continue in East Jerusa-lem. This, in turn, set off the Palestinians. Some in the United States also raised fair questions about whether it was wise to buy a ninety-day freeze for negotiations that might well lead nowhere. I wasn't happy either—I confided to Tony Blair that I found it to be "a nasty business"—but it felt like a sacrifice worth making.

Under all this pressure, however, the deal started to unravel almost immediately, and by the end of November it was effectively dead. In December 2010, I spoke at the Saban Forum, a conference that brings together leaders and experts from across the Middle East and the United States. I pledged that America would stay engaged and keep pressing both sides to grapple with the core issues, even if it was through a return to "proximity talks." We would push both the Israelis and the Palestinians to lay out their positions on the toughest questions with real specificity, and then we would work to narrow the gaps, including by offering our own ideas and bridging proposals when appropriate. Since my husband put forward the "Clinton Parameters" a decade before, the United States had been reluctant to push any specific plans or even a substantive framework. "Peace cannot be imposed from outside," was a frequent saying, and true. But now we would be more aggressive in setting the terms of the debate.

President Obama followed through on this commitment in the spring of 2011 by declaring in a speech at the State Department, "We believe the borders of Israel and Palestine should be based on the 1967 lines with mutually agreed swaps, so that secure and recognized borders are established for both states."

Netanyahu unhelpfully chose to focus on the reference to "1967 lines" and ignore the "agreed swaps," and another highly personal standoff between the two heads of state resulted. The Palestinians, meanwhile, escalated their plan to petition the United Nations for statehood. George Mitchell stepped down that summer, and I spent much of the rest of 2011 trying to keep the situation from deteriorating from deadlock into disaster.

It wasn't easy. By then Hosni Mubarak, the most prominent champion for peace among the Arab states, had fallen from power in Egypt. Unrest was spreading across the region. Israelis faced a new and unpredictable strategic landscape. Some Palestinians wondered if they should be protesting in the streets like the Tunisians, Egyptians, and Libyans. The prospects for a return to serious negotiations seemed further away than ever. A window of opportunity that had opened with the inauguration of President Obama in early 2009 seemed to be closing.

Throughout those difficult days I often thought back to our long discussions in Washington, Sharm el-Sheikh, and Jerusalem. I hoped that one day the constituencies for peace among both peoples would grow so strong and loud that their leaders would be forced to compromise. In my head I heard the deep and steady voice of my slain friend Yitzhak Rabin: "The coldest peace is better than the warmest war."

15

The Arab Spring: Revolution

They're sitting on a powder keg and if they don't change, it's going to explode." I was exasperated. It was the first week of January 2011, and we were planning another trip to the Middle East. This time I wanted to go beyond the usual agenda of official meetings and private cajoling about needed political and economic reforms in the Arab world. Jeff Feltman, Assistant Secretary for Near Eastern Affairs, my top advisor on the region, agreed. Trying to drive change in the Middle East could feel like banging your head against a brick wall, and Jeff had been doing it for years, under several administrations. Among other roles, he had served as Ambassador to Lebanon during some of its most tumultuous recent history, including the assassination of Prime Minister Rafic Hariri in 2005 that triggered the Cedar Revolution and the withdrawal of Syrian troops, as well as the war between Israel and Hezbollah in 2006. These experiences would serve Jeff well in the weeks to come as we tried to stay one step ahead of a wave of upheaval that would sweep the region. The period ahead would be fluid and confusing even for experienced diplomats.

I turned to two of my speechwriters, Megan Rooney and Dan Schwerin. "I'm tired of repeating the same old things every time I go there," I told them. "I want to say something that really breaks through this time." The upcoming annual Forum for the Future conference in Doha, the capital of energy-rich Qatar, would provide an opportunity for me to deliver a message to many of the Middle East's most influential royals, political leaders, business tycoons, academics, and civil society activists. Many of them would be gathered in the same room at the same time. If I wanted to make the case that the region's status quo was unsustainable, this was the place to do it. I told Megan and Dan to get to work.

Of course, I was not the first American official to push for reform. In 2005, Secretary of State Condoleezza Rice went to Egypt and made a remarkable admission: for more than half a century, the United States had chosen to pursue "stability at the expense of democracy" and "achieved neither." That would be true no longer, she promised. Four years later in President Obama's major speech in Cairo, he too called for democratic reforms.

Yet for all the words delivered in public and even more pointed words in private, and despite the persistent efforts of people from all walks of life to make their countries more prosperous and free, by early 2011, much of the Middle East and North Africa remained locked in political and economic stagnation. Many countries had been ruled for decades under martial law. Across the region corruption at every level, especially at the top, was rampant. Political parties and civil society groups were nonexistent or tightly restricted; judicial systems were far from free or independent; and elections, when they were held, were often rigged. This sorry state of affairs was dramatized anew in November 2010, when Egypt held flawed Parliamentary elections that nearly eliminated the token political opposition.

A landmark study published in 2002 by leading Middle Eastern scholars and the United Nations Development Program was as troubling as it was revealing. The Arab Human Development Report painted a devastating portrait of a region in decline. Despite the Middle East's oil wealth and strategic trading location, unemployment was more than double the global average, and even higher for women and young people. A growing number of Arabs lived in poverty, crowded into slums without sanitation, safe water, or reliable electricity, while a small elite gained increasing control over land and resources. It was also not surprising that Arab women's political and economic participation was the lowest in the world.

Despite its problems, most of the region's leaders and power brokers seemed largely content to carry on as they always had. And despite the best intentions of successive American administrations, the day-to-day reality of U.S. foreign policy prioritized urgent strategic and security imperatives such as counterterrorism, support for Israel, and blocking Iran's nuclear ambitions over the long-term goal of encouraging internal reforms in our Arab partners. To be sure, we did press leaders to reform, because we believed that would eventually provide greater long-term stability and inclusive prosperity. But we also worked with them on a wide range of security concerns and never seriously considered cutting off our military relationships with them.

This was a dilemma that had confronted generations of American policymakers. It's easy to give speeches and write books about standing up for democratic values, even when it may conflict with our security interests, but when confronted with the actual, real-world trade-offs, choices get a lot harder. Inevitably, making policy is a balancing act. Hopefully we get it more right than wrong. But there are always choices we regret, consequences we do not foresee, and alternate paths we wish we had taken.

I talked with enough Arab leaders over the years to know that for many of them, it wasn't a simple matter of being content with how things were; they accepted that change would come but only slowly. I looked for ways to build personal relationships and trust with them, to better grasp the cultural and social views that influenced their actions, and, when possible, push for more rapid change.

All of this was on my mind as 2011 dawned and I prepared once again to visit the Middle East. I had spent much of 2009 and 2010 working with President Hosni Mubarak of Egypt and King Abdullah II of Jordan to bring the Israeli and Palestinian leaders together for direct peace talks, only to see them fall apart after three rounds of substantive negotiations. Time and again I had told both sides that the status quo was unsustainable and that they needed to make the necessary choices that would lead to peace and progress. Now I was thinking the same thing about the entire region. If Arab leaders, many of whom were America's partners, failed to embrace the need for change, they risked losing control of their increasingly young and alienated populations and opening the door to unrest, conflict, and terrorists. That's the argument I wanted to make, without too many of the usual diplomatic niceties diluting the message.

As we planned a trip around the theme of economic, political, and environmental sustainability, events unfolded on the ground that raised the stakes even higher.

The pro-Western government in Lebanon was teetering on the verge of collapse under intense pressure from Hezbollah, a heavily armed Shiite militia with significant influence in Lebanese politics. On January 7,

I flew to New York to discuss the crisis with Lebanese Prime Minister Saad Hariri, the son of the assassinated former leader, Rafic Hariri; and King Abdullah of Saudi Arabia, both of whom were visiting the United States.

At the same time, reports were coming in of street protests in Tunisia, a former French colony on the Mediterranean coast of North Africa between Libya and Algeria that had been ruled for decades by the dictator Zine el Abidine Ben Ali. For the many European tourists who flocked to its beaches and cosmopolitan hotels, it was easy to ignore the dark side of Ben Ali's Tunisia. Women enjoyed more rights there than in many other Middle Eastern nations, the economy was more diversified, and extremists were not welcome. But the regime was ruthless, repressive, and corrupt, and beyond the glitzy tourist destinations, many people lived in poverty and despair.

The unrest had begun with a single heartbreaking incident on December 17, 2010. A twenty-six-year-old Tunisian man named Mohamed Bouazizi was selling fruit from a small cart in Sidi Bouzid, a poor provincial city south of the capital, Tunis. Like so many others in Tunisia, he was part of the underground economy and struggled to make enough money to provide for his family. Bouazizi did not have an official permit to sell his produce, and on that day he had an altercation with a female police officer that left him humiliated and desperate. Later that day he set himself on fire in front of the local government offices. That act galvanized protests across Tunisia. People took to the streets, protesting corruption, indignity, and lack of opportunity. On social media they passed around lurid tales of Ben Ali's corruption, some derived from reports by U.S. diplomats about the regime's excesses over the years, which had been released by WikiLeaks not long before the protests began.

The regime responded to the protests with excessive force, which only fueled public outrage. Ben Ali himself visited Bouazizi in the hospital, but the gesture did little to quell the growing unrest, and the young man died a few days later.

On January 9, as I flew from Washington to Abu Dhabi for the start of my trip, which would take me from the United Arab Emirates (UAE) to Yemen, Oman, and Qatar, security forces in Tunisia intensified their crackdown on protesters. Several people were killed. Most observers saw it as yet another example of a familiar cycle of repression in a region that had become numb to such convulsions.

The UAE is a tiny but influential Persian Gulf nation that has grown exceedingly wealthy because of its extensive oil and natural gas reserves. The government, under the leadership of Crown Prince Mohammed bin Zayed Al Nahyan, was investing in solar power as a way of diversifying its economy and hedging against future volatility in the global oil market, a rare instance of foresight and smart planning in a petrostate. At the high-tech Masdar Institute in the desert about twenty miles outside of Abu Dhabi, I spoke to a group of graduate students about the region's shrinking oil supplies and declining water tables. "The old strategies for growth and prosperity will no longer work," I said. "For too many people in too many places, the status quo today is unsustainable."

No place in the region seemed to represent my warnings better than Yemen, at the foot of the Arabian Peninsula. The contrast between its dusty and medieval capital, Sanaa, and the sleek and modern UAE cities of Abu Dhabi and Dubai could not have been starker. Yemen, a tribal society that had been ruled since 1990 by a strongman named Ali Abdullah Saleh, was plagued by violent separatist insurgencies, an influx of al Qaeda–linked terrorists, widespread unemployment, dwindling water supplies, dreadful child survival statistics, and, counterintuitively, a surging population that was expected to double in the next twenty years. Yemen's population is one of the most heavily armed and least literate on earth.

America's relationship with President Saleh was emblematic of the dilemma at the heart of our Middle East policy. He was corrupt and autocratic, but he was also committed to fighting al Qaeda and keeping his fractious country together. The Obama Administration decided to hold our noses, increase our military and development aid to Yemen, and expand our counterterrorism cooperation. Over a long lunch at his palace, I talked with Saleh about how we could work more closely together on security. I also pressed him on human rights and economic reforms. He was not so much interested in hearing that as he was in showing me the antique rifle that had been a gift from General Norman Schwarzkopf. He was also adamant that I see the Old City of Sanaa before leaving and insisted that I take a tour.

The Old City is right out of the *Arabian Nights*, a jumble of mudbrick buildings whose façades are covered with decorative alabaster work, almost like gingerbread houses. Crowds of curious onlookers watched from spice shops and cafés as we passed. Most of the women wore veils, either headscarves called *hijab* or the more extensive face coverings called *niqab*. The men wore large curved daggers at their belts, and quite a few carried Kalashnikov rifles. Many of the men were chewing khat leaves, the Yemeni narcotic of choice. I was in a wide armored SUV that could barely fit through the narrow streets. The car came so close to some of the walls of the shops and houses that if the windows had been open, I could have reached inside.

My destination was the Mövenpick Hotel, which sits on a rise overlooking the city, where I met with a large group of activists and students, part of Yemen's vibrant civil society. I opened our meeting with a message intended not just for Yemenis but for people across the Middle East. "The next generation of Yemenis will be hungry for jobs, health care, literacy, education and training that connect them to the global economy, and they will be seeking responsive democratic governance that reaches and serves their communities." The entire region had to figure out how to offer young people a vision for a future of opportunity resting on a foundation of stability and security. My remarks set off an energetic exchange of ideas and venting by the crowd. Students who had studied abroad spoke passionately about why they had returned home to help build their country. Despite their frustration over repression and corruption, they were still hopeful that progress was possible.

One young woman in the crowd was named Nujood Ali, who successfully fought for a divorce at age ten. She had been forced to marry a man three times her age who had made her drop out of school. This wasn't uncommon in Yemen, but to Nujood, it felt like a prison sentence. Desperate to escape what quickly became an abusive marriage and to reclaim her dream of an education and an independent life, she boarded a bus and made it to the local courthouse. Everyone towered above her and paid no attention until a judge asked the young girl why she was there. Nujood said she wanted a divorce. A lawyer named Shada Nasser came to her rescue. Together they shocked Yemen and the world by fighting in court—and winning. I suggested that Nujood's story should inspire Yemen to end child marriage once and for all.

The next day provided more contrasts when I went on to Oman, whose ruler, Sultan Qaboos bin Said Al Said, had made wiser choices over the years that helped his country build a modern society while remaining true to its culture and traditions. "Let there be learning, even under the shade of trees," he had proclaimed. In the 1970s the entire country had three primary schools, which educated fewer than a thousand boys and no girls. In 2014, Oman has universal primary education, and more women than men graduate from the country's universities. Oman is a monarchy, not a democracy, but it has shown what is possible when a leader focuses on education, empowers women and girls, and puts people at the center of its development strategy. In 2010, the UN Development Programme ranked Oman as the world's most improved country in human development since 1970.

That same day, January 12, as Lebanese Prime Minister Hariri was in Washington preparing to meet with President Obama, his government fell apart amid factional infighting, a curse stalking every Lebanese government that has tried to balance the interests and agendas of its mixed citizenry of Sunnis, Shiites, Christians, and Druze. Meanwhile violence was escalating on the streets of Tunisia. It didn't feel like a full-blown crisis yet, but there was definitely a sense that the region was starting to shake.

My final stop was Doha, Qatar, for the speech to the regional conference that we had been working on so intently. Early on the morning of January 13, I walked into a crowded meeting room full of Arab leaders and outlined the region's challenges as bluntly as I could: unemployment, corruption, a sclerotic political order that denied citizens their dignity and universal human rights. "In too many places, in too many ways, the region's foundations are sinking into the sand," I said, echoing the themes I had highlighted over the course of the trip. Offering a direct challenge to the assembled leaders, I continued, "You *can* help build a future that your young people will believe in, stay for, and defend." If not, "those who cling to the status quo may be able to hold back the full impact of their countries' problems for a little while, but not forever."

Few Arab leaders are accustomed to hearing criticism delivered publicly and directly. Although I understood their feelings and customs, I thought it important that they take seriously how quickly the world was changing around them. If I had to be a little undiplomatic to do that, so be it. "Let us face honestly that future. Let us discuss openly what needs to be done. Let us use this time to move beyond rhetoric, to put away plans that are timid and gradual, and make a commitment to keep this region moving in the right direction," I said in closing. After I was finished the American journalists traveling with me were buzzing about how blunt my words had been. I wondered if any actions would follow.

The next day, with demonstrations in Tunisia swelling, Ben Ali fled the country and sought refuge in Saudi Arabia. Protests that had begun with a dispute over a fruit cart had grown into a full-fledged revolution. I had not expected events to underscore my "sinking into the sand" warning so quickly or dramatically, but now the message was undeniable. Yet as significant as these events were, none of us expected what happened next.

=====

The protests in Tunisia proved contagious. Thanks to satellite television and social media, young people across the Middle East and North Africa had a front-row seat to the popular uprising that toppled Ben Ali. Emboldened, they began turning private criticisms of their governments into public calls for change. After all, many of the same conditions that drove frustration in Tunisia were present across the region, especially with regard to corruption and repression.

On January 25, protests in Cairo against police brutality grew into massive demonstrations against the authoritarian regime of Hosni Mubarak. Tens of thousands of Egyptians occupied Tahrir Square in the heart of the city and resisted efforts by the police to force them to disperse. Day after day the crowds in the square grew, and they became focused on a single goal: driving Mubarak from power.

I had known Mubarak and his wife, Suzanne, for nearly twenty years. He was a career Air Force officer who had risen through the ranks to become Vice President under Anwar Sadat, the Egyptian ruler who fought the Yom Kippur War with Israel in 1973 and later signed the Camp David Accords. Mubarak was injured in the extremist attack that assassinated Sadat in 1981, but he survived, became President, and cracked down hard on Islamists and other dissidents. He ruled Egypt like a pharaoh with nearly absolute power for the next three decades.

Over the years I spent time with Mubarak. I appreciated his consistent support for the Camp David Accords and a two-state solution for Israelis and Palestinians. He tried harder than any other Arab leader to convince Yasser Arafat to accept the peace agreement negotiated by my husband in 2000. But, despite his partnership with the United States on key strategic matters, it was disappointing that after so many years in power his regime still denied the Egyptian people many of their fundamental freedoms and human rights and was badly mismanaging the economy. Under Mubarak's rule, a country known to historians as the "breadbasket of antiquity" struggled to feed its own people and became the world's largest importer of wheat.

In May 2009, Mubarak's twelve-year-old grandson died suddenly from an undisclosed health problem. The loss seemed to shatter the aging leader. When I called Suzanne Mubarak to offer my sympathy, she told me the boy had been "the President's best friend."

For the Obama Administration, the protests in Egypt presented a delicate situation. Mubarak had been a key strategic ally for decades, yet America's ideals were more naturally aligned with the young people calling for "bread, freedom, and dignity." When asked by a journalist about the protests on that first day, I sought to offer a measured response that reflected our interests and values, as well as the uncertainty of the situation, and avoided throwing further fuel on the fire. "We support the fundamental right of expression and assembly for all people, and we urge that all parties exercise restraint and refrain from violence," I said. "But our assessment is that the Egyptian Government is stable and is looking for ways to respond to the legitimate needs and interests of the Egyptian people." It would turn out that the regime was certainly not "stable," but few observers could have predicted just how fragile it actually was.

On January 28, President Obama joined a meeting of the national security team in the White House Situation Room and asked us for recommendations about how to handle events in Egypt. The debate around the long table went back and forth. We delved once more into questions that had bedeviled U.S. policymakers for generations: How should we balance strategic interests against core values? Can we successfully influence the internal politics of other nations and nurture democracy where it has never flowered before, without incurring negative unintended consequences? What does it mean to be on the right side of history? These were debates we would have throughout the so-called Arab Spring.

Like many other young people around the world, some of President Obama's aides in the White House were swept up in the drama and idealism of the moment as they watched the pictures from Tahrir Square on television. They identified with the democratic yearnings and technological savvy of the young Egyptian protesters. Indeed Americans of all ages and political stripe were moved by the sight of people so long repressed finally demanding their universal human rights, and repulsed by the excessive force the authorities used in response. I shared that feeling. It was a thrilling moment. But along with Vice President Biden, Secretary of Defense Bob Gates, and National Security Advisor Tom Donilon, I was concerned that we not be seen as pushing a longtime partner out the door, leaving Egypt, Israel, Jordan, and the region to an uncertain, dangerous future.

The arguments for throwing America's weight behind the protesters went beyond idealism. Championing democracy and human rights had been at the heart of our global leadership for more than half a century. Yes, we had from time to time compromised those values in the service of strategic and security interests, including by supporting unsavory anti-Communist dictators during the Cold War, with mixed results. But such compromises were harder to sustain in the face of the Egyptian people demanding the very rights and opportunities we had always said they and all peoples deserved. While before it had been possible to focus on the Mubarak who supported peace and cooperation with Israel and hunted terrorists, now it was impossible to ignore the reality that he was also a heavy-handed autocrat who presided over a corrupt and calcified regime.

And yet many of the same national security interests that had led every previous administration to maintain close ties with Mubarak remained urgent priorities. Iran was still attempting to build a nuclear arsenal. Al Qaeda was still plotting new attacks. The Suez Canal remained a vital trade route. Israel's security was as essential as ever. Mubarak had been a partner in all these areas, despite anti-American and anti-Israeli sentiments among his own people. His Egypt served as a linchpin of peace in a volatile region. Were we really ready to walk away from that relationship after thirty years of cooperation?

Even if we did decide that was the right choice, it was far from clear how much influence we could actually have on events on the ground. Contrary to popular belief among many in the Middle East, the United States has never been an all-powerful puppet master able to achieve any outcome we desire. What if we called for Mubarak to step down, but then he refused and managed to stay in power? What if he did step down and was succeeded by a lengthy period of dangerous disorder or by a successor government no more democratic and actively opposed to our interests and security? Either way, our relationship would never be the same and our influence in the region would erode. Other partners would see how we treated Mubarak and lose trust and confidence in their relationships with us.

Historically, transitions from dictatorship to democracy are fraught with challenges and can easily go terribly wrong. In Iran in 1979, for example, extremists hijacked the broad-based popular revolution against the Shah and established a brutal theocracy. If something similar happened in Egypt, it would be a catastrophe, for the people of Egypt as well as for Israeli and U.S. interests.

Despite the size of the protests in Tahrir Square, they were largely leaderless, driven by social media and word of mouth rather than a coherent opposition movement. After years of one-party rule, Egypt's protesters were ill prepared to contest open elections or build credible democratic institutions. By contrast, the Muslim Brotherhood, an eighty-year-old Islamist organization, was well positioned to fill a vacuum if the regime fell. Mubarak had driven the Brotherhood underground, but it had followers all over the country and a tightly organized power structure. The group had renounced violence and made some efforts to appear more moderate. But it was impossible to know how it would behave and what would happen if it gained control.

These arguments gave me pause. Along with the Vice President, Gates, and Donilon, I counseled caution. If Mubarak falls, I told the President, "it all may work out fine in twenty-five years, but I think the period between now and then will be quite rocky for the Egyptian people, for the region, and for us." But I knew the President wasn't comfortable sitting by and doing nothing while peaceful protesters were beaten and killed in the streets. He needed a path forward that urged Egypt toward democracy but avoided the chaos of an abrupt regime collapse.

On *Meet the Press* on Sunday, January 30, I tried to set out a sustainable approach. "Long-term stability rests on responding to the legitimate needs of the Egyptian people, and that is what we want to see happen," so I said that we hoped to see a "peaceful, *orderly* transition to a democratic regime." My using the word *orderly* rather than *immediate* was intentional, although unpopular in some quarters of the White House. Some on the President's team wanted me to at least foreshadow Mubarak's departure, if not call for it. I, however, thought it was crucial that the rhetoric from me and others in the administration help Egypt achieve the reforms most of the protesters sought with a soft landing rather than a hard thud.

When I spoke with Egyptian Foreign Minister Ahmed Aboul Gheit that week, I urged the government to show restraint and demonstrate that it would be responsive to the demands of the people. "It's going to be challenging for President Mubarak to make the case that he's heard people after thirty years unless he holds free and fair elections and doesn't try to engineer his successor," I told Aboul Gheit. "That is not tomorrow's business," he responded. "Tomorrow's business is to pacify the people and settle them down." But he agreed to pass along my concerns.

Mubarak, however, wasn't listening. Even as unrest escalated and the regime's control of the country appeared to be slipping, he delivered a defiant speech late on the evening of January 29 in which he fired many of his Cabinet Ministers but refused to resign or limit his own term in office.

I recommended to President Obama that he dispatch an envoy to talk with Mubarak in person and persuade him to announce a strong package of reforms, including an end to the country's repressive emergency law that had been in effect since 1981, a pledge not to run in the elections already planned for September, and an agreement not to put forward his son Gamal as his successor. These steps might not satisfy everyone, but they would be significant concessions and give the protesters a chance to organize ahead of the elections.

For this delicate assignment, I suggested Frank Wisner, a retired senior diplomat who had served as Ambassador to Egypt from 1986 to 1991 and had developed a strong personal relationship with Mubarak. They had spent many hours together discussing the region and the world. Like his great friend Richard Holbrooke, Wisner cut his diplomatic teeth in Vietnam before representing our country in hotspots all over the world. In addition to Egypt, he served as Ambassador in Zambia, the Philippines, and India before retiring in 1997. I thought that if any American could get through to Mubarak, it would be Wisner. But some in the White House were skeptical of Wisner and his mission. They were ready to cut Mubarak loose. President Obama was losing patience, but he ultimately agreed with me to give diplomacy one more chance.

Wisner met with Mubarak on January 31 and delivered our message. Mubarak listened but didn't give an inch. He was stressed, maybe even bewildered by what was happening around him, but he was in no way ready to give up his power. Like so many autocrats before him, he had come to view himself as inseparable from the state. Mubarak was enough of a realist to know he couldn't sit in his palace and ignore the protests altogether. So he sent out his newly appointed Vice President, the longtime intelligence chief Omar Suleiman, to propose a national dialogue about possible reforms. Two days earlier Mubarak had selected Suleiman to fill the long-vacant Vice Presidency as a half-hearted attempt to calm the protests. Neither the promise of a national dialogue nor the appointment of a Vice President placated anyone.

That night the military also released a remarkable statement declaring that it would not use force against the Egyptian people and recognizing the legitimacy of the protesters' rights and demands. This was an ominous sign for Mubarak. If the military abandoned him, there was no way he could remain in power.

The first day of February saw more huge protests. That afternoon in the White House Situation Room, the national security team once again debated what to do. Halfway through our discussion, we received news that Mubarak was going on television to address the nation. We turned to the large video screens and waited to see what the embattled leader would say. Mubarak looked old and tired but sounded defiant. He promised not to run in the September election, to seek reforms to the Constitution, and to ensure a "peaceful transfer of power" before the end of his term. But he did not lift the emergency law or say that his son would not run in his place, nor did he offer to begin handing over any of his absolute powers. Mubarak had actually come around to much of what Wisner had asked of him, but it was too little, too late—both for the crowds in the streets and the team in the Situation Room.

"That's not going to cut it," President Obama said, visibly frustrated. Then he called Mubarak and said the same thing. We debated whether the President should make a public statement declaring that he was done waiting for Mubarak to do what was right. Once again senior Cabinet officials, including me, counseled caution. We warned that if the President appeared to be too heavy-handed, it might backfire. But other members of the team appealed once again to the President's idealism and argued that events on the ground were moving too quickly for us to wait. He was swayed, and that evening he went before the cameras in the Grand Foyer of the White House. "It is not the role of any other country to determine Egypt's leaders. Only the Egyptian people can do that," President Obama said. "[But] what is clear—and what I indicated tonight to President Mubarak—is my belief that an orderly transition must be meaningful, it must be peaceful, and it must begin *now*." When Press Secretary Robert

Gibbs was asked at his briefing the next day to define "now," his answer left little room for doubt. "Now means yesterday," he said.

Things in Cairo got worse. Regime supporters came out in force and clashed violently with protesters. Men wielding clubs and other weapons swept through Tahrir Square on camels and horses, cracking heads. I called Vice President Suleiman to make it clear that such violent repression was absolutely unacceptable. The Egyptian leadership did not repeat this tactic in the following days. On February 4, I spoke once again to Foreign Minister Aboul Gheit. In earlier conversations he had come across as confident and upbeat. Now he couldn't hide his frustration, even desperation. He complained that the United States was unceremoniously shoving Mubarak out the door without considering the consequences. Listen to what the Iranians are saying, he warned. They are eager to take advantage of Egypt's potential collapse. His fear of an Islamist takeover was visceral. "I have two granddaughters, one six and the other eight," he told me. "I want them to grow up to be like their grandmother and like you. Not wearing a *niqab* like in Saudi Arabia. This is the fight of my life."

His words stayed with me as I flew to Germany to address the Munich Security Conference, a key gathering of leaders and thinkers from across the international community. For all our talk about supporting democracy, what did that really mean? Surely more than just one election, one time. If Egypt's women saw their rights and opportunities rolled back under a newly elected government, was that democracy? What about if minorities like Egypt's Coptic Christians were persecuted or marginalized? If Mubarak was going to leave the presidency and Egypt was going to begin a transition, then these questions about what would happen next would become relevant and pressing.

In Munich, as in Doha a month before, I made the case for political and economic reforms across the Middle East. "This is not simply a matter of idealism," I said. "It is a strategic necessity. Without genuine progress toward open and accountable political systems, the gap between people and their governments will only grow, and instability will only deepen." Of course, these transitions would look different and proceed at different speeds in each country, depending on their unique circumstances. But no nation could ignore the aspirations of their people forever.

At the same time, I warned, we should be clear-eyed about the risks inherent in any transition. Free and fair elections would be necessary, but not sufficient. Functioning democracies require the rule of law, an independent judiciary, a free press and civil society, respect for human rights, minority rights, and accountable governance. In a country like Egypt, with a long history of authoritarian rule, it would take strong, inclusive leadership and sustained effort from across society, as well as international support, to put these building blocks of democracy in place. No one should expect them to appear overnight. My words that day may have sounded out of tune with the hope and optimism many felt watching the protests in Cairo, but they reflected the challenges I saw ahead.

At the same conference in Munich, Wisner, as a private citizen and no longer playing any role for the administration, appeared via satellite to offer his personal opinion on the situation. This distressed the White House, which thought it had his assurance that he would not discuss his mission publicly. Wisner made waves by saying Mubarak shouldn't go immediately but should oversee a transition. His comments came across as contradicting the President, and the White House was annoyed that Wisner had overstepped his brief. The President called me to express his unhappiness about the "mixed messages" we were sending. That's a diplomatic way of saying he took me to the woodshed. The President knew events in Egypt were not in America's control, but he wanted to do right by both our interests and our values. So did I. I knew Mubarak had stayed too long and done too little. But beyond getting rid of him, the people in Tahrir Square seemed to have no plan. Those of us who favored the stodgy-sounding "orderly transition" position were concerned that the only organized forces after Mubarak were the Muslim Brotherhood and the military.

By February 10, hundreds had been killed in clashes with security forces. The violence fed the protesters' rage and their demands that Mubarak resign. Rumors swirled that he would finally bow to the pressure. Expectations ran high as Mubarak delivered yet another address to the nation. This time he announced the transfer of some of his powers to Vice President Suleiman, but still he refused to step down or accept the need for a transition in which he relinquished power. The crowds in Tahrir Square were infuriated.

The next day, February 11, Mubarak finally accepted defeat. Vice President Suleiman, looking worn and drawn, appeared on television and announced that the President had stepped down and ceded all his powers to the military leadership. An Army spokesman read a statement pledging to "conduct free and fair presidential elections" and answer "the legitimate demands of the people." Mubarak himself did not speak, instead quietly departing Cairo for his residence on the Red Sea. Unlike Ben Ali in Tunisia, he did not flee the country, staying true to his defiant promise, "I will die in Egypt." That last act of stubbornness left him exposed to prosecution and retribution, and he has spent the following years under house arrest, in court, or in the hospital as his health reportedly declined.

About a month later I visited Cairo and walked through Tahrir Square myself. My security team was nervous about what we were heading into; it was a complete unknown. But as Egyptians thronged around me, the overwhelming message was one of warmth and hospitality. "Thank you for coming," several people said. "Welcome to the new Egypt!" others shouted. They were proud of the revolution they had won.

Then I met with a number of the students and activists who had played leading roles in the demonstrations. I was curious to hear about their plans to move from protests to politics and how they planned to influence the writing of a new Constitution and contest the upcoming elections. I found a disorganized group not prepared to contest or influence anything. They had no experience in politics, no understanding about how to organize parties, run candidates, or conduct campaigns. They didn't have platforms and showed little interest in forming them. Instead they argued among themselves, blamed the United States for a variety of sins, and were largely dismissive of electoral politics. "Have you considered forming a political coalition and joining together on behalf of candidates and programs?" I asked. They just looked at me blankly. I came away worried that they would end up handing the country to the Muslim Brotherhood or the military by default, which in the end is exactly what happened.

The acting head of state was Mubarak's Defense Minister, Field Marshall Mohamed Tantawi, who had promised to preside over a smooth transition to a democratically elected civilian government. When I met him in Cairo, he was so tired he could barely hold his head up. The shadows under his eyes reached practically down to his mouth. He was a professional soldier through and through, whose bearing and appearance reminded me of General Ashfaq Parvez Kayani in Pakistan. Both men were committed nationalists, devoted to the military cultures that produced them, and uneasy with both their dependence on aid from the

United States and the political and economic threats they perceived to their respective militaries' enormous powers. As Tantawi and I talked about his plans for the transition, I could see him choosing his words carefully. He was in a difficult position, trying to save his beloved Army from the wreckage of the Mubarak regime, protect the people, as the Army had promised to do, and do right by the former leader who had nurtured his career. In the end Tantawi followed through on his promise to hold elections. And when his preferred candidate, former Prime Minister Ahmed Shafik, narrowly lost to Mohamed Morsi of the Muslim Brotherhood, he allowed the result to stand.

Throughout the delicate transition process, the United States tried to walk a tightrope, promoting our democratic values and strategic interests without taking sides or backing particular candidates or factions. Yet despite our efforts to play a neutral and constructive role, many Egyptians viewed America with distrust. Supporters of the Muslim Brotherhood accused us of having propped up the Mubarak regime and suspected that we would collude with the military to keep them from power. Their opponents feared the prospect of Islamist rule and alleged that the United States had conspired with the Brotherhood to force out Mubarak. I wasn't sure how we could be accused of both aiding and foiling the Muslim Brotherhood, but logic never gets in the way of a good conspiracy theory.

When I returned to Egypt in July 2012, I found the streets of Cairo once again seething with protests. But this time they weren't directed at the government—they were directed at me. Crowds gathered outside my hotel, and as we drove into its parking garage through the side entrance, people banged on our vehicles. Egyptian police did nothing to stop them, and my Diplomatic Security agents were forced to push the crowd back themselves, something they ordinarily wouldn't do. Once inside my room more than a dozen stories up, I could hear the din of angry anti-American chants. My security and staff spent an anxious night prepared to evacuate the hotel if required. Despite warnings of more protests in Alexandria, I insisted we stick to the plan and fly there the next day to officially open a renovated American Consulate. After the event, as we left to get into our cars, we were forced to walk near the angry crowd. Toria Nuland, my intrepid spokeswoman, was hit in the head by a tomato (she took the blow gracefully), and a man pounded his shoe against my car's window as we pulled out heading to the airport.

In Cairo, along with separate meetings with Morsi and the generals, I sat down with a group of concerned Coptic Christians at the U.S. Embassy. They were deeply anxious about what the future held for them and their country. It was a very emotional, personal conversation.

One of the most moving scenes from the revolution in Tahrir Square was when Christian protesters formed a protective circle around their Muslim comrades during the call to prayer. The reverse happened when the Christians celebrated a Mass. Sadly, that spirit of unity had not lasted. Just a month after the fall of Mubarak, there were reports from the city of Qena that a group of Salafists had cut off the ear of a Coptic Christian schoolteacher and burned his house and car. Other attacks followed. Morsi's election only heightened fears in the Christian community.

In our meeting, one of the more agitated participants brought up an especially outrageous canard. He accused my trusted aide Huma Abedin, who is Muslim, of being a secret agent of the Muslim Brotherhood. This claim had been circulated by some unusually irresponsible and demagogic right-wing political and media personalities in the United States, including members of Congress, and now it had turned up in Cairo. I wasn't going to let that stand and told him in no uncertain terms how wrong he was. After a few minutes of conversation the embarrassed accuser apologized and asked why a member of the U.S. Congress would make such an assertion if it wasn't true. I laughed and said that unfortunately plenty of falsehoods are circulated in Congress. After the meeting Huma went right up to the man, politely introduced herself, and offered to answer any questions he had. It was a characteristically gracious move on her part.

Privately I was furious at the attacks on Huma by several ignorant House members. So I was grateful to Senator John McCain, who had gotten to know her over the years, when he went to the floor of the Senate and made his own disdain clear: "When anyone, not least a member of Congress, launches vicious and degrading attacks against fellow Americans on the basis of nothing more than fear of who they are, in ignorance of what they stand for, it defames the spirit of our nation, and we all grow poor because of it. Our reputations, our character, are the only things we leave behind when we depart this earth. And unjust acts that malign the good name of a decent and honorable person, is not only wrong, it is contrary to everything we hold dear."

Several weeks later, with Huma sitting at his side at the White House's annual Iftar dinner to break the Ramadan fast, President Obama also defended her, saying, "The American people owe her a debt of gratitude—because Huma is an American patriot, and an example of what we need in this country—more public servants with her sense of decency, her grace and her generosity of spirit. So, on behalf of all Americans, we thank you so much." The President of the United States and one of our nation's most renowned war heroes make quite a one-two punch. It was a real testament to Huma's character.

In our meeting I told the Coptic leaders that the United States would stand firmly on the side of religious freedom. All citizens should have the right to live, work, and worship as they choose, whether they be Muslim or Christian or from any other background. No group or faction should impose its authority, ideology, or religion on anyone else. America was prepared to work with the leaders that the Egyptian people chose. But our engagement with those leaders would be based on their commitment to universal human rights and democratic principles.

Unfortunately the months and years that followed proved that my early concerns about the difficulties of democratic transitions were well-founded. The Muslim Brotherhood consolidated its power but failed to govern in a transparent or inclusive fashion. President Morsi clashed frequently with the judiciary, sought to marginalize his political opponents rather than build a broad national consensus, did little to improve the economy, and allowed the persecution of minorities, including the Coptic Christians, to continue. But he did surprise some skeptics by upholding the peace treaty with Israel and by helping me negotiate a cease-fire in Gaza in November 2012. Once again the United States faced our classic dilemma: Should we do business with a leader with whom we disagreed on so many things in the name of advancing core security interests? We were back on the high wire, performing the balancing act without easy answers or good options.

In July 2013, with millions of Egyptians again protesting in the streets, this time against the overreaches of the Morsi government, the military under Tantawi's successor, General Abdul-Fattah el-Sisi, stepped in a second time. They removed Morsi and began an aggressive new crackdown on the Muslim Brotherhood.

As of 2014, the prospects for Egyptian democracy do not look bright. Sisi is running for President with only token opposition, and he appears to be following in the classic mold of Middle Eastern strongmen. Many Egyptians seem tired of the chaos and ready for a return to stability. But, there is little reason to believe that restored military rule will be any more sustainable than it was under Mubarak. To do so it will have to be more inclusive, more responsible for the needs of the people, and eventually, more democratic. In the end, the test for Egypt and other countries across the Middle East will be whether they can build credible democratic institutions that uphold the rights of every citizen while providing security and stability in the face of old enmities across faith, ethnic, economic, and geographic divides. That will not be easy, as recent history has shown, but the alternative is to watch the region keep sinking into the sand.

======

King Abdullah II of Jordan managed to stay ahead of the wave of unrest that washed away other governments in the region during the Arab Spring. Jordan held credible legislative elections and began cracking down on corruption, but the economy remained stagnant, in large measure because Jordan is one of the world's most energy-starved nations. Roughly 80 percent of its energy came from natural gas delivered via pipelines from Egypt. But after the fall of Mubarak and the rise of instability in the Sinai, those pipelines, which also carried gas to Israel, became the frequent target of attacks and sabotage, interrupting the flow of energy into Jordan.

Costly government subsidies were keeping the price of electricity from spiraling out of control, but as a result the country's public debt was ballooning. The King faced a difficult dilemma: cut the subsidies, let energy prices rise, and face the wrath of the people, or maintain the subsidies and run the risk of financial meltdown.

One obvious answer lay to the east, in Iraq, where the United States was helping the government of Prime Minister Nouri al-Maliki rebuild its wrecked oil and gas industry. A less obvious and more controversial source of energy lay to the west, in Israel, which had just discovered extensive natural gas reserves in the eastern Mediterranean. The two countries had been at peace since the signing of a historic treaty in 1994, but Israel remained deeply unpopular among the Jordanian public, a majority of whom were of Palestinian origin. Given all his other troubles, could the King risk more protests by pursuing a major new trade deal with Israel? Could he afford not to? Over lunch with the King at the State Department in January 2012, and in follow-up discussions with his Foreign Minister Nasser Judeh, I urged them to start talking to the Israelis—in secret if necessary.

With U.S. support, Jordan began negotiating with both Iraq and Israel. An agreement with Iraq was signed in 2013 that, with the construction of a pipeline from southern Iraq to Aqaba on the Red Sea, should provide Jordan 1 million barrels per day of crude oil and more than 250 million cubic feet of natural gas. After a year of secret talks with the Israelis, a deal was announced in early 2014 to use Israeli natural gas from the eastern Mediterranean to fuel a power plant on the Jordanian side of the Dead Sea. The King was not wrong to have been cautious; representatives of the Muslim Brotherhood in Jordan slammed the agreement with the "Zionist entity" as "an attack on the Palestinian cause." But it promised a future of greater energy security for Jordan and a new source of cooperation for two neighbors in a region of enormous challenges.

━━━

Perhaps our most delicate balancing act in the Middle East was with our partners in the Persian Gulf: Bahrain, Kuwait, Qatar, Saudi Arabia, and the UAE. The United States had developed deep economic and strategic ties to these wealthy, conservative monarchies, even as we made no secret of our concerns about human rights abuses, especially the treatment of women and minorities, and the export of extremist ideology.

Every U.S. administration wrestled with the contradictions of our policy toward the Gulf. The choices were never harder than after 9/11. Americans were shocked that fifteen of the nineteen hijackers and Osama bin Laden himself hailed from Saudi Arabia, a nation that we had defended in the 1991 Gulf War. And it was appalling that money from the Gulf continued funding extremist madrassas and propaganda all over the world.

At the same time, these governments shared many of our top security concerns. Saudi Arabia had expelled bin Laden, and the kingdom's security forces had become strong partners in the fight against al Qaeda. Most of the Gulf states shared our worries about Iran's march toward a nuclear weapon along with its aggressive support of terrorism. These tensions were rooted in an ancient sectarian split within Islam: Iran is predominantly Shiite, while the Gulf states are predominantly Sunni. Bahrain is an exception. There, as in Iraq under Saddam, an elite Sunni minority rules over a Shiite majority. In Syria the situation is reversed.

To support our shared security interests over the years and help deter Iranian aggression, the United States sold large amounts of military equipment to the Gulf states, and stationed the U.S. Navy's 5th Fleet in Bahrain, the Combined Air and Space Operations Center in Qatar, and maintained troops in Kuwait, Saudi Arabia, and the UAE, as well as key bases in other countries.

When I became Secretary I developed personal relationships with Gulf leaders both individually and as a group through the Gulf Cooperation Council, a political and economic association of the Gulf countries. We created a U.S.-GCC security dialogue to intensify our cooperation. Most of the focus of our discussions was on Iran and counterterrorism, but I pressed leaders on the need to open up their societies, respect human rights, and offer more opportunities to their young people and women.

Occasionally, as in an egregious case of child marriage in Saudi Arabia, I was able to make some headway. I learned about an eight-year-old girl whose father forced her to marry a fifty-year-old man in exchange for about $13,000. Saudi courts rejected pleas from her mother to stop the marriage, and it did not look like the government was going to inter-vene. I knew that embarrassing governments with public condemnation can backfire, making them dig their heels in deeper. Instead of calling a press conference to condemn the practice and demand action, I looked for a way to persuade the Saudis to do the right thing and still save face. Quietly reaching out through diplomatic channels, I offered a simple but firm message: "Fix this on your own and I won't say a word." The Saudis appointed a new judge who quickly granted a divorce. It was a lesson I've learned all over the world: There's a time to get on a soapbox—and I've been on quite a few—but sometimes the best way to achieve real change, in diplomacy and in life, is by building relationships and understanding how and when to use them.

I responded differently to the ban on women driving in Saudi Arabia. In May 2011, a Saudi woman activist posted a video online of her driv-ing a car and was subsequently arrested and detained for nine days. In June, a few dozen women across Saudi Arabia took the wheel in protest. I spoke with Saudi Foreign Minister Prince Saud al-Faisal on the phone and raised my personal concern on the issue. In this case I also spoke out publicly, calling the women "brave," expressing how moved I was by their actions. When another group of women again protested the ban on October 26, 2013, some opponents falsely pointed to the date—my birthday—as proof that the protests were organized outside Saudi Arabia. Unfortunately for the kingdom and its women, the ban continues.

When I traveled to Saudi Arabia in February 2010, I balanced my itinerary between security talks with the King and a visit to a women's university in Jeddah. Both were memorable in their own way.

I was greeted at the airport in Riyadh, the capital, by Prince Saud al-Faisal, a seventy-year-old Princeton-educated royal who had served as the kingdom's Foreign Minister since 1975. Like most Saudis I met, he alternated between wearing tailored bespoke suits and long flowing robes with a kaffiyeh headdress. I appreciated spending time with the Prince, who understood the forces, representing tradition and modernity, that were competing for ascendancy in the region.

King Abdullah, who was in his eighties, had invited me to visit him at his desert camp an hour outside of town, and in a first for me, he sent his personal luxury tour bus to pick us up. The bus was lavishly appointed, and the Prince and I sat across the aisle from each other in plush leather seats as we drove through the countryside. I noticed a number of encampments filled with camels. The Prince and I started a funny conversation about the popularity of the kingdom's camel population, which seems to stem from both practical and sentimental reasons. He discussed the long history nomads had with their camels but told me that he personally didn't like them. I was surprised—imagine an Australian hating koala bears or a Chinese loathing pandas—but then I haven't had to spend too much time around camels myself, and I've heard they can be ornery.

Soon we arrived at what had been described to us as a desert "camp," but which turned out to be a massive air-conditioned tent pitched over a palace with marble floors and gilded bathrooms, surrounded by trailers and helicopters. The dignified monarch in long black robes was waiting for us. Contrary to some of my American colleagues, who like to get right down to business, I usually start my side of an official conversation with small talk as a signal of my respect and friendship. So I continued with the camel theme. "I want you to know, Your Majesty, that His Highness thinks camels are ugly," I said, gesturing to Prince Saud. The King smiled. "I think His Highness was not being fair to camels," he said. The King,

the Prince, and I bantered for a while, and then he invited our entire traveling party, consisting of nearly forty people including the press corps, to
join him for an elaborate lunch. He walked me down what seemed like
an endless buffet table, with two stewards trailing behind with our trays.
There were dozens of dishes, ranging from local favorites like lamb and
rice to lobster and paella. The journalists and staff, for whom meals on
the road are often catch-as-catch-can, looked like they'd died and gone to
foodie heaven. Waiters hovered nearby, ready to refill our plates. I sat next
to the King at the head of a long U-shaped table with a giant flat-screen
television in the middle of the hollow space prominently positioned so the
King could watch soccer and off-road racing while he ate. He turned the
volume up very loud so that no one else in the crowded room could hear
what we discussed. I leaned in and we began to talk.

We spent four hours together that afternoon, delving into the region's
challenges, from Iran to Iraq to the Israelis and Palestinians. The King
spoke forcefully about the need to prevent Iran from acquiring a nuclear
weapon and urged us to take a harder line with Tehran. He expressed his
hope that more Saudi students would be allowed to study in the United
States, which had become more difficult since 9/11. It was a productive
meeting, and it signaled that our partnership was on firm footing. The
differences between our cultures, values, and political systems are vast,
but working together where possible advances America's interests.

The next day I got a firsthand reminder of how complicated this all
is. Huma's mother, Dr. Saleha Abedin, is vice dean at Dar Al-Hekma, a
women's university in Jeddah, where I had arranged to hold a town hall
discussion with the students. As I walked into the auditorium, I saw the
crowd of young women, all with their hair covered under *hijabs* and a
few with their faces covered as well.

In Arabic, *Dar Al-Hekma* means "The House of Wisdom," and I
talked to the students about how much wisdom there is in making sure
that girls as well as boys have access to education. I quoted the Egyptian
poet Hafez Ibrahim, who wrote, "A mother is a school. Empower her
and you empower a great nation," and I talked about my own experiences with all-women's education at Wellesley. The students peppered me
with probing questions about everything from Iran's nuclear ambitions
to the plight of the Palestinians and the prospects for health care reform
in America. One of them asked me what I thought of Sarah Palin and
if I'd move to Canada if she ever became President. (No, I said, I would

not flee.) These women might have limited opportunities to participate publicly in their ultraconservative society, but there was nothing limited about their intelligence, energy, and curiosity.

Throughout the entire event, one of the female security officers, who was covered head to toe in black with two tiny slits for her eyes, kept vigilant watch on all the Americans. She was not going to let any of the male staff or journalists get anywhere near these students. As I was wrapping up onstage, she approached Huma and whispered to her in Arabic, "I would love to have a picture with her." When I finished, Huma pulled me aside and pointed to this shrouded woman. "Should we go to a private room to do it?" I asked, out of respect for her modesty. She nodded, and we ducked into a small office. Then, just as we were about to take the photo, the woman pulled off her veil, revealing a huge smile. The camera snapped, and the veil came back down. Welcome to Saudi Arabia.

Almost exactly a year later the delicate balance of our relationships in the Gulf threatened to unravel. The wave of popular protests that started in Tunisia and crashed into Egypt did not stop there. The call for political reform and economic opportunity spread across the entire Middle East. No country was untouched. Yemen was almost torn apart, and President Saleh eventually was forced to leave office. Libya descended into civil war. The governments in Jordan and Morocco made cautious but real reforms. In Saudi Arabia the Royal Family opened their deep pockets in an attempt to placate citizens with more generous social welfare programs.

Bahrain, as the home base for the U.S. Navy in the Persian Gulf, was an exceptionally complicated case for us. In this least wealthy of the Gulf monarchies, demonstrations took on a sectarian cast, with the majority Shiites protesting against their Sunni rulers. In mid-February 2011, crowds demanding democratic reforms and equality for all Bahrainis, regardless of sect, gathered at a major traffic intersection in central Manama called the Pearl Roundabout. Events in Tunisia and Egypt left security forces across the region on edge, and a few early incidents of excessive force in Manama brought more angry citizens into the streets.

Around 3 A.M. on Thursday, February 17, a handful of protesters camped out in the Pearl Roundabout were killed in a police raid, sparking widespread outrage. But the Sunni leaders in Bahrain and in neighboring Gulf countries did not see the largely Shiite protests as a popular outpouring for democracy; they saw the hidden hand of Iran. They worried that their large adversary across the water was fomenting unrest in order to weaken their governments and improve its own strategic position. Given Iran's track record, this was not an unreasonable fear. But it clouded their perception of the legitimate grievances of their people and hastened the use of force.

I got on the phone with the Bahraini Foreign Minister Sheikh Khalid bin Ahmed al Khalifa to express my concern about the violence and the possibility of events spiraling out of control. The next day would be crucial, and I hoped his government would take steps to avoid further violence around the funerals and Friday prayer services, which had become times of mobilization across the region. Responding to peaceful protests with force was a recipe for more trouble. "This is a misreading of the world we are in, which is becoming a much more complicated environment," I said. "I want you to hear it from me. We do not want any violence that allows outside interference in your internal affairs. In order to avoid this, there has to be effort at genuine consultations." We both knew that "outside interference" was code for Iran. My point was that excessive force could lead to instability that Iran would be able to exploit, which was the very thing his government was trying to avoid.

The Foreign Minister sounded worried, and his answers only heightened my concern. He said that the police action had not been planned, blamed the protesters for starting the violence, and promised that his government was committed to dialogue and reform. "These deaths were catastrophic," he said. "We are at the brink of a sectarian abyss." That was a chilling phrase. I told him that I was sending Jeff Feltman to Bahrain immediately. "We will come with suggestions, trying to be helpful and productive during this difficult time. I'm not saying there is an easy answer. Your situation is particularly challenging because of the sectarian situation you face. I have no doubt you have a big neighbor interested in this matter in a way other countries do not."

Spurred to action by fears of growing violence and encouraged by Jeff, who spent a lot of time on the ground in Manama over the following weeks, the Bahraini Crown Prince tried to organize a national dialogue to address some of the concerns of the protesters and ease the tensions gripping the country. The Crown Prince was a moderate who understood the need for reform and was the ruling family's best chance to reconcile the competing factions in the country. Behind the scenes Jeff was working to broker an understanding between the Royal Family and the more moderate leaders of the Shiite opposition. But the protests kept growing, and by March, protesters were calling for an end to the monarchy altogether. Clashes with police were getting bigger and more violent. It seemed as if the government was losing control, and conservative members of the Bahraini ruling family were putting pressure on the Crown Prince to abandon his mediation efforts.

On Sunday, March 13, our defense attaché at the embassy in Riyadh reported unusual troop movements in Saudi Arabia that might be heading toward Bahrain. Jeff called the UAE Foreign Minister Sheikh Abdullah bin Zayed Al-Nahyan, or AbZ, as he was often referred to, who confirmed that a military intervention was about to be launched. Bahrain's government was going to invite its neighbors in to help provide security. They had not seen the need to inform the United States, as they did not intend to ask our permission or entertain any entreaties to stop. The next day thousands of Saudi troops crossed the border into Bahrain with some 150 armored vehicles. About five hundred police from the UAE followed.

I was concerned about this escalation and worried about a bloodbath if Saudi tanks started rolling through the barricaded streets of Manama. And the timing could not have been worse. At that very moment we were deep into diplomatic negotiations to build an international coalition to protect Libyan civilians from an impending massacre by Colonel Muammar Qaddafi, and we were counting on the UAE and other Gulf nations to play key roles. The Arab League had voted on March 12 to request that the UN Security Council impose a no-fly zone in Libya, and their active participation in any military operation would provide legitimacy in the region. Otherwise the international community might not be able to act. After Iraq and Afghanistan, we weren't going to risk looking like we'd launched another Western intervention in a Muslim country.

I was in Paris for meetings on Libya, as was AbZ, so we arranged to meet at my hotel. On the way in, he was asked by a reporter about the situation in Bahrain. "The Bahrain Government asked us yesterday to look at ways to help them to defuse the tension," he said. I was worried exactly the opposite was about to happen. The next day the King of Bahrain declared a state of emergency. I spoke with the Saudi Foreign Minister and urged him to hold off using force to clear the protesters. Just give Jeff a little more time to make negotiations work, I said. Even twenty-four hours might make a difference. We were close to a deal with the major Shiite political party to pull back from the key areas of the city in exchange for the government affirming the right to peaceful protest and starting a good-faith dialogue. Saud al-Faisal was implacable. The protesters needed to go home and let normal life resume, he said. Only then could we talk about a deal. He blamed Iran for stirring up trouble and supporting radicals. It was time to end the crisis and return stability to the Gulf, he said.

Early on March 16, security forces moved in to clear the Pearl Roundabout. Riot police supported by tanks and helicopters clashed with protesters and used tear gas to evict them from their makeshift camp. Five people were killed. The arrival of the Saudi troops and this new crackdown further inflamed Shiite opinion across the country. Under pressure from hard-liners in both camps, the negotiations between the opposition and the Crown Prince collapsed.

I was in Cairo meeting with the Egyptian transitional authorities and was dismayed by the reports coming in from Bahrain. In an interview with the BBC, I spoke candidly about my concerns. "The situation in Bahrain is alarming," I said. "We have called on our friends in the Gulf—four of whom are assisting the Bahrain security efforts—to force through a political solution, not a security standoff."

"So what leverage do you still have on countries like Bahrain and Saudi Arabia?" the BBC's Kim Ghattas asked. "They're your allies. You train their armies. You supply them with weapons. And yet when the Saudis decided to send troops into Bahrain—and I believe Washington made clear it wasn't pleased about that—they said, 'Don't interfere. This is an internal GCC matter.'" It was true, and it was frustrating.

"Well, they are on notice as to what we think," I replied. "And we will intend to make that very clear publicly and privately, and we will do everything we can to try to move this off the wrong track, which we believe is going to undermine long-term progress in Bahrain, to the right track, which is the political and economic track."

Those might sound like reasonable words—and they were—but they were more pointed than how we usually speak in public about the Gulf countries. My message was heard loud and clear in the Gulf. In Riyadh and Abu Dhabi, our partners were angry and offended.

On March 19, I was back in Paris putting the final touches on the Libya coalition. With Qaddafi's forces closing in on the rebel stronghold of Benghazi, UN-backed air operations were imminent. I spoke once again with AbZ and emphasized that America remained committed to our partnership, as I did personally. There was a long silence on the phone and the line went dead. Had things gotten that bad, I wondered? Then we were reconnected. "Did you hear me?" I asked. "I was listening!" he responded. "Good, I was talking and talking and then there was a long silence, and I thought, what have I done here?" He laughed. But then he got serious again and delivered a sharp blow. "Frankly, when we have a situation with our armed forces in Bahrain, it's hard to participate in another operation if our armed forces' commitment to Bahrain is questioned by our main ally," he said. In other words, forget about Arab participation in the Libya mission.

This was turning into a disaster. I had to fix it, fast. But how? There were no good options here. Our values and conscience demanded that the United States condemn the violence against civilians we were seeing in Bahrain, full stop. After all, that was the very principle at play in Libya. But if we persisted, the carefully constructed international coalition to stop Qaddafi could collapse at the eleventh hour, and we might fail to prevent a much larger abuse—a full-fledged massacre.

I told AbZ that I wanted to reach a constructive understanding. He asked if we could meet in person. "I am hearing you now, and we want a way out. And you know we are keen to take part in Libya," he said. A few hours later, just after 6 P.M. in Paris, I sat down with him and told him that I could craft a statement that would stay true to our values without being insulting to them. I hoped that would be enough to convince the Emiratis to rejoin the mission in Libya. If not, we were prepared to go forward without them.

That evening I held a press conference at the stately home of the U.S. Ambassador in Paris. I spoke about Libya and stressed that Arab leadership in the air campaign was crucial. Then I turned to Bahrain. "Our goal is a credible political process that can address the legitimate aspirations of all the people of Bahrain, starting with the Crown Prince's dialogue, which all parties should join." Bahrain had the right to invite in forces from neighboring countries, I added, and we welcomed word from the Gulf countries that they would provide a major aid package for economic and social development. "We have made clear that security alone cannot resolve the challenges facing Bahrain," I continued. "Violence is not and cannot be the answer. A political process is. We have raised our concerns about the current measures directly with Bahraini officials and will continue to do so."

The differences in tone and substance from what I said in Cairo were relatively small, and I felt comfortable that we had not sacrificed our values or credibility. Few, if any, outside observers even noticed any change at all. Soon the Arab jets were flying over Libya.

I wished we had better options in Bahrain and more leverage to produce a positive outcome. We continued to speak out in the months that followed, emphasizing that mass arrests and brute force were at odds with the universal rights of Bahrain's citizens and would not make legitimate calls for reform go away. We also continued to work closely with the government of Bahrain and with its Gulf neighbors on a range of issues.

In November 2011, in a speech at the National Democratic Institute in Washington, I addressed some of the questions that had arisen about America and the Arab Spring. One that we heard often was: Why does America promote democracy one way in some countries and another way in others? In short, why do we call on Mubarak to give up power in Egypt and mobilize an international military coalition to stop Qaddafi in Libya, while retaining relations with Bahrain and other Gulf monarchies?

The answer, I said, began with a very practical point. Circumstances varied dramatically from country to country, and "it would be foolish to take a one-size-fits-all approach and barrel forward regardless of circumstances on the ground." What was possible and made sense in one place might not be possible or wise in another. It was also true, I said, that America has many important national interests in the region, and they will not always align perfectly, despite our best efforts. "We'll always have to walk and chew gum at the same time." That was certainly true in Bahrain. America will always have imperfect partners who doubtless view us as imperfect too, and we'll always face imperatives that drive us to make imperfect compromises.

———

I saw this in February 2012 when I returned to Tunisia, where the convulsions of the Arab Spring had begun. The riot police were gone. There was no more pepper spray in the air. The din of protest had quieted. A moderate Islamist party had won a plurality of the votes in an open, competitive, and credible election. Its leaders promised to embrace freedom of religion and full rights for women. The United States pledged significant financial support, and we began working to boost trade and investment that would get the economy going again. The new government faced many challenges, and the years ahead would be rocky, but there was reason to hope that, in Tunisia at least, the promise of the Arab Spring might actually be realized.

I wanted to talk to the young people who had provided the emotional core of the revolution and who stood to gain the most if democracy took root in Tunisia. About two hundred of them met with me in the Palais du Baron d'Erlanger, a center for Arab and Mediterranean music perched on a cliff above the sea. I spoke about the hard work of making a transition to democracy and about the role their generation could play. Then I took questions. A young lawyer asked for the microphone. "I think that there exists among many young people in Tunisia and across the region a deep feeling of mistrust towards the West in general and the United States in particular. And many observers partly explain the surge of extremism in the region and in Tunisia by this skepticism," he said. "And even among the mainstream of moderate and pro-Western youth, there is a sense of despair and fatalism when it comes to the possibility of building a real and lasting partnership that is based on mutual interests. So is the United States aware of this issue? And how do you think we can address it?"

He had just put his finger on one of our biggest challenges. And I understood that the distrust he and so many others felt was connected to the compromises we had to make in the Middle East. "We are aware of it," I responded. "We regret it. We feel that it doesn't reflect the values or the policy of the United States." I tried to explain why America had worked with autocrats in the region for so long, from Ben Ali in Tunisia to Mubarak in Egypt to our partners in the Gulf. "You deal with the governments that are in place. And yes, we did. We dealt with the governments that were in place, just like we deal with the governments elsewhere. Right now, we're in a big argument with Russia and China because they won't agree to the Security Council resolution to help the poor people in Syria. But we don't stop dealing with Russia and China across a whole range of issues because we have serious disagreements with them. So I think part of it is to recognize the reality that governments have to deal with, and to look at the whole picture."

I knew this wasn't very satisfying, but it was the truth. America will always do what it takes to keep our people safe and advance our core interests. Sometimes that means working with partners with whom we have deep disagreements.

But there is another part of the big picture that is often lost, a truth about America that is easy to miss amid the daily headlines of one crisis or another. The United States has sacrificed enormous amounts of blood and treasure to help other people around the world achieve their own freedom. Looking around at the open and engaged young Tunisians, I rattled off a string of examples, including how America helped the people of Eastern Europe emerge from behind the Iron Curtain and nurtured democracies across Asia. "I will be the first to say we, like any country in the world, have made mistakes. I will be the first to say that. We've made a lot of mistakes. But I think if you look at the entire historical record, the entire historical record shows we've been on the side of freedom, we've been on the side of human rights, we've been on the side of free markets and economic empowerment." The young lawyer nodded and sat down.

16

Libya: All Necessary Measures

Mahmoud Jibril was late.

It was March 14, 2011, little more than a month after the fall of Hosni Mubarak in Egypt. Attention had already shifted to the next crisis in the region, this time in Libya, a country of some 6 million people located between Egypt and Tunisia along the Mediterranean coast of North Africa. Protests against the authoritarian regime of longtime Libyan dictator, Colonel Muammar Qaddafi, had turned into a full-scale rebellion after he used extreme force against the demonstrators. Now Jibril, a Libyan political scientist with a PhD from the University of Pittsburgh, was on his way to meet with me on behalf of the rebels fighting Qaddafi's forces.

I had flown through the night and arrived in Paris early that morning to meet with the Foreign Ministers of the Group of 8 leading industrialized countries—France, Germany, Italy, Japan, the United Kingdom, Canada, Russia, and the United States—to discuss ways to stop Qaddafi from slaughtering his own people. (Russia was expelled from the group in 2014, after the invasion of Crimea, and it went back to being the G-7, as it was before 1998.) Joining us were Ministers from several Arab countries who were calling for robust international action to protect Libyan civilians, especially from Qaddafi's air force. When I arrived I spent most of the day locked in intense discussions with European and Arab leaders concerned that Qaddafi's superior forces were poised to overwhelm the rebels. When I met with French President Nicolas Sarkozy, he urged the United States to support international military intervention to stop Qaddafi's advance toward the rebel stronghold of Benghazi in eastern Libya. I was sympathetic, but not convinced. The United States had spent the previous decade bogged down in long and difficult wars in Iraq and Afghanistan, and before we joined yet another conflict, I wanted to be sure we had thought through the implications. Would the international community, including Libya's neighbors, unite behind this mission? Who were these rebels we would be aiding, and were they prepared to lead Libya if Qaddafi fell? What was the endgame here? I wanted to meet Mahmoud Jibril face-to-face to discuss these questions.

My suite in the grand old Westin-Vendôme on rue de Rivoli looked out over the Tuileries Garden, and from the window I could see the Eiffel Tower lit up against the Parisian sky. The beauty and color of Paris were a long way from the horror unfolding in Libya.

It had started in a now-familiar way. The arrest of a prominent human rights activist in Benghazi in mid-February 2011 had sparked protests that soon spread across the country. Libyans, inspired by what they had seen in Tunisia and Egypt, began demanding a say in their own government. Unlike in Egypt, where the Army refused to fire on civilians, Libyan security forces unleashed heavy weapons on the crowds. Qaddafi turned loose foreign mercenaries and thugs to attack demonstrators. There were reports of indiscriminate killings, arbitrary arrests, and torture. Soldiers were executed for refusing to fire on their fellow citizens. In response to this violent crackdown, protests morphed into armed rebellion, especially in parts of the country that had long chafed at Qaddafi's quixotic rule.

In late February, the UN Security Council, shocked by Qaddafi's brutal response, called for an immediate end to the violence and unanimously approved a resolution to impose an arms embargo on Libya, freeze the assets of key human rights violators and members of the Qaddafi family, and refer the Libyan case to the International Criminal Court. The ICC eventually charged Qaddafi, his son Saif al-Islam Qaddafi, and the military intelligence chief Abdullah al-Senussi with crimes against humanity. The United States also imposed sanctions of its own and moved to provide emergency humanitarian aid to Libyans in need. At the end of February, I traveled to the UN Human Rights Council in Geneva to remind the international community that it had a responsibility to protect universal rights and to hold violators accountable. I said that Qaddafi had "lost the legitimacy to govern," and "the people of Libya have made themselves clear: It is time for Qaddafi to go—now, without further violence or delay." A few days before, in the same chamber in the Palais des Nations, the Libyan delegation had dramatically renounced their allegiance to Qaddafi and declared their support for the rebels. "Young people in my country today are with their blood writing a new chapter in the history of struggle and resistance," one diplomat said.

A week later the rebels in Benghazi formed a transitional governing council. Armed militias across the country made gains against the regime, including in the western mountains. But then Qaddafi unleashed firepower they could not match. His tanks rolled through town after town. The resistance started to crumble, and Qaddafi pledged to hunt down and exterminate all who opposed him. The situation was increasingly desperate. That's why Jibril was coming to plead his case.

As I waited for him to arrive, I thought about Muammar Qaddafi, one of the most eccentric, cruel, and unpredictable autocrats in the world. He cut a bizarre and sometimes chilling figure on the world stage, with his colorful outfits, Amazonian bodyguards, and over-the-top rhetoric. "Those who do not love me do not deserve to live!" he once said. Qaddafi seized power in a coup in 1969 and ruled Libya, a former Italian colony, with a mix of new-age socialism, fascism, and personality cult. Although the country's oil wealth kept the regime afloat, his capricious governance hollowed out Libya's economy and institutions.

As a state sponsor of terrorism, client of the Soviet Union, and proliferator of weapons of mass destruction, Qaddafi became a top enemy of the United States in the 1980s. In 1981, *Newsweek* put him on its cover with the headline "The Most Dangerous Man in the World?" President Reagan called him the "mad dog of the Middle East" and bombed Libya in 1986 in retaliation for a terrorist attack in Berlin that killed American citizens, which Qaddafi had planned. Qaddafi claimed one of his children died in the air strikes, which further strained relations.

In 1988, Libyan agents planted the bomb that destroyed Pan Am Flight 103 over Lockerbie, Scotland, killing 270 people. Thirty-five of the passengers killed on that flight were students from Syracuse University in upstate New York, and I got to know some of their families when I represented them in the U.S. Senate. In my eyes, Qaddafi was a criminal and a terrorist who could never be trusted. Many of his Arab neighbors agreed. Most of them had tangled with him over the years. At one point he had even plotted to assassinate the King of Saudi Arabia.

When Condoleezza Rice met Qaddafi in Tripoli in 2008, she found him to be "unstable," with a "slightly eerie fascination" with her person-ally. In 2009 he made a stir in New York when he spoke at the UN Gen-eral Assembly for the first time in his forty-year rule. He brought along a large Bedouin tent but was told he could not pitch it in Central Park. At the UN he was given fifteen minutes to speak but rambled on for a full hour and a half. His bizarre diatribe included rants about the Ken-nedy assassination and the possibility that swine flu was really a biological weapon designed in a laboratory. He suggested that Israelis and Palestin-ians live together in a single state called "Isratine" and that the UN move its headquarters to Libya to reduce jet lag and avoid the risk of terrorist attacks in New York. In short, it was a bizarre performance—but, for Qaddafi, typical.

Despite all this, in recent years Qaddafi had tried to show the world a new face, giving up his nuclear program, mending fences with the inter-national community, and contributing to the fight against al Qaeda. Sadly any hope that he was mellowing into something resembling a statesman in his old age evaporated as soon as the protests started. Then it was back to the old murderous Qaddafi.

All of this—the defiant dictator, the attacks on civilians, the peril-ous position of the rebels—led me to consider what many of my foreign counterparts were debating: Was it time for the international community to go beyond humanitarian aid and sanctions and take decisive action to stop the violence in Libya? And if yes, what role should the United States play to advance and protect our interests?

Just a few days earlier, on March 9, I had joined the rest of President Obama's national security team in the White House Situation Room to discuss the crisis in Libya. There was little appetite for direct U.S. inter-vention. Defense Secretary Robert Gates believed that the United States did not have core national interests at stake in Libya. The Pentagon told us that the most talked-about military option, a no-fly zone like the one we had maintained in Iraq during the 1990s, was unlikely to be enough to tip the balance toward the rebels. Qaddafi's ground forces were just too strong.

The next day I testified before Congress and argued that this was not a time for America to rush unilaterally into a volatile situation: "I'm one of those who believes that absent international authorization, the United States acting alone would be stepping into a situation whose consequences are unforeseeable. And I know that's the way our military feels." Too often, other countries were quick to demand action but then looked to America to shoulder all the burdens and take all the risks. I reminded Congress, "We had a no-fly zone over Iraq. It did not prevent Saddam Hussein from slaughtering people on the ground, and it did not get him out of office."

Retired General Wesley Clark, an old friend who led the NATO air war in Kosovo in the 1990s, summed up the argument against intervention in an op-ed in the *Washington Post* on March 11: "Whatever resources we dedicate for a no-fly zone would probably be too little, too late. We would once again be committing our military to force regime change in a Muslim land, even though we can't quite bring ourselves to say it. So let's recognize that the basic requirements for successful intervention simply don't exist, at least not yet: We don't have a clearly stated objective, legal authority, committed international support or adequate on-the-scene military capabilities, and Libya's politics hardly foreshadow a clear outcome."

The very next day a development in Cairo began to change the calculus. After more than five hours of deliberation and debate, the Arab League, representing twenty-one Middle Eastern nations, voted to request that the UN Security Council impose a no-fly zone in Libya. The Arab League had previously suspended the Qaddafi government's membership, and now it recognized the rebel council as the legitimate representative of the Libyan people. These were major steps by an organization previously known as a club for autocrats and oil barons. One of the prime movers was the Egyptian diplomat Amr Moussa, who was serving as the Arab League's Secretary-General but had his eye on the upcoming Presidential elections in Egypt. This no-fly zone resolution was, in part, his bid for support from the revolutionary factions that had helped drive out Mubarak. The Gulf monarchs went along, in part to show their own restive populations that they were on the side of change. And, of course, they all hated Qaddafi.

If the Arabs were willing to take the lead, perhaps an international intervention was not impossible after all. Certainly it would put pressure on Russia and China, who might otherwise be expected to veto any Western-backed action at the UN Security Council. But the Arab League statement used the term *humanitarian action* and did not explicitly mention military force. I wondered if Amr Moussa and the others were really prepared to back what it would take to stop Qaddafi from massacring his people.

AbZ, the Foreign Minister of the UAE, a powerful behind-the-scenes player at the Arab League, was in Paris when I arrived. We met in my hotel before the G-8 dinner, and I pressed him on how far the Arab commitment went. Were they prepared to see foreign planes dropping bombs on Libya? Even more important, were they prepared to fly some of those planes themselves? From the Emiratis, at least, the answer to both questions was a surprising yes.

The Europeans were even more gung ho. I got an earful about military intervention from Sarkozy. He is a dynamic figure, always full of ebullient energy, who loves being at the center of the action. France, a former colonial power in North Africa, had been close to Ben Ali in Tunisia, and the revolution there had caught Sarkozy flat-footed. The French had not been players in Egypt. So this was their chance to jump into the fray supporting the Arab Spring, demonstrating that they too were on the side of change. Sarkozy was also influenced by the French public intellectual Bernard-Henri Lévy, who had hitched a ride in a vegetable truck from the Egyptian border to see for himself what was happening. They were both genuinely moved by the plight of the Libyan people suffering at the hands of a brutal dictator, and they made a persuasive case that something had to be done.

When I saw British Foreign Secretary William Hague at dinner that night, he pressed the case for action. If Hague thought military action in Libya was necessary, that counted for a lot. I knew that he, like me, was wary of making such decisions without confidence in the rationale, strategy, and endgame.

Back at the hotel I met with our Ambassador to Libya, Gene Cretz, and our newly appointed Special Representative to the Libyan rebels, Chris Stevens, who had earlier served as Deputy Chief of Mission and Chargé d'affaires in Tripoli. Cretz was a colorful character, a brash and funny diplomat from upstate New York. When his secret cables to Washington describing Qaddafi's excesses were published by WikiLeaks, Cretz had faced threats and intimidation in Tripoli, and in late December 2010, I made the decision to bring him back to Washington for his own safety. By late February 2011, with the revolution heating up, our remaining diplomatic staff evacuated. Many left on a ferry to Malta that hit unusually high and heavy seas, but thankfully everyone made it to safety.

Stevens was another talented diplomat with long experience in the region. A blond-haired, charismatic Californian who spoke both French and Arabic, he had served in Syria, Egypt, Saudi Arabia, and Jerusalem. Chris devoured old Libyan histories and memoirs and delighted in sharing obscure historical trivia and cracking jokes in the local dialect. I asked Chris to return to Libya to make contact with the rebel council in their stronghold of Benghazi. It was a challenging and dangerous mission, but America needed to be represented there. Chris agreed and accepted the assignment. His mother liked to say that he had sand in his shoes, always moving and running and working, seeking out new challenges and adventures across the Middle East. After years of experience in the field, he understood that the difficult and dangerous places are where America's interests are most at stake and where it's most important that we're represented with skilled and subtle diplomacy. Later in the spring he and a very small team arrived in Benghazi on board a Greek cargo ship, like a 19th-century envoy, and got right to work building relationships with the civilian and military leaders of the rebellion. He did such an impressive job I would later ask the President to nominate him to succeed Cretz as our Ambassador to Libya.

Finally, around 10 P.M., Jibril arrived at the Westin in Paris accompanied by Bernard-Henri Lévy, who had helped arrange the meeting. They made quite a pair, the rebel and the philosopher. Hard to tell who was who. Jibril appeared more like a technocrat than a firebrand. He was small and bespectacled, with thinning hair and a stern demeanor. Lévy, by contrast, cut a dramatic and stylish figure, with long wavy hair and his shirt open practically down to his navel. He has been quoted as saying, "God is dead but my hair is perfect." (To that I'd say, I think God is alive, but I'd love to have perfect hair!)

I found Jibril to be impressive and polished, especially for the representative of a rebel council on the verge of annihilation. He had served as head of the National Economic Development Board under Qaddafi before defecting to join the revolution and seemed to understand how much work would be necessary to rebuild a country devastated by decades of cruelty and mismanagement. He told us that hundreds of thousands of civilians in Benghazi were in imminent danger as the regime's forces marched toward the city, raising the specters of the genocide in Rwanda and ethnic cleansing in the Balkans. He pleaded for international intervention.

As Jibril spoke, I tried to take his measure. We had learned the hard way in Iraq and elsewhere that it's one thing to remove a dictator and another altogether to help a competent and credible government take his place. If the United States agreed to intervene in Libya, we would be making a big bet on this political scientist and his colleagues. Over four decades Qaddafi had systematically removed anyone who might pose a threat to his rule and pulverized Libya's institutions and political culture. So we were unlikely to find a perfect George Washington waiting in the wings. All things considered, Jibril and those he represented might well be the best we could hope for.

Afterward I reported to the White House what I had heard in Paris and my progress with our international partners. Our NATO allies were prepared to take the lead in any military action. The Arab League would support it, and some would even actively participate in combat operations against an Arab neighbor—a telling sign of how far Qaddafi had gone. I believed we could wrangle the votes in the Security Council to back a strong resolution. We had managed to get the Russians and Chinese on board with tough sanctions against North Korea and Iran in 2009 and 2010, and I believed we could do the same now. And, based on my meeting with Jibril, I thought there was a reasonable chance the rebels would turn out to be credible partners.

The National Security Council remained divided on the wisdom of intervening in Libya. Some, including UN Ambassador Susan Rice and National Security Council aide Samantha Power, argued that we had a responsibility to protect civilians and prevent a massacre if we could. Defense Secretary Gates was firmly opposed. A veteran of the conflicts in Iraq and Afghanistan and a realist about the limits of American power, he did not think our interests in Libya justified the sacrifice. We all knew the consequences of intervention were unpredictable. But Qaddafi's troops were now a hundred miles from Benghazi and closing fast. We were looking at a humanitarian catastrophe, with untold thousands at risk of being killed. If we were going to stop it, we had to act now.

The President decided to move forward with drawing up military plans and securing a UN Security Council resolution. But there were two key stipulations. First, because the Pentagon had assured us that a no-fly zone by itself would be little more than a symbolic gesture, we would need to secure UN backing for more robust military action if necessary: the authority to use "all necessary measures" to protect civilians. Second, the

President wanted to keep U.S. involvement limited, so our allies would have to shoulder much of the burden and fly most of the sorties. These conditions would require extensive additional diplomacy, but Susan and I both thought it was possible and started working the phones.

The next day at the Security Council in New York, the Russians offered a weak resolution calling for a cease-fire that I thought was actually a ploy to muddy the waters and blunt the building momentum for a no-fly zone. Unless we could convince them not to veto our stronger resolution, it was dead in the water. Beyond Russia, we were also concerned about China, which had veto power as well, and several nonpermanent members.

On the morning of March 15, I flew from Paris to Cairo to meet with Amr Moussa and emphasize how important it was that the Arab League come out strongly for military intervention and agree to actively participate. This policy had to be recognized as being driven by Libya's neighbors, not the West, or it wasn't going to work. Moussa confirmed that Qatar and the UAE were prepared to contribute planes and pilots to the effort, a major step forward. Later Jordan would step up as well. I knew this support would make it easier to convince wavering Security Council members in New York.

Qaddafi made our job easier when he went on television on March 17 and warned the citizens of Benghazi, "We are coming tonight, and there will be no mercy." He pledged to go house by house looking for "traitors" and told Libyans to "capture the rats." By then I was in Tunisia and called Russian Foreign Minister Sergey Lavrov. He had previously told me that Russia was dead set against a no-fly zone, but since then several nonpermanent members of the Security Council had gotten on board with our resolution. Now it was important to assure the Russians that this would not be like Iraq or Afghanistan and to be clear about our intentions. "We don't want another war," I told Lavrov. "We don't want to put troops on the ground." But, I explained, "Our goal is to protect civilians from brutal and indiscriminate attacks. The no-fly zone is necessary, but insufficient. We need additional measures. Time is critical."

"I take your point about not seeking another war," he responded. "But that doesn't mean that you won't get one." However, he added, the Russians had no interest in protecting Qaddafi or seeing him slaughter his people. I explained that our resolution would incorporate the Russian proposal for a cease-fire, but that it had to also authorize a forceful response if Qaddafi refused to stop his advance. "We can't vote in favor," Lavrov said. "But we will abstain and it will pass." That was all we needed. In this context an abstention was nearly as good as a yes vote. In later discussions, especially about Syria, Lavrov claimed he had been misled about our intentions. That struck me as disingenuous since Lavrov, as a former Ambassador to the UN, knew as well as anyone what "all necessary measures" meant.

Next I called Luís Amado, the Foreign Minister of Portugal, a non-permanent member of the Security Council. Even if we avoided a veto, we still needed to be sure we had a majority, and the more votes we got, the stronger the message to Qaddafi would be. "I wanted to reiterate that the United States has no interest, or intention, or planning of any kind of using ground troops or a ground operation," I told Amado. "We believe passing this resolution will give a big wake-up call to Qaddafi and the people around him. This could clearly influence the actions that he takes in the next days." He listened to my arguments and then agreed to vote yes. "Don't worry, we'll be there," he told me.

President Obama called South African President Jacob Zuma and made the same case to him. Susan lobbied her counterparts in New York. The French and British were working hard as well. In the end the final vote was 10 to 0, with five abstentions; Brazil, India, China, and Germany joined Russia in sitting out the vote. We now had a strong mandate to protect Libyan civilians with "all necessary measures."

Almost immediately, there were difficulties and drama.

President Obama was very clear with our team and our allies that the United States would participate in a military operation to enforce the UN resolution, but only in a limited way. A key first step for enforcing a no-fly zone would be knocking out Qaddafi's air defense system, and the United States was better equipped to do that than any of our partners. But the President wanted allied air forces to take the lead as soon as possible, and he was adamant that there would be no U.S. troops deployed. "No boots on the ground" became a mantra. All of that meant that we needed a broad and well-coordinated international coalition that could step in and take over after U.S. cruise missiles and bombers cleared the way. I soon found out that getting all our allies to work together as a team on this would be harder than any of us anticipated.

Sarkozy was eager to take the lead. In the run-up to the UN vote, he had been the most vocal advocate for international military action, and now he saw his chance to reassert France's role as a major world power. He invited a wide range of European and Arab nations to Paris for an emergency summit on Saturday, March 19, to discuss implementation of the UN resolution. Conspicuously not invited, however, was our NATO ally Turkey. There were already tensions between Sarkozy and Turkish Prime Minister Erdoğan because of France's objections to Turkey joining the EU. Then Erdoğan had emerged as a voice of caution on Libya, and Sarkozy worked to exclude him from the coalition. The snub infuriated Erdoğan and turned him even more decidedly against intervention.

When I spoke with Turkish Foreign Minister Davutoğlu I tried to ease some of the hurt feelings. "I first want to tell you that I pushed very hard for you to be invited," I said. As I feared, Davutoğlu was quite upset. "We are expecting action through NATO and suddenly in Paris, there is a meeting and we are not invited," he complained, with good reason. Was this a French crusade or an international coalition? I explained that the summit had been organized by the French but that we were pushing hard for the military operation itself to be run by NATO.

In Paris I delivered President Obama's message about our expectation that others would step up. Just after landing, I checked in by phone with AbZ. As described earlier, this turned into a very difficult conversation, as he threatened to pull the UAE out of the Libya operation because of U.S. criticism of their actions in Bahrain.

Then, before the official meeting even began, Sarkozy pulled me and British Prime Minister David Cameron aside and confided that French warplanes were already headed toward Libya. When the larger group found out that France had jumped the gun, it caused an uproar. Italian Prime Minister Silvio Berlusconi, who was just as strong-willed and eager for the spotlight as Sarkozy, was particularly incensed. There is an informal belief that old colonial powers should take the lead in addressing crises in their former dominions. That's why, later, France was the one to send troops to Mali and the Central African Republic. In the case of Libya, a former Italian colony, Berlusconi felt that Italy should be out front, not France. What's more, because of its strategic location jutting out into the Mediterranean, Italy provided the natural launching pad for most of the air sorties into Libya. It had already started opening a number of air force bases to allied jets. Now Berlusconi felt upstaged by Sarkozy, and he threatened to walk out of the coalition and close access to his country's bases.

Beyond the bruised egos, though, Berlusconi and others had good reason to be concerned. We had learned in the Balkans and Afghanistan that coordinating a multinational military operation is complicated. Unless there are clear lines of command and control, with everyone working together to implement the same strategy, it can devolve into dangerous confusion. Imagine if a dozen different nations sent warplanes to Libya without coordinating with one another on flight plans, targets, and rules of engagement. It would be pandemonium in the sky, with the real possibility of a mishap resulting in the loss of life.

Because we had the most capabilities, the United States started out in the lead coordinating role. The next logical step was to have NATO organize the intervention. The Alliance already had an integrated military command and experience coordinating in previous conflicts. Sarkozy did not like that idea. For starters, it might mean less glory for France. But he also thought making Libya a NATO mission would alienate the Arab world, whose leadership had helped sway opinion before the UN vote. Qatar and the UAE had pledged to send planes to help enforce the no-fly zone—would they do so under the banner of NATO? What's more, NATO operates by consensus, which means any one member, including Turkey, could block action. We had worked very hard at the UN to secure language authorizing "all necessary measures" to protect civilians so that we could do more than prevent Qaddafi's planes from attacking rebel towns—it was crucial that we be able to stop his tanks and troops on the ground before they reached Benghazi. Some called that a "no-drive zone." But Erdoğan and others were drawing the line at a pure no-fly zone with no air-to-ground strikes. Sarkozy feared that if NATO ran the mission, we would end up watching as Benghazi burned.

The Paris meeting ended without an agreement on what should happen after the initial American-led phase of intervention. But with Qaddafi's forces on the move and French jets already in the air, there was no time for hesitation. I went before the cameras and announced, "America has unique capabilities and we will bring them to bear to help our European and Canadian allies and Arab partners stop further violence against civilians, including through the effective implementation of a no-fly zone." A few hours later U.S. Navy warships in the Mediterranean fired more than a hundred cruise missiles, targeting air defense systems inside Libya and at a large column of armored vehicles approaching Benghazi. President Obama, who was traveling in Brazil, said, "I want the American people to know that the use of force is not our first choice and it's not a choice that I make lightly." But, he went on, "actions have consequences, and the writ of the international community must be enforced. That is the cause of this coalition."

Over the next seventy-two hours Libya's air defenses were successfully destroyed and the people of Benghazi were saved from imminent devastation. President Obama was later unfairly criticized as "leading from behind" in Libya. That's a silly phrase. It took a great deal of leading— from the front, the side, and every other direction, to authorize and accomplish the mission and to prevent what might have been the loss of tens of thousands of lives. No one else could have played the role we did, both in terms of the military capability to land a decisive first blow against Qaddafi's forces and the diplomatic capacity to build and hold together a broad coalition.

Unfortunately relations inside the Alliance went from bad to worse over the next few days. On Monday, only two days after the Paris summit, representatives gathered at NATO headquarters in Brussels to try to work out the differences. But the meeting soon descended into acrimony, with the French Ambassador storming out of the room. Both sides were doubling down. As feared, the Turks were insisting on narrow parameters for a NATO mission, and the French were refusing to give up control. On Monday evening President Obama called Erdoğan to explain again the importance of "all necessary measures" and underscore that this would not include sending ground forces for an invasion. He later spoke to Sarkozy, who was willing to let NATO take over the no-fly zone if the French, British, and others could continue the more aggressive no-drive zone on their own. From our perspective, setting up two parallel missions was fraught with potential difficulties. But we agreed with Sarkozy that we couldn't give up the ability to target Qaddafi's ground forces, as they threatened to exterminate rebel communities.

On Monday night a terrifying incident heightened the stakes for all of us. An F-15 Strike Eagle fighter piloted by two U.S. airmen, Major Kenneth Harney and Captain Tyler Stark, suffered a mechanical failure over eastern Libya around midnight. Just after dropping a five-hundred-pound bomb on their target, the jet went into a tailspin. The two airmen ejected, but a tear in Stark's parachute sent him off course. Harney was rescued soon afterward by a U.S. search-and-rescue team, but Stark was missing. I was worried sick thinking about this twenty-seven-year-old from Littleton, Colorado, lost in the Libyan desert.

Amazingly Stark was found by friendly Libyan rebels from Benghazi, who called a local English teacher to come and talk to him. It turned out the teacher, Bubaker Habib, had close ties to the staff of the U.S. Embassy. Our staff had all left the country, but Bubaker kept their numbers and was able to reach the State Department Operations Center. Over the course of a call with Ops, with State relaying information to the Pentagon, Stark's rescue was arranged. In the meantime Bubaker drove him to a hotel in Benghazi, where he was treated by doctors for torn tendons in his knee and ankle. Bubaker later told *Vanity Fair* that he instructed the rebels, "We have an American pilot here. If he gets caught or killed it's the end of the mission. Make sure he is safe and sound." The Libyans thanked Stark profusely, expressing their gratitude for the U.S. intervention that was protecting them from Qaddafi's troops.

In Washington all of us let out a huge sigh of relief. At the same time, I was beginning to see the contours of a possible compromise that might break the deadlock among our allies. If Turkey agreed not to veto action to enforce the no-drive zone—it didn't have to participate, just abstain from blocking it—then we could convince France to give NATO full command and control.

NATO Secretary-General Anders Fogh Rasmussen reported to me that he had spoken to the Turks and had heard that the Arabs would not object to participating in a NATO-led mission, which was one of Sarkozy's big concerns. As it turns out, AbZ happened to be in Davutoğlu's office in Ankara when Rasmussen called. Davutoğlu handed the phone over to the Emirati and let him express his consent directly. Word from Qatar and the Arab League was also positive. "Did you share that with France?" I asked Rasmussen. He replied, "Their response was that it's one thing what the Arabs say in private and another thing what they do publicly." I said I would talk with Davutoğlu myself and see if we could get the Arabs to go on the record with their support.

When I reached Davutoğlu, I stressed that the United States agreed that NATO should now take over command and control. "We want the handover to be as smooth as possible. We need a unified command in a single theater of operations. We need to ensure all aspects including the civilian protection mission are integrated." That meant having both the no-fly zone and the no-drive zone. Davutoğlu agreed. "There should be one command and control and it should be under NATO," he said. "It's important for the people of Libya. If there is a UN umbrella and under that NATO is doing the operation no one will see this as crusaders or East versus West."

I also called French Foreign Minister, Alain Juppé. "I think we are ready to accept the compromise under certain conditions," he told me. If NATO was going to run the military operation, France wanted to set up a separate diplomatic committee made up of all the nations contributing forces, including the Arabs, to provide policy guidance. It was a modest gesture, I thought, and one we should be able to accommodate.

To seal the deal, I convened a conference call with the French, Turks, and British. "I believe we have an understanding among us. But I just want to be sure. It's crucial we're all on the same page on NATO's responsibility to enforce the no-fly zone and protect civilians in Libya." Then I carefully walked through the compromise. By the end of the call, we were all in agreement. "Bravo!" exclaimed Juppé as we hung up.

Soon NATO assumed formal command and control of what became known as Operation Unified Protector. The United States continued to provide vital intelligence and surveillance information that helped guide the air strikes, as well as midair refueling that allowed allied aircraft to stay in the skies over Libya for long stretches of time. But the vast majority of combat sorties would be flown by others.

The military campaign in Libya lasted longer than any of us had hoped or expected, although we never went down the slippery slope of putting troops on the ground, as some had feared. At times the coalition frayed and there was a fair amount of hand-holding and arm-twisting needed to keep all our partners on board. But by late summer 2011, the rebels had pushed back the regime's forces. They captured Tripoli toward the end of August, and Qaddafi and his family fled into the desert. The revolution had succeeded, and the hard work of building a new country could begin.

———

In mid-October, with Tripoli liberated but Qaddafi still on the loose, I decided to visit Libya myself to offer America's support to the new transitional government. With the country awash in shoulder-fired surface-to-air missiles, it was too dangerous to fly our usual blue-and-white 757 with "The United States of America" emblazoned from tip to tail, so the Air Force provided a C-17 military transport plane equipped with defensive countermeasures for the morning flight from Malta to Tripoli.

Just before we took off, a photographer for *Time* magazine, Diana Walker, saw me checking my BlackBerry and snapped a quick shot. Her photo, to everyone's surprise, became an internet sensation many months later and the basis for a "meme" known as "Texts from Hillary." The idea was simple: an internet user would pair the photo of me holding my phone with a picture of another famous person holding a phone and add funny captions to narrate the texts we supposedly sent back and forth. The first one posted showed President Obama lounging on a couch, with the caption "Hey Hil, Watchu doing?" The imagined response from me: "Running the world." Eventually I decided to get in on the fun myself. I submitted my own version full of internet slang: "ROFL @ ur tumblr! g2g—scrunchie time. ttyl?" That roughly translated to "Love your site." I also invited the creators of Texts from Hillary, two young PR professionals in Washington named Adam Smith and Stacy Lambe, to visit me at the State Department. We posed for a photograph of all three of us checking our phones at the same time.

At the time Walker took that photo, however, fun was the furthest thing from my mind. I was preparing for what promised to be a grueling day in a war-torn capital with a new government that had little hold on power and even less experience running a country.

After landing safely, the door of the C-17 opened and I looked out from the top of the plane's stairs and saw a crowd of armed and bearded militia fighters waiting below. They were from Zintan, a battle-scarred town in Libya's mountainous northwest that had been one of the major flash points of the revolution. Under the uneasy power-sharing arrangement between the various militias now in control of Tripoli, the Zintan brigade had responsibility for the airport. My security detail was as nervous as I had ever seen them. I took a deep breath and started to walk down the stairs. To my surprise the militia fighters started chanting, "God is Great!" and "USA!" They waved and cheered and held up their hands in the "V for victory" sign. Soon I was mobbed by these exuberant and exultant men from the mountains. Several handed their automatic rifles to comrades to hold while they squeezed next to me for a picture; others patted my back or shook my hand. Kurt Olsson, the head of my security detail, remained unflappable, but I imagine he came away with a few new gray hairs.

The men took their guns and piled into SUVs and pickup trucks mounted with heavy weapons and escorted my motorcade through the city, aggressively boxing out other traffic and waving excitedly whenever they were alongside my car. The streets of Tripoli were covered with revolutionary graffiti, some lampooning Qaddafi and others celebrating rebel slogans and victories. Soon we arrived at the offices of a large Islamic charity that the new government was using as its makeshift headquarters.

After meeting with the Chairman of the National Transitional Council of Libya, Mustafa Abdul Jalil, I made my way to the office of Jibril, the rebel leader I had met in Paris who was now the interim Prime Minister. He greeted me with a broad smile, and I said, "I am proud to stand here on the soil of a free Libya."

In meetings with Jalil and Jibril we discussed the many challenges facing the new government. At the top of their list was the continuing threat from Qaddafi and his loyalists. I assured them that NATO would continue its mission to protect Libyan civilians until the former dictator was found and fully defeated. Then I raised another concern.

Any government's first responsibility is to provide security and ensure law and order. This was going to be a big challenge in Libya. Unlike in Egypt, where the military and security forces had remained largely intact after the fall of Mubarak, in Libya there was now a major vacuum. And, as friendly and high-spirited as the militia fighters from Zintan had been, the presence of so many independent armed groups in Tripoli and across the country was not sustainable. It was crucial to bring all the militias together in a single army under the control of civilian authorities, establish the rule of law, prevent score-settling and vigilante justice, and round up the loose weapons now flooding the country. The United States was prepared to help the new government in all these areas, but it was going to take leadership from them to make it work. Jibril and the others nodded in agreement and pledged to make it a priority.

After our meetings I sped off to a town hall discussion with students and civil society activists at Tripoli University. Qaddafi had done all that he could to discourage the emergence of volunteer groups, NGOs, independent media, and government watchdogs that make up civil society. I hoped they were willing and able to play a positive role in Libya's next phase. History had shown that it was one thing to remove a tyrant and quite another to build a new government that delivers for its people. Democracy would face serious challenges in Libya. Would the country's future be shaped by the arms of its militias or the aspirations of its people?

One after another, the students and activists stood up and asked thoughtful and practical questions about how to build a new democracy. "We have no political parties," observed one young woman studying to become an engineer. She asked how Libyans should "encourage our people to involve more in the political life, considering that we have elections in a matter of two years or less and we have to elect our parliaments and our president." Another young woman, a medical student, stood up. "We are very new to this democracy," she began. "What steps do you think we can take to root the freedom of speech into the Libyan identity?" These young people desperately wanted to live in a "normal country," with access to the global economy and all the rights they knew people in America and around the world had enjoyed for so long. And, in contrast to some of the young people I had met next door in Egypt, they were eager to put aside their differences, learn lessons from the outside, and get involved in the political process. Free Libya had a long way to go—they were starting basically from scratch—but these young people impressed me with their thoughtfulness and determination to build it.

Before leaving Tripoli I stopped by a local hospital to visit with civilians and fighters wounded in the revolution against Qaddafi. I talked with young men who had lost limbs and doctors and nurses overwhelmed by the casualties they had seen. I promised that the United States would provide medical support and even fly some of the most challenging cases to hospitals in America.

My final visit was to the compound of our Ambassador to Libya, Gene Cretz, which had been turned into a makeshift embassy. During the revolution, regime thugs had ransacked and burned our actual embassy (all U.S. personnel had already evacuated), so now our returned diplomatic staff was camped out in Gene's living room. I marveled at the toughness and resolve of these brave American diplomats. We heard gunshots in the distance, and I wondered whether it was fighting or celebration. The embassy staff seemed quite used to it by now. As I shook each of their hands, I thanked them for all their incredible work and sacrifices.

Leaving Tripoli, the C-17 lifted off steep and fast. So much had happened in the nine months since I went to Doha to warn the leaders of the

Middle East that if they did not embrace reform their region was going to sink into the sand.

Libya held its first elections in the summer of 2012. By all accounts, despite security concerns, the voting was well run and relatively free of irregularities. After more than forty years without political participation under Qaddafi, about 60 percent of Libyans, a broad cross-section of society, went to the polls to elect their representatives and then took to the streets in celebration.

I was worried that the challenges ahead would prove overwhelming for even the most well-meaning transitional leaders. If the new government could consolidate its authority, provide security, use oil revenues to rebuild, disarm the militias, and keep extremists out, then Libya would have a fighting chance at building a stable democracy. If not, then the country would face very difficult challenges translating the hopes of a revolution into a free, secure, and prosperous future. And, as we soon learned, not only Libyans would suffer if they failed.

17

Benghazi: Under Attack

On September 11, 2012, Ambassador Chris Stevens and Information Management Officer Sean Smith were killed in a terrorist attack on our diplomatic compound in Benghazi, Libya. Two CIA officers, Glen Doherty and Tyrone Woods, were killed hours later during an attack on the Agency's nearby compound.

Sean Smith had joined the State Department after six years in the Air Force and served for a decade at our embassies and consulates in Pretoria, Baghdad, Montreal, and The Hague.

Tyrone Woods was known to his friends in the Navy SEALs and later the CIA as "Rone." He served multiple tours in Iraq and Afghanistan. In addition to being an experienced combat veteran, he also earned distinction as a registered nurse and certified paramedic. He and his wife, Dorothy, had three sons, including one born just a few months before he died.

Glen Doherty, who went by "Bub," was a former SEAL as well and an experienced paramedic. He too had deployed to some of the most dangerous places on earth, including Iraq and Afghanistan, always putting his life on the line to safeguard other Americans. Both Tyrone and Glen had committed their skills and experience to protecting CIA personnel in Libya.

Ambassador Chris Stevens, the only one of the four I had the privilege of knowing personally, was a talented diplomat and an engaging and extraordinarily warm human being. When I asked him in the spring of

2011 to undertake the dangerous mission to make contact with the Libyan rebel leadership in Benghazi during the revolution, and later to return to Libya as Ambassador after the fall of Qaddafi, he quickly accepted. Chris understood the risks and recognized how challenging it would be to help pull together a shattered country, but he knew that America had vital national security interests at stake. His long experience in the region and talent for delicate diplomacy made him a natural choice.

Losing these fearless public servants in the line of duty was a crushing blow. As Secretary I was the one ultimately responsible for my people's safety, and I never felt that responsibility more deeply than I did that day.

Sending those who serve our nation into harm's way is one of the hardest choices our country and leaders ever have to make. Far and away my greatest regret from those years is that not all of them returned home safely. I often think about the families who lost loved ones serving our country. The gravity of the mission and the gratitude of our nation may provide some solace, but in the end there is nothing any of us can say or do to fill the holes left behind.

The truest way to honor them is to improve our ability to protect those who carry on their work and prevent future losses.

═══

From my first day leading the State Department, I was aware that terrorists could strike any of our more than 270 diplomatic posts around the world. It had happened too many times before, and those hell-bent on attacking America would never stop trying. In 1979, fifty-two American diplomats were taken hostage in Iran and held captive for 444 days. The Hezbollah attacks on our embassy and Marine barracks in Beirut in 1983 killed 258 Americans and more than a hundred others. In 1998, al Qaeda bombed our embassies in Kenya and Tanzania, killing more than two hundred people, including twelve Americans. I vividly remember standing next to Bill at Andrews Air Force Base when the remains of those who had fallen returned home.

All told, terrorists have killed sixty-six American diplomatic personnel since the 1970s and more than a hundred contractors and locally employed staff. Four U.S. Ambassadors were murdered in terrorist attacks between 1973 and 1979 alone. Since 2001 there have been more than one hundred assaults on U.S. diplomatic facilities around the world and nearly two dozen direct attacks on diplomatic personnel. In 2004, gunmen killed nine people, including five locally employed staff in an attack on our consulate in Jeddah, Saudi Arabia. In May 2009, a roadside bomb in Iraq killed Terry Barnich, the Deputy Director of our Transition Assistance Team. In March 2010, Lesley Enriquez, a pregnant twenty-five-year-old consular officer in Juarez, Mexico, was shot to death, along with her husband. In August 2012, USAID officer Ragaei Said Abdelfattah was killed by a suicide bomber in Afghanistan. As of 2014, 244 of America's diplomats have fallen in our nation's history while serving overseas.

Diplomacy, by its very nature, must often be practiced in dangerous places where America's national security hangs in the balance. We have to weigh the imperatives of our national security against the sacrifices required to safeguard it. As Secretary of State I was responsible for nearly seventy thousand employees, and I deeply admired those who volunteered to accept the risks that come with carrying our flag where it is needed most. Every day as they walk into work the men and women of the State Department pass the names of those 244 fallen diplomats inscribed in marble in the lobby of the Harry S Truman Building. It's a constant reminder of the risks that come with representing the United States around the world. I was heartened—though not surprised—to learn from the Department that after major attacks against the United States, applications to the Foreign Service went up. People want to serve our country, even when it means being in harm's way. Nothing speaks more to the character and dedication of those who represent our country around the world.

The events of September 2012, and the choices made in the days and weeks before and since, throw into sharp relief some of the toughest dilemmas of American foreign policy—and the heartbreaking human stakes of every decision we make. Our diplomats must balance the necessity of engaging in difficult and dangerous settings with the need to stay safe and secure. As a country, we have to do more to protect them, without preventing them from doing their important jobs. We need to stay open to the world in a time when any provocation can spark anti-American riots across the globe and far-flung terrorist groups continue to plot new attacks. Ultimately these challenges boil down to this: Are we willing to shoulder the burdens of American leadership in a perilous age?

Part of the answer came from the independent investigation into the Benghazi attacks, which noted, "The total elimination of risk is a non-starter for U.S. diplomacy, given the need for the U.S. government to be present in places where stability and security are often most profoundly lacking and host government support is sometimes minimal to non-existent."

While we can and must work to reduce the danger, the only way to eliminate risk entirely is to retreat entirely and to accept the consequences of the void we leave behind. When America is absent, extremism takes root, our interests suffer, and our security at home is threatened. There are some who believe that is the better choice; I am not one of them. Retreat is not the answer; it won't make the world a safer place, and it's just not in our country's DNA. When faced with setbacks and tragedies, Americans have always worked harder and smarter. We strive to learn from our mistakes and avoid repeating them. And we do not shrink from the challenges ahead. That is what we must continue to do.

The events of that September occurred in what is often called the "fog of war," with information hard to come by, and conflicting or incomplete reports making it difficult to tell what was actually happening on the ground, especially from thousands of miles away in Washington. To a frustrating degree, that fog persisted so long, in part because of continuing turmoil in Libya. And despite the best efforts of officials from across our government—including the White House, the State Department, the military, the intelligence community, the FBI, an independent Accountability Review Board, and eight Congressional committees—there will never be perfect clarity on everything that happened. It is unlikely that there will ever be anything close to full agreement on exactly what happened that night, how it happened, or why it happened. But that should not be confused with a lack of effort to discover the truth or to share it with the American people. I am grateful to the many dedicated professionals who have worked tirelessly to answer all the questions they could to the best of their abilities.

What follows is based on a combination of my own personal experience and information learned over the following days, weeks, and months thanks to several exhaustive investigations, especially the work of the independent review board charged with determining the facts and pulling no punches. While there has been a regrettable amount of misinformation, speculation, and flat-out deceit by some in politics and the media, more than a year later in-depth reporting from a number of reputable sources continues to expand our understanding of these events.

━━━━━

While the morning of September 11, 2012, began like many others, there are few dates as meaningful to our country. On every 9/11 since 2001, I think back to that terrible day. I was not even a year into representing New York in the Senate when it was devastated by the attacks on the Twin Towers. That day, which started with hundreds fleeing down the stairs of the Capitol Building and ended with hundreds of members standing on those very same steps singing "God Bless America" in a moving display of unity, shaped my unrelenting focus on helping New York recover and securing it against future attacks. With those memories flooding back, I left home for the State Department.

After the short drive to the office, the first order of business, as always, was to receive the daily briefing on intelligence and national security developments, including the latest reports of terrorist threats around the world. This briefing is given every day to senior officials across our government. It is prepared by a team of dedicated career intelligence analysts who work overnight before fanning out across Washington before dawn every morning to hand-deliver and orally present their reports.

The past few months had been a tumultuous time across the Middle East and North Africa. The civil war in Syria was escalating, sending refugees streaming into Jordan and Turkey. In Egypt the ascension of the Muslim Brotherhood and tensions with the military raised questions about the future of the Arab Spring. Al Qaeda's affiliates in North Africa, Iraq, and the Arabian Peninsula continued to threaten regional security.

On September 8, an inflammatory fourteen-minute video that purported to be a trailer for a full-length movie called *Innocence of Muslims* was aired on an Egyptian satellite TV network widely available across the Middle East. According to several press accounts, the film depicts a "buffoonish caricature of the prophet Muhammad," using "slurs about him that are often repeated by Islamophobes," even comparing him to a donkey. One press report claims that in the film the Prophet is "accused of homosexuality and child molestation." Many Egyptian viewers were outraged, and, fueled by the internet, that rage quickly spread across the

Middle East and North Africa. Although the U.S. government had absolutely nothing to do with the video, many blamed America.

The anniversary of 9/11 added another potentially combustible element and, like every year, prompted our intelligence and security officials to proceed with extra caution. Yet the intelligence community, as they've testified since, relayed no actionable intelligence about specific threats against any U.S. diplomatic post across the Middle East and North Africa.

Later that morning I walked from my office down the hall to the Treaty Room to officially swear in Gene Cretz, who had recently returned from service in Libya, as our new Ambassador to Ghana. Around the same time, half a world away in Cairo, young men began gathering in the street outside the U.S. Embassy as part of a protest organized by hard-line Islamist leaders against the insulting video. The crowd swelled to more than two thousand people shouting anti-American slogans and waving black jihadi banners. Some demonstrators climbed the walls and ripped apart a large American flag, replacing it with a black flag. Egyptian riot police eventually arrived, but the protest continued. Thankfully none of our people were injured in the melee. Journalists and others in the crowd using social media recorded angry comments about the video. One young man said, "This is a very simple reaction to harming our prophet." Another insisted, "This movie must be banned immediately and an apology should be made."

This was not the first time that provocateurs had used offensive material to whip up popular outrage across the Muslim world, often with deadly results. In 2010, a Florida pastor named Terry Jones announced plans to burn the Quran, Islam's holy text, on the ninth anniversary of 9/11. His threats were picked up and amplified by extremists setting off widespread protests. At that time I was surprised that one firebrand in Gainesville, Florida, with a tiny church could cause so much trouble. But the consequences of his threat were all too real. Secretary of Defense Bob Gates personally called Jones and told him that his actions endangered the lives of American and Coalition soldiers and civilians in Iraq and Afghanistan. Jones agreed to hold off, and the anniversary came and went. Then in March 2011, he went back on his word and burned a Quran. Bob's warnings proved tragically prescient, as an angry mob in Afghanistan set fire to a UN office and killed seven people. Deadly protests erupted again in February 2012 after U.S. troops inadvertently burned religious texts at Bagram Air Force Base in Afghanistan. Four Americans died. Now Jones was helping promote this new video insulting the Prophet Muhammad and there was a real danger of history repeating itself.

With an eye on the developing situation in Cairo, I headed to the White House to meet with Defense Secretary Leon Panetta and National Security Advisor Tom Donilon. When I returned to my office, I huddled with senior State Department leaders throughout the afternoon, closely monitoring reports from our embassy. Our Ambassador to Egypt, Anne Patterson, happened to be back in Washington for consultations, and she stayed in constant contact with her Deputy Chief of Mission and worked the phones to pressure the Egyptian authorities to get control of the situation. We were all relieved when further violence was avoided.

We learned later that as events unfolded in Cairo, in neighboring Libya Ambassador Chris Stevens was visiting the country's second largest city, Benghazi.

A lot had happened in Libya since my visit to Tripoli in October 2011. Two days after I left Libya, Colonel Muammar Qaddafi was captured and killed. The first Parliamentary elections were held in early July 2012, and the transitional government handed over power to a new General National Congress in August in a ceremony that Chris cited as the highlight of his time in the country. Chris and his team worked closely with Libya's new leaders as they grappled with the significant challenges of setting up a democratic government and providing security and services in a country hollowed out by decades of tyranny. Militia fighters, like those who had greeted me at the airport and guarded my motorcade a year earlier, would have to be brought under the authority of the central government. There were loose weapons to collect, elections to organize, and democratic institutions and processes to establish. Law and order remained a real problem.

In February 2012, I sent Deputy Secretary Tom Nides to Tripoli and then welcomed interim Prime Minister Abdurrahim El-Keib to Washington in March. We offered to help the government secure its borders, disarm and demobilize the militias, and reintegrate former fighters into the security services or civilian life. In July Deputy Secretary Bill Burns followed up with another visit. I stayed in touch with leaders in the Libyan government by phone, including an August call with Libyan General National Congress President Mohammed Magariaf, and received regular updates from our teams in Washington and Tripoli on efforts across the U.S. government to assist the new Libyan government. There was preliminary progress on demobilization, demilitarization, and reintegration, as well as efforts to secure and disable loose weapons throughout Libya, but so much remained to be done. Specialists from the Defense Department and State Department border security experts worked closely with their Libyan counterparts. On September 4, 2012, we designated Libya eligible for the Global Security Contingency Fund, a joint Defense and State initiative pooling resources and expertise to address the wide variety of challenges the Libyan government faced.

Chris was at the center of all this activity, and he knew better than anyone how many challenges remained for Libya. On Monday, September 10, he left the U.S. Embassy in Tripoli and flew four hundred miles east to Benghazi, where we maintained a temporary diplomatic post with rotating staff. Benghazi is a port city on the Mediterranean Sea with a population of more than 1 million people, mostly Sunni Muslims, and large African and Egyptian minorities. Its varied architecture, a mix of age-weathered buildings and construction projects abandoned half-completed, reflects a history of conquest and conflict by competing Arab, Ottoman, and Italian rulers, as well as the quixotic ambitions and long, slow decay of the Qaddafi regime. Benghazi had been a hotbed of dissidents, and both the 1969 revolution that brought Qaddafi to power and the 2011 revolution that unseated him began in the city. Chris knew Benghazi well from his time as our representative to the rebel Transitional National Council, which was based there during the 2011 uprising, and he was widely liked and admired.

U.S. Ambassadors are not required to consult or seek approval from Washington when traveling within their countries, and rarely do. Like all Chiefs of Mission, Chris made decisions about his movements based on the security assessments of his team on the ground, as well as his own judgment. After all, no one had more knowledge or experience in Libya than he did. He was well aware of the lawlessness in Benghazi, including a series of incidents earlier in the year against Western interests. Yet he also understood Benghazi's strategic importance in Libya and decided that the value of a visit outweighed the risks. He brought along two security officers, so there were five Diplomatic Security (DS) agents at the compound in Benghazi at the time of the attack. With State Department officer Sean Smith, there was a total of seven Americans on-site.

We would subsequently learn that upon arriving in Benghazi, Chris received a briefing from local CIA personnel, who were based at a second, larger compound less than a mile away. Its existence and mission were closely guarded secrets, but there was an understanding between security officials in both agencies that in an emergency, a CIA rapid-response team would deploy to the State Department compound to provide extra protection. Chris's first day ended with dinner with members of the city council at a hotel in town.

On Tuesday, the eleventh anniversary of 9/11, Chris held all of his meetings within the State compound. In the late afternoon, after the mob had gathered at our embassy in Cairo, he met with a Turkish diplomat. When Chris walked him out afterward, there were no signs of anything out of the ordinary. At around 9 P.M. both Chris and Sean retired for the night.

About forty minutes later, without warning, dozens of armed men appeared at the gates of the compound, overwhelmed the local Libyan guards, and streamed inside. They set fires as they went.

Alec, the DS agent manning the compound's tactical operations center, saw the mob on closed-circuit television, heard the sounds of gunfire and an explosion, and sprang into action. He activated the compound's alert system, established contact with U.S. security officials at the embassy in Tripoli, and, as had been practiced, alerted the well-armed CIA team stationed nearby to request their immediate assistance.

The other four DS agents reacted exactly as they were trained to do. Scott, the Agent in Charge, moved Chris and Sean, two men he would nearly lose his own life protecting that night, to a fortified safe haven within the compound's main house. The remaining three agents scrambled to collect their heavier weapons and tactical gear, but quickly found themselves pinned down in two separate buildings elsewhere on the compound.

Scott kept watch from inside the safe haven, his M4 rifle at the ready, while Chris borrowed his phone to make a series of calls to local contacts and to his Deputy, Greg Hicks, at the embassy in Tripoli. They heard men rampaging through the rest of the house and banging on the steel gate of the safe haven. Then, unexpectedly, the attackers withdrew. They doused the building with diesel fuel and set it on fire. The diesel gave off a thick, black, acrid smoke that quickly filled the air. Soon Chris, Sean, and Scott were struggling to see and breathe.

Their only hope was to make it to the roof. There was an emergency exit that offered a chance of escape. Crawling on his hands and knees,

Scott led the way. His eyes and throat burning, he managed to reach the exit grille and throw it open. But when he crawled through it and turned around, Chris and Sean were not right behind him as they had been only moments before. They were lost in the blinding smoke. To this day I am haunted by the thought of what those excruciating minutes in the burning building must have felt like.

Scott searched desperately, reentering the building multiple times, calling out their names without success. Finally, near collapse, he climbed a ladder to the roof. The other DS agents heard his hoarse voice crackle through the radio with a chilling message: the Ambassador and Sean were missing.

When the crowd of armed attackers, having ransacked most of the compound, started to recede, the three agents who had been pinned down were finally able to reach the main building. They provided first aid to Scott, who was suffering from severe smoke inhalation and other wounds, and then they retraced his steps back through the window into the safe haven. By now it was impossible to see anything inside because of the smoke, but they refused to give up the search, making numerous attempts to find Chris and Sean, crawling on the floor and feeling their way around. When one of them attempted to open the front door of the building, part of the ceiling collapsed.

From the moment the CIA station learned their fellow Americans were under attack, a response team prepared to launch a rescue. They could hear explosions in the distance and quickly assembled their weapons and prepared to deploy. Two vehicles of armed officers left the CIA post for the diplomatic compound about twenty minutes after the attack had begun. Until late October, when the Agency publicly acknowledged its presence in Benghazi, the existence of the CIA station was a secret, so in the immediate aftermath of the attack these officers received no public recognition. But all of us at the State Department were immensely grateful for the way our CIA colleagues responded that night.

When the CIA team arrived, they split up to secure the compound and joined the DS agents in the search of the burning building. Soon they made a terrible discovery. Sean was dead, apparently from smoke inhalation. His body was carefully carried out of the ruined building. There was still no sign of Chris.

My first word of the attack came around that time, when Steve Mull rushed down the hall to my office from the State Department's Operations Center. Steve, a thirty-year veteran of the Foreign Service, widely respected for his diplomatic and logistical skills, was in his final weeks as the Department's Executive Secretary, preparing to take up his next post as Ambassador to Poland. Among other responsibilities, the "Exec Sec" is tasked with managing the flow of information between Washington and the Department's hundreds of posts around the world. Troubling reports from across the Middle East had filled this day. But even against that backdrop, as soon as I saw the look in Steve's eyes, I could tell something was terribly wrong. All he knew at that point was that our Benghazi compound was under attack.

My thoughts immediately went to Chris. I had personally asked him to take on the assignment of Ambassador to Libya, and I shuddered to think that he and our other people on the ground were now in grave danger.

I picked up the secure phone on my desk and hit the button that instantly connected me to the White House, to National Security Advisor Tom Donilon. President Obama learned of the attack during an Oval Office meeting with Secretary of Defense Leon Panetta and Chairman of the Joint Chiefs Marty Dempsey, a no-nonsense straight shooter. After hearing the news the President gave the order to do whatever was necessary to support our people in Libya. It was imperative that all possible resources be mobilized immediately. The CIA outpost was already responding, but he wanted any assets that could be deployed pressed into service. When Americans are under fire, that is not an order the Commander in Chief has to give twice. Our military does everything humanly possible to save American lives—and would do more if they could. That anyone has ever suggested otherwise is something I will never understand.

Learning of the attack was a punch in the gut, but in the middle of an ongoing crisis, I didn't have time to process the flood of emotions—there was too much to do. I directed our State operations team, led by Under Secretary Pat Kennedy, to work with the embassy in Tripoli to get our people to safety and to break down the doors of the Libyan government if necessary to demand more support. I also called CIA Director David Petraeus since the Agency maintained the nearby post with a heavy security force. We also had to get ready for the possibility of other assaults elsewhere. Our embassy in Cairo had already been targeted. Now Benghazi was under attack. Where would be next? Pat was a forty-year veteran of the Foreign Service, having served eight Presidents from both parties. Some mistook his mild manner and penchant for cardigans and sweater vests as a sign of softness, but Pat was as tough as they came. He was calm amid the commotion and assured me that everything that could be done was being done. He was no stranger to fluid events, having served during some of the worst attacks on State Department personnel and property, and as a young Foreign Service officer had a small role supporting the families of the six American diplomats who ultimately escaped Iran after our embassy there was overrun in 1979 (dramatized in the film *Argo*).

In Tripoli a plane was quickly chartered, and a group of seven military and intelligence personnel began prepping for rapid deployment to Benghazi. Additional options were limited. The Pentagon had Special Operations forces standing by in Fort Bragg, North Carolina, but they would take several hours to muster and were more than five thousand miles away. Our civilian leaders and uniformed commanders, including the Chairman of the Joint Chiefs of Staff and others from his team, have repeatedly testified under oath both in public and in closed classified hearings that assets were immediately mobilized, but none could quickly reach Libya. Critics have questioned why the world's greatest military force could not get to Benghazi in time to defend our people. Part of the answer is that, despite having established United States Africa Command in 2008, there just wasn't much U.S. military infrastructure in place in Africa. Unlike in Europe and Asia, the U.S. military footprint in Africa is nearly nonexistent. Additionally our military is not deployed globally with the mission of maintaining forces at the ready to defend diplomatic posts. Tethering our forces to more than 270 embassies and consulates worldwide is a mission our military leaders have testified the Pentagon is simply not equipped to handle. Those are the facts, though not everyone accepts them and some insist on repeatedly questioning the actions of our military. For instance, weeks after the attack there was a sensational report that an American AC-130 gunship was sent to Benghazi but later waved off. The Pentagon undertook a comprehensive look into the accusation. Not only was there no gunship nearby, but there was no gunship on or near the entire continent of Africa. The closest gunship was over a thousand miles away in Afghanistan. This is but one of the false accusations made by those all too willing to misinform.

Another asset that some critics assert would have made a difference was called FEST. After the embassy bombings in East Africa in 1998, an interagency Foreign Emergency Support Team was deployed; it was trained and equipped to help restore secure communications, respond to biohazards, and provide other support to crippled diplomatic facilities. But this team was not an armed reaction force capable of intervening in an active fight, and they too were based thousands of miles away, in Washington.

Many Americans and even members of Congress were surprised to learn that there were no U.S. Marines assigned to our Benghazi compound. In fact Marines are assigned to only a little over half of all our diplomatic posts around the world, where their primary mission is the protection and, if necessary, the destruction of classified materials and equipment. So while there were Marines stationed at our embassy in Tripoli, where nearly all of our diplomats worked and which had the capability to process classified material, because there was no classified processing at the diplomatic compound in Benghazi, there were no Marines posted there.

There was also no live video feed out of the compound in Benghazi for anyone back in Washington to monitor. Some larger embassies around the world do have this capability, but Benghazi was a temporary facility without sufficient broadband access. It did have closed-circuit cameras and a video recording system on-site, not unlike a home DVR, but U.S. security officials would not gain access to this footage until weeks later, when Libyan authorities recovered the equipment and turned it over to American officials. So officials in the Diplomatic Security Command Center in Virginia trying to monitor the rush of events in real time had to rely on a single open phone line, listening to their colleagues in Tripoli and Benghazi. They could hear some of what was happening, but the picture was agonizingly incomplete.

To help fill this gap, one asset that could be quickly brought to bear was an unarmed and unmanned surveillance drone that was already flying a mission elsewhere over Libya. The drone was redirected to Benghazi and arrived on station roughly ninety minutes after the attack began, providing U.S. security and intelligence officials another way to monitor what was happening on the ground.

Around that time the Operations Center reported that gunfire at the compound had subsided and our security forces were attempting to locate missing personnel. That was a chilling phrase. Much of the mob had withdrawn, but for how long? Fighters and looters were still milling about nearby. The team decided that staying any longer would put more American lives at risk. Despite the ongoing efforts to find Chris, who was still missing in the burning main building, their only choice was to evacuate back to the CIA's more heavily guarded facility less than a mile away.

Reluctantly the five DS agents piled into an armored vehicle. The drive was short—only a few minutes—but harrowing. They took heavy and sustained fire on the street almost immediately and sped past a crowd of fighters clustered around a roadblock. Two tires blew out and the armored glass shattered, but they kept pressing forward. Possibly tailed by two unknown vehicles, they crossed into the median and then into oncoming traffic. A few minutes later they reached the CIA post. The wounded received medical support, and the others took up defensive positions. The CIA response team followed shortly afterward, carrying Sean Smith's body. Chris was still missing.

On the seventh floor of the State Department, everyone was doing everything we could think to do. State officials at all levels were talking to their counterparts across the government. U.S. officials in Washington and Libya were working with the Libyans to restore security and help with the search for our Ambassador. I called the Department's senior leadership back together to take stock and discuss next steps. I also spoke again with the White House. The CIA post was now coming under fire from small arms and rocket-propelled grenades. Everyone there braced for another swarm of attackers, but they did not materialize. The shooting continued sporadically before finally stopping.

The Operations Center reported that a hard-line Islamist militia called Ansar al-Sharia was claiming responsibility for the attack, though they would later retract it. It was something to take seriously. In the days that followed, U.S. intelligence analysts took a hard look at the attacks to try to determine how they began and who participated in them. But until then, we had to assume and plan for the worst—the possibility of further attacks against U.S. interests in the region.

Our embassy in Tripoli was twisting every arm they could find, but I wasn't satisfied with what we were getting from the Libyans. I called Libyan President Magariaf, and as I would do in other conversations that week, put in the starkest of terms the possibility of additional attacks. I wanted to make sure that he and others understood the urgency of the situation and did not assume the threat had passed. Magariaf was deeply apologetic. I thanked him for his concern but made it crystal clear that we needed more than regret: We needed immediate action to protect our people in Benghazi and Tripoli.

Meanwhile the plane with U.S. security reinforcements from Tripoli landed at the airport in Benghazi. Their goal was to locate vehicles and get to the CIA post as quickly as possible. But by now the airport was full of Libyan security officials and militia leaders who insisted on assembling a large armored motorcade to escort the Americans. Our frustrated team, anxious to help their colleagues, was held for hours until Libyan forces felt confident enough to leave the airport and head to the CIA post.

In Washington I convened a conference call with eight senior Department leaders and Deputy Chief of Mission Greg Hicks in Tripoli. Greg was one of the last people to talk to Chris before he disappeared, and with the Ambassador missing, he was now assuming formal responsibility for the safety of every American in the country. It had been a long night, and I was worried about how our team in Tripoli was holding up. I also wanted them to know what was being done from Washington, by the military, the CIA, and other parts of the government. Greg told me that as a precaution, he thought we should evacuate the embassy in Tripoli to an alternative compound, and I agreed. We talked about the search for Chris, whom we both cared about deeply. Things were not looking good, and I could hear the pain in Greg's voice. I asked him to pass along my prayers to his entire team and to stay in close contact.

I headed to the Operations Center for a secure videoconference between various government agencies and the White House Situation Room, officials from the National Security Council, the CIA, the Department of Defense, the Joint Chiefs of Staff, and other agencies. This was a Deputies meeting that did not include Principals, but protocol was the last thing on my mind. I downloaded to the group my discussions with Greg and President Magariaf, and I stressed how critical it was to get our people out of Benghazi as quickly and safely as possible.

Back in my office I told the team it was time to make a public statement. So far, I had been single-mindedly focused on coordinating across our government and mobilizing resources for our people on the ground. But reports about events in Benghazi were swirling in the press, and the American people deserved to hear directly from me about what was going on, even if we had only limited information. State Department practice was to hold off on issuing any statement until we could confirm the fate of all our personnel—but we still couldn't locate Chris. I decided it was important to be as forthcoming as possible as quickly as possible. I issued a statement confirming the loss of one of our officers, condemning the attack, and pledging to work with partners around the world to protect American diplomats, posts, and citizens.

Not long after talking with me, Greg and his team at the embassy received a startling phone call. It was from the same cell phone that Chris had used in the final moments before he disappeared in the smoke-filled safe haven. But this wasn't Chris. A man speaking Arabic said that an unresponsive American matching the Ambassador's description was now at a local hospital. He offered no further information or assurances. Could this really be Chris? Or was this report a trap to lure our people out of the CIA complex and into the open? We had to find out. Greg asked a local contact to go to the hospital and investigate. Remarkably this person was the same Libyan who helped rescue our downed Air Force pilot a year earlier.

An amateur video surfaced days later that showed a crowd of looters and onlookers wandering through the smoldering compound after our team evacuated. A group of Libyans, never identified, found Chris's body amid the clearing smoke and, although they did not know his identity, took him to a local hospital. They reportedly arrived at the emergency room shortly after 1 A.M. Doctors spent forty-five minutes attempting to resuscitate him, but at around 2 A.M. they declared Chris dead from smoke inhalation. Later the Prime Minister of Libya called Greg in Tripoli with the news. He called it the saddest phone call of his life. Absolute confirmation came when Chris's body was brought to American personnel at the airport in Benghazi the next morning. I knew that Chris was likely dead, but until confirmation there was still a chance that he might somehow have survived. Now that hope was gone.

━━━

With our DS agents at the heavily fortified CIA post and our reinforcements from Tripoli on the ground at the airport, I decided to move from the office to my home in northwest Washington, only minutes away from Foggy Bottom. I knew the days ahead were going to be taxing on us all, with the entire Department looking to me to lead them through this shocking tragedy while keeping everyone focused on what lay ahead. When I became Secretary the Department outfitted my house with all the secure communications and other equipment necessary to work as easily from there as I could from the office.

I got on the phone with President Obama and gave him the latest up-dates. He asked me how our people were holding up and reiterated that he wanted all necessary steps taken to protect our diplomats and citizens in Libya and across the region. I agreed and gave him my assessment of where we stood. I did not believe this crisis was over. We could expect more unrest to come, if not in Libya, then somewhere else.

The reinforcement team from Tripoli finally made it from the airport to the CIA outpost, providing their exhausted colleagues with a tremen-dous sense of relief. It did not last long.

Within minutes of the team's arrival, mortar fire was heard. The first shells missed, but the next hit their target with devastating force, killing the two CIA security personnel, Glen Doherty and Tyrone Woods, and seriously wounding others, including one of our DS agents, David.

The tragedy in Benghazi had now been compounded immeasurably. We needed to get the rest of our people—nearly three dozen in all, be-tween State's five DS agents and the CIA personnel—out of that city before we lost anyone else.

About an hour later Libyan government security forces, who had dispersed when the CIA post was hit by the mortar attack, returned to provide escort to the airport. A first planeload of Americans took off at 7:30 A.M. A second plane evacuated the rest, including the bodies of Sean Smith, Glen Doherty, Tyrone Woods, and Chris Stevens, which had ar-rived from the hospital. By noon all U.S. personnel from Benghazi were finally in Tripoli.

=====

In Washington, I kept thinking about the horror of what had happened. For the first time since 1979, a U.S. Ambassador had been killed in the line of duty. Four Americans were dead. Our compound in Benghazi was a smoking ruin, our CIA post abandoned. And there was no telling what would happen next, or where.

I braced myself for the day that lay ahead. I knew how essential it would be to lead with strength a reeling Department while remaining focused on ongoing threats. But first I needed to call the families of those we'd lost. They needed to know how much our Department and the nation honored their loved ones' service, that our hearts were broken at their loss. These would not be easy calls to make, but they were a solemn responsibility.

After checking in for any updates with General Dempsey, I sat down at my desk in the State Department and called Chris's sister, Anne Stevens, a doctor at Seattle Children's Hospital. She had been up most of the night talking with Chris's colleagues at the State Department and passing news to the rest of the Stevens family. Even exhausted and in shock, she was still able to focus on what her brother would have wanted. "I hope this will not prevent us from continuing to support the Libyan people, from moving ahead," she told me. Anne knew how committed Chris was to helping build a new Libya out of the wreckage of the Qaddafi regime and how important that was to American interests. He had fallen in love with the Middle East as a young Peace Corps volunteer teaching English in Morocco and went on to represent the United States as a Foreign Service officer all over the region. Everywhere he went, he won friends for the United States and made other people's hopes his own. I told Anne that he would be remembered as a hero by many nations.

In the weeks that followed I was awed by the grace and dignity with which the Stevens family coped with their grief and the harsh spotlight of history. After I left office we stayed in touch, and I was proud to support their efforts to launch the J. Christopher Stevens Virtual Exchange Initiative, which will use technology to connect young people and educators across the Middle East and the United States. It is a fitting way to honor Chris's memory and to carry forward the work he cared about so much.

I then called Sean Smith's wife, Heather, who lived in the Netherlands with the couple's two young children, and expressed my condolences for the loss of her husband. It was an enormous shock. He and Heather had made plans to go on vacation after his tour. Like Chris Stevens, Sean Smith was committed to America's engagement around the world and proud to serve. In the aftermath of the attack in Benghazi, Heather also expressed her belief that her husband wouldn't have wanted America to pull back from the world or live in fear.

That was an important sentiment to remember on September 12. Overnight, protests against the offensive internet video had continued to spread from Egypt across the Middle East. About two hundred angry Moroccans gathered outside our consulate in Casablanca. In Tunisia police had to use tear gas to disperse a crowd outside the U.S. Embassy. In

Sudan, Mauritania, and Egypt similar demonstrations were taking place outside American outposts. After what had happened in Benghazi the day before, everyone was on edge, and we treated each incident as if it might quickly spiral out of control.

I convened another videoconference with the exhausted but determined team still in Tripoli. They had done extraordinary work over the previous twenty-four hours, and I wanted to thank them personally and let them know that though they were thousands of miles from home, they were not alone.

Next I wanted to speak directly to the American people and the world. I felt the heavy burden of explaining the unexplainable to a country that had woken up to news of another bloody 9/11. Emotions were running very high. A number of my aides, who had known and loved Chris Stevens, were in tears. I took a quiet moment alone in my office to compose myself and think about what I wanted to say. Then I walked down the hall to the Treaty Room, where the press corps was assembled.

As the cameras snapped away, I laid out the facts as we knew them—"heavily armed militants" had assaulted our compound and killed our people—and assured Americans that we were doing everything possible to keep safe our personnel and citizens around the world. I also offered prayers for the families of the victims and praise for the diplomats who serve our country and our values all over the world. Chris Stevens had risked his life to stop a tyrant, then given his life trying to help build a better Libya. "The world needs more Chris Stevenses," I said.

With Anne Stevens's plea to carry forward Chris's commitment to the future of Libya still in my ears, I explained to the American people that "this was an attack by a small and savage group—not the people or Government of Libya," and that we would not turn our back on a country we had helped liberate. I also assured them that while we were still working to determine the exact motivations and methods of those who had carried out the attacks, we would not rest until they were found and brought to justice.

After my remarks I headed to the White House, where President Obama was preparing to address the nation himself. Standing just outside the Oval Office, we discussed whether he could come to Foggy Bottom right after his statement to comfort Chris's and Sean's grieving colleagues. I told him it would mean a great deal to a Department still very much in shock. We walked out into the Rose Garden, where the President told the world, "No acts of terror will ever shake the resolve of this great nation, alter that character, or eclipse the light of the values that we stand for."

After the President spoke I raced back to the Department. Though he suggested I ride over with him, I wanted to make sure everything was in place for this impromptu visit. Usually a Presidential visit takes weeks to orchestrate. This one would be on the fly.

When he arrived, we walked together through the lobby and I showed him where the names of diplomats who have fallen in the line of duty are inscribed in marble. He later signed the condolence book for those we had just lost.

On almost no notice, hundreds of State Department employees had gathered in the building's inner courtyard, including many from the Bureau of Near Eastern Affairs, where Chris Stevens had spent his career, as well as the Information Resource Management Bureau, where Sean Smith worked. The hastily arranged sound system wouldn't work, so I set the microphone on the ground and went ahead introducing the President. He spoke movingly for twenty minutes about how much the work of our diplomats means to America's national security and to our values. He urged the men and women of the State Department to honor the memory of those we lost by redoubling our efforts to represent the best traditions of our great nation. I could see on their faces how it meant the world to them, and to the many others watching through their windows overlooking the courtyard. When he was finished, I brought him over to meet some of Chris's colleagues in Near Eastern Affairs, who had been working practically nonstop since the crisis began. Later that afternoon I went to their offices and the office where Sean's colleagues worked to express my sorrow and gratitude. I felt enormously proud to serve this President, to lead this team, and to be part of the State Department family.

═══

The turmoil in the region continued to rage. Over the coming days and weeks we faced wave after wave of unrest that threatened our people and posts in a dozen countries and resulted in the deaths of scores of protesters, though thankfully no additional American lives were lost.

On Thursday, September 13, demonstrators breached the gates of the U.S. Embassy in Yemen. Yet more violent clashes continued in Cairo. In India as many as 150 people were arrested outside our consulate in

Chennai. On Friday the tensions grew even worse. Thousands of Tunisians besieged our embassy in Tunis, destroying vehicles and defacing buildings while staff was barricaded inside. An American school across the street was burned and looted. I called Tunisian President Moncef Marzouki, who promised to send his personal guards to disperse the protesters and protect our American and Tunisian staff. In Khartoum thousands of Sudanese swarmed over the walls of our embassy and tried to raise a black flag. Pakistani protesters took to the streets in Islamabad, Karachi, and Peshawar. There were demonstrations as far away as Indonesia and the Philippines. Even in Kuwait, a wealthy country that the United States helped liberate in the first Gulf War, people were arrested trying to scale the walls of our embassy. The spark lit in Cairo on September 8 was now a full-on wildfire, continuing to spread and threaten American posts and personnel in its path.

Throughout those difficult days my team and I were in constant touch with the governments of the countries wracked by protests. I had tense conversations with regional leaders who needed to hear exactly how serious this was. I also worked with the Pentagon to make sure extra Marines were dispatched to Tunisia, as well as to Sudan and Yemen.

I know there are some who don't want to hear that an internet video played a role in this upheaval. But it did. Pakistani protesters even beat an effigy of Terry Jones, the Florida pastor associated with the film. And American diplomats, far from the politics of Washington, felt the impact up close.

What about the attack in Benghazi? In the heat of the crisis we had no way of knowing for sure what combination of factors motivated the assault or whether and how long it had been planned. I was clear about this in my remarks the next morning, and in the days that followed administration officials continued to tell the American people that we had incomplete information and were still looking for answers. There were many theories—but still little evidence. I myself went back and forth on what likely happened, who did it, and what mix of factors—like the video—played a part. But it was unquestionably inciting the region and triggering protests all over, so it would have been strange not to consider, as days of protests unfolded, that it might have had the same effect here, too. That's just common sense. Later investigation and reporting confirmed that the video was indeed a factor. All we knew at that time with complete certainty was that Americans had been killed and others were still in danger. Why we were under attack or what the attackers were thinking or doing earlier that day was not at the forefront of anyone's mind. All that mattered to us was saving lives. Nothing else made a difference.

However, there were journalists still on the ground in Benghazi asking questions. The *New York Times* reported, "Interviewed at the scene on Tuesday night, many attackers and those who backed them said they were determined to defend their faith from the video's insults." Reuters also had a reporter on the ground that night, who wrote, "The attackers were part of a mob blaming America for a film they said insulted the Prophet Muhammad." The *Washington Times* also interviewed residents in Benghazi and said, "Heavily armed militants had hijacked what was initially a peaceful protest outside the U.S. diplomatic mission. The demonstrators were protesting a film that insulted Islam's prophet, Muhammad. They were quickly joined by a separate group of men armed with rocket-propelled grenades."

More than a year later, in December 2013, the *New York Times* published the most comprehensive account to date of what happened in Benghazi based on "months of investigation" and "extensive interviews with Libyans in Benghazi who had direct knowledge of the attack there and its context." The investigation concluded that, "Contrary to claims by some members of Congress, it was fueled in large part by anger at an American-made video denigrating Islam." The *Times* found that, "Anger at the video motivated the initial attack," and "there is no doubt that anger over the video motivated many attackers."

There were scores of attackers that night, almost certainly with differing motives. It is inaccurate to state that every single one of them was influenced by this hateful video. It is equally inaccurate to state that none of them were. Both assertions defy not only the evidence but logic as well. As the *New York Times* investigation found, the reality "was different, and murkier, than either of those story lines suggests."

Regardless, there was no question that the unrest threatening other U.S. embassies and consulates around the world was related to the video. So over the course of those difficult days, I did what I could to publicly address the widespread anger in the Muslim world. As a person of faith myself, I understand how hurtful it can be when your beliefs are insulted. But no matter how wronged one might feel, resorting to violence is never justified. The world's great religions are strong enough to withstand petty insults, and our individual faith should be as well.

On the evening of September 13, I hosted the State Department's annual Eid al Fitr reception marking the end of Ramadan, Islam's holy month of fasting. Among a warm and diverse crowd, I emphasized that we knew the killers in Benghazi did not speak for the more than 1 billion Muslims around the world. Then the Libyan Ambassador to the United States came forward to say a few words. He grew emotional remembering his friend Chris Stevens, whom he had known for years. They had played tennis and eaten traditional Libyan food together and spent hours talking about the future. Chris was a hero, he said, who never stopped believing in the potential of the Libyan people to emerge from the shadow of dictatorship.

He wasn't the only one who felt that way. Tens of thousands of Libyans poured into the streets of Benghazi to mourn Chris, who they knew as a steadfast champion of their revolution. The images were striking. One young woman, her head covered and her eyes haunted with sadness, held up a handwritten sign that said, "Thugs and killers don't represent Benghazi nor Islam." Others said, "Chris Stevens was a friend to all Libyans," and "We want justice for Chris."

In Tripoli the country's leaders publicly condemned the attack and organized a memorial service for Chris. "He gained the trust of the Libyan people," President Magariaf told the mourners. The government fired top security officials responsible for Benghazi and, on September 22, issued an ultimatum to Ansar al-Sharia and other militias across the country: Disarm and disband in forty-eight hours or face the consequences. As many as ten major armed groups complied. Taking matters into their own hands, the people of Benghazi overran the headquarters of Ansar al-Sharia and many of the militia's members fled the town. "You terrorists, you cowards, go back to Afghanistan," people chanted.

———

Throughout this sad period, the families of our fallen colleagues were always on my mind. I wanted to be sure that we did everything possible to comfort and accommodate them. I asked Chief of Protocol Capricia Marshall to make this her mission. Complicating matters was the fact that Tyrone Woods's and Glen Doherty's real jobs working for the CIA were still secret, and would remain so for six more weeks. Nobody was permitted to even talk about it with their families, who may or may not have known the truth of their loved ones' missions at the time.

I asked Deputy Secretary of State Bill Burns, America's highest-ranking Foreign Service officer, who was traveling abroad, to meet the plane carrying the remains of our fallen and accompany them from Germany back to Washington. Bill is as balanced and stoic as they come, but that is a journey no one should ever have to take.

Normally the remains of Americans who are killed serving our country go through Dover Air Force Base in Delaware, where casualties from Iraq and Afghanistan return. But I wanted to be sure that the families and our colleagues from the State Department had a chance to be present for their arrival, if they wanted to be. So with help from Leon Panetta and his Pentagon team, we routed the plane from Germany to Andrews Air Force Base in Maryland before proceeding to Dover, just as was done in 1998 after the East Africa embassy bombings.

On Friday afternoon, three days after the attacks, President Obama, Vice President Biden, Secretary of Defense Leon Panetta, and I met the families at Andrews. Sean Smith and Tyrone Woods both had small children. Seeing them there, knowing they would grow up without their fathers, was almost more than I could bear. All four men had loved ones who were devastated by their sudden loss. In a situation like that, there are no sentiments that can provide much comfort or understanding. All you can do is offer a human touch, a kind word, a gentle embrace. The room was crowded with more than sixty family members and close friends, and every person carried his or her own private grief. They were united by the heroism and service of those they loved, and the grief they felt for lost husbands, sons, fathers, and brothers.

We walked out to a large open hangar off the tarmac, where thousands of friends and colleagues had gathered under a giant American flag. It was an extraordinary outpouring of support and respect. Everyone stood in somber silence as U.S. Marines in crisp blues and whites slowly carried the four flag-draped coffins from the transport plane to waiting hearses and then saluted the fallen. A military chaplain offered a prayer.

When it was my turn to speak, I paid tribute to the service and sacrifice of the four patriots we had lost and tried to reflect both the pride and sorrow their colleagues and I felt. I also wanted to honor the work of diplomacy that Chris Stevens had so exemplified, and I talked about the remarkable scenes of sympathy and solidarity we had seen in Libya since his death. They were testaments to the impact Chris had there. I also read aloud a letter from Mahmoud Abbas, the President of the Palestinian Authority, who worked closely with Chris when he served in Jerusalem and fondly recalled his energy and integrity. Abbas deplored his murder as "an act of ugly terror." Finally, with protests continuing across the region, I once again addressed the ongoing unrest and anti-Americanism rocking the Middle East that had begun with a video before taking on a life of its own. "The people of Egypt, Libya, Yemen and Tunisia did not trade the tyranny of a dictator for the tyranny of a mob," I said. The violence needed to stop. We could expect more difficult days to come, but the United States would not retreat from the world or our responsibilities of global leadership. We would "wipe away our tears, stiffen our spines, and face the future undaunted."

President Obama added his own sober words of eulogy. When he finished, I squeezed his hand. He put his arm around my shoulder. The Marine Band played "America the Beautiful." Never had the responsibilities of office felt so heavy.

═══════

As Secretary of State, I was accountable for the safety of almost seventy thousand people at the Department and USAID and our more than 270 posts around the world. When something went wrong, as it did in Benghazi, it was my responsibility. And that responsibility included making sure that we determined where the gaps had been in the Department's systems and security procedures and that we did everything possible to reduce the risks of another tragedy in the future. We had learned from Beirut in 1983, from Kenya and Tanzania in 1998, from September 11, 2001, and now it was time to learn from the tragedy in Benghazi. That learning process needed to start with figuring out what went wrong.

Whenever there is a loss of life of State Department personnel overseas, law requires that an Accountability Review Board be stood up to investigate. Since 1988 there have been nineteen such investigations. Thomas Pickering was chosen to serve as Chair of the Benghazi review board. Pickering is a retired senior Foreign Service officer with an impeccable record who has represented the United States all over the world, including in many difficult posts such as El Salvador during that country's civil war, Israel during the start of the first intifada, and Russia in the early years after the fall of the Soviet Union. Tom is tough, smart, and blunt. To honor and protect the Department he loved, he would spare no criticism wherever he found error. If anyone could lead a credible investigation and find the answers to our many questions, it was Ambassador Pickering.

Retired Admiral Mike Mullen, a former Chairman of the Joint Chiefs of Staff and a widely respected, straight-talking Navy man, served as Pickering's partner. They were joined by a distinguished group of public servants with long experience in diplomacy, management, and intelligence. The five-person board was tasked with getting to the bottom of what happened.

I announced the investigation on September 20, just a few weeks after the attacks. That was faster than many previous investigations had launched, but it was important to move as quickly as possible. I ordered everyone at the State Department to cooperate fully and urged the board to leave no stone unturned. They had unfettered access to anyone and anything they thought relevant to their investigation, including me if they had chosen to do so. Though most previous review board reports were not made available to the public, I wanted to release as many as possible without compromising any security sensitivities.

As the investigation got under way, I also took steps to address a number of pressing vulnerabilities that couldn't wait for the official report. I ordered an immediate and thorough review of our diplomatic security posture around the world. I asked the Department of Defense to partner with us in forming joint security assessment teams to carefully scrutinize embassies and consulates in dangerous countries, sending teams of Special Forces and Diplomatic Security specialists to more than a dozen high-risk nations. I worked with General Dempsey and Secretary Panetta to dispatch additional Marine Security Guards to bolster security at high-threat posts, and asked Congress to fund additional Marines going forward, hire additional Diplomatic Security agents, and address physical vulnerabilities at our facilities overseas. I named the first Deputy Assistant Secretary of State for High-Threat Posts in the Bureau of Diplomatic Security.

When the Accountability Review Board finished its report, Ambassador Pickering and Admiral Mullen briefed me on its findings. They didn't pull a single punch. Their investigation was hard-hitting, finding systemic problems and management deficiencies in both the Bureau of Diplomatic Security and the Bureau of Near Eastern Affairs. They found poor coordination between the offices handling diplomatic security and the offices guiding policy and relations with the host government. Security was not viewed as a "shared responsibility," and there was confusion about who on the ground, beyond the Ambassador himself, was actually empowered to make decisions. With more than 270 posts around the world, each with its own technical challenges and requirements, day-to-day questions about security rarely rose to the top levels of the Department, and, as a result, there was inadequate leadership in regard to matters of security.

Though security upgrades had been made to the Benghazi compound—including extending the height of the outer wall with masonry concrete and barbed wire; installing external lighting, concrete vehicle barriers, guard booths, and sandbag emplacements; hardening wooden doors with steel and reinforced locks; and adding equipment to detect explosives—the review board determined that these precautions were simply inadequate in an increasingly dangerous city. A focus of the investigation and Congressional inquiries was on the question of whether requests made by security officials on the ground in Libya were denied by their supervisors in Washington. The review board found that personnel in Benghazi did not feel that their security requests were "a high priority for Washington" and that "Embassy Tripoli did not demonstrate strong and sustained advocacy with Washington for increased security." At the embassy, and in the relevant bureaus and offices charged with making decisions about security, there was "confusion over who, ultimately, was responsible and empowered to make decisions." Communications between Washington and Tripoli took the form of phone calls, emails, and cables. Millions of these documents are sent every year by posts to headquarters, by headquarters to posts, between posts, and so on. They are used for everything from summarizing what's happening in a country to announcing personnel changes. Every cable written to headquarters is sent over the Ambassador's name and addressed to the Secretary of State. Every cable written by headquarters goes out over the name of the Secretary of State to the Ambassador. That might not make a whole lot of sense, but it's been the practice of the State Department for as long as anyone can remember. Obviously no Secretary can read or write these more than 2 million cables a year, and Ambassadors aren't writing—or even aware of—every cable that comes in or out of their embassy. Only a fraction are actually meant for the Secretary's eyes. The bulk of them are meant for the other recipients, sometimes numbering in the hundreds.

Some critics have taken advantage of this procedural quirk to say that security requests reached my desk. But that's not how it works. It shouldn't. And it didn't. Security matters are handled by officials responsible for security. It's rare that such a cable would come to the Secretary of State's desk. First, that's not what the sender intended. An agent in Islamabad isn't writing to me personally, asking for more ammunition. Second, it wouldn't make sense. The professionals charged with security should be the ones making security decisions. Third, it's just plain impossible for any Secretary of any Cabinet agency to take that on, not only because of the volume but because it's just not their expertise, nor is it mine. I had confidence in Diplomatic Security because they were ably protecting our posts in dangerous places all over the world, including highly volatile countries such as Afghanistan and Yemen.

Another major finding of the review board was that the Department relied too heavily on local Libyan security. Under the Vienna Convention on Diplomatic Relations of 1961, host governments have primary responsibility for providing security to diplomatic facilities in their countries. But in fractured postrevolutionary Libya, the government had limited capacity, with militias filling many of its functions. So the Department had contracted with members of a local militia vetted by the CIA to be present at the compound at all times, and also contracted unarmed local security guards to man the entry points. As became evident during the attacks, there were fatal weaknesses in their abilities and willingness to fulfill their security duties against fellow Libyans when they were most needed.

The review board also noted that the State Department faced a "struggle to obtain the resources necessary to carry out its work," something we faced in a time of shrinking budgets across the entire government. I spent four years making the case to Congress that adequately funding our diplomats and development experts was a national security priority, and we had many great partners and champions on the Hill. But it was a continuing challenge. The review board called for "a more serious and sustained commitment from Congress to support State Department needs, which, in total, constitute a small percentage both of the full national budget and that spent for national security."

In its final analysis, the review board found that "U.S. personnel on the ground in Benghazi performed with courage and readiness to risk their lives to protect their colleagues, in a near impossible situation." Despite the flaws in our security systems, the investigation concluded that "every possible effort was made to rescue and recover Ambassador Stevens and Sean Smith" and that "there simply was not enough time for armed U.S. military assets to have made a difference." The report praised the administration's "timely" and "exceptional" coordination during the crisis itself and found no delays in decision making and no denials of support from Washington or from the military. It said our response saved American lives, and it did.

The review board made twenty-nine specific recommendations (twenty-four unclassified) to address the deficiencies it found in areas such as training, fire safety, staffing, and threat analysis. I agreed with all twenty-nine and immediately accepted them. I asked Deputy Secretary Tom Nides to head a task force to ensure that all of the recommendations would be implemented quickly and completely and to take a number of additional steps above and beyond the recommendations. We would take a top-to-bottom look at how the State Department makes decisions about where, when, and whether people operate in high-threat areas and how we respond to threats and crises.

Tom and his team got right to work translating each of the recommendations into sixty-four specific action items. They were assigned to bureaus and offices with specific timelines for completion. In addition we initiated an annual high-threat post review to be chaired by the Secretary of State and ongoing reviews by the Deputy Secretaries to ensure that pivotal questions about security would reach the highest levels. We also began regularizing protocols for sharing information with Congress so that their resource decisions were continually informed by our security needs on the ground.

I pledged that I would not leave office until every recommendation was on its way to implementation. By the time I left, we had met that goal. By then the State Department was working with Congress and the Department of Defense to increase the number of Marine Security Detachments at U.S. diplomatic facilities, had reviewed and begun upgrading fire and life safety equipment requirements abroad, started equipping all overseas facilities with more modern surveillance cameras, created 151 new Diplomatic Security positions with Congressional support, and enhanced the Department's security training efforts.

As a former Senator I understand and have a great deal of respect for the oversight role that Congress is meant to play. Over my eight years serving on Capitol Hill, I exercised that responsibility many times when I believed there were tough questions that needed answers. So being responsive and transparent with lawmakers was a priority starting immediately after the attacks. I decided to go up to Capitol Hill the week after the attacks to brief the entire House and Senate on what we knew at that point, along with the Director of National Intelligence James Clapper, Deputy Secretary of Defense Ashton Carter, Vice Chairman of the Joint Chiefs of Staff Admiral James "Sandy" Winnefeld Jr., and other senior officials from the intelligence and law enforcement communities. Many members of Congress were left unsatisfied with the answers they heard that day; some were outright angry. We ourselves were frustrated by not having every answer, but that didn't deter us from sharing what we knew. Though the briefing was scheduled for only an hour, I remained in the Senate's secure chamber for more than two and a half hours, until every single Senator who had a question was able to ask it.

Over the months that followed, senior officials, most of them nonpartisan career professionals, from the State Department, the Department of Defense, the CIA, the FBI, and other intelligence agencies appeared on more than thirty occasions before eight different Congressional committees, submitted thousands of pages of documents, and answered questions as quickly and fully as possible.

In January I spent more than five hours testifying before the Senate and the House of Representatives, answering what must have been more than a hundred questions from dozens of members as best I could, given what we knew at the time. Though the end of my term was near, I told the Senators and Congressmen that I was determined to leave the State Department and our country safer and stronger. Addressing the attacks in Benghazi, I stated, "As I have said many times, I take responsibility, and nobody is more committed to getting this right." The United States has a vital role to play as a global leader, I reminded the lawmakers, and when America is absent, especially from unstable environments, there are consequences. That's why I sent Chris Stevens to Libya in the first place; it's also why he wanted to be there. It was our responsibility, I said, to make sure that the men and women on the front lines always have the resources they need and to do everything we can to reduce the risks they face. America could not and would not retreat.

Some of the members of Congress asked thoughtful questions aimed at applying the hard lessons we had learned and improving future operations. Others remained fixated on chasing after conspiracy theories that had nothing to do with how we could prevent future tragedies. And some only showed up because of the cameras. They had skipped closed hearings when there wasn't a chance of being on TV.

Much attention focused on what Susan Rice, our Ambassador to the United Nations, said on various Sunday-morning talk shows on September 16, five days after the attacks in Benghazi. In response to questions, Susan cautioned that the facts about what happened in Benghazi were still unclear and that an investigation was pending. But, she said, according to the best information currently available, the attacks were "initially a spontaneous reaction to what had just transpired hours before in Cairo, almost a copycat of—of the demonstrations against our facility in Cairo, which were prompted, of course, by the video. What we think then transpired in Benghazi is that opportunistic extremist elements came to the consulate as this was unfolding."

Critics accused her of trumping up tales of a protest that never happened in order to cover up the fact that this had been a successful terrorist attack on President Obama's watch. They obsessed over the question of who in the government prepared Susan's "talking points" that morning and hoped to find evidence of heavy-handed political malfeasance by the White House. Susan stated what the intelligence community believed, rightly or wrongly, at the time. That was the best she or anyone could do. Every step of the way, whenever something new was learned, it was quickly shared with Congress and the American people. There is a difference between getting something wrong, and committing wrong. A big difference that some have blurred to the point of casting those who made a mistake as intentionally deceitful.

Many also fixate on the question of why I didn't go on TV that morning, as if appearing on a talk show is the equivalent of jury duty, where one has to have a compelling reason to get out of it. I don't see appearing on Sunday-morning television as any more of a responsibility than appearing on late-night TV. Only in Washington is the definition of talking to Americans confined to 9 A.M. on Sunday mornings. The days and hours in between simply don't count. I don't buy that.

The American people need to be kept informed of what's happening. That's our responsibility. I wanted the American people to hear directly from me. That's why I spoke publicly first thing in the morning after the attack. And two days later at Andrews Air Force Base. And countless times in the weeks and months that followed, through statements, press interviews, and press conferences.

The extensive public record now makes clear that Susan was using information that originated with and was approved by the CIA. The earliest drafts of the talking points written and circulated by the Agency said, "We believe based on currently available information that the attacks in Benghazi were spontaneously inspired by the protests at the U.S. Embassy in Cairo." That assessment didn't come from political operatives in the White House; it came from career professionals in the intelligence community. It was written by intelligence officials for use by members of the House Permanent Select Committee on Intelligence, Democrats and Republicans alike, who asked David Petraeus at the end of a briefing on Benghazi on Friday the 14th what part of what they heard behind closed doors they were allowed to say on television. The points were not designed to be an exhaustive account of every piece of intelligence; they were merely meant to help already briefed Congressmen make public statements while staying clear of classified or sensitive material. None of the intelligence officials working on that request had any idea the talking points would be used two days later by Susan. This is another conspiracy theory that flies in the face of facts—and reason.

I was asked about this repeatedly during my Congressional testimony. "I personally was not focused on talking points. I was focused on keeping our people safe," I responded. At one point, during some particularly tendentious questioning, the exchange grew heated. Afterward some of my words were taken out of context for political purposes, so it's worth repeating my full answer that day:

With all due respect, the fact is we had four dead Americans. Was it because of a protest? Or was it because of guys out for a walk one night who decided they would go kill some Americans? What difference at this point does it make? It is our job to figure out what happened and do everything we can to prevent it from ever happening again, Senator. Now, honestly I will do my best to answer your questions about this, but the, the fact is that people were trying in real time to get to the best information. The [intelligence community] has a process, I understand, going with the other committees to explain how these talking points

*came out. But, you know to be clear, it is from my perspective, less
important today looking backwards as to why these militants decided
they did it, than to find them and bring them to justice, and then maybe
we'll figure out what was going on in the meantime.*

In yet another example of the terrible politicization of this tragedy, many
have conveniently chosen to interpret the phrase "What difference at this
point does it make?" to mean that I was somehow minimizing the tragedy
of Benghazi. Of course that's not what I said. Nothing could be further
from the truth. And many of those trying to make hay of it know that,
but don't care. My point was simple: If someone breaks into your home
and takes your family hostage, how much time are you going to spend
focused on how the intruder spent his day as opposed to how best to rescue
your loved ones and then prevent it from happening again? Many of these
same people are a broken record about unanswered questions. But there
is a difference between unanswered questions and unlistened to answers.

Coming in the heat of a tight Presidential campaign less than two
months before Election Day, maybe it's naïve of me to think the death of
four Americans wouldn't have been used for political purposes. Politics
only muddied the context and obscured many of the facts. One of the best
parts of being Secretary of State was experiencing four years in a place
where partisan politics was almost entirely absent from our work.

Those who exploit this tragedy over and over as a political tool minimize the sacrifice of those who served our country. I will not be a part of
a political slugfest on the backs of dead Americans. It's just plain wrong,
and it's unworthy of our great country. Those who insist on politicizing
the tragedy will have to do so without me.

———

As Secretary I got to know many of the Diplomatic Security officers stationed all over the world, and I was extraordinarily grateful for their
service and professionalism. The two agents who headed up my own
protective detail, first Fred Ketchem and then Kurt Olsson, were unflappable and indefatigable. I trusted them with my life.

Although the five agents in Benghazi on September 11 were vastly
outnumbered, they performed heroically and put their own lives on the
line to protect their colleagues. David, the agent critically wounded in the

mortar attack at the CIA base, spent months recovering at Walter Reed Medical Center. I called him during his stay and told him that when he was healthy enough, I wanted to host him and his colleagues and properly honor them for their service.

On the morning of January 31, 2013, my second-to-last day as Secretary of State, the Treaty Room was filled with family and friends of the five agents. David was still in a wheelchair, but he made it. Members of the Stevens family were there as well, to show their appreciation for how much these men had done to protect Chris. It was my honor to pay tribute to their courage and professionalism. They represented the strength and spirit of a great nation. I presented each agent with the State Department's Heroism Award. There were tears in people's eyes as they watched. It was a reminder that on that terrible night, we saw the best and worst of humanity, just as we had eleven years before.

Memories of Benghazi will stay with me always, and they will shape the way America's diplomats do their jobs in the future. But we should remember Chris Stevens, Sean Smith, Glen Doherty, and Tyrone Woods as much for how they lived as for how they died. They all volunteered to serve their country where security was far from assured because those were the places where American interests and values were most at stake and they were most needed.

18

Iran: Sanctions and Secrets

The Sultan of Oman has a flair for the dramatic.

We were sitting over a lavish lunch in a palace designed by the Sultan himself in Oman's capital city of Muscat, near the tip of the Arabian Peninsula, when I heard the familiar strains of John Philip Sousa's "Liberty Bell" march. Sultan Qaboos, dressed in a long flowing robe with a ceremonial dagger on his belt and a colorful turban on his head, smiled and looked up. On a balcony above us, partially hidden by a screen, was part of the Royal Oman Symphony Orchestra. It was a typical gesture for a shrewd and gracious leader who valued his relationship with the United States, loved music, and used his absolute power to modernize his country over four decades of rule.

What the Sultan had to say was even more dramatic. It was January 12, 2011, just days before the Arab Spring would upend the chessboard of Middle East geopolitics. I had just come from Yemen, Oman's troubled southern neighbor, and was headed to a regional conference in Qatar to warn leaders that without economic and political reform, their regimes would "sink into the sand." But today the Sultan's focus was on Iran.

The standoff over Iran's illicit nuclear program was escalating, and it posed an urgent threat to regional and global security. Since 2009 the Obama Administration had pursued a "dual-track" strategy of pressure and engagement, but negotiations between Iran and the five permanent members of the UN Security Council (the United States, Russia, China,

Britain, and France), plus Germany—the so-called P5+1—were going nowhere. The prospects of armed conflict, possibly including an Israeli strike to knock out Iranian nuclear facilities like the ones carried out against Iraq in 1981 and Syria in 2007, were mounting.

"I can help," the Sultan said. He was one of the few leaders seen by all sides as an honest broker, with close ties in Washington, the Gulf states, and Tehran. He proposed hosting secret direct talks between the United States and Iran to resolve the nuclear issue. Previous attempts to engage Iran's theocratic regime had failed, but the Sultan thought there might be a chance for him to facilitate a breakthrough. Secrecy would be necessary to prevent hard-liners on all sides from derailing talks before they had a chance to get going. Was I willing to explore the idea?

On the one hand, there was no reason to trust the Iranians and every reason to believe they would exploit any opportunity for delay and distraction. New negotiations could turn into a rabbit hole that would buy the Iranians time to race closer to their goal of a nuclear weapon that would threaten Israel, their neighbors, and the world. Any concessions we offered as part of these talks could undo years of careful work to build an international consensus for tough sanctions and increased pressure on the regime in Tehran. On the other hand, the Sultan's offer could be our best chance to avoid conflict or the unacceptable prospect of a nuclear-armed Iran. Our failure to pursue diplomacy could end up fraying the broad international coalition we had built to impose and enforce sanctions on Iran.

———

While it is hard to believe, given all that has happened since, Iran was once a Cold War ally of the United States. The country's monarch, the Shah, owed his throne to a 1953 coup supported by the Eisenhower Administration against a democratically elected government thought to be sympathetic to Communism. It was a classic Cold War move for which many Iranians never forgave America. Our governments enjoyed close relations for more than twenty-five years—until, in 1979, the autocratic Shah was overthrown by a popular revolution. Shiite fundamentalists led by Ayatollah Ruhollah Khomeini soon seized power and imposed their theocratic version of an Islamic republic on the Iranian people. Iran's new rulers were implacably opposed to America, calling us "the Great Satan." In November 1979, Iranian radicals stormed the U.S. Embassy in Tehran and held fifty-two Americans hostage for 444 days. It was an appalling breach of international law and a traumatic experience for our country. I remember watching nightly news reports in Little Rock counting the number of days the hostages had been held captive as the crisis went on and on without an end in sight. It became even more tragic when a rescue mission by the U.S. military ended with the crash of a helicopter and a transport plane in the desert that killed eight servicemembers.

The Iranian Revolution led to decades of state-sponsored terrorism. The Iranian Islamic Revolutionary Guard and Hezbollah, which served as an Iranian proxy, carried out attacks across the Middle East and the world. Their crimes included the bombings in Beirut, Lebanon, of the U.S. Embassy in April 1983, which killed sixty-three people, including seventeen Americans; the attack on the U.S. Marine barracks that October, which killed 241 Americans; and the 1996 bombing of Khobar Towers in Saudi Arabia that killed nineteen U.S. Air Force personnel and wounded hundreds of others. Iran also targeted Jews and Israelis, including bombing an Israeli cultural center in Buenos Aires, Argentina, in 1994, killing eighty-five people and injuring hundreds more. On a regular basis the State Department designated Iran as the world's "most active state sponsor of terrorism" and documented its links to bombings, kidnappings, hijackings, and other acts of terrorism. Iranian rockets, automatic weapons, and mortars were also being used to kill U.S. troops as well as our partners and civilians in Iraq and Afghanistan.

Given this history, the prospect of a nuclear-armed Iran represented a serious security threat to Israel, Iran's neighbors in the Gulf, and, by extension, the world, which is why the UN Security Council had passed six resolutions since 2006, calling on Iran to cease its weapons program and abide by the Nuclear Nonproliferation Treaty. Like more than 180 other nations, Iran is a signatory to the Treaty, which gives countries the right to nuclear energy for peaceful purposes but requires those with existing nuclear weapons to pursue disarmament and those without nuclear weapons to foreswear acquiring them. Allowing Iran to acquire a nuclear weapon in violation of this treaty could open the floodgates on proliferation, first in the Middle East among its Sunni-led rivals, and then around the world.

We knew Iran had worked for years to develop the technology and materials necessary to build a bomb, despite condemnation and pressure from the international community. In early 2003, Iran possessed about a hundred centrifuges for enriching uranium, one of the two ways to fuel nuclear weapons, the other being plutonium. Centrifuges spin at incredibly fast speeds, enriching uranium to a high enough level that it can be used to build a bomb. This is a difficult and precise process that requires thousands of centrifuges. Over the next six years, with the international community divided and Iran denying access and information to the International Atomic Energy Agency (IAEA), it steadily expanded its program. By the time President Obama took office, Iran had about five thousand centrifuges. Despite Iran's leaders' claims that their nuclear program was intended for purely peaceful scientific, medical, and commercial purposes, their scientists were working in secret in hardened bunkers built deep inside mountains, enriching uranium at levels and quantities that led reasonable people to harbor well-founded suspicions of their intentions.

For a brief period in the late 1990s, there was hope that Iran might choose a different course. In 1997, Iranians elected as President a relative moderate, Mohammad Khatami, who said in an American TV interview that he wanted to tear down the "wall of mistrust" between Iran and the United States. The Clinton Administration was understandably wary in the wake of the Khobar Towers attack, but Bill responded with cautious reciprocal steps, including mentioning Iran in a video message marking Eid al Fitr, the feast at the end of the Muslim holy month of Ramadan. "I hope that the day will soon come when we can enjoy once again good relations with Iran," he said. The administration sent out a number of diplomatic feelers in an attempt to start a dialogue, including a letter delivered via our mutual friend the Sultan of Oman. In 2000, Secretary of State Madeleine Albright offered a more public olive branch by formally apologizing for the American role in the 1953 Iranian coup and easing certain economic sanctions. But Iran never followed through, in part because hard-liners restrained Khatami's ability to act.

That groundwork may have helped encourage Khatami to reach out after the 9/11 attacks in the hopes of cooperating with the United States in Afghanistan, which shares a border with Iran. But President Bush's speech in 2002, in which he named Iran, Iraq, and North Korea an "Axis of Evil," ended any chance of further dialogue between our countries at that time. The Europeans then took the lead on negotiating with Iran over its nuclear program, but those talks fell apart after Khatami was replaced in 2005 by Mahmoud Ahmadinejad, a Holocaust denier and provocateur who threatened to wipe Israel off the map and insulted the West at every turn.

As a Senator representing New York during the Bush years, I advocated for increasing pressure on the regime in Tehran and its proxies, voting to impose sanctions on Iran and to formally designate the Revolutionary Guard as a terrorist organization. As I stated again and again, "We cannot, we should not, we must not permit Iran to build or acquire nuclear weapons." Yet without a broad international consensus, unilateral U.S. sanctions did little to curb Iranian behavior.

In a 2007 essay in the journal *Foreign Affairs*, I argued, "The Bush Administration refuses to talk to Iran about its nuclear program, preferring to ignore bad behavior rather than challenge it." And, "If Iran does not comply with its own commitments and the will of the international community, all options must remain on the table." Without being specific, "options" could be read as including potential military action, but I emphasized that the first choice should be diplomacy. After all, if the United States could negotiate with the Soviet Union at the height of the Cold War, with thousands of their missiles pointed at our cities, we should not be afraid to talk with other adversaries such as Iran under appropriate conditions. This was a delicate balancing act—raising the prospect of military action while also pushing for diplomacy and restraint—but it was hardly novel. Effective foreign policy has always involved the use of both sticks and carrots, and finding the right balance between the two is more art than science.

During the heat of the 2008 Presidential primaries, I jumped on Senator Obama's statement in a debate that he would meet with the leaders of Iran, Syria, Venezuela, Cuba, and North Korea "without precondition" during the first year of a new administration. Return to diplomacy, I said, engage with these countries, but don't promise to reward them with a high-profile Presidential meeting unless we get something in return. In response his campaign accused me of toeing the Bush line and refusing to talk to our adversaries. None of this was particularly illuminating for voters, but that's life on the campaign trail. I also caused a bit of a stir in April 2008 when I warned Iran's leaders that if they launched a nuclear attack on Israel on my watch, the United States would retaliate and "we would be able to totally obliterate them." That got Tehran's attention, and Iran actually filed a formal protest at the UN.

After President Obama asked me to be Secretary of State, we started talking about crafting a more effective approach toward Iran. Our goal may have been straightforward—prevent Iran from developing nuclear weapons—but the path to achieve it was anything but.

By early 2009, Iran appeared to be on the rise in the Middle East. The U.S.-led invasion of Iraq had removed Iran's nemesis Saddam Hussein and put in place a Shiite government more to its liking. U.S. power and prestige in the region were at a low. Hezbollah had fought Israel to a bloody stalemate in Lebanon in 2006, and Hamas was still firmly in control of the Gaza Strip after a two-week Israeli invasion in January 2009. Sunni monarchs in the Gulf watched in fear as Iran built up its military, extended its influence, and threatened to dominate the strategically vital Strait of Hormuz. Inside Iran the regime's iron grip was unchallenged, and it enjoyed booming oil exports. President Ahmadinejad was a bellicose peacock strutting on the world stage. But the real authority rested with the Supreme Leader, Ayatollah Ali Khamenei, who succeeded Khomeini in 1989 and made no secret of his hatred for America. The hard-line Revolutionary Guard was amassing such significant power within Iran, including vast economic holdings, that the country appeared to be moving toward a military dictatorship under the veneer of clerical leadership. I made some waves when I noted this trend during a trip to the Gulf.

Faced with this difficult landscape, President Obama and I were determined to use both engagement and pressure to present Iran's leaders with a clear choice: If they complied with their treaty obligations and addressed the international community's concerns about their nuclear program, then they could benefit from improved relations. If they refused, they would face increased isolation and even more painful consequences.

One of President Obama's first gestures was to send two private letters to Ayatollah Khamenei offering a new diplomatic opening. He also recorded video messages aimed directly at the Iranian people. Like my husband's efforts a decade before, these feelers were met with a stone wall in Tehran. None of us were under any illusions that Iran was going to change its behavior simply because a new American President was willing to talk. But we believed that the effort to engage would strengthen our hand in seeking tougher sanctions if Iran rejected our overtures. The rest of the world would see that the Iranians, not the Americans, were the intransigent ones, and that would make them more likely to support increasing pressure on Tehran.

An early avenue we explored was possible cooperation on Afghanistan. After all, back in 2001, in the early days of the war, there had been exploratory talks about working together to stem the drug trade and stabilize the country. Since then, however, Iran had played a much less constructive role. In the lead-up to a major international conference on Afghanistan organized by the UN at The Hague at the end of March 2009, I had to decide whether to support the UN's extending an invitation to Iran. After consulting with NATO allies, I described the upcoming conference as "a big tent meeting with all the parties who have a stake and an interest in Afghanistan." That left the door open for Iran; if they showed up, it would be our first direct encounter.

Tehran ended up sending a Deputy Foreign Minister to The Hague, whose speech included some positive ideas for collaboration. I did not meet with the Iranian diplomat, but I did send Jake Sullivan to speak with him to raise the prospect of direct engagement on Afghanistan.

Jake also hand-delivered a letter requesting the release of three Americans being detained in Iran: a retired FBI agent named Robert Levinson, a graduate student named Esha Momeni, and an American journalist of Iranian Japanese descent named Roxana Saberi. Roxana was arrested in Tehran and accused of espionage only days after I took office in January 2009. After a hunger strike and persistent lobbying by the United States and others, she was released in May. She came to see me at the State Department soon after and told me about her harrowing ordeal. Robert Levinson is still being held. Esha Momeni, who had been out on bail but barred from leaving the country, was allowed to return to the United States in August 2009.

At the same conference at The Hague, Richard Holbrooke had a brief exchange with the Iranian diplomat at an official lunch, though the Iranians later denied the encounter took place.

The second half of 2009 turned out to be full of unexpected developments that dramatically reshaped the international debate about Iran.

First came the Iranian elections. In June, Ahmadinejad was declared the winner of a Presidential vote that was, by all accounts, deeply flawed if not totally rigged. Large crowds gathered in the streets of Tehran and throughout the country to protest the results. It was a surprising moment, as the Iranian middle class demanded the democracy that the 1979 revolution had promised but never delivered. The protests gained strength and were known as the Green Movement. Millions of Iranians took to the streets in an unprecedented display of dissent, many even calling for an end to the regime. Security forces responded with brutal violence. Citizens marching peacefully were beaten with batons and arrested en masse. Political opponents were rounded up and abused, and several people were killed. People around the world were horrified by video footage of a young woman shot dead in the street. The violence was shocking, but the repression was in keeping with the regime's abysmal human rights record.

Within the Obama Administration we debated how to respond. "We are monitoring the situation as it unfolds in Iran, but we, like the rest of the world, are waiting and watching to see what the Iranian people decide," I announced as the protests picked up steam but before the worst of the crackdown. "We obviously hope that the outcome reflects the genuine will and desire of the Iranian people."

Contacts in Iran urged us to stay as quiet as possible. They worried that if the United States spoke out in support of the demonstrators, or overtly tried to insert ourselves into the situation, it would allow the regime to dismiss the protests as a foreign plot. Many of our intelligence analysts and Iran experts agreed. Still there was a strong temptation to stand up and proclaim our support for the Iranian people and our disgust with the heavy-handed tactics of the regime. That felt like the appropriate role for America to play, in keeping with our democratic values.

After listening to all the arguments, the President grudgingly decided that we would better serve the aspirations of the Iranian people by not putting the United States in the middle of the crisis. It was a difficult, clear-eyed tactical call. It was not, as some commentators speculated at the time, because the President cared more about engaging with the regime than standing up to it. This was about doing what we believed was the right thing for the protesters and for democracy, nothing more. Behind the scenes my team at the State Department stayed in constant contact with activists in Iran and made an emergency intervention to prevent Twitter from shutting down for maintenance, which would have deprived protesters of a key communications tool.

In retrospect I'm not sure our restraint was the right choice. It did not stop the regime from ruthlessly crushing the Green Movement, which was exceedingly painful to watch. More strident messages from the United States would probably not have prevented the outcome and might even have hastened it, but there's no way of knowing now if we could have made a difference. I came to regret that we did not speak out more force-fully and rally others to do the same. In the aftermath of the crackdown in Iran, I resolved to step up efforts to provide pro-democracy activists with tools and technology to evade government repression and censor-ship. Over the next few years we invested tens of millions of dollars and trained more than five thousand activists around the world.

By September, with Khamenei and Ahmadinejad back firmly in con-trol in Tehran, there was a new flash point. For more than a year, Western intelligence agencies had been monitoring what was believed to be a secret Iranian enrichment facility under construction beneath the mountains near the city of Qom, southwest of Tehran. After the debacle of faulty intelligence about weapons of mass destruction in Iraq, there was under-standable caution in jumping to conclusions regarding Iran, but this was a deeply troubling development. The facility was just months away from completion and, if finished, would enhance Iran's ability to build a nuclear bomb because of its protected location. When the Iranians discovered that we were aware of their deception, they scrambled to cover it up. On September 21, 2009, they delivered a low-key letter to the IAEA admitting the existence of a small pilot project near Qom that had somehow never been mentioned before.

We decided to expose the truth on our own terms. That week world leaders were gathered for the annual meeting of the UN General As-sembly in New York. We knew that public disclosure of Iran's secret enrichment facility near Qom would cause an uproar—one we hoped to use to our advantage. President Obama was set to chair a meeting of the Security Council on nuclear security, and P5+1 negotiators were about to open a new round of talks with the Iranians. We had to choreograph carefully the disclosure with our British and French allies to maximize our leverage with both the Iranians and those countries predisposed to give them the benefit of the doubt, especially Russia and China. If handled deftly, this explosive revelation could tip the diplomatic balance against Iran and help move us toward tougher international sanctions.

In President Obama's suite at the Waldorf Astoria hotel, we huddled to plot our strategy. One option was to have the President make a dramatic presentation of the intelligence about the Qom facility at the Security Council. That would have conjured up memories of both the famous confrontation between U.S. Ambassador to the UN Adlai Stevenson and his Russian counterpart during the Cuban Missile Crisis and the infamous presentation by Secretary of State Colin Powell about Iraqi weapons of mass destruction. Neither was a precedent we wanted to repeat. We also wanted to be sure we had fully coordinated with our allies and briefed the IAEA, the Russians, and the Chinese in advance. So we decided against the UN Security Council route.

On the afternoon of September 23, President Obama, National Security Advisor Jim Jones, and I met in the Waldorf for an hour with Russian President Dmitry Medvedev, his Foreign Minister Sergey Lavrov, and his National Security Advisor Sergei Prikhodko and presented the evidence about Qom. In the first meeting between the two Presidents that spring in London, Medvedev had admitted that Russia had underestimated Iran's nuclear program, but this new information about Iranian deception still shocked the Russians. It was the only time in the four years I served as Secretary that I can remember seeing the steely Lavrov appear flustered and at a loss for words. Afterward Medvedev surprised the press by talking tougher on Iran than they'd ever heard before: "Sanctions rarely lead to productive results—but in some cases sanctions are inevitable." Reporters peppered the White House staff with questions about what had caused the noticeable change in Russian rhetoric, but we weren't ready to go public yet with the Qom news.

Plans took shape for an announcement two days later at the G-20 summit in Pittsburgh, where many of the same world leaders would travel from New York. When the time came, President Obama stepped to the podium alongside British Prime Minister Gordon Brown and French President Nicolas Sarkozy. "The size and configuration of this facility is inconsistent with a peaceful program," President Obama declared. "Iran is breaking rules that all nations must follow."

Events were moving quickly now. On the first day of October, representatives of the P5+1 met in Geneva with an Iranian delegation. I sent Under Secretary of State Bill Burns to represent the United States and meet privately with the Iranian negotiator. Under growing international pressure, Iran agreed to allow IAEA inspectors to visit the secret site near Qom, which they did later that month.

The other item on the agenda in Geneva was the Tehran Research Reactor, which was given to Iran by the United States in the 1960s to produce medical isotopes to be used in diagnosis and treatment of diseases. Over the summer of 2009, Iran reported that it was running out of the nuclear fuel rods needed to power the reactor and produce the isotopes.

While Iran did have a supply of low-enriched uranium, it did not have the higher-enriched uranium required for the fuel rods, so it asked the IAEA for assistance in meeting their fuel needs on the open market. This request caught the eye of American nuclear experts, including the State Department's Bob Einhorn, who began working on a creative plan to solve several problems at once. What if Iran sent all, or at least a significant percentage, of its uranium stockpile abroad, and in return got back fuel rods that could power the research reactor but could not be used for a bomb? That would answer their legitimate needs while setting back their weapons program many months, perhaps up to a year. If the Iranians accepted, we'd have time to work toward a more comprehensive deal that would answer all our concerns about the nuclear program. If they refused, then their true ambitions would be exposed. In August I had discussed the idea with Russia's Lavrov and argued that transferring low-enriched uranium out of Iran would reduce tensions in the region. I hoped that if the United States and Russia worked together to show unity, it would force the Iranians to respond. He agreed, saying, "We should look at this request seriously. We are ready in principle to participate with you."

Now, in the Geneva talks, it was time to put the proposal on the table and see how the Iranians would react. During a lunch break Burns suggested to the chief Iranian negotiator, Saeed Jalili, that they have a direct discussion apart from the bigger group. When Jalili agreed, Burns outlined the terms we were offering. Jalili knew he was facing a united international community and an undeniably fair and reasonable offer. He had no choice but to agree. Einhorn and the Iranian deputy negotiator went over the details point by point. The Iranians accepted all of it, with one proviso: nothing could be said publicly until after they'd gone back to Tehran and shared the agreement with their superiors.

When the negotiators reconvened later in the month at the IAEA in Vienna, the Iranians had changed their tune. Jalili's discussions in Tehran had not gone well. Hard-liners in the government were dead set against the deal. Now the Iranians were saying they were willing to give up a smaller amount of low-enriched uranium, and they wanted to store it in a remote part of Iran rather than send it abroad, both of which were unacceptable. It would defeat the whole purpose of denying them enough enriched uranium to make a bomb. The IAEA urged them to return to the terms of the original agreement, but without success. The Vienna meetings ended in failure. The deal was dead.

As President Obama had promised during his campaign, we had tried to engage Iran. Now, he decided, it was time to ramp up the pressure and sharpen the choice facing Iran's leaders. To impose real consequences, however, we would need the rest of the world to join us.

Susan Rice, our Ambassador to the UN, reported that finding the votes for a strong resolution in the Security Council would be a hard lift. I was hearing the same thing from my foreign counterparts. "We don't think this is the time to discuss sanctions against Iran," Chinese Foreign Minister Yang told me in January 2010. "Once sanctions become the order of the day, it might be difficult to resume talks for a considerable period of time." Yes, China and Russia agreed in principle that Iran should not be allowed to develop or possess nuclear weapons; they just weren't willing to do much to stop it.

Nonetheless I believed that with the wind now at our backs, it was worth trying to overcome this opposition and push tough new sanctions through the Security Council. Throughout the spring of 2010 we worked aggressively to round up the votes. I threw myself into it, with a wide-ranging diplomatic effort that reminded me of backroom negotiations in the Senate, with all the horse trading, arm-twisting, vote counting, alternating appeals to principle and self-interest, and hard-ball politics that go into passing major legislation.

While attention generally focuses on the five permanent members of the Security Council because we each have the power to veto any resolution, there are actually another ten seats on the Council that rotate among other nations selected for two-year terms by the General Assembly. To be adopted, a Security Council resolution must avoid a veto but also garner nine votes out of fifteen total members. That made small countries with rotating seats such as Uganda and Lebanon very important. And it was why I spent time over my four years courting nations that didn't normally play a big role in international affairs, such as Togo, but whose votes I knew we would need at pivotal times.

Assembling nine votes among fifteen skittish Council members proved to be tricky. In one of my many strategy sessions with Britain's David Miliband during this period, he made the point that it was not enough to convince China to hold off on vetoing the resolution; we needed affirmative support in order to bring other undecided votes along. "On our number counting, it otherwise seems dicey," he said. "There is danger if they abstain that we may lose Nigeria, Uganda, Brazil, Turkey." I was doing my own counting and did not believe we would lose Uganda or Nigeria. Brazil and Turkey would be another story. "And it is still an open question if the Russians will vote for the resolution if the Chinese abstain," David continued. "We believe they will," I responded, "but the cost might be a weaker resolution." On it went.

In mid-April I made my pitch to Yoweri Museveni, President of Uganda. Ahmadinejad was due in Uganda the next day, as part of Iran's diplomatic counterattack designed to block new sanctions, so it was crucial that I got to Museveni first to secure his agreement. It helped that I had known him since 1997, when I first visited his country, and that my husband and I had kept in touch with him since. I reminded him that the Obama Administration had tried to engage with Iran and that the international community had made good-faith offers. Iran had rejected every entreaty, defied the international community, and continued to enrich uranium at high levels. I also warned that if diplomacy failed, the result might be military action, which no one wanted to see. This would prove to be a compelling argument for many wavering countries. "We want to work with you to send the most powerful message to Iran and demonstrate that there still is time for Iran to change its behavior," I said.

Museveni was circumspect. "I will tell [Ahmadinejad] two things," he said. "First, we uphold the right of all countries to access nuclear energy for electricity and other uses, and second, we are totally against proliferation of nuclear weapons. This is the message I will put in my written speech for the banquet. I will encourage him to open his country to inspection if he has nothing to hide." I pressed the point: "If you have your experts look at the IAEA report where they lay out the issues, it is hard not to have suspicions." "I agree with you," he replied. "For Iran to have nuclear weapons, that means Saudi Arabia and Egypt will have to do the same. That affects us directly and we can't support that. I will have a frank discussion with the President." In the end Uganda voted for the sanctions.

As Miliband rightly observed, China represented the key vote. If we could convince Beijing to come around, the rest of the Security Council would likely fall into place. In New York, Susan Rice and her team were working with other delegations on language for the sanctions resolution. The Chinese and Russians kept trying to weaken the terms. We made some concessions, but we saw no point in passing another toothless resolution. In April, President Obama invited leaders from around the world to Washington for a summit on nuclear security. He took the opportunity to sit down with Chinese President Hu Jintao to talk about Iran. I listened as the two Presidents went back and forth in a side room off the main Convention Center floor. China had extensive commercial ties with Tehran and depended on Iranian oil to fuel its rapid industrial growth. President Hu agreed that Iran should not acquire nuclear weapons, but he was leery of any steps that felt too aggressive. Finally the two Presidents agreed to back "substantial" measures, without clarifying exactly what that would mean.

Not long afterward I followed up with Chinese State Councilor Dai Bingguo. China was still blocking important elements of the draft sanctions resolution, especially meaningful measures on finance and banking activity directly tied to Iran's illicit nuclear activities. "I must say, China's response, while having evolved helpfully, still falls short of the reciprocal effort we expected from President Hu's conversation with President Obama," I told Dai. "We need to act in a quick and unified manner through a meaningful resolution if we are to reduce the growing risk of conflict in the region and give space for a political solution." I said that lack of international unity and resolve would undermine the interests China was seeking to protect, including maintaining stability in the Middle East, keeping oil prices stable, and protecting the recovery of the global economy. "We want to avoid events that will escape our control," I added.

Dai admitted that he too was dissatisfied, but he remained optimistic. For the moment, so was I. We kept talking to the Chinese and the Russians. The gaps were narrowing, and it felt as though we were getting close to an agreement that would impose the strictest sanctions in history.

But then, just when our goal was in sight, events took another unexpected turn. On May 17, 2010, in a triumphant press conference in Tehran, the Presidents of Brazil, Turkey, and Iran announced they had reached an agreement for Iran to swap low-enriched uranium for reactor fuel rods. Superficially their deal resembled the offer Iran had spurned the previous October. But in fact it was deeply flawed. The deal did not account for the fact that Iran had continued to enrich uranium for several months since the earlier proposal and the transfer of the same amount of uranium would now leave it with a significant stockpile. Unlike in the October agreement, Iranians would retain ownership of the uranium they sent abroad and reserved the right to pull it back at any time. Most troubling, though, was the fact that Iran continued to proclaim its right to enrich uranium to higher levels, and there was nothing in this new agreement to stop it or even to indicate that it would discuss the matter with the IAEA or P5+1. In short, this agreement would address Iran's need to find fuel rods for its research reactor, but it would do precious little to answer the world's concerns about its illegal weapons program. Given the timing, I was sure it was an Iranian attempt to derail our push for sanctions at the UN—and there was a good chance it would succeed.

Ever since the October 2009 agreement collapsed, Turkey and Brazil had been making noises about revisiting it. Both countries held rotating seats on the UN Security Council and were eager to exercise increased influence on the world stage. They were prime examples of the "emerging powers" whose rapid economic growth was fueling big ambitions for regional and global clout. They also happened to have two confident leaders in Luiz Inácio Lula da Silva of Brazil and Recep Tayyip Erdoğan of Turkey, both of whom considered themselves to be men of action able to bend history to their will. Once they had set their sights on brokering a solution on Iran, there was little that could dissuade them from trying, even if only lackluster—or even counterproductive—results emerged.

The United States and the other permanent members of the Security Council reacted cautiously to Brazil and Turkey's early efforts. After so much duplicity, we worried that Iran might exploit the good intentions of Brazil and Turkey in order to protect its nuclear program and fracture the growing international consensus against it. Our concerns grew as it became clear that the Iranians had no intention of stopping their enrichment activities and were suggesting they would give up their uranium in small batches rather than in one big shipment, as originally envisioned. Over time that would mean they would never be without enough nuclear material to build a bomb.

In early March 2010, I visited Lula in Brasília. I explained why this would be a bad outcome and tried to dissuade him from pursuing it, but Lula would not be deterred. He rejected my view that Iran was only playing for time. During my visit I explained publicly, "The door is open for negotiation. We never slammed it shut. But we don't see anybody even in the far-off distance walking toward it." I went on: "We see an Iran that runs to Brazil, an Iran that runs to Turkey, an Iran that runs to China, telling different things to different people to avoid international sanctions."

President Obama followed up with a letter to Lula in April underscoring our concerns: "Iran appears to be pursuing a strategy that is designed to create the impression of flexibility without agreeing to actions that can begin to build mutual trust and confidence." He conveyed the same message to Erdoğan in Turkey. Meanwhile, lending credence to our argument, Iran pledged to continue enriching uranium. Their only goal seemed to be to derail the sanctions drive at the UN.

With Lula set to visit Tehran, I called Brazilian Foreign Minister Celso Amorim and urged him to see the Iranian efforts for what they were, "an elaborate dance." But he was full of confidence for what could be achieved. Finally I grew exasperated and exclaimed, "There has to be an end to the process. At some point, there has to be a day of reckoning." Amorim argued that it might be easier for the Iranians to make a deal with Brazil and Turkey than with the United States. I doubted something positive could come from the meeting and worried that it was happening at a particularly precarious time because we were finally close to an agreement with the Chinese and Russians on the text of a new sanctions resolution at the UN. Neither Moscow nor Beijing were particularly enthusiastic about the process, and I sensed that if they saw an opportunity to bolt and give Iran more time, they would take it in a flash.

That was my immediate concern when I saw the news that Lula, Erdoğan, and Ahmadinejad had reached an agreement. In case there was any doubt, Amorim confirmed it at a press conference. "This plan is a route for dialogue and takes away any grounds for sanctions," he said.

When we spoke afterward, the Foreign Ministers of Brazil and Turkey both tried to sell me on the merits of the deal. They reported on their tough eighteen-hour negotiations and tried to convince me that they had succeeded. I think they were surprised that their triumph was being greeted with such skepticism. But I wanted to see action from Iran, not more words. "We have a saying that the proof is in the pudding," I told Amorim. "I agree that the tasting of the pudding is key, but there must be time to get the spoon out and have time to try it," he replied. To that I replied, "This pudding has been in for over a year now!"

The urgent question now was whether we could hold together the sanctions resolution in the face of this new gambit. We had an agreement in principle with China and Russia, which I hurried to announce as soon as possible after the press conference in Tehran. But until votes were actually cast in New York, nothing was set in stone. When Beijing issued a cautious statement welcoming the Brazil-Turkey deal, I could feel the ground beginning to shift. Fortunately I was scheduled to fly to

China a few days later for high-level talks with the Chinese leadership. Iran would be at the top of the agenda, alongside North Korea and the South China Sea.

Over a long dinner with Dai Bingguo at the Diaoyutai Guesthouse, we talked through the issue. I walked through our objections to the Brazil-Turkey proposal and reminded Dai of the long record of Iranian double-dealing, including the deception at Qom. It was time to resolve any remaining issues with the text of the sanctions resolution, I said. As usual, Dai was thoughtful but firm, with his eye on both the sweep of history and the bottom line. China was uncomfortable with the international community imposing penalties on states except in the most egregious instances, and it certainly did not want any of its commercial interests threatened by sanctions. Compounding their reluctance, only a year earlier we had gone through a similar exercise when seeking to impose tougher sanctions on North Korea. So we were asking them to hold their nose and go along for the second time in as many years.

I reminded Dai that China's main interest in the Middle East was stability, which ensured the steady flow of oil. If our push for sanctions at the UN failed, there would continue to be the potential for military confrontation. That could spike the price of oil and wreak havoc with the global economy. Alternatively, if China chose to reduce its commercial ties to Iran, we could help it find other sources of energy. In the end, I was blunt. This is important to us, I told Dai. If we're going to build a cooperative relationship, as Presidents Obama and Hu had pledged, then we need China to be with us at the Security Council.

By the conclusion of the evening, I felt I had put the process back on track. I cemented that impression in discussions over the next few days with President Hu and Premier Wen. The drive toward new sanctions could continue. "We are pleased with the cooperation that we've received. We have a P5+1 consensus," I announced after my meetings in Beijing. All that was left to do was work out the fine print. "There is a recognition on the part of the international community that the agreement that was reached in Tehran a week ago between Iran, Brazil and Turkey only occurred because the Security Council was on the brink of publicly releasing the text of the resolution that we have been negotiating for many weeks. It was a transparent ploy to avoid Security Council action."

The vote in New York was set for June 9. Susan and her team were still going back and forth with the Chinese on the final list of specific

Iranian companies and banks to sanction, and we were mounting a final push to get more of the nonpermanent members of the Security Council on board. At a minimum we wanted to see abstentions rather than nays.

Meanwhile I had to attend a meeting of the Organization of American States in Lima, Peru. It turned out to be a fortuitous detour. China's Ambassador to the United States, Zhang Yesui, was also in town to attend the OAS meeting, and I invited him to my hotel for a drink. I hoped we could settle the sanctions list once and for all. The J. W. Marriott in Lima is perched atop the Costa Verde cliffs, with a striking view of the Pacific. When Ambassador Zhang arrived, I led him over to a quiet table in the bar where we could talk. I had been visiting with members of the State Department press corps, who were enjoying pisco sours, a local favorite that mixes Peruvian liquor with lime juice, egg whites, and bitters, and many of the reporters remained at the bar. They had no idea that negotiations were going on right under their nose. At one point an ebullient Mark Landler of the *New York Times* approached our table bearing two pisco sours. Who says diplomacy can't be effective and fun at the same time? I smiled and accepted. Zhang politely followed suit. And there, over Peruvian cocktails, we reached a final understanding on the sanctions designations.

The UN Security Council passed Resolution 1929 by a vote of 12 to 2. It imposed the strictest sanctions in history on Iran, targeting the Revolutionary Guard, arms sales, and financial transactions. Only Turkey and Brazil, still unhappy about their failed diplomatic maneuver, voted no. Lebanon abstained after last-minute outreach by me, Vice President Biden, and Transportation Secretary Ray LaHood, a prominent Lebanese American. I had called Lebanese President Michel Suleiman hours before from Colombia and urged him not to vote no, which he was inclined to do based on his political necessities at home. I knew he was navigating some difficult decisions, and I was pleased with the abstention.

The resolution was far from perfect—securing consensus with Russia and China had required compromises—but I was proud of what we had achieved. During the Bush years Iran had managed to play the world's great powers against one another and avoided serious international sanctions for its misdeeds. The Obama Administration changed that.

Despite our success, I knew this was just the beginning. The UN resolution opened the door for much tougher additional unilateral sanctions by the United States and other countries. We had coordinated with Congressional leaders throughout this process, and soon Congress approved a law that would hit even harder at Iran's economy. I was also talking to our European partners about new steps they would take as well.

Even as the pressure built, we kept the offer of engagement on the table. In December 2010, I traveled to Bahrain for a conference on security in the Persian Gulf. We knew that a delegation of Iranian diplomats was also expected to attend. Despite the brief contacts made at previous summits by Richard Holbrooke and Jake Sullivan, I had never yet come face-to-face with an Iranian counterpart. I decided to use the opportunity to send a message. In the middle of my speech at a gala dinner in a Ritz-Carlton ballroom, I paused and said, "At this time, I would like to address directly the delegation at this conference from the government of the Islamic Republic of Iran." The room grew still. The Iranian Foreign Minister Manouchehr Mottaki was sitting just a few seats away. "Nearly two years ago, President Obama extended your government a sincere offer of dialogue. We are still committed to this offer," I said. "You have the right to a peaceful nuclear program. But with that right comes a reasonable responsibility: that you follow the treaty you signed, and fully address the world's concern about your nuclear activities. We urge you to make that choice—for your people, your interests, and our shared security."

Afterward, as dinner was breaking up and everyone was shaking hands, I called out to Mottaki, "Hello, Minister!" He muttered something in Farsi and turned away. A few minutes later we ran into each other again, outside in the driveway. I offered another friendly greeting, and again he refused to reply. I smiled to myself. In his first inaugural address, President Obama had told Iran and other pariah states that we would "extend a hand if you are willing to unclench your fist." Mottaki had just demonstrated how hard this was to achieve. But, in fairness, we *had* just successfully campaigned around the world to impose crippling sanctions on his country. Engagement and pressure. Carrots and sticks. This was the nature of diplomacy, and we were playing a long game.

———

This was the backdrop against which, in January 2011, the Sultan of Oman made his offer to me of secret direct talks with Iran. Engagement through the P5+1 process had stalled. Intercession by well-intentioned third parties had also failed. Again and again Iran had proven to be intransigent and untrustworthy. Yet there was reason to think that, despite all this, the Sultan might actually be able to deliver. After all, he had done it in the case of the imprisoned American hikers.

Back in July 2009, three young Americans were arrested by Iranian security forces while hiking in the mountainous border area between northern Iraq and Iran and charged with espionage. Joshua Fattal, Shane Bauer, and Sarah Shourd were living and working among the Kurds of northern Iraq, and there was no reason to suspect them of being spies. From Washington it was impossible to know exactly what happened or even whether or not the trio had strayed across the border. But the incident echoed the kidnapping of two American journalists near the border between China and North Korea just a few months before and posed an immediate problem. As in North Korea, we had no diplomatic relations with Iran and no embassy in Tehran to provide assistance. We had to rely on the Swiss as our formal "protecting power" to represent us. But the Iranians initially refused to grant consular access to the Swiss diplomats, meaning nobody was allowed to visit the detained Americans, as required under the Vienna Convention that governs diplomatic relations among nations. I made a public appeal for the hikers' release, which I repeated frequently over the following months, and enlisted the Swiss to send private messages as well.

We stayed in close touch with the hikers' distraught families, and in November, I invited them to my office at the State Department so we could meet in person. It took months for the Swiss Ambassador in Tehran to get into the notorious Evin Prison to see the three Americans. They had been held for months without formal charges or access to legal representation. With the help of the Swiss, the mothers of the hikers were given visas to travel to Iran just after Mother's Day. I met with them again before they left and sent my prayers with them to Tehran. They were permitted a tearful reunion with their children but were not allowed to bring them home. The whole scene was used by Iran as a publicity stunt.

Throughout this ordeal I tried every back channel we could find to persuade the Iranians to release the hikers. I asked Jake Sullivan to take on the project. At a conference in Kabul, Afghanistan, in the summer of 2010, I sent Jake to hand the Iranian Foreign Minister a message about the hikers, just as we had done the year before in The Hague for the other detained Americans. But the key contact was in Oman. One of the Sultan's top advisors approached Dennis Ross, President Obama's top Iran advisor, and offered to serve as a go-between.

The Omanis were as good as their word. In September 2010, Sarah Shourd was released on bail. Once she left Iran, I called the Sultan to thank him and see what could be done about the remaining two hikers (it would take another year to win their release as well). "We are always ready to do what's right to help," the Sultan told me. His comment was still in my head as we sat and talked in January 2011.

Freeing a detained hiker was a far cry from facilitating sensitive talks about the future of Iran's nuclear program. But the Sultan had shown he could get results. So I listened carefully to his proposal for a new substantive back channel, and I asked if we could be sure that the Iranian side would actually be authorized to negotiate in good faith. After all, we'd invested lots of time in the P5+1 process, only to see the agreement made in the room overruled back in Tehran. The Sultan couldn't make any promises, but he wanted to try. I agreed that if we proceeded, absolute secrecy would be needed. We didn't want another circus with lots of posturing for the press and political pressure from back home. Even under the best of circumstances, this was a long shot. But it was worth testing. I told the Sultan I would talk with President Obama and my colleagues in Washington but that we should begin thinking about how to put his plan into motion.

For the next several months, we proceeded cautiously. There were real concerns about whom we would be talking to and what their motivations were. President Obama was wary, but interested. He called the Sultan himself at one point to probe the viability of the diplomatic channel. We kept the circle small. Bill Burns, Jake, and I worked with a tight team at the White House that included Tom Donilon, by then the National Security Advisor; his Deputy, Denis McDonough; Dennis Ross, until his departure in November 2011; and Puneet Talwar, the national security staff's Senior Director for Iran, Iraq, and the Gulf States. The Omanis passed messages back and forth with us about how talks might take shape and what kind of delegation would be sent. To no one's surprise, it was difficult to get straight answers out of the Iranians on even the simplest questions.

In the fall our confidence about proceeding took a hit when U.S. law enforcement and intelligence agencies uncovered an Iranian plot to assassinate the Saudi Ambassador in Washington. An Iranian national was arrested at the airport in New York and confessed to an elaborate scheme right out of a show like *24* or *Homeland*. It involved attempting to recruit a Mexican drug cartel to bomb a restaurant where the Ambassador was known to eat. Fortunately the Mexican hit man turned out to be an informant for the U.S. Drug Enforcement Administration. We had evidence suggesting the conspiracy was conceived, sponsored, and directed by senior officials in Iran. Not long after, the chief of Iran's Navy unnerved global markets by warning that it could close the Strait of Hormuz at any time, which would choke off much of the world's oil supplies.

At this point, in October 2011, I decided to return to Muscat and pay a second visit to the Sultan. He was still keen to get talks going and suggested that we send an advance team to Oman to discuss the logistical issues in person, since passing messages wasn't going so well. I agreed, so long as the Iranians were serious, and the Sultan could provide us with assurances that they would speak for the supreme leader. I also urged the Sultan to convey a stern warning to the Iranians about the Strait of Hormuz. After the conversation, we began making secret arrangements to send Jake and Puneet and a small team to begin these conversations. Senator John Kerry talked to an Omani close to the Sultan and kept us informed of what he heard.

For the delicate first meeting with the Iranians, Jake was not the most experienced diplomat at the State Department I could have chosen, but he was discreet and had my absolute confidence. His presence would send a powerful message that I was personally invested in this process. In early July 2012, Jake quietly left one of my trips in Paris and caught his own flight to Muscat. His destination was such a closely held secret that other members of my traveling team, colleagues who worked with him around the clock both at home and on the road, assumed that he had a family emergency of some kind and were worried about him. Remarkably they did not learn of his true mission until reading about it in the press more than a year later.

Once on the ground in Oman, Jake and Puneet slept on the couch at an empty embassy house. The Iranian advance team came with a series of demands and preconditions, none of which was acceptable. They were there, which was something in and of itself, but clearly skittish, perhaps reflecting an ambivalent and divided leadership back in Tehran. Jake reported his impression that the Iranians weren't yet ready to engage seriously. We agreed to keep the channel open and to wait and see if conditions improved.

Throughout this period, even as we pursued this secret avenue of engagement, we worked steadily to increase international pressure on the Iranian regime and counter its aggressive ambitions. One priority was to expand our military partnerships in the Gulf and deploy new military resources across the region to reassure our partners and deter Iranian aggression. We stayed in close and constant coordination with Israel and took unprecedented steps to protect its military superiority over any potential rivals. I asked Andrew Shapiro, my longtime Senate aide and now Assistant Secretary of State for Political-Military Affairs, to help make sure Israel was equipped with highly advanced weapons systems like the F-35 Joint Strike Fighter. We worked with the Israelis to develop and build a multilayered air defense network that included upgraded versions of the Patriot missiles originally deployed in the 1991 Gulf War, new advanced early warning radar, antirocket batteries called "the Iron Dome," and other systems to protect against ballistic missiles known as "David's Sling" and the "Arrow-3 Interceptor." During the conflict with Hamas in Gaza in late 2012, the Iron Dome proved effective in protecting Israeli homes and communities.

I also spent many hours with Israeli Prime Minister Benjamin Netanyahu discussing our dual-track strategy and trying to convince him that sanctions could work. We agreed that a credible threat of military force was important—which is why President Obama and I repeatedly said "All options are on the table"—but we had different views on how much we should telegraph in public. I told him that President Obama was serious when he said we would not allow Iran to acquire a nuclear bomb and that "containment" was not our policy. Containment might have worked with the Soviet Union, but given Iran's ties to terrorism and the volatility of the region, we didn't think a nuclear-armed Iran was any more acceptable—or containable—than the Israelis did. So all options really were on the table, including military force.

In addition to our work with the Israelis, the Obama Administration also increased America's own sea and air presence in the Persian Gulf and deepened our ties to the Gulf monarchies, who viewed Iran with great alarm. I worked with the Gulf Cooperation Council on a dedicated ongoing security dialogue, and we conducted joint military exercises with

GCC members. Convincing Turkey to host a major radar installation also helped us build a new missile defense system that would protect our allies in Europe from a possible Iranian attack.

Even as we shored up our defenses, we also went on the offense to increase pressure on Iran in the hopes of changing its leaders' calculus. Through legislation and executive action, the Obama Administration and Congress worked together to pile on tougher and tougher sanctions, all building on the original Security Council measures put in place in the summer of 2010. Our goal was to put so much financial pressure on Iran's leaders, including on the military's growing number of business ventures, that they would have no choice but to come back to the negotiating table with a serious offer. We would go after Iran's oil industry, banks, and weapons programs. And we would enlist insurance companies, shipping lines, energy traders, financial institutions, and many other actors to cut Iran off from global commerce. Most of all, I would make it my mission to convince the top consumers of Iran's oil to diversify their supplies and buy less from Tehran. With each one who agreed, Iran's coffers took another big hit. Iran's lifeblood was its oil; it was the world's third largest exporter of crude, which brought in much-needed hard currency. So we did everything we could to make it harder for Iran to do business, particularly around oil.

The Europeans were essential partners in this effort, and when all twenty-seven members of the European Union agreed to impose a full boycott of Iranian oil, it was a huge blow. Bob Einhorn, the expert who helped craft the original October 2009 Tehran Research Reactor swap plan, and Under Secretary of Treasury David Cohen went to work finding the most creative and effective ways to enforce all our new sanctions. Freezing the assets of Iranian banks made it impossible for Iranian tankers to buy insurance on the international market and cut off access to global financial networks. It was a full-court press.

Under a new law signed by President Obama in December 2011, other countries had to demonstrate every six months that they were meaningfully reducing consumption of Iranian oil or face sanctions themselves. To put this into practice, I turned to our newly created Bureau of Energy Resources, headed by Carlos Pascual. Everywhere Iran tried to sell its oil, our team was there, offering up alternative suppliers and explaining the financial risks of conducting a transaction with a global pariah. Iran's major customers faced difficult choices with significant economic consequences. Thankfully many of them showed far-sighted leadership by embracing the opportunity to diversify their energy portfolios.

We were just as active in places like Angola, Nigeria, South Sudan, and the Persian Gulf, encouraging Iran's competitors to pump and sell more of their own oil, to keep the market balanced and prevent damaging price spikes. Iraq's resurgent oil industry, long a U.S. priority, proved invaluable. But the most crucial new supplies came from our own backyard. As American domestic oil and gas production increased dramatically, thanks to new technologies and exploration, our energy imports plummeted. This took pressure off the global market and made it easier to exclude Iran, as other nations could rely on the supply America no longer required.

The biggest consumers of Iranian oil, and the hardest to convince to turn off the spigot, were in Asia. China and India, in particular, depended on Iranian oil to meet their rapidly expanding energy needs. The advanced economies of South Korea and Japan were also highly dependent on imported oil. Japan faced an added burden because of the meltdown of the Fukushima nuclear plant and the resulting moratorium on nuclear power. Nonetheless the Japanese pledged to cut their consumption of Iranian oil significantly, a courageous commitment under the circumstances.

India, by contrast, initially publicly refused Western entreaties to reduce their reliance on Iranian oil. In our private conversations Indian leaders agreed that peace in the Middle East was important and were acutely aware that 6 million Indians lived and worked in the Gulf and could be vulnerable to political or economic instability. At the same time, though, India's fast-growing economy depended on a steady supply of energy, and they worried that their energy needs were so great that there was no viable way to meet them without Iranian oil. Left unsaid was another reason for their reluctance: India, which had championed the "nonaligned movement" during the Cold War and still prized its "strategic autonomy," simply hated to be told what to do. The more loudly we urged them to change course, the more likely they were to dig in their heels.

In May 2012, I visited New Delhi to make the case in person. I argued that maintaining a unified international front was the best way to persuade Iran to return to the negotiating table, achieve a diplomatic solution to the impasse, and avoid a destabilizing military conflict. I outlined the advantages of a diversified energy supply and talked about potential alternatives to Iran available on the market. I also assured the Indians that, if they took positive steps, we would make clear that it was their decision, however they chose to characterize it. All we cared about was the end result, not beating our chest. That seemed to make a difference. When Minister of External Affairs S. M. Krishna and I went out to talk to the media, we were of course asked about the Iran issue. I deferred to Krishna to answer first. "Given our growing demand, it is natural for us to try and diversify our sources of imports of oil and gas to meet the objective of energy security," he said. "Since you asked a specific question about Iran, it remains an important source of oil for us, although its share in our imports are declining, which is well known. Ultimately, it reflects the decision that refineries make based on commercial, financial and technical considerations." That was good enough for me. I promised Krishna that I would send Carlos and his team of experts to Delhi to help speed those "totally non-Iran-related" decisions.

In the end our efforts led to every major Iranian customer, even the most reluctant, agreeing to reduce their purchases of Iran's oil. The result was dramatic. Inflation in Iran soared by more than 40 percent, and the value of the Iranian currency declined dramatically. Oil exports declined from 2.5 million barrels of crude each day in early 2012 to around 1 million, which resulted in a loss of more than $80 billion in revenue.

Iranian oil tankers sat idle, with no markets to visit and no foreign investors or insurance companies willing to back them, and Iranian jets rusted in their hangars, with no replacement parts available. Big multinational companies like Shell, Toyota, and Deutsche Bank began pulling out of Iran. Even Ahmadinejad, who long tried to deny that sanctions would have any effect, began complaining about the "economic assault."

For years I had been talking about "crippling sanctions," and now it was coming true. Bibi Netanyahu told me he liked the phrase so much that he had adopted it as his own. I took pride in the coalition we assembled and the effectiveness of our efforts, but no pleasure in the hardship that Iran's people suffered because of their leaders' choice to continue defying the international community. We made every effort to ensure that the sanctions didn't deprive Iranians of food, medicines, and other humanitarian goods. And I looked for opportunities to emphasize that our quarrel was with the government of Iran, not its citizens, including in an interview broadcast in Farsi on Voice of America's *Parazit* program,

Iran's equivalent of *The Daily Show*. The people of Iran deserved a better future, but that would not be possible unless their leaders changed course.

Through it all, Iran remained defiant. It continued to be linked to new terrorist plots around the world, in Bulgaria, Georgia, and Thailand. Tehran worked to undermine neighboring governments and incited unrest from Bahrain to Yemen and beyond. It poured money and weapons into Syria to prop up its ally Bashar al-Assad and support his brutal crackdown against the Syrian people. Eventually it sent in Revolutionary Guard trainers and Hezbollah fighters to further bolster Assad. And, of course, it continued to advance its nuclear program in violation of Security Council resolutions and refused to engage in good faith with the P5+1. In public President Obama and I stressed that the window for diplomacy was still open but that it would not remain so forever. In private we maintained some hope that the Omani channel would ultimately yield progress. The more pressure we mounted and the more the Iranian economy crumbled, the more incentive Tehran had to reconsider its posture.

═══

That's exactly what started happening toward the end of 2012, just as my time at the State Department began to draw to a close. Iran's economy, regional position, and international reputation were all in shambles. President Ahmadinejad's second term was a disaster, and his political standing at home had collapsed, along with his once close relationship with the Supreme Leader and other powerful conservatives and clerics who truly held the levers of power in Iran. Meanwhile the Omanis indicated that the Iranians were finally getting ready to move forward on the long-awaited secret talks. They wanted to send a Deputy Foreign Minister to meet with my Deputy Bill Burns in Muscat. We agreed.

In March 2013, a few weeks after my term as Secretary ended, Bill and Jake returned to Oman to see what this new opening might yield. The answer was still disappointing. The Iranians seemed to be struggling with what to do. Some elements of their government clearly favored serious engagement, but other powerful forces were holding the negotiators back. Once again our team came home with the impression that the time was not yet ripe for a breakthrough.

Then events intervened once more. That spring Iran geared up for new elections to replace Ahmadinejad as President. It was hard to believe it had already been four years since massive protests filled the streets of Tehran after the previous vote. Since then the regime had been ruthless in driving political opposition underground and stamping out dissent. In keeping with this record, the authorities handpicked every candidate in the 2013 race and disqualified anyone not deemed conservative or loyal enough. They even barred Ali Akbar Hashemi Rafsanjani, a leader of the 1979 revolution, former President, and influential cleric, because he was perceived to present a challenge to the regime. The eight candidates who made it through all had close ties to the Supreme Leader and solid regime credentials. In short, the powers that be in Iran were playing it as safe as possible.

Saeed Jalili, the country's dogmatic nuclear negotiator, was seen as the Ayatollah's preferred choice and therefore the presumed front-runner. He campaigned on vacuous slogans about "Islamic development" and avoided talking much about the failing economy or questioning Iran's disastrous foreign policy. Out among the people, there seemed to be little interest or excitement for the election, which was the regime's goal. But frustration was not hard to find. Western media quoted a forty-year-old garage owner outside Qom, the city with the secret nuclear facility unmasked in 2009, grumbling about the economy: "I love Islam, but how do we fix 100 percent inflation? I'll vote for anybody with a good plan, but until now I haven't seen any candidate with clear ideas for the future."

Then, in the final days before the June election, something remarkable happened. In the middle of the regime's carefully orchestrated election, these frustrations burst into public view, and the contradictions and failures of the regime's policies were suddenly being questioned before the entire country. In an explosive nationally televised debate, Jalili's opponents went after him aggressively for his mismanagement of the country's nuclear policy and the terrible toll it had taken on the economy. "Being conservative does not mean being inflexible and stubborn," said Ali-Akbar Velayati, a former Foreign Minister with a reputation as a hard-liner. "We can't expect everything and give nothing," Mohsen Rezaei, a former senior commander in the Islamic Revolutionary Guard, piled on, questioning the mantra of resistance against the world. "Do you mean that we have to resist and keep people hungry?" he asked. Jalili tried to defend his stonewalling at the most recent P5+1 talks—"They wanted to exchange a jewel for candy," he protested—and invoked the Supreme Leader in his defense. But that didn't stop the attacks. Hassan

Rouhani, a former chief nuclear negotiator himself and the closest person to a moderate in the race because of his talk of "constructive interaction with the world," slammed Jalili for allowing Iran to be sanctioned at the UN Security Council. "All of our problems stem from this," he said. "It's good to have centrifuges running, providing people's lives and sustenance are also spinning." Iranians watching at home must have been in a state of shock. They had rarely been allowed to witness a debate like this before.

On Election Day, in June 2013, Iranians turned out in surprisingly large numbers and elected Rouhani in a landslide. This time there would be no attempt to reverse the results or steal the election. Crowds gathered in the streets chanting, "Long live reform." Rouhani took office in August and immediately began making conciliatory statements toward the international community and even tweeted good wishes on Rosh Hashanah, the Jewish New Year.

I was now a private citizen, but I watched all this with great interest and a healthy dose of skepticism. The Supreme Leader still held all the real power, especially when it came to the nuclear program and foreign policy. He had allowed Rouhani's election and was so far tolerating all this talk of a new direction, even quietly defending the new President against attacks from unsettled hard-liners, all of which perhaps meant that he understood how unsustainable the regime's policies had become. But there was no reason yet to believe that he had fundamentally decided to change course on any of the core issues at the heart of Iran's belligerence toward its region and much of the world.

But behind the scenes, after the election of Rouhani, the Omani channel was heating up. The Sultan was the first foreign leader to visit Rouhani in Tehran. President Obama sent another letter and this time got a positive response. In Muscat, Bill and Jake, who was by this time Vice President Biden's National Security Advisor, resumed meeting with Iranian officials, who were finally empowered to negotiate from the highest levels. Maintaining strict secrecy was more important than ever, to preserve Rouhani's fragile credibility back home. Relatively quickly the outlines of a preliminary deal began to take shape. Iran would halt advances in its nuclear program and allow new inspections for six months in exchange for modest sanctions relief. That would open a window for intense negotiations to address the international community's concerns and resolve all outstanding issues. Under Secretary of State for Political Affairs Wendy Sherman, an experienced negotiator and the first woman to hold that position, joined the discussions in Oman and helped hammer out the details.

The teams also discussed the possibility of a historic face-to-face meeting between Presidents Obama and Rouhani in New York at the UN General Assembly in late September. At the very last minute, however, the Iranians failed to deliver on the meeting, an indication that divisions and misgivings continued inside the regime. But the two leaders did speak on the phone—as Rouhani's limousine was driving him to the airport for his flight home. It was the first such conversation since 1979. My successor, Secretary Kerry, met with the new Iranian Foreign Minister, Javad Zarif, and the administration began briefing key allies about the progress achieved in the secret talks. Israeli Prime Minister Netanyahu warned in a speech to the UN that Rouhani was a "wolf in sheep's clothing."

In October, the secret Oman channel began to merge with the official P5+1 process in Geneva that Wendy Sherman had been leading for the United States. Bill and Jake participated, but they took elaborate measures to stay out of sight of the press, including staying at a separate hotel and going in and out of service entrances.

In November, Secretary Kerry flew to Geneva twice in the hopes of pushing the negotiations over the finish line. There were still big concerns to work out: Would Iran stop all enrichment of uranium, or could it be allowed to continue enriching to a level far below what was needed for a bomb? For Rouhani, maintaining even a low level of enrichment provided him important political cover. But the Israelis and others thought that such a concession would set a dangerous precedent. Then there was the question of how much sanctions relief to provide. Again some were against giving any ground unless Iran took irreversible and verifiable steps to dismantle its nuclear program. Bibi scoffed that the P5+1 was preparing to offer Iran the "deal of the century" on a silver platter.

Kerry and Wendy pressed ahead with President Obama's backing and, along with our partners, managed to fashion a compromise. Iran agreed to eliminate its stockpile of higher-enriched uranium and continue enriching only to 5 percent (far below weapons grade); keep thousands of centrifuges offline, including all of its next-generation centrifuges; allow intrusive inspections; and stop work on new facilities, including a plutonium reactor. In return the international community would provide several billion dollars in sanctions relief, mostly from previously frozen Iranian assets. From the White House President Obama hailed the deal as "an important first step toward a comprehensive solution" and credited years of patient diplomacy and pressure.

When we came into office back in 2009, the international community was fractured, diplomacy was stalled, and the Iranians were marching steadily toward a nuclear weapon. Our dual-track strategy of engagement and pressure reversed those trends, united the world, and finally forced Iran back to the negotiating table. I remained skeptical that the Iranians would deliver a final comprehensive agreement; I had seen too many false hopes dashed over the years to allow myself to get too optimistic now. But this was the most promising development in a long time, and it was worth testing to see what could be achieved.

Although it took five years to get this initial deal, the hardest work was still ahead. All the tough issues that had bedeviled Iran's relationship with the international community are still unresolved. And even if the nuclear issue was eventually satisfactorily settled by an enforceable agreement, Iran's support for terrorism and its aggressive behavior in the region would remain a threat to the national security of the United States and our allies.

Going forward, Iran's leaders—its Supreme Leader in particular—face real choices about the future. At the time of the Iranian Revolution in 1979, Iran's economy was nearly 40 percent larger than Turkey's; in 2014 this is reversed. Is the country's nuclear program worth beggaring an illustrious civilization and impoverishing a proud people? If Iran had a nuclear weapon tomorrow, would that create even one more job for a country where millions of young people are out of work? Would it send one more Iranian to college or rebuild the roads and ports still crumbling from the war with Iraq a generation ago? When Iranians look abroad, would they rather end up like North Korea or South Korea?

19

Syria: A Wicked Problem

"History is a somber judge—and it will judge us all harshly if we prove incapable of taking the right path today," said Kofi Annan as he looked around the table at the Ministers who had answered his invitation to come to Geneva's Palais des Nations at the end of June 2012 in hopes of resolving the bloody civil war raging in Syria.

Kofi had been through his share of difficult diplomatic negotiations. As the seventh Secretary-General of the United Nations, from 1997 to 2006, the soft-spoken Ghanaian had won the Nobel Peace Prize. "Collectively, you have the potential to wield tremendous power and to change the direction of this crisis," he told us. "By being here today, you suggest the intention to show that leadership." Yet, as Kofi knew well, opinion in the room was sharply divided over what kind of leadership was actually needed.

The crisis began in early 2011, when Syrian citizens, inspired in part by the successful peaceful protests in Tunisia and Egypt, took to the streets to demonstrate against the authoritarian regime of Bashar al-Assad. As in Libya, security forces responded with excessive force and mass detentions, which in turn eventually led some Syrians to take up arms to defend themselves and, eventually, to try to topple Assad. It was a lopsided fight, however, and by June 2011, the regime had killed about 1,300 people, including children. (As of early 2014, estimates put the total killed at more than 150,000, but that is likely too low.)

In early 2010, about a year before the maelstrom began in Syria, I recommended that the President nominate Robert Ford, an experienced diplomat who had served across the Middle East, most recently in Iraq, as the first U.S. Ambassador to Syria in more than five years. It was not an easy decision. The United States had withdrawn our Ambassador to signal displeasure with the Syrian regime, and returning one might be taken as an endorsement of Assad. But I thought then, and continue to believe now, that we are generally better served by having an Ambassador on the ground, even with regimes we strongly oppose, to deliver messages and serve as our eyes and ears.

President Obama agreed with my recommendation and nominated Robert in February 2010. He was held up by the Senate because of opposition, not to him personally (his credentials were stellar) but to the idea of sending an Ambassador to Syria at all. Just after Christmas the President used his Constitutional authority to make appointments during the Congressional recess to put Robert in place. He arrived in Damascus in January 2011, just in time to get settled before the demonstrations began. Protests escalated in March, and security forces opened fire and killed protesters in Daraa. Assad deployed the Army. Government forces laid siege to Daraa at the end of April, deploying tanks and conducting sweeps of houses.

The United States strongly condemned all violence against civilians. As a result Ambassador Ford and our embassy team faced harassment and threats, including one serious incident in July 2011, when pro-government protesters breached the embassy compound, smashed windows, sprayed graffiti, and attacked Robert's residence.

Despite the danger, he went to Hama, the scene of an infamous 1982 massacre, to meet with protesters and express American solidarity and sympathy with those calling for democratic reform. As Robert drove into the city, residents covered his car with flowers. He visited a hospital where people injured by Syrian security forces were being treated, and he tried to learn more about the protesters, what their objectives were and how to establish ongoing contact with them. That visit established Robert's status as our lead in working with the opposition. Many of the same Senators who had blocked his confirmation were so impressed with his courage and intelligence that they voted to confirm him in early October. This was another example of an experienced diplomat taking risks to get out from behind the embassy's walls to do the job right.

Despite an international outcry over the violence in Syria, Russia and China vetoed a modest resolution at the UN Security Council in October 2011 that would have condemned Assad's human rights abuses and demanded that peaceful protests be allowed to proceed. Russia had long-standing political ties with Syria, dating back to the Cold War, including an important naval base on Syria's Mediterranean coast, and there were religious ties between Syria's Orthodox Christians and the Russian Orthodox Church. Russia was determined to retain its influence and steadfastly backed the Assad regime.

Bashar al-Assad is the son of Hafez al-Assad, who seized control of Syria in 1970 and served as its leader for thirty years until his death in June 2000. A trained ophthalmologist, Bashar was groomed as his father's successor only after his older brother's death in a car accident in 1994, and he assumed the presidency following his father's death. Bashar's wife, Asma, had a career in investment banking before becoming First Lady. A 2005 profile of the couple said, "They seemed the essence of secular Western-Arab fusion." But, as the article noted, this image was a "mirage," as the high hopes for the new Syrian ruler turned into "a pattern of empty promises, nasty oratory and bloody tactics." As unrest spread across the Middle East, it was these "empty promises" and unrealized hopes that motivated many of the protests of the Syrian people.

Assad and his ruling clique were Alawites, a Shiite sect closely aligned with Iran that had ruled over the Sunni majority in Syria for decades, going back to the French mandate after World War I. Alawites made up 12 percent of the country. The rebels were predominantly Sunnis, who constituted more than 70 percent of the population, while the Kurds made up 9 percent. Another 10 percent of Syrians are Christians, and approximately 3 percent are Druze, a sect originating from Shiite Islam with elements of Christianity, Judaism, and other beliefs. As the crisis unfolded, one of the biggest challenges we faced was helping the opposition unite across the country's many religious, geographic, and ideological lines.

In October 2011, the Arab League demanded a cease-fire in Syria and called on the Assad regime to pull its troops back from the major cities, release political prisoners, protect access for journalists and humanitarian workers, and begin a dialogue with the protesters. Most predominantly Sunni Arab countries, especially Saudi Arabia and the other Gulf states, backed the rebels and wanted Assad gone. Under pressure from his neighbors, Assad nominally agreed to the Arab League plan, but then almost immediately disregarded it. Regime forces continued killing protesters in the following days. In response the Arab League suspended Syria's membership.

In December, the Arab League tried again. As before, Assad agreed to their plan. This time, though, Arab monitors were sent to Syria's battle-scarred cities. Unfortunately even the presence of this international monitoring team did little to calm the violence, and once again it quickly became clear that Assad had no intention of keeping his word. In late January 2012, the Arab League pulled the observers out in frustration and asked the UN Security Council to back its call for a political transition in Syria that would require Assad to hand over power to a Vice President and establish a government of national unity.

By this point the regime's Army was using tanks to shell residential suburbs of Damascus. The rebels' determination to resist at all costs was hardening; some were becoming radicalized, and extremists were joining the fight. Jihadist groups, including some with ties to al Qaeda, began trying to exploit the conflict to advance their own agendas. Refugees were fleeing across Syria's borders in large numbers into Jordan, Turkey, and Lebanon. (As of 2014, there were more than 2.5 million refugees from the Syrian conflict.)

At the end of January 2012, I attended a special session of the Security Council in New York to hear the Arab League's report and debate how to respond. "We all have a choice," I told the Council. "Stand with the people of Syria and the region or become complicit in the continuing violence there."

A new resolution supporting the Arab League's peace plan ran into the same trouble as previous attempts. The Russians were implacably opposed to anything that might constitute pressure on Assad. The year before, they had abstained in the vote to authorize a no-fly zone over Libya and to take "all necessary measures" to protect civilians and then chafed as the NATO-led mission to protect civilians accelerated the fall of Qaddafi. Now, with Syria in chaos, they were determined to prevent another

Western intervention. Assad's regime was too strategically important to them. Libya was "a false analogy," I argued in New York. The resolution did not impose sanctions or support the use of military force, focusing instead on the need for a peaceful political transition. Still the Russians weren't having any of it.

I spoke with Russian Foreign Minister Sergey Lavrov from my plane on the way to the Munich Security Conference and then met there with him in person. I told him we needed a unified message from the international community. Moscow wanted the resolution to be tougher on the rebels than on the regime. Lavrov pressed me on what would happen when Assad refused to comply. Would the next step be a Libya-style intervention? No, I responded. The plan was to use this resolution to pressure Assad to negotiate. "He'll only get the message when the Security Council speaks with one voice. We have gone very far in clarifying this isn't a Libya scenario. There is not any kind of authorization for force or intervention or military action."

The Russian rhetoric about upholding sovereignty and opposing foreign intervention rang particularly hollow given their track record elsewhere. In 2008 and 2014, Putin did not hesitate to send troops into Georgia and Ukraine, violating the sovereignty of those countries, simply because it suited his interests.

As Lavrov and I talked in Munich, there was a surge in violence in Syria. Regime forces targeted Homs, the country's third largest city and a cradle of the rebellion, with a barrage of shelling that killed hundreds. It was the bloodiest day in the conflict thus far.

I told Lavrov that every word in the resolution in New York had been thoroughly debated. We had made concessions, while keeping the minimum of what we hoped would end the violence and begin a transition. Now it was time to vote. The resolution would be called to the floor that day.

"But what is the endgame?" Lavrov asked. Sitting there in Munich, I could not predict every step to come, and I knew it would be a mistake to minimize the challenges Syrians would face after Assad. But I was sure about one thing: if we did not begin a peace process, the endgame would be grim indeed. There would be more bloodshed, hardening defiance from those whose families were being brutalized and whose homes were being bombed, and a greater likelihood that a full-blown civil war would attract extremists, possibly resulting in a failed state, with different areas of the country controlled by warring factions, including terrorist groups. Every additional day of repression and violence made it more difficult for Syrians to reconcile and rebuild and increased the risk of instability and sectarian conflict spreading from Syria across the region.

A few hours after my meeting with Lavrov, the Security Council convened and called for a vote. I went before the press corps in Munich, saying, "Are we for peace and security and a democratic future, or are we going to be complicit in the continuing violence and bloodshed? I know where the United States stands, and we will soon find out where every other member of the Security Council stands." Even after the bloodiest day yet in Syria, Russia and China used their veto power to prevent the world from condemning the violence. To block this resolution was to bear responsibility for the horrors on the ground. It was, as I said later, despicable.

As predicted, the situation kept getting worse. The UN and the Arab League named Kofi Annan as their Joint Special Envoy on Syria at the end of February. His mandate was to convince the regime, the rebels, and their respective foreign backers to agree on a political resolution to the conflict.

To support this new diplomatic track, I helped pull together a meeting of like-minded countries to consider other avenues for increasing pressure on the regime and providing humanitarian assistance to suffering civilians, since our first choice was blocked at the UN. We supported diplomacy, but we weren't going to just wait for it. The roster of those who felt equally compelled to act kept swelling, and we ultimately had more than sixty nations come together in Tunisia at the end of February for what became known as the Friends of the Syrian People. We formed a sanctions working group to cut off Assad's access to funds (although the Russians and Iranians were quite effective in replenishing his coffers), pledged to send emergency supplies to refugees fleeing the violence, and increased training of Syrian civilian opposition leaders.

Behind the scenes there was a lot of talk in Tunis about funneling weapons to the rebels to begin evening the odds against the regime's Army and its Iranian and Russian backers. Our partners in the Gulf were watching Sunni rebels and civilians being slaughtered live on Al Jazeera, and they were increasingly impatient. Saudi Foreign Minister Prince Saud al-Faisal said he thought supplying weapons was "an excellent idea." I understood his frustration at how things were going and the desire to shift the military balance on the ground. But there were also reasons to be wary of further militarizing the situation and accelerating the spiral to full-scale civil war. Once guns went into the country, they would be hard to control and could easily fall into the hands of extremists.

Assad's backers had no such worries. Iranian forces from the Revolutionary Guard and its elite paramilitary unit, the Quds Force, were already in Syria supporting Assad and the Syrian military. The Iranians were playing a key advisory role, accompanying Syrian forces to the field and helping the regime organize its own paramilitary forces. Militants from Hezbollah, Iran's proxies in Lebanon, also joined the fight on behalf of the Syrian regime. The combined Iranian-Hezbollah presence was critical to the regime's grasp on power.

I asked Prince Saud if he thought Assad would cooperate with a plan to end the violence and commence a political transition, if we could convince the Russians to agree on one. He did not think so, he said, because Assad's family would never permit him. Led by his mother, he was under constant pressure to uphold his family's position and follow his father's brutal example of how to suppress an uprising. That was a reference to when Hafez al-Assad infamously destroyed the city of Hama in 1982 in retaliation for another uprising.

In Riyadh, at the end of March, I met with Prince Saud and King Abdullah and participated in the first meeting of a new strategic partnership between the United States and all six Gulf countries. Much of the focus was on the threat from Iran, but we also discussed the need to do more to support the rebels in Syria. Late that night I flew to Istanbul, where I met with representatives from Turkey, Saudi Arabia, the UAE, and Qatar and heard the same messages about the need to get arms to the rebels.

I was in a difficult position. On the one hand, the United States was not prepared to join such efforts to arm the rebels, but we also didn't want to splinter the anti-Assad coalition or lose leverage with the Arab countries. "Some will be able to do certain things, and others will do other things," I said carefully in Riyadh. "So when we talk about assistance, we are talking about a broad range of assistance. Not every country will do the same." That was as close as I could get to publicly acknowledging what was a fait accompli: Certain countries would increase their efforts to funnel arms, while others would focus on humanitarian needs. (As of April 2014, the

United States had pledged more than $1.7 billion in such assistance and is the largest donor of aid for displaced Syrians.)

March 2012 marked the one-year anniversary of the uprising in Syria, and the UN estimated that the death toll by then stood at more than eight thousand. Kofi Annan was methodically meeting with all the players, including Assad himself, trying to thread the diplomatic needle and end the conflict before the casualties mounted any higher. In the middle of the month he unveiled a six-point plan. It was similar to what the Arab League had tried earlier in the year. Kofi called on the Assad regime to pull back its military forces and silence their heavy weapons, allow peaceful demonstrations and access to Syria for humanitarian aid and journalists, and begin a political transition that addressed the legitimate aspirations and concerns of the Syrian people. In an effort to win Russian agreement, he proposed that the UN Security Council ratify his plan in a less weighty "statement" rather than a full resolution. That helped reassure Moscow that it would not be used as a legal basis for military intervention later on. The Western powers went along because it meant finally getting the Security Council on record. In the statement the Council called for a cease-fire and directed Kofi to "facilitate a Syrian-led political transition to a democratic, plural political system . . . including through commencing a comprehensive political dialogue between the Syrian government and the whole spectrum of the Syrian opposition."

Now that it had gotten on board with the statement, Russia leaned on Assad to accept Kofi's terms, which he did at the end of March. We had seen how much his word meant, so no one was counting on a cease-fire actually taking hold. As the April 10 deadline approached, the violence showed no signs of slowing. Syrian military forces even fired into Turkey and Lebanon, which raised the specter of a wider regional conflict. But then some measure of quiet did come. The cease-fire was never full or comprehensive, but there was a lull in the fighting. Like the Arab League before it, the UN dispatched teams of observers to monitor conditions on the ground.

Again, however, despite his pledges, Assad never took any credible steps to implement the rest of Kofi's plan, and the fragile cease-fire soon began to unravel. After about a month Kofi reported "serious violations," and in late May there was a massacre of more than a hundred villagers in Houla, half of them children. Russia and China continued to prevent the Security Council from compelling compliance with the six-point plan or attaching any consequences for violations. It now looked as if their earlier assent had been little more than posturing intended to ease international condemnation.

I began encouraging Kofi to take another tack. Perhaps he should organize an international conference to focus on transition planning. Without further diplomatic progress, the tattered cease-fire would collapse completely, and we'd be left back at square one. In the first weeks of June, Kofi visited me in Washington, and we spoke often by phone as he shuttled between Moscow, Tehran, Damascus, and other capitals in the region. He agreed that it was time to take the next diplomatic steps and began formulating plans for a summit at the end of June.

In mid-June, increasing violence forced the UN to suspend its observer patrols. I accompanied President Obama to the G-20 meeting in Los Cabos, Mexico, where we sat down with Russian President Putin for about two hours. Syria was the principal topic of discussion.

President Obama outlined our position: Either the international community could sit on the sidelines and watch Syria be torn apart by civil and proxy warfare, with all the resulting negative consequences for regional stability, or Russia could use its influence to encourage a viable political solution. Putin claimed that he had no particular love for Assad, who was causing Moscow quite a headache, and he also professed to have no real leverage with Damascus. I think he personally identified with the challenges Assad faced from internal opposition, and he warned about the growing threat from extremists among the opposition and pointed to how messy transitions had become in Libya, Egypt, and, of course, Iraq.

These were all convenient rationalizations for blocking action while continuing to supply Assad with money and arms. Even though I did not trust Russia's actions or words, I knew we had no alternative but to exhaust every diplomatic option. "Go back to the Russians and say your team is going to lay down a transition plan, and Russia can be part of the discussion or left on the sidelines," I advised Kofi after the Putin meeting. As the date of his proposed conference in Geneva approached, I worked closely with Kofi to develop specific language that we hoped might be able to gain consensus. In a curtain-raising opinion piece in the *Washington Post*, he made his expectations clear. He wanted Syria's neighbors and the world's great powers to "commit to act in unison to end the bloodshed and implement the six-point plan, avoiding further militarization of the conflict." He added, "I expect all who attend Saturday's meeting to agree that a Syrian-led transition process must be achieved in accordance with clear principles and guidelines."

On the day before the start of the summit, I urged Kofi to stand by the principles he was proposing: "I understand the tweak here, the clarification there. I can live with that. But the core idea that has to come out of the meeting is that the international community, including Russia and China, are united behind a political transition that would go to a democratic future. That's sacrosanct. The details can be batted around but we have to keep that core." Kofi thought that, in the end, the Russians would get on board. "They said change can come but it must be orderly," he told me. I was not as optimistic, but agreed we had to test.

════

I arrived in Geneva shortly after 1:00 in the morning of June 30 after a flight from Russia, where I had attended an economic conference of Asian-Pacific nations. Over a long dinner in St. Petersburg, I had pressed Lavrov on the need to support Kofi's efforts and bring the conflict to an end. I knew the Russians would never be comfortable explicitly calling for Assad to leave office, but, with our help, Kofi had crafted an elegant solution. He was proposing the establishment of a transitional unity government exercising full executive power, which would be broadly inclusive but exclude "those whose continued presence and participation would undermine the credibility of the transition and jeopardize stability and reconciliation." That was code for excluding Assad. The Russians wanted words that papered over the difference between us (Assad must go) and them (we're not going to force him to go) and leave it up to the Syrians to sort out.

Lavrov took a hard line. He claimed Russia wanted a political resolution, but he wouldn't agree to anything that might make that possible. I pointed out that if we failed to reach an agreement the next day in Geneva based on Kofi's proposal for an orderly transition, the UN-led diplomatic effort would collapse, extremists would gain ground, and the conflict would escalate. The Arabs and the Iranians would pour in even more weapons. Sectarian tensions and a growing flood of refugees would further destabilize Syria's neighbors, especially Lebanon and Jordan. I still believed the Assad regime would eventually fall, but it would take much more of the Syrian state and the region with it. Such a scenario wouldn't serve Russia's interests or preserve its influence. But Lavrov wouldn't budge. Boarding my plane to Switzerland, I knew we'd have to continue pressing the Russians and working to get everyone else on board with a text.

In Geneva I met first with British Foreign Secretary William Hague and French Foreign Minister Laurent Fabius to take stock of what we wanted to achieve at the conference. Hague and I then talked with Hamad bin Jassim of Qatar, and Turkish Foreign Minister Davutoğlu, who pushed us to consider supporting the rebels with military aid regardless of the outcome in Geneva. They knew the United States and Britain were not prepared to do that but wanted to be heard nonetheless.

UN Secretary-General Ban Ki-moon presided over the opening session of the meeting of what he called (optimistically) the Action Group on Syria with Foreign Ministers from the five permanent members of the Security Council, along with Turkey, Iraq, Kuwait, Qatar, and the European Union. Neither Iran nor Saudi Arabia was invited.

At the start of the meeting, Kofi outlined his goals: "We are here to agree on guidelines and principles for a Syrian-led political transition that meets the legitimate aspirations of the Syrian people. And we are here to agree on actions that each and every one of us must take to turn these objectives into reality on the ground, including consequences for noncompliance." He presented a document that would enshrine the transition he was proposing.

I welcomed Kofi's plan to pave the way for a democratic transition and "a post-Assad future." The United States shared his goal of a democratic, pluralistic Syria that would uphold the rule of law and respect the universal rights of all its people and every group, regardless of ethnicity, sect, or gender. We also agreed that it was important to maintain the integrity of the Syrian state and its institutions, particularly enough of the security infrastructure to prevent the kind of chaos we had seen in Iraq after the fall of Saddam Hussein and the disbanding of the Iraqi Army and government. For a new agreement actually to be implemented, I said, it would need a UN Security Council resolution "imposing real and immediate consequences for non-compliance." In addition nations with influence on the warring parties would have to pressure them to accept and support the transition. That meant that Russia should use its clout with the regime, while the Arabs and the West would do the same with the rebels to get them all on board.

We preferred stronger language than what Kofi was suggesting on certain points (for example, we would have liked a more direct reference to Assad's departure), but, in the interest of simplicity and consensus, we agreed to accept the document as it was written, and we urged all other nations to follow suit.

The public portion of international meetings like this is typically scripted. Each country and organization states its position, and it can be rather boring. The action generally starts when the cameras leave. That's what happened here.

We left the ceremonial hall and crowded into a long rectangular room with Kofi and Ban Ki-moon at the head and the Ministers, each with a single aide, arranged on each side of two facing tables. Emotions ran high; at one point Ministers were shouting at one another and even pounding the table. Eventually the commotion settled into a running argument between me and Lavrov. That's where this had always been headed.

Eventually it seemed as if the Russians might accept a transitional governing body, if we could get the language right. Lavrov balked at Kofi's phrase excluding those who would "undermine the credibility of the transition and jeopardize stability and reconciliation." I offered a new formulation to break the deadlock. The transitional governing body would include members of both the government and the opposition chosen "on the basis of mutual consent." Finally the Russians agreed.

It's easy to get lost in the semantics, but words constitute much of a diplomat's work, and I knew they would shape how the rest of the world received our agreement and how it was understood on the ground in Syria. I offered "mutual consent" as a way out because, in practice, there was no way Assad would pass such a test; the opposition would never consent to him. We retained the phrase "full executive powers" to describe the mandate for the proposed transitional governing body; that meant Assad and his cronies would be stripped of their authority. To strengthen our case, I made sure the agreement explicitly put the Syrian security and intelligence services, along with "all governmental institutions," under the control of the transitional governing body and called for "top leadership that inspires public confidence" (another standard Assad would never meet).

I insisted that we should go next to the Security Council and pass what's called a Chapter VII resolution, which would authorize tough sanctions in the event of noncompliance. Lavrov was noncommittal on that, but he agreed to use Russia's influence to support Kofi and his plan and joined all of us in signing on the dotted line of what we had negotiated. Then we all went out to explain it to the world.

Trouble started almost right away. The press missed the intent and plain meaning of "mutual consent" and read it as an admission that Assad could stay in power. The *New York Times* filed a gloomy report under the headline "Talks Come Up with Plan for Syria, but Not for Assad's Exit." Lavrov did his best to fuel this interpretation. "There is no attempt to impose any kind of a transition process," he told the press. "There are no prior conditions to the transfer process and no attempt to exclude any group from the process." That was technically true but blatantly misleading.

Kofi dismissed Lavrov's spin. "I will doubt that the Syrians—who have fought so hard for their independence, to be able to say how they're governed and who governs them—will select people with blood on their hands to lead them," he said. I backed him up: "What we have done here is to strip away the fiction that [Assad] and those with blood on their hands can stay in power. The plan calls for the Assad regime to give way to a new transitional governing body that will have full governance powers." Over time the opposition and civilians in Syria came to see the Geneva Communiqué for what it was: a blueprint for Assad's departure.

It was a bad summer for Syria. After signing the agreement in Geneva, the Russians ultimately refused to back the Chapter VII resolution at the UN or exert any real leverage with Assad. Although disappointing, their behavior was hardly surprising.

In August, Kofi resigned in disgust. "I did my best and sometimes the best is not always good enough," he told me. "I don't know what else you could've done, given the intransigence of the Russians on the Security Council," I replied. And I told him, "I can't imagine how we could've done any more than what we did. At least in Geneva we had a framework, but they were just immovable." Meanwhile the casualties in Syria climbed into the tens of thousands, and the crisis spun further out of control.

I was growing increasingly frustrated but kept at it. When we ran into the Russian-made brick wall at the UN, I kept pressing forward along non-UN tracks, holding more meetings of the Friends of the Syrian People, which by now had expanded to about a hundred nations. The challenge was to convince all the parties—Assad and his Russian and Iranian backers on the one side, the rebels and the Arab states on the other—that a final decisive military victory was impossible and they should focus on reaching a diplomatic solution. That was going to take a great deal of carefully and consistently applied pressure. The United States and our partners steadily ratcheted up sanctions on the Assad regime. We froze their assets, imposed travel bans, and restricted trade. The Syrian economy was in free-fall. But with Russia and Iran bankrolling Assad's war effort, the fighting continued unabated.

Assad kept escalating the use of air power and began firing Scud missiles to overwhelm the rebels, which killed even more civilians. The opposition, despite efforts by the Europeans, Arabs, and the United States, remained in disarray. We provided rebels with "nonlethal" aid, including communications gear and rations, starting in March 2012, but we held the line against contributing arms and training. There were many voices, particularly among the Syrian opposition, crying out for us to support them as we had supported the Libyan rebels. But Syria was not Libya.

The Assad regime was much more entrenched than Qaddafi, with more support among key segments of the population, more allies in the region, a real Army, and far more robust air defenses. Unlike in Libya, where the rebel Transitional National Council had controlled large swaths of territory in the east, including Benghazi, the country's second largest city, the opposition in Syria was disorganized and diffuse. It struggled to hold territory and to coalesce around a single command structure. And, of course, there was one other crucial difference: Russia was blocking any move at the UN on Syria, in large measure to prevent a replay of Libya.

In the early days of the fighting many had assumed Assad's fall was inevitable. After all, the previous leaders of Tunisia, Egypt, Libya, and Yemen were all gone. It was hard to imagine that, after so much bloodshed and getting a taste of freedom, the Syrian people would just settle down and agree to accept dictatorial rule once again. But now, in the second year of civil war, it seemed increasingly possible that Assad would hang on, even if it meant tearing the country apart and fomenting destructive sectarian strife. Syria could be doomed to a long and bloody stalemate. Or it could become a failed state, with the structure of government collapsing and chaos ensuing. And the longer the conflict dragged on, the more danger there was that the instability would destabilize vulnerable neighbors, like Jordan and Lebanon, and the more likely it was that extremists would build support inside Syria.

I started referring to Syria as a "wicked problem," a term used by planning experts to describe particularly complex challenges that confound standard solutions and approaches. Wicked problems rarely have a right answer; in fact, part of what makes them wicked is that every option appears worse than the next. Increasingly that's how Syria appeared. Do nothing, and a humanitarian disaster envelops the region. Intervene militarily, and risk opening Pandora's box and wading into another quagmire, like Iraq. Send aid to the rebels, and watch it end up in the hands of extremists. Continue with diplomacy, and run head-first into a Russian veto. None of these approaches offered much hope of success. But we had to keep at it.

As it became clear that the Geneva effort was stalemated, I and others on the Obama national security team began exploring what it would take to stand up a carefully vetted and trained force of moderate Syrian rebels who could be trusted with American weapons. There are real risks to such an approach. In the 1980s, the United States, Saudi Arabia, and Pakistan armed Afghan rebels called mujahideen who helped end the Soviet occupation of their country. Some of those fighters, including Osama bin Laden, went on to form al Qaeda and turned their sights on targets in the West. Nobody wanted a repeat of that scenario.

But if rebels could be vetted and trained effectively, it would be helpful in a number of ways. First, even a relatively small group might be able to give a big psychological boost to the opposition and convince Assad's backers to consider a political solution. Hezbollah gave credence to this view on the other side, when they helped shift the war in Assad's favor by deploying only a few thousand hard-core fighters.

Second, and more immediately, our action—or inaction—had consequences for our relationships with our regional partners. It wasn't a secret that various Arab states and individuals were sending arms into Syria. But the flow of weapons was poorly coordinated, with different countries sponsoring different and sometimes competing armed groups. And a troubling amount of matériel was finding its way to extremists. Because the United States was not part of this effort, we had less leverage to corral and coordinate the arms traffic. I had heard this firsthand in difficult conversations around the Gulf. If, however, America was willing finally to get in the game, we could be much more effective in isolating the extremists and empowering the moderates inside Syria.

One of the prime worries about Syria—and one of the reasons it was a wicked problem—was the lack of any viable alternatives to Assad on the ground. He and his allies could plausibly argue, like Louis XV of France, "Après moi, le déluge." (After Assad, chaos.) The power vacuum in Iraq after the fall of Saddam and the disbanding of the Iraqi Army offered a cautionary tale. But if the United States could train and equip a reliable and effective moderate rebel force, it could help hold the country together during a transition, safeguard chemical weapons stockpiles, and prevent ethnic cleansing and score settling.

But could it be done? The key would be thoroughly vetting the rebel fighters to ensure we first weeded out the extremists and then maintained close intelligence sharing and operational coordination with all our partners.

In Iraq and Afghanistan the United States spent considerable energy training local soldiers, trying to mold them into a cohesive national army capable of providing security and defeating insurgencies. General David Petraeus, who commanded the U.S. military effort in both countries before becoming Director of the Central Intelligence Agency in 2011, knew firsthand how hard this could be. Despite some successes, the Iraqi and Afghan security forces were still struggling to find their footing. But through his experience in those countries, Petraeus had learned a lot about what worked and what didn't.

I invited Petraeus to my house in Washington for lunch on a Saturday afternoon in July to discuss whether it was possible to vet, train, and equip moderate opposition fighters. If he thought this kind of effort could be accomplished in Syria, that would mean a lot. He had already given careful thought to the idea, and had even started sketching out the specifics and was preparing to present a plan.

Our military's top brass, reluctant to get involved in Syria, consistently offered dire projections of the forces that would be required to overcome Assad's advanced air defenses and conduct a Libya-style no-fly zone. But Secretary of Defense Panetta had become as frustrated as I was with the lack of options in Syria; he knew from his own time leading the CIA what our intelligence operatives could do.

In mid-August, I headed to Istanbul to consult with President Abdul-

71

President Obama and I tour the Sultan Hassan Mosque in Cairo, Egypt, in June 2009. Later that day President Obama gave a speech at Cairo University and offered an ambitious and eloquent recalibration of America's relationship with the Islamic world.

72

Reconnecting with Nujood Ali, a young Yemeni girl who successfully fought for a divorce at age ten, during my January 2011 visit to Sanaa, Yemen. In our town hall meeting with young people and activists, I suggested that Nujood's story should inspire Yemen to end child marriage once and for all.

TOP: I walk with Special Envoy for Middle East Peace George Mitchell to President Obama's remarks in the White House Rose Garden on September 1, 2010, as direct peace talks begin between the Israelis and Palestinians. BOTTOM: That night President Obama hosted a working dinner in the Old Family Dining Room of the White House. From left to right (closest to camera): King Abdullah II of Jordan, President Obama, and President Hosni Mubarak of Egypt. From left to right (farthest from camera): me, Prime Minister Benjamin Netanyahu of Israel, President Mahmoud Abbas of the Palestinian Authority, and Quartet Special Envoy Tony Blair.

75

On September 2, 2010, I hosted the first of three rounds of direct talks between Palestinian Authority President Mahmoud Abbas and Israeli Prime Minister Benjamin Netanyahu at the State Department. Afterward, I joined them and Special Envoy George Mitchell for a chat in my office before leaving them alone to talk.

76

As was so often the case, I am the only woman in the room in this January 2011 meeting of the Gulf Cooperation Council in Doha, Qatar. The next day, I would warn Arab leaders, "In too many places, in too many ways, the region's foundations are sinking into the sand." I am sitting between UAE Foreign Minister Abdullah bin Zayed Al-Nahyan (left) and Qatari Prime Minister Hamad bin Jassim (right).

77

Standing in the Situation Room with President Obama, National Security Advisor Tom Donilon, Treasury Secretary Tim Geithner, and Director of National Intelligence Jim Clapper (all seated), as we watch Egyptian President Hosni Mubarak try to answer the demands of protesters on February 1, 2011. His announcement was too little, too late.

I shake hands with an Egyptian girl in Cairo's Tahrir Square, the heart of the Arab Spring, on March 16, 2011.

After Muammar Qaddafi fled Tripoli, I decided to visit Libya to offer America's support to the new transitional government and urge them to restore security as soon as possible. Posing with a group of exuberant Libyan militia fighters after landing in Tripoli in October 2011.

I swear in Chris Stevens as the new U.S. Ambassador to Libya in the State Department's Treaty Room on May 14, 2012, as his father, Jan Stevens, looks on. Chris was a dedicated public servant who was committed to helping build a new Libya out of the wreckage of the Qaddafi regime.

81

Protesters tear down the U.S. flag at our embassy in Cairo on September 11, 2012, after an offensive video about the Prophet Muhammad sparked anger across the Muslim world.

82

President Obama signs a condolence book in front of the State Department's memorial wall one day after the horrific attacks in Benghazi, Libya. The President visited the Department to comfort the grieving colleagues of Ambassador Chris Stevens and Sean Smith.

83

With President Obama and Chaplain Colonel J. Wesley Smith at Joint Base Andrews, Maryland, on September 14, 2012, as we prepare to receive and honor the remains of our colleagues killed in Benghazi.

84

I appear before the Senate Foreign Relations Committee in January 2013 to testify about the attack on our compound in Benghazi.

85

With Sultan Qaboos of Oman in Muscat in October 2011. The Sultan helped us bring home three American hikers detained in Iran and open a secret diplomatic channel to discuss Iran's nuclear program.

86

Speaking at a UN Security Council meeting on the crisis in Syria in New York City in January 2012. Russia blocked UN actions to address the terrible violence in Syria even as the situation deteriorated. The death toll continues to rise, and millions have been forced from their homes.

87

With President Obama in his hotel suite in Phnom Penh, Cambodia, we discuss whether I should fly to the Middle East to try to broker a cease-fire between Israel and Hamas in Gaza. Standing behind us (from left to right): my Director of Policy Planning Jake Sullivan, Deputy National Security Advisor Ben Rhodes, and National Security Advisor Tom Donilon.

Negotiating with Egyptian President Mohamed Morsi in Cairo in November 2012, in an attempt to end the violence in Gaza. Morsi helped me negotiate a cease-fire between Israel and Hamas that holds to this day.

President Obama and I crash a meeting in Copenhagen, Denmark, during the
UN Climate Change Conference in December 2009. We interrupted Chinese
Premier Wen Jiabao, Brazilian President Lula da Silva, Indian Prime Minister
Manmohan Singh, and South African President Jacob Zuma at the crowded
table.

Norwegian Foreign Minister Jonas Gahr Støre and I discuss the impacts of
climate change aboard the Arctic Research Vessel *Helmer Hanssen* during a trip
up a fjord off the coast of Tromsø, Norway, in June 2012.

Touring an exhibition of old and new cookstoves alongside Dr. Kalpana Balakrishnan, a cookstove researcher, during a visit to Chennai, India, in July 2011. I championed the use of clean-burning cookstoves around the world instead of more traditional, dirty stoves that burn wood or solid fuel and release toxic fumes that contribute to the deaths of millions of people every year, especially women and children.

92

After landing in Haiti only four days after the devastating earthquake in January 2010, I sit in a tent with Haitian Prime Minister Jean-Max Bellerive, Haitian President René Préval, U.S. Ambassador to Haiti Ken Merten, my Counselor and Chief of Staff Cheryl Mills, USAID Administrator Raj Shah, and Lieutenant General Ken Keen to discuss Haiti's emergency response and recovery.

93

Protesters greet me outside the airport in Port-au-Prince in January 2011, during Haiti's contested elections a year after the earthquake. Haitians had suffered so much, and they deserved to have their votes counted and a peaceful transfer of power, which is what they finally got.

94

Bill and I are surrounded by Haitian workers at the grand opening ceremony of the new Caracol industrial park in Haiti in October 2012. The Caracol project was the centerpiece of our efforts to restart Haiti's economy, in keeping with a broader trend in our development work around the world of shifting our focus from aid to investment.

Speaking about internet freedom at the Newseum in Washington in January 2010. I put nations such as China, Russia, and Iran on notice that the United States would promote and defend an internet where people's rights are protected and that is open to innovation, interoperable all over the world, secure enough to hold people's trust, and reliable enough to support their work.

UNITED NATIONS
FOURTH WORLD CONFERENCE ON WOMEN
BEIJING, 4-15 SEPTEMBER 1995

Nearly twenty years after my September 1995 speech in Beijing at the UN's Fourth World Conference on Women, women's rights remain "unfinished business" in the 21st century. As Secretary I focused on defending the freedoms enshrined in the Universal Declaration of Human Rights and making them real in the lives of people all over the world.

With Melanne Verveer after swearing her in as the first Ambassador-at-Large for Global Women's Issues. Melanne helped me weave a "full participation agenda" into the fabric of American foreign policy.

One of our first steps in advancing human rights was rejoining the UN Human Rights Council. I address the Council in Geneva, Switzerland, in December 2011, advocating for the rights of LGBT people around the world.

In September 2012, I watch from 10,000 miles away in Timor-Leste as Bill delivers the speech that earned him the title "Secretary of Explaining Things" at the Democratic National Convention in Charlotte, North Carolina. There was no CNN and limited internet, but we managed to pull up the video on our Ambassador's home computer.

Deputy Secretaries Tom Nides (left) and Bill Burns and Under Secretary Pat Kennedy (right) join me as I say farewell to the amazing men and women of the State Department on my last day, February 1, 2013. I walked out the same entrance I had entered four years earlier, proud of all the work we had accomplished.

lah Gül, Prime Minister Erdoğan, and Foreign Minister Davutoğlu. Turkey was deeply troubled by what was happening across its border and trying to cope with the massive influx of refugees from Syria, some of whom I met while there, as well as periodic incidents of cross-border violence, including Syria's shooting down a Turkish fighter jet over the Mediterranean. The loss of that plane was a dramatic reminder that this crisis could explode into a regional conflict at any moment. In my meetings I affirmed that the United States and the rest of our NATO allies were committed to Turkey's security against Syrian aggression.

Although there had been continuous consultations between us and the Turks since the conflict started, I thought we should intensify operational planning by our militaries in order to prepare contingency plans. What would it take to impose a no-fly zone? How would we respond to the use or loss of chemical weapons? How could we better coordinate support for the armed opposition? The Turks agreed, and two days later Davutoğlu and I got on the phone to discuss our thinking with the Foreign Ministers of Great Britain, France, and Germany.

I returned to Washington reasonably confident that if we decided to begin arming and training moderate Syrian rebels, we could put in place effective coordination with our regional partners. By now interagency planning was in high gear, and Petraeus presented the plan to the President. He listened carefully and had a lot of questions. He worried that arming the rebels was not likely to be enough to drive Assad from power and that with all the weapons already flowing into the country from Arab nations, our contributions would hardly be decisive. And there were always unintended consequences to consider. The story of the mujahideen in Afghanistan remained a powerful cautionary tale never far from anyone's mind. The President asked for examples of instances when the United States had backed an insurgency that could be considered a success.

These were very reasonable concerns, but Petraeus and I argued that there was a big difference between Qatar and Saudi Arabia dumping weapons into the country and the United States responsibly training and equipping a nonextremist rebel force. And getting control of that mess was a big part of our plan's rationale. What's more, the goal was not to build up a force strong enough to defeat the regime. Rather the idea was to give us a partner on the ground we could work with that could do enough to convince Assad and his backers that a military victory was impossible. It wasn't a perfect plan, by any means. In fact, the best I could say for it was that it was the least bad option among many even worse alternatives.

Despite high-level support from the National Security Council, some in the White House were skeptical. After all, the President had been elected in large part because of his opposition to the war in Iraq and his promise to bring the troops home. Getting entangled in any way in another sectarian civil war in the Middle East was not what he had in mind when coming into office. And the President thought we needed more time to evaluate the Syrian opposition before escalating our commitment.

The risks of both action and inaction were high. Both choices would bring unintended consequences. The President's inclination was to stay the present course and not take the significant further step of arming rebels.

No one likes to lose a debate, including me. But this was the President's call and I respected his deliberations and decision. From the beginning of our partnership, he had promised me that I would always get a fair hearing. And I always did. In this case, my position didn't prevail.

With the plan to arm the rebels dead in the water, I threw myself back into the diplomatic push, trying to further isolate and pressure the regime while addressing the humanitarian catastrophe. In August 2012, UN Secretary-General Ban Ki-moon had appointed Lakhdar Brahimi, an experienced diplomat from Algeria, to succeed Kofi Annan. He and I met and talked often, right up until my tenure ended. At a meeting of the Friends of the Syrian People in September, I announced additional aid to help get food, water, blankets, and critical medical services to people suffering in Syria. I also pledged increased support for civilian opposition groups, including satellite-linked computers, telephones, cameras, and training for more than a thousand activists, students, and independent journalists. As more parts of Syria slipped free from the regime's control, we would also help local opposition groups provide essential services, such as reopening schools and rebuilding homes. But all of these steps were Band-Aids. The conflict would rage on.

=====

By the time I departed the State Department in early 2013, tens of thousands of Syrians had been killed. Millions more had fled. International diplomacy had reached a standstill. Our fears were being realized as extremists were eclipsing the more moderate leaders of the Free Syrian Army.

In March 2013, little more than a month after I left office, troubling reports started coming in from around Aleppo that the Assad regime had begun using chemical weapons for the first time. This had been a major concern for two years. Syria was believed to maintain some of the biggest stockpiles of mustard gas, sarin, and other chemical weapons in the world. Throughout 2012, we had received sporadic reports that regime forces were moving or mixing chemical agents. In response both President Obama and I issued stark warnings. In August 2012, President Obama said that moving or using chemical weapons was a red line for the United States. The clear implication was that if the regime crossed that line, actions, potentially including military force, would be taken. In 2012, that threat seemed to be an effective deterrent, and Assad backed down. So if these new reports about chemical weapons were true, the conflict in Syria had just taken a very dangerous turn.

The President again said that the use of chemical weapons would be a game changer, but U.S. intelligence agencies were not yet ready to say with any certainty that an attack had actually happened. More investigation was needed. In June 2013, in a low-key statement, the White House confirmed that it finally felt confident that chemical weapons had indeed been used on a small scale on multiple occasions, killing up to 150 people. The President decided to increase aid to the Free Syrian Army. On background, administration officials told the press they would begin supplying arms and ammunition for the first time, reversing the President's decision the previous summer.

Then, in August 2013, the world was shocked by images of a massive new chemical attack in opposition neighborhoods around Damascus. The reported death toll would climb to more than 1,400 men, women, and children. This was a major escalation and a blatant violation of both the President's red line and long-standing international norms. Pressure began building immediately for a robust response from the United States. Secretary of State Kerry took the lead in condemning the attack, calling it a "moral obscenity." President Obama said, "We cannot accept a world where women and children and innocent civilians are gassed on a terrible scale." Americans wondered whether military action was imminent.

Some commentators and members of Congress asked why the President cared so much about chemical weapons when Assad had been killing so many people with conventional weapons. Chemical weapons are in a category by themselves. They have been banned by the international community since the 1925 Geneva Protocol and 1993 Chemical Weapons Convention because they are gruesome, indiscriminate, and inhumane. As President Obama explained, "If we fail to act, the Assad regime will see no reason to stop using chemical weapons. As the ban against these weapons erodes, other tyrants will have no reason to think twice about acquiring poison gas, and using them. Over time, our troops would again face the prospect of chemical warfare on the battlefield. And it could be easier for terrorist organizations to obtain these weapons, and to use them to attack civilians."

As the White House geared up for action, Prime Minister David Cameron lost a vote in the British Parliament to authorize the use of force in Syria. Two days later President Obama announced his intent to order air strikes to deter and degrade future use of chemical weapons by the Assad regime. But in a move that surprised many in Washington, the President said he would seek authorization from Congress, which was in recess, before acting. Suddenly Congress was plunged into a fierce debate about what to do. Parallels were drawn with the run-up to the war in Iraq. Worst-case scenarios and slippery slopes were invoked. The President's plan for a limited strike to uphold a crucial global norm seemed to get lost in the bluster. As the days went by, the tide of public opinion began to turn against the White House. Vote counters in Congress began predicting that the President might lose, which would deal a serious blow to U.S. prestige and credibility. I watched the back-and-forth with consternation. Syria had become even more of a wicked problem. I supported the President's efforts with Congress and urged lawmakers to act.

During this time, I spoke with Secretary Kerry and White House Chief of Staff Denis McDonough about ways to strengthen the President's hand abroad, especially in advance of his trip later that week to the G-20 summit in St. Petersburg, where he'd see Vladimir Putin. Not wanting Putin to be able to hold the contentious Congressional debate over the President, I suggested to Denis that the White House find some way to show bipartisan support ahead of the vote. Knowing that Senator Bob Corker, the leading Republican on the Senate Foreign Relations Committee, was no fan of Putin's, my advice to Denis was that he be enlisted to help send a message. The idea was to use a routine committee hearing that week to hold a vote on the authorization to use military force that the President would win. Denis, always open to ideas and very familiar with the ways of Congress from his time serving on Capitol Hill, agreed. Working with Corker, the White House got the vote. While not the world's most significant statement, it was enough to telegraph to Putin that we were not as divided as he hoped. Denis called back a few days later to see if I had any other ideas, and said that the President wanted to call me the next day. Knowing how much he had on his plate, I told Denis the President shouldn't feel it was necessary. But Denis said that POTUS (the President of the United States) was going to call, and we spoke the next day about the state of play of his Congressional efforts and other ongoing developments on the international stage.

In a fortuitous coincidence, I was scheduled to go to the White House in person on September 9 for an event about illegal wildlife trafficking. At the State Department I had learned that African forest elephants were nearing extinction. While unfortunate on its own, what caught my attention was one of the reasons behind it: terrorists and armed groups like Al Shabaab and the Lord's Resistance Army had entered the illegal ivory trade as a means of funding their illicit and destabilizing activities across Central Africa. When I left government and joined Bill and Chelsea at the Clinton Foundation, Chelsea and I began working with leading conservation groups to organize a global response that would "stop the killing, stop the trafficking, and stop the demand." Thanks in part to our lobbying, the White House also saw this as an important issue, and President Obama signed an executive order in the summer of 2013 to step up antitrafficking efforts. Now the White House was holding a conference to plan next steps, and they wanted Chelsea and me to be there. Of course, all anyone in the rest of the world wanted to hear about was Syria.

That morning, at a press conference in London, Secretary Kerry was asked if there was anything Assad could do to prevent military action. "Sure," Kerry replied, "he could turn over every single bit of his chemical weapons to the international community in the next week—turn it over, all of it without delay and allow a full and total accounting for that. But he isn't about to do it and it can't be done." Although Kerry's answer may have reflected conversations he was having with allies and the Russians, it sounded to the world like an offhand remark. A State Department spokesperson downplayed it as "a rhetorical argument." The Russians, however, seized on Kerry's comment and embraced it as a serious diplomatic offer.

When I arrived at the White House at 1 P.M., top administration officials were debating how to respond. I was given a briefing, and then I went into the Oval Office to talk with the President. It was strange being back in that familiar room for the first time since I'd stepped down seven months earlier, once again discussing an urgent international crisis. I told the President that if the votes for action against Syria were not winnable in Congress, he should make lemonade out of lemons and welcome the unexpected overture from Moscow.

There were reasons to be cautious, of course. This latest diplomatic ploy by the Russians could be just another delaying tactic to keep Assad in power at all costs. The large chemical weapons supply wasn't good for them either, with its own restive Muslim population. But the prospect of eliminating Assad's chemical weapons stockpile was worth the risk, especially since the President was facing a potentially damaging standoff with Congress. This wouldn't end the civil war or do much to help civilians caught in the crossfire, but it would remove a serious threat to Syrian civilians, neighbors including Israel, and the United States itself. As the conflict worsened and instability increased, so too would the chances that these chemical weapons would be used again against Syrian civilians or transferred to Hezbollah or stolen by other terrorists.

I told the President that I still believed it was crucial to pursue a diplomatic solution that would end the conflict. I knew exactly how hard this would be. After all, I had been trying since March 2011. But the road map we had signed in Geneva the previous year still offered a path forward. Maybe cooperation on chemical weapons would create momentum for broader progress. It was unlikely, but worth testing.

The President agreed and asked me to make a statement. Outside the Oval, I huddled with Ben Rhodes, the President's Deputy National Security Advisor and top foreign policy speechwriter, scribbling new language at the top of my remarks on ivory trafficking. Like Denis McDonough, Rhodes was one of the President's aides whom I had come to trust and value over the years. He had also grown close with members of my team, and they would reminisce about how far we'd all come since the bad old days of the 2008 primary campaign, and how they missed working together. Now I was glad once again to have his advice on how to send just the right message to the world.

When I walked into the wildlife event in the White House auditorium, it was packed with more cameras and journalists than had probably ever reported on elephant poaching before. I started with Syria: "If the regime immediately surrendered its stockpiles as was suggested by Secretary Kerry and the Russians, that would be an important step. But this cannot be another excuse for delay or obstruction, and Russia has to support the international community's efforts sincerely or be held to account." I also stressed that it was the President's threat to use force that spurred the Russians to look for a way out.

The White House decided to put off the vote in Congress to give diplomacy a chance to work. Secretary Kerry flew to Geneva and hammered out the details for removing chemical weapons with Lavrov. Just a month later, the UN agency charged with implementing the deal, the Organisation for the Prohibition of Chemical Weapons, was awarded the Nobel Peace Prize. It was quite a vote of confidence. Remarkably, as of this writing, the agreement has held, and the UN is making slow but steady progress dismantling Assad's chemical weapons arsenal, despite extraordinarily difficult circumstances. There have been delays, but more than 90 percent of Syria's chemical weapons had been removed by late April 2014.

In January 2014 Special Representative Brahimi convened a second UN conference on Syria in Geneva with the goal of implementing the agreement I had negotiated back in June 2012. For the first time representatives from the Assad regime sat down face-to-face with members of the opposition. But talks failed to produce any progress. The regime refused to engage seriously on the question of a transitional governing body, as mandated by the original agreement, and their Russian allies stood faithfully behind them. Meanwhile the fighting on the ground continued unabated.

The humanitarian tragedy unfolding in Syria is heartbreaking. As usual, innocent women and children are bearing the brunt of the suffering. Extremists continue to gain ground, and intelligence officials in the United States and Europe warn that they could pose a threat well beyond Syria. In February 2014, CIA Director John Brennan reported, "We are concerned about the use of Syrian territory by the Al Qaeda organization to recruit individuals and develop the capability to be able not just to carry out attacks inside of Syria, but also to use Syria as a launching pad." Director of National Intelligence James Clapper put an even finer point on it, saying that at least one extremist group in Syria "does have aspirations for attacks on the [American] homeland." With a bloody stalemate continuing in Syria, this danger will only grow, and the United States and our allies will not be able to ignore it. More moderate members of the Syrian opposition also recognize the threat posed by the extremists trying to hijack their revolution, and some have launched efforts to drive them out of rebel-held territory. But that will be an uphill battle, requiring a diversion of arms and men away from the fight against Assad. In April 2014, there were reports that the United States would provide additional training and arms to certain rebel groups.

As Kofi Annan said at the first Geneva summit, "History is a somber judge." It is impossible to watch the suffering in Syria, including as a private citizen, and not ask what more could have been done. That's part of what makes Syria and the broader challenge of an unstable Middle East such a wicked problem. But wicked problems can't paralyze us. We need to keep urgently seeking solutions, however hard they are to find.

20

Gaza: Anatomy of a Cease-fire

The motorcade pulled over to the side of the dusty highway between Ramallah and Jerusalem. Security agents scrambled out of their armored vehicles and peered down the road, back toward the heart of the West Bank. Others looked up at the sky. Israeli intelligence had just shared reports that a rocket might have been fired by Palestinian extremists in the Gaza Strip. There was no way to know for sure where it was headed. American officials in the motorcade who had been riding in a standard-issue van quickly piled into one of the several heavily armored cars that provided better protection from a blast. With everyone situated we were back on the road, headed toward Jerusalem.

In the days before Thanksgiving 2012, the Holy Land once again felt like a war zone. I left a high-level summit in Asia and flew to the Middle East on an emergency diplomatic mission to try to stop an air war between Israel and Hamas in Gaza from escalating into a much more deadly ground war. To do that I would have to broker a cease-fire between implacable and distrustful adversaries against the backdrop of a region in turmoil. After four years of frustrating diplomacy in the Middle East, this would be a crucial test of America's leadership.

Nearly four years earlier, the Obama Administration had come into office mere days after the end of another conflict in Gaza, one also precipitated by rocket fire into Israel. In early January 2009, the Israeli military launched a ground invasion of Gaza to stop rockets being launched by militants across the border. After nearly two weeks of brutal urban fighting that left about 1,400 people dead in Gaza, Israel pulled back and resumed a de facto siege of the Palestinian enclave. For the next few years, persistent but low-level violence continued across the border. More than one hundred rockets were fired into southern Israel in both 2009 and 2010, as well as occasional mortar attacks. In some cases Israeli jets would retaliate with air strikes. This situation was far from acceptable, but by the standards of the region it was considered a relatively quiet time. But starting in 2011, as the extremists rearmed and much of the Middle East was swept by revolution, the violence escalated. Hundreds of rockets hit Israel that year. The pace accelerated in 2012. On November 11, Israeli Defense Minister Ehud Barak warned about potential Israeli action against terrorist factions in Gaza after more than a hundred rockets hit southern Israel in a twenty-four-hour period, injuring three Israelis.

Since 2007, Gaza had been ruled by Hamas, the extremist Palestinian group founded in the late 1980s during the first intifada and designated by the United States as a foreign terrorist organization in 1997. Its stated goal was not an independent state in the Palestinian territories, but the destruction of Israel altogether and the establishment of an Islamic emirate in the territory between the Jordan River and the Mediterranean Sea. For years it drew financial and military support from Iran and Syria, and, after the death of Yasser Arafat in 2004, it competed with the more moderate Fatah Party of Mahmoud Abbas for leadership of the Palestinian cause. After winning legislative elections in 2006, Hamas seized control of the Gaza Strip from Abbas and the Palestinian Authority in 2007, and it held on to power despite the 2009 war. Hamas and its foreign backers spent their money on arms smuggling to rebuild their stocks, while Gaza's economy continued to decline and its people continued to suffer.

Then the upheaval of the Arab Spring shook up the Middle East chessboard, and Hamas found itself navigating a changed landscape. In Syria, its traditional patron, the Alawite dictator Bashar al-Assad, engaged in a brutal crackdown against the largely Sunni population. Hamas, a Sunni organization, abandoned its headquarters in Damascus. At the same time, the Muslim Brotherhood, a Sunni Islamist party with ties to

Hamas, rose to power in postrevolutionary Egypt, across the border from Gaza. For Hamas, it was like one door opening just as another one was closing. Complicating matters further, Hamas faced growing competition at home from other extremist groups, in particular Palestinian Islamic Jihad, equally intent on fighting Israel but not burdened by any responsibility to govern Gaza or deliver results to the people.

With Israel enforcing a blockade of Gaza by sea and keeping tight control of its northern and eastern borders, the main point of resupply for Hamas came through the short southern border with Egypt's Sinai Peninsula. Under Mubarak the Egyptians were reasonably strict about smuggling and generally worked well with Israel, although Hamas found success digging tunnels beneath the border and into Egyptian territory. After Mubarak fell and the Muslim Brotherhood rose to power in Egypt, crossing the Gaza border became easier.

At the same time, Egyptian authorities started to lose control of the Sinai Peninsula. The 23,000-square-mile desert region juts out into the Red Sea from the eastern banks of the Suez Canal. The Sinai is famous for its role in the Bible and its strategic location as a land bridge between Africa and Asia. It was invaded by Israel twice, once in 1956 during the Suez Crisis and again in 1967 during the Six Day War. Under the terms of the 1979 Camp David Accords, Israel returned Sinai to Egypt, and an international peacekeeping force including U.S. troops arrived to maintain the truce. Sinai is also home to nomadic and restive Bedouin tribes long marginalized by Cairo. These tribes took advantage of the chaos triggered by the Egyptian Revolution by asserting their autonomy and demanding more economic support from the government and greater respect from government security forces. As the Sinai descended into lawlessness, extremists with links to al Qaeda began to see it as a safe haven.

In one of my first meetings with the new Egyptian President, Mohamed Morsi, I asked, "What are you going to do to prevent al Qaeda and other extremists from destabilizing Egypt and, in particular, the Sinai?" His response was "Why would they do that? We have an Islamist government now." Expecting solidarity from terrorists was either quite naïve or shockingly sinister. "Because you will never be pure enough," I explained. "I don't care what your positions are. They will come after you. And you'll have to protect your country and your government." He would hear none of it.

By August 2012, the threat posed by the situation in the Sinai was undeniable. One Sunday evening, a group of some thirty-five armed and masked militants attacked an Egyptian Army outpost near the border with Israel and killed sixteen soldiers as they were sitting down to eat dinner. The extremists then stole an armored vehicle and a truck, loaded it with explosives, and headed toward Israel. The truck exploded as they barreled through the border fence at the Kerem Shalom crossing. Israeli air strikes then destroyed the armored vehicle. The confrontation lasted only about fifteen minutes, but it badly shook both Egypt and Israel. After the tragedy, with U.S. support, Egypt increased efforts to fight militants in Sinai, including with the use of air power. But the area remained highly unstable.

Then, in late October, two more events occurred in quick succession that demonstrated how truly complicated and unstable the situation had become.

On October 23, the Emir of Qatar, Sheikh Hamad bin Khalifa al-Thani, visited Gaza at the invitation of Hamas. It was the first time a head of state had gone to the isolated enclave since Hamas took control in 2007, and both sides played up the symbolism. The Emir drove in from Egypt in a lavish motorcade of about fifty black Mercedes-Benzes and armored Toyotas, and Hamas greeted him with all the pomp and circumstance it could muster. Ismail Haniya, the Hamas Prime Minister, declared that the Qatari visit marked the end of the "political and economic siege that was imposed on Gaza" and introduced his wife in her first public appearance. For his part, the Emir pledged $400 million in development aid, more than Gaza received from all other international donors combined. He was accompanied by his wife, Sheikha Moza, and his cousin Hamad bin Jassim al-Thani, or HBJ as we called him, who served as Qatar's Prime Minister and Foreign Minister.

For Haniya and Hamas, this was an opportunity to get out from behind the shadow of Palestinian Authority President Mahmoud Abbas, recognized by the international community as the legitimate leader of the Palestinian people, and to show that their future was bright despite any estrangement from Syria and Iran. For Qatar, it was a chance to revel in a newfound regional influence and stake a claim as the Arab world's chief backer of the Palestinian cause. For Israel, it was a source of growing concern. For the United States, which continued to view Hamas as a dangerous terrorist organization, Qatar was a conundrum that illustrated the complexity of dealing with the Middle East during this turbulent time.

Geographically Qatar looks like a small finger extending into the Persian Gulf from Saudi Arabia. At just over 4,400 square miles, it's less than half the size of Vermont, but it is blessed with extensive reserves of oil and natural gas and, per capita, is one of the wealthiest countries in the world. There are only about a quarter of a million Qatari citizens, but many times that number of foreign workers are imported to keep the country running. Sheikh Hamad deposed his father to become Emir in 1995 and soon set about raising Qatar's profile. Under his governance, the booming capital city of Doha came to rival Dubai and Abu Dhabi as regional hubs of trade and culture, and its satellite television network Al Jazeera became the most influential source of news in the Middle East and a platform for Qatar to influence the entire region.

Like its Gulf neighbors, Qatar had little in the way of democracy or respect for universal human rights, but it has maintained strong strategic and security ties with the United States, and it hosts a major U.S. Air Force installation. This balancing act was put to the test across the Gulf during the Arab Spring.

The Emir and HBJ maneuvered to take advantage of the regional upheaval and position Qatar as a champion of the revolutions. Their goal was to turn their small nation into a major power in the Middle East by backing the Muslim Brotherhood and other Islamists across the region. The other Gulf monarchies feared that such a course would invite instability at home, but the Qataris saw a chance to build influence with the new players emerging on the scene and to champion their conservative cultural views, along with distracting attention from their own lack of reform at home.

Using the soft power of Al Jazeera and their bottomless checkbook, the Emir and HBJ bankrolled Morsi in Egypt, funneled weapons to Islamist rebels in Libya and Syria, and built new ties to Hamas in Gaza. Qatari fighter jets also helped enforce the no-fly zone in Libya. Everywhere you turned in the Middle East in those days, you saw the hand of Qatar. It was an impressive diplomatic tour de force, and in some instances Qatar's efforts aligned with our own. But other Arab nations and Israel saw Qatar's support for Islamist forces and extremist elements as posing a growing threat. The Emir's visit to Gaza crystallized the problem. (In 2013, with Islamists in retreat in Egypt and elsewhere, the Emir abdicated in favor of his son, and HBJ was replaced by a low-profile former Deputy Interior Minister. Relations among the Gulf states reached a nadir in March 2014, when Saudi Arabia, Bahrain, and the UAE withdrew their Ambassadors from Qatar.)

Within hours of the Emir's visit to Gaza, explosions rocked a weapons factory in Khartoum, Sudan. Sudanese officials said that four warplanes had flown in from the east and bombed the factory, killing two people. They pointed the finger squarely at Israel. It was not the first time. Over the previous four years the Sudanese had accused Israel of conducting several air strikes against targets in their country. Just that September, a shipment of rockets and munitions bound for Gaza was destroyed south of Khartoum. The Israelis declined to comment about the factory explosion, but a senior Defense Ministry official noted that Sudan "is supported by Iran, and it serves as a route for the transfer, via Egyptian territory, of Iranian weapons to Hamas and Islamic Jihad terrorists."

Sudan certainly had a checkered history with terrorism. It harbored Osama bin Laden in the early 1990s, and in 1993, the State Department designated it a state sponsor of terrorism. Sudan also maintained close ties with both Iran and Hamas. Shortly after the explosion at the weapons factory, two Iranian warships visited Port Sudan. Hamas leader Khaled Meshal visited Khartoum a few weeks later.

Taken together, all of these regional factors—rocket fire from Gaza, instability in the Sinai, Qatari power plays, Iranian meddling, smuggling from Sudan—made for an intensely combustible situation in the fall of 2012. In November, the cauldron boiled over.

═══

On November 14, 2012, I was with Secretary of Defense Leon Panetta and Joint Chiefs of Staff General Martin Dempsey in Perth, Australia, for annual consultations with our Australian allies in a conference center in Kings Park, overlooking the city and the Swan River. As our afternoon session was breaking up, Panetta got word that Israeli Defense Minister Barak was urgently trying to reach him. Panetta stepped into a kitchen area to take the secure call from Jerusalem. After lunch, he joined General Dempsey and me on a patio to share Barak's report. I could tell from his face that things were about to get complicated. The Israeli military was about to launch a major air campaign against militants in Gaza. The bombing runs would start imminently.

From peaceful Perth, the prospect of another war in the Middle East felt a million miles away (actually about seven thousand), but this was deadly serious. I told Panetta and Dempsey that the Israeli response was understandable. The Hamas rockets were becoming increasingly advanced and accurate, to the point of even threatening Tel Aviv, forty miles from the border. Residents there hadn't faced air-raid warnings since the first Gulf War in 1991, when Saddam Hussein launched Scud missiles at Israel. Every country has the right to defend itself, and no government could be expected to accept such provocation. Still any escalation in violence was going to make the situation that much harder to contain, and no one wanted to see a repeat of the all-out war that raged only four years earlier.

The first major round of air strikes killed Ahmed Jabari, a terrorist accused of planning many attacks against Israelis over the years. Over the next two days people on both sides were killed. The front page of the *New York Times* on November 16 was dominated by dramatic side-by-side photographs of funerals in Gaza City and Jerusalem.

According to Israel, during that week more than 1,500 rockets were fired from Gaza. Six Israelis, four civilians and two soldiers, were killed, and more than two hundred were injured. Many Israeli families were forced to evacuate their homes in southern areas near Gaza as rockets continued to rain down from the sky. Hundreds of Palestinians were reportedly killed in the air campaign the Israeli military called Operation Pillar of Defense.

I received frequent updates from Ambassador Dan Shapiro and his team at our embassy in Tel Aviv and from our experts back in Washington. Deputy Secretary Bill Burns, who had served as the Department's top Middle East official under Colin Powell, once again gathered information for me. Bill and I agreed that there was a limited window in which diplomacy might be able to head off further escalation of the conflict.

I called Egyptian Foreign Minister Mohamed Amr to see if there was anything Egypt could do to ratchet down the tensions. "We can't accept this," Amr said of the Israeli air strikes. Though Mubarak had been replaced as President by Morsi, a leader of the Muslim Brotherhood, I hoped Egypt would remain a key intermediary and voice for peace. I appealed to Amr's sensitivity about Egypt's stature. "I think your role in this is very important and I urge you to do everything you can to deescalate the situation," I said, telling him that Egypt had to talk to Hamas and urge them to cease bombing Israel. Israel was only acting in self-defense, I argued, and "there is no country on earth that can sit by and absorb rockets being fired at their people." Amr agreed to try. "I hope both of us can do something to stop this craziness," he said. "We need to work together in a close effort."

As I traveled across Australia, from Perth to Adelaide, and then to Singapore, President Obama and I stayed in close contact, coordinating the pressure we were placing on our Middle Eastern counterparts. He leaned on Morsi and consulted with Prime Minister Netanyahu and Prime Minister Erdoğan, urging all sides to push for a cease-fire. As we compared notes, we considered whether more direct engagement made sense. Should I fly to the Middle East to try to end the violence?

Neither of us was sure my going was the wisest course. For starters, he and I had serious business to attend to in Asia. After a quick stop in Singapore, I was planning to meet President Obama in Thailand and then travel to Burma with him for a historic visit intended to bolster that country's nascent democratic opening. Then we were to go to Cambodia for a big summit of Asian leaders that was expected to be dominated by delicate diplomacy over the South China Sea. Personal attention counts for a lot in Asia, so leaving now would come at a cost.

That wasn't all: The President was understandably wary of our taking on a direct mediation role in the middle of another messy conflict in the Middle East. If we tried to broker a cease-fire and failed, as seemed quite likely, it would sap America's prestige and credibility in the region. There was even a good chance that direct U.S. engagement would set back the cause of peace by raising the profile of the conflict and prompting both sides to stiffen their negotiating positions. That was the last thing he or I wanted or America needed.

I continued as planned with the Asia trip, spending as much time as possible on the phone with key Middle Eastern leaders and concerned European allies. On every call I argued that the best path forward would be a simultaneous cease-fire between Israel and Hamas.

The stakes were high. The Israeli Cabinet had called up seventy-five thousand reservists for a possible ground invasion of Gaza. As feared, this was shaping up as a replay of the January 2009 war, which had taken a horrendous toll on the people of Gaza and on Israel's reputation globally. It was imperative to resolve the crisis before it became a ground war. The only good news was that the Iron Dome air defense system that we had helped build to protect Israel from rockets was working even better than expected. The Israeli military reported the Iron Dome had a success rate of more than 80 percent for all rockets it targeted. Even if that was a generous estimate, the success rate was astonishing. Still, one rocket from Gaza hitting its targets was one too many, and the Israelis were determined to go after the stockpiles and launch sites in Gaza.

When I joined President Obama in Bangkok on November 18, I reported that my telephone diplomacy was running into a difficult reality: Neither side wanted to be seen blinking first. He was finding the same thing with his calls. This is why I kept pushing the idea of a simultaneous cease-fire, with both sides stepping back from the brink at the same time.

"Hamas is trying to propose conditions before a cease-fire. Israel will never accept that and we have no more than forty-eight hours before Israel might launch a ground offensive, which will be devastating," I warned Qatar's HBJ an hour after arriving in Bangkok.

The President and I paid a quiet private visit to the ailing King of Thailand in a Bangkok hospital and walked together around the famous Wat Pho temple, home to Thailand's largest gold "reclining Buddha" statue, more than 150 feet long. Despite the surroundings, our conversation kept coming back to Gaza. There was no doubt in either of our minds that Israel had a right to defend itself. But we also knew that a ground invasion could be catastrophic for all concerned.

Two days later the situation was so dire that I decided to raise again with the President the idea of my leaving Asia and flying to the Middle East to personally intervene in the conflict. It was fraught with risk, but even if we failed, the danger of an impending wider war was now too great to hold anything back. First thing that morning, I went upstairs to the President's suite in the elegant old Raffles Hotel Le Royal in Phnom Penh, Cambodia. He was still in the shower, so I waited for a few minutes. As he drank his morning coffee, we talked over what to do. He remained wary. What were the chances that my going would actually stop the violence? Would it look like we were undercutting Israel? What might be the unintended consequences of putting America in the middle of this mess? We discussed all those questions and more. In the end we agreed that peace in the Middle East was a compelling national security priority; it was crucial to avoid another ground war in Gaza; and there was no substitute for American leadership.

The President wasn't 100 percent there yet, but he agreed that I should start getting ready to go. Huma and our traveling team began scrambling to work out the logistics of diverting from Cambodia to Israel, not exactly your typical route. It was only two days before Thanksgiving, and there was no telling how long this would take, so I encouraged anyone from the staff who needed to get home to hitch a ride back to the States with the President on Air Force One.

Later that morning the President and I huddled one more time in a makeshift "hold room" in Phnom Penh's massive Peace Palace conference center. In a small space cordoned off by pipes and drapes, we went over the pros and cons one more time. Jake Sullivan, Tom Donilon, and Ben Rhodes joined us for a final go-round. Donilon was nervous, having been burned too many times over the years by misadventures in the Middle East, but eventually he agreed I should go. The President listened to all the arguments and then made his decision. It was time to act. We might not succeed, but we sure were going to get caught trying.

The President said he would call both Morsi and Bibi from Air Force One on the way back to Washington to try to make more headway before I touched down. His parting advice was familiar encouragement. Just as when we negotiated the fate of the blind human rights dissident Chen Guangcheng, the President's message was clear: "Don't screw up!" I wasn't planning to.

=====

On the eleven-hour flight from Cambodia to Israel, I thought long and hard about the complexities of the crisis. You couldn't understand what was going on in Gaza without also understanding the path these rockets had taken before they were launched, winding their way from Iran through Sudan and ultimately to Hamas, and what those links meant for regional security. You also had to understand the increasingly significant role technology played. The rockets were getting more and more sophisticated, but so were Israel's air defenses. Which would prove decisive? Then you had to consider how the conflict in Syria was creating friction between Sunni Hamas and its longtime Shiite patrons in Damascus and Tehran, at the same time that the Sunni Muslim Brotherhood was rising in Cairo and the Syrian civil war continued to unfold. What about the growing instability in the Sinai and the pressure it was putting on the new Egyptian government? Israel was heading toward elections, and

Netanyahu's coalition was far from stable. How would Israel's domestic politics influence his stance on Gaza? All these questions and many more would be swirling as I tried to negotiate a cease-fire.

From the plane I called German Foreign Minister Guido Westerwelle, who was in Jerusalem conducting his own consultations. "I'm sitting here in the hotel you will stay in—we just had a rocket alarm and had to leave our rooms," he told me. "You can't imagine how nervous the situation is."

At nearly 10 P.M. on November 20, we landed at Ben Gurion International Airport in Tel Aviv and drove the thirty minutes to Netanyahu's office in Jerusalem. I went right upstairs and sat down with the Prime Minister and a small group of our aides. The Israelis told us they had already begun talks with the Egyptians, who were representing Hamas, but they were foundering on long-standing and difficult issues regarding Israel's embargo of Gaza, freedom of movement for its people, fishing rights off the coast, and other existing tensions. Bibi and his team were very pessimistic that any deal could be reached. They said they were serious about launching a ground invasion into Gaza if nothing changed. They would give me some time, but not much. I was now on the clock.

As the hours went by, the Prime Minister's staff kept wheeling in carts of food, stacked high with grilled cheese sandwiches and tiny éclairs. Comfort food in the midst of high stress, though nobody was looking at his or her watch. I appreciated the fact that Bibi and his team held nothing back around me. They interrupted and contradicted one another, even the Prime Minister.

Netanyahu was under a lot of pressure to invade. Opinion polls in Israel strongly favored such a step, especially among Bibi's Likud base. But Israeli military commanders were warning of high numbers of casualties, and Netanyahu was also concerned about the regional consequences. How would Egypt react? Would Hezbollah begin attacking from Lebanon? He also knew that the military had achieved most of its goals within the first few hours of sustained air strikes, especially degrading Hamas's long-range rocket capabilities, and that Iron Dome was doing a good job protecting Israeli citizens. Bibi didn't want a ground war, but he was having trouble finding an exit ramp that would allow Israel to disengage and deescalate without making it seem as if it was backing down in the face of continued Hamas defiance, which would only invite more violence later. Meanwhile Mubarak was gone and the Israelis didn't trust the new Muslim Brotherhood government in Cairo. That made the role of the

United States even more crucial. At least one Israeli official later told me that this was the hardest choice Netanyahu had faced as Prime Minister.

I said I was going to fly to Cairo the next day, and I wanted to bring with me a document that I could present to President Morsi as the basis for final negotiations. The key, I thought, was to be sure to have a few points where the Israelis would be willing to make concessions if pressed, so Morsi could feel as if he had gotten a good deal for the Palestinians. We went round and round on the specifics without finding a formula that would work.

We broke up the meeting after midnight, and I headed to the iconic eighty-year-old King David Hotel for a few hours of restless sleep. It seemed more likely than not that this diplomatic mission would fail and Israeli troops would enter Gaza. In the morning I drove to Ramallah to consult with Abbas. Though his influence here was limited, I didn't want to exclude him and in any way lend legitimacy to Hamas in the inter-Palestinian power struggle. I also knew that the Palestinian Authority continued to pay salaries and stipends to thousands of people in Gaza, despite Hamas rule, so it would be helpful to have Abbas's support for a cease-fire.

By this time the Palestinian Authority headquarters in Ramallah was familiar ground to me. Known as the Mukataa, it was originally built as a British fort in the 1920s and became famous in 2002, when the Israeli Army besieged the compound with Yasser Arafat and his top aides trapped inside and eventually destroyed most of it. In 2012, there were few signs of that violent history. The complex had been rebuilt and now included Arafat's limestone mausoleum, where a Palestinian honor guard stood watch as visitors came to pay their respects.

It had been a difficult year for Abbas. His popularity was sagging, and the economy in the West Bank was slowing. After the Israeli settlement moratorium expired in late 2010 and he pulled out of direct negotiations, Abbas had decided to petition the UN to recognize Palestine as an independent state. He had staked his career on the idea that statehood could be achieved through peaceful means—as opposed to the Hamas vision of armed struggle—and the failure of negotiations severely undercut his political position. Abbas felt he needed to find another nonviolent avenue to press forward if he was going to keep his hold on power and continue to offer a viable alternative to the extremists. A symbolic vote at the UN was unlikely to do much for the everyday life of Palestinians, but sticking it to Israel on the world stage and exposing its growing isolation would bolster Abbas at home—and, the Palestinians argued, might encourage Israel to make concessions. The problem was that going to the UN ran counter to the crucial idea that peace could be achieved only by negotiations between the parties, with compromises from both sides. Unilateral actions, whether it was a Palestinian statehood bid at the UN or Israeli settlement construction in the West Bank, eroded trust and made it harder to foster those compromises.

Throughout 2011, we unsuccessfully tried to convince Abbas to abandon his petition, while also working to make sure there would not be enough votes in the Security Council to move it forward. (We wanted to avoid having to use our veto if possible.) At the same time, I began working with the EU's Cathy Ashton and Tony Blair on a framework for restarting direct negotiations based on terms of reference President Obama had outlined in his May 2011 speech. There was a flurry of diplomacy at the UN General Assembly in September 2011, but it was not enough to dissuade Abbas from submitting his petition and forcing the issue. Thanks to our behind-the-scenes cajoling, it went nowhere in the Security Council. All Abbas got for his troubles—besides strained relations with the United States and Israel—was membership at UNESCO, the UN cultural agency. He pledged to return in 2012 and try again.

Now Hamas was upstaging Abbas with its headline-grabbing resistance to Israel and making him look tired and weak to his people. I think he was grateful for my visit but depressed by his situation. After a rather desultory discussion, he agreed to back my peacemaking efforts and wished me well in Cairo.

Then it was back to Jerusalem for another discussion with Netanyahu. His advisors had called in the middle of the night and asked us to return for another meeting before leaving for Cairo. We went issue by issue, carefully calibrating how far the Israelis could bend without breaking and gaming out how things might go with the Egyptians. By the end of the meeting we had a strategy in place and I had Israeli-approved language to bring to Egypt as a basis for negotiations.

Then I headed to the airport. While we were en route, word came of a bus bombing in Tel Aviv, the first in years. Dozens of people had been hurt. It was an ominous reminder of the urgency of my mission.

Midafternoon on November 21, I arrived at the Presidential Palace in

Cairo where I had met with Mubarak so many times before. The building and household staff were the same, but now the Muslim Brotherhood was in charge. So far Morsi had upheld the Camp David Peace Treaty with Israel, which had been a cornerstone of regional stability for decades, but how long would that last if Israel invaded Gaza again? Would he seek to reaffirm Egypt's traditional role as mediator and peacemaker and establish himself as an international statesman? Or would he move to exploit popular anger and position himself as the one man in the Middle East who could stand up to Israel? We were about to put him to the test.

Morsi was an unusual politician. History had thrust him from the back room to the big chair. In many ways he was in over his head, trying to learn how to govern from scratch in a very difficult setting. Morsi clearly loved the power of his new position and thrived on the dance of politics (until it later consumed him). I was relieved to see that, in the case of Gaza at least, he seemed more interested in being a dealmaker than a demagogue. We met in his office with a small group of his advisors and began going through the document I had brought from Israel's Prime Minister, line by line.

I encouraged Morsi to think about Egypt's strategic role in the region and his own role in history. He spoke solid English, having earned his PhD from the University of Southern California in materials science in 1982 and taught at California State University, Northridge, until 1985. He scrutinized every phrase of the text. "What does this mean? Has this been translated right?" he asked. At one point he exclaimed, "I don't accept this." "But you proposed it in one of your early drafts," I responded. "Oh, we did? OK," he agreed. He even overruled Foreign Minister Amr at one point in the negotiations and offered a key concession.

The proposal was brief and to the point. At an agreed-upon "zero hour," Israel would halt all hostilities in Gaza, from land, sea, and air, and the Palestinian factions would stop rocket launches and all other attacks along the border. Egypt would act as guarantor and monitor. The tricky part was what would come next. When would the Israelis loosen restrictions at the border crossings so Palestinians could get in food and supplies? How could Israel be sure Hamas wasn't rebuilding its rocket arsenal? We proposed that these complicated issues "be dealt with after twenty-four hours from the start of the cease-fire." That was intentionally vague, the idea being that Egypt could facilitate substantive talks once the fighting ended. Netanyahu had given me the running room to negotiate which issues were specifically mentioned in this clause, and I needed it. Morsi pressed on a few points, and we revised the list several times, eventually settling on the following: "Opening the crossings and facilitating the movements of people and transfer of goods and refraining from restricting residents' free movements and targeting residents in border areas and procedures of implementation shall be dealt with after twenty-four hours from the start of the cease-fire."

Throughout the negotiations the Egyptians were on the phone with the leaders of Hamas and other Palestinian extremist factions in Gaza, including some who were actually sitting in the offices of the Egyptian intelligence services across town. Morsi's team, new to governing, was tentative with the Palestinians and seemed uncomfortable twisting their arms to get a deal done. We kept reminding the Muslim Brotherhood men that they now represented a major regional power, and it was their responsibility to deliver.

I updated President Obama frequently and spoke to Netanyahu several times. He and Morsi wouldn't speak directly to each other, so I served as the conduit for a high-stakes game of telephone negotiations, while Jake and our formidable Ambassador in Cairo, Anne Patterson, were drilling down on some of the trickier details with Morsi's advisors.

Netanyahu was intent on gaining U.S. and Egyptian help to block new weapons shipments into Gaza. He didn't want to end the air strikes and then find himself back in this untenable position in another year or two. When I pressed Morsi on that point, he agreed it would be in Egypt's security interests as well. But he, in turn, wanted a commitment to reopen Gaza's borders to humanitarian aid and other goods as soon as possible, plus greater freedom of movement for Palestinian fishing boats off the coast. Netanyahu was willing to be flexible on these points if he received assurances on the weapons and the rockets stopped. With each turn of the discussion, we inched closer and closer to an understanding.

After hours of intense negotiation we hammered out an agreement. The cease-fire would go into effect at 9 P.M. local time, just a few hours away. (It was an arbitrary time, but we needed to come up with a clear answer to the basic question "When will the violence stop?") But before we could declare victory, there was one more piece of business to attend to. We had agreed that President Obama would call Bibi, both to personally ask him to agree to the cease-fire and to promise increased American assistance cracking down on weapons smuggling into Gaza. Was this political cover so Bibi could tell his Cabinet and his voters he had called off the invasion because Israel's most important ally had begged him? Or did he take some personal satisfaction from making the President jump through hoops? Either way, if this was what it would take to seal the deal, we needed to get it done.

Meanwhile my team anxiously watched the clock. It was now after 6:00 in Cairo on the night before Thanksgiving. Air Force regulations about crew rest were going to kick in soon, which would mean we wouldn't be able to take off until the next day. But if we left soon, under the wire, we might just make it back in time for people to spend the holiday with their families. Any snags, and the only turkey we'd be eating for Thanksgiving would be the Air Force's famous turkey taco salad. Of course, this wasn't the first holiday threatened by the crazy demands of international diplomacy, and no one on my team complained; they just wanted to get the job done.

Finally all the pieces were in place, the call was made, and we received the go-ahead from Jerusalem and Washington. Essam al-Haddad, Morsi's national security advisor, got down on his knees to thank God. Foreign Minister Amr and I walked downstairs to a jam-packed press conference and announced that a cease-fire had been agreed to. It was absolute pandemonium in there, with emotions running high. Amr spoke of "Egypt's historic responsibility toward the Palestinian cause" and also its "keenness to stop the bloodshed" and preserve regional stability. The new Muslim Brotherhood government would never seem as credible again as it did that day. I thanked President Morsi for his mediation and praised the agreement, but cautioned, "There is no substitute for a just and lasting peace" that "advances the security, dignity, and legitimate aspirations of Palestinians and Israelis alike." So our work was far from over. I pledged that "in the days ahead, the United States will work with partners across the region to consolidate this progress, improve conditions for the people of Gaza, and provide security for the people of Israel."

As our motorcade raced through the streets of Cairo that night, I wondered how long—or even if—the cease-fire would hold. The region had seen so many cycles of violence and dashed hopes. It would take only a few extremists and a rocket launcher to reignite the conflict. Both sides would have to work hard to preserve the peace. And even if they succeeded, there would be difficult talks over the coming days about all the complex issues we had deferred in the agreement. I could easily be back here soon, trying to put the pieces together again.

At 9 P.M., as scheduled, the skies above Gaza grew quiet. But in the streets below thousands of Palestinians celebrated. Hamas leaders, who had narrowly avoided another devastating Israeli invasion, declared victory. In Israel, Netanyahu adopted a somber tone and speculated that it was still "very possible" that he would be forced to launch "a much harsher military operation" if the cease-fire did not hold. Yet despite these contrasting reactions, it seemed to me that the two most important strategic outcomes of the conflict boded quite well for Israel. First, for the time being at least, Egypt remained a partner for peace, which had been in serious doubt since the fall of Mubarak. Second, the success of Iron Dome in shooting down incoming rockets had reinforced Israel's "qualitative military edge" and exposed the futility of Hamas's military threats.

When we got to the plane, I asked Jake if the agreement was still holding. I was only half joking. He said yes, and I settled in for the long flight home.

As it turned out, the cease-fire held better than anyone expected. In 2013, Israel enjoyed the quietest year in a decade. Later, one senior Israeli official confided to me that his government had been forty-eight hours away from launching a ground invasion of Gaza and that my diplomatic intervention was the only thing standing in the way of a much more explosive confrontation. Of course, I continue to believe that over the long run nothing will do more to secure Israel's future as a Jewish democratic state than a comprehensive peace based on two states for two peoples.

PART SIX

The Future We Want

21

Climate Change:
We're All in This Together

N o! No! No!" the Chinese official said, waving his arms across the doorway. The President of the United States was barging uninvited into a closed meeting with the Premier of China—and there was no way to stop him.

When you're a senior official representing the United States abroad, let alone the President or Secretary of State, every movement is carefully planned and every door opens on cue. You get used to being whisked through busy city centers in motorcades, bypassing customs and security at the airport, and never having to wait for an elevator. But sometimes protocol breaks down and diplomacy gets messy. That's when you have to improvise. This was one of those times.

President Obama and I were looking for Premier Wen Jiabao in the middle of a large international conference on climate change in Copenhagen, Denmark. In December 2009, that charming city was cold, dark, and uncharacteristically tense. We knew that the only way to achieve a meaningful agreement on climate change was for leaders of the nations emitting the most greenhouse gases to sit down together and hammer out a compromise—especially the United States and China. The choices and trade-offs confronting us would be difficult. New clean energy technologies and greater efficiencies might allow us to cut emissions while creating jobs and exciting new industries, and even help emerging economies leapfrog the dirtiest phases of industrial development. But there was no getting around the fact that combating climate change was going to be a hard political sell at a time when the world was already reeling from a global financial crisis. All economies ran primarily on fossil fuels. Changing that would require bold leadership and international cooperation.

But the Chinese were avoiding us. Worse, we learned that Wen had called a "secret" meeting with the Indians, Brazilians, and South Africans to stop, or at least dilute, the kind of agreement the United States was seeking. When we couldn't find any of the leaders of those countries, we knew something was amiss and sent out members of our team to canvass the conference center. Eventually they discovered the meeting's location.

After exchanging looks of "Are you thinking what I'm thinking?" the President and I set off through the long hallways of the sprawling Nordic convention center, with a train of experts and advisors scrambling to keep up. Later we'd joke about this impromptu "footcade," a motorcade without the motors, but at the time I was focused on the diplomatic challenge waiting at the end of our march. So off we went, charging up a flight of stairs and encountering surprised Chinese officials, who tried to divert us by sending us in the opposite direction. We were undeterred. *Newsweek* later described us as "a diplomatic version of Starsky and Hutch."

When we arrived outside the meeting room, there was a jumble of arguing aides and nervous security agents. Robert Gibbs, the White House Press Secretary, got tangled up with a Chinese guard. In the commotion the President slipped through the door and yelled, "Mr. Premier!" really loudly, which got everyone's attention. The Chinese guards put their arms up against the door again, but I ducked under and made it through.

In a makeshift conference room whose glass walls had been covered by drapes for privacy against prying eyes, we found Wen wedged around a long table with Indian Prime Minister Manmohan Singh, Brazilian President Luiz Inácio Lula da Silva, and South African President Jacob Zuma. Jaws dropped when they saw us.

"Are you ready?" said President Obama, flashing a big grin. Now the real negotiations could begin.

═══

It was a moment that was at least a year in the making. In our 2008 campaigns both Senator Obama and I highlighted climate change as an urgent challenge for our country and the world, and we offered plans to curb emissions, improve energy efficiency, and develop clean energy technologies. We tried to level with the American people about the hard choices to come while avoiding the old false choice between the economy and the environment.

The problems posed by global warming were evident, despite the deniers. There was a mountain of overwhelming scientific data about the damaging effects of carbon dioxide, methane, and other greenhouse gases. Thirteen of the top fourteen warmest years on record have all come since 2000. Extreme weather events, including fires, heat waves, and droughts are measurably on the rise. If this continues, it will cause additional challenges, displacing millions of people, sparking competition over scarce resources such as fresh water, and destabilizing fragile states.

Once in office, President Obama and I agreed that climate change represented both a significant national security threat and a major test of American leadership. We knew that the United Nations would hold a major climate conference at the end of our first year in office and that it would be an opportunity to galvanize broad international action. So we began laying the groundwork.

This was part of a bigger story about how our foreign policy had to change. During the Cold War, Secretaries of State could focus nearly exclusively on traditional issues of war and peace, such as nuclear arms control. In the 21st century we've also had to pay attention to the emerging global challenges that affect everyone in our interdependent world: pandemic diseases, financial contagion, international terrorism, transnational criminal networks, human and wildlife trafficking—and, of course, climate change.

Movement on the domestic front began quickly in 2009, as the new Obama Administration started working with Congress on ambitious "cap-and-trade" legislation that would create a market for pricing, buying, and selling carbon emissions, while also taking direct action through federal agencies like the Environmental Protection Agency (EPA) and passing legislation that provided incentives to generate more solar and wind power. There was a lot of excitement when a bill passed the House of Representatives in June with the leadership of Congressmen Henry

Waxman from California and Ed Markey from Massachusetts, but it quickly got bogged down in the Senate.

Internationally, we had tough going. From the start I knew it would take creative and persistent diplomacy to build a network of global partners willing to tackle climate change together. Building this kind of coalition, especially when the policy choices involved are so difficult, is much harder than herding cats. The first step was embracing the international negotiations process called the United Nations Framework Convention on Climate Change, which allowed all participating nations to discuss this shared challenge at a single venue. The goal was to gather everyone in Copenhagen in December 2009 and try to strike a deal between the developed and developing countries.

I needed an experienced negotiator with expertise in climate and energy issues to lead this effort, so I asked Todd Stern to become Special Envoy for Climate Change. I knew Todd from his work in the 1990s as a negotiator on the Kyoto Accord, which Vice President Al Gore championed and Bill signed but the Senate never ratified. Beneath a calm demeanor, Todd is a passionate and dogged diplomat. During the years of the Bush Administration he worked diligently on climate and energy issues at the Center for American Progress. Now he would have to use all his skill to cajole reluctant nations to come to the negotiating table and compromise. I wanted to give him as much of a running start as possible, so I brought him with me on my first trip to Asia. If we didn't convince China, Japan, South Korea, and Indonesia to adopt better climate policies, it would be nearly impossible to reach a credible international agreement.

In Beijing, Todd and I visited the high-tech gas-fired Taiyanggong Thermal Power Plant, which emits half the carbon dioxide of a coal-powered plant and uses a third of the water. After getting a look at the state-of-the-art turbines manufactured by General Electric, I spoke to a Chinese audience about the economic opportunities that come from addressing the challenges of climate change. Their government had begun making huge investments in clean energy, especially in solar and wind, but was refusing to commit to any binding international agreements on emissions. Todd spent many hours then and later trying to convince them to change their minds.

Our early focus on China was no accident. Thanks to its tremendous economic growth over the past decade, China was quickly becoming the world's largest overall emitter of greenhouse gases. (Chinese officials were always quick to point out that their country's per capita emission rate still lagged far behind that of the industrialized West, particularly the United States. Although on that score, too, they are rapidly catching up.) China was also the largest and most influential of a new group of regional and global powers, including Brazil, India, Indonesia, Turkey, and South Africa, who were gaining international clout more for their expanding economies than their military might. Their cooperation would be essential for any comprehensive agreement on climate change.

Each in its own way, these countries were grappling with the implications of their growing weight and influence. For example, China had moved hundreds of millions of people out of poverty since Deng Xiaoping opened it to the world in 1978, but in 2009, 100 million people still lived on less than a dollar per day. The Communist Party's commitment to raising incomes and decreasing poverty relied on increasing industrial output. That posed a stark choice: Could China afford to tackle climate change while so many millions were still so poor? Could it follow a different development path, relying on more efficient and renewable energy, that would still decrease poverty? China was not the only nation struggling with this question. When you govern a country that has deep inequalities and poverty, it's understandable to believe you can't afford to restrain your growth just because 19th- and 20th-century industrial powers polluted their way to prosperity. If India could improve the lives of millions of its citizens by accelerating industrial growth, how could it afford to choose a different path? The answers given by these countries as to whether they would be part of combating climate change, even though they hadn't caused it, would determine the success or failure of our diplomacy.

With this in mind, Todd and I went together to India in the summer of 2009. After proudly showing us around one of the greenest buildings near Delhi and offering me a flowered garland, Environment Minister Jairam Ramesh surprised us during our public speeches by throwing down a rhetorical gauntlet. Taking steps to address climate change should be the responsibility of wealthy countries like the United States, he declared, not emerging powers like India that had more pressing domestic challenges to worry about. In our private conversation, Ramesh reiterated that India's per capita emissions were below that of developed countries, and he argued that there was no legitimate basis for international pressure being put on India in the run-up to Copenhagen.

But it was a stubborn fact that it would be impossible to stop the rise in global temperatures if these rapidly developing countries insisted on playing by the old rules and pumping massive amounts of carbon into the atmosphere. Even if the United States somehow reduced our emissions all the way to zero tomorrow, total global levels still would be nowhere near where they need to be if China, India, and others failed to contain their own emissions. What's more, the same poor people the Indian Minister was concerned about helping would be the ones most vulnerable to the ravages of climate change. So in my response to his comments I said that the United States would do its part to develop clean technologies that would drive economic growth and fight poverty while also reducing emissions. But, I emphasized, it was crucial for the whole world to embrace this as a shared mission and responsibility. This was a debate that would continue in the following months, shape the negotiating positions when countries gathered for the UN's climate conference in Denmark that December, and provoke the secret meeting the President and I crashed.

———

Copenhagen is a picturesque city, full of cobblestoned streets and parks. But when I arrived in the dead of winter in the middle of a swirling snowstorm just past 3 A.M. on December 17, 2009, it was bitterly cold and the negotiations had gone into deep freeze. In just two days the conference would end, and it seemed as if this opportunity for action would slip through the world's fingers.

On one side of the debate were the emerging powers, or as I began to think of them, the "emerging emitters," considering their quickly growing share of total carbon dioxide output. Most of them were seeking to avoid a binding agreement that would limit their growth. On another side were the Europeans, still hoping to extend the Kyoto Accord that had placed big burdens on rich nations but essentially had given large developing countries like China and India a free pass. Many poor and small countries, especially the island nations, were desperate for an agreement that would help them stave off or at least mitigate the climate changes they were already experiencing.

The United States was pushing for what we considered a realistic achievable outcome: a diplomatic agreement agreed to by leaders (rather than a legal treaty ratified by Parliaments and enforceable by courts), which would commit every major nation, developed and developing alike, to take substantive steps to curb carbon emissions and report transparently on their progress—neither of which had ever happened before. We didn't expect every country to take the same steps or even cut emissions by an equal amount, but we were seeking an agreement requiring every country to assume some responsibility to reduce emissions.

One of my first meetings in Copenhagen was with the Alliance of Small Island States. It is estimated that global sea levels rose by 6.7 inches over the course of the 20th century. As Arctic ice continues to melt, sea levels will continue to rise at an increasing rate and threaten the very existence of some of these small countries. In 2012, when I visited the Cook Islands for a meeting of the Pacific Island Forum, leaders there told me that climate change was the single greatest threat facing their nations.

Islands and low-lying nations are on the front lines of this struggle, but the rest of us are not far behind. About 40 percent of all humankind lives within sixty miles of a coast. Sprawling cities near coastal deltas, including those of the Mississippi, Nile, Ganges, and Mekong rivers, are at particular risk. We have to project forward and think about what will happen as climate change continues and sea levels keep rising. What will happen to those billions of people if their homes and cities become unlivable? Where will they go? Who will provide assistance?

Imagine the violence that could follow in the wake of more severe droughts and extreme food and water shortages in fragile states, or the effects on global commerce as farms and infrastructure are destroyed in floods and storms. What will be the impact on global trade and stability as the gap between rich and poor countries widens further? When I met in Copenhagen with Ethiopian Prime Minister Meles Zenawi, who emerged as a spokesperson for some of the countries most vulnerable to the effects of climate change and least able to manage them, he told me that the world was expecting a lot from us, and that this was a moment for American leadership.

Despite all the high hopes leading up to this conference, and perhaps to a degree because of them, things went badly from the start. Interests collided, nerves frayed, and compromise appeared out of reach. We needed to change the dynamic somehow. Early in the morning on December 17, I called a press conference. Our team at the conference hall found a large room with stadium-style seating, and when I arrived there were hundreds of journalists from all over the world packed in and eager for any bit of news that might herald a break in the deadlock. I told the crowd that the United States was prepared to lead a collective effort by developed countries to mobilize $100 billion annually by 2020 from a combination of public and private sources to help the poorest and most vulnerable nations mitigate the damage from climate change—if we could also reach a broad agreement on limiting emissions.

The idea began with the Europeans, particularly British Prime Minister Gordon Brown, who had proposed a similar deal in the summer. Prior to my arrival in Copenhagen, Todd and Deputy National Security Advisor Mike Froman recommended that I have it in my back pocket in case we needed to jump-start negotiations. By offering a concrete commitment, I hoped to breathe new life into the talks, put pressure on China and the other "emerging emitters" to respond, and win support from developing countries who would welcome this new assistance. The journalists and delegates started buzzing immediately, and many were thrilled. The Danish Prime Minister captured the changing mood when he said, "There's a feeling among negotiators that now we have to go into business, and now we have to be flexible, and now we have to try as hard as we can to make real compromises."

But the good feelings didn't last long. The fundamentals of the impasse remained firmly in place. That night, with President Obama not yet in Copenhagen, I joined other world leaders for a contentious debate that stretched late into the night in a small and overheated room. The Chinese weren't giving an inch; neither were the Indians and Brazilians. Some of the Europeans were letting the perfect be the enemy of the good—and the possible. We emerged, frustrated and tired, sometime around 2:00 in the morning, still without an agreement. Exhausted Presidents and Prime Ministers rushed for the exit, only to find a traffic jam of motorcades and security vehicles. So we stood there in what amounted to the world's most unusual taxi line. Patience began to wear thin. Here we all were, hungry and sleepy, with nothing to show for our efforts. No previous climate conference had included so many leaders at the highest level, and yet we were no closer to reaching an agreement. Finally President Sarkozy of France could take no more. He rolled his eyes and with a look of extreme exasperation, he declared, in English, "I want to die!" We all knew what he meant.

What a difference a day makes. Sitting next to President Obama in the small leaders' meeting he and I had just forced our way into, I hoped that we might finally be getting somewhere. I looked across the table at Wen Jiabao, then at the leaders of India, Brazil, and South Africa. They represented about 40 percent of the world's population, and their place at this table symbolized a profound shift in global influence. Countries that just a few decades before had been marginal players in international affairs were now making crucial decisions.

Watching the body language of these leaders, I was glad that President Obama had decided to come to Denmark. He had originally been scheduled to land in Copenhagen on Friday morning, the final day of negotiations. We had hoped to have a deal ready for his arrival, but the deadlocked negotiations made that impossible. Back at the White House his advisors grew nervous. Given how stuck the talks were, was it even worth the President's time to make the trip? This was another case when I thought we had to "get caught trying." I called the President and assured him that his personal intervention might provide the push we needed to break the impasse. He agreed, and Air Force One soon touched down in freezing Copenhagen.

Now here we were, making a last-ditch effort. Among the sticking points was this: If nations agreed to cut their emissions, how would those commitments be monitored and enforced? The Chinese, always allergic to outside scrutiny, were resisting any robust reporting requirements or verification mechanisms. The Indians, however, were more amenable. The country's soft-spoken Prime Minister, Manmohan Singh, was gently pushing back against the Chinese objections. President Jacob Zuma of South Africa, who had been one of our most strident critics in earlier meetings, was also more constructive and conciliatory.

We could feel the momentum in the room shifting, and we weren't the only ones. In a surprising display, one of the other members of the Chinese delegation, a talented diplomat with whom we generally had very cordial relations, started loudly scolding the far more senior Premier. He was quite agitated by the prospect that a deal might actually be at hand. Wen, embarrassed, instructed his interpreter not to translate the outburst. Trying to get the meeting back on track, President Obama, in his cool and calm way, asked Wen what the other Chinese official said. The Premier looked at us and said, "It is not important."

In the end, after lots of cajoling, debating, and compromising, the leaders in that room fashioned a deal that, while far from perfect, saved the summit from failure and put us on the road to future progress. For the first time all major economies, developed and developing alike, agreed to make national commitments to curb carbon emissions through 2020 and report transparently on their mitigation efforts. The world began moving away from the division between developed and developing countries that had defined the Kyoto agreement. This was a foundation to build on.

That's what the President and I told our European friends when we met to debrief them. Crammed into another small room, Brown, Sarkozy, Angela Merkel of Germany, Fredrik Reinfeldt of Sweden, Lars Rasmussen of Denmark, and José Manuel Barroso of the European Commission listened carefully to President Obama. They wanted a legal treaty out of Copenhagen and didn't like our compromise. However, they reluctantly agreed to support it since there was no viable alternative. The Europeans were right that we didn't achieve everything we wanted at Copenhagen. But that's the nature of compromise.

In the months that followed, dozens of nations, including all the major developing countries, did in fact submit proposed plans for limiting emissions. And they are, as best as we can tell, acting to implement those plans. We built on this foundation in follow-on conferences over the next four years in Cancun, Durban, and Doha, all leading to another gathering in Paris in 2015 with the hope of achieving an even stronger agreement applicable to all.

═══

After Copenhagen, I began looking for ways to keep making progress, even if political opposition in Congress and disagreements with China and others on the world stage made it difficult to achieve the kind of sweeping reforms we needed to combat climate change. As a girl in Illinois, I played my share of softball, and one of the lessons that stuck with me was that if you try to hit only home runs, you'll end up popping out more often than not. But if you also go for singles and doubles, even walks, they can add up to something even bigger.

That was the idea behind the Climate and Clean Air Coalition I announced in February 2012, with the purpose of reducing what's called "super pollutants." More than 30 percent of global warming is attributed to these particles, including methane, black carbon, and hydrofluorocarbons (HFCs), which are produced by animal waste, urban landfills, air conditioning units, burning fields, cooking fires, and oil and gas production, among other things. The pollutants are also highly damaging to people's respiratory health. The good news is that these greenhouse gases disperse in the atmosphere more quickly than carbon dioxide, so an aggressive effort to reduce them can slow the rate of climate change more quickly. According to one study, "A sharp reduction in emissions of shorter-lived pollutants beginning in 2015 could offset warming temperatures by up to 50 percent by 2050."

Doing that would buy the world precious time to develop new technologies and the political will to deal with the tougher carbon problems. I started talking to like-minded governments, especially the Scandinavians, about what we could do. We decided to form a public-private partnership consisting of governments, businesses, scientists, and foundations. I held an event at the State Department with the Environmental Ministers from Bangladesh, Canada, Mexico, and Sweden, the Ambassador from Ghana, and the Administrator of the U.S. Environmental Protection Agency, Lisa Jackson, to launch the Climate and Clean Air Coalition. In 2014, there are thirty-seven country partners and forty-four nonstate partners, and the Coalition is making important strides toward reducing methane emissions from oil and gas production and black carbon from diesel fumes and other sources. Addressing waste management in cities from Nigeria to Malaysia, reducing black carbon from brick production in places like Colombia and Mexico, and curtailing methane emissions in Bangladesh and Ghana may fly under the radar, but steps like these are making a difference in the global effort to address climate change.

One of my partners in this effort was Norwegian Foreign Minister Jonas Gahr Støre. He invited me to visit Norway and see firsthand the effects of climate change on shrinking Arctic glaciers. I arrived in the picturesque Norwegian city of Tromsø, which sits north of the Arctic Circle, in June 2012. In the summer the temperatures there climbed into the 40s and daylight lingered nearly all night. Jonas and I boarded the Arctic Research Vessel *Helmer Hanssen* for a trip up a fjord to get a closer look at the melting ice. The air was so clean and crisp, I could hardly believe it. The mountains, still mostly snow-covered, seemed to jut up right out of the icy water. Jonas pointed to the receding glaciers with concern. Summer thaws were now leaving parts of the Arctic Ocean ice-free for weeks at a time. In fact, glaciers were retreating almost everywhere around the world, including in the Alps, Himalayas, Andes, and Rockies and in Alaska and Africa.

Alaska is warming at twice the rate of the rest of the United States, and erosion, melting permafrost, and rising waters are already forcing some communities along the coast to relocate further inland.

In 2005, I joined Senator McCain and two other Republican Senators, Lindsey Graham and Susan Collins, for a trip to Whitehorse, Canada, and Barrow, Alaska, the northernmost point of the United States. We met with scientists, local leaders, and First Nations elders to hear from them about the effects of climate change. Flying over the vast coniferous forests of the Yukon, I could see huge brown swaths of dead spruce trees, killed off by infestations of bark beetles that had moved north because of warmer temperatures, especially the milder winters. Those dead trees became kindling for forest fires that the Canadians told us were happening more frequently. We could see the smoke for ourselves as it billowed up from a nearby blaze.

Virtually everyone I spoke to on that trip had a personal wake-up call about what was happening. A tribal elder recounted how he had returned to a lake where he had fished as a boy only to find it dried up. I met lifelong participants in dogsled races who told me they no longer even needed to wear gloves. In Barrow the sea used to freeze all the way up to the North Pole beginning in November. Now, residents told us, they found slush instead of ice. At Kenai Fjords National Park, rangers showed us the measurements of the shrinking glaciers. It had gotten so bad that you couldn't even see the ice from the visitors' center built a few decades earlier to showcase the stunning view.

Seven years later, in Norway, I was seeing even more evidence of the steady march of climate change. I liked Jonas and admired his passion for protecting his country's precious ecosystem. Unfortunately there was only so much Norway could do on its own. So he threw himself into the intense diplomacy needed to bring all the Arctic powers together. He and I discussed our shared efforts at the Arctic Council, the international organization responsible for setting out the rules for protecting the region. Tromsø is now home to its permanent headquarters. The Council includes all the key players: the United States, Canada, Denmark, Finland, Iceland, Norway, Russia, and Sweden. I shared Jonas's commitment to the Council, and in 2011 I became the first U.S. Secretary of State to attend one of its formal meetings, which was held in Nuuk, the remote capital

of Greenland. One of my allies in pushing greater American involvement in the Arctic Council was the Republican Senator from Alaska Lisa
Murkowski. She made the trip with Secretary of the Interior Ken Salazar
and me. I signed the first legally binding international agreement among
the eight Arctic states, putting in place plans for search-and-rescue missions for ships in distress. That was a start, hopefully paving the way for
future cooperation on climate change, energy, and security.

The melting ice was opening up new opportunities for shipping and
oil and gas exploration across the Arctic, setting off a scramble for resources and territorial rights. Some of the energy reserves could be enormous. Russian President Vladimir Putin had cast his eyes on the region
and directed his military to return to a number of old Soviet bases in
the Arctic. In 2007, a Russian submarine even deposited a Russian flag
on the floor of the ocean near the North Pole. Russia's moves raised the
prospect of an arms race in the region and the "militarization" of Arctic
relations. Stephen Harper, the Prime Minister of Canada, has said that to
"defend national sovereignty" in the Arctic, his country needs "forces on
the ground, ships in the sea and proper surveillance." China, too, is eager
to gain influence in the region. It's hungry for energy and excited by the
prospects of new shipping routes that could cut the travel time between
ports in Shanghai and Hong Kong and markets in Europe by thousands
of miles. China has launched several Arctic research expeditions, built its
own research center in Norway, expanded investments in Nordic countries, signed a trade agreement with Iceland, and gained observer status
at the Arctic Council.

Jonas and I discussed the need to prevent this latter-day gold rush
from overwhelming the Arctic's fragile ecosystem and accelerating climate change. Increased economic activity was inevitable and could be
conducted responsibly, if we were careful. But more ships, more drilling,
and more military forces in the region would only accelerate the environmental damage. Just imagine the impact of an oil spill in the Arctic
like the one that hit the Gulf of Mexico in 2010. If we let the Arctic turn
into the Wild West, the health of the planet and our own security would
be at risk.

In the future, I hope that the Arctic Council is able to reach agreement
on how to protect and use the Arctic. This challenge may not galvanize
public opinion today, but it's one of the most important long-term issues
we face.

Despite a strong call to action from President Obama in his second in-augural address, a serious, comprehensive response to climate change remains stymied by entrenched political opposition at home. The reces-sion may have helped cut our total emissions, but it also made it harder to mobilize the political will to drive more meaningful change. When the economy is hurting and people are looking for jobs, many other concerns fade into the background. And the old false choice between promoting the economy and protecting the environment surfaces once again. One exception has been the rapid transformation from coal to natural gas in the generation of electricity. Burning natural gas emits only about half the greenhouse gases that coal does, so long as methane is prevented from leaking from the gas wells, although its production carries other environ-mental risks. To take full advantage of our large resource of natural gas, states and the federal government will need to provide better regulations, more transparency, and rigorous enforcement.

I wish we had achieved more to combat climate change during the first four years of the Obama Administration. Losing the Congress set us back a lot because the Republican majority, unlike conservative parties in other countries, has made denying climate change and opposing even economically beneficial responses to it a central part of its platform. But we can't get discouraged by the size of the problem or the stubbornness of the opposition. We have to keep taking practical steps that actually work. In our meeting in Copenhagen, the Prime Minister of Ethiopia told me that the world was looking to the United States to lead the way on climate change. I believe this is both a responsibility we should accept and an opportunity we should seize. After all, we're still the largest economy and the second-largest emitter of carbon dioxide. The more serious the effects of climate change, the more important it will be for us to lead. The crucial innovations that will help meet this challenge, whether new clean energy technologies, carbon sequestration techniques, or ways to increase our energy efficiency, are most likely to come from our scientists and laboratories. And changing the way we produce and conserve energy can make a large contribution to our economy.

Despite their hard-line stance in international settings, China's leaders are taking important steps at home to invest in clean energy and begin ad-dressing their environmental problems. Over the years we've seen growing grassroots pressure from the Chinese people on issues of pollution, air quality, and clean water. In January 2013, in Beijing and more than two dozen other cities in China the air quality from pollution grew so bad— twenty-five times greater in Beijing than any U.S. city would consider a safe level—that people referred to it as an "airpocalypse." Our embassy in Beijing played an essential role in publicly providing information about pollution, including hourly updates via Twitter. The situation grew so dire that the Chinese leadership recognized pollution as a threat to the country's stability and started to monitor it and publicly release their own numbers on air quality.

In June 2013, President Obama and President Xi signed an agreement to work together on eliminating some "super pollutants," the hydrofluo- rocarbons that come largely from air conditioning units. This was the first agreement between the United States and China to do something specific on climate change. If these steps succeed, it may help to convince China that concerted global action on climate change is in its long-term interest. An understanding between the United States and China will be essential for a global agreement.

The next big international milestone will come in Paris in 2015, when the process that began in Copenhagen will hopefully culminate in a new legal agreement on emissions and mitigation that is applicable to every country in the world. Reaching that goal won't be easy, as we've learned, but it does represent a real opportunity for progress.

America's ability to lead in this setting hinges on what we ourselves are willing to do at home. No country will fall in line just because we tell them to. They want to see us taking significant steps of our own— and we should want the same thing. The failure to pass a comprehen- sive climate bill through the Senate in 2009 made our negotiating job at Copenhagen much harder. To succeed in Paris, we need to be able to show real results at home. President Obama's June 2013 Climate Action Plan is an important step in the right direction, and despite Congres- sional gridlock, the President is moving forward with strong executive actions. Since 2008, we've nearly doubled production of clean renewable energy from wind, solar, and geothermal sources; improved fuel effi- ciency for vehicles; and for the first time begun measuring greenhouse gas emissions from our largest sources. In 2012, U.S. carbon emissions fell to the lowest level in twenty years. But there's a lot more to do. Building a broad national consensus on the urgency of the climate threat and the imperative of a bold and comprehensive response will not be easy, but it is essential.

The most important voices to be heard on this issue are those of the many people whose lives and livelihoods are most at risk from climate change: tribal elders in Alaska watching their fishing holes dry up and the land below their villages erode away; the leaders of island nations trying to raise the alarm before their homes are submerged forever; military planners and intelligence analysts preparing for future conflicts and crises caused by climate change; and all those families, businesses, and communities who have been assaulted by extreme weather. At the conference in Copenhagen in 2009 the most compelling pleas for action came from the leaders of the small island nations, confronting the loss of their land to rising ocean levels. "If things go business as usual," one said, "we will not live, we will die. Our country will not exist."

22

Jobs and Energy:
A Level Playing Field

Algeria is one of those complicated countries that forces the United States to balance our interests and values. It has been an important ally in the fight against al Qaeda and was a potential stabilizing force in North Africa as Libya and Mali descended into chaos. But it also has a poor human rights record and a relatively closed economy.

Both because we need to continue our security cooperation and because it's the right thing to do, the United States sought to encourage improvements in human rights and a more open economy in Algeria. When the government decided to solicit foreign bids to build power plants and modernize its energy sector, I saw an opportunity for advancing prosperity in Algeria and seizing an opportunity for American business. General Electric was competing for the more than $2.5 billion contract. Too often I had seen risk-averse U.S. corporations avoid emerging or challenging markets, while Asian and European companies scooped up contracts and profits. State-owned or -controlled enterprises were especially difficult competitors because they played by their own rules, with unlimited resources and little compunction about violating international norms on bribery and corruption. With growth at home still too slow and unemployment still too high, we couldn't afford to leave good opportunities on the table or put up with unfair competition. So GE's move to compete in

Algeria represented a bold step by a flagship American company, with the potential to yield economic benefits back home and strategic benefits in North Africa.

In October 2012, I went back to Algiers to urge the government to continue political reforms, expand security cooperation in Mali, and consider the GE deal. President Abdelaziz Bouteflika greeted me on a red carpet outside the Mouradia Palace, a sprawling white villa with Moorish-style arches. Behind him rows of Algerian cavalry stood at attention, in their traditional red tunics and green pants. After the seventy-five-year-old Bouteflika walked me past the honor guard into the palace, we spent three hours together, in a wide-ranging dialogue that touched on subjects ranging from the effects of climate change to threats from al Qaeda. I also asked about GE and I left Algiers optimistic that the company would be given a fair shot to win the contract.

Less than a year later GE won the contract to help build six natural gas power plants, which are expected to increase Algeria's electricity-generating capacity by about 70 percent. Over the next few years GE will build generators and giant turbines for these plants in Schenectady, New York, and Greenville, South Carolina, supporting thousands of manufacturing jobs. As a local union representative in Schenectady told the *Times-Union*, "It shows the world we are still No. 1 in world-class power manufacturing." To me, it also reconfirmed an insight that guided much of our work at the State Department over the previous four years: Because energy and economics are increasingly at the heart of our strategic challenges, they must also be at the heart of American diplomacy.

When I became Secretary in 2009, I focused on two big questions about the global economy: Could we sustain and create good jobs at home and help speed our recovery by opening new markets and boosting exports? And were we going to let China and other relatively closed markets continue to rewrite the rules of the global economy in a way that would surely disadvantage our workers and companies? The answers would go a long way toward determining whether America would continue to lead the world's economy and whether we would restore prosperity for our own people.

Traditionally trade, energy, and international economics have not been priorities for Secretaries of State. After all, we have a U.S. Trade Representative and Secretaries of Commerce, Energy, and the Treasury. But the global financial crisis made that division impractical. It was clearer than ever that America's economic strength and our global leadership were a package deal. We would not have one without the other.

I called our efforts "economic statecraft," and urged our diplomats around the world to make it a priority. We had diplomatic posts in more than 270 cities around the world, many of them with resident economic officers. I wanted to use these resources to create new opportunities for growth and shared prosperity. Over the next four years we stood up to protectionism and mercantilism, went to bat for American companies and workers, sought to attract more direct foreign investment into our country, and worked to capitalize on the energy revolution that was helping to drive our domestic recovery and reshape the global strategic landscape.

=====

America had worked for decades to create a global economy of free and fair, open and transparent trade and investment, with clear rules of the road that would benefit everyone.

The current global trading system doesn't fully meet that standard. It is distorted not only by barriers to entry in developing and emerging economies, but by the power of special interests in developed countries, including the United States. Just as it isn't fair for other countries to keep our products and services out of their markets, or to demand bribes or steal our intellectual property in return for access to them, it isn't fair to use our patent laws to deny life-saving generic medicines to poor people in low-income countries. (The work of the Clinton Health Access Initiative to lower prices and increase volume for AIDS medicines proves that there are ways to save lives and protect legitimate economic interests.) To make trade fairer as well as freer, developing countries have to do a better job of improving productivity, raising labor conditions, and protecting the environment. And in the United States we have to do a better job of providing good jobs to those who are displaced by trade.

Currently the United States is negotiating comprehensive agreements with eleven countries in Asia and in North and South America, and with the European Union. We should be focused on ending currency manipulation, environmental destruction, and miserable working conditions in developing countries, as well as harmonizing regulations with the EU. And we should avoid some of the provisions sought by business interests, including our own, like giving them or their investors the power to sue foreign governments to weaken their environmental and public health rules, as Philip Morris is already trying to do in Australia. The United States should be advocating a level and fair playing field, not special favors.

Despite all its problems, a more open trading system has lifted more people out of poverty in the last thirty-five years than at any comparable time in history. And there is less imbalance in our trade with the countries we do have agreements with, like Canada and Mexico, than with those we don't, like China. Making an open system work better will help more people than state capitalism, petro capitalism, currency manipulation, and corrupt deal making ever will.

Meanwhile, I was determined to do everything I could to help American businesses and workers seize more of the legitimate opportunities already available. We faced strong headwinds from countries that wanted a different system altogether.

China had become the leading exponent of an economic model called "state capitalism," in which state-owned or state-supported companies used public money to dominate markets and advance strategic interests. State capitalism, as well as a range of new forms of protectionism involving barriers behind borders—such as unfair regulations, discrimination against foreign companies, and forced technology transfers—posed a growing threat to the ability of American businesses to compete in key markets. These policies ran directly counter to the values and principles we had worked to embed in the global economy. We believed an open, free, transparent, and fair system with clear rules of the road would benefit everyone.

Though China was the largest offender when it came to new forms of protectionism and state capitalism, it was hardly alone. By 2011, sovereign wealth investment funds, which are owned and run by governments, often with revenue from exports of oil and natural gas, had grown to control roughly 12 percent of all investment worldwide. Increasingly, state-owned and state-supported enterprises were operating not just in their home markets but around the globe, sometimes in secrecy, often lacking the transparency and accountability that shareholders and regulations ensure. We were seeing hybrid companies masquerading as commercial actors that were actually controlled by states and acting with strategic consequences, such as Russia's Gazprom.

As a Senator I warned that China, a member of the World Trade Organization, "needs to be convinced to play by the rules in the global marketplace," and I was concerned that the Bush Administration's laissez-faire philosophy led them to take a hands-off approach. In 2004, I was approached by executives at a storied New York company, Corning Glass, with a problem that highlighted the challenges we faced. Established in 1851, Corning, a glass manufacturer headquartered in Corning, New York, was famous for supplying the scratch-resistant "gorilla glass" used by more than thirty-three major brands of smartphones, tablets, and notebooks, including Apple's iPhone. Corning also produced advanced liquid crystal displays in computer monitors and televisions, as well as optical fiber and cables for the communications industry, clean filters for diesel engines, and a wide range of other innovative products. They spent more than $700 million a year on research. Their technology and products were so good that competitors in China felt they needed an unfair advantage to compete. So they asked their friends in the Chinese government to either block Corning from entering the market altogether or slap their fiber optics with absurdly high tariffs. There were also blatant attempts to steal the company's intellectual property.

This wasn't fair, and it was also a threat to the future of a company that employed thousands of New Yorkers. In April 2004, I invited the Chinese Ambassador to my Senate office and sent a pointed letter to the Chinese Minister of Trade. I also made every attempt possible to enlist the Bush Administration to back me up. After failing to get much attention from the White House, I raised the Corning matter directly with President Bush at the dedication of my husband's Presidential library in Little Rock, Arkansas. "This is a great American company being threatened," I told him. "Your administration needs to help me help them." President Bush agreed to look into the problem, and he did. In December China dropped the discriminatory tariff. Allowed to compete on a level playing field, Corning's business thrived.

Other American companies face similar challenges. In October 2009, new Chinese postal laws came into effect requiring domestic operating permits for express delivery service companies. The move was widely seen as a plan for the Chinese government to expand its own express delivery service by the state-controlled China Post. The major American delivery companies, FedEx and UPS, had been doing business in China for years. Before 2009, FedEx had permission to operate in fifty-eight locations there, and UPS in thirty. Both companies feared that the Chinese government would issue them severely restrictive licenses. Our U.S. Ambassadors in Beijing, first Jon Huntsman and then Gary Locke (as a former Commerce Secretary, Gary understood exactly how important this was), raised the issue with the Chinese government, but to no avail. Fred Smith, the CEO of FedEx, eventually called me to ask for my help.

I brought the matter up directly with Wang Qishan, the Vice Premier responsible for the economy and someone I had come to know and respect. Secretary of Commerce John Bryson and I followed up in a joint letter. After our efforts the Chinese informed FedEx that they had finally granted licenses, but only to eight cities in China, and just five for UPS. That was a start, but nowhere near good enough. I delivered another message to Vice Premier Wang. Eventually the Chinese pledged that over the course of a three-year interim period, they would grant permits for the remaining cities. The embassy reported back that the Chinese officials were surprised by the sustained U.S. government response to the issue at such a senior level. As of this writing, both companies have been able to maintain their operating status in China. The Chinese have stood by their promise to increase licenses, but both companies remain concerned about the potential for growth in the future.

I was prepared to keep fighting for individual American companies, but given the scope of the challenge, we needed to think bigger. In the summer of 2011, I decided to make it clear that the United States intended to stand up for a fair global economic system. I headed to Hong Kong, an island of entrepreneurial capitalism attached to China's still evolving state-dominated economy. Hong Kong seemed like the perfect place to make the argument for a level playing field and a common set of global economic rules. I had first visited the city in the 1980s, when I accompanied Bill on a trade mission to promote Arkansas's businesses and exports. This time I was trying to sell more than soybeans. I was selling the American model of free markets for free people. It had taken a beating in the eyes of the world during the financial crisis, and a growing number of nations were giving a fresh look to the Chinese model of state capitalism and autocracy, which continued to produce impressive economic growth at home. In a speech at the Shangri-La Hotel, in front of a large crowd of business leaders from across the region, I made my case.

"We must start with the most urgent task before us: realigning our economies in the wake of the global financial crisis," I said. "This means pursuing a more balanced strategy for global economic growth." Developed nations like the United States would need to build more at home and sell more abroad (which would create jobs and jump-start our recovery and help increase growth in the rest of the world), while rapidly developing countries in Asia and elsewhere that had accumulated large savings would need to buy more—and strengthen and update their financial and trade policies to ensure a more level economic playing field and greater stability in global markets.

I acknowledged the challenges faced by developing economies that still had to lift hundreds of millions of people out of poverty. China often argued that this imperative outweighed any obligation to play by established international rules for business, labor, and human rights practices. But I countered that China and other emerging economies had benefited greatly from the international system the United States had helped create, including their membership in the World Trade Organization, and now they needed to take their share of responsibility for upholding it. Besides, that was actually the best way to ensure continued growth and prosperity and to help even more people climb out of poverty and into the middle class in developed and developing countries alike.

After all, Malaysian manufacturers wanted access to markets overseas as much as American manufacturers did. Indian firms wanted fair treatment when they invested abroad, just as we did. Chinese artists wanted to protect their creations from piracy. Every society seeking to develop a strong research and technology sector needed intellectual property protections because, without them, innovation would entail higher risk and bring fewer rewards. And I explicitly rejected the idea that there could be one set of rules for the major industrialized economies like the United States and another for emerging markets like China. "Enough of the world's commerce takes place with developing nations that leaving them out of the rules-based system would render the system unworkable," I said. "And ultimately, that would impoverish everyone."

Unfortunately, much of the attention that day was not on trade but on a drama unfolding thousands of miles away, back in Washington, one that threatened to undermine my argument and the world's confidence in American economic leadership.

In mid-May 2011, the U.S. government had reached its debt ceiling, and the President and Congress had only a limited time to raise it or risk defaulting on America's debts, which would have catastrophic consequences for us and the global economy. Despite the high stakes, this was a difficult issue for many to understand. To many Americans, it sounded like Congress was debating whether to give itself permission to spend a lot of money and rack up new debts. But that wasn't it at all. The real question was whether Congress would vote to pay debts it had already run up in spending bills it had already passed into law. The vast majority of countries don't require an extra step like this, so it was also hard for people around the world to comprehend what was happening.

Some in Congress were actually arguing that, for the first time in history, we should refuse to pay our debts and let our country default, despite all the consequences for the global economy and for America's credibility and leadership. From every continent, foreign leaders were expressing grave concerns. China, which had invested more than a trillion dollars in U.S. government securities, was particularly nervous. The state-owned newspaper *Xinhua* reflected the prevailing attitude when it wrote: "Given the United States' status as the world's largest economy and the issuer of the dominant international reserve currency, such political brinksmanship in Washington is dangerously irresponsible." When this scenario played out a second time, in 2013, the Chinese went further. They started talking about a "de-Americanized world" and suggested it was time to look for a different reserve currency besides the dollar. Of course, because China owned so much of our debt, they were in a strong position to make that outcome more likely.

When I arrived in Hong Kong, the crisis had reached a fever pitch. I awoke to the headline "US Debt Talks Down to Wire as Parties Battle" in the local English-language newspaper. At the Hong Kong Government House, Chief Executive Donald Tsang greeted me with his customary smile and bow tie but asked the questions that were on everyone's mind in Asia and around the world: What is going on in Washington? Could they still trust the U.S. economy? I heard the same questions at a reception with business leaders before my speech.

The answer I gave was, of course, yes. I said that I was confident a deal would be reached. Privately I crossed my fingers and hoped it was true.

The entire experience was a reminder of how closely the rest of the world watches how we make decisions at home and how central America's economic strength and political resolve are to our global leadership. The full faith and credit of the United States should never be in doubt, and the Secretary of State shouldn't have to publicly reassure people in other nations that we'll pay our debts. Period.

My toughest sell, however, was still ahead. I drove across the bridge into China's Shenzhen Province, to meet with my Chinese counterpart,

State Councilor Dai Bingguo. The Chinese were following our political dysfunction with a mix of bewilderment, concern, and anticipation. Of course, they didn't want anything truly awful to happen because they understood how interdependent our economies had become. But the more paralyzed the United States looked, the better China would look to the world. The Chinese could say to potential partners, You can't count on the Americans, but you can always count on us. Dai seemed to enjoy dwelling on America's fiscal woes, adopting a somewhat sardonic tone about our political gridlock. I wasn't having any of it. "We could spend the next six hours talking about China's domestic challenges," I countered. I left my meeting with Dai even more convinced that America had to avoid these self-inflicted wounds and get our own house in order.

Despite the ongoing drama in Washington, I used my speech in Hong Kong to put down a marker about the importance of following globally accepted economic rules of the road. But we needed to do more than talk. In his 2012 State of the Union address, President Obama declared, "I will not stand by when our competitors don't play by the rules." The administration was already bringing trade enforcement cases against China at nearly twice the rate of the Bush Administration. Now there would be a special new Trade Enforcement Unit to go after unfair trading practices wherever they damage our interests and the operation of free markets. And when other nations provided unfair financing for their exports, the United States would offer matching support to our firms.

———

A lot of good American jobs depend on a level playing field with rules that are clear, fair, and followed. On average, every $1 billion of goods we export supports between 5,000 and 5,400 jobs, and those jobs pay between 13 and 18 percent more than non-export-related jobs. In 2010 President Obama set a target of doubling America's exports over five years. The administration worked hard to improve and ratify trade agreements with South Korea, Colombia, and Panama that were negotiated under President Bush, and also launched new trade talks with many of the nations of the Pacific Rim, as well as with the EU.

I made export promotion a personal mission. During my travels I often made a pitch for an American business or product, like GE in Algeria. For example, in October 2009, I visited the Boeing Design Center in Moscow because Boeing had been trying to secure a contract for new planes with the Russians. I made the case that Boeing's jets set the global gold standard, and, after I left, our embassy kept at it. In 2010, the Russians agreed to buy fifty 737s, for almost $4 billion, which translated into thousands of American jobs. And our efforts weren't just on behalf of big companies like Boeing or GE—we also advocated for small and medium-sized businesses across our country trying to go global.

We got creative with initiatives like Direct Line, which allowed our Ambassadors to host phone calls or video chats with American businesses eager to break into new markets. The U.S. Ambassador to Spain hosted a call with thirty companies to discuss the protection of intellectual property rights, for instance, while our Ambassador to Chile hosted one on renewable energy opportunities there.

The State Department worked with the Commerce Department as well as state and local officials on a program called SelectUSA, which President Obama launched in June 2011, to attract more foreign direct investment into our country, which already supported more than 5 million American jobs, including 2 million in manufacturing. The early results were encouraging. In October 2013, President Obama highlighted 220 new jobs at an Austrian company's auto-parts plant in Cartersville, Georgia, and a $600 million investment in Wichita, Kansas, by the Canadian company Bombardier.

One little-noticed but quite effective tool was State's aviation diplomacy. During my four years, our experts negotiated fifteen Open Skies Agreements with nations all over the world, bringing the total number to more than a hundred. These agreements opened new routes to U.S. air carriers. According to independent estimates, the direct connection between Memphis and Amsterdam had a $120 million annual impact on Tennessee's economy and supported more than 2,200 local jobs. And when American Airlines started flying direct to Madrid, it had a $100 million annual impact on the Dallas–Fort Worth economy.

Since 2009, U.S. exports have increased by 50 percent, which means they've grown four times as fast as the economy as a whole. All these sales overseas have contributed about $700 billion to our total economic output and are responsible for as much as a third of our economic growth, supporting an estimated 1.6 million private-sector jobs. Though millions of Americans are still out of work, these are meaningful results.

Lowering barriers to access for American companies was a big part of our efforts. So was raising standards in foreign markets on key issues like labor rights, environmental protection, the behavior of state-owned enterprises, and intellectual property. Companies in the United States already met these standards, but those of many other countries didn't. We needed to level the playing field and improve a lot of lives around the world along the way. For too long we'd seen companies closing factories and leaving the United States because they could do business more cheaply in foreign countries where they didn't have to pay workers a living wage or abide by U.S. rules on pollution. Using diplomacy and trade negotiations to raise standards abroad could help change that calculus.

I felt particularly passionate about improving working conditions around the world. Over the years I met workers, many of them women and even children, who labored under atrocious conditions. The most heartbreaking were victims of human trafficking and forced labor that amounts to modern-day slavery.

One day in July 2012, I met with a number of women workers and activists in Siem Reap, Cambodia, along with a local representative of an organization called the Solidarity Center, which is funded in part by the AFL-CIO to improve labor rights around the world. The Cambodian women told me about the many challenges they faced. Too many employers used various forms of coercion to force workers to stay on the job for long hours, sometimes under unsafe conditions. Many children were still forced to tend fields, bake bricks, and beg in the street. Children from rural villages were being trafficked to cities for sexual exploitation, often by foreign men who might pay thousands of dollars for virgin girls or to engage in other forms of child sex tourism. Too many police at every level were poorly trained, if at all, to address these problems or to protect survivors, and too many public officials looked the other way or, worse, profited from the trade in human beings.

When I was in Siem Reap in 2010, I visited a shelter and recovery center for survivors of human trafficking run by a courageous woman named Somaly Mam. Trafficked into a brothel as a little girl, she was raped and abused repeatedly before finally escaping. In 1996, she started a movement to rescue other trafficked girls and support them as they rebuilt their lives as she had. By 2010 her organization, funded in part by the State Department, operated three shelters across Cambodia that provided safety and caring, along with rehabilitation and vocational training, to reintegrate survivors into society.

The girls I met were shockingly young to be survivors of such terrible crimes, but I saw how the love and nurturing they were receiving had put light back in their eyes. Some eagerly showed me around, while others, who were shyer, cautiously watched to see what the fuss was about.

The crime of human trafficking is not limited to Cambodia, or Southeast Asia. Nearly 30 million people around the world are in modern-day slavery of one form or another, trapped in prostitution or laboring in fields or factories or on fishing boats. The United States is not immune. In 2010 six "recruiters" were indicted in Hawaii in the largest human trafficking case ever charged in U.S. history. They had coerced four hundred Thai workers into farm labor by confiscating their passports and threatening to have them deported if they complained.

As Secretary I appointed Lou CdeBaca, a decorated former federal prosecutor, to ramp up our global antitrafficking efforts and to produce reports on enforcement of antitrafficking laws in 177 countries. I also asked Lou to take a look at our own country, something the Department had never done before, because I thought it was important to hold ourselves to the same high standards we expected from others. By law, the findings of those reports triggered sanctions on countries failing to make progress, so they became a powerful diplomatic tool to encourage concrete action.

In addition to trafficking, I was also concerned about the unscrupulous, even criminal employers, aided and abetted by governments, who exploited their workers, adults and children alike. That's one of the reasons I strongly support the right of workers to organize unions. After decades of struggle, workers in America formed unions strong enough to protect their rights and secure such advances as the eight-hour day and the minimum wage, achievements that helped create and sustain the American middle class.

In many countries around the world, unions are still suppressed and workers have few, if any, rights. This is bad for them and it's bad for American workers too, because it creates unfair competition that drives down wages for everyone. Contrary to what some governments and employers might think, research shows that respecting workers' rights leads to positive long-term economic outcomes, including higher levels of foreign direct investment. Bringing more workers into the formal economy and giving them fair protections has positive ripple effects for society. Inequality declines while mobility increases. Taxes are paid. Countries and communities are stronger and better able to meet the expectations and aspirations of their people. The flipside is also true: Denying workers their rights costs societies dearly in lost productivity, innovation, and growth. It undermines the rule of law and plants the seeds of instability. And it's bad for us when foreign workers are too poor to buy U.S. products.

Back in 1999, I explored some of these questions in a speech at the Sorbonne in Paris called "Globalization into the Next Millennium." Would greater economic interdependence lead to greater growth, stability, and innovation for people around the world? Or would it merely lead to a "race to the bottom" of the economic ladder for billions of people? Would it help to expand opportunities for all citizens, or reward only those of us already lucky enough to have the skills to navigate the Information Age? I suggested that it was time to tackle "runaway global capitalism's worst effects" and "put a human face on the global economy, giving workers everywhere a stake in its success, equipping them to reap its rewards," while providing "social safety nets for the most vulnerable." A decade later the urgency of these concerns had only heightened.

The State Department had long had a bureau dedicated to democracy, human rights, and labor, although the last part sometimes was neglected. I wanted to change that, and so did my Assistant Secretary, Michael Posner, a human rights activist who had helped found the Fair Labor Association in the 1990s. Under Mike's leadership, the United States stepped up its support for training programs and workshops on international labor standards for union organizers, employers, and government officials. We sponsored exchanges so that labor academics from around the world could learn from one another, helped police and prosecutors go after human trafficking and forced labor, launched new diplomatic dialogues with labor ministries, and signed agreements with key countries like Vietnam and China to provide technical assistance on a range of labor issues, from mine safety to social security.

In a town hall meeting in Dhaka, Bangladesh, in May 2012, a labor activist asked me what Bangladeshis could do to improve rights and conditions for workers, especially in their country's booming garment industry. "We face all kinds of obstructions with the police, goons, thugs, and false allegations in court," she said. "And, in fact, one of our leaders, Aminul Islam, was very brutally murdered."

This was an issue I had raised forcefully with the Bangladeshi government because I thought that the case of the murdered trade union leader was a real test for the country's justice system and the rule of law. In responding to the question, I also turned to the broader question of labor rights in a developing economy:

> *There are strong forces that oppose workers being organized. We have this in my own country. You go back to the 19th and the early 20th century when labor unions were just getting started, there were goons, there were thugs, there were killings, there were riots, there were terrible conditions. We passed laws at the beginning of the 20th century against child labor, against too many hours for people to work, but that took time. It took time to develop a sense of political will to address those issues. So you are beginning that, and it's a very important struggle. . . . You are doing very important work. Do not be discouraged or intimidated. You deserve to have the support of your government and your society.*

Then I explained some of the efforts we were making around the world to stand up for labor rights:

> *We have worked from Colombia to Cambodia with the owners of factories and other enterprises to help them understand how they can continue to make a very good profit while treating their workers right. . . . It's a part of becoming a middle-class country. Workers deserve to have their labor respected and fairly paid for. Factory owners deserve to have what they pay for, which is an honest day's work for the wages that they pay. So there is a way to accommodate those interests, and we've seen it, and we can continue to work with you to try to achieve it.*

———

One area where economics and geopolitics come together most potently—and where U.S. leadership is most needed—is energy. Many of the international challenges I dealt with over my four years directly or indirectly sprang from the world's insatiable hunger for energy and the shifting dynamics created by new sources and supplies coming online. Consider how often energy played a role in the events discussed in this book: the bitter dispute over oil between Sudan and South Sudan; competing claims in the

South and East China Seas that were as much about control of resources under the seafloor as commerce on the water's surface; the extensive effort to sanction Iran's oil exports; and, of course, the international effort to cut greenhouse gas emissions and address the challenge of climate change.

Energy has always been an important factor in international affairs, but a number of developments have lent it new significance in recent years: growing economies in China, India, and other emerging markets have generated huge new demand; technological innovations have opened up previously inaccessible sources of oil and natural gas and made renewables like wind and solar cost-effective, creating new energy players to compete with traditional petro-powers like Russia and Saudi Arabia; and the urgency of combatting climate change has provided an incentive to develop clean alternatives to fossil fuels and improve efficiency.

The scramble for new energy resources had the potential to lead to more conflict or more cooperation around the world. I thought that, with the right strategy and tools, the United States could help steer away from the former and toward the latter. To help us do that effectively, I created a bureau at the State Department dedicated to energy diplomacy, and asked Ambassador Carlos Pascual to run it. He and his team worked closely with the Department of Energy, which had invaluable technical expertise but less of a global reach. Much of our energy diplomacy was focused on five broad challenges.

First, we tried to help resolve disputes between countries that either laid claim to the same resources or had to cooperate to utilize them. For example, recall that South Sudan has extensive oil reserves while its northern neighbor Sudan does not. But Sudan does have refining and shipping facilities, which the South lacks. That means the two countries, despite ongoing hostility, need to work together.

Second, we worked to discourage the use of energy supplies by one nation to dominate or intimidate another. Russia's bullying of Ukraine and other European countries with natural-gas price gouging and supply cutoffs is a good example.

Third, we implemented sanctions targeting Iran's oil industry and worked with partners around the world to significantly reduce their imports of Iranian crude oil and bring new supplies online elsewhere.

Fourth, we promoted clean energy sources like solar, wind, hydro, geothermal, and natural gas (which isn't perfect but is cleaner than coal) that could help us slow the effects of climate change.

Fifth, we worked to prevent or mitigate the so-called resource curse by promoting transparency and accountability in extractive industries, and working with partner governments to invest resource income responsibly and avoid corruption. No country has suffered more from the resource curse than Nigeria. When I visited in 2009 and 2012, I stressed the urgency of Nigerians tackling corruption and investing revenues to improve millions of lives, not swell personal fortunes. Nigeria could be a G-20 member and an influential global voice if it made the hard choice to overcome the curse.

While we were pursuing all this work abroad, there were also exciting developments at home. American innovation was at the forefront of unlocking new energy supplies, whether it was hard-to-reach oil and gas or cutting-edge renewables. In 2013, the United States reportedly surpassed both Saudi Arabia and Russia to lead the world in oil and gas production. And electricity generation from wind and solar more than doubled between 2009 and 2013.

The boom in domestic energy production, especially in natural gas, created major economic and strategic opportunities for our country.

Expanded energy production created tens of thousands of new jobs, from oil rigs in North Dakota to wind turbine factories in South Carolina. Cheap and plentiful natural gas is helping drive down costs for energy-intensive manufacturers and giving the United States a big competitive advantage over places like Japan and Europe, where energy prices remain much higher. Researchers project that all the ripple effects from our domestic energy revolution could create up to 1.7 million permanent jobs by 2020 and add between 2 and 4 percent to our annual gross domestic product. The shift to natural gas is also helping lower carbon emissions, because it's cleaner than coal. Greater domestic production is reducing our dependence on foreign oil, easing a major strategic burden, and freeing up supplies elsewhere to help our European allies lessen their dependence on Russia.

There are legitimate climate change concerns about the new extraction practices and their impact on local water, soil, and air supplies. Methane leaks in the production and transportation of natural gas are particularly worrisome. So it's crucial that we put in place smart regulations and enforce them, including not drilling when the risks are too high.

If we approach this challenge responsibly and make the right investments in infrastructure, technology, and environmental protection, America can be the clean energy superpower for the 21st century. That means creating a positive environment for private-sector innovation and risk-taking, with targeted tax incentives, a commitment to research and development, and policies that encourage rather than undercut the transition to clean, renewable sources of energy. And it means investing in the infrastructure of the future, including next-generation power plants to produce electricity more cleanly, smarter grids to deliver it more effectively, and greener buildings to use it more efficiently. China and others are already racing forward with big bets on renewables. We cannot afford to cede leadership in this area, especially since American innovation holds the key to the next generation of advances, and our capacity to employ them at home and in our hemisphere is almost limitless. Our economic recovery, our efforts against climate change, and our strategic position in the world all will improve if we can build a bridge to a clean energy economy.

—————

When grappling with some of these big global trends in energy and economics, it can be easy to forget how much they affect the daily lives of individuals and families around the world. One example that really brought this home for me was the simple but overlooked issue of cookstoves. It combined concerns about energy, the environment, economics, and public health at a local level. And it demonstrated how a creative, 21st-century approach to development and diplomacy could solve problems and improve lives in unexpected ways.

If you've ever built a campfire or tried to cook outdoors, you likely know what it feels like when the wind changes direction and black smoke fills your lungs. It can bring tears to your eyes. Now imagine if, instead of being a rare outdoor activity, this was something you experienced daily, inside your own home. That's what happens to 3 billion people around the world who gather every day around open fires or old and inefficient stoves in small kitchens and poorly ventilated houses. Women labor over these hearths for hours, often with their babies strapped to their back, and they spend hours more gathering wood for fuel. The food they prepare is different on every continent, but the air they breathe is the same: a toxic mix of chemicals released by burning wood or other solid fuel that can reach two hundred times the amount the EPA considers safe. As the women cook, smoke fills their lungs, and the toxins begin poisoning them and their children. The black carbon, methane, and other "super pollutants" released in this smoke also contribute to climate change.

The results of daily exposure are devastating. The World Health Organization released data in March 2014 showing that household air pollution was responsible for 4.3 million premature deaths in 2012, more than double the number of deaths from malaria and tuberculosis combined. That makes this dirty smoke one of the worst health risks in the developing world. Although people have cooked over open fires and dirty stoves for all of human history, we now know that it is slowly killing millions of people.

I asked Kris Balderston, my Special Representative for Global Partnerships, to lead an effort to tackle this under-the-radar but deeply troubling and consequential challenge. And in September 2010, at the annual meeting of the Clinton Global Initiative, I launched the Global Alliance for Clean Cookstoves with nineteen founding partners from governments, business, international institutions, academia, and philanthropy. The Alliance decided to pursue a market-based approach to persuade companies to build clean, efficient, and affordable stoves and fuels. We set an ambitious goal: 100 million homes adopting new clean stoves and fuels by 2020. We knew how difficult this would be, from the technical challenge of designing cheap, safe, clean, and durable stoves to the logistical challenge of distributing them all over the world and the social challenge of convincing consumers to actually embrace them. But we hoped that technological breakthroughs and growing private-sector engagement would allow us to succeed. On behalf of the U.S. government, I announced a pledge of $50 million to get the effort going.

I was delighted by the speed and scope of the progress we made around the world. More than 8 million clean cookstoves were distributed in 2012, more than double the number in 2011 and ahead of projections toward the goal of 100 million. By the end of 2013 the Alliance had grown to include more than eight hundred partners, and the U.S. government had boosted its commitment to $125 million.

Since leaving the State Department, I have continued my work with the Alliance as an Honorary Chair. There are projects in Bangladesh, China, Ghana, Kenya, Nigeria, and Uganda, with efforts beginning in India and Guatemala as well. The Alliance now supports thirteen testing centers across the world and has spearheaded new global standards for cookstoves, giving manufacturers, distributors, and buyers guidelines for cleanliness, safety, and efficiency standards. This is a crucial step in building a viable market that will deliver clean stoves to consumers who will actually use them.

======

In difficult economic times, there is an inherent tension between our desire to lift other people around the world out of poverty and into the middle class and our need to protect our own hard-pressed middle class. If global economics were a zero-sum game, then the rise of other markets and the growth of other countries' middle classes would always come at our own expense. But it doesn't have to be. I believe our own prosperity depends on having partners to trade with and that our fortunes are inextricably linked to those of the rest of the world. And I am convinced that, as long as the competition is fair, the more people around the world who leave poverty and join the middle class, the better it will be for America.

This belief is rooted in my own experiences growing up in a middle-class American family. After World War II my dad, Hugh Rodham, opened a small drapery fabric business. He worked long hours and sometimes employed day laborers. He often enlisted my mother, my brothers, and me to help with the silkscreen printing. My parents believed in self-reliance and hard work, and they made sure we kids learned the value of a dollar and appreciated the dignity of a job well done.

I had my first paying job, other than babysitting, when I was thirteen. I worked for the Park Ridge Park District three mornings a week supervising a small park a few miles from my house. Since Dad left for work early in our only car, I had to walk to work, pulling a wagon filled with balls, bats, jump ropes, and other supplies back and forth. From that year on, I always had summer and holiday jobs. They helped pay my college and law school costs. I was grateful for the sacrifices my parents made to give us opportunities they never had, and Bill and I worked hard to pass on to Chelsea many of these same values, including a strong work ethic. We felt this was particularly important because she was growing up in such unusual circumstances, first in a Governor's Mansion and then in the White House. If my parents were alive today, they'd be incredibly proud of what a strong, principled, and hardworking woman their granddaughter has become. I know I am.

The world has changed a lot since I was growing up, but the American middle class remains the greatest economic engine in history and the heart of the American Dream. Its success is rooted in the basic bargain that if you work hard and play by the rules, you will prosper; that if you innovate, if you create and build, there is no limit on what you can achieve. The middle class has always been defined as much if not more by the values and aspirations we share as by the goods we purchase.

My time as Secretary of State coincided with another great movement of people into the middle class, but this time it was happening in other countries, as hundreds of millions climbed out of poverty for the first time. The projections are staggering. The global middle class is expected to double in size by 2035, to as many as 5 billion. Two-thirds of all Chinese, more than 40 percent of all Indians, and half the population of Brazil are all expected to make it into the middle class. For the first time in history most people on earth are projected to be middle class rather than poor by 2022.

This explosive growth raises questions about our planet's capacity to sustain the level of consumption we've come to identify with middle-class life, especially when it comes to automobiles, energy, and water. Climate change, scarce resources, and local pollution will force us to make dramatic changes in patterns of production and consumption. But if we do it well the changes will create new jobs, new businesses, and a better quality of life. That means the rise of a global middle class will be good for the world. It will also be good for Americans. As wages and incomes rise elsewhere, there'll be more people able to buy our goods and services and less incentive for companies to outsource our jobs. After years of stagnant incomes and declining social and economic mobility, we need it.

Middle-class people around the world are also more likely to share our values. People everywhere typically want the same things out of life: good health, a decent job, a safe community, and the chance to provide education and opportunities to their children. They care about dignity, equality of opportunity, and due process before a fair judicial system. When people manage to climb into the middle class, and the immediate needs of survival are less pressing, they also tend to demand accountable governance, efficient services, better education, better health care, a clean environment, and peace. And most of them find the siren song of political extremism less appealing. The global middle class is a natural constituency for America. It's in our interest to see it grow to include more people. We should do everything we can to expand it at home and around the world.

23

Haiti: Disaster and Development

F our days after the earthquake in Haiti, the only working runway at the airport in Port-au-Prince was a jumble of activity. As I walked down the stairs of our U.S. Coast Guard C-130 cargo plane, I saw pallets of supplies sitting untouched on the tarmac. Planes with more emergency relief circled overhead, waiting their turn to land. The terminal itself was dark and abandoned, glass from its shattered windows strewn over the ground. Traumatized families had taken refuge on the airport grounds. Few Haitians wanted to be indoors after the earthquake, especially as aftershocks continued, and there weren't nearly enough safe structures left in the country to provide shelter for the more than 1 million people who lost their homes.

The 7.0-magnitude earthquake that devastated Haiti on January 12, 2010 killed more than 230,000 people in a country of 10 million and injured at least 300,000 more. Haiti was already the poorest country in the Western Hemisphere. Now it faced a staggering humanitarian disaster. The need for both immediate relief and long-term reconstruction in Haiti would test our aid capabilities and underscore the importance of pioneering a new approach to international development for the 21st century.

By my side that day in Haiti was Cheryl Mills, my indefatigable Counselor and Chief of Staff, and Dr. Raj Shah, the new head of the U.S. Agency for International Development, who had been sworn in only nine days earlier. Cheryl had been spearheading a review of our Haiti policy for the past year, and when the earthquake struck, she moved quickly to organize a massive response across the U.S. government. The State Department set up a twenty-four-hour-a-day crisis task force in the Ops Center to stay on top of the flood of information, requests for help, and offers of assistance. Consular officers worked around the clock to track down the whereabouts of an estimated forty-five thousand American citizens in Haiti and responded to nearly 500,000 inquiries from concerned friends and loved ones.

In the middle of that first night we learned that the United Nations mission in Haiti could not locate many of its people. By the morning we learned that the head of the UN mission, his principal Deputy, and 101 other UN workers had been killed, tragic losses for all of us that dramatically reduced the ability of the international community to muster and coordinate a response to the disaster.

Almost nobody was able to get into Haiti in the first forty-eight hours. The world was lining up to send aid, and there was no system for getting it in or distributing it once it arrived. The destruction of Port-au-Prince's port forced shipping cargo to land more than a hundred miles from the capital. The road connecting the Dominican Republic to Haiti was unnavigable, and other roads across the country were impassable. Only a small number of air traffic controllers were left at the damaged airport to manage the stream of planes trying to deliver aid. It was a mess.

When I got the news of the earthquake, I was in Hawaii on my way to Asia for a four-nation tour. As soon as I realized the extent of the damage in Haiti, I canceled the trip and headed back to Washington to oversee relief efforts. A number of Asian leaders were disappointed, but they all understood the urgency of the crisis, and many offered to help in any way they could.

My head was full of memories dating back to the first time I visited Haiti in 1975 as part of my honeymoon with Bill. We experienced the tension between the beauty of the place—the people, the colors, the food, the art—and the poverty and weakness of its institutions. One of the most memorable experiences of our trip was meeting a local voodoo priest named Max Beauvoir. Surprisingly he had studied at the City College of New York and the Sorbonne and had degrees in chemistry and biochemistry. He invited us to attend one of his ceremonies. We saw Haitians "seized with spirits" walk on hot coals, bite the heads off live chickens, and chew glass, spit out the shards, and not bleed. At the end of the ceremony, the people claimed the dark spirits had departed.

We also saw the infamous security forces of dictator "Baby Doc" Duvalier strut around town with their mirror sunglasses and automatic weapons. At one point we saw Baby Doc himself drive by, headed for his palace—the same Presidential Palace that would fall in the earthquake thirty-five years later.

When I got back to Washington after the earthquake, I did not think it made sense for me to go to Port-au-Prince right away. After watching and participating in emergency responses to disasters over the years, I had learned that one of the most important responsibilities for public officials is to avoid getting in the way of first responders and rescue workers. We did not want to tax Haiti's already overwhelmed systems or divert any of its limited resources to support a high-level visit when the priority was saving as many lives as possible.

But two days after the earthquake Cheryl spoke with Haiti's President René Préval, and he told her that the only outsider that he trusted was me. "I need Hillary," he said. "I need her. And no one else." It was a reminder of how important personal relationships can be, even at the highest levels of diplomacy and government.

On Saturday, January 16, I flew to Puerto Rico, where a Coast Guard cargo plane was waiting. It would have an easier time than my 757 negotiating the tricky landing at the damaged airport. When we arrived in Port-au-Prince Ambassador Ken Merten was waiting on the tarmac.

His team at the embassy was doing incredible work. One embassy nurse, whose own home was destroyed, worked nonstop for almost forty-eight hours in a makeshift surgical trauma unit to tend to seriously injured Americans who showed up at the embassy seeking help. A security officer, who, along with members of the local guard force, went searching for missing U.S. staff, found two injured colleagues whose home had fallen into a deep ravine. They carried the couple by foot for six hours on a makeshift gurney of ladders and garden hoses until they reached the embassy health unit.

But we suffered the loss of a number of our embassy personnel and their family members in Haiti, including Victoria DeLong, a Cultural Affairs Officer, and the wife and young children of Andrew Wyllie, a decorated State Department officer working with the United Nations.

Our embassy team was working closely with our staff back in Washington to coordinate offers of assistance. We successively tested an innovative idea with Google and a number of telecommunications companies to collect and map requests for emergency assistance—many of which came in via an SMS text hotline—which were then shared with rescue teams on the ground.

Experts from across the U.S. government were trying to get into Haiti to help. The Federal Emergency Management Agency swung into action, sending doctors and public health specialists from USAID, the Department of Health and Human Services, and the Centers for Disease Control and Prevention. The Federal Aviation Administration sent a portable airport control tower. Six search-and-rescue teams made up of firefighters, police officers, and engineers arrived from California, Florida, New York, and Virginia.

Next to Ambassador Merten on the tarmac was Lieutenant General Ken Keen, the Deputy Commander of U.S. Southern Command, who had been in Haiti on a planned visit when the earthquake hit. They were standing on the back porch of the Ambassador's residence when the ground started to shake. Thankfully the residence was largely undamaged and quickly became a gathering place for embassy personnel and Haitian government ministers, as well as General Keen's link back to U.S. Southern Command in Miami as he managed the military's role.

Coast Guard officers were America's first boots on the ground. Eventually more than twenty thousand U.S. civilian and military personnel were directly involved in search and rescue. They restored airports and seaports, provided life-saving health and medical service, and met basic survival needs of the Haitian people. The hospital ship USNS *Comfort* treated hundreds of patients. U.S. forces were welcomed and cheered, and the people and their government begged them not to leave. Soldiers who served in Haiti between multiple deployments to Iraq and Afghanistan marveled at what a refreshing change it was to feel so wanted on foreign soil.

I saw another familiar face on the runway: National Security Council Chief of Staff Denis McDonough. He had caught a military jet the day before to help coordinate the complex relief effort. He was literally soaked in sweat in a polo shirt and khakis helping direct traffic on the tarmac. His presence spoke volumes about President Obama's personal commitment to Haiti. I had stood with the President in the White House two days before, when he publicly pledged U.S. assistance. It was the first time I ever saw President Obama fighting to control his emotions.

My first order of business was to confer with President Préval. We met in a tent on the airport grounds. Immediately I could see why Cheryl thought it was so important that I come in person. The destruction of Préval's country and the despair of his people were etched on his face.

When the earthquake hit, Préval and his wife were arriving at their private home on a hillside. They watched their house collapse in front of their eyes. His office at the Presidential Palace was also severely damaged. Préval couldn't find several of his ministers. Others were severely injured or dead. According to reports, 18 percent of Haitian civil servants were killed in Port-au-Prince, twenty-eight of the twenty-nine government buildings were destroyed, and members of the Cabinet and legislators were missing or confirmed dead. The situation was dire and the government crippled.

When Préval first became President, he had little political experience, but by the time the quake hit he had become adept in the deal-making culture of Haitian politics. Still, he remained naturally reserved and found it difficult, even in the aftermath of the quake, to go out among his people, who wanted to see, touch, and talk to their leader.

Sitting in the tent with Préval, I tried to gauge how he was holding up in the face of such an overwhelming catastrophe. We had urgent business to conduct. The international relief effort was choking on the bottleneck of the airport. I proposed that the U.S. military take over operations there as soon as possible so that aid could begin flowing. Préval wasn't sure. Like all nations, Haiti prized its sovereignty. And even in an emergency, memories of previous U.S. military interventions were not easily dismissed. I assured him that our troops would not be there to patrol the streets or replace the UN forces working to restore law and order. This was just about getting the airport working again and making sure planes landed and supplies got distributed. Cheryl and our team had prepared a legal agreement for Préval to sign to give the U.S. military temporary responsibility for the airport and port. We walked through it line by line. He recognized that Haiti needed all the help it could get, but he also understood that other countries and his political opponents would criticize him for "selling out" to the Americans. It was one of many painful decisions he would have to make in the days ahead.

Préval signed the agreement. He was putting his personal trust in me as much as in our country. He looked me in the eye and said, "Hillary, I need you to be Haiti for Haiti, because right now we can't do it." I told Préval he could count on America, and me. "We will be here today, tomorrow and for the time ahead as long as you want us." Soon, with U.S. help, the airport and seaport began handling ten times more cargo, and aid began reaching the people in Haiti who needed it most.

At a second, larger meeting with American and international aid groups, Préval was less cooperative. He disagreed sharply with the recommendation to set up large camps to shelter hundreds of thousands of homeless Haitians. Presciently he worried that if we built these camps, Haiti would never get rid of them; instead he asked that we give people tents and tarps to stay in their own neighborhoods. But the UN team argued that it would be much harder to distribute food and water if people were dispersed. Camps would be much more efficient, which is why they are part of the standard international response to disasters.

When we flew out of Port-au-Prince later that day, we packed as many people as we could onto the plane, bringing two dozen Haitian Americans to safety. Cheryl and I talked about all the work that lay ahead. If we were going to live up to my promise to Préval—to be Haiti for Haiti—this wasn't going to be a quick relief effort. We had to be ready for a long haul.

———

In times of emergency Americans' first instinct is to help. None of us who lived through the dark days after 9/11 will ever forget how people across the country lined up to give blood. We saw the same generosity on display after Hurricane Katrina, when families in Houston and other communities opened their homes to displaced residents of New Orleans, and after Superstorm Sandy, when people came together to help New Jersey and New York. When the earthquake hit Haiti, the State Department worked with a technology company called mGive to enable Americans to make donations directly to the Red Cross via text message. The effort raised more than $30 million in less than three weeks from more than 3 million Americans. All told, Americans wound up contributing $1 billion to help Haitians after the quake.

For our country, stepping up in an emergency is not just the right thing to do. It's also a smart strategic move. In the aftermath of a disaster like the

Asian tsunami of 2004, when we provided extensive humanitarian relief, we built up valuable reservoirs of goodwill. In Indonesia, the epicenter of tsunami damage, about eight in ten people said our emergency assistance improved their view of the United States, and approval of America more than doubled from an Iraq-era low of 15 percent in 2003 to 38 percent in 2005. We saw the same phenomenon in 2011, when the United States rushed to provide assistance to Japan after its earthquake, tsunami, and nuclear meltdown known as the "triple disaster." Approval of America among the Japanese soared from 66 percent all the way to 85 percent, the highest among any nation polled.

While many of us respond to urgent needs in a crisis, it can often be harder to summon the resolve to step up and help when it comes to slow-motion tragedies like poverty, hunger, and disease rather than dramatic, attention-grabbing emergencies like a tsunami. Helping Haiti in the immediate aftermath of a devastating earthquake was one thing. But what about before the disaster, when Haiti was plagued by the worst poverty in the Americas? Or afterward, when it faced years of difficult rebuilding? What role should the United States play in those efforts?

Americans have always been charitable. In the early days of our nation, Alexis de Tocqueville wrote about the "habits of the heart" that made our democracy possible and brought frontier families together to raise barns and sew quilts. My mother was one of tens of thousands of Americans who sent care packages to hungry families in Europe after World War II. They included staples like powdered milk, bacon, chocolate, and SPAM. I am continuously impressed by the philanthropic spirit of the so-called Millennial Generation. According to one study, nearly three-quarters of all young people in America volunteered for a nonprofit organization of some kind in 2012.

Yet in debates about foreign aid, especially long-term assistance rather than short-term relief, many Americans ask why we should be generous abroad when there is so much work to do at home in our own country. In a time of tight budgets and big domestic challenges, there are certainly hard choices to make, but it's helpful to be clear about the facts. Polls show that Americans significantly overestimate the percentage of the federal budget allocated to foreign aid. In November 2013, a Kaiser Family Foundation survey found that, on average, Americans believe that 28 percent of the federal budget is spent on foreign assistance, and more than 60 percent of people say that's too much. But in reality we spend less than 1 percent of the budget on foreign aid. When people learn the truth, opposition is cut in half.

For decades, there has been a philosophical tension in our approach to international development. Should foreign assistance be purely altruistic, to help alleviate suffering wherever the need is greatest, or is it intended as part of our strategy to compete for hearts and minds in extended ideological struggles like the Cold War? Or to address the despair and alienation that fuel current radicalism and insurgency? President Kennedy inspired a generation with his call to service in "a struggle against the common enemies of man: tyranny, poverty, disease, and war itself," as he put it in his inaugural address. Yet he never lost sight of the strategic context. The idea for the Peace Corps began with a brief campaign speech at 2:00 in the morning at the University of Michigan in October 1960. "How many of you who are going to be doctors are willing to spend your days in Ghana?" he asked the crowd of students who had gathered in the middle of the night to hear him speak. "On your willingness to do that, not merely to serve one year or two years in the service, but on your willingness to contribute part of your life to this country, I think will depend the answer whether a free society can compete." Even at 2 A.M. he was thinking about how development might advance the interests of the United States.

I've always thought the debate between "aid for aid's sake" and "aid for strategic ends" was somewhat beside the point. We need to do both. President Obama and I were committed to elevating development alongside diplomacy and defense as core pillars of American power, but inside the administration we had many of these same debates. As the White House began putting together the first Presidential Policy Directive on development, I argued that we needed to draw a clear link between our aid work and U.S. national security. There were some development professionals who disagreed with that view, but the President eventually accepted the premise that natural disasters, poverty, and disease in other countries were also threats to U.S. strategic interests.

Haiti provided a prime example. Helping the country get back on its feet made sense for both humanitarian and strategic reasons.

It was impossible not to be moved by the plight of poor Haitians crowded into the slums of Port-au-Prince, with few economic or educational opportunities and a series of corrupt, erratic, and dictatorial governments. The Haitian people have enormous talent and perseverance, but they have had to endure crushing poverty and disappointment that would sap anyone's spirit. It should offend our conscience to see children growing up so close to our shores in such dire conditions.

And allowing a bastion of poverty, drug trafficking, and political instability to fester just seven hundred miles from Florida—a little more than the distance between Washington and Atlanta—is a dangerous proposition. Every year waves of refugees flee Haiti trying to make it to the United States through dangerous, shark-infested waters in rickety boats and rafts. Compared to military intervention and caring for massive influxes of desperate refugees, smart development assistance is a bargain.

Even before the earthquake Haiti was a priority for me. When I became Secretary I asked Cheryl to take a fresh look at our policy toward Haiti and come up with a strategy for high-impact economic development that would make a difference in the lives of Haitians. I also saw this as an opportunity to road-test new approaches to development that could be applied more broadly around the world. After all, despite its challenges, Haiti had many important ingredients for success. It was not riven by religious or sectarian divides. It shares an island with a stable and democratic country, the Dominican Republic, and enjoys proximity to the United States. It has big diaspora communities in both the United States and Canada. In short, Haiti has so much going for it that other desperately poor countries do not. If we could help Haitians build on these advantages, they could unlock great potential.

On the day the earthquake hit in January 2010, Cheryl and her team were finalizing a report to send to the White House with a full set of recommendations for Haiti, based on priorities laid out by the Haitians themselves. In the following weeks everyone's focus was on emergency response. But soon it would be time to think about long-term reconstruction and development needs. So I told Cheryl to dust off her report and get to work.

=====

The challenge of "building back better," a phrase borrowed from my husband and his work with President George H. W. Bush after the Asian tsunami in 2004, was daunting. The earthquake was a disaster of unprecedented scope that devastated Haiti's economic center and much of its productive infrastructure, including the main port and airport, power lines and substations, and important trunk roads. Préval and his Prime Minister, Jean-Max Bellerive, recognized early on that Haiti required bold economic development strategy that would use recovery funds to create lasting improvements in the lives of the Haitian people. They had plenty of prescriptions to choose from as Haiti became the focal point of an ongoing debate about development and the role foreign aid can play in stimulating an economy and improving a government.

What emerged was a development strategy crafted by the Haitian government that served as a guide for reconstruction. Two of its central tenants, to create economic opportunity in regions called growth corridors outside of congested Port-au-Prince and to expand jobs in agriculture and light manufacturing, became hallmarks of U.S. assistance to Haiti.

The idea of letting the local government set priorities and guide the development was not exactly new. In his celebrated speech launching the Marshall Plan in 1947, George Marshall argued that, "It would be neither fitting nor efficacious for this Government to undertake to draw up unilaterally a program designed to place Europe on its feet economically." But Marshall's wisdom was often overlooked in the following decades. Donor nations and NGOs swooped into developing countries with their own plans and ideas. That impulse was understandable, considering that local governments often required expert advice, but it often led to unintended consequences. Aid workers in the field sometimes griped about the "10,000-mile screw driver" with which officials back in Washington or various European capitals tried to micromanage development efforts. Plans that sounded good on the drawing board foundered when applied in the real world, and without local cooperation and buy-in they didn't translate.

Eventually the international development community rediscovered General Marshall's guidance as the principle of "country ownership," and we put it at the heart of our efforts in Haiti and around the world. Country ownership meant that for us, as much as possible, we would work with local officials and national ministries on the needs they identified, to help them build up their capacities and ensure a coherent, unified approach with all donors and organizations working together toward those ends, rather than in parallel or in competition. Our development model could not be formulaic. What works in Papua New Guinea may not work in Peru. We had to go case by case, country by country, even village by village, to analyze needs, assess opportunities, and tailor investments and partnerships to maximize our impact.

In Haiti and elsewhere, the primary vehicle for our development work would be USAID, an agency filled with determined public servants but plagued by years of dwindling resources and drifting focus. In the 1990s Republicans in Congress led by Senator Jesse Helms of North Carolina called for abolishing USAID altogether, arguing that the end of the Cold War had removed the strategic rationale for large-scale foreign aid. Although Helms failed to dismantle the agency, he was able to drastically reduce its budget. Lost in the debate were the real consequences of pulling back and letting problems fester, especially in places like Afghanistan. When the United States walked away after the Soviet withdrawal in 1989, we created the space for the Taliban to emerge. It was a costly error.

Interestingly, near the end of my husband's presidency Senator Helms came to support Bill's initiative to forgive the debts of poor countries if they put all the savings into health care, education, or economic development. A lot of the credit for that goes to Bono, lead singer of U2, who proved surprisingly persuasive with the cantankerous Senator.

The Bush Administration had its own take on development. The President's brand of "compassionate conservatism" led him to invest in new development programs outside of the existing bureaucracy of USAID that have made huge impacts, especially in sub-Saharan Africa. The Millennium Challenge Corporation provided generous assistance to countries that met certain standards and made reforms on corruption and governance. President Bush's Emergency Plan for AIDS Relief built clinics, distributed drugs, and saved lives all over Africa. It was an amazing success.

When I became Secretary, rebuilding and refocusing USAID was a top priority. Without reforms, including reducing our reliance on outside contractors and increasing our ability to innovate and execute, we were in danger of being outpaced and outclassed by other countries. Many European nations had excellent development programs that operated with more local involvement and much lower overhead than typical USAID efforts. China was spending huge sums across the developing world. We might not have thought highly of their methods, which prioritized extracting resources and bringing in their own people rather than adding value, increasing employment, and protecting the environment, but there was no disputing the scale and scope of their engagement. As I found all over the world, few people could identify tangible symbols of American aid, but in many nations people drove by a Chinese-built stadium or on a superhighway every day. We didn't want to emulate their approach or discount the value of less visible projects, especially ones that boosted crop yields and prevented unnecessary deaths from AIDS, TB, and malaria. But we did need to keep improving and innovating so that American development programs would remain the most respected in the world.

To run USAID we found a thoughtful and talented young man at the Department of Agriculture, Dr. Rajiv Shah. A trained doctor and health economist who had run major programs at the Gates Foundation, Raj soon became a valued partner who shared our commitment to reforming the agency and elevating development within our foreign policy.

The Obama Administration proposed doubling foreign assistance by 2014, but just as important, we planned to reform how that money was spent, making sure less was diverted to salaries and overhead for for-profit contractors and more went directly into programs on the ground. I also wanted to reverse the "brain drain" at USAID by increasing the number of development professionals and making it once again an exciting and fulfilling place to work.

Raj and I agreed that to succeed, USAID needed a new emphasis on innovation, investment, and self-sufficiency. We began looking for new ways to identify and support the best development ideas from outside government that could help us solve problems around the world, especially market-driven solutions that would empower people and encourage creativity. USAID launched "Grand Challenges" competitions—contests to support potentially game-changing innovations. We also created a venture capital–style fund to invest in big ideas that could yield big results. The first round of financing supported projects like solar lighting in rural Uganda and mobile health services in India. New partnerships with the National Science Foundation and the National Institutes of Health began connecting American scientists working on development research with their counterparts around the world. New science fellowships allowed us to bring in more researchers, engineers, and physicians to work with USAID. In 2008 USAID spent roughly $127 million to support research and development. By 2014 that number was up to $611 million.

Starting in 2011, Raj and I began discussing a centerpiece project for this innovation agenda: a state-of-the-art development laboratory run by USAID in partnership with research universities, NGOs, the tech community, and U.S. corporations. After three years of preparation I was proud to join Raj in early April 2014 to help launch what is now called the U.S. Global Development Lab. It will focus on breakthrough solutions in water, health, nutrition, energy, education, and climate change, with the goal of helping 200 million people in the first five years.

Another major push was to find new ways to stimulate private-sector investment in developing countries. American companies often struggle to navigate the complicated array of U.S. agencies involved in international investment and trade, including the Overseas Private Investment Corporation (OPIC), the State Department, USAID's Development Credit Authority, the Trade and Development Agency, and the Export-Import Bank. Before I left office, I presented President Obama with a plan to build up OPIC into a full-scale "development finance institution" that could mobilize resources from across the government to incentivize private-sector investments that would require no additional taxpayer money. Other countries have these kinds of institutions; we should too. It's good for American businesses and for our partner countries.

While we improved our own development capacities, it was also crucial to help our partners improve theirs. I was especially concerned about corruption and poorly functioning tax systems in developing countries we were trying to help. Foreign aid is a hard enough sell under the best of circumstances, but it's even more difficult when elites in our partner countries do everything they can to avoid doing their fair share. That was something I saw all over the world, and it outraged me. When a country makes reforms to improve tax collection, expand transparency, and fight corruption, it can ignite a virtuous cycle. Taxpayers can see what they're getting for their money. Higher revenues allow governments to provide better services and pay decent wages to public employees. All this, in turn, creates a more attractive climate for both foreign investors and development donors and puts countries on the path toward self-sufficiency.

═══

Helping rebuild Haiti would be a major test for USAID and for how well we could work with the Haitian government while increasing its capacities, and coordinating with all our international partners, including governments, NGOs, and institutions.

I began calling leaders around the world right after the earthquake, starting with the Foreign Ministers of France, Brazil, Canada, and the

Dominican Republic. At a Haiti Donors Conference in the spring of 2010 the United States began the process of allocating more than $3.5 billion in assistance, and we encouraged other nations to follow our example. All told, the conference yielded in excess of $9 billion in government pledges for long-term development, in addition to substantial commitments from the private sector. Every country in our hemisphere got involved. I was especially glad to see that the Dominican Republic, which shares the island of Hispaniola with Haiti and has not always gotten along with its neighbor, went above and beyond to help. We even cooperated with Cuba and Venezuela.

UN Secretary-General Ban Ki-moon had asked Bill to serve as his Special Envoy to Haiti starting in May 2009, a position he held until 2013. Then President Obama asked him and former President George W. Bush to lead a postearthquake campaign that raised tens of millions of dollars to start new enterprises and increase employment. By Bill's side was Dr. Paul Farmer, a cofounder of the organization Partners in Health, whom Bill had asked to become the UN Deputy Special Envoy in August 2009. Partners in Health started working in Haiti in 1983, developing a unique model of providing quality care with limited resources to poor people in rural areas. After the earthquake Paul and his team managed to build a full-fledged teaching hospital, Hôpital Universitaire de Mirebalais, in Mirebalais, Haiti, which is also the country's largest solar-powered building.

The international relief and reconstruction effort did a lot of good, especially in the immediate aftermath of the quake, but there were shortcomings in the efforts. Tens of thousands of relief personnel set up camp in what felt like a city under siege, and they were not always well coordinated. Too many well-meaning NGOs clogged the pipelines. And, in a heartbreaking case of unintended consequences, the cholera epidemic that broke out in the fall of 2010 likely started with Nepalese peacekeepers brought in by the UN.

USAID missed the mark in some important places. The hospital referral networks that one of our health experts designed never materialized, largely due to bureaucratic infighting. On energy, the United States built a power plant and did repairs, but our grander plans of energy transformation have not yet come to fruition.

There were, however, important successes. As of January 2013, 7.4 million cubic meters of rubble had been removed, one third of it by the U.S.

government. The number of Haitians living in tent camps declined from a high of 1.6 million to less than 200,000. More than 300,000 people have found safer housing thanks to USAID-funded programs. And the cholera response and vaccinations led by the Centers for Disease Control (CDC) helped drive down the fatality rate of the cholera epidemic from 9 percent to just over 1 percent. The United States supported 251 primary care and fifty-two secondary care sites across Haiti, which were estimated to reach the health care needs of nearly 50 percent of the Haitian population. We helped nearly ten thousand farmers access improved seeds and fertilizer and introduced new techniques for better productivity. Rice yields have more than doubled, and corn yields have more than quadrupled.

The primary goal of our long-term development strategy in Haiti was to jump-start the economy, create jobs that would pay people decent wages, and reduce dependence on foreign assistance over time. A center-piece of our efforts was a $300 million industrial park at Caracol, in the northern part of Haiti, funded jointly by the State Department, USAID, the Haitian government, and the Inter-American Development Bank. It quickly became a global effort, with a Korean textile company, Sae-A Trading Co., committing to build and run a factory there to make T-shirts and other items for Wal-Mart, Kohl's, and Target. When I visited for the October 2012 dedication, 1,050 Haitians already worked there, with more expected to be hired soon.

The Caracol project was in keeping with a broader trend in our development work around the world. We were shifting our focus from aid to investment. In the 1960s, when President Kennedy created USAID, official development assistance from countries like the United States represented 70 percent of the capital flows going into developing countries. Since then, even though countries have actually increased development budgets, official development assistance represents just 13 percent of those capital flows. That's mainly due to surging private investment and trade in emerging markets, which is good news. Given this shift, it made sense to refocus our approach to development so we can better harness market forces and make smart public-sector investments that could catalyze sustainable economic growth.

The United States was not abandoning traditional aid, such as sacks of rice or cases of medicines. That kind of assistance is still a vital tool, especially as part of an emergency response to a disaster. But through investment we sought to break the cycle of dependence that aid can create by helping countries to build their own institutions and their own capacity to deliver essential services. Aid chases need; investment chases opportunity.

By the end of 2013, just over a year after it opened, the industrial park at Caracol was providing jobs to about 2,000 Haitians. There were six private-sector tenants, a million square feet of leased factory and office space, and $26 million in annual exports. Over the course of 2014 employment and exports are on track to more than double as manufacturers move into newly completed factories. It also has a modern waste water treatment facility, a new electric grid providing reliable power to surrounding towns for the first time, as well as new housing, schools, and health clinics.

In a 2013 column in the *Financial Times*, Haiti's Prime Minister Laurent Lamothe noted that the majority of Haitian families make around $700 a year in subsistence agriculture and are "never certain if heavy rains may wash away their harvest." So when Caracol opened, fifty applications came in for every job. "A single mother in Caracol now earns an average annual salary of $1,820 in her first ever wage job," Lamothe wrote. "If she advances to become a line supervisor, she can earn up to 50 per cent more. Previously unemployed, she now can afford to send her kids to school, pay for a mobile phone and 24/7 electricity and have some discretionary income to save. She also benefits from paid vacation, health care and one of the best worker rights and worker safety regimes in the world."

The day that the Caracol industrial park was dedicated in October 2012 was an occasion for all of us who had lived through Haiti's darkest days to celebrate a little good news, and no one deserved applause more than Préval himself. By that point, however, he had been out of office for more than a year, and his relationship with the new President was far from warm.

The ill will dated back to the November 2010 elections, just ten months after the earthquake. The official government tally and an independent count by the Organization of American States (OAS) reached different conclusions about which candidates should advance to a run-off. Many Haitians, who had already endured so much, were outraged that after all they had endured their votes might not be counted. The streets were soon full of loud and unruly protests.

I decided to go to Haiti to meet with Préval and the candidates to see if there could be a peaceful resolution that would avoid a crisis when there was so much work still to be done in the aftermath of the earthquake. Préval's preferred candidate, who the OAS said had actually finished third, complained that the international community was pushing him out of the race. I insisted that just wasn't the case. After all, I explained, people tried to push me out of the race when I ran for President in 2008. Just as President Obama and I did, he and the other two candidates had to respect the voters' preference. "Look, I've run in elections," I said. "I've won two, and I've lost a big one. So I know how it feels. But what's more important is that democracy be protected." Unlike a professional diplomat or an academic or businessperson, I could put myself in these candidates' shoes. Elections can be painful. Democracy is tough. In some places you can be killed because you want to run or you want to vote, or you can be imprisoned and bankrupted. You have to understand the risks that people are taking, the worries they have, their need to feel respected.

I met with Préval at his temporary residence. We sat close together in plush chairs, practically knee-to-knee. I started talking about what it means to think not just for tomorrow but for the long term. I told him that this was his defining moment. He was either going to be remembered as a President no different from all the Haitian leaders in history who refused to listen to their people, or he was going to be remembered as the President who allowed democracy to take root. He had to choose. "I'm talking to you not only as your friend, but as someone who loves my country and had to do a lot of hard things, too," I said. "Do the hard thing, because the hard thing is going to ultimately be in the best interests of your country and in your best interests, even though you won't feel that way until you're able to step back and look back." He ended the meeting saying, "Well, you've given me a lot to think about. I'll see what I can do."

Shortly afterward Préval and all three candidates accepted the OAS results. The celebrated musician Michel Martelly, widely known as "Sweet Micky," won the run-off, and Préval retired. Usually the winner of an election receives all the kudos. But in this case I thought the hero of the hour was the man who stepped down gracefully, even with his country still reeling from an unimaginable catastrophe. It was the first time in Haitian history that any President peacefully turned over power to someone from an opposing party.

This was a very good sign for the country's future. The link between sustainable development and good governance is well established. That's why we put it at the heart of many of our aid programs, most notably the Millennium Challenge Corporation. Haiti's troubles on both fronts provided a case in point. And we had a counterexample readily available. Chile was hit by an even more powerful earthquake just a month after Haiti. But unlike Haiti, Chile had the infrastructure, resources, and governing institutions to withstand such a devastating event and respond quickly and effectively. To "build back better" Haiti needed to do more than clean up the rubble and get the economy going again. It needed a strong democracy and an accountable, responsive government. A peaceful transfer of power was a crucial first step.

I was pleased to see Préval at the Caracol ribbon-cutting event, but I wondered how he and Martelly would interact. To my surprise and delight, Martelly acknowledged Préval and brought him up onstage. Then they raised their hands together in celebration. It was a simple gesture, familiar to Americans. But no two Presidents had ever done that in Haiti—mainly because there have been so few peaceful transitions. It left me believing that Haiti was, finally, despite all of the struggles, on a better path.

═══

In the international development business, it's easy to get frustrated and fatalistic. But step back and look at the sweep of history, and you realize just how remarkable our country's contributions have been. Just in my lifetime the United States has helped eradicate smallpox and reduce polio and malaria. We helped save millions of lives through immunizations, life-saving treatment for AIDS, and oral rehydration therapy that greatly reduced the deaths of infants and children. We helped educate millions of young people and provided significant support to once impoverished countries that have flourished and become generous donors themselves, such as South Korea. Americans should take pride in these achievements, which have not only helped humanity but have also helped our nation project our values and strengthen our leadership in the world.

24

21st-Century Statecraft:
Digital Diplomacy in a Networked World

My government can go to hell!" declared the young woman defiantly. I had asked a pro-democracy activist from Belarus if she was worried about facing repercussions when she returned home from TechCamp, a training session the State Department organized in neighboring Lithuania in June 2011. We used these sessions to help civil society groups from across the region learn how to use technology to advance their work and avoid persecution. Among the countries to emerge from the old Soviet Union, Belarus had one of the most repressive regimes. But this woman wasn't afraid, she told me. She had come to Lithuania to learn new skills that would help her stay one step ahead of the censors and secret police. I liked her style.

There were about eighty other activists from eighteen countries crammed into a small room in Vilnius for two eleven-hour days of training. For the most part, they weren't wide-eyed idealists or technology evangelists. These were dissidents and organizers who were eager for *any* new tools that would help them express their views, organize, and circumvent censorship. A team of experts from the State Department was on hand to explain how activists could protect their privacy and anonymity online and thwart restrictive government firewalls. We also had executives from Twitter, Facebook, Microsoft, and Skype.

Some of the activists talked about how the Syrian regime of Bashar al-Assad monitored the hashtags used by opposition Twitter users and then flooded the network with spam using the same tags to thwart those trying to follow the opposition. Was there anything they could do to prevent that? Others wanted help mapping demonstrations and crackdowns in real time during crises.

That evening I took members of my delegation out to dinner at a local restaurant in Vilnius. Over Lithuanian beer, I asked how they thought the day had gone. Alec Ross, my Senior Advisor for Innovation, was particularly pleased. In 2008, Alec had helped the Obama campaign's outreach to Silicon Valley and the broader technology industry. When I became Secretary, I asked him to help me move the State Department into the 21st century. I myself am not the most tech-savvy person—although I surprised my daughter and my staff by falling in love with my iPad, which I now take everywhere I travel—but I understood that new technologies would reshape how we practiced diplomacy and development, just as they were changing how people everywhere communicated, worked, organized, and played.

We discussed how these tools were in and of themselves value-neutral. They could be forces for bad as easily as for good, just as steel can be used to build hospitals or tanks and nuclear power can either energize a city or destroy it. We had to act responsibly to maximize technology's benefits—while minimizing the risks.

Technology was opening up new avenues to help solve problems and promote America's interests and values. We would focus on helping civil society across the world harness mobile technology and social media to hold governments accountable, document abuses, and empower marginalized groups, including women and young people. I'd seen firsthand how innovations were lifting people out of poverty and giving them more control over their own lives. In Kenya farmers saw their income grow by as much as 30 percent after they started using cell phones for mobile banking technology and learning how better to protect crops from pests. In Bangladesh more than 300,000 people signed up to learn English on their mobile phones. There were nearly 4 billion cell phones in use in the developing world, many of them in the hands of farmers, market vendors, rickshaw drivers, and others who'd historically lacked access to education and opportunity. Various studies have found that a 10 percent increase in the penetration rate for mobile phones in a developing country can lead to an increase in GDP per capita of between 0.6 and 1.2 percent. That translates to billions of dollars and countless jobs.

However, we'd also seen the darker side of the digital revolution. The same qualities that made the internet a force for unprecedented progress—in its openness, its leveling effect, its reach and speed—also enabled wrongdoing on an unprecedented scale. It's well known that the internet is a source for nearly as much misinformation as information, but that's just the beginning. Terrorists and extremist groups use the internet to incite hate, recruit members, and plot and carry out attacks. Human traffickers lure new victims into modern-day slavery. Child pornographers exploit children. Hackers break into financial institutions, retailers, cell phone networks, and personal email accounts. Criminal gangs as well as nations are building offensive cyber warfare and industrial espionage capabilities. Critical infrastructure like power grids and air traffic control systems are increasingly vulnerable to cyber attack.

Like other sensitive government agencies, the State Department was frequently the target of cyber attacks. Department officials had to fend off intrusions in their email and increasingly sophisticated phishing attempts. When we first arrived at State, these attempts were similar to the fraudulent emails many Americans experience at home on their personal computers. Just as the broken English of the infamous Nigerian bank scam tips off most users, the often sloppy early attempts to penetrate our secure systems were easy to spot. But by 2012, the sophistication and fluency had advanced considerably, with attackers impersonating State Department officials in an attempt to dupe their colleagues into opening legitimate-looking attachments.

When we traveled to sensitive places like Russia, we often received warnings from Department security officials to leave our BlackBerrys, laptops—anything that communicated with the outside world—on the plane, with their batteries removed to prevent foreign intelligence services from compromising them. Even in friendly settings we conducted business under strict security precautions, taking care where and how we read secret material and used our technology. One means of protecting material was to read it inside an opaque tent in a hotel room. In less well-equipped settings we were told to improvise by reading sensitive material with a blanket over our head. I felt like I was ten years old again, reading covertly by flashlight under the covers after bedtime. On more than one occasion I was cautioned not to speak freely in my own hotel room. And it wasn't just U.S. government agencies and officials who were targets. American companies were also in the crosshairs. I fielded calls from frustrated CEOs complaining about aggressive theft of intellectual property and trade secrets, even breaches of their home computers. To better focus our efforts against this increasingly serious threat, I appointed the Department's first Coordinator for Cyber Issues in February 2011.

Around the world, some countries began erecting electronic barriers to prevent their people from using the internet freely and fully. Censors expunged words, names, and phrases from search engine results. They cracked down on citizens who engaged in nonviolent political speech, and not just during periods of unrest and mass protest. One of the most prominent examples was China, which, as of 2013, was home to nearly 600 million internet users but also some of the most repressive limits on internet freedom. The "Great Firewall" blocked foreign websites and particular pages with content perceived as threatening to the Communist Party. Some reports estimate that China employed as many as 100,000 censors to patrol the web. For ten months starting in 2009 the government even shut down the internet altogether in the northwest province of Xinjiang after riots among the ethnic Uighur population.

That June, young Iranians used websites and social media to get their message out during protests after disputed elections. The brutal shooting of a twenty-six-year-old woman named Neda Agha-Soltan by pro-government paramilitary forces was captured on grainy cell phone footage, uploaded to the web, and shared far and wide via Twitter and Facebook. Within hours millions of people watched Neda die in a pool of blood on a Tehran street. *Time* magazine described it as "probably the most widely witnessed death in human history." The video helped galvanize global outrage on behalf of the protesters.

Just five days earlier, State Department officials who were tracking the online efforts of the Iranian opposition made a troubling discovery. Twitter was planning to shut down its global service for preplanned maintenance at a time that would be the middle of the day in Tehran. Jared Cohen, a twenty-seven-year-old member of our Policy Planning Staff, had contacts at Twitter. In April he had organized a trip to Baghdad for Jack Dorsey, one of the cofounders of the company, and other technology executives. He quickly reached out to alert Dorsey to the disruption the shutdown could cause to Iranian activists. As a result Twitter delayed its maintenance until the middle of the following night. In a blog post the company noted the reason for the delay was "the role Twitter is currently playing as an important communication tool in Iran."

But the Iranian government also proved adept at using these new technological tools for its own purposes. Their Revolutionary Guard stalked protest leaders by tracking their online profiles. When some Iranians living overseas posted criticism of the regime, their family members in Iran were singled out for punishment. The authorities eventually shut down the internet and mobile networks altogether. They also relied on more conventional means of intimidation and terror. In the face of the brutal crackdown, the protests crumbled.

I was appalled by what happened in Iran and by the persecution of online activists in authoritarian states all over the world. I turned to Dan Baer, our Deputy Assistant Secretary for Democracy, Human Rights and Labor whom I had recruited from Georgetown, where he was a professor researching and teaching about the intersection between ethics, economics, and human rights. I asked Dan to work with Alec and his team to find ways we could help. They told me there were powerful emerging technologies we could fund that would help dissidents circumvent government surveillance and censorship. Our investments could play a pivotal role in taking such tools to scale and making them accessible to the activists who needed them most. But there was a catch: Criminals and hackers could also use these tools to avoid detection. Our own intelligence and law enforcement agencies would have a hard time keeping up. Could we be opening up a Pandora's box of illicit online activity? Was it worth the risk to empower and protect the activists?

I took those concerns seriously. The implications for our national security were real. It was not an easy call. But I decided that striking a blow for free expression and association around the world was worth the risk. Criminals would always find ways of exploiting new technologies; that was no reason to sit on our hands. I gave the green light to move ahead. Our team got to work, and by the time I visited Lithuania in 2011, we had invested more than $45 million in tools to help keep dissidents safe online and trained more than five thousand activists worldwide, who turned around and trained thousands more. We worked with designers to create new apps and devices, such as a panic button that a protester could press on a phone that would signal to friends that he or she was being arrested, while simultaneously erasing all of their personal contacts.

=====

This technology agenda was part of efforts to adapt the State Department and U.S. foreign policy to the 21st century. During the transition period before I became Secretary, I read an essay in the journal *Foreign Affairs* titled "America's Edge: Power in the Networked Century" by Anne-Marie Slaughter, the dean of the Woodrow Wilson School of Public and International Affairs at Princeton. Her concept of networks keyed off the architecture of the internet, but it was bigger than that. It had to do with all the ways people were organizing themselves in the 21st century, collaborating, communicating, trading, even fighting. In this networked world, she explained, diverse and cosmopolitan societies would have significant advantages over homogeneous and closed societies. They'd be better positioned to take advantage of expanding commercial, cultural, and technological networks and capitalize on the opportunities presented by global interdependence. This was good news, she argued, for the United States, with our multicultural, creative, hyperconnected population.

In 2009, more than 55 million Americans were immigrants or the children of immigrants. These first- or second-generation Americans were valuable links back to their home countries and also significant contributors to our own country's economic, cultural, and political life. Immigration helped keep the U.S. population young and dynamic at a time when many of our partners and competitors were aging. Russia, in particular, faced what President Putin himself has called a "demographic crisis." Even China, because of its "One Child Policy," was headed toward a demographic cliff. I only wish that the bipartisan bill passed in the Senate in 2013 reforming our immigration laws could pass the House.

While I maintained a healthy respect for traditional forms of power, I agreed with Anne-Marie's analysis of America's comparative advantage in a networked world. Here was an answer to all the hand-wringing about decline that was rooted in both America's oldest traditions and our newest innovations. I asked Anne-Marie to take a leave from Princeton and join me at the State Department as Director of Policy Planning, our internal think tank. She also helped lead a top-to-bottom review of the

State Department and USAID that we called the Quadrennial Diplomacy and Development Review. It was inspired by the Pentagon's Quadrennial Defense Review, which I became familiar with as a member of the Senate Armed Services Committee, and it aimed to map out exactly how we would put smart power into practice and use what I started calling "21st-Century Statecraft." This included harnessing new technologies, public-private partnerships, diaspora networks, and other new tools, and it soon carried us into fields beyond traditional diplomacy, especially energy and economics.

The State Department's Bureau of Public Affairs established a digital division to amplify our messaging across a wide range of platforms, including Twitter, Facebook, Flickr, Tumblr, and Google+. By 2013 more than 2.6 million Twitter users followed 301 official feeds in eleven languages, including Arabic, Chinese, Farsi, Russian, Turkish, and Urdu. I encouraged our diplomats at embassies around the world to develop their own Facebook pages and Twitter accounts, to go on local TV, and to engage in every other way they could. Just as important, I wanted them to listen to what people in their countries were saying, including on social media. In an era in which security concerns often limited contact with foreign citizens, social media offered a way to hear from the people directly, even in relatively closed societies. More than 2 billion people were now online, nearly a third of humankind. The internet had become the public space of the 21st century, the world's town square, classroom, marketplace, and coffeehouse, so America's diplomats needed to be there, too.

When Mike McFaul, a professor of political science at Stanford and a Russia expert at the National Security Council, was preparing to move to Moscow as our new Ambassador, I told him that he'd have to find creative ways to get around government obstacles and communicate directly with the Russian people. "Mike, remember these three things," I said, "be strong, engage beyond the elites, and don't be afraid to use every technology you can to reach more people." Mike soon found himself harassed and vilified by the Kremlin-controlled media. I made a point of calling him on an open line one night and, speaking very clearly so all the eavesdropping Russian spies could hear, I told him what a good job he was doing.

Mike became an avid user of social media, eventually attracting more than seventy thousand followers on Twitter and becoming one of Russia's ten most influential online voices, based on numbers of mentions by other users and readership. Many Russians knew him primarily as @McFaul, and they were intrigued by his surprising candor and willingness to mix it up with all comers. In between explaining U.S. policies and shining a spotlight on some of the Kremlin's abuses, Mike posted a steady diet of personal thoughts and photos. Russians got to see the U.S. Ambassador as a human being, enjoying the Bolshoi Ballet, showing visiting relatives around Red Square, and recovering from a broken finger injured in a basketball game. In one official meeting not long after that incident, Prime Minister Dmitry Medvedev asked about Mike's hand. When he began to tell the story behind the injury, Medvedev just waved him off. "I know all about it," he said. "I read about it on the internet."

Early in his tenure Mike got into a heated back-and-forth on Twitter with the Russian Foreign Ministry. The Swedish Foreign Minister Carl Bildt, who has more than 250,000 followers, chimed in with a tweet of his own: "I see that Russia MFA [Ministry of Foreign Affairs] has launched a twitter-war against US Ambassador @McFaul," he wrote. "That's the new world—followers instead of nukes. Better." I think Mike would be the first to agree.

===

If the hyperconnectivity of the networked world played to America's strengths and offered opportunities to exercise smart power to advance our interests, it also presented significant new challenges to our security and our values.

This became painfully apparent in November 2010, when the online organization WikiLeaks and several media outlets around the world began publishing the first of more than 250,000 stolen State Department cables, many of which contained sensitive observations and intelligence from our diplomats in the field.

A junior military intelligence officer stationed in Iraq, Private Bradley Manning, downloaded the secret cables from a Department of Defense computer and gave them to WikiLeaks and its Australian leader, Julian Assange. Some celebrated Manning and Assange as champions of transparency who were carrying on a noble tradition of exposing government wrongdoing, comparing them to Daniel Ellsberg's leaking of the Pentagon Papers during the Vietnam War. I didn't see it that way. As I said at the time, people of good faith understand the need for sensitive diplomatic communications, to protect both the national interest and the global common interest. Every country, including the United States, must be able to have candid conversations about the people and nations with whom they deal. And the thousands of stolen cables generally showed America's diplomats doing their jobs well, often in difficult circumstances.

The cables also provided intriguing color. For instance, one discussed a diplomat's meeting with a Central Asian Minister who showed up drunk to a meeting, "slouching back in his chair and slurring all kinds of Russian participles," while another described the scene at a wedding in Dagestan, Russia, where guests threw $100 bills at child dancers as a "microcosm of the social and political relations of the North Caucasus." Diplomats often provided insight into world leaders, such as one cable on the Zimbabwean despot Robert Mugabe that noted "his deep ignorance on economic issues (coupled with the belief that his 18 doctorates give him the authority to suspend the laws of economics)."

The publication of these reports had the unintended consequence of showing how hard our Foreign Service officers were working, and what keen observers and talented writers many of them were. But some of the unvarnished comments also damaged relationships our diplomats had carefully built over many years. Our diplomats routinely reported on conversations with human rights activists and dissidents, business leaders, even officials of foreign governments who could face persecution and retribution if their names became public.

In the immediate aftermath of the leaks I condemned the illegal disclosure of classified information. "It puts people's lives in danger, threatens our national security, and undermines our efforts to work with other countries to solve shared problems," I said. Then I turned to face the diplomatic fallout from aggrieved allies and outraged partners.

I asked Under Secretary of State for Management Pat Kennedy to set up a task force to analyze the leaks cable by cable and determine exactly what information was compromised and the consequences of those disclosures to our interests, our personnel, and our partners. We rushed to develop a process to identify at-risk sources and, if needed, help them get to safety.

On the night before Thanksgiving 2010, I started making what would be dozens of calls from my house in Chappaqua. First up was my friend Kevin Rudd, the Australian Foreign Minister and former Prime Minister. We began with a discussion of our usual topics of interest, led by North Korea. "The other point I want to raise is WikiLeaks," I told him.

Our Ambassador to Australia had already briefed Rudd that some of our confidential discussions about the region, including China's activities, might have been compromised. In response the Australian government had established their own task force to deal with the situation. "It could be a real problem," he said. "It's a dreadful fallout," I agreed. "We deeply regret it and feel blind-sided." I promised to do all we could to help with the damage control.

It would be a long Thanksgiving holiday, working the phones and offering apologies. Over the coming days I spoke with many Foreign Ministers, one Prime Minister, and one President. These calls covered other issues as well, but in every conversation I explained the impending release of the secret cables and asked for their understanding. Some were angry and hurt; others saw an opportunity to gain leverage with the United States and tried to exploit it. But most were gracious. "I appreciate that you called yourself," said German Foreign Minister Guido Westerwelle. Chinese Foreign Minister Yang was consolatory, saying, "I can't predict the reaction of the public, but it's important for both sides to deepen mutual trust. That's the magic word for the China-U.S. bilateral relationship." One leader even joked, "You should see what we say about you."

The in-person conversations were harder. In the first week of December I attended a summit of the Organization for Security and Cooperation in Europe in Astana, Kazakhstan, along with many other world leaders. Silvio Berlusconi, the Italian Prime Minister whose antics described in a number of leaked cables were now being ridiculed on the front pages of Italian newspapers, was especially upset. "Why are you saying these things about me?" he asked when we sat down together. "America has no better friend," he insisted. "You know me, I know your family." He launched into an impassioned story about how his father used to take him to the graveyards of American soldiers who had sacrificed on behalf of Italy. "I've never forgotten it," he said. Berlusconi was no stranger to bad publicity, as bulging files of scandalous press clippings could attest. But the way he was regarded by his peers, and by the United States in particular, mattered a great deal to him. And this was embarrassing.

I apologized, yet again. No one wished these words had stayed secret more than I did. Understandably that wasn't enough to assuage him. He asked me to stand with him in front of the cameras and offer a strong statement about the importance of the U.S.-Italian relationship, which I did. For all of Berlusconi's foibles, he genuinely loved America. Italy was also a key NATO ally whose support we needed around the world, including in the upcoming military campaign in Libya. So I did everything I could to reestablish a measure of trust and respect.

Eventually my team and I reached nearly every leader mentioned prominently in a secret cable. Our full-court press seemed to minimize the lasting harm. And in some cases the honesty of our apology may even have added new depth to some relationships. Others were beyond repair.

In Libya, Ambassador Gene Cretz's searing reports on Colonel Muammar Qaddafi made him persona non grata in Tripoli. He was even threatened by some of Qaddafi's thugs, prompting me to recall him to the United States for his own safety. In neighboring Tunisia it was the dictator who had to flee. The publication of secret U.S. reports about the corruption of the regime helped fuel growing popular frustration that eventually blossomed into a revolution that chased Ben Ali from office.

In the end the diplomatic fallout from WikiLeaks was bad, but not crippling; however, it did foreshadow another, much more serious breach of a far different nature, which occurred after I left office. Edward Snowden, a contractor at the National Security Agency (NSA), which is chiefly responsible for monitoring foreign communications, stole a massive batch of highly secret files and passed them to journalists. Snowden fled first to Hong Kong and then to Russia, which granted him asylum. His leaks revealed some of America's most sensitive classified intelligence programs. There was outrage around the world that the United States allegedly was monitoring the personal cell phone calls of partners such as German Chancellor Angela Merkel and Brazilian President Dilma Rousseff. There was also concern that terrorists and criminals would change their own communications practices now that they knew more about the sources and methods used by the U.S. intelligence community.

Most of the attention back home, however, focused on how various NSA data collection programs might affect American citizens. In particular, scrutiny focused on the bulk collection of telephone records, not the content of the conversations or the identities of callers but a database of phone numbers, and the time and duration of calls, that could be examined if there was a reasonable suspicion that a particular number was associated with terrorism. President Obama has since called on Congress to implement a number of reforms so the government will no longer keep such data.

While continuing to defend the need for foreign surveillance and intelligence operations, the President welcomed a public debate about how to balance security, liberty, and privacy a dozen years after 9/11. It's hard to imagine similar conversations taking place in Russia or China. Ironically, just a few weeks before the Snowden story hit, the President had given a major speech about national security policy in which he said, "With a decade of experience now to draw from, this is the moment to ask ourselves hard questions—about the nature of today's threats and how we should confront them. . . . The choices we make about war can impact—in sometimes unintended ways—the openness and freedom on which our way of life depends."

Living in the public eye for so many years has given me a deep appreciation of privacy and the need to protect it. And although the technologies at issue are new, the challenge of balancing liberty and security is not. Way back in 1755 Benjamin Franklin wrote, "Those who would give up essential Liberty, to purchase a little temporary Safety, deserve neither Liberty nor Safety." With liberty and security, it's not that the more you have of one, the less you have of the other. In fact I believe they make each other possible. Without security, liberty is fragile. Without liberty, security is oppressive. The challenge is finding the proper measure: enough security to safeguard our freedoms, but not so much (or so little) as to endanger them.

As Secretary of State I focused on protecting privacy, security, and liberty on the internet. In January 2010 Google announced that it had discovered Chinese authorities trying to break into the Gmail accounts of dissidents. The company said it would respond by rerouting Chinese traffic to its Hong Kong servers outside the "Great Firewall." The government in Beijing reacted with anger. Suddenly we were in the middle of a whole new kind of international incident.

For some time I had been working on a speech staking out America's commitment to internet freedom; now it seemed more important than ever to sound the alarm about online repression. On January 21, 2010, I went to the Newseum, a high-tech Washington museum on the history and future of journalism, and made the case for the "freedom to connect." I argued that the same rights we cherished in our homes and public squares—to assemble, to speak, to innovate, to advocate—existed online.

For Americans, this idea was rooted in the First Amendment, whose words were carved in fifty tons of Tennessee marble on the front of the Newseum. But the freedom to connect was not just an American value. The Universal Declaration of Human Rights confirms that all people everywhere have the right "to seek, receive and impart information and ideas through any media and regardless of frontiers."

I wanted to put nations like China, Russia, and Iran on notice that the United States would promote and defend an internet where people's rights are protected and that is open to innovation, interoperable all over the world, secure enough to hold people's trust, and reliable enough to support their work. We would oppose attempts to restrict access or to rewrite the international rules governing the structure of the internet, and would support activists and innovators trying to subvert repressive firewalls. Some of these countries wanted to replace the multi-stakeholder approach to internet governance established in the 1990s, which brings together governments, the private sector, foundations, and citizens, and supports the free flow of information within a single global network, and instead centralize control in the hands of governments alone. They wanted each government to be able to make its own rules, creating national barriers in cyberspace. This approach would be disastrous for internet freedom and commerce. I directed our diplomats to push back against these attempts in every forum, no matter how small.

The speech caused a stir, especially online. Human Rights Watch called it "groundbreaking." I certainly hoped that we had begun a conversation that would change how people thought about freedom on the internet. Most of all, I wanted to make sure that the United States was leading the way on the frontiers of human rights in the 21st century, just as we had in the 20th.

25

Human Rights: Unfinished Business

When I was growing up in Park Ridge, Illinois, I attended Sunday school at our Methodist church every week. My parents were both people of faith, but they expressed it in different ways, and I sometimes struggled to reconcile my father's insistence on self-reliance and my mother's concerns about social justice. In 1961 a dynamic new youth minister named Don Jones arrived at our church, and he helped me better understand the role I wanted faith to play in my own life. He taught me to embrace "faith in action" and to open my eyes to injustice in the wider world beyond my sheltered middle-class community. He gave me lots of books to read, and took our youth group to visit black and Hispanic churches in Chicago's inner city. We found a lot in common with the girls and boys in those church basements, despite our very different life experiences. It was in those discussions that I first became interested in learning more about the Civil Rights Movement. For me and my classmates, Rosa Parks and Dr. Martin Luther King were names we occasionally saw in a newspaper headline or overheard while our parents watched the nightly news. For many of the kids I met through those church trips, however, they were sources of hope and inspiration.

One day Don announced that he wanted to take us to hear Dr. King speak in Chicago. It wasn't hard to persuade my parents to give me permission to go, but some of my friends' parents thought Dr. King was a "rabble-rouser" and wouldn't let their kids attend. I was excited but unsure of what to expect. When we got to Orchestra Hall and Dr. King began to speak, I was transfixed. The speech was entitled "Remaining Awake through a Revolution," and he challenged all of us that evening to stay engaged in the cause of justice and not to slumber while the world changed around us.

Afterward I stood in a long line to shake Dr. King's hand. His grace and piercing moral clarity left a lasting impression on me. I was raised with a deep reverence for the virtues of American democracy. In the view of my rock-ribbed anti-Communist, Republican father, the fact that we had the Declaration of Independence and the Bill of Rights and the Soviets didn't was a defining feature of the ideological struggle of the Cold War. The promises that our founding documents made about freedom and equality were supposed to be sacrosanct. Now I was realizing that many Americans were still denied the rights I took for granted. This lesson and the power of Dr. King's words lit a fire in my heart, fueled by the social justice teachings of my church. I understood as I never had before the mission to express God's love through good works and social action.

I was equally inspired by my early encounters with Marian Wright Edelman. A 1963 graduate of Yale Law School, she was the first African American woman admitted to the Mississippi Bar and worked as a civil rights lawyer for the NAACP in Jackson. When I heard Marian speak during my first semester at Yale, she opened a door for me to a life dedicated to legal, social, and political advocacy for human rights, especially for women and children.

One of my first jobs after law school was working for Marian at the Children's Defense Fund. She asked me to help investigate a mystery: In many communities, a surprising number of young children were not in school. We knew from the census that they lived there, so what was going on? As part of a nationwide survey, I went door to door in New Bedford, Massachusetts, talking to families. We found some kids staying home to care for younger siblings while parents worked. Others had dropped out to work themselves in order to help support their families. But mostly we found children with disabilities who were staying home because there weren't adequate accommodations for them at the public schools. We found blind and deaf children, children in wheelchairs, children with developmental disabilities, and children whose families couldn't afford the treatment they needed. I remember meeting a girl in a wheelchair on the small back porch of her house, where we sat and talked under a grape arbor. She so wanted to go to school, to participate and learn—but it didn't seem possible.

Along with many partners across the country, we collected the data from our survey and sent it to Washington, and Congress eventually enacted legislation declaring that every child in our country is entitled to an education, including those with disabilities. For me, it was the beginning of a lifelong commitment to children's rights. I also remained committed to the cause of people with disabilities, and at the State Department I appointed the first Special Advisor for International Disability Rights to encourage other governments to protect the rights of people with disabilities. I was proud to stand with President Obama at the White House when he declared that the United States would sign the United Nations Convention on the Rights of Persons with Disabilities, which is modeled on the Americans With Disabilities Act and would be our first new human rights treaty of the 21st century. And I was dismayed when a handful of Republican Senators managed to block its ratification in December 2012, despite impassioned pleas from former Republican Senate Majority Leader and disabled war hero Bob Dole.

======

One of my first opportunities to take a stand on behalf of human rights with the whole world watching came in September 1995. As First Lady I was leading the U.S. delegation to the Fourth World Conference on Women in Beijing, where I was slated to give a major speech to representatives from 189 countries, as well as thousands of journalists and activists.

"What do you want to accomplish?" Madeleine Albright asked me as I worked on a draft with Lissa Muscatine, my talented speechwriter. "I want to push the envelope as far as I can on behalf of women and girls," I replied. I wanted my speech to be simple, vivid, and strong in its message that women's rights are not separate from or a subsidiary of the human rights every person is entitled to enjoy.

During my travels as First Lady, I had seen firsthand the obstacles that women and girls faced: how restrictive laws and customs kept them from pursuing an education or health care or participating fully in their nations' economies and politics; how even in their own homes they endured violence and abuse. I wanted to shine a bright spotlight on these obstacles and encourage the world to begin tearing them down. I also wanted to speak for the women and girls seeking education, health care, economic independence, legal rights, and political participation—and to strike the right balance between seeing women as victims of discrimination and seeing women as agents of change. I wanted to use my voice to tell the stories not only of the women I had met but also of the millions of others whose stories would not be heard unless I and others told them.

The heart of the speech was a statement that was both obvious and undeniable but nonetheless too long unsaid on the world stage. "If there is one message that echoes forth from this conference," I declared, "let it be that human rights are women's rights and women's rights are human rights, once and for all."

I offered a list of abuses, including domestic violence, forced prostitution, rape as a tactic or prize of war, genital mutilation, and bride burning, all violations of women's rights and also of human rights, and went on to urge that the world should condemn them with one voice. I talked about some of the remarkable women I had met: new mothers in Indonesia who came together regularly in their village to discuss nutrition, family planning, and baby care; women in India and Bangladesh who used microfinance loans to buy milk cows, rickshaws, thread, and other materials to start thriving small businesses; the women in South Africa who helped lead the struggle to end apartheid and were now helping to build a new democracy.

My speech ended with a call to action for all of us to return to our countries and renew our efforts to improve educational, health, legal, economic, and political opportunities for women. When the last words left my lips, the delegates leaped from their seats to give me a standing ovation. As I exited the hall, women hung over banisters and raced down escalators to shake my hand.

My message had resonated with the women in Beijing, but I could never have predicted how far and wide the impact of this twenty-one-minute speech would stretch. For nearly twenty years women around the world have quoted my words back to me, or asked me to sign a copy of the speech, or shared personal stories about how it inspired them to work for change.

Most important, all 189 nations represented at the conference agreed to an ambitious and detailed Platform for Action that called for the "full and equal participation of women in political, civil, economic, social and cultural life."

Back at the White House I gathered my team together and said that I wanted to get right to work building on what we had accomplished in Beijing. We began holding regular strategy sessions. Sometimes we'd meet in the Map Room on the first floor of the Residence, where President Franklin Roosevelt tracked the progress of our military in World War II. Most of the maps were long gone (I located one of FDR's originals showing the positions of Allied Armies in Europe in 1945 and hung it over the fireplace), but it still felt like a good place to plan a global campaign. This time we weren't fighting fascism or Communism, but our goal was big and bold: advancing the rights and opportunities of half the world's population.

In this context you could look at a map of the world in a number of ways. It was easy to see one problem after another. Throw a dart at the map, and you were likely to hit a country where women faced violence and abuse, an economy where women were denied the chance to participate and prosper, or a political system that excluded women. It was no coincidence that the places where women's lives were most undervalued largely lined up with the parts of the world most plagued by instability, conflict, extremism, and poverty.

This was a point lost on many of the men working across Washington's foreign policy establishment, but over the years I came to view it as one of the most compelling arguments for why standing up for women and girls was not just the right thing to do but also smart and strategic. The mistreatment of women was certainly not the only or even the chief cause of our problems in Afghanistan, where the Taliban banished girls from school and forced women to live in medieval conditions, or in Central Africa, where rape became a common weapon of war. But the correlation was undeniable, and a growing body of research showed that improving conditions for women helped resolve conflicts and stabilize societies. "Women's issues" had long been relegated to the margins of U.S. foreign policy and international diplomacy, considered at best a nice thing to work on but hardly a necessity. I became convinced that, in fact, this was a cause that cut to the heart of our national security.

There was another way to look at the map. Instead of problems, you could see opportunities. The world was full of women finding new ways to solve old problems. They were eager to go to school, own land, start a business, and run for office. There were partnerships to form and leaders to nurture, if we were willing to step up. I encouraged our government, the private sector, the NGO community, and international institutions to take up this challenge and to see women not as victims to be saved but as partners to be embraced.

I had two Chiefs of Staff in the White House who were indispensable traveling companions on my journey. Maggie Williams, who worked with me at the Children's Defense Fund in the 1980s, is a terrific communicator and one of the most creative and decent people I've ever met. She helped set the course for my time as First Lady and remained a close friend and confidante ever since. Melanne Verveer was Maggie's Deputy in the first term and then her successor in the second. We've always had a real mutual admiration society. Melanne and her husband, Phil, had studied at Georgetown with Bill, and she had gone on to be a star on Capitol Hill and at People for the American Way. Her energy and intellect are simply unstoppable, and her passion for working on behalf of women and girls is unmatched.

The years that followed Beijing saw exciting progress. In many countries laws that once permitted unequal treatment of women and girls were repealed. The United Nations created a new body called UN Women, and the Security Council passed resolutions recognizing the crucial role of women in peacemaking and security. Researchers at the World Bank, the International Monetary Fund (IMF), and other institutions expanded their study of the untapped potential of women to drive economic growth and social progress. As women gained the chance to work, learn, and participate in their societies, their economic, social, and political contributions multiplied.

Yet despite this progress, women and girls still comprise the majority of the world's unhealthy, unfed, and unpaid. At the end of 2013, women held less than 22 percent of all seats in Parliaments and Legislatures around the world. In some places women cannot open a bank account or sign a contract. More than a hundred countries still have laws that limit or prohibit women's participation in the economy. Twenty years ago, American women made 72 cents on the dollar. Today it's still not equal. Women also hold a majority of lower wage jobs in this country and nearly three quarters of all jobs in fields that rely on tips like waiters, bartenders, and hairstylists—which pay even less than average hourly work. Meanwhile, only a small percentage of Fortune 500 CEOs are women. In short, the journey toward full participation for women and girls is far from over.

Faced with these grim facts, it can be easy to get discouraged. In the White House after Beijing, at times when I felt daunted by the scope of the challenges we were trying to overcome, I often found myself looking for comfort to a portrait of Eleanor Roosevelt that I kept in my office. The example she set as a fearless First Lady and a courageous fighter for human rights inspired and fortified me. After Franklin Roosevelt's death and the end of World War II, Eleanor represented the United States as a delegate to the new United Nations and helped shape its development. During the first meeting of the UN General Assembly, in London in early 1946, she joined the sixteen other women delegates in publishing "an open letter to the women of the world," in which they argued that "women in various parts of the world are at different stages of participation in the life of their community," but "the goal of full participation in the life and responsibilities of their countries and of the world community is a common objective toward which the women of the world should assist one another." Eleanor's language of "full participation," echoed in the Beijing Platform for Action nearly fifty years later, has always resonated with me.

So have many of her other words. "A woman is like a tea bag," she once observed wryly. "You never know how strong she is until she's in hot water." I love that and, in my experience, it's spot on. In 1959, by which time Eleanor was a revered elder stateswoman near the end of her life, she used one of her newspaper columns to issue a call to action to the American people: "We have not yet succeeded in our democracy in giving every one of our citizens equal freedom and equal opportunity, and that is our unfinished business." As I dove deeper into my work on behalf of women and girls around the world, I started describing the quest for equal rights and full participation for women as the "unfinished business" of our time. It was a reminder to audiences—and to me—just how far we still had to go.

=====

Eleanor Roosevelt's greatest achievement was the Universal Declaration of Human Rights, the first binding international agreement on the rights of humankind. In the aftermath of World War II and the Holocaust, many nations were pressing for a statement of this kind to help ensure that we would prevent future atrocities and protect the inherent humanity and dignity of all people. The Nazis were able to pursue their crimes because they were able progressively to constrict the circle of those defined as humans. This cold, dark region of the human soul, where people withdraw first understanding, then empathy, and finally even the designation of personhood from another human being, was not, of course, unique to Nazi Germany. The impulse to dehumanize has reappeared throughout history, and it was precisely this impulse that the drafters of the Universal Declaration hoped to restrain.

They discussed, they wrote, they revisited, revised, and rewrote. They incorporated suggestions and revisions from governments, organizations, and individuals around the world. It is telling that even in the drafting of the Universal Declaration there was a debate about women's rights. The initial version of the first article stated, "All men are created equal." It took women members of the Commission, led by Hansa Mehta of India, to point out that "all men" might be interpreted to exclude women. Only after long debate was the language changed to say, "All human beings are born free and equal in dignity and rights."

At 3:00 in the morning on December 10, 1948, after nearly two years of drafting and one last long night of debate, the president of the UN General Assembly called for a vote on the final text. Forty-eight nations voted in favor, eight abstained, none dissented, and the Universal Declaration of Human Rights was adopted. It made clear that our rights are not conferred by governments; they are the birthright of all people. It does not matter what country we live in, who our leaders are, or even who we are. Because we are human, we therefore have rights. And because we have rights, governments are bound to protect them.

During the Cold War, America's devotion to human rights made our country a source of hope and inspiration for millions of people around the world. But our policies and practices did not always match our ideals. At home it took the courage of a woman who refused to give up her seat on a public bus, a preacher who refused to shut up about the "fierce urgency of now," and so many others who refused to put up with segregation and discrimination, to force America to recognize the civil rights of all our citizens. Around the world our government often prioritized security and strategic interests over concerns about human rights, supporting odious dictators if they shared our opposition to Communism.

Throughout the history of American foreign policy, there has been a running debate between so-called realists and idealists. The former, it is argued, place national security ahead of human rights, while the latter do the opposite. Those are categories that I find overly simplistic. No one should have any illusions about the gravity of the security threats America faces, and as Secretary I had no higher responsibility than to protect our citizens and our country. But at the same time, upholding universal values and human rights is at the core of what it means to be American. If we sacrifice those values or let our policies diverge too far from our ideals, our influence will wane and our country will cease to be what Abraham Lincoln called the "the last best hope of earth." Moreover, defending our values and defending our interests are often in less tension than it may sometimes appear. Over the long term, repression undermines stability and creates new threats, while democracy and respect for human rights create strong and stable societies.

As you've seen throughout this book, however, there are times when we do have to make difficult compromises. Our challenge is to be clear-eyed about the world as it is while never losing sight of the world as we want it to become. That's why I don't mind that I've been called both an idealist and a realist over the years. I prefer being considered a hybrid, perhaps an idealistic realist. Because I, like our country, embody both tendencies.

One of my favorite examples of how support for human rights advances our strategic interests comes from the 1970s, when the United States under President Gerald Ford signed the Helsinki Accords with the Soviet Union. Some commentators in the West dismissed the human rights provisions in the agreements as the height of idealist folly, not worth the paper they were printed on. The Soviets would obviously disregard them.

Then something unexpected happened. Behind the Iron Curtain activists and dissidents felt empowered to begin working for change because the Helsinki Accords gave them cover to talk about human rights. Communist officials were caught in a bind. They couldn't condemn a document the Kremlin had signed, but if they enforced its provisions the entire authoritarian system would break down. In the years that followed, the shipyard workers of Solidarity in Poland, reformers in Hungary, and demonstrators in Prague all seized on the fundamental rights defined at Helsinki. They held their governments to account for not living up to the standards to which they had agreed. Helsinki proved to be a Trojan horse that contributed to the fall of Communism. There was nothing "soft" about that.

I tried never to forget the wisdom of Helsinki and the strategic impact human rights can have. Any time I needed a reminder, I just looked over at that portrait of Eleanor Roosevelt, which I still kept near my desk.

In late 1997, two years after the conference in Beijing, the United Nations invited me to help kick off commemorations of the fiftieth anniversary of the Universal Declaration of Human Rights. On December 10, which had become known as Human Rights Day, I went to UN headquarters in New York and delivered a speech about our shared responsibility to carry the Declaration's legacy forward into the new millennium. I praised the progress the world had made since 1948, but noted, "We have not expanded the circle of human dignity far enough. There are still too many of our fellow men and women excluded from the fundamental rights proclaimed in the Declaration, too many whom we have hardened our hearts against—those whose human suffering we fail fully to see, to hear, and to feel." In particular I called attention to the women and girls around the world who were still systematically denied their rights and shut out from opportunities to participate in their societies. "The full enfranchisement of the rights of women is unfinished business in this turbulent century," I said, echoing Eleanor's phrase. "It is because every era has its blind spots that we must see our own unfinished business now while we stand on the threshold of a new millennium with even greater urgency. We must rededicate ourselves to completing the circle of human rights once and for all."

═══

When I became Secretary of State in 2009, I was determined to put this "unfinished business" at the top of America's diplomatic to-do list. Melanne Verveer was one of my first calls. She had spent the previous eight years running Vital Voices, an organization she and I had started with Madeleine Albright to find and support emerging women leaders around the world. I asked Melanne to serve as the first Ambassador-at-Large for Global Women's Issues and to help me craft a "full participation agenda" and weave it into the fabric of American foreign policy and national security. We had to push tradition-bound bureaus and agencies to think differently about the role of women in conflicts and peacemaking, economic and democratic development, public health, and more. I didn't want her office to be the only place where this work was done; rather I wanted it to be integrated into the daily routine of our diplomats and development experts everywhere.

The State Department and USAID launched a wide range of global and regional initiatives, including programs to help women entrepreneurs gain access to training, markets, finance, and credit; a partnership with some of America's top women's colleges and universities to identify, mentor, and train women in public service around the world; and efforts to help more women use mobile technology for everything from secure banking to documenting gender-based violence. Melanne tirelessly traveled the world, finding local partners and ensuring that these efforts took root in communities as well as capitals. I liked to joke with her that she might be the only person I knew with more frequent-flier miles than I. (If only the Air Force offered them!)

Many years ago on a trip across Africa I was struck that everywhere I went I saw women laboring in the fields, women carrying water, women fetching firewood, women working at market stalls. I was talking to some economists, and I asked them, "How do you evaluate the contributions that women make to the economy?" One of them replied, "We don't, because they don't participate in the economy." He meant the formal economy of offices and factories. But if women across the world all of a sudden stopped working one day, those economists would quickly discover that women actually contribute quite a lot to the economy, as well as to the peace and security of their communities.

I encountered this attitude all over the world. I can't tell you how many times I sat across the table from some President or Prime Minister whose eyes glazed over whenever I raised the issue of women's rights and opportunities in his country. I quietly kept track of how many women leaders or advisors ever joined those meetings. It wasn't hard to do, because there were hardly any.

My most egregious interaction with a clueless leader was in the remote Southeast Asian island nation of Papua New Guinea in November 2010. It's a mysterious and bountiful country on the verge of progress, but plagued by one of the highest rates of violence against women in the world. According to one estimate, 70 percent of women in Papua New Guinea will be victims of rape or physical violence in their lifetime. At our joint press conference, Prime Minister Sir Michael Somare was asked by an American reporter what his response was to these troubling statistics. Somare claimed the problems were "exaggerated by people who write about us." Yes, he admitted, there were some cases of violence, but he added, "I have been around for a long time and I know that men and the women, sometimes there are fights, arguments do take place, but it's nothing very brutal." There were laws in place, he said. "We have cases where people are drunk. . . . A person cannot control when he's under the influence of liquor." I was taken aback, to say the least, and even the jaded American press corps was speechless. Afterward, as you can imagine, Melanne and I got right to work on new programs and partnerships with civil society in Papua New Guinea, trying to amplify women's voices and provide them with new platforms for participation. I am pleased that in May 2013, a new Prime Minister, Peter O'Neill, formally apologized to the women of his country for the violence and promised to toughen criminal penalties.

Even at home in Washington our work on behalf of women was often seen as a parenthetical exercise, somehow separate from the important work of foreign policy. In one *Washington Post* article about our efforts with women in Afghanistan, an unnamed senior administration official sniffed, "Gender issues are going to have to take a backseat to other priorities. . . . There's no way we can be successful if we maintain every special interest and pet project. All those pet rocks in our rucksack were taking us down." I wasn't surprised the official was afraid to be named making a comment like that. Melanne and I started calling her shop the Pet Rock Office and kept on working.

I have to admit, I grew tired of watching otherwise thoughtful people just smile and nod when I brought up the concerns of women and girls. I'd been championing these issues on the world stage for nearly twenty years, and sometimes it felt like all I was doing was preaching to the choir. So I decided to redouble our efforts to make a case strong enough to convince skeptics based on hard data and clear-eyed analysis that creating opportunities for women and girls across the globe directly supports everyone's security and prosperity, and should be part of our diplomacy and development work.

Melanne's team began combing through all the data that had been collected by institutions such as the World Bank and the IMF. They quickly learned that some aspects of women's participation were well studied, especially the benefits of bringing more women into the workforce and the obstacles that held them back, but others were significantly under-researched. In many parts of the world there was a lack of reliable and regular data on even the basic facts about the lives of women and girls, such as whether they had birth certificates, at what age they had their first child, how many hours of paid and unpaid work they did, or whether they owned the land they farmed.

I've always believed that good decisions in government, in business, and in life are based on evidence rather than ideology. This is especially true when it comes to policies that will affect millions of people. You have to do the research and run the numbers; that's how we minimize risk and maximize impact. And these days we keep statistics on every-thing we care about, from RBIs in baseball to ROI in business. There's a saying in management circles: "What gets measured gets done." So if we were serious about helping more girls and women achieve their full potential, then we had to get serious about gathering and analyz-ing the data about the conditions they faced and the contributions they made. We needed not only more data but also better data. We needed to make it accessible to researchers and policymakers so it could help them make good decisions. The State Department launched a number of new initiatives to fill the data gaps, working with the UN, the World Bank, the Organization for Economic Co-operation and Development, and others.

(In general I was surprised how many people in Washington operated in an "evidence-free zone," where data and science were disregarded. A senior advisor to President Bush was once quoted disparaging what he called "the reality-based community" of people who "believe that solu-tions emerge from your judicious study of discernible reality." I've always thought that's exactly how to solve problems. The Bush aide went on, "That's not the way the world really works anymore. . . . We're an empire now, and when we act, we create our own reality." That attitude helps explain a lot of what went wrong in those years.)

We didn't have to wait for all these projects to bear fruit to start trum-peting the data we already had, especially on women and the economy. And you didn't have to look far. In the early 1970s, American women held 37 percent of all jobs in the United States, compared to 47 percent in 2009. The productivity gains attributable to this increase accounted for more than $3.5 trillion in GDP growth over four decades.

The story has played out in less developed economies as well. For example, Latin America and the Caribbean steadily increased women's participation in the labor market starting in the 1990s. The World Bank has estimated that extreme poverty in the region decreased by 30 percent as a result of recent gains.

These and similar findings add up to a compelling case that it is in everyone's interest to increase women's participation in the economy and to tear down the barriers that still hold them back. In September 2011 I assembled all the data I could and made this argument at a summit of Asian-Pacific leaders in San Francisco. "To achieve the economic expansion we all seek, we need to unlock a vital source of growth that can power our economies in the decades to come," I told the delegates. "And that vital source of growth is women. With economic models straining in every corner of the world, none of us can afford to perpetuate the barriers facing women in the workforce."

I was delighted when the Prime Minister of Japan Shinzo Abe announced that increasing women's economic participation would be a pillar of his ambitious new economic agenda. It was dubbed "womenomics." He detailed plans to improve access to affordable child care and extend parental leave to encourage more women to enter the workforce. Abe also asked the country's biggest businesses to each appoint at least one woman executive. We need more far-sighted leadership like that at home and around the world.

Another area where we focused our efforts was the role of women in making and keeping peace. We had seen so many inspiring examples of women around the world making unique contributions to ending conflicts and rebuilding shattered societies in Liberia, Colombia, Rwanda, Northern Ireland, and elsewhere. I remember vividly my visit to a fish and chips restaurant in Belfast in 1995, where I had a chance to sit and drink tea with both Catholic and Protestant women who were tired of the Troubles and eager for peace. While they may have attended different churches on Sunday, seven days a week they all said a silent prayer for the safe return of a child from school or a husband from an errand in town. One of them, Joyce McCartan, who founded the Women's Drop-In Center in 1987 after her seventeen-year-old son was shot and killed, said: "It takes women to bring men to their senses."

When women participate in peace processes, they tend to focus discussion on issues like human rights, justice, national reconciliation, and economic renewal that are critical to making peace. They generally build coalitions across ethnic and sectarian lines and are more likely to speak up for other marginalized groups. They often act as mediators and help to foster compromise.

Yet despite all that women tend to bring to the table, more often than not they're excluded. Of the hundreds of peace treaties signed since the early 1990s, fewer than 10 percent had any women negotiators, fewer than 3 percent had any women signatories, and only a small percentage included even a single reference to women. So it's not too surprising that more than half of all peace agreements fail within five years.

I spent years trying to get generals, diplomats, and national security policymakers in our own country and around the world to tune in to this reality. I found sympathetic allies at the Pentagon and in the White House, including Under Secretary of Defense for Policy Michèle Flournoy and Admiral Sandy Winnefeld, Vice Chairman of the Joint Chiefs of Staff. State, USAID, and Defense got to work on a plan that would change the way diplomats, development experts, and military personnel interact with women in conflict and postconflict areas. There would be new emphasis on stopping rape and gender-based violence and empowering women to make and keep peace. We called it a National Action Plan on Women, Peace, and Security.

In December 2011, President Obama issued an executive order launching the plan. Flournoy and Winnefeld joined me at Georgetown to explain it to the public. Looking at the Admiral in his crisp Navy uniform at an event about women as peacemakers, I hoped we had finally turned a corner, at least in our country.

As my term as Secretary drew to a close, I wanted to be sure that the changes we had made to knit gender issues into every aspect of U.S. foreign policy wouldn't disappear after I left. In any bureaucracy, institutionalizing reforms is difficult, and that was certainly true at the State Department. Over several months we worked with the White House to prepare a Presidential Memorandum that would make Melanne's position of Ambassador-at-Large for Global Women's Issues permanent and ensure that her successors reported directly to the Secretary of State. It took some pressing to get this through the White House system, but luckily my former Deputy Secretary Jack Lew had become President Obama's Chief of Staff, so we had a very well-placed ally. On January 30, 2013, one of my last days in office, I had lunch with President Obama in his private dining room off the Oval Office, and, as I was leaving, he stopped me to watch him sign the memorandum. He could not have given me a better send-off.

=====

Our work on behalf of women and girls around the world was embedded in a broader human rights agenda aimed at defending the freedoms enshrined in the Declaration of Human Rights and making them real in the lives of people all over the world.

In 2009, there was no denying that our country's approach to human rights had gotten somewhat out of balance. On his second full day in office President Obama issued an executive order prohibiting the use of torture or official cruelty by any U.S. official and ordered the closure of Guantánamo Bay (a goal that has not yet been achieved). He pledged to put human rights back at the heart of our foreign policy.

As I've described, the United States became a champion of freedom on the internet and stepped up aid to dissidents trying to evade censors and bypass firewalls. We advocated on behalf of journalists thrown in jail for exposing inconvenient truths about repressive regimes, helped survivors of human trafficking step out of the shadows, and made the case for workers' rights and fair labor standards. Behind these headlines was the daily work of diplomacy: pressing foreign governments, supporting dissidents, engaging civil society, and making sure that our own government kept human rights front and center in all policy deliberations.

One of our first steps was to rejoin the UN Human Rights Council, a forty-seven-member body created in 2006 to monitor abuses around the world. It replaced the UN Human Rights Commission, which Eleanor Roosevelt had helped establish and lead in the late 1940s. Over time it had become a laughingstock as notorious human rights violators like Sudan and Zimbabwe were elected as members. The new organization faced the same problems; even Cuba won a seat. The Bush Administration refused to participate, and the Council seemed to spend most of its time condemning Israel. So why join? It wasn't that the Obama Administration didn't see the Council's flaws, but we decided that participating would give us the best chance to be a constructive influence and put it on a better track.

The Council continued to have serious problems, but it proved to be a useful platform for advancing our agenda. When Muammar Qaddafi was using extreme violence against civilians in Libya in early 2011, I went to the Council in Geneva to rally the world against his atrocities. While there I spoke out against a continuing bias against Israel. I also urged the Council to move beyond a decade-long debate over whether insults to religion should be banned or criminalized. "It is time to overcome the false divide that pits religious sensitivities against freedom of expression and pursue a new approach based on concrete steps to fight intolerance wherever it occurs," I said.

For years some Muslim-majority nations at the Council had pushed resolutions opposed by the United States and others that would have threatened freedom of expression in the name of preventing "defamation" of religion. This was not just a theoretical exercise, considering the firestorms that erupted periodically when someone around the world published a cartoon or posted a video online denigrating the Prophet Muhammad. I thought we could break the impasse by recognizing that tolerance and freedom are both core values that need protecting. To reach a compromise, we needed a partner willing to move past the charged political and ideological questions clouding the debate.

We found that partner in the Organization of Islamic Cooperation, which represents nearly sixty nations. Its chair, the Turkish diplomat and scholar Ekmeleddin İhsanoğlu, was a thoughtful man whom I had met in the 1990s, when he was the director of the Research Centre for Islamic History, Art and Culture in Istanbul. İhsanoğlu agreed to work with me on a new resolution at the Human Rights Council that would take a strong stand for freedom of expression and worship and against discrimination and violence based upon religion or belief, while avoiding the broad prohibitions on speech called for in the former "defamation" resolutions. Our teams in Geneva began hammering out the text, and in late March 2011 the Council unanimously adopted it.

Religious freedom is a human right unto itself, and it is also wrapped up with other rights, including the right of people to think what they want, say what they think, associate with others, and assemble peacefully without the state looking over their shoulders or prohibiting them from doing so. The Universal Declaration of Human Rights makes clear that each of us is born free to practice any religion, to change our religion, or to have none at all. No state may grant these freedoms as a privilege or take them away as a punishment.

Every year the State Department publishes a report detailing cases of religious persecution around the world. For example, in Iran authorities repress Sufi Muslims, evangelical Christians, Jews, Bahais, Sunnis, Ahmadis, and others who do not share the government's religious views. We also tracked a troubling resurgence of anti-Semitism in parts of Europe; in countries like France, Poland, and the Netherlands swastikas were spray-painted on Jewish tombs, schools, synagogues, and kosher shops.

In China the government cracked down on unregistered "house churches" and the Christians who worshipped in them, as well as Uighur Muslims and Tibetan Buddhists. On my first trip to China as Secretary, in February 2009, I attended a service in one of these house churches to send a message to the government about religious freedom.

Our interest in protecting religious liberty and the rights of minorities went beyond a moral argument. There were also important strategic considerations, particularly in societies in transition. When I visited Egypt in 2012, the Coptic Christians wondered whether they would be accorded the same rights and respect as all Egyptians by their new government. In Burma ethnic Rohingya Muslims continue to be denied full citizenship and equal opportunities for education, employment, and travel. What Egypt, Burma, and other countries decide on protections for these religious minorities will have a major impact on the lives of their people and will go a long way toward determining whether these countries are able to achieve stability and democracy. History teaches us that when the rights of minorities are secure, societies are more stable and everyone benefits. As I said in Alexandria, Egypt, in the hot tumultuous summer of 2012, "Real democracy means that every citizen has the right to live, work, and worship as they choose, whether they are man or woman, Muslim or Christian, or from any other background. Real democracy means that no group or faction or leader can impose their will, their ideology, their religion, their desires on anyone else."

═══

Over the years, I have often returned to an argument from my speech at the UN marking the fiftieth anniversary of the Universal Declaration of Human Rights: "Here we are at the very close of the 20th century, a century that has been scorched by war time and time again. If the history of this century teaches us anything, it is that whenever the dignity of any individual or group is compromised by the derogation of who they are, of some essential attribute they possess, then we all leave ourselves open to nightmares to come." I urged that we learn the lesson and extend the circle of citizenship and human dignity to include everyone without exception.

When I said those words, I had in mind not only the women and girls around the world who continued to be marginalized in so many ways but other "invisibles," from religious and ethnic minorities to people with disabilities to lesbian, gay, bisexual, and transgender (LGBT) people. When I look back on my time as Secretary, I'm proud of the work we did to extend the circle of human dignity and human rights to include people historically excluded.

In January 2011, the world learned about David Kato. He was a gay activist in Uganda, well known in that country and in international advocacy circles. He had been threatened many times, including on the front page of a Ugandan newspaper, which had published a photo of David and others under the words "HANG THEM." Eventually someone followed through on the threats. David was killed in what police said was a robbery but was more likely an execution.

Like many people in Uganda and around the world, I was appalled that the police and government had done little to protect David after the public calls for his murder. But this was about more than police incompetence. The Ugandan Parliament was considering a bill to make being gay a crime punishable by death. A high-ranking government official—the Minister of Ethics and Integrity, no less—gave an interview in which he said dismissively, "Homosexuals can forget about human rights." LGBT people in Uganda were routinely harassed and attacked, and the authorities did virtually nothing to stop it. When I raised these issues with Ugandan President Yoweri Museveni, he ridiculed my concerns. "Oh, Hillary, here you go again," he would say. David's death wasn't an isolated incident; it was the result of a nationwide campaign to suppress LGBT people by any means necessary, and the government was part of it.

I asked for a briefing on David's life and work and read an interview he gave in 2009 in which he said he wanted to be "a good human rights defender, not a dead one, but an alive one." He had that opportunity stolen from him, but others were continuing his work, and I wanted the United States to be firmly in their corner.

Abuse of LGBT people is by no means exclusive to Uganda. As of this writing, more than eighty countries worldwide, from the Caribbean to the Middle East to South Asia, have in one way or another made it a crime to be LGBT. People are jailed for having same-sex relationships, for wearing clothes that go against typical gender norms, or simply for saying that they are LGBT. Uganda's neighbor Kenya has been sending gay men to prison for years. In northern Nigeria gay men can still face death by stoning. In Cameroon in 2012, a man was sent to jail simply for sending a text to another man that expressed romantic love. I was deeply troubled when Nigerian President Goodluck Jonathan and Uganda's Museveni both signed harsh, repressive antihomosexuality bills in early 2014. Homosexuality was already criminalized in both countries, but the new Nigerian law provides for a prison sentence of fourteen years for engaging in a same-sex relationship and ten years for LGBT advocacy, and some acts under the new Ugandan law are punishable by a life sentence.

The regime of Vladimir Putin in Russia has enacted a series of anti-gay laws, prohibiting the adoption of Russian children by gay couples or any couples from countries that allow same-sex marriage, and making it a crime to promote gay rights or even discuss homosexuality around children. When I pressed Russian Foreign Minister Sergey Lavrov to do more to protect the rights of LGBT people, the normally cool and restrained diplomat turned nasty. Russians don't have a problem with homosexuals, he told me, just with their "propaganda." "Why do 'these people' have to go around flaunting it? Russians shouldn't have to put up with that." Lavrov was contemptuous of the idea of being "on the right side of history" on this issue; that was just "sentimental nonsense." I tried to explain the steps we were taking to repeal "Don't Ask Don't Tell" and open up our military to LGBT service members, and I asked my Defense Department traveling representative Admiral Harry Harris to elaborate. The Russian side of the table started snickering. "Oh, he is gay?" one of them asked in a stage whisper. Harry isn't and couldn't care less about Russian jibes, but I was appalled that my sophisticated Russian counterparts were casually and cruelly parroting offensive talking points.

The dismal state of LGBT rights around the world had been on the U.S. human rights radar for some time. Since 1993, when reporting instructions were changed to include sexual orientation, the State Department has highlighted abuses faced by LGBT communities around the world in its annual Human Rights Report and has raised the issue in our dealings with other governments, as I did with Lavrov and Museveni and others. We also did quite a bit of outreach to LGBT populations through PEPFAR, which not only helped save millions of lives but brought people who had been isolated into the public sphere.

But I decided our human rights efforts needed an upgrade. There was too much evidence that the climate for LGBT people was deteriorating in many parts of the world. This was in stark opposition to the remarkable progress in other places, including the United States. It was a terrible irony: In some parts of the world life for LGBT people was better than ever; in others it had never been worse.

Meanwhile, I looked for ways to make progress closer to home, by better supporting the LGBT members of the State Department family. In earlier generations talented members of the Foreign Service had been forced to resign when their sexual orientation became known. Those days were gone, but there were still plenty of rules in place that made life harder for our LGBT colleagues. So in 2009, I extended the full range of legally available benefits and allowances to same-sex domestic partners of Foreign Service staff serving abroad. In 2010, I directed that the State Department's equal employment opportunity policy explicitly protect against discriminatory treatment of employees and job applicants based on gender identity. We also made it easier for Americans to change the sex listed on their passport and made it possible for same-sex couples to obtain passports under the names recognized by their state through their marriage or civil union. To support the antibullying movement started by the columnist Dan Savage, I recorded an "It Gets Better" video that went viral. I don't know if my words of comfort and encouragement reached any at-risk teenagers, but I hope they did.

I supported the State Department's annual Pride event, hosted by a group called GLIFAA, Gays and Lesbians in Foreign Affairs Agencies. As the name suggests, these are LGBT people who work in U.S. foreign affairs, so they have a strong professional stake in improving the climate for LGBT people abroad, as well as here at home. The annual Pride celebration they organized at State was at once joyful and purposeful. At the 2010 Pride celebration, after recapping some of the progress we'd made together in the past year, I turned to the terrible harms still being suffered by LGBT people worldwide. "These dangers are not gay issues—this is a human rights issue," I said. The room burst into whoops and cheers. I went on: "Just as I was very proud to say the obvious more than fifteen years ago in Beijing, that human rights are women's rights and women's rights are human rights, let me say today that human rights are gay rights and gay rights are human rights, once and for all." Again loud, sustained applause. Of course, I had hoped that my remarks would be well received, but I was surprised by the passionate reaction from the crowd. Clearly this was something people had been waiting to hear even more fervently than I had realized. Later Dan Baer, an active member of GLIFAA, confirmed this. "You need to say this to the world," he told me.

With that the work began on one of the most memorable speeches I delivered as Secretary of State.

Most of my major speeches as Secretary were, naturally, thick with foreign policy. They laid out multiyear, multipronged strategies on complex issues. Often they included carefully worded caveats, encoded warnings, and at least a few instances of diplomatic jargon. My speechwriters worked hard to make every one accessible to the broadest possible audience, but the fact remained: Foreign policy speeches tend to be wonky, and their most fervent listeners and readers are foreign policy professionals, whether government officials, think tank experts, or journalists on the beat.

I wanted this speech to be different. I wanted it to mean something to LGBT people in lots of different circumstances—not just the activists on the front lines, fluent in the argot of human rights, but also the bullied teenager in rural America, or Armenia or Algeria, for that matter. I wanted it to be simple and direct—the exact opposite of the over-the-top, darkly suggestive language you hear in many antigay jeremiads. I wanted it to at least have a chance at convincing dubious listeners, so it needed to be reasonable and respectful, without backing a millimeter away from its defense of human rights. Most of all, I wanted it to send a clear message to the leaders of countries everywhere: Protecting their LGBT citizens was part of their human rights obligations, and the world was watching to make sure they'd meet them.

Before we started writing the speech, I wanted to figure out where I'd give it, since on a topic this sensitive the location and occasion would matter more than usual. It was early 2011. I had travel scheduled to just about every region of the world in the coming months. Would one of those trips be the right one? I was going to Africa in August, and we briefly considered going to Uganda and giving the speech in David Kato's memory, but ruled that out pretty quickly. I wanted to avoid at all costs suggesting that antigay violence is just an African problem rather than a global problem, or giving local bigots an excuse to complain about U.S. bullying. I wanted the only story to be the message of the speech itself.

We looked at the calendar; maybe we should choose a significant date rather than a significant location. The 2011 Pride celebration in June? No—if I gave the speech in the United States, it wouldn't be the speech I envisioned. The press would cover it from a domestic political angle, if they covered it at all. (Talking about LGBT rights during Pride Month isn't exactly newsworthy.) It just wouldn't make the same impact.

Eventually Jake Sullivan and Dan Baer both had the same idea: I should deliver the speech in Geneva, at the headquarters of the UN Human Rights Council. If my goal was to firmly place LGBT rights within the international community's framework of human rights, there was no better place to do it.

So we had a place. What about a date? We decided on the first week of December, to mark the anniversary of the signing of the Universal Declaration of Human Rights, just as I had done back in 1997. The historical significance was meaningful; more practically, I was already scheduled to be in Europe that week for meetings at NATO headquarters in Brussels. Adding a stop in Geneva would be easy.

Writing the speech wasn't easy. I wanted to refute the most egregious myths that antigay zealots spread as truth, including those that government Ministers had said in all seriousness to me when I pressed them to treat LGBT people humanely. My speechwriter Megan Rooney researched the most outlandish examples. There were so many: that gay people were mentally ill child abusers; that God *wanted* us to reject and isolate them; that poor countries couldn't afford to care about human rights; that these countries didn't have any LGBT people at all. That's what Iranian President Mahmoud Ahmadinejad told an audience at Columbia University in 2007, "In Iran, we don't have homosexuals, like in your country." I'd heard similar things in private many times.

In our first draft we listed five common myths and then debunked them one by one. The speech evolved quite a bit over several successive drafts, but we ended up sticking with that basic structure throughout. I knew the speech needed to be exceedingly calm and measured if it had any chance of changing anyone's mind, so many of my edits were aimed at that; for example, "five myths" became "five issues." I thought it was important to acknowledge that many views on LGBT people are rooted in religious and cultural traditions that hold great meaning in people's lives and shouldn't be treated contemptuously. "I come here before you with respect, understanding and humility," I wrote. The strength of the ideas were undiminished by the more measured language.

I told Megan to go back to my 1995 Beijing speech and use that as a model. After all, what I wanted to do here was very similar: name the ugly things happening to this group of people and declare that they are human rights violations, for the simple fact is that these people are human beings. That was it: no complex arguments, no thundering rhetoric, just a few unadorned assertions that were long overdue.

There were a few strategic questions we needed to answer. First: Should we "name and shame" countries that had taken steps in the wrong direction? An early draft of the speech called out Uganda, among others. I decided that was a mistake. Any list would be incomplete; plus I knew that any country singled out for criticism would feel obligated to respond, most likely defensively and angrily. After all, the United States has made strides, but we still have work to do on equality for LGBT Americans. I wanted this speech to make leaders think, not lash out.

Instead, we looked for examples of non-Western countries that had made great progress on LGBT rights. What better way was there to refute the myth that supporting LGBT people was a Western, colonialist practice? Happily there were many to choose from. In the end I praised Mongolia, Nepal, South Africa, India, Argentina, and Colombia and quoted the former President of Botswana.

The second question: How should we advertise the speech? If we said it was about LGBT human rights, we knew some people—exactly the people we wanted to reach—would stay away. So we decided to bill it simply as a human rights speech marking the anniversary of the Universal Declaration, and leave it at that.

In the weeks leading up to the speech, once most of it was set, I kept my ears open for stories and ideas worth adding. At a meeting at the White House the Commandant of the Marine Corps shared an anecdote about the repeal of Don't Ask Don't Tell. "I was against it and I said so at the time," he told me. "But once it happened I saw that my fears were unfounded." The Marines had embraced the change with proud professionalism, he added. Into the speech it went. My Legal Advisor Harold Koh suggested adding something about the importance of empathy, walking in someone else's shoes. It ended up being one of the loveliest parts of the speech.

Finally, we left for Europe. Switzerland was to be the third country in a five-country tour, one country per day. In Germany I led the U.S. delegation at a conference on Afghanistan. In Lithuania, I attended a meeting of the Organization for Security and Cooperation in Europe. When we finally arrived at our small, charming hotel in Vilnius, many of my staff headed to the hotel bar for a late dinner of Lithuanian specialties. But Megan and Jake were too nervous about the next day's remarks to relax. They headed to her hotel room, sat on the floor, and with Dan Baer (who was already in Geneva) on speakerphone, went through every line of the speech. They finished just before dawn.

Early the next morning I learned that the White House had finally approved a policy change that we had been discussing. From now on, the United States would take into account the LGBT human rights record of a country when appropriating foreign aid. This kind of policy has a real chance of influencing the actions of other governments. I was looking forward to adding it to the speech.

On December 6, we flew into Geneva and headed to the Palace of Nations. It was looking even more palatial than usual. The building is impressive enough on a normal day; built to be the headquarters for the League of Nations, it opened in 1936, a last gasp of optimism before Europe disintegrated. Here many of the great questions of 20th-century diplomacy were arbitrated, from nuclear disarmament to the independence of nations emerging from colonialism. Its corridors and chambers are always crowded, but on this day it was thronged with people.

I walked onto the stage and began.

Today, I want to talk about the work we have left to do to protect one group of people whose human rights are still denied in too many parts of the world today. In many ways, they are an invisible minority. They are arrested, beaten, terrorized, even executed. Many are treated with contempt and violence by their fellow citizens while authorities empowered to protect them look the other way or, too often, even join in the abuse. They are denied opportunities to work and learn, driven from their homes and countries, and forced to suppress or deny who they are to protect themselves from harm.

Some in the audience had a curious look on their faces. Where was this going?

"I am talking about gay, lesbian, bisexual and transgender people," I continued.

I was proud to deliver every word of that speech, but a few lines in particular stand out in my memory. Remembering David Kato, I spoke directly to all the other brave LGBT activists fighting uphill battles in lonely, dangerous places worldwide: "You have an ally in the United States of America. And you have millions of friends among the American people."

Remembering all the conversations I'd had with foreign leaders who threw up their hands and said, "Our people hate gays, they support these laws, what can we do?," I spoke directly to those officials: "Leadership, by definition, means being out in front of your people when it is called for. It means standing up for the dignity of all your citizens and persuading your people to do the same."

And in an echo of my speech in Beijing and my words at the State Department a year earlier, I said, "Like being a woman, like being a racial, religious, tribal, or ethnic minority, being LGBT does not make you less human. And that is why gay rights are human rights, and human rights are gay rights."

I woke up the following morning to my first indication that the speech had broken through: the hairdresser who styled my hair that morning, who was gay, theatrically fell to his knees in gratitude. I laughed and told him to get up, for heaven's sake. My hair, as usual, couldn't wait.

The ripples created by the speech were bouncing around the globe and back, and my phone was soon crowded with messages. A huge number of people had watched the speech online. I was gratified, for many reasons. Though I had expected a few of the African delegates in the audience that day to walk out, they did not. And as I've seen from the many pictures and videos people have sent me from Pride events around the world, the words "gay rights are human rights" have been blazoned on countless posters, banners, and T-shirts. I was proud that America had once again stood up for human rights, just as we had on so many previous occasions.

Late in my term, I received a letter from a Foreign Service officer stationed in Latin America that has become a treasured possession: "I write you not as an employee of the Department of State writing to the Secretary, but as a husband and as a father writing to thank you, as an individual, for all you have done for our family over the past four years. I had long dreamt of being a Foreign Service Officer, but had never seriously considered it until you became our Secretary of State. The moment that you directed the Department to recognize same-sex spouses as family members, the one thing that had been holding me back was suddenly no longer standing in the way." He went on to describe the joy of having his husband of seven years be able to join him at his foreign post and that, as a result, they were able to welcome twins into the world as well. He even enclosed a photo of their happy family. "What was hardly imaginable three years ago . . . that we'd be diplomats for our country, that our relationship would be recognized by the government, that we'd be able to be fathers, has all come true."

=====

When I left the State Department in 2013 and began working at the Clinton Foundation in New York, I knew that I wanted to continue working on "the great unfinished business of the 21st century." The fast-approaching twentieth anniversary of the Fourth World Conference on Women in Beijing helped focus my thinking. I was proud of how much had been accomplished in that time. Yet there was no doubt that we were still a long way from the goal of "full and equal participation."

Melanne had started an academic center on women, peace, and security at Georgetown University, for which I agreed to serve as honorary founding chair. Now that we weren't flying around the globe every other day, we found ourselves talking and thinking more about the sweep of history and the future of the movement to which we had devoted so many years. I called Maggie Williams and asked her to come strategize with us. Along with Chelsea and our great team at the Clinton Foundation, including Jen Klein and Rachel Vogelstein, who both had played key roles at the State Department, we came up with a new plan.

At the annual meeting of the Clinton Global Initiative in New York in September 2013, I announced that the Clinton Foundation would mobilize a broad effort to evaluate the progress women and girls had made since Beijing and to chart the path forward to achieve full and equal participation for women and girls. I said it was time for a clear-eyed look at how far we'd come, how far we still had to go, and what we planned to do about this unfinished business.

With partners like the Gates Foundation, we began work on a digital "global review" of the status of women and girls in time for the twentieth anniversary of Beijing in September 2015. I wanted everyone to be able to see the gains we'd made, as well as the gaps that remained. We'd present easily accessible information that could be shared and put to use by advocates, academics, and political leaders to design reforms and drive real change.

I also wanted to build on the Platform for Action the world endorsed in Beijing and lay out a 21st-century agenda to accelerate full participation for women and girls around the world, including in areas that were still over the horizon in 1995. For example, none of us in Beijing could have imagined the ways in which the internet and mobile technology would transform our world or comprehended what it would mean to have 200 million fewer women than men online in the developing world. Closing that "digital divide" would open up vast new opportunities for economic and political participation.

Eventually we started calling our new initiative No Ceilings: The Full Participation Project. The name was a playful echo of the "18 million cracks in the glass ceiling" that became famous at the end of my Presidential campaign, but it meant much more than that. You didn't have to be at the highest levels of politics or business; women and girls everywhere still faced all sorts of ceilings that held back their ambitions and aspirations and made it harder, if not impossible, for them to pursue their dreams.

Not long after I announced No Ceilings, I heard a surprising story. Stephen Massey, a colleague from the Clinton White House, happened to be in Beijing and wandered into a bookstore. It was a large and modern shop, but quiet and nearly empty. Then Stephen could hardly believe his ears. Over the store's loudspeakers he heard a familiar phrase: "Human rights are women's rights and women's rights are human rights, once and for all." It was my voice. They were playing a recording of the speech throughout the store. What a difference twenty years makes! In 1995, the Chinese government had shut down the closed-circuit television feed carrying my remarks. Now those controversial words had become "background music" for shoppers, part of the fabric of everyday life. Stephen whipped out his smartphone, recorded a video, and emailed it home. When I saw it, I had to laugh. Was that really a good way to sell books? In China?

The message of Beijing and the lifetime of work it represented had become so much a part of my identity it was practically written into my DNA. I was glad that it had permeated into the culture, in places that had once been hostile. The cause of protecting and expanding human rights is as urgent and compelling as ever, and further progress is unlikely without continued American leadership.

———

In February 2014, the Human Rights Campaign (the other HRC!) invited my daughter, Chelsea, to speak at a conference on gay rights. In her remarks she offered a new twist on a familiar phrase. "My mother has often said that the issue of women is the unfinished business of the 21st century," she said. "That is certainly true. But so too are the issues of LGBTQ rights the unfinished business of the 21st century." Of course she's right, and I could not be more proud of her strong stand on behalf of equality and opportunity for all people.

Earlier I described the work of American foreign policy as a relay race. Leaders are handed the baton and asked to run our leg as ably as we can and put the next runner in the best possible position to succeed. Well, families are like that too. From the moment I first held Chelsea in my arms in the hospital in Little Rock, I knew my mission in life was to give her every opportunity to thrive. As she's grown up and stepped out into the world in her own right, my responsibilities have changed. And now that she's expecting a child of her own, I'm preparing for a new role that I've looked forward to for years: grandmother. And I've found myself thinking a lot about my relationship with my own mom, as an adult as well as in childhood, and what lessons I learned from her.

When I became Secretary of State, Mom was just about to turn ninety. She had been living with us in Washington for the past few years, ever since being alone in her apartment overlooking the zoo on Connecticut Avenue became too much. Like so many Americans of my generation, I felt both blessed to have these extra years with an aging parent and very responsible for making sure she was comfortable and well-cared for. Mom gave me so much unconditional love and support when I was growing up in Park Ridge; now it was my turn to support her. Of course I never would have let her hear me describe it that way. Dorothy Howell Rodham was a fiercely independent woman. She couldn't bear the thought of being a burden to anyone.

Having her so close became a source of great comfort to me, especially in the difficult period after the end of the 2008 campaign. I'd come home from a long day at the Senate or the State Department, slide in next to her at the small table in our breakfast nook, and let everything just pour out.

Mom loved mystery novels, Mexican food, *Dancing with the Stars* (we actually managed to get her to a taping of the show once), and most of all her grandchildren. My nephew Zach Rodham's school was just five minutes away, and he came over many afternoons to visit her. Spending time with Fiona and Simon Rodham, her youngest grandchildren, was a precious delight for her. For Chelsea, her grandmother was one of the most important figures in her life. Mom helped Chelsea navigate the unique challenges of growing up in the public eye and, when she was ready, encouraged her to pursue her passion for service and philanthropy. Even in her nineties, Mom never lost her commitment to social justice, which did so much to mold and inspire me when I was growing up. I loved that she was able to do the same for Chelsea. And I'm not sure if I ever saw Mom happier than at Chelsea's wedding. She proudly walked down the aisle on Zach's arm and exulted over her joyful, radiant granddaughter.

Mom's own childhood was marked by trauma and abandonment. In Chicago her parents fought frequently and divorced when she and her sister were young. Neither parent was willing to care for the kids, so they were put on a train to California to live with their paternal grandparents in Alhambra, a town near the San Gabriel Mountains east of Los Angeles. The elderly couple was severe and unloving. One Halloween, after Mom was caught trick-or-treating with school friends, a forbidden activity, she was confined to her room for an entire year, except for the hours she was in school. She wasn't allowed to eat at the kitchen table or play in the yard. By the time Mom turned fourteen, she could no longer bear life in her grandmother's house. She moved out and found work as a housekeeper and nanny for a kind-hearted woman in San Gabriel who offered room and board plus $3 a week and urged her to attend high school. For the first time she saw how loving parents care for their children—it was a revelation.

After graduating high school, Mom moved back to Chicago in the hopes of reconnecting with her own mother. Sadly she was spurned yet again. Heartbroken, she spent the next five years working as a secretary before she met and married my father, Hugh Rodham. She built a new life as a homemaker, spending her days lavishing love on me and my two younger brothers.

When I got old enough to understand all this, I asked my mother how she survived abuse and abandonment without becoming embittered and emotionally stunted. How did she emerge from this lonely early life as such a loving and levelheaded woman? I'll never forget how she replied. "At critical points in my life somebody showed me kindness," she said. Sometimes it would seem so small, but it would mean so much—the teacher in elementary school who noticed that she never had money to buy milk, so every day would buy two cartons of milk and then say, "Dorothy, I can't drink this other carton of milk. Would you like it?" Or the woman who hired her as a nanny and insisted that she go to high school. One day she noticed that Mom had only one blouse that she washed every day. "Dorothy, I can't fit into this blouse anymore and I'd hate to throw it away. Would you like it?" she said.

Mom was amazingly energetic and positive even into her nineties. But her health started to fail her; she had trouble with her heart. By the fall of 2011, I was growing worried about leaving her alone. On the evening of October 31, another Halloween, I was preparing to leave for London and Turkey. My team was already on board the airplane at Andrews waiting for me to arrive so we could take off. That's when I got the call that Mom had been rushed to George Washington University Hospital. I quickly canceled the trip and sped there. Bill, Chelsea, and Marc rushed down from New York, and my brothers and their wives, Hugh and Maria and Tony and Megan, arrived as quickly as they could. Mom was a fighter her entire life, but it was finally time to let go. I sat by her bedside and held her hand one last time. No one had a bigger influence on my life or did more to shape the person I became.

When I lost my father in 1993, it felt too soon, and I was consumed with sadness for all the things he would not live to see and do. This was different. Mom lived a long and full life. This time I wept not for what she would miss but for how much I would miss her.

I spent the next few days going through her things at home, paging through a book, staring at an old photograph, caressing a piece of beloved jewelry. I found myself sitting next to her empty chair in the breakfast nook and wishing more than anything that I could have one more conversation, one more hug.

We held a small memorial service at the house with close family and friends. We asked Reverend Bill Shillady, who married Chelsea and Marc, to officiate. Chelsea spoke movingly, as did many of Mom's friends and our family. I read a few lines from the poet Mary Oliver, whose work Mom and I both adored.

Standing there with Bill and Chelsea by my side, I tried to say a final good-bye. I remembered a piece of wisdom that an older friend of mine shared in her later years that perfectly captured how my mother lived her life and how I hoped to live mine: "I have loved and been loved; all the rest is background music."

I looked at Chelsea and thought about how proud Mom was of her. Mom measured her own life by how much she was able to help us and serve others. I knew if she was still with us, she would be urging us to do the same. Never rest on your laurels. Never quit. Never stop working to make the world a better place. That's our unfinished business.

EPILOGUE

"Where did Hillary go?" the President asked, looking around. He was in the middle of a short speech about democracy in Burma, standing on the porch of Aung San Suu Kyi's house in Rangoon. "Where is she?"

It was November 2012, and we were on our final trip together as President and Secretary of State. I waved from off to the side and caught his eye. "There she is," he said. As he thanked me, I thought about how far we had come from that day more than four years earlier in Dianne Feinstein's living room. Like our entire last trip together, it was a moment of bittersweet nostalgia, of satisfaction in what we had accomplished, delight in the partners we had become, and sadness that it would soon be over.

Just two weeks earlier the President had won reelection. Unlike in 2008, this time I hadn't been able to campaign for him. By law and tradition, Secretaries of State stay out of domestic politics. The Democratic National Convention in Charlotte, North Carolina, was the first I had missed since 1976. In 2008, the convention in Denver had offered me a chance to endorse President Obama and help unify Democrats after the long primary campaign. But during the 2012 convention I was half a world away, representing our country on a diplomatic mission to Asia.

On the night my husband addressed the convention and formally nominated the President, I was in Timor-Leste, Asia's newest country, which had won its long struggle for independence from Indonesia in 2002.

After a day of diplomacy in the capital of Dili, just before flying to Brunei for a meeting and dinner with Sultan Hassanal Bolkiah, I stole away for a few private moments in the residence of our Ambassador. There was no CNN and only limited internet bandwidth, but Philippe Reines had managed to connect to his TiVo back in Washington, so we could watch a delayed recording of Bill's just-completed speech on the Ambassador's home computer. I sat down to watch while the rest of my team crowded behind me.

I had to smile when I saw him take the stage in front of the enthusiastic crowd. It had been sixteen years since Bill's last campaign, but he still loved the excitement of a great political moment. Like a country lawyer laying out the facts for a jury, he explained how deeply damaged our economy and global standing had been in 2009 and how the Obama Administration had begun turning things around. At the end of his speech he addressed the question of American decline and renewal. "For more than two hundred years, through every crisis, we've always come back," he said. "People have predicted our demise ever since George Washington was criticized for being a mediocre surveyor with a bad set of wooden false teeth. And so far, every single person that's bet against America has lost money because we always come back. We come through every fire a little stronger and a little better." After Bill finished, President Obama unexpectedly appeared onstage to thank him. As the two Presidents embraced, the crowd went wild. Watching from some ten thousand miles away, I was full of pride for the former President I married, the current President I served, and the country we all loved.

═══

After wrapping up our day in Burma, President Obama and I boarded Air Force One for the flight to Cambodia, where we would attend the East Asia Summit and ASEAN Leaders Meeting. It would be another crucial test for our pivot strategy. At the same time, the conflict in Gaza between Israel and Hamas was boiling over, and we had to decide whether I would break off from the trip to fly there to try to broker a cease-fire. With so much to talk about, the President asked me to join him in his office at the front of Air Force One.

I sat in front of his large wooden desk as we discussed the delicate diplomacy ahead. Despite all that was going on, we started reminiscing. These four years had changed us in ways neither of us could have predicted. We had seen and done things together that helped us better understand ourselves, each other, and the world as we never could have before.

But even with all of our time together I didn't see coming what happened next. "Would you consider staying on as Secretary of State?" the President asked.

Ever since I had accepted the job, I had told myself, "One term, that's it," and had often said so publicly as well. As much as I loved being Secretary of State, I was looking forward to leaving public life and spending more time with my family, reconnecting with friends, and doing the everyday things I missed. It would be nice to stay in one time zone, without having to add or subtract five, ten, fourteen hours wherever I happened to wake up.

But just like four years before, I felt the tug of my "service gene," that voice telling me there is no higher calling or more noble purpose than serving your country. When the President of the United States asks you to step up to the plate, how can you say no? And there was so much unfinished business. The summit in Cambodia and the conflict in Gaza were just two examples. What would happen to democracy in Burma? Or our secret negotiations with Iran? How would we counter the growing challenge from Putin in Russia?

But diplomacy is a relay race, and I was nearing the end of my leg. "I'm sorry, Mr. President," I said. "But I can't."

═══

A few months later we said our good-byes. I had lunch with President Obama in his private dining room off the Oval Office. Over fish tacos we discussed a twenty-page memo I had prepared with recommendations for his second term, both building on what we had started and new initiatives. On the way out we paused in the Oval Office. Tearing up, I hugged the President and told him again how much our work and friendship meant to me. And that I'd be on call if he ever needed me.

On February 1, 2013, my final day in Foggy Bottom, I sat down at the desk in the small cherry-paneled inner office for the last time and wrote John Kerry a letter. I left it in the same place I had found Condi's note to me four years before that. Then I signed my letter of resignation to the President. For the first time in twenty years, after serving as First Lady, Senator, and Secretary of State, I no longer had any role in government.

My final act was to go down to the lobby—where I had been greeted on my first day back in 2009—to say good-bye to the men and women of the State Department and USAID. Thanking them seemed inadequate for all their dedicated service, but I did my best. Once again I saw the marble walls with the etched names of the colleagues we had lost, those who had fallen serving our country. I said a quiet prayer for them and their families. Filling the large lobby were so many people I had come to love and respect. I was glad they would continue serving the United States with intelligence, persistence, and courage.

In the coming years, Americans will have to decide whether we are prepared to learn from and call on the lessons of our history and rise once more to defend our values and interests. This is not a summons to confrontation or to a new Cold War—we've learned painfully that force should be our last resort, never our first. Instead, it's an appeal to stand firmly and united in pursuit of a more just, free, and peaceful world. Only Americans can decide this.

In the end, our strength abroad depends on our resolve and resilience at home. Citizens and leaders alike have choices to make about the country we want to live in and leave to the next generation. Middle-class incomes have been declining for more than a decade, and poverty has increased as almost all the benefits of growth have gone to those at the very top. We need more good jobs that reward hard work with rising wages, dignity, and a ladder to a better life. Investments to build a truly 21st-century economy with more opportunity and less inequality. An end to the political dysfunction in Washington that holds back our progress and demeans our democracy. That means more of our neighbors and fellow citizens must be empowered to participate fully in both our economy and our democracy. That is the only way to restore the American Dream and ensure our long-term prosperity and continued global leadership.

It won't be easy to do that in our current political atmosphere. But to quote from one of my favorite movies, *A League of Their Own*: "It's supposed to be hard. . . . The hard is what makes it great." Doing what's hard will continue to make our country great.

I wrote this book over the course of 2013 and early 2014, mostly from a cozy, sun-drenched third-floor study in our home in Chappaqua, New York. There's a thick carpet and a comfortable chair, and I can look out through the windows into the treetops. I finally had time to read, catch up on sleep, go on long walks with my husband and our dogs, see more of my family, and think about the future.

In early 2014, Bill and I got some wonderful news that we'd been eagerly waiting to hear: we were going to be grandparents. We were both beyond happy for Chelsea and Marc and unabashedly giddy at the prospect. When Chelsea was born, I was full of nerves—despite all the books I had read and my work at Yale's Child Study Center, I was unprepared for the sheer miracle and responsibility of parenthood. I prayed that I would be a good enough mother and I quickly came to feel that having a child is like letting "your heart go walking around outside your body," as the writer Elizabeth Stone put it. It was wonderful and terrifying all at the same time. All these years later, as I look forward to a grandchild, there is nothing but excitement and anticipation. And I recall what Margaret Mead said, that children keep our imaginations fresh and our hearts young, and drive us to work for a better future.

Now, more than ever, the future is very much on my mind. Over the past year, as I've traveled around our country once again, the one question I'm asked more than any other is: Will I run for President in 2016?

The answer is, I haven't decided yet.

But whenever someone brings it up, I'm honored by the energy and enthusiasm of those encouraging me to run, and even more by their belief that I can provide the leadership our country needs.

Right now I believe we should be focused on the work to be done in our country that can't wait until 2016. Many of our fellow Americans who were hit hard by the Great Recession haven't recovered. Too many young people are burdened with bigger student debt and smaller job prospects. There's also an important election in 2014 that will decide control of Congress and have real consequences for our economy and our future. It's not one we can afford to look past or sit out.

Recently, Bill and I took another of our long walks, this time with our three dogs, near our home. It had been an unseasonably long winter, but spring was finally peeking through the thaw. We walked and talked, continuing a conversation that began more than forty years ago at Yale Law School and hasn't stopped yet.

We both know I have a big decision in front of me.

Having run for President before, I understand exactly how challenging it is on every front—not only on candidates but on their families as well. And having lost in 2008, I know that nothing is guaranteed, nothing can be taken for granted. I also know that the most important questions anyone considering running must answer are not "Do you want to be President?" or "Can you win?" They are "What's your vision for America?" and "Can you lead us there?" The challenge is to lead in a way that unites us again and renews the American Dream. That's the bar, and it's a high one.

Ultimately, what happens in 2016 should be about what kind of future Americans want for themselves and their children—and grandchildren. I hope we choose inclusive politics and a common purpose to unleash the creativity, potential, and opportunity that makes America exceptional. That's what all Americans deserve.

Whatever I decide, I will always be thankful for the chance to represent America around the world. I have learned anew the goodness of our people and the greatness of our nation. I feel blessed and grateful. Our future is so full of possibility. And for me and my family that includes looking forward to a new addition—another American who deserves the best possible future we can offer.

But for this day, at least, I just wanted to stretch my legs and enjoy the spring. Everywhere around me there was new life. There have been too few quiet moments like this over the years. And I want to savor them. The time for another hard choice will come soon enough.

ACKNOWLEDGMENTS

The motto of the Clinton Foundation is "We're all in this together." It's a simple statement of unity in a world full of division. As I've discovered, it's also an apt description of what it takes to write a book. I'm indebted to everyone who helped me through four years at the State Department and more than a year of writing and editing. And the easiest choice I made was to ask Dan Schwerin, Ethan Gelber, and Ted Widmer to become my book team. I could not have been more fortunate as we labored day and night.

Dan Schwerin started with me in the Senate and came to State as one of my speechwriters. He's been my essential partner, toiling with me over phrases and pages, capturing my thoughts and helping me wrestle them into coherence. He's not only a talented writer, but also a wonderful colleague. Ethan Gelber is the "indispensable man" who managed a sprawling writing and editing process, making sense of my scribbles, clarifying my memories, and keeping me sane as the drafts piled up. I never could have done it without him. Ted Widmer, an accomplished historian and valued collaborator, offered context and perspective and a much-needed dose of humor and humanity.

Huma Abedin, Cheryl Mills, Philippe Reines, and Jake Sullivan, who gave so much to me and to our country during our years at the State Department, were essential advisors, inspirers, and willing fact-checkers throughout the process. I also relied on the assistance and counsel of

Kurt Campbell, Lissa Muscatine, and Megan Rooney, who generously read drafts and offered advice.

Thanks to Simon & Schuster, especially Chief Executive Officer Carolyn Reidy and my publisher and editor, Jonathan Karp. I've now done five books with Carolyn, and it was once again a delight. Jonathan, who provided the right combination of encouragement and criticism, has a well-deserved reputation as a caring and constructive editor. I also appreciate the entire team: Irene Kheradi, Jonathan Evans, Lisa Erwin, Pat Glynn, Gina DiMascia, Ffej Caplan, Inge Maas, Judith Hoover, Philip Bashe, Joy O'Meara, Jackie Seow, Laura Wyss, Nicholas Greene, Michael Selleck, Liz Perl, Gary Urda, Colin Shields, Paula Amendolara, Seth Russo, Lance Fitzgerald, Marie Florio, Christopher Lynch, David Hillman, Ellie Hirschhorn, Adrian Norman, Sue Fleming, Adam Rothberg, Jeff Wilson, Elina Vaysbeyn, Cary Goldstein, Julia Prosser, and Richard Rhorer.

Once again, I'm grateful to the incomparable Bob Barnett, my attorney and guide through the publishing world, who was ably assisted by contract attorney Michael O'Connor.

One of the best parts of writing this book was the chance to reconnect and reminisce with friends and colleagues. My thanks to everyone who shared memories, notes, and perspectives, including Caroline Adler, Dan Baer, Kris Balderston, De'Ara Balenger, Jeremy Bash, Dan Benaim, Dan Benjamin, Jarrett Blanc, Johnnie Carson, Sarah Davey, Alex Djerassi, Bob Einhorn, Dan Feldman, Jeff Feltman, David Hale, Amos Hochstein, Fred Hof, Sarah Hurwitz, Jim Kennedy, Caitlin Klevorick, Ben Kobren, Harold Koh, Dan Kurtz-Phelan, Capricia Marshall, Mike McFaul, Judith McHale, George Mitchell, Dick Morningstar, Carlos Pascual, Nirav Patel, John Podesta, Mike Posner, Ben Rhodes, Alec Ross, Dennis Ross, Frank Ruggiero, Heather Samuelson, Tom Shannon, Andrew Shapiro, Anne-Marie Slaughter, Todd Stern, Puneet Talwar, Tomicah Tilleman, Melanne Verveer, Matthew Walsh, and Ashley Woolheater. Also to Clarence Finney and his industrious archivists, and John Hackett, Chuck Daris, Alden Fahy, Behar Godani, Paul Hilburn, Chaniqua Nelson, and the careful reviewers at the State Department and the National Security Council.

I was fortunate to serve alongside a committed senior team: Deputy Secretaries of State Bill Burns, Jack Lew, Tom Nides, and Jim Steinberg, Ambassador to the UN Susan Rice, USAID Administrator Raj Shah,

Global AIDS Coordinator Eric Goosby, MCC CEO Daniel Yohannes, and OPIC President and CEO Elizabeth Littlefield.

I will always have a special place in my heart for the entire "S Family," pictured in photo 10, the dedicated Foreign Service officers and civil servants who take such great care of Secretaries, including Nima Abbaszadeh, Daniella Ballou-Aares, Courtney Beale, Christopher Bishop, Claire Coleman, Jen Davis, Linda Dewan, Sheila Dyson, Dan Fogarty, Lauren Jiloty, Brock Johnson, Neal Larkins, Joanne Laszczych, Laura Lucas, Joe Macmanus, Lori McLean, Bernadette Meehan, Lawrence Randolph, Maria Sand, Jeannemarie Smith, Zia Syed, Nora Toiv, and Alice Wells, as well as the Executive Secretariat and the incredible Line team.

Thanks to the senior leadership of the State Department, USAID, PEPFAR, and MCC, including Dave Adams, Tom Adams, Elizabeth Bagley, Joyce Barr, Rick Barton, John Bass, Bob Blake, Eric Boswell, Esther Brimmer, Bill Brownfield, Susan Burk, Piper Campbell, Philip Carter, Maura Connelly, Michael Corbin, Tom Countryman, Heidi Crebo-Rediker, PJ Crowley, Lou CdeBaca, Ivo Daalder, Josh Daniel, Glyn Davies, Eileen Donahoe-Chamberlain, Jose Fernandez, Alonzo Fulgham, Phil Goldberg, David Goldwyn, Phil Gordon, Rose Gottemoeller, Marc Grossman, Michael Hammer, Lorraine Hariton, Judy Heumann, Christopher Hill, Bob Hormats, Rashad Hussain, Janice Jacobs, Roberta Jacobson, Bonnie Jenkins, Suzan Johnson Cook, Kerri-Ann Jones, Beth Jones, Paul Jones, Declan Kelly, Ian Kelly, Laura Kennedy, Pat Kennedy, Robert King, Reta Jo Lewis, Carmen Lomellin, Princeton Lyman, Dawn McCall, Ken Merten, Steve Mull, Toria Nuland, Maria Otero, Farah Pandith, Nancy Powell, Lois Quam, Stephen Rapp, Julissa Reynoso, Anne Richard, John Robinson, Miguel Rodriguez, Hannah Rosenthal, Eric Schwartz, Barbara Shailor, Wendy Sherman, Dan Smith, Tara Sonenshine, Don Steinberg, Karen Stewart, Ann Stock, Ellen Tauscher, Linda Thomas-Greenfield, Arturo Valenzuela, Rich Verma, Phil Verveer, Jake Walles, Pamela White, and Paul Wohlers.

I want especially to single out the brave and dedicated Diplomatic Security officers who kept me and our people safe around the world. During my tenure, my DS teams were led by Fred Ketchum and Kurt Olsson.

Throughout this journey, a committed band of tireless aides and advisors has supported the book and all the rest of my work while I raced to finish. Thanks to Monique Aiken, Brynne Craig, Katie Dowd, Oscar Flores, Monica Hanley, Jen Klein, Madhuri Kommareddi, Yerka Jo, Marisa McAuliffe, Terri McCullough, Nick Merrill, Patti Miller, Thomas Moran, Ann O'Leary, Maura Pally, Shilpa Pesaru, Robert Russo, Marina Santos, Lona Valmoro, and Rachel Vogelstein.

Thanks again to President Obama for putting his trust in me and giving me the chance to represent our country, and to Vice President Biden and the National Security Council staff for their partnership.

Finally, thanks, as always, to Bill and Chelsea for a year's worth of patient listening and careful reading of draft after draft, helping me distill and explain four jam-packed years. Once again, they gave me the invaluable gifts of their support and love.

INDEX

Abbas, Mahmoud (Abu Mazen):
  as Arafat's successor, 309, 472
  and cease-fire, 482–83
  Chris Stevens remembered by, 406
  and Gaza, 472, 474, 482–83
  and Goldstone Report, 318
  and Palestinian statehood, 311, 326,
    328, 482–83
  and peace process, 301–2, 309–11, 312,
    313, 316, 318–19, 322, 323–28
  and settlement construction, 316, 318,
    319, 328
  and West Bank, 309–11, 322
Abbaszadeh, Nima, 599
Abdelfattah, Ragaei Said, 384
Abdullah, Abdullah, 143, 144
Abdullah, King of Saudi Arabia, 314,
  315, 334, 353–54, 453
Abdullah II, King of Jordan, 323, 333,
  350–51
Abe, Shinzo, 571
Abedin, Huma, 2, 11, 15, 49, 348–49, 354,
  355, 597
Abedin, Saleha, 354
Aboul Gheit, Ahmed, 341–42, 344
Acheson, Dean, 20–21, 31–32

Acheson, Eldie, 20
Action Group on Syria, 457–59
Adams, Dave, 599
Adams, Gerry, 224
Adams, Henry, 13
Adams, Tom, 599
Adler, Caroline, 598
Afghan High Peace Council, 168
Afghanistan:
  and al Qaeda, 146, 148, 153, 175, 188,
    461
  Bush Administration focus on, 43, 132,
    137, 142
  Coalition forces in, 159, 199, 374
  COIN in, 138
  Constitution of, 151, 152, 153, 158,
    167
  corruption in, 145, 149
  economic development in, 149, 155–56,
    167
  ending war in, 150–51, 162, 164–67
  geography of, 130
  international conferences on, 153, 166
  international contact group in, 140
  and Iran, 140, 419, 422
  nation-building in, 138

Afghanistan (*cont.*)
NATO forces in, 133, 140, 159, 198, 213, 422
Northern Alliance in, 131, 154
Northern Distribution Network, 237–39
Pakistani border with, 131–32, 146, 155–56, 171, 198, 199, 233, 237
Soviet withdrawal from (1989), 21, 131, 147, 178, 186, 233, 461, 537
Special Operations in, 193
supply lines to, 231, 233, 237–39, 243
Taliban in, 130–32, 133, 138, 141, 143, 145, 148, 152, 153–55, 163–64, 175, 537
terrorism in, 188–89, 418
trade with Pakistan, 155–58
training local soldiers in, 462, 463
transition in, 45, 145, 147, 159, 166, 167
troops coming home from, 148–49, 199, 237
troop surges in, 129–30, 131–35, 138, 140, 147, 153, 159
USAID in, 141
U.S.–led invasion of, 131, 175
U.S. security interests in, 137
war in, 25, 73, 129, 142, 145, 147, 150–51, 156, 162, 164–67, 364
women's rights sought in, 152–53, 158, 562, 569
Afghan National Security Forces, 132, 146, 166
AFL-CIO, 517
Af-Pak, 132; *see also* Afghanistan; Pakistan
Africa, 269–99
agriculture in, 278–79
and China, 270–72, 276, 288
conflict and chaos in, 279
corruption in, 272, 276, 277, 281
and democracy, 272, 273, 277
economic growth in, 269–70
HIV/AIDS in, 291–93, 295, 537
natural resources in, 270–71
and resource curse, 277, 522

U.S. relationship with, 269–72, 277–78
wildlife trafficking in, 467, 468, 469
women's work in, 568
see also specific nations
African Growth and Opportunity Act (AGOA), 276
African Union, 200, 271, 272, 296
and Somalia, 287, 288, 289
and South Sudan, 283
surveillance drones of, 289
Agha-Soltan, Neda, 548
Ahmadinejad, Mahmoud, 419, 421, 422, 424, 428, 431, 441, 442, 580
Aiken, Monique, 600
Air Force One, 39, 592
Ai Weiwei, 63
Akihito, Emperor of Japan, 47
Alaska:
and global warming, 502, 503, 506
purchase of, 14
Albright, Madeleine, 31, 55, 63, 68, 104, 419, 560, 567
Algeria, jobs in, 507–8, 516
Ali, Nujood, 336
Aliyev, Ilham, 240
Al Jazeera, 318, 452, 475
Alliance of Small Island States, 497
Al-Nahyan, Crown Prince Mohammed bin Zayed, 335
Al-Nahyan, Sheikh Abdullah bin Zayed (AbZ), 357, 358–59, 368, 373, 376
al Qaeda, 340, 351, 386
and Afghanistan, 146, 148, 153, 175, 188, 461
counterterrorism against, 188–90
drone strikes against, 183–84
and Islamist extremists, 473
kidnapping for ransom, 200
in Pakistan, 138, 148, 164, 171, 183, 186–87
and propaganda, 201
and September 11 attacks, 132, 148, 163, 171, 172–74, 175, 183, 197
and "Sunni Awakening," 136
and Syria, 450, 469

and Taliban, 131, 151, 158, 163, 164
U.S. embassies bombed (1998) by, 131,
   171, 383, 406
U.S. intelligence about, 199
Al Shabaab, 175, 199, 278, 286–89, 290,
   467
al-Zawahiri, Ayman, 200
Amado, Luís, 372
Amendolara, Paula, 598
American Airlines, 516
American Israel Public Affairs
   Committee, 320
Americans with Disabilities Act, 560
Amorim, Celso, 261, 431
Amr, Mohamed, 477–78, 484, 486
Angola, oil from, 276, 440
Annan, Kofi, 447, 452, 454–59, 470
Ansar al-Sharia, 395, 404
APEC (Asia-Pacific Economic
   Cooperation), 44, 112, 243
Aquino, Benigno III, 60
Arab Human Development Report,
   332
Arab-Israeli War (1948), 325
Arab League, 314
   and Libya, 213, 357, 367–68, 370, 371,
      376
   and Syria, 449–50, 452, 454
Arab Peace Initiative (2002), 314, 315
Arab Spring, 49, 121, 200, 227, 272,
   331–62, 472, 475
   and Persian Gulf nations, 351–60
   protests in Egypt, 338, 339–46, 347–49,
      355, 364, 386
   protests in Tunisia, 334, 337, 338, 355,
      360, 364
   and transitions to democracy, 360–62
   U.S. policy debates in, 339, 360
Arafat, Yasser, 303, 304, 309, 311, 312,
   324, 338, 472, 482
Arctic Circle:
   melting glaciers, 497, 501–3
   protection of, 503
   and Russia, 239, 503
Arctic Council, 502–3

Arias, Óscar, 266–67
Aris, Michael, 103
Armenia:
   and Azerbaijan, 219, 240
   independence of, 219
   and Turkey, 218–20
ASEAN (Association of Southeast Asian
   Nations), 44, 46, 52, 76, 78, 121
   U.S.–ASEAN Leaders Meeting,
      113
ASEAN Treaty of Amity and
   Cooperation, 113
Ashton, Cathy, 222–23, 241, 483
Asia-Pacific region:
   China's roles in, 67, 73–74
   and democracy, 60, 62, 63–64, 99
   India's role in, 59–60
   nationalism in, 111–12
   pivot in, 39, 45–64, 79, 99, 112, 121
   as priority, 29, 43, 45–46
   territorial disputes in, 74–76, 78–79
   and TPP, 77–78, 254
   trade in, 74, 515
   tsunami (2004), 533, 535
   U.S. leadership role in, 43–44, 46, 52,
      60, 61, 67, 73, 79
   see also specific nations
Asia Society, New York, 46–47, 70,
   163–64, 166
Aso, Taro, 48
Assad, Bashar al-, 470, 472, 546
   and Arab League, 449–50
   and chemical weapons, 465–66, 469
   Iranian support for, 442, 453, 460
   Russian support for, 236, 243, 449,
      450–51, 455, 459–61
   street protests against, 447–48,
      450–52
   and transition, 453, 454, 455, 456,
      458–59, 461–62, 463
Assad, Hafez al-, 449, 453
Assange, Julian, 552
Astor, Jacob and Ava, 81
Atatürk, Mustafa Kemal, 214, 215
Aung San, 102–3, 104, 105, 109, 119

Australia:
  and China, 43
  U.S. alliance with, 44
Azerbaijan, 219, 240

Bachelet, Michelle, 261, 262
Bader, Jeff, 45
Baer, Dan, 549, 579, 580, 582, 598
Bagley, Elizabeth, 599
Bahrain, 351, 352, 373, 434, 442
  and Arab Spring, 355–60
  and Qatar, 476
Baker, James A. III, 31, 315
Balderston, Kris, 524, 598
Balenger, De'Ara, 598
Balkans, 220–23, 240, 369, 374
Ballou-Aares, Daniella, 599
Banda, Joyce, 279
Bangladesh:
  and climate change, 501
  technology in, 546
  worker rights in, 519–20
Ban Ki-moon, 457, 458, 464, 540
Barak, Ehud, 81, 304, 318, 321, 327, 472,
  476
Barnett, Bob, 598
Barnich, Terry, 384
Barr, Joyce, 599
Barroso, José Manuel, 500
Bartholomew, Patriarch, 217
Barton, Rick, 599
Bash, Jeremy, 598
Bashe, Philip, 598
Bashir, Omar al-, 271
Bass, John, 599
Bauer, Shane, 435, 436
Bayh, Evan, 134
BBC World Service, 108
Beale, Courtney, 599
Beauvoir, Max, 528–29
Bedouin tribes, in Sinai, 473
Begin, Menachem, 323
Bellerive, Jean-Max, 536
Ben Ali, Zine el Abidine, 334, 338, 346,
  361, 368, 555

Benghazi, see Libya
Benaim, Dan, 598
Benjamin, Dan, 189, 190, 598
Bergdahl, Bowe, 158
Berlin Wall, fall of, 206
Berlusconi, Silvio, 373–74, 554
Bhutto, Benazir, 176–78, 184
  assassination of, 178, 197
  Daughter of Destiny, 177
Bhutto, Zulfikar Ali, 177
Biden, Joe, 55, 192, 196, 444, 600
  and Afghanistan, 129, 130, 138, 146
  and campaigns, 9, 11, 17
  and Middle East, 319–20, 340, 341,
    405, 433
  and Russia, 231–32, 234
  and Vice Presidency, 10, 22–23
Bildt, Carl, 552
bin Abdulaziz al-Saud, Prince Saud al-
  Faisal, 352, 353, 358, 452, 453
bin Laden, Osama:
  CIA's location of, 191–92, 195
  death of, 164, 165, 196–97, 199
  and drone strikes, 183
  SEAL operation against, 170–71,
    193–97
  search for, 131, 171, 174, 187, 191, 195
  and September 11 attacks, 171, 174,
    351
  and terrorism, 131, 154, 461
Bishop, Christopher, 599
Blair, Tony, 30, 207, 208, 323, 329, 483
Blake, Bob, 599
Blake, Stephen, 106, 108
Blanc, Jarrett, 598
Boehner, John, 94
Boeing Aviation, 516
Bolkiah, Sultan Hassanal, 592
Bombardier, 516
Bono, 297, 537
Borisov, Boyko, 212–13
Bosnia, 138, 150, 164, 213, 220–21
Boswell, Eric, 599
Botswana, 277
Bouazizi, Mohamed, 334

Bouteflika, Abdelaziz, 508
Boxer, Barbara, 279
Bo Xilai, 85, 86
Brahimi, Lakhdar, 464, 469
Brazil:
    biofuels in, 255
    and climate change, 495, 498, 499
    economic growth in, 255, 259–61, 430, 495
    financial crisis in, 247
    and Iran, 427–33
    middle class in, 526
    and UN, 427–28, 430
Brennan, John, 251, 469
Brimmer, Esther, 599
Britain, see United Kingdom
Brothers to the Rescue, 258
Brown, Gordon, 207–8, 223, 425, 498, 500
Brownfield, Bill, 599
Bryson, John, 512
Bulgaria, 212–13, 442
Burk, Susan, 599
Burma, 101–26
    and China, 105, 110–12, 116
    and democracy, 60–61, 80, 102, 104, 112, 114, 117, 122, 125–26
    foreign investment in, 124
    geography of, 103
    government reforms in, 112, 114, 116, 118, 120, 121, 123–24
    Hillary Clinton's travel to, 114–21, 591, 592
    independence of, 104, 120
    and India, 116
    Irrawaddy River in, 110–12
    Myitsone Dam project in, 110–12
    nationalism in, 111
    and North Korea, 104, 107, 120
    President Obama's visit to, 124–25
    progress in, 79–80, 121–22, 123–24, 126
    religious discrimination in, 575
    sanctions against, 105, 109, 112
    U.S. relationship with, 108, 109–10, 121–22
    in World War II, 103–4

Burns, Bill, 598
    and Asia-Pacific, 29, 87, 90
    and Benghazi, 388, 405
    and Gaza cease-fire, 477
    and Iran, 425, 426, 436, 442, 444
    and Russia, 231
Bush, Barbara, 3, 10
Bush, George H. W., 3, 286, 315, 535
Bush, George W., 184, 228, 297
    and Afghanistan, 43, 132, 137, 142
    and compassionate conservatism, 537
    and Haiti, 540
    and PEPFAR, 291–93, 537
    and September 11 attacks, 173
Bush, Laura, 152, 297
Bush Administration (W.), 24, 41, 131–32, 139, 433, 573
    and development programs, 537
    and Europe, 205, 215
    Iraq as focus of, 43, 131, 134–35, 148, 205, 207, 419, 424, 425
    and Israel, 309, 315
    and Latin America, 247–48, 250, 253, 254
    and "Pathways to Prosperity," 254
    and Russia, 236, 237
    and terrorism, 131, 174–75, 178, 419
    and trade, 510–11, 515
Bush Doctrine, 25
Byrd, Robert, 173

Cairo (dog), 193
Calderón, Felipe, 247, 249–50, 252
Cambodia:
    Hillary Clinton's visit to, 61
    human trafficking in, 517–18
    restrictions in, 61
    working conditions in, 517
Cameron, David, 208, 373, 466
Cameroon, 577
Campbell, Kurt, 43, 78, 598
    and Burma, 108, 109, 114, 118, 123, 124–25
    and Chen, 86, 87–88, 89, 90, 92, 93, 94–97, 99, 100

Campbell, Piper, 599
Camp David Accords, 338
Canada:
  and Arctic Council, 502, 503
  and climate change, 501, 502
  and electricity, 256
  First Nations in, 502, 506
  and NATO, 211
  and Pacific Alliance, 254
  trade with, 246, 510
Caplan, Ffej, 598
Cardoso, Fernando Henrique, 255, 260,
  261
Carson, Johnnie, 273, 279–80, 287, 288,
  598
Carter, Ashton, 411
Carter, Jimmy, 5, 55
Carter, Philip, 599
Carter, Rosalynn, 10
Caspian Sea, natural gas in, 240–41
Castro, Fidel, 257, 258, 262, 264, 265
Castro, Raul, 258, 262, 264, 265
CdeBaca, Lou, 518, 599
Center for Strategic Counterterrorism
  Communications, 189, 200
Centers for Disease Control (CDC), 541
Central African Republic, coup in, 272
Chavez, Hugo, 257, 258–59, 263–64
Chechnya, 229
Chemical Weapons Convention (1993),
  466
Chen Guangcheng, 79, 83–100, 480
Chiang Kai-shek, 96
Children's Defense Fund, 3, 559–60, 563
Chile:
  and Cuba, 261–62
  democracy in, 261
  earthquake in, 544
  economic growth in, 255
  and electricity, 256
  and Pacific Alliance, 254
China, 65–82
  and Africa, 270–72, 276, 288
  and AIDS, 69
  antidemocratic movement in, 63

antipollution protests in, 111
and Arctic research, 503
assertiveness of, 73–74, 78–80
and Burma, 105, 110–12, 116
censorship in, 64, 66, 100
and Chen, 79, 83–100, 480
and climate change, 491–92, 494–95,
  496, 498, 499, 500, 504–5
demographic crisis in, 550
economic growth of, 495, 508, 513, 521
and energy, 494, 504–5, 521
foreign policy of, 73, 432
Hillary Clinton's travel to, 66–73, 432
investments in developing nations,
  537–38
investments in U.S., 514
and Iran, 424–25, 427–29, 431, 433,
  440
labor issues in, 519
and Laos, 61
and Libya, 370
middle class in, 526
and Mongolia, 61, 62–63, 64
National Museum, 96
Nixon in, 65, 68, 69, 93, 121, 313
and North Korea, 54, 55, 56, 58
and pollution, 504–5
postal laws of, 511–12
religious discrimination in, 575
rise of, 42, 47, 52, 60, 64, 67, 70, 73, 94,
  100
and Russia, 243, 245
and South China Sea, 74–76, 78–79,
  113–14
sovereignty of, 88
state capitalism in, 510, 512–13
Strategic and Economic Dialogue
  with, 72–73, 75–76, 84–85, 89, 92,
  93–94, 97, 99
and Syria, 449, 452, 454
and technology, 548, 556, 557
and Tibet, 68
trade with, 42–44, 510, 511–12, 513,
  515
USA Pavilion in, 71

U.S. relationship with, 46, 47, 65–66, 68, 72–73, 80, 88, 92, 95, 97–100, 432, 554

U.S. students in, 97

and women's rights, 66, 68–69, 104

Christopher, Warren M., 23, 31, 41

Churchill, Winston, 228

CIA:

and Benghazi attacks, 382, 389–92, 395–98, 404, 409, 413

and bin Laden, 191–92, 195

and counterterrorism, 184, 187–90

officers' deaths in line of duty, 187–88

civil rights, 558–59, 565

Clapper, James, 196, 411, 469

Clark, Wesley, 367

Climate Action Plan, 505

Climate and Clean Air Coalition, 500–501

climate change, 491–506

cap-and-trade, 493–94

and consumption levels, 526

Copenhagen conference on (2009), 491–92, 494, 496–500, 504, 506

denying, 504

and emerging powers, 495, 496, 498

and energy generation, 504–5

and greenhouse gas emissions, 521

and island nations, 496, 497, 506

Kyoto Accord, 494, 496, 500

Paris conference (2015), 505

and quality of life, 526

and rising sea levels, 497

super pollutants, 500–501, 504–5

U.S. leadership in, 496–98, 504, 505–6

Clinton, Bill, 600

and Africa, 276, 277, 286, 292, 297

and "building back better," 535–36

and campaigns, 3, 4, 8, 9, 11, 12, 47, 591–92

and China, 65, 67, 68, 73

and Colombia, 253

and development programs, 535–36, 537

and Haiti, 540

and Holbrooke, 162

and Hillary Clinton's speeches, 5, 6

and Hillary Clinton as Secretary of State, 16, 34

and Hurricane Katrina, 3

and Kyoto Accord, 494

and McGovern campaign (1972), 249

and Middle East, 302–3, 304, 329, 338

and national security, 137

and Northern Ireland, 224–25

and North Korea, 55–56

reelection of, 187

and September 11 attacks, 173

statue in Kosovo, 222

and Suu Kyi, 105

and Vietnam, 77

wedding of Hillary Clinton and, 80

Clinton, Chelsea, 6, 9, 16, 58, 66, 173, 467, 600

and Bhutto, 176, 177, 184

gay rights speech of, 586

and her grandmother, 587, 589

and Mandela, 294, 297

wedding of, 80–82, 587, 588

work ethic of, 525

Clinton, Hillary Rodham:

"America's Pacific Century," 45–46

and Democratic Conventions, 9, 10–11, 591–92

as First Lady, 10, 27, 39, 49, 131, 137, 138, 152, 176, 177, 260, 303, 560–62, 563

and Gaza cease-fire, 471, 478–87

and grandparenthood, 595

in individual negotiations, see specific names

learning from defeat, 7, 596

major speeches by, see Clinton, Hillary Rodham, speeches

and McGovern campaign (1972), 249

and nuclear arms treaty, 234–35

and presidential races (2008), 3–5, 8–9, 42; (2016), 595–96

and primaries (2008), 1–2, 3–4, 5–7, 8, 10, 15, 420

Clinton, Hillary Rodham (*cont.*)
  as Secretary of State, *see* Secretary of State, U.S.
  as Senator, 3, 10, 13, 14, 15, 17, 39, 42, 131, 136, 137, 143, 152, 172, 174, 420, 551
  and September 11 attacks, 172–74
  travels of, *see specific nations*
  wedding of Bill and, 80
  and wildlife trafficking, 467, 468–69
Clinton, Hillary Rodham, speeches:
  on Afghan peace prospects, 162–64, 166
  in Africa, 272, 273–74, 277, 296
  at Asia Society, 46–47, 70, 163–64, 166
  on Benghazi attack, 400, 412–13
  on counterterrorism, 200
  on democracy, 575
  on free markets, 512–13, 515
  "Globalization into the Next Millennium," 519
  on human rights, 575–76, 583
  on internet freedom, 556–57
  on Israel/Palestine, 320–21, 329
  on Latin America, 254–55
  on LGBT, 579–84
  on Middle East challenges, 337, 360, 434
  at Munich Security Conference, 344–45
  nominating Obama, 9, 10–11
  in Northern Ireland, 225
  to primary campaign staff (2008), 5–7
  at World Conference on Women, Beijing, 560–62, 581, 583
  at World Economic Forum, Davos (1998), 49
Clinton Administration:
  and al Qaeda, 131
  economic plan of, 187
  and gun control, 250
  and Latin America, 247, 252–53, 258
  and NATO, 211
  and North Korea, 53
  see also Clinton, Bill

Clinton Foundation, 16, 253, 467, 584–85
Clinton Global Initiative, 16, 285, 524, 584
Clinton Health Access Initiative (CHAI), 290–91, 292
Cohen, David, 439
Cohen, Jared, 548
COIN, 135–36, 138
Cold War, 32, 85, 163, 214, 231, 262, 340, 417, 420, 449, 565
  and Cuba, 247, 257, 424
  domino theory in, 267
  end of, 206, 207, 211, 213, 537
  foreign policy in, 493, 534
  ideological struggle of, 559
  nonaligned movement in, 440
Coleman, Claire, 599
Collins, Susan, 134, 502
Colombia, 252–53
  mass transit in, 255
  and Pacific Alliance, 254
  Plan Colombia, 247, 253
  and pollution, 501
  trade agreement with, 254, 515
Community of Democracies, 63
Congo (DRC), 279–82
Congress, U.S.:
  and children with disabilities, 560
  and climate change, 493–94, 500, 504, 505
  and counterterrorism, 183
  and debt default, 513–15
  and funding, 409, 410
  and immigration laws, 550
  and land bomb removal, 61
  oversight role of, 411–14
  political brinksmanship in, 514, 515
Connelly, Maura, 599
cookstoves, 523–25
Corbin, Michael, 599
Corker, Bob, 466–67
Corning, 511
Costa Rica, hydropower in, 255
Côte d'Ivoire, 272, 295
Countryman, Tom, 599

Craig, Brynne, 600
Crebo-Rediker, Heidi, 599
Cretz, Gene, 368, 369, 380, 387, 555
Crimea, Russian invasion of, 212, 227,
    230, 236, 239–42, 363
Crocker, Ryan, 165, 166
Crouse, Timothy, 8
Crowley, Joe, 105
Crowley, PJ, 599
Cuba, 261–65, 540
    and Cold War, 247, 257, 424
    Damas de Blanco ("Ladies in White")
        in, 265
    embargo against, 265
    and OAS, 257–58, 262–64
    U.S. relationship with, 248, 264–65
Cui Tiankai, 88–90, 92, 93, 95, 97

Daalder, Ivo, 599
Dačić, Ivica, 223
Dai Bingguo, 69–70, 72, 79, 82, 515
    and Chen, 91, 92–93, 94, 95
    and Iran, 429, 432
Dalai Lama, 68
Daniel, Josh, 599
Darfur, genocide in, 271, 283
Daris, Chuck, 598
Davey, Sarah, 598
Davies, Glyn, 599
Davies, Glyn, 599
Davis, Jen, 599
Davutoğlu, Ahmet, 217, 218, 219–20,
    321–22, 373, 376–77, 457, 463
Dayton Peace Accords, 138
de Klerk, F. W., 293–94
DeLong, Victoria, 529
Democratic National Conventions:
    (1992), 8, 9
    (1996), 9
    (2004), 2
    (2008), 9, 10–11, 591
    (2012), 591–92
Democratic Party: party unity in, 5, 8, 9, 10
Democratic Republic of Congo (DRC),
    279–82

Dempsey, Martin, 392, 407, 476–77
Deng Xiaoping, 72, 73, 495
Denmark, 502
Dewan, Linda, 599
DiMascia, Gina, 598
Diplomatic Security Service, 35, 394
Direct Line, 516
disabilities, people with, 559–60
Djerassi, Alex, 598
Dlamini-Zuma, Nkosazana, 296
Doctors Without Borders, 125, 208
Doe, Samuel, 275
Doherty, Glen, 382, 398, 404–5, 415
Dole, Bob, 560
Dolo, Adolphus ("General Peanut
    Butter"), 274
Dominican Republic, 535, 540
Donahoe-Chamberlain, Eileen, 599
Donilon, Tom, 23, 196
    and Benghazi, 388, 392
    and Egypt, 340, 341
    and Gaza, 480
    and Latin America, 265
    and National Security Council, 45,
        192, 436
    and Omani back channel, 436
Dorsey, Jack, 548
Dougherty, Jill, 7
Dowd, Katie, 600
Duvalier, "Baby Doc," 529
Dyson, Sheila, 599

Eagleburger, Lawrence, 31
East Africa, U.S. embassies bombed in
    (1998), 131, 171, 383, 406
East China Sea, 74, 79, 521
Edelman, Marian Wright, 559
Egypt:
    Coptic Christians in, 348, 349, 575
    disorganization in, 346
    elections in, 332, 347
    Hillary Clinton's travels to, 346–48,
        484–87
    Innocence of Muslims aired in, 386–88,
        399, 401–3, 405, 412, 574

Egypt (*cont.*)
  and Israel/Palestine, 322, 325, 349, 477, 481, 484–87
  military rule in, 350
  and Muslim Brotherhood, 341, 345, 346, 347–49, 351, 386, 472–73, 477, 481, 484–86
  peaceful protests in, 200–201, 447
  and terrorism, 474
  transition sought for, 344–45, 347–50, 379, 455, 460
  U.S. relationship with, 340
  violent protests in, 338, 339–46, 347–49, 355, 364, 386
Einhorn, Bob, 426, 439, 598
Eisenhower Administration, 417
Ekho Moskvy, 229–30
Elbegdorj, Tsakhiagiin, 62
Elizabeth II, queen of England, 226
El-Keib, Abdurrahim, 388
Ellsberg, Daniel, 552
El Salvador, 254, 256, 406
Emanuel, Rahm, 17, 23, 138, 316, 320
energy, 520–23
  and cookstoves, 523–25
  and economics, 508–9
  electricity, 256, 494, 504
  extraction practices, 522–23
  and jobs, 515–20
  and resource curse, 277, 522
Energy and Climate Partnership of the Americas, 255–56
Engole, John Robert, 293
Enriquez, Lesley, 250
Entebbe raid (1976), 307
Environmental Protection Agency (EPA), 493, 501
Erdoğan, Recep Tayyip, 215, 216–18, 322, 374, 375, 430–31, 463, 478
Erwin, Lisa, 598
Espinosa, Patricia, 250, 251, 252, 266
Eurasian Union, 239
European Union, 44, 575
  and Afghanistan, 140
  and Balkans, 223

  and climate change, 498, 500
  energy sources for, 240–42
  and financial crisis, 210, 213
  and Iran, 439
  and NATO, 205, 211–14, 242
  Nobel Peace Prize to, 214
  and the Quartet, 323
  and Turkey, 219
  and Ukraine, 240, 241
  U.S. relationship with, 205–7
Evans, Jonathan, 598
Export-Import Bank, 539

Fabius, Laurent, 208–9, 457
Fahy, Alden, 598
Fair Labor Association, 519
Fallows, James, 121
Fang Lizhi, 85
FARC, 252–53
Farmer, Paul, 540
Fattal, Joshua, 435, 436
Fayyad, Salam, 310
Federal Emergency Management Agency (FEMA), 530
FedEx, 511–12
Feed the Future, 279
Feingold, Russ, 134, 279
Feinstein, Dianne, 2, 17
Feldman, Dan, 160, 161, 598
Feltman, Jeff, 331, 356–57, 598
Fernandez, Jose, 599
FEST (Foreign Emergency Support Team), 393–94
Finland, 502
Finny, Clarence, 598
First Amendment, 557
First Nations, 502, 505
Fitzgerald, Lance, 598
Fleming, Sue, 598
Flores, Oscar, 600
Florio, Marie, 598
Flournoy, Michèle, 132, 572
Fogarty, Dan, 599
Foley, Tom, 30
Ford, Betty, 10

Ford, Gerald R., 566
Ford, Robert, 448–49
Foreign Policy (magazine), 45
Forum for the Future, 331, 337
Fox, Vicente, 247
France:
    and Iran, 424–25
    and Libya, 213, 368, 372–77
    and Syria, 463
    and Turkey, 219
    U.S. soldiers buried in, 206
Franklin, Benjamin, 556
Freedom House, 60, 256
Friends of the Syrian People, 452, 459–60,
    464
Froman, Mike, 498
Fu, Bob, 95
Fulgham, Alonzo, 599
Funes, Mauricio, 256

G-7, 363
G-8, 363, 368
Gandhi, Sonia, 59
Gao Yaojie, 69
García Márquez, Gabriel, 252
Gates, Robert M.:
    and Afghanistan, 129, 130, 133, 147,
        148, 155
    and bin Laden operation, 170, 171,
        191, 192
    and counterterrorism, 190
    as Defense Secretary, 24–25
    and Egypt, 340, 341, 387
    and Libya, 366, 370
    and North Korea, 56–57, 58
Gates Foundation, 292, 584
Gaza Strip, 307, 314, 471–87
    cease-fire negotiated in, 304–5, 306,
        471, 477–87
    elections in, 472
    ground invasion threatened, 481, 482,
        484, 487
    Hamas in, 310, 313, 421, 438, 472–74,
        475, 477–79, 481–83, 487
    humanitarian aid in, 485

Israeli air strikes into, 476–77, 485
Israeli siege of, 305, 321, 472, 473, 474,
    481, 484
and Qatar, 474–76, 479
rockets fired from, 304–5, 312, 471,
    472, 476, 477–79, 480, 484, 485,
    487
weapons smuggling into, 485–86
zero hour in, 484, 485–87
Gazprom, 239, 241
Gbowee, Leymah, 274
Gehry, Frank, 33
Geithner, Tim, 72–73, 84, 94, 97–98
Gelber, Ethan, 597
General Electric (GE), 494, 507–8, 516
Geneva Protocol (1925), 466
Genghis Khan, 62
Georgia:
    Russian invasion of, 229, 231, 236, 239,
        451
    terrorism in, 442
Germany:
    Berlin Wall in, 206
    and global financial crisis, 210
    and Syria, 463
    U.S. relationship with, 205
Ghana:
    and climate change, 501
    President Obama's trip to, 270
Ghattas, Kim, 358
Gibbs, Robert, 187, 344, 492
Gilani, Yousaf Raza, 155
Gillard, Julia, 44, 50
Giuliani, Rudy, 172
GLIFAA (Gays and Lesbians in Foreign
    Affairs Agencies), 578–79
Global Alliance for Clean Cookstoves,
    524–25
Global Counterterrorism Forum, 189,
    200
global economy:
    dollar as reserve currency, 514
    in emerging economies, 513
    and energy, 508–9
    free markets in, 512–13

global economy (*cont.*)
  international trade, 233, 235, 242,
    509–11, 513, 515–17, 525
  middle class, 525–26
  and U.S. debt default, 513–15
  U.S. exports, 516–17
  and workers' rights, 518–20
Global Security Contingency Fund, 389
Global Trends 2025: A Transformed World
    (NIC), 25
global warming, *see* climate change
Glynn, Pat, 598
Godani, Behar, 598
Goldberg, Phil, 599
Goldstein, Cary, 598
Goldstone, Richard, 318–19
Goldwyn, David, 599
Goodwin, Doris Kearns, 13
Google, 556
Goosby, Eric, 291, 599
Gorbachev, Mikhail, 212
Gordon, Phil, 220, 599
Gore, Al, 8, 54, 55, 494
Gore, Tipper, 8
Gottemoeller, Rose, 234, 599
Graham, Lindsey, 134, 502
Greeley, Horace, 13
Greene, Nicholas, 598
Gross, Alan, 264
Grossman, Marc, 163, 165, 166, 599
Guantánamo Bay, 22, 158, 165, 573
Guinea-Bissau, coup in, 272
Gül, Abdullah, 215, 462–63
Gulf Cooperation Council, 352, 358–60,
    438–39
Gulf War (1991), 351, 438, 477

Habib, Bubaker, 376
Hackett, John, 598
Haddad, Essam al-, 486
Hague, William, 208, 368, 457
Haiti, 527–44
  agriculture in, 541, 542
  Caracol project in, 541–42, 544
  and democracy, 247

development plan for, 535–41, 544
earthquake in, 208, 527–32, 535–36
elections in, 542–43
Hillary Clinton's travel to, 542–44
poverty in, 533, 534–35
refugees from, 535
sovereignty of, 531
UN mission in, 247, 260
USAID in, 527, 530, 537–41
voodoo in, 528–29
Hale, David, 598
Hamas, 304–5, 309–10, 313, 315, 421, 438,
    472–74, 476–79, 481–83, 487
Hammer, Michael, 599
Haniya, Ismail, 474
Hanley, Monica, 600
Hanssen, Robert, 41
Hariri, Rafic, 331, 334
Hariri, Saad, 334, 337
Hariton, Lorraine, 599
Harney, Kenneth, 375–76
Harper, Stephen, 503
Harris, Harry, 577
Haughey, Sharon, 226
Havel, Václav, 101, 211–12
Hayes, Jeff, 158
HEAL Africa, 282
Heaney, Seamus, 224
Helms, Jesse, 537
Helsinki Accords, 566–67
Henley, William Ernest, "Invictus," 296
Heumann, Judy, 599
Hezbollah:
  in Iran, 418, 442
  Israel attacked by, 312, 331, 421
  in Lebanon, 312, 313, 333, 383, 418,
    421, 453
  in Syria, 453, 461, 468
Hicks, Greg, 390, 396–97
Hilburn, Paul, 598
Hill, Christopher, 599
Hillman, David, 598
Hirschhorn, Ellie, 598
Hochstein, Amos, 598
Hof, Fred, 598

Holbrooke, Richard, 40, 231, 342
  and Afghanistan/Pakistan, 28, 29,
    132, 139–42, 143, 149, 150–51, 155,
    157–59, 169, 175, 182, 189
  and Bosnia, 138, 150, 164
  and Dayton Peace Accords, 138
  death of, 161–62
  heart attack of, 159–61
  and Iran, 422, 434
  To End a War, 150
Holder, Eric, 190, 251
Hollande, François, 208
Honduras:
  elections in, 266, 267–68
  Hillary Clinton's travel to, 256, 259–60,
    263
  ouster of Zelaya in, 265–68
Hong Kong:
  and international trade, 512–13, 514,
    515
  and internet communication, 556
Hoover, Judith, 598
Hormats, Bob, 599
Hu Jintao, 69, 72, 74, 85, 92
  and Iran, 429, 432
  and transition, 86, 96
  and U.S.–China relationship, 73, 95
human rights, 558–89
  civil rights, 558–59, 565
  and Helsinki Accords, 566–67
  human trafficking, 517–18, 547, 573
  and "invisibles," 576
  LGBT, 576–84
  people with disabilities, 559–60
  religious freedom, 574–75
  State Department reports on, 574–75,
    577–78
  and UN, 111, 364–65, 557, 564–65, 567,
    573–74, 575–76, 580
  Universal Declaration, 557, 564–65,
    567, 573, 580
  women's rights, 66, 68–69, 152–53, 158,
    560–64, 567–73, 584–85
  workers' rights, 517, 518–20
Human Rights Campaign, 586

Human Rights Watch, 557
Hungarian Revolution, 566
Huntsman, Jon, 511
Hurricane Katrina, 3, 532
Hurwitz, Sarah, 598
Hussain, Rashad, 599
Hussein, Saddam, 134, 191, 352, 367, 421,
    457, 462, 477
Hussein bin Talal, King of Jordan, 323

Ibrahim, Hafez, 354
Iceland, 502, 503
İhsanoğlu, Ekmeleddin, 574
immigration laws, 550
India:
  and Burma, 116
  and climate change, 495–96, 498, 499
  economic growth in, 440, 495, 521
  and energy security, 441, 521
  Hillary Clinton's travel to, 440–41
  and Iran, 440
  middle class in, 526
  and Pakistan, 59, 140, 156, 171, 178,
    185, 186
  strategic autonomy of, 440
  U.S. relationship with, 58–60
Indonesia:
  and climate change, 494, 495
  democracy in, 60, 215
  East Asia Summit in, 113–14
  economic growth in, 495
  Hillary Clinton's travel to, 51–52, 113
  tsunami in (2004), 533, 535
  U.S.–ASEAN meeting in, 113
  U.S. relationship with, 46
Innocence of Muslims (video), 386–88, 399,
    401–3, 405, 412, 574
Insulza, José Miguel, 259
Inter-American Development Bank, 541
International Atomic Energy Agency
    (IAEA), 419, 424–26, 428, 430
International Criminal Court (ICC), 278,
    364
International Monetary Fund (IMF), 112,
    563, 569

International Red Cross, 304, 532
internet, 546–57
  censorship of, 546, 548, 549
  and First Amendment, 557
  influence of, 49, 402–3, 406
  multistakeholder approach to, 557
  networking via, 550–52
  terrorists' use of, 547, 555
  "Texts from Hillary" on, 378
  Twitter, 423, 546, 548–49, 551–52
  as value-neutral, 546
"Invictus" (Henley), 296
Iran, 416–46
  and Afghanistan, 140, 419, 422
  in Axis of Evil, 419
  and Egypt, 344
  elections in, 422, 442–44
  Green Movement in, 422–24
  Hezbollah in, 418, 442
  hikers imprisoned by, 435–36
  hostage rescue attempt in (1980), 170,
    192, 195
  hostages taken in (1979), 383, 393,
    417–18
  and internet, 423, 548–49, 557
  and Israel, 307, 308, 312, 314, 417
  nuclear program of, 217, 218, 233, 260,
    332, 340, 351, 354, 416–17, 418–19,
    420–21, 424–34, 436, 438, 442, 443,
    444–46
  and oil, 421, 439–41, 521
  and provocation, 355–56, 358
  Quds Force, 453
  Revolutionary Guard, 418, 420, 421,
    442, 443, 453, 549
  Revolution in, 418, 419, 443, 446
  sanctions against, 231, 233, 235, 243,
    420, 425–34, 438, 439–42, 444–46
  Shah of, 341, 417
  smart power applied in, 34
  and Sultan of Oman, 416–17, 419,
    434–48, 442, 444–45
  and Syria, 314, 442, 452–53, 456,
    460
  Tehran Research Reactor, 425, 439

  and terrorism, 351, 417–18, 437, 438,
    442, 446, 472, 476
  theocracy in, 341, 575
  and Turkey, 217, 260
Iraq:
  in Axis of Evil, 419
  Bush Administration focus on, 43, 131,
    134–35, 148, 205, 207, 419, 424, 425
  "Clear, hold, and build" policy in, 136
  COIN in, 135
  Hillary Clinton's vote on, 134–35,
    136–37
  and Israel, 417
  lessons learned in, 134, 137, 138, 455,
    457, 462
  no-fly zone in, 366, 367
  oil and gas in, 350–51, 440
  Special Operations in, 193
  "Sunni Awakening" in, 136, 138, 352
  and terrorism, 418
  training local soldiers in, 462
  U.S. diplomat killed in, 384
  U.S. invasion of, 205, 207, 421
  war in, 25, 45, 73, 136, 148, 229, 364,
    461, 464, 466
Iraq Resolution (2002), 136–37
Iraq Study Group, 134
Ireland:
  Good Friday Agreement, 224–25, 226,
    313
  Northern, 224–26
Irish Republican Army, 224
Islam:
  Eid al Fitr, 404, 419
  and extremists, 313, 473, 475–76
  and restrictions on women, 130–31,
    352–53, 354–55
  split within, 352
Israel:
  Arab-Israeli War (1948), 325
  and Arab Peace Initiative (2002), 314,
    315
  birth rate in, 312
  and Camp David Accords, 338, 473,
    484

and cease-fire, 349
establishment of (1948), 304
and Gaza, *see* Gaza Strip
and Golan Heights, 314
and Goldstone Report, 318
Hezbollah attacks on, 312, 331, 421
Hillary Clinton's travels to, 302–3,
    305–6, 319, 480–82, 483
and intifada, 301, 308, 407, 472
and Iran, 307, 308, 312, 314, 417
Iron Dome defense system in, 306, 438,
    478–79, 480, 487
and Jerusalem, 317–19, 320, 321, 328,
    330
as Jewish homeland, 304, 306, 487
and Jordan Valley, 325–26
MDA in, 303–4
military edge of, 438, 487
natural gas reserves in, 350–51
and Oslo Peace Accords, 301, 303, 305,
    307
and Palestine, 301–30
public image of, 478
and self-defense, 477–78, 479, 486, 487
and settlement construction, 315–23,
    327–28
Six Day War, 301, 473
and Sudan, 476
and Syria, 312, 313, 314, 417, 468
and terrorism, 303, 308, 340, 473, 483
and Turkey, 218, 314, 321–22
and two-state solution, 305–6, 307, 311,
    320, 325, 338, 487
and West Bank settlements, 308–11,
    317–18, 482
and Yom Kippur War, 338
Italy:
    and Libya, 373–74
    U.S. relationship with, 554–55
    U.S. soldiers buried in, 554

Jabari, Ahmed, 477
Jackson, Lisa, 501
Jacobs, Janice, 599
Jacobson, Roberta, 599

Jahjaga, Atifete, 223
Jalil, Mustafa Abdul, 379
Jalili, Saeed, 426, 443, 444
Japan:
    and Afghanistan, 153, 166
    and climate change, 494
    Clintons' first visit to, 47–49
    democracy in, 60, 61
    economy of, 47–48, 571
    Fukushima nuclear plant in, 48, 440,
        533
    Hillary Clinton's town hall meetings
        in, 49–50
    and Iran, 440
    Maritime Self-Defense Force, 48
    and South China Sea, 74, 75
    U.S. alliance with, 44, 46, 75
    "womenomics" in, 571
Jarrett, Valerie, 125
Jassim al-Thani, Hamad bin (HBJ), 457,
    474, 475, 479
Jefferson, Thomas, 31
Jenkins, Bonnie, 599
Jiang Zemin, 67, 72
Jibril, Mahmoud, 363, 364, 365, 369–70,
    379
Jiloty, Lauren, 599
Jo, Yerka, 600
jobs, 515–20
    and developing economies, 520, 542
    and energy production, 522–23
    and foreign investment, 516
    and international trade, 507–8, 515–17
    and working conditions, 517–20
Johnson, Brock, 599
Johnson, Lady Bird, 10
Johnson Cook, Suzan, 599
Johnson Sirleaf, Ellen, 275
Joint Special Operations Command, 191
Jonathan, Goodluck, 577
Jones, Beth, 599
Jones, Don, 558
Jones, James, 23, 45, 129, 138, 148, 265,
    425
Jones, Kerri-Ann, 599

Jones, Paul, 599
Jones, Stephanie Tubbs, 5
Jones, Terry, 387–88, 402
Jordan:
    and energy sources, 350–51
    and Israel/Palestine, 310, 322, 325–26,
        350–51
    and Libya, 371
    reforms in, 355
    and Syria, 450, 456, 461
Judeh, Nasser, 351
Juppé, Alain, 208–9, 377

Kabila, Joseph, 280–81
Kansi, Mir Aimal, 188
Kantor, Mickey, 30
Karp, Jonathan, 598
Karzai, Hamid, 16, 142–46, 147, 152–55,
        160, 162
    and elections, 143–45
    and Taliban, 145, 153–55, 164–66
    and transition, 167–69
Kato, David, 576, 583
Kayani, Ashfaq Parvez, 346
Kazakhstan, 237, 238
Keen, Ken, 530
Kelly, Declan, 599
Kelly, Ian, 599
Kennedy, Jacqueline Bouvier, 10
Kennedy, Jim, 5, 598
Kennedy, John F., 163–64, 534, 541
Kennedy, Laura, 599
Kennedy, Pat, 392–93, 553, 599
Kennedy, Paul, 25, 47
Kennedy, Ted, 5
Kenya:
    elections in, 278
    Hillary Clinton's travel to, 276–79
    LGBT in, 577
    technology in, 546
    U.S. embassy bombed in, 131, 383,
        406
Kenya Agricultural Research Institute,
        278
Kenyatta, Uhuru, 278

Kerry, John, 21, 77, 167, 466, 593
    and Afghanistan, 144
    and Iran, 445
    and New START, 234
    and Syria, 465, 467, 469
Ketchem, Fred, 414, 599
Key, John, 44
Khalifa, Sheikh Khalid bin Ahmed al,
        356
Khalifa al-Thani, Sheikh Hamad bin,
        474
Khama, Seretse, 277
Khamenei, Ayatollah Ali Hojatolislam,
        421, 424, 443–44, 446
Khar, Hina Rabbani, 199
Khatami, Mohammad, 419
Kheradi, Irene, 598
Khomeini, Ayatollah Ruholla, 417, 421
Khrushchev, Nikita, 207
Khyber Pass, 156
Kibaki, Mwai, 278
Kiir, Salva, 284, 285
Kikwete, Jakaya, 279
Kim Il-sung, 55
Kim Jong Il, 55–56
Kim Jong Un, 61
King, Rev. Martin Luther King Jr.,
        558–59
King, Robert, 599
Kipling, Rudyard, 103
Kirk, Ron, 276
Kissinger, Henry A., 31, 65, 69, 93, 322
Klein, Jen, 584, 600
Koh, Harold, 87, 89, 91, 99, 183, 581, 598
Kohl, Helmut, 209
Kommareddi, Madhuri, 600
Kony, Joseph, 290
Korean War, 214
Kosovo, 211, 213, 221–23, 367
Kouchner, Bernard, 208
Krishna, S. M., 441
Kurtz-Phelan, Dan, 598
Kuwait, 351
Kyoto Accord, 494, 496, 500
Kyrgyzstan, 237, 238

labor rights, 517, 518–20
LaHood, Ray, 433
Lamothe, Laurent, 542
Landler, Mark, 433
Langdon, Ross, 291
Lantos, Tom, 105, 110
Laos, 61
Larkins, Neal, 599
Latin America, 246–68
    combined economy of, 254
    democracies in, 254, 256, 257, 259, 264
    economic growth in, 255
    Energy and Climate Partnership of the
        Americas, 255–56
    and OAS, 256–59, 262–64, 266, 542–43
    "Pathways to Prosperity" in, 254
    U.S. relationship with, 246–48, 251
    wealth gap in, 254–55
    women as leaders in, 256, 261, 571
    see also specific nations
Laszczych, Joanne, 599
Lavrov, Sergey, 231, 232, 244, 577
    and Asia-Pacific, 243
    and Iran, 425, 426
    and Libya, 371–72
    and Syria, 451–52, 456–57, 458–59, 469
leadership, definition of, 583
Lebanon:
    Cedar Revolution in, 331
    crisis in, 333–34, 337
    Hezbollah in, 312, 313, 333, 383, 418,
        421, 453
    and Syria, 450, 454, 456, 461
    and UN, 427, 433
    U.S. facilities attacked in (1983), 383,
        406, 418
Lee, Euna, 54, 56
Lee, Matt, 98
Lee Myung-bak, 53, 58
Leghari, Begum Nasreen, 177
Leghari, Farooq Ahmad Khan, 177
Letterman, David, 231
Levinson, Robert, 422
Lévy, Bernard-Henri, 368, 369
Lew, Jack, 29–30, 149, 572, 598

Lewis, Reta Jo, 599
LGBT rights, 576–84
Liberia:
    civil war in, 274
    women activists in, 274–75
Libya, 363–81
    "all necessary measures" against,
        370–71, 372, 374–75, 450
    and Arab League, 213, 357, 367–68,
        370, 371, 376
    attacks in Benghazi, 382–83, 385,
        390–404, 411–14
    civil war in, 355, 364–65, 366
    elections in, 380, 381, 388
    "fog of war" in, 385
    Hillary Clinton's travel to, 377–80
    investigations into Benghazi attacks in,
        385–96, 406–14
    journalists in, 403
    law and order needed in, 379, 388
    military campaign in, 377
    NATO forces in, 213–14, 370, 373–77,
        450
    no-drive zone in, 376, 377
    no-fly zone in, 235, 357, 366–67, 370,
        371, 372, 374, 377, 450, 462, 475
    Qaddafi in, 357, 358, 359, 360, 363–75,
        379, 460, 555
    and terrorism, 365–66
    transitional government in, 365, 370,
        377, 379–81, 388–89, 404, 455, 460
    UN embargo on, 364, 370
    U.S. staff evacuated from, 368, 380
    Zintan brigade in, 378–79
Lieberman, Avigdor, 308
Lincoln, Abraham, 13, 14, 566
Ling, Laura, 54, 56
Li Shuxian, 85
Lithuania, 545–46, 549
Littlefield, Elizabeth, 599
Liu Xiaobo, 63, 97
Livni, Tzipi, 306
Lobo, Porfirio, 268
Locke, Gary, 87, 91, 95, 511–12
Lomellin, Carmen, 599

Lord's Resistance Army (LRA), 290, 467
Louis XV, King of France, 462
Love, Reggie, 2, 11
Lucas, Laura, 599
Lugar, Richard, 234
Lula da Silva, Luiz Inácio, 255, 259–60,
    261, 263, 430–31, 492
Luzzatto, Tamera, 173
Lyman, Princeton, 599
Lynch, Christopher, 598

Maas, Inge, 598
Maathai, Wangari, 276
Machel, Graça, 294, 297
Machel, Samora, 294
Macmanus, Joe, 599
Madagascar, 272
Magariaf, Mohammed, 388, 395, 396, 404
Magaziner, Ira, 292
Malawi, agriculture in, 279
Malaysia:
    democracy in, 60
    and South China Sea, 113
    strategic importance of, 46
    waste management in, 501
Mali, 272
Maliki, Nouri al-, 350
Malta, law center in, 200
Mandela, Nelson, 101, 119, 123, 275,
    293–98
    aging and death of, 296–97
    legacy of, 295, 297–98
    Nobel Peace Prize to, 298
Manning, Bradley, 552
Manning, Greg, 173
Manning, Lauren, 173, 197
Mansour, Mullah Akhtar Muhammad,
    154–55
Mao Zedong, 73, 207
Mardenfeld, Debbie, 173–74, 197
Marine One (helicopter), 147
Markey, Ed, 494
Marshall, Capricia, 27–28, 404, 598
Marshall, George C., 32, 536
Marshall Plan, 536

Martelly, Michel, 543, 544
Merten, Ken, 599
Marton, Kati, 139, 160–61
Marzouki, Moncef, 402
Massey, Stephen, 585
Mbeki, Thabo, 295
McAuliffe, Marisa, 600
McCain, John, 11, 77, 134, 348, 502
McCall, Dawn, 599
McCartan, Joyce, 571
McChrystal, Stanley, 133, 138
McConnell, Mitch, 104, 105, 107
McCullough, Terri, 600
McDonough, Denis, 28, 436, 466–67, 468,
    530
McFaul, Mike, 243, 551–52, 598
McGovern, George, 249
McGuinness, Martin, 224, 226
McHale, Judith, 179–80, 598
McHugh, John, 134
McLean, Lori, 599
McRaven, Bill, 191, 192, 193–94, 197
Mead, Margaret, 595
Mead, Walter Russell, 122, 196
Medvedev, Dmitry, 230–36, 238, 244, 245,
    425, 552
Meehan, Bernadette, 599
Mehta, Hansa, 565
Merkel, Angela, 16, 209–11, 500, 555
Merrill, Nick, 600
Merten, Ken, 529–30
Mexico:
    and climate change, 501
    drug cartels in, 247, 249–52
    economic growth in, 255
    environmental programs in, 255
    financial crisis in, 247
    independence of, 248–49
    Mérida Initiative in, 247, 250
    and Pacific Alliance, 254
    trade with, 246, 510
    U.S. consulates attacked in, 249–50,
    384
    U.S. relationship with, 248–52
Mezvinsky, Marc, 80, 81

mGive, 532

Micheletti, Roberto, 265–68

Michiko, Empress (Japan), 47, 48–49

middle class, 525–26

Middle East, 301–30
   Arab-Israeli War (1948), 325
   Arab Spring, 49, 121, 200, 272, 331–62,
     472
   and Camp David Accords, 338, 473,
     484
   economic decline in, 332
   economic reforms in, 344
   energy sources in, 350–51
   Hillary Clinton's travels to, 331,
     333–37, 479–87
   Islamic split in, 352
   and Oslo Peace Accords, 301, 303, 305,
     307
   peace efforts in, 28, 31, 43, 81, 308, 310,
     311–14, 315, 323–30, 333
   and the Quartet, 323
   and Saban Forum, 329
   Six Day War, 301, 473
   and transitions to democracy,
     361–62
   violent reactions to offensive video in,
     386–88, 399–400, 401–3, 406, 412
   Yom Kippur War, 338
   see also specific nations
midterm elections:
   (1994), 187
   (2006), 136
   (2010), 234
Mikulski, Barbara, 17

Miliband, David, 207, 427–28

Millennium Challenge Corporation, 537,
   544

Miller, Patti, 600

Mills, Cheryl, 27, 28, 86, 87, 123, 527–28,
   531–32, 535, 597

Milošević, Slobodan, 138, 141, 150, 221

Mindszenty, Cardinal József, 85, 87

Missionaries of Charity, 58

Mitchell, Derek, 109–10, 112, 118, 121,
   123

Mitchell, George, 28, 29, 598
   and Israel/Palestine, 313–18, 319, 322,
     324, 325, 326, 329
   and Northern Ireland, 225, 313–14, 326

Mobutu Sese Seko, 280

Mogadishu, Somalia, 195, 286

Mohamud, Hassan Sheikh, 289

Momeni, Esha, 422

Mongolia, U.S. relationship with, 61–64

Moran, Thomas, 600

Morningstar, Richard, 240, 598

Morocco:
   reforms in, 355
   street protests in, 399

Morsi, Mohamed, 347, 348, 349, 473, 475,
   477–78, 482, 484–86

Mother Teresa, 58–59

Motsoaledi, Aaron, 291

Mottaki, Manouchehr, 434

Moussa, Amr, 367–68, 371

Mubarak, Gamal, 342, 343

Mubarak, Hosni, 347, 361
   fall from power, 200, 329, 341, 342–46,
     348, 350, 360, 363, 367, 473, 481, 487
   and Israel/Palestine, 319, 323, 325, 329,
     333, 340
   and violent protests, 338–45

Mubarak, Suzanne, 338, 339

Mugabe, Robert, 273

Mull, Steve, 391–92, 599

Mullen, Mike, 129, 147, 148, 196, 407

Munich Security Conference, 344–45, 451

Munter, Cameron, 198

Murkowski, Lisa, 503

Muscatine, Lissa, 30, 560, 598

Museveni, Yoweri, 428, 576, 577

Musharraf, Pervez, 178, 184

Muslim Brotherhood:
   and anti-U.S. protests, 347–49
   and Arab Spring, 386
   and Gaza, 475, 477, 481, 484–86
   and Jordan, 351
   and Qatar, 475
   rise to power, 472–73
   and transition, 341, 345, 346, 349, 477

Mutombo, Dikembe, 280
Myanmar, *see* Burma

Nagorno-Karabakh, 219
Nalbandian, Edward, 219–20
Napolitano, Janet, 190, 251
Nasr, Vali, 155
Nasser, Shada, 336
National Action Plan on Women, Peace
    and Security, 572
National Building Museum, Washington,
    5–6
National Democratic Institute, 360
National Institutes of Health, 538
National Intelligence Council, 25
National Science Foundation, 538
National Security Agency (NSA), 244,
    555
National Security Council, 22, 146, 190,
    370, 464
NATO, 211–14, 242
    and Afghanistan, 133, 140, 159, 198,
        213, 422
    expansion of, 212
    in Kosovo, 222, 367
    in Libya, 213–14, 370, 373–77, 450
    and September 11 attacks, 205
    and Washington Treaty, 205
Nelson, Chaniqua, 598
Netanyahu, Benjamin "Bibi," 306–8
    and elections, 306
    and Gaza, 478, 481–82, 484–87
    and Iran, 307, 308, 438, 441, 445
    and Jerusalem, 317–18, 320, 321, 328
    and peace process, 301–2, 313, 316, 319,
        322, 323–29
    and settlement construction, 315–16,
        317–20
    and two-state solution, 317
Netanyahu, Benzion, 307
Netanyahu, Yonatan, 307
Newseum, 556–57
New START (New Strategic Arms
    Reduction Treaty), 234, 243
New York University, 89, 97, 99

New Zealand, 44
Nides, Tom, 30, 198–99, 388, 410, 598
Nigeria:
    oil from, 276, 440
    and resource curse, 522
    and UN, 427–28
    waste management in, 501
Nigerian bank scam, 547
Nixon, Richard M., and China, 65, 68, 69,
    93, 121, 313
Nixon Administration, 136
Nkoana-Mashabane, Maite, 296
No Ceilings: The Full Partnership
    Project, 585
Norman, Adrian, 598
Northern Distribution Network, 237–39
Northern Ireland, 224–26, 326
    Good Friday Agreement, 224–25, 226,
        313
    Hillsborough Agreement, 226
    Vital Voices Conference in, 224, 571
North Korea, 53–58, 79
    in Axis of Evil, 419
    and Burma, 104, 107, 120
    Cheonan incident, 56
    and DMZ, 57
    nuclear capability of, 53–55
    repression in, 61
    sanctions against, 55, 57, 235, 432
Norway, melting glaciers in, 501–2
Nossel, Suzanne, 33
Nuland, Toria, 347, 599
Nye, Joseph, 33

Obama, Barack, 600
    and Afghanistan/Pakistan, 129–30,
        132, 141, 145, 146–49, 159, 237
    and Africa, 270, 288, 290, 292
    and Asia-Pacific, 45, 54, 55, 56, 74, 77,
        112–14, 116, 121–22, 124–25
    and bin Laden operation, 170, 192,
        193–94, 196–97
    and climate change, 491–93, 499–500,
        504–5
    as Commander in Chief, 392

and counterterrorism, 190
and Europe, 206, 214, 220
and financial recession, 210
and foreign investment, 516
and foreign trade, 515
and Haiti, 530–31, 534, 538
and Holbrooke, 162
Hillary Clinton working with, 18–19, 51
and Latin America, 248, 249, 251, 253, 254, 257, 259, 262–63, 264, 265
and Mandela, 296–97
and Middle East, 332, 335, 339, 343, 370, 372, 373, 375, 392, 397–98, 400–401, 455, 461, 463–67, 472, 478, 480, 483
oath of office, 19
and "the Obama effect," 206
and Pakistan, 198
as President-elect, 11–19
and presidential race (2008), 3–4, 5, 6, 8, 10
and primaries (2008), 1–2, 3–4, 8, 15, 22, 420
reelection of, 591
and Russia, 230, 232–34, 235, 236, 238, 242, 243–44
and Secretary of State offer to Hillary Clinton, 12, 15–18, 19, 420
Senate campaign of, 2
West Point speech by, 147–49, 159, 163
Obama, Michelle, 8, 9, 297
Obama, Sasha and Malia, 8
Obama Administration:
Cabinet and team members, 22–25
and China, 68, 432
and drone strikes, 183–84, 185
and Iran, 416, 419, 420, 421, 423–25, 427–29, 433–34, 436, 438–39, 442, 445–46
and Israel/Palestine, 304–5, 306, 313, 315–17, 320, 321, 322, 326–27
Presidential Policy Directives, 534
and reelection, 591–92

Oberly, Kay, 34
O'Connor, Michael, 598
Odinga, Raila Amolo, 278
O'Leary, Ann, 600
Oliver, Mary, 589
Olmert, Ehud, 301, 305, 306
Olsson, Kurt, 378–79, 414, 599
Oman:
    Hillary Clinton's travel to, 334, 336–37
    and Iran, 416–17, 419, 434–38, 442, 444–45
Omar, Mullah, 130, 157, 158, 165
O'Meara, Joy, 598
O'Neill, Peter, 569
One World Clean Energy, 295
Open Skies Agreements, 516
Operation Cast Lead, 304
Operation Eagle Claw, 192, 193
Operation Neptune Spear, 194
Operation Pillar of Defense, 477
Operation Tomodachi, 48
Operation Unified Protector, 377
Organization for Economic Co-operation and Development, 570
Organization for Security and Cooperation, 554
Organization of American States (OAS), 256–59, 262–64, 266, 268, 433, 542–43
Organization of Islamic Cooperation, 140, 574
Ortega, Daniel, 263
Orwell, George, 103, 110
Oslo Peace Accords, 301, 303, 305, 307
Otero, Maria, 599
Ottoman Empire, 214
Overseas Private Investment Corporation (OPIC), 539

Pacific Alliance, 254
Pacific Island Forum, 497
Pahlavi, Mohammad Reza Shah, 341, 417

Pakistan:
  Afghanistan border with, 131–32, 146,
    155–56, 171, 198, 199, 233, 237
  al Qaeda in, 138, 148, 164, 171, 183,
    186–87
  bin Laden in, 164, 165, 192, 193
  counterterrorism in, 189
  drone attacks in, 183–84, 185
  economic hardship in, 176, 198
  Hillary Clinton's travel to, 176–77
  and India, 59, 140, 156, 171, 178, 185,
    186
  ISI, 154, 171
  soldiers killed by U.S. forces in (2011),
    198–99
  sovereignty of, 171, 186, 197, 198–99
  Taliban in, 131, 151, 154, 156, 164, 171,
    175, 178, 181, 186, 198, 237
  terrorism in, 59, 176, 180–81, 182–87,
    188, 197, 199
  trade with Afghanistan, 155–58
  USAID in, 141, 182
  U.S. relationship with, 18, 171,
    176, 178–80, 181–82, 185–87, 193,
    197–99
Palestinian Territories:
  birth rate in, 312
  and Camp David Accords, 338, 473,
    484
  and cease-fire, 349
  and East Jerusalem, 317, 319, 320, 328
  and elections, 309
  and Fatah, 309, 472
  flag of, 301, 325
  and Gaza, see Gaza Strip
  and Hamas, see Hamas
  Hillary Clinton's travel to, 482–83
  and Israel, 301–30
  and Palestinian Authority, 474
  and statehood, 304, 311, 312, 326, 328,
    329, 482–83
  and terrorism, 304, 308, 315, 472
  and two-state solution, 305–6, 307, 311,
    320, 325, 338, 487
  and West Bank, 308–11, 317–18, 322

Palestinian Authority (PA), 308–11, 315,
    472, 474, 482–83
Palestinian Islamic Jihad, 473, 476
Palestinian Liberation Organization,
    309
Palin, Sarah, 11, 354
Pally, Maura, 600
Panama, trade agreement with, 254,
    515
Pan Am Flight 103, Lockerbie, 365
Pandith, Farah, 599
Panetta, Leon:
  and Afghanistan/Pakistan, 167, 184,
    188
  and Benghazi, 405, 407
  and bin Laden operation, 191, 192,
    196
  and CIA, 187–89
  and counterterrorism measures,
    187–90
  as Defense Secretary, 44, 167
  and Middle East unrest, 388, 392, 462,
    476–77
  and New Zealand ships, 44
Papua New Guinea, 568–69
Parks, Rosa, 558, 565
Partners in Health, 540
Pascual, Carlos, 252, 439, 441, 598
Pastrana, Andrés, 252
Pataki, George E., 172
Patel, Nirav, 598
Patterson, Anne, 388, 485
Paulson, Hank, 43, 72
Peace Corps, 277, 534
Pelosi, Nancy, 11
PEPFAR (President's Emergency Plan
    for AIDS Relief), 291–93, 537, 578
Peres, Shimon, 305–6
Perl, Liz, 598
Persian Gulf, 351–60, 361
  and Arab Spring protests, 355
  Gulf Cooperation Council, 352,
    358–60, 438–39
  Gulf War (1991), 351, 438, 477
  and Iran, 421

and Muslim Brotherhood, 475
and oil, 440
and Syria, 450, 452, 453, 462
U.S. military support in, 352, 355, 438
see also specific nations
Peru:
mass transit in, 255
and Pacific Alliance, 254
Pesaru, Shilpa, 600
Petraeus, David, 41
and Afghanistan/Pakistan, 133,
139–40
and CIA, 392, 413
and COIN, 135–36, 138
and Iraq, 133–34, 135–36
and Syria, 462–63
Philip Morris, 510
Philippines:
elections in, 60
and South China Sea, 74, 75, 113
U.S. alliance with, 44, 75, 113
Pickering, Thomas, 406–7
Pinochet, Augusto, 261
Pitsuwan, Surin, 52
Podesta, John, 16, 598
Poehler, Amy, 231
Poland:
shale gas extraction in, 241
Solidarity in, 566
Porat, Yochai, 303
Posner, Michael, 112, 519, 598
Powell, Colin, 31, 41, 135, 425, 477
Powell, Nancy, 599
Power, Samantha, 370
Prague Spring, 566
Pray the Devil Back to Hell
(documentary), 275
presidential elections:
(2008), 3, 8–11, 16
(2012), 591
(2016), 595–96
Préval, René, 529, 531–32, 536, 542–43,
544
Prikhodko, Sergei, 425
Prosser, Julia, 598

Putin, Vladimir, 212, 228–30
and Central Asia, 237, 238–39
and Crimea, 227, 236, 241–42
and Eurasian Union, 239
Hillary Clinton's meetings with,
229–30, 242–44
and KGB, 231
and LGBT, 577
return to power, 235–36, 238–39
and Russian expansionism, 236, 239,
244–45, 503
and Syria, 455, 466–67
and term limits, 230
and Ukraine, 241, 451

Qaboos, Sultan of Iran, 416
Qaddafi, Muammar, 357, 358, 359, 360,
363–75, 379, 460, 555
capture and death of, 388
fall from power, 381, 383, 450
Qaddafi, Saif al-Islam, 364
Qatar, 351
and Al Jazeera, 318
Forum for the Future conference in,
331, 337
and Gaza, 474–76, 479
geography of, 475
Hillary Clinton's travel to, 334
influence of, 475
and Libya, 371, 376
and Syria, 453, 463
Taliban in, 164–65, 166, 168
U.S. relationship with, 475
Quadrennial Diplomacy and
Development Review, 551
Quam, Lois, 599
Quartet, 323
Qureshi, Shah Mahmood, 180–81, 199

Rabbani, Burhanuddin, 154
Rabin, Leah, 303
Rabin, Yitzhak, 303, 305, 323, 324, 330
Rafsanjani, Ali Akbar Hashemi, 443
Ramesh, Jairam, 495
Randolph, Lawrence, 599

Rapp, Stephen, 599
Rasmussen, Anders Fogh, 212, 376, 500
Reagan, Nancy, 10
Reagan, Ronald, 207, 234, 365
Redelfs, Arthur, 250
Reid, Harry, 17, 144, 234
Reidy, Carolyn, 598
Reines, Philippe, 12–13, 232, 592, 597
Reinfeldt, Fredrik, 500
religious freedom, 574–75
Reynoso, Julissa, 599
Rezaei, Mohsen, 443
Rhodes, Ben, 114, 468, 480, 598
Rhorer, Richard, 598
Rice, Condoleezza, 31, 35, 231, 262, 332, 366, 593
Rice, Susan, 598
    and Iran, 428, 432–33
    and Libya, 370, 371, 372, 412–13
    and North Korea, 54
    as UN Ambassador, 23–24, 54, 412, 427
Richard, Anne, 599
Ride, Sally, 309
Riedel, Bruce, 132
Riedel review, 141, 151, 153, 157
Robinson, John, 599
Robinson, Peter, 225
Rodham, Dorothy, 6, 67, 81, 586–89
Rodham, Hugh (brother), 252, 588
Rodham, Hugh (father), 525, 587
Rodham, Tony (brother), 588
Rodriguez, Miguel, 599
Romney, Mitt, 94, 307
Rooney, Megan, 331–32, 580, 581, 582, 598
Roosevelt, Eleanor, 111, 179, 564, 567, 573
Roosevelt, Franklin D., 81, 562, 564
Roosevelt, Theodore, 2
Rosenthal, Hannah, 599
Ross, Alec, 546, 549, 598
Ross, Dennis, 314, 436, 598
Rothberg, Adam, 598
Rouhani, Hassan, 443–45
Rousseff, Dilma, 260–61, 555

Roy, Stapleton, 46
Rudd, Kevin, 43–44, 553–54
Ruggiero, Frank, 157–58, 162, 164–65, 598
Rumsfeld, Donald, 205
Russia, 227–45
    anti-gay laws in, 577
    and Arctic Council, 502, 503
    attacks on the press in, 229, 230
    Boeing Design Center, Moscow, 516
    and Central Asia, 237, 238–39
    and China, 243, 245
    and Crimea, 212, 227, 230, 236, 239–42, 363
    demographic crisis in, 550
    economy of, 229
    elections in, 235–36
    as energy source, 219, 229, 239–41, 242, 521
    expansionism in, 211, 229, 236, 239, 244–45, 503
    and Georgia, 229, 231, 236, 239, 451
    Hillary Clinton's radio interview in, 229–30
    and Iran, 233, 243, 424–25, 427–29, 431, 433
    and Libya, 370, 371–72, 450–51
    and Mongolia, 61–62
    and Northern Distribution Network, 237–39
    and North Korea, 55
    nuclear treaty with, 233, 234, 243
    and the Quartet, 323
    reset with, 231–38, 243–44
    re-Sovietization of, 239, 241–42, 245
    and Syria, 236, 243, 449, 450, 452, 454–57, 458, 459–61, 466–69
    and technology, 557
    and Turkey, 219
    and Ukraine, 227, 239–42, 451, 521
    U.S. relationship with, 230–32, 237–38, 243–45
Russo, Robert, 600
Russo, Seth, 598
Rwanda, genocide in, 369

Saberi, Roxana, 422
Sadat, Anwar, 323, 338
Said al Said, Sultan Qaboos bin, 336
Salazar, Ken, 503
Salcido Ceniceros, Jorge Alberto, 250
Saleh, Ali Abdullah, 335, 355
Salisbury, Lord, 208
Sall, Macky, 273
Samuelson, Heather, 598
Sand, Maria, 599
Santos, Juan Manuel, 253
Santos, Marina, 600
Sarkozy, Nicolas, 208, 209, 364, 368,
    372–75, 425, 500
Saturday Night Live, 231
Saudi Arabia:
    and Bahrain, 357–59
    child marriage in, 352
    as Custodian of the Two Holy
        Mosques, 315
    and energy resources, 521
    Hillary Clinton's travel to, 353–55
    Iran assassination plot against, 437
    Khobar Towers bombing (1996), 418,
        419
    and Qatar, 476
    and September 11 attacks, 351
    social welfare programs in, 355
    and Syria, 450, 453, 463
    U.S. consulate attacked in, 384
    U.S. relationship with, 351, 354
    women restricted in, 352–53, 354–55
Savage, Dan, 578
Schell, Orville, 46–47
Schumer, Chuck, 17, 172–73
Schwartz, Eric, 599
Schwarzkopf, Norman, 335
Schwerin, Dan, 331–32, 597
SCIF (Sensitive Compartmented
    Information Facility), 35
Scott (DS agent in Benghazi), 390–91
SEALs:
    and bin Laden, 164, 170–71, 174,
        193–97
    intelligence work of, 199

Secretary of State:
    air travel of, 39–41; see also specific
        nations
    avoiding domestic politics, 591
    confirmation hearing, 30, 34–35
    economic statecraft of, 509
    and employee security, 384–85, 393–94,
        406–10, 411
    and foreign policy architecture, 33
    former Secretaries, 31–32
    Hillary Clinton's last day as, 593–94
    job offer of, 12–18, 19
    office suite of, 35
    passing the baton of, 593–94
    and public opinion, 179
    roles of, 21–22, 33–34, 508–9, 515–16,
        566, 591
    as senior Cabinet post, 15, 68
    and smart power, 33–34, 45, 153, 290,
        551, 552
    transition team for, 30–31
    working with the President, 18–19
    see also State Department, U.S.
Seeds of Peace, 304
SelectUSA, 516
Selleck, Michael, 598
Senegal:
    constitutional crisis in, 272–74
    Hillary Clinton's speech in, 272
Senussi, Abdullah al-, 364
Seow, Jackie, 598
September 11 attacks:
    and al Qaeda, 132, 148, 163, 171,
        172–74, 175, 183, 197
    anniversaries of, 386–87, 390, 400
    and bin Laden, 171, 174, 351
    and Bush Administration, 131, 178,
        419
    and emergency relief, 173, 532
    and European support, 205
    and failed states, 286
    and Ground Zero, 172, 174
    and Iran, 419
    9/11 Commission, 174
    and Saudi Arabia, 351

September 11 attacks (*cont.*)
   and Victims Compensation Fund, 174
   and War on Terror, 174–75, 189, 197, 228
Serbia, 221–23
Seward, William Henry, 13–14
Shafik, Ahmed, 347
Shah, Rajiv, 527, 538–39, 598
Shaheen, Jeanne, 279
Shailor, Barbara, 599
Shalit, Gilad, 315
Shannon, Tom, 262–63, 265, 267–68, 598
Shapiro, Andrew, 438, 598
Shapiro, Dan, 477
Sharon, Ariel, 312
Sheikh Ahmed, Sharif, 287–88, 289
Sherman, Wendy, 444–45, 599
Shields, Colin, 598
Shillady, Rev. William, 81, 588
Shinseki, Eric, 148
Shourd, Sarah, 435, 436
Shultz, George, 31, 35
Shwe Mann, 117, 122
Sikorski, Rados_aw, 240, 241
Sinai Peninsula, 473–74, 476
Singapore, and South China Sea, 113
Singh, Manmohan, 59, 492, 499
Sinn Féin, 224
Sisi, Abdul-Fattah el-, 349–50
Six Day War, 301, 473
Slaughter, Anne-Marie, 550, 598
Smith, Chris, 95
Smith, Dan, 599
Smith, Fred, 512
Smith, Jeannemarie, 599
Smith, Sean, 382, 389, 390–91, 395, 398, 399, 401, 405, 410, 415
Smith, Stephen, 43–44
Snowden, Edward, 244, 555–56
Solidarity Center, 517
Somalia, 286–91
   Al Shabaab in, 175, 199, 278, 286–89, 290, 467
   "Black Hawk Down" incident in, 286
   as classic failed state, 286

   elections in, 287, 289
   Mogadishu in, 195, 286
   pirates based in, 286, 288
   and terrorism, 286–87, 288, 289, 290–91
   transitional government in, 289
Somaly Mam, 517
Somare, Sir Michael, 568–69
Sonenshine, Tara, 599
South Africa:
   apartheid in, 295
   and climate change, 495, 499
   economic growth in, 495
   HIV/AIDS in, 291–93, 295
   and Mandela, 119, 293–98
   Robben Island in, 294
South China Sea, 74–76, 78–79, 113–14, 521
Southern Corridor pipeline, 240
South Korea:
   Cheonan incident, 56
   and climate change, 494
   democracy in, 60
   and DMZ, 57
   Hillary Clinton's travel to, 50–51, 53–58
   and Iran, 440
   trade agreement with, 515
   U.S. alliance with, 44, 46
South Sudan, 283–86
   independence of, 283
   oil in, 283–84, 285, 440, 520, 521
Soviet Union:
   collapse of, 227, 228, 407, 567
   withdrawal from Afghanistan (1989), 21, 131, 147, 178, 186, 233, 461, 537
   see also Russia
Stark, Tyler, 375–76
State Department, U.S.:
   academic exchanges supported by, 221, 336, 354
   Accountability Review Board, 406–10
   aviation diplomacy, 516
   Bureau of Energy Resources, 439

Cabinet post, 15, 68; *see also* Secretary
  of State
career professionals in, 26–30, 135, 414
and chain of command, 374, 408–9
counterterrorism in, 199–200
and democratic values vs. security
  interests, 333, 335, 340, 349, 351,
  359–62, 384, 534, 549, 566
diplomats who died overseas, 34, 188,
  250, 382–84, 398–401, 405–6, 415,
  529, 594
energy diplomacy, 521–22
and federal budget, 24, 26, 199, 409,
  533–34
forward-deployed diplomacy in, 45
and frozen conflicts, 219–29
Heroism Award, 415
and human rights, *see* human rights
and international development, 534, 539
investigations into Benghazi attacks,
  385–96, 406–14
and jobs, 516–17
and LGBT rights, 578–79
and religious prosecution, 574–75
and SelectUSA, 516
and transitions from dictatorship
  to democracy, 341, 343, 344, 349,
  361–62, 379–80
and 21st-century statecraft, 545–57
wicked problems in, 461, 470
and WikiLeaks, 252, 334, 368, 552–55
Steen, Florence, 6
Steinberg, Don, 599
Steinberg, Jim, 29, 41, 43, 598
Steiner, Michael, 158
Stern, Todd, 494–95, 498, 598
Stevens, Anne, 399, 400
Stevens, Chris:
  in Benghazi attacks, 382–83, 390–92,
    394–97, 410
  and CIA briefing, 389–90
  death of, 397, 398–99
  memories of, 399, 400, 401, 404–6, 415
  as Special Representative/Ambassador,
    368, 369, 388, 389, 411

Stevenson, Adlai E., 424
Stewart, Karen, 599
Stilwell, "Vinegar Joe," 103
St. John, Gregory, 173
Stock, Ann, 599
Stone, Elizabeth, 595
Støre, Jonas Gahr, 501, 502, 503
Strait of Hormuz, 421, 437
Sudan:
  civil war in, 284
  Comprehensive Peace Agreement,
    283
  and Darfur genocide, 271, 283
  and South Sudan, 283–86, 520, 521
  terrorism in, 476
  U.S. Embassy in, 402
Suez Canal, 340, 473
Suharto, Indonesian President, 51
Suleiman, Michel, 433
Suleiman, Omar, 343, 344, 345
Sullivan, Jake, 30, 159, 580, 582, 598
  and Burma, 114
  and Chen, 83, 86, 87, 91, 97, 100
  and Gaza, 480, 485, 487
  and Iran, 422, 434, 435–36, 437, 444
Summit of the Americas:
  (1994), 247, 248
  (2009), 248
  (2010), 253, 259
"Sunni Awakening," 136, 138, 352
Sun Tzu, *The Art of War,* 47
Superstorm Sandy, 532
Supreme Court, U.S., 184
Suu Kyi, Aung San, 104, 591
  Congressional Gold Medal to, 123
  and government reforms, 112, 116, 120
  and Hillary Clinton's visits, 101–3, 115,
    118–20
  and the Irrawaddy, 110, 111
  and Parliament, 61, 118–19, 120, 122
  Presidential Medal of Freedom to, 105
  and President Obama, 114, 125
  release from house arrest, 108–9, 117
  travel to U.S., 121–24
  and Yettaw, 106–8

Sweden, and climate change, 501, 502
Switzerland:
  diplomacy conducted via, 435
  and Turkey, 219–20
Syed, Zia, 599
Syria, 352, 447–70, 546
  Alawites in, 449, 472
  cease-fire in, 454–55
  chemical weapons used in, 465–69
  civil war in, 386, 447, 453–55, 460, 464, 468, 472
  disorganized opposition in, 460
  extremists in, 450, 461–62, 465, 469, 475
  as failed state, 460
  Free Syrian Army, 465
  Hama massacre (1982), 448, 453
  Hezbollah in, 453, 461, 468
  humanitarian aid to people of, 361, 452, 453–54
  and Iran, 314, 442, 452–53, 456, 460
  and Israel, 312, 313, 314, 417, 468
  proxy warfare in, 455
  refugees from, 450, 463, 464
  and Russia, 236, 243, 449, 450, 452, 454–57, 458, 459–61, 466–69
  sanctions against, 452, 460
  six-point plan for, 454–55, 457
  street protests in, 447–48, 450–52
  and terrorism, 450, 469–70, 472
  training rebels in, 461–64
  transition in, 453, 454, 455–59, 469
  weapons supplied to, 452–53, 456, 457, 461, 463
  as wicked problem, 461–64, 466, 470

Taban, Anngrace, 284–86
Taban, Bishop Elias, 284–86
Taiwan, democracy in, 60
Taliban:
  in Afghanistan, 130–32, 133, 138, 141, 143, 145, 148, 152, 153–55, 163–66, 175, 537
  and al Qaeda, 131, 151, 158, 163, 164
  and A-Rod contact, 157–58, 162, 164–65

  and bin Laden's death, 164
  negotiation with, 156–58, 164–67, 168–69
  in Pakistan, 131, 151, 154, 156, 164, 171, 175, 178, 181, 186, 198, 237
  propaganda of, 141
  in Qatar, 164–65, 166, 168
  tortures by, 130–31
Talwar, Puneet, 436, 437, 598
Tantalus, 324
Tantawi, Mohamed, 346–47
Tanzania:
  agriculture in, 279
  U.S. embassy bombed in, 131, 383, 406
Tauscher, Ellen, 17, 234, 599
Taylor, Charles, 274, 275
Taylor, Jewel, 274
technology, 545–57
  cyber attacks, 547–48
  and government surveillance, 549–50
  and Israeli defense, 480
  male vs. female users of, 585
  mobile phones, 546–47, 548
  and Newseum, 556–57
  and privacy, 547–50, 552–53, 555–57
  and Snowden, 555–56
  TechCamp, 545–46
  WikiLeaks, 252, 334, 368, 552–55
  see also internet
Thaçi, Hashim, 223
Thailand, 44, 113, 442, 479
Than Shwe, 52, 106, 107–8, 116
Thatcher, Margaret, 207, 307
Thein Sein:
  and elections, 122
  Hillary Clinton's meetings with, 115, 116–18, 120, 124
  and Myitsone Dam, 111
  as President of Burma, 108–9, 116–17, 123
  and reforms, 118, 120, 121, 122, 123
  and Suu Kyi, 109, 116, 117, 123, 125
Thomas-Greenfield, Linda, 599

Tibet, 68

Tilleman, Tomicah, 598

Timor-Leste, 591–92

Titanic, 81

Tocqueville, Alexis de, 533

Toiv, Nora, 599

Trade and Development Agency, 539

Trans-Pacific Partnership (TPP), 77–78, 254

Treasury Department, U.S., and terrorist financing, 190

Truman, Harry S, 20, 22, 32, 304

Truman Administration, 32

Tsang, Donald, 514

Tubman, Harriet, 14

Tunisia:
  elections in, 360
  peaceful transition in, 360–61, 460
  street protests in, 334, 337, 338, 355, 360, 364, 447
  U.S. Embassy besieged in, 399, 402–3

Turkey, 214–20
  and Armenia, 218–20
  and climate change, 495
  economic growth in, 430, 446, 495
  and France, 373
  and Greece, 218
  and Iran, 217, 260, 427–33
  and Israel, 218, 314, 321–22
  and Libya, 373, 375, 376
  and Southern Corridor pipeline, 240
  and Syria, 450, 453, 454, 462–63
  and the UN, 427–28, 430
  U.S. relationship with, 218, 439
  and Zero Problems, 217, 218, 219

21st-century statecraft, 545–57
  use of term, 551
  see also technology

Twitter:
  in Iran, 423, 548–49
  in Russia, 551–52
  and State Department, 551
  in Syria, 546

U2, 8

Uganda:
  clinic in, 293
  LGBT in, 576
  military training in, 289–90
  and the UN, 427–28

Ukraine:
  and European Union, 240, 241
  Orange Revolution in, 240
  and Russia, 227, 239–42, 451, 521

United Arab Emirates (UAE), 200, 334–35, 351
  intervention in Bahrain, 357–59, 373
  and Libya, 371, 373
  and Qatar, 476
  and Syria, 453

United Kingdom:
  economic recession in, 207
  Good Friday Agreement, 224–25, 226, 313
  and Iran, 424–25
  and Kenya, 278
  and Libya, 213, 375
  and Syria, 463, 466
  U.S. relationship with, 205

United Nations (UN):
  and Afghanistan, 140, 144, 165
  Chapter VII resolution in, 458–59
  and chemical weapons, 469
  and climate change, 493, 494
  and Crimea, 242
  and Cuba, 258
  and emerging powers, 430
  and Global Counterterrorism Forum, 189, 200
  and Goldstone Report, 318
  and Haiti, 247, 260
  and human rights, 111, 364–65, 557, 564–65, 567, 573–74, 575–76, 580
  International Women's Day, 131
  and Iran, 233, 416–17, 418, 424–25, 427–29, 431–33, 435, 439, 442, 444–45
  and Libya, 235, 364, 366, 370–74
  and Middle East, 318, 326–30

United Nations (UN) (*cont.*)
  and North Korea, 54, 55, 56, 57, 107
  Nuclear Nonproliferation Treaty, 418
  P5+1 nations, 416–17, 424, 425, 430,
    432, 435, 436, 442, 443, 445
  and Palestine, 482–83
  peacekeeping missions of, 260, 282
  and the Quartet, 323
  rotating seats in, 427
  Security Council resolutions, 427
  and Syria, 236, 449, 450–52, 454–55,
    457–59, 469
  UN Women, 261, 282, 563, 564, 570
  U.S. Ambassador to, 23–24, 412, 427
United States:
  and Arctic Council, 502
  and climate change, 491–92, 496–98,
    504, 505–6
  and debt default, 513–15
  drones used by, 183–84, 185
  drug markets in, 250–51
  embassies bombed in East Africa
    (1998), 131, 171, 383, 406
  energy production in, 440, 522–23
  financial crisis in (2008), 73
  and foreign policy, *see* State
    Department, U.S.
  full faith and credit of, 514
  and humanitarian aid, 532–34, 544
  and human trafficking, 517–18, 573
  immigrants in, 550
  interagency competition in, 190
  and international trade, 509–10, 515
  and laws of war and self-defense,
    183
  leadership roles of, 482, 496–98, 504,
    505–6, 512
  LGBT in, 578–81
  and Obama, *see* Obama, Barack
  and the Quartet, 323
  refugees in embassies of, 79, 84, 85, 87
  rumors of decline, 25–26, 47, 52, 73–74
  Trade Enforcement Unit, 515
  use of torture in, 573
  volunteerism in, 533

  women and the economy in, 570–71
  see also Secretary of State; State
    Department
United States Africa Command, 393
Universal Declaration on Human Rights,
  111, 364–65, 557, 564–65, 567, 573,
  575–76, 580, 581
UPS, 511–12
Urda, Gary, 598
Uribe, Álvaro, 252, 253
U.S.–Afghan Women's Council, 152
USAID (U.S. Agency for International
  Development), 26, 61, 277, 406, 551
  and Afghanistan/Pakistan, 141, 182
  creation of, 541
  Development Credit Authority, 539
  "Grand Challenges" competitions, 538
  and Haiti, 527, 530, 537–41
  and women's programs, 568
U.S. Army:
  10th Mountain Division, 143
  Night Stalkers, 193
U.S. Coast Guard, 530
U.S.–EU Energy Council, 214, 241
U.S. Global Development Lab, 539
U.S. Navy:
  7th Fleet, 48
  and North Korea, 107
  SEALs, 164, 170–71, 174, 193–97, 199
USNS *Comfort,* 530
USS *Cole,* 171
USS *Fitzgerald,* 113
USS *George Washington,* 57
USS *Impeccable,* 75
Uzbekistan, 237, 238

Valenzuela, Arturo, 599
Valmoro, Lona, 49, 600
Vaysbeyn, Elina, 598
Velayati, Ali-Akbar, 443
Venezuela:
  and Haiti, 540
  and OAS, 258–59, 263
  state-controlled economy of, 254,
    259

Verma, Rich, 234, 599
Verveer, Melanne, 563, 567–68, 569, 572,
      584, 598
Verveer, Phil, 599
Vienna Convention on Diplomatic
      Relations (1961), 409, 435
Vietnam:
   Hillary Clinton's travel to, 61, 76–79
   labor issues in, 519
   restrictions in, 61
   and South China Sea, 74, 75, 78, 113
   strategic importance of, 46
   U.S. relationship with, 77
Vietnam War, 61, 136
Vilsack, Tom, 278
Vital Voices, 224, 567, 571
Vogelstein, Rachel, 584, 600
Voice of America, 108, 180, 441

Wade, Abdoulaye, 272–73
Walker, Diana, 378
Walles, Jake, 599
Walsh, Matthew, 598
Wang, Bob, 84, 87, 88
Wang Lijun, 85–86
Wang Qishan, 512
Warner, John, 136
Warsaw Pact, 211
Washington, George, 167–68, 592
Waxman, Henry, 493–94
Webb, Jim, 105, 107–8
Wellington Declaration, 44
Wells, Alice, 599
Wen Jiabao:
   and Chen, 88
   and climate change conference, 491,
      492, 499
   and Iran, 432
   and South China Sea, 113, 114
   and transition, 86, 96
   and U.S.-China relationship, 47, 72,
      92, 95–96
Wesley, John, 18
Westerwelle, Guido, 481, 554
White, Pamela, 599

White, Ryan, 291
White, Stanford, 81
Widmer, Ted, 597
WikiLeaks, 252, 334, 368, 552–55
Wilberforce, William, 208
wildlife trafficking, 467, 468–69
Williams, Maggie, 563, 584
Willson, Jeff, 598
Winnefeld, James "Sandy" Jr., 411,
      572
Wisner, Frank, 342, 345
Wohlers, Paul, 599
women's rights, 560–64, 567–73
   in Afghanistan, 152–53, 158, 562
   in Africa, 568
   in China, 66, 68–69
   gender-based violence in Democratic
      Republic of Congo (DRC), 279–82
   and Hillary Clinton's Beijing speech,
      66, 560–62, 583, 584–85
   Islam's restrictions on women, 130–31,
      352–53, 354–55
   in Japan, 571
   and the UN, 261, 282, 563, 564, 570
Woods, Tyrone, 382, 398, 404–5, 415
Woolheater, Ashley, 598
workers' rights, 517, 518–20
World Bank, 563, 569, 570, 571
World Conference on Women, Beijing
      (1995), 66, 104, 560–62, 584–85
World Economic Forum, Davos, 49
World Health Organization, 524
World Trade Center (1993) bombing,
      176
World Trade Organization, 233, 235,
      242, 510, 513
Wyllie, Andrew, 529
Wyss, Laura, 598

Xi Jinping, 505

Yang Jiechi, 54–55, 69, 70–72, 79, 107,
      114, 427, 554
Yanukovych, Viktor, 227, 241
Yao Ming, 71

Yavuz, Elif, 290–91
Yeltsin, Boris, 212, 228
Yemen:
 and Arab Spring, 355
 counterterrorism in, 189
 Hillary Clinton's travel to, 334,
  335–36
 unrest in, 442, 460
Yettaw, John, 106–8
Yohannes, Daniel, 599
Yom Kippur War, 338
Yousef, Ramzi, 176
Yudhoyono, Susilo Bambang, 51–52, 60,
 106

Zakaria, Fareed, 276, 277
Zambia, Hillary Clinton's travel to,
 271
Zardari, Asif Ali, 160, 162, 176, 177–79,
 184, 197, 198
Zarif, Javad, 445
Zazi, Najibullah, 175
Zelaya, Manuel, 257, 259, 263, 265–68
Zenawi, Meles, 497
Zhang Yesui, 433
Zhou Enlai, 65, 93
Zimbabwe, 273
Zoellick, Robert, 75
Zuma, Jacob, 291, 295, 372, 492, 499

PHOTO CREDITS

30. AP Photo/Saul Loeb, Pool
31. AP Photo/Saul Loeb, Pool
32. AP Photo/Saul Loeb, Pool
33. Official White House Photo by Pete Souza
34. Official White House Photo by Pete Souza
35. Official White House Photo by Pete Souza
36. REUTERS/Jerry Lampen
37. SHAH MARAI/AFP/Getty Images
38. Department of State
39. J. SCOTT APPLEWHITE/AFP/Getty Images
40. ROBERT F. BUKATY/AFP/Getty Images
41. AP Photo/K. M. Chaudary
42. Diana Walker/TIME
43. Official White House Photo by Pete Souza
44. Official White House Photo by Pete Souza
45. TRIPPLAAR KRISTOFFER/SIPA/Newscom
46. Chip Somodevilla/Getty Images
47. Michael Nagle/Getty Images
48. REUTERS/Larry Downing
49. KCSPresse/Splash News/Newscom
50. Brendan Smialowski/Getty Images
51. Department of State
52. BRENDAN SMIALOWSKI/AFP/Getty Images
53. SAUL LOEB/AFP/Getty Images
54. AP Photo/RIA-Novosti, Alexei Nikolsky, Pool
55. HARAZ N. GHANBARI/AFP/Getty Images
56. © Philippe Reines
57. AP Photo/Mandel Ngan, Pool
58. AP Photo/Eraldo Peres
59. © TMZ.com/Splash News/Corbis
60. STR/AFP/Getty Images
61. AP Photo/Pablo Martinez Monsivais, Pool
62. REUTERS/Glenna Gordon/Pool
63. ROBERTO SCHMIDT/AFP/Getty Images
64. AP Photo/Khalil Senosi
65. AP Photo/Jacquelyn Martin, Pool
66. Photo by Susan Walsh, Pool/Getty Images
67. AMOS GUMULIRA/AFP/Getty Images
68. Charles Sleicher/Danita Delimont Photography/Newscom
69. AP Photo/Jacquelyn Martin, Pool
70. © Sara Latham
71. Official White House Photo by Pete Souza

72. © Stephanie Sinclair/VII/Corbis
73. Astrid Riecken/Getty Images
74. Official White House Photo by Pete Souza
75. Department of State
76. MARWAN NAAMANI/AFP/Getty Images
77. Official White House Photo by Pete Souza
78. PAUL J. RICHARDS/AFP/Getty Images
79. REUTERS/Kevin Lamarque
80. Department of State
81. STR/AFP/Getty Images
82. Official White House Photo by Pete Souza
83. Official White House Photo by Pete Souza
84. Chip Somodevilla/Getty Images
85. KEVIN LAMARQUE/AFP/Getty Images
86. Mario Tama/Getty Images
87. Official White House Photo by Pete Souza
88. AP Photo/Egyptian Presidency
89. Official White House Photo by Pete Souza
90. AP Photo/Saul Loeb, Pool
91. © Kris Balderston
92. AP Photo/Julie Jacobson, Pool
93. Allison Shelley/Getty Images
94. AP Photo/Larry Downing, Pool
95. Andrew Harrer/Bloomberg via Getty Images
96. Courtesy of the William J. Clinton Presidential Library
97. *Washington Post*/Getty Images
98. AP Photo/Anja Niedringhaus
99. © Nicholas Merrill
100. MANDEL NGAN/AFP/Getty Images

Visiting a recovery centre for survivors of human trafficking in Siem Reap, Cambodia, in 2010.